Health and Welfare
during Industrialization

A National Bureau
of Economic Research
Project Report

Health and Welfare during Industrialization

Edited by Richard H. Steckel and Roderick Floud

The University of Chicago Press

Chicago and London

RICHARD H. STECKEL is professor of economics at Ohio State University and a research associate of the National Bureau of Economic Research. RODERICK FLOUD is provost of London Guildhall University and a research associate of the National Bureau of Economic Research.

The University of Chicago Press, Chicago 60637
The University of Chicago Press, Ltd., London
© 1997 by the National Bureau of Economic Research
All rights reserved. Published 1997
Printed in the United States of America
06 05 04 03 02 01 00 99 98 97   1 2 3 4 5
ISBN: 0-226-77156-3 (cloth)

Library of Congress Cataloging-in-Publication Data

Health and welfare during industrialization / edited by Richard H. Steckel and Roderick Floud.
        p.   cm. — (A National Bureau of Economic Research project report)
    Includes bibliographical references and index.
    ISBN 0-226-77156-3 (cloth : alk. paper)
    1. Public health—Economic aspects.   2. Industrialization—Health aspects.   3. Quality of life.   4. Stature—Economic aspects.
    I. Steckel, Richard H. (Richard Hall), 1944–   . II. Floud, Roderick.   III. Series.
    RA427.H39 1997
    338.4′33621—dc21   96-38157
                                                                                          CIP

Relation of the Directors to the
Work and Publications of the
National Bureau of Economic Research

1. The object of the National Bureau of Economic Research is to ascertain and to present to the public important economic facts and their interpretation in a scientific and impartial manner. The board of Directors is charged with the responsibility of ensuring that the work of the National Bureau is carried on in strict conformity with this object.

2. The President of the National Bureau shall submit to the Board of Directors, or to its Executive Committee, for their formal adoption all specific proposals for research to be instituted.

3. No research report shall be published by the National Bureau until the President has sent each member of the Board a notice that a manuscript is recommended for publication and that in the President's opinion it is suitable for publication in accordance with the principles of the National Bureau. Such notification will include an abstract or summary of the manuscript's content and a response form for use by those Directors who desire a copy of the manuscript for review. Each manuscript shall contain a summary drawing attention to the nature and treatment of the problem studied, the character of the data and their utilization in the report, and the main conclusions reached.

4. For each manuscript so submitted, a special committee of the Directors (including Directors Emeriti) shall be appointed by majority agreement of the President and Vice Presidents (or by the Executive Committee in case of inability to decide on the part of the President and Vice Presidents), consisting of three Directors selected as nearly as may be one from each general division of the Board. The names of the special manuscript committee shall be stated to each Director when notice of the proposed publication is submitted to him. It shall be the duty of each member of the special manuscript committee to read the manuscript. If each member of the manuscript committee signifies his approval within thirty days of the transmittal of the manuscript, the report may be published. If at the end of that period any member of the manuscript committee withholds his approval, the President shall then notify each member of the Board, requesting approval or disapproval of publication, and thirty days additional shall be granted for this purpose. The manuscript shall then not be published unless at least a majority of the entire Board who shall have voted on the proposal within the time fixed for the receipt of votes shall have approved.

5. No manuscript may be published, though approved by each member of the special manuscript committee, until forty-five days have elapsed from the transmittal of the report in manuscript form. The interval is allowed for the receipt of any memorandum of dissent or reservation, together with a brief statement of his reasons, that any member may wish to express; and such memorandum of dissent or reservation shall be published with the manuscript if he so desires. Publication does not, however, imply that each member of the Board has read the manuscript, or that either members of the Board in general or the special committee have passed on its validity in every detail.

6. Publications of the National Bureau issued for informational purposes concerning the work of the Bureau and its staff, or issued to inform the public of activities of Bureau staff, and volumes issued as a result of various conferences involving the National Bureau shall contain a specific disclaimer noting that such publication has not passed through the normal review procedures required in this resolution. The Executive Committee of the Board is charged with review of all such publications from time to time to ensure that they do not take on the character of formal research reports of the National Bureau, requiring formal Board approval.

7. Unless otherwise determined by the Board or exempted by the terms of paragraph 6, a copy of this resolution shall be printed in each National Bureau publication.

(Resolution adopted October 25, 1926, as revised through September 30, 1974)

Contents

Acknowledgments

The papers in this volume were presented at a conference held in Cambridge, Massachusetts, on 21–22 April 1995. We thank Martin Feldstein and the National Bureau of Economic Research for their support of the conference, and we are grateful to Robert Fogel and Claudia Goldin for their advice and encouragement. Local arrangements for the conference were skillfully handled by Kirsten Foss Davis and the NBER conference department. The editors are indebted to Mark Fitz-Patrick and Cristina McFadden of the NBER publications department and to Anita Samen of the University of Chicago Press for their help in preparing the book for publication. We also recognize the valuable contributions of numerous discussants or reviewers, including John Brown, Ivan Franca, Robert Gallman, Timothy Guinnane, Michael Haines, Jane Humphries, John Komlos, Robert Margo, Emily Mechner, Rebecca Menes, Joel Mokyr, Clayne Pope, Irwin Rosenberg, Nevin Scrimshaw, Peter Temin, Peter Timmer, and two anonymous referees.

Introduction

Richard H. Steckel and Roderick Floud

The changing state of human welfare during industrialization has long been a staple of debate among scholars. Current views on the subject can be traced back to mid-nineteenth-century England, when Marx and Engels claimed that industrialization impoverished the working class, and authors such as Charles Dickens penned tales of woe set in miserable factories, workhouses, and cities. While historians of thought ponder the theoretical structure of marxist philosophy and audiences suffer with Oliver Twist, the arduous work of discovering what actually happened during industrialization has been turned over to economic historians. Students of the quantitative and qualitative history of living standards are advancing knowledge on the subject. They are collecting evidence on the quality of life in the past, exploring mechanisms of causation, and appraising trends, fluctuations, and class differences in welfare.

Although the standard of living debate is liveliest in England, every country that had industrialized by the early twentieth century has been the object of study and review. Economic historians have extended national income series for many countries into the nineteenth century, and the results have been compared with alternative measures of the quality of life. Moreover, new methods and new sources of data have been brought to bear on these questions during the past two decades. Thus, a standard of living debate of some sort exists for each early industrializer. No single study, however, has attempted to assemble evidence, investigate patterns, and draw conclusions on health and welfare in numerous countries.

This volume brings together nine essays that examine a wide range of evidence on health and welfare during industrialization and its aftermath in eight

Richard H. Steckel is professor of economics at Ohio State University and a research associate of the National Bureau of Economic Research. Roderick Floud is provost of London Guildhall University and a research associate of the National Bureau of Economic Research.

countries: the United States, England, Sweden, the Netherlands, France, Germany, Japan, and Australia. The goal is to place the standard of living debate in comparative international perspective by examining several indicators of the quality of life, especially real per capita income and health, but also real wages, education, and inequality. The authors employ traditional measures of health such as life expectancy at birth and mortality rates but make extensive use of vast amounts of data recently collected on stature, which measures nutritional status. The papers also contribute to the standard of living debate within each country. The collection of country studies is introduced by Stanley Engerman's survey, which places the standard of living debate in international perspective.

The value of the project as a whole exceeds the sum of the individual studies because the countries under examination are diverse by region of the world, timing of industrialization, nature of government policy, pace of change, and cultural circumstances. By comparing and contrasting the experiences of these countries from a broad perspective of indicators, it may be possible to generalize about the ways that industrialization influenced human welfare. The number of countries under study is modest, but pronounced patterns can emerge in small samples, and we expect to define a larger research agenda.

It is an open question whether the course of national welfare during the various industrialization experiences was governed largely by idiosyncratic factors and the cumulative influence of historical accidents that affected countries unequally—such as major wars or the acquisition and settlement of new territories—or whether general tendencies and similar causal structures prevailed. Aligning the results for particular countries by time period and by stage of industrialization establishes a common framework for study. From this structure more can be learned about the significance of government policy for the course of economic growth and human welfare, the role of transportation and trade in spreading diseases that were detrimental to welfare, and the ways that public health measures helped offset the undesirable side effects for health created by congested arrangements for living and work.[1]

Methodology

Some differences of opinion in standard of living debates stem from alternative ways of defining the problem. Although material indicators such as per capita income or real wages have predominated, the literature encompasses measures as far ranging as stress on the family and psychological adjustments required for adapting to an urban-industrial way of life. While it is assumed that several of the measures used in this volume are well known (real per capita income, real wages, life expectancy, and literacy) and require no introduction

---

1. We note that the mechanisms underlying relationships between trade and health and between urbanization and health may have been complex. Both trade and urbanization may have raised incomes, something beneficial per se for health, while spreading disease. In addition, these processes may have had consequences for the distribution of income and health.

or special explanation, this chapter includes a methodology section for readers who may be unfamiliar with anthropometric measures such as stature and the body mass index. In the past two decades numerous studies by economic historians have used stature to investigate health aspects of the standard of living.[2] In addition, the concluding section on health and welfare includes a brief introduction to the problem of welfare assessment using alternative measures.

Anthropometric Measures

There is a long tradition among human biologists and nutritionists of using stature to assess health aspects of human welfare (Tanner 1981). The realization that environmental conditions influenced growth stimulated interest in human growth studies in the 1820s. Auxological epidemiology (auxology is the study of human growth) arose in France, where Villermé studied the stature of soldiers; in Belgium, where Quetelet measured children and formulated mathematical representations of the human growth curve; and in England, where Edwin Chadwick inquired into the health of factory children. Charles Roberts judged the fitness of children for factory employment by using frequency distributions of stature and other measurements, such as weight-for-height and chest circumference. Franz Boas identified salient relationships between the tempo of growth and height distributions and in 1891 coordinated a U.S. national growth study, which he used to develop national standards for height and weight. The twentieth century has witnessed a worldwide explosion of growth studies (Eveleth and Tanner 1976, 1990).

These studies have shown, among many other things, that two periods of intense activity characterize the growth process following birth (Tanner 1978). The increase in height, or velocity, is greatest during infancy, falls sharply, and then declines irregularly into the preadolescent years. During adolescence, velocity rises sharply to a peak that equals approximately one-half of the velocity during infancy then declines rapidly and reaches zero at maturity. The adolescent growth spurt begins about two years earlier in girls than in boys, and during their spurt girls temporarily overtake boys in average height. As adults, males are taller than females primarily because they have approximately two additional years of growth prior to adolescence.

The height of an individual reflects the interaction of genetic and environmental influences during the period of growth (Waterlow and Schürch 1994). According to Eveleth and Tanner (1976, 222),

> Such interaction may be complex. Two genotypes which produce the same adult height under optimal environmental circumstances may produce different heights under circumstances of privation. Thus two children who would be the same height in a well-off community may not only be smaller under poor economic conditions, but one may be significantly smaller than the other. . . . If a particular environmental stimulus is lacking at a time when

---

2. For the most recent survey of this literature, see Steckel (1995).

it is essential for the child (times known as "sensitive periods") then the child's development may be shunted as it were, from one line to another.

Although genes are important determinants of individual height, studies of genetically similar and dissimilar populations under various environmental conditions suggest that differences in average height across most populations are largely attributable to environmental factors. In a review of studies covering populations in Europe, New Guinea, and Mexico, Malcolm (1974) concluded that differences in average height between populations are almost entirely the product of the environment. Using data from well-nourished populations in several developed and developing countries, Martorell and Habicht (1986) reported that children from Europe or of European descent, from Africa or of African descent, and from India or the Middle East have similar growth profiles. Far Eastern children or adults are an exception that may have a substantial genetic basis; well-off Japanese, for example, reach, on average, the 15th height percentile of the well-off in Britain (Tanner et al. 1982). Important for interpreting stature in the United States is the fact that Europeans and people of European descent and Africans and people of African descent who grew under good nutritional circumstances have nearly identical stature (Eveleth and Tanner 1976, appendix).[3]

Height at a particular age reflects an individual's history of *net* nutrition, or diet minus claims on the diet made by maintenance, work (or physical activity), and disease. The synergy between malnutrition and illness may further reduce the nutrition left over for growth (Scrimshaw, Taylor, and Gordon 1968). Poorly nourished children are more susceptible to infection, which reduces the body's absorption of nutrients. The interaction implies that analyses of stature must recognize not only inputs to health such as diet and medical care but also work effort and related phenomena such as methods of labor organization. Similarly, researchers must attempt to understand ways that exposure to infectious disease may have placed claims on the diet.[4] For example, Sophia Twarog's paper on nineteenth-century Germany in this volume argues that early termination or complete lack of breast-feeding impaired infant health because a nutritious diet (breast milk) was replaced by starchy paps and gruels that were often contaminated or fed with contaminated utensils.[5]

Studies of nutrition and health in the past have identified many instances in which dietary intake was important for health and human growth. Thomas McKeown (1976) has been one of the foremost proponents of the thesis that

3. To compare health status in situations where genetic differences are relevant, stature can be converted into percentiles of the appropriate (ethnic, regional, or country specific) height standards.

4. An alternative view of stature is the "small but healthy" paradigm emphasized by Sukhatme (1982), Seckler (1982), and others, in which it is claimed that many individuals adapt with low costs to nutritional deprivation. For critiques of this view, see James (1987), Martorell (1989), and Dasgupta (1993).

5. Most women in Württemburg did not breast-feed at all, largely for cultural reasons. Those that did (in Schwarzwald Kreis) worked heavily and produced insufficient milk.

improving diets were significant for the long-term decline of mortality rates in nineteenth-century Europe. In this vein, Robert Fogel (1994) estimated that diets in late-nineteenth-century France were so poor that the bottom fifth of the labor force was either incapable of work or could put forth less than three hours of light work per day. Richard Steckel (1986) reported that dietary deficiencies, especially of protein, significantly retarded growth among American slave children while improved access to food stimulated growth among teenagers.

The sensitivity of growth to deprivation depends on the age at which it occurs. For a given degree of deprivation, the adverse effects may be proportional to the velocity of growth under optimal conditions (Tanner 1966). Thus, young children and adolescents are particularly susceptible to environmental insults. The return of adequate nutrition following a relatively short period of deprivation may restore normal height through catch-up growth.[6] If conditions are inadequate for catch-up, individuals may still approach normal adult height by an extension of the growing period by as much as several years. Prolonged and severe deprivation results in stunting, or a reduction in adult size.

Figure 1 is a useful organizing device for exploring the relationship of height to living standard. Stature is a function of proximate determinants such as diet, disease, and work intensity during the growing years, and as such it is a measure of the consumption of basic necessities that incorporates demands placed on one's biological system. Because family income heavily influences purchases of basic necessities such as food and medical care, stature is ultimately a function of access to resources and environmental sanitation. It is noteworthy that stature may be diminished by consumption of products, such as alcohol or drugs, that are harmful to health, but excessive consumption of food, while leading to rapid growth, may impair health in later life. Public health measures, personal hygiene, and the disease environment affect the incidence of disease that places claims on nutrition. In addition, human growth may have functional consequences for health, labor productivity, mental development, and personality, which in turn may influence socioeconomic conditions.

Numerous sources of evidence exist for stature, including records on military recruits, slaves, convicts, and Southern oath takers who swore allegiance to the Union. Among these, the military records are the most abundant and widely used in this volume, but good use is also made of data about schoolchildren, convicts, and national guardsmen. Minimum height standards, age and height heaping, ethnic differences in growth potential, and selectivity biases among those measured complicate the interpretation of stature from these sources, but researchers have devised techniques to address these problems. For example, volunteer armies often applied minimum height standards that varied with personnel needs, but flexible enforcement of the standards eroded

---

6. Ingestion of toxic substances, such as alcohol or tobacco, in utero or in early childhood may create permanent stunting regardless of subsequent nutritional conditions.

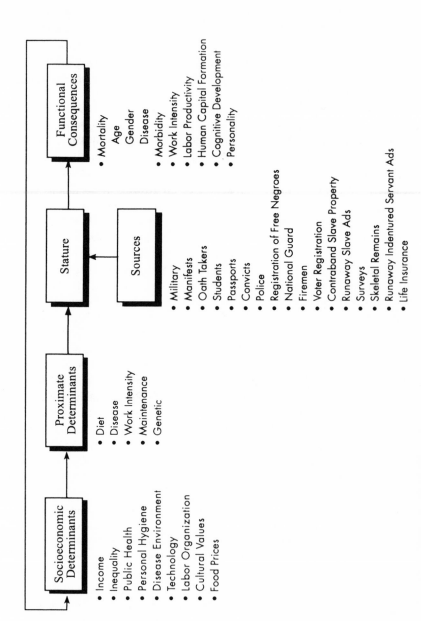

Fig. 1   Relationships involving stature

Socioeconomic Determinants
- Income
- Inequality
- Public Health
- Personal Hygiene
- Disease Environment
- Technology
- Labor Organization
- Cultural Values
- Food Prices

Proximate Determinants
- Diet
- Disease
- Work Intensity
- Maintenance
- Genetic

Stature

Sources
- Military
- Manifests
- Oath Takers
- Students
- Passports
- Convicts
- Police
- Registration of Free Negroes
- National Guard
- Firemen
- Voter Registration
- Contraband Slave Property
- Runaway Slave Ads
- Surveys
- Skeletal Remains
- Runaway Indentured Servant Ads
- Life Insurance

Functional Consequences
- Mortality
  - Age
  - Gender
  - Disease
- Morbidity
- Work Intensity
- Labor Productivity
- Human Capital Formation
- Cognitive Development
- Personality

the lower tail of the height distribution. Assuming that the underlying distribution was normal, or Gaussian, Wachter and Trussell (1982) devised techniques such as the Quantile Bend Estimator and the Reduced-Sample Maximum Likelihood Estimator to identify the height below which standards were applied and to compensate for those omitted. In situations where normality may not hold, such as small samples (less than a few hundred observations), Komlos and Kim (1990) proposed a restricted sample estimator based on the mean estimated from the upper portion of the distribution unaffected by changes in height minimums. These techniques are unnecessary in the case of conscript armies, in which all or nearly all the young-adult male population was measured. The papers in this volume on Sweden (Sandberg and Steckel) and on France (Weir) utilize conscript records, which also have the advantage of nearly complete representation of the male population and its various socio-economic classes and geographic divisions.

Heaping, or concentrations of measurements at whole feet or meters, at even-numbered ages or units, and at ages or units ending in zero plagues many data sources, including some modern studies. Simulations suggest that these problems were relatively minor for estimates of sample means, primarily because their effects are largely self-canceling (Fogel et al. 1983). Rounding by the U.S. military during World War II probably biased average heights by approximately 0.5 cm below the actual mean. In any event, rounding practices that were uniform over time and across space would not distort comparisons of relative height averages. In addition, smoothing techniques help to overcome heaping irregularities that contaminate the picture of the growth profile.

After such measurement issues have been dealt with, it is possible to compare stature with other indicators. Because real GNP per capita is the most widely used indicator of living standards, it is particularly useful to compare and contrast this measure with stature (Steckel 1983, 1995; Floud 1994). Income is a potent determinant of stature that operates through diet, disease, and work intensity, but one must recognize that other factors such as personal hygiene, public health measures, and the disease environment affect illness, while work intensity is a function of technology, culture, and methods of labor organization.[7] In addition, the relative price of food, cultural values such as the pattern of food distribution within the family, methods of food preparation, and tastes and preferences for foods may also be relevant for net nutrition. Yet influential policymakers view higher incomes for the poor as the most effective means of alleviating protein-energy malnutrition in developing countries

7. Empirical models of the relationship between a country's per capita GNP and average height are discussed below. More elaborate models would consider a lagged relationship between income and stature, both at the household and the aggregate (national) level. E.g., adult stature is a function of average income in each year from conception to maturity, and growth is more sensitive to income levels at ages when growth is ordinarily high, i.e., during early childhood and adolescence. For an application of this idea, see Brinkman, Drukker, and Slot (1988).

(World Bank 1993, 75).[8] Extremely poor families may spend two-thirds or more of their income on food, but even a large share of their very low incomes purchases inadequate calories. Malnutrition associated with extreme poverty has a major impact on height, but at the other end of the income spectrum expenditures beyond those needed to satisfy calorie requirements purchase largely variety, palatability, and convenience.

Gains in stature associated with higher income are not limited to developing countries. Within industrialized countries, height rises with socioeconomic class (Eveleth and Tanner 1990, 199). These differences in height are related to improvements in diet, reductions in physical workloads, reduced exposure to pathogens (through sewage disposal, cleaner water supply, and improved housing), and better health care. Expenditures on health services rise with income, and there is a positive relationship between health services and health (Fuchs 1972).

At the individual level, extreme poverty results in malnutrition, retarded growth, and stunting. Higher incomes enable individuals to purchase a better diet, and height increases correspondingly; but once income is sufficient to satisfy caloric requirements, individuals often consume foods that also satisfy many vitamin and mineral requirements. Height may continue to rise with income because individuals purchase a more complete diet or better housing and medical care. As income increases, consumption patterns change to realize a larger share of genetic potential, but environmental variables are powerless after individuals attain the maximum capacity for growth.[9] The limits to this process are clear from the fact that people who grew up in very wealthy families are not physical giants.

While the relationship between height and income is nonlinear at the individual level, the relationship at the aggregate level depends on the distribution of income. Average height may differ for a given per capita income depending on the fraction of people with insufficient income to purchase an adequate diet or to afford medical care. Because the gain in height at the individual level increases at a decreasing rate as a function of income, one would expect average height at the aggregate level to rise, for a given per capita income, with the degree of equality of the income distribution (assuming that there are people who have not reached their genetic potential).

The empirical relationship between average height and per capita income has been studied by linking data from late-twentieth-century national height studies with per capita GNP. Despite the large number of factors that may influence average height at a given level of per capita income, the simple correlations between a country's average height and the logarithm of its per capita

8. Development economists have debated the effects of income on the diets of the poor. See Behrman and Deolalikar (1987).

9. Of course, it is possible that higher incomes could purchase products such as alcohol, tobacco, or drugs that impair health.

income are in the range of 0.82 to 0.88 (Steckel 1983, 1995).[10] Regression estimates of height on per capita income and other variables indicate that the elasticity of height with respect to the log of per capita income (at sample means) is 0.27 for adolescents and 0.19 for adults, and the elasticity of height with respect to the Gini coefficient (at sample means) is −0.041 for adolescents and −0.086 for adults.

A strong association between stature and per capita income also existed a century earlier. In a study of European countries in the late nineteenth and early twentieth centuries, Floud (1994) found a height-income relationship similar to that observed in more recent data. Although the height-income relationship has been less well studied in eras before the late nineteenth century, the available evidence points to diverse outcomes, including a strong association (see papers in this volume by Weir on France, by Drukker and Tassenaar on the Netherlands, and by Honda on Japan), a weak relationship, and possibly a negative correlation. Certainly counterexamples (countries with populations taller than their income alone would suggest) can be found, including Ireland in the early nineteenth century and America in the late colonial and early national periods (Mokyr and Ó Gráda 1988; Nicholas and Steckel 1992; Costa and Steckel, chap. 2 in this volume). It has also been noted that taller populations of the eighteenth and nineteenth centuries tended to live in rural, isolated, and less commercial regions (Komlos 1989; Sandberg and Steckel 1988; Shay 1986; Margo and Steckel 1983). Given that a nonlinear relationship between height and income has been found in the past century and that the height-income relationship could shift over time, we conclude that heights and income measure different but related aspects of the quality of life.

Stature is only one of several biological indicators of nutritional status. Medical researchers have shown that relative body weight is a useful predictor of illness and mortality risks (James and Ralph 1994). Although investigators use various measures of weight to height, including weight divided by height and weight divided by the cube of height, the most widely used measure is the body mass index (BMI). Defined as weight in kilograms divided by the square of height in meters, BMI is easy to calculate and highly correlated with other indicators of obesity such as skinfold thickness (Keys et al. 1972).

Height and BMI measure different aspects of nutritional status. Stature measures the history of net nutrition from conception to the time of measurement (in the case of a child) or until the age that adult height was attained. In contrast, BMI reflects current levels of nutrition since the numerator (weight) may change rapidly relative to the denominator (height). BMI is similar to stature, however, in that it reflects the balance between dietary intakes and claims on those intakes made by maintenance, work, and disease.

---

10. The log specification fits about as well as a quadratic or cubic polynomial, and given these results the log is preferred on grounds of simplicity.

The value of height and weight in forecasting health has been established in longitudinal studies of child growth in developing countries (Martorell 1985). In two West African villages, children who died were significantly smaller and lighter than the survivors (Billewicz and McGregor 1982). Consistent with these studies, Gerald Friedman (1982) reported that shorter slaves were more at risk of death in Trinidad. Adult BMI is also a useful indicator of the chances of developing chronic diseases later in life. A Norwegian study of adult men shows that the mortality risk was a U-shaped function of BMI, where men whose BMI was in the range 21–29 had the lowest chances of death (Waaler 1984). A similar U-shaped pattern between BMI and subsequent mortality risk applied to Union Army veterans (Costa 1993). The paper in this volume by Costa and Steckel investigates the relationship between BMI and health in the United States during the late nineteenth and early twentieth centuries.

Health and Welfare

Real per capita income remains, however, the most widely used measure of the standard of living. With conceptual origins in the seventeenth century, national income accounts became generally available only in the mid-twentieth century when the Great Depression and World War II created needs for evaluating policy and planning military efforts. Although economists recognize the great contributions of the national accounts, current research momentum has shifted to alternatives or supplements that address shortcomings of per capita income as a welfare measure or that provide insights into the quality of life in time periods or among groups for which conventional measures cannot be calculated.

When national income accounting methodology emerged as an important subject in the 1930s, economists such as Kuznets (1941), Davis (1945), and Bennett (1937) urged the creation of welfare measures that would reflect the satisfaction of consumers. In particular, Kuznets proposed several refinements to GNP that would incorporate nonmarket activities, occupational costs, leisure, costs of urban living, and inequality. However, the emergency created by the Great Depression did not allow time to ponder carefully or incorporate these refinements. Policymakers understandably gave high priority to rapid deployment of a system of accounts that would be helpful in designing policies to combat the number one problem, unemployment. Thus, the Commerce Department adopted a narrow approach to the standard of living by focusing on the value of final goods and services.

A revival of interest in social accounting occurred in the 1970s, when urban sprawl, pollution, congestion, and crime stimulated interest in broad welfare measures. Seeking a better measure of consumption or welfare, Nordhaus and Tobin (1973) adjusted GNP for capital services, leisure, nonmarket work, and disamenities. Others extended these ideas to international comparisons using inequality as an ingredient in welfare (Kakwani 1981). International organizations and economists, concerned with the slow progress of the poor in developing countries, proposed a basic human needs approach to living standards that advocated minimum amounts of food, clothing, shelter, water, and sanitation (Adelman and Morris 1973; Chenery et al. 1974).

The papers in this volume utilize some of these new approaches to assessing welfare, which will be grouped for purposes of discussion into multiple indicators and adjustments to GNP. There is no general agreement within the profession on the suitability of alternative approaches, and here we do not attempt to resolve these larger questions. Instead, the papers try various methods employed in the literature and compare their implications. For example, in the cases of Sweden and France all indicators of the standard of living rose during industrialization, which leaves little doubt that the quality of life improved for the vast majority of people. Other countries, such as the United States and the United Kingdom, experienced cycles or fluctuations in some indicators, which raises questions about methods and weights in drawing conclusions about the course of welfare. In these cases, summary statements about the direction and extent of welfare change require an explicit scheme for weighting the indicators.

A multiple indicator approach to the standard of living has a tradition within the United Nations. By the 1950s, the United Nations had outlined a component approach that included indicators such as nutrition, health, consumption, and housing (United Nations 1954). This method recognizes the difficulty and complexity of measuring the quality of life and accepts the shortcomings of any single indicator. All the papers in this volume utilize the multiple indicator approach, and some authors supplement their analyses with additional methods. Standard indicators such as per capita GDP, life expectancy, stature, and literacy are widely used, but several papers also use measures such as meat consumption and urbanization. Several papers make use of the Human Development Index, discussed below, but some authors prefer a general discussion of indicators over an explicit weighting scheme.

The United Nations' multiple indicator approach has evolved over time, and a recent version takes the form of the Human Development Index, or HDI (United Nations Development Programme [UNDP] 1990). Designed as a minimal measure of the standard of living, this index has three components, which are given equal weight: longevity (measured by life expectancy, X_1), educational attainment (measured by the literacy rate, X_2), and access to resources (measured by the log of per capita GDP, X_3).[11] Comparisons are made across countries by selecting maximum and minimum values for the indicators and defining a deprivation measure that places a country on a scale of zero to one. Specifically, if I_{ij} is the deprivation indicator for country j with respect to indicator i, where $I_{ij} = (\max X_{ij} - X_{ij})/(\max X_{ij} - \min X_{ij})$ and the average level of deprivation for country j is given by $I_j = (I_1 + I_2 + I_3)/3$, then $(\text{HDI})_j = (1 - I_j)$.

---

11. The log formulation was inspired by arguments for declining marginal utility of income.

Critiques of HDI have clarified several of its attributes and suggested refinements (UNDP 1993, 104–13). It is a minimal measure that distinguishes among levels of deprivation rather than gradations of opulence. It incorporates essential aspects of the standard of living—health, education, and income—but is not comprehensive. Important aspects of the quality of life, such as equality, political and religious freedom, and opportunities for social and economic mobility are not included. One may also question the choice of indicators. Per capita GDP is a logical choice for access to resources, and life expectancy at birth represents the state of health, but education often includes more than basic literacy.[12] The choice of equal weights has attracted criticism, but defenders note that components of the measure tend to be positively correlated, and therefore alternative but reasonable choices for weights would give similar results.

HDI can be adapted for use in economic history by defining maximum and minimum values that encompass the range of historical experience and by substituting alternative indicators where appropriate or where the data ordinarily used are lacking. Although the individual papers in this volume employ various values, the range often chosen for the literacy rate is zero to 100 percent and that for per capita GDP is approximately $410 in 1987 prices (the cost of a subsistence diet) to $4,861 in 1987 prices (the upper bound chosen by the United Nations, which was inspired by the poverty-level income of the industrial countries in the Luxembourg Income Study).[13] Limits for life expectancy at birth are 30 years (roughly the lower end of experience for national populations in the preindustrial and early industrial period) to 80 years (approximately the highest observed in the world today). Additional calculations sometimes use other ranges or make use of different indicators. In situations where adequate mortality data are lacking, as in the United States, life expectancy is replaced by adult male stature, where the limits are 156 cm (taken from possibly the shortest population ever measured, the Bundi of New Guinea) to 180 cm (approximately the highest average stature in the world today).

Researchers dissatisfied with cardinal weighting schemes have proposed ordinal measures for intercountry comparisons of quality of life. The paper by Costa and Steckel on the United States employs the Borda rule to rank welfare outcomes over time.[14] This procedure gives each alternative outcome a point

---

12. A modified HDI measures education by literacy and years of schooling. Unfortunately, the latter are often unavailable for historical settings.

13. Stigler's (1945) subsistence diet (largely wheat flour, cabbage, and pancake flour, supplemented by spinach and pork liver) cost $59.88 in 1944, which amounted to approximately $140 in 1970 prices and $410 in 1987 prices.

In 1994 the United Nations (UNDP 1994) suggested a new method for calculating the deprivation index for per capita GDP, which was based on a threshold that discounted income values above the global average in that year ($5,120). Since the per capita incomes in the countries under study in this volume did not reach that level until well into the twentieth century, we believe that the earlier method employed here is preferable for historical research.

14. For a discussion and application, see Dasgupta (1993, 108–16).

equal to its rank within each index. For example, suppose there are three criteria—income, life expectancy, and literacy—and they rank i, j, and k, respectively, for a particular time period, then the Borda score is $i + j + k$. Rankings are arranged from the worst (lowest) to the best (highest) score.

Among some countries studied in this volume, income and health trends diverged (the United States and Britain) or gains in health were largely unrelated to gains in income (Sweden). These examples raise the question of whether per capita income adequately incorporates the value of health status. To the extent that per capita income fails to include the value of health, it is important to have methods for appraising its contribution to welfare change.

An early attempt to adjust estimates of income uses age-specific mortality rates and their shadow prices as determined from a model of consumer choice (Usher 1973, 1980). Under the strong assumptions that utility is separable, consumption is constant across all ages, and utility functions take the form $U_t = \sum_{i=0}^{t-1} C_i^\beta / (1 + r)^i$, where β is the elasticity of annual utility, U_t, with respect to consumption C_t in period t and r is the subjective discount rate, Usher derived a measure of the contribution of gains in life expectancy to economic growth. After defining $\hat{C}(t)$ to be the consumption level at which one would be as well-off with the mortality rates of some base year, T, as one was with the actual consumption level, $C(t)$, and the mortality rates of that year, he shows that $\hat{C}(t) = C(t)[L(t)L(T)]^{1/\beta}$ where $L(t)$ is an index of survival rates. Therefore, $G_{\hat{c}} = G_c + (1/\beta)G_L$, and the value of improvements in health is given by the difference between the growth rates of $\hat{C}(t)$ and $C(t)$.

In contrast with Usher's shadow prices, Thaler and Rosen (1976) used market information on wages across occupations with various health risks to measure the value of life. In this approach, workers demand premiums in the form of equalizing wage differentials to offset the risks of employment in more hazardous jobs. They estimated that workers were willing to pay 2–4 percent of their annual income to reduce the risk of death by 0.001. Viscusi (1978) placed the risk premium at approximately 5 percent. No comparable work has been done for the past, but pending historical research one might venture to assume that the risk premium remained constant over time. Comparisons of growth rates in per capita income with mortality rate changes suggest trade-offs that workers would have been willing to make.

Each method for appraising welfare has strengths and shortcomings, which suggests the need for careful consideration of their implications. While single measures have the advantage that comparisons are easily made over time and across countries, they also have the liability of excluding or failing to incorporate fully some aspects important to the quality of life. Among these, per capita income is the most comprehensive, but it is not always available in the past and it may fail to capture the value of health, education, and other important dimensions of living standards. The value of health can be estimated enroute to adjusting GDP, but approaches now available also have problems. In particular, it may be difficult to estimate the extent to which expenditures on health are already included in GNP. The multiple indicator approach incorporates a vast array of information relevant to the quality of life, but a summary statement on welfare requires a set of relative weights for the indicators. Weights can be chosen, as in HDI, but they are subject to debate. To the extent that the conclusions of the various methods agree, however, our confidence in the interpretation of history is strengthened, and where they differ, we can define an agenda for research.

References

Adelman, Irma, and Cynthia Taft Morris. 1973. *Economic growth and social equity in developing countries.* Stanford, Calif.: Stanford University Press.

Behrman, Jere R., and Anil B. Deolalikar. 1987. Will developing country nutrition improve with income? A case study for rural South India. *Journal of Political Economy* 95:492–507.

Bennett, M. K. 1937. On measurement of relative national standards of living. *Quarterly Journal of Economics* 51:317–35.

Billewicz, W. Z., and I. A. McGregor. 1982. A birth-to-maturity longitudinal study of heights and weights in two West African (Gambian) villages, 1951–1975. *Annals of Human Biology* 9:309–20.

Brinkman, Henk Jan, J. W. Drukker, and Brigitte Slot. 1988. Height and income: A new method for the estimation of historical national income series. *Explorations in Economic History* 25:227–64.

Chenery, Hollis, Montek S. Ahluwalia, C. L. G. Bell, John H. Duloy, and Richard Jolly. 1974. *Redistribution with growth.* Oxford: Oxford University Press.

Costa, Dora L. 1993. Height, weight, wartime stress, and older age mortality: Evidence from the Union Army records. *Explorations in Economic History* 30:424–49.

Dasgupta, Partha. 1993. *An inquiry into well-being and destitution.* New York: Oxford University Press.

Davis, Joseph S. 1945. Standards and content of living. *American Economic Review* 35:1–15.

Eveleth, Phyllis B., and J. M. Tanner. 1976. *Worldwide variation in human growth.* Cambridge: Cambridge University Press.

———. 1990. *Worldwide variation in human growth,* 2d ed. Cambridge: Cambridge University Press.

Floud, Roderick. 1994. The heights of Europeans since 1750: A new source for European economic history. In *Stature, living standards, and economic development,* ed. John Komlos, 9–24. Chicago: University of Chicago Press.

Fogel, Robert W. 1993. New sources and new techniques for the study of secular trends in nutritional status, health, mortality, and the process of aging. *Historical Methods* 26:5–43.

———. 1994. Economic growth, population theory, and physiology: The bearing of long-term processes on the making of economic policy. *American Economic Review* 84:369–95.

Fogel, Robert W., Stanley L. Engerman, Roderick Floud, Gerald Friedman, Robert A. Margo, Kenneth Sokoloff, Richard H. Steckel, T. James Trussell, Georgia Villaflor, and Kenneth W. Wachter. 1983. Secular changes in American and British stature and nutrition. *Journal of Interdisciplinary History* 14:445–81.

Friedman, Gerald C. 1982. The heights of slaves in Trinidad. *Social Science History* 6:482–515.

Fuchs, Victor R. 1972. The contribution of health services to the American economy. In *Essays in the economics of health and medical care,* ed. Victor R. Fuchs, 3–38. New York: National Bureau of Economic Research.

James, W. P. T. 1987. Research relating to energy adaptation in man. In *Chronic energy deficiency: Consequences and related issues,* ed. Beat Schürch and Nevin S. Scrimshaw, 7–36. Lausanne, Switzerland: International Dietary Energy Consultancy Group.

James, W. P. T., and A. Ralph, eds. 1994. The functional significance of low body mass index (BMI). *European Journal of Clinical Nutrition* 48 (Suppl. 3): 1–202.

Kakwani, Nanak. 1981. Welfare measures: An international comparison. *Journal of Development Economics* 8:21–45.

Keys, Ancel, Flaminio Fidanza, Martti J. Karvonen, Noboru Kimura, and Henry L. Taylor. Indices of relative weight and obesity. *Journal of Chronic Disease* 25:329–43.

Komlos, John. 1989. *Nutrition and economic development in the eighteenth-century Habsburg monarchy.* Princeton, N.J.: Princeton University Press.

Komlos, John, and Joo Han Kim. 1990. Estimating trends in historical heights. *Historical Methods* 23:116–20.

Kuznets, Simon. 1941. *National income and its composition, 1919–1938.* New York: National Bureau of Economic Research.

Malcolm, L. A. 1974. Ecological factors relating to child growth and nutritional status. In *Nutrition and malnutrition: Identification and measurement,* ed. Alexander F. Roche and Frank Falkner, 329–52. New York: Plenum.

Margo, Robert A., and Richard H. Steckel. 1983. Heights of native-born whites during the antebellum period. *Journal of Economic History* 43:167–74.

Martorell, Reynaldo. 1985. Child growth retardation: A discussion of its causes and its relationship to health. In *Nutritional adaptation in man,* ed. Kenneth Blaxter and J. C. Waterlow, 13–29. London: John Libbey.

———. 1989. Body size, adaptation and function. *Human Organization* 48:15–19.

Martorell, Reynaldo, and Jean-Pierre Habicht. 1986. Growth in early childhood in developing countries. In *Human growth: A comprehensive treatise,* vol. 3, ed. Frank Falkner and J. M. Tanner, 241–62. New York: Plenum.

McKeown, Thomas. 1976. *The modern rise of population.* London: Edward Arnold.

Mokyr, Joel, and Cormac Ó Gráda. 1988. Poor and getting poorer? Living standards in Ireland before the famine. *Economic History Review* 41:209–35.

Nicholas, Stephen, and Richard H. Steckel. 1992. Tall but poor: Nutrition, health, and living standards in pre-famine Ireland. NBER Working Paper Series on Historical Factors in Long Run Growth, no. 39. Cambridge, Mass.: National Bureau of Economic Research.

Nordhaus, William D., and Tobin, James. 1973. Is growth obsolete? In *The measurement of economic and social performance,* ed. Milton Moss, 509–64. New York: National Bureau of Economic Research.

Sandberg, Lars G., and Richard H. Steckel. 1988. Overpopulation and malnutrition rediscovered: Hard times in nineteenth-century Sweden. *Explorations in Economic History* 25:1–19.

Scrimshaw, N. S., C. E. Taylor, and J. E. Gordon. 1968. *Interactions of nutrition and disease.* WHO Monograph Series, no. 52. New York: United Nations.

Seckler, David. 1982. Small but healthy: A basic hypothesis in the theory, measurement and policy of malnutrition. In *Newer concepts in nutrition and their implications for policy,* ed. P. V. Sukhatme, 127–37. Pune: Maharashtra Association for the Cultivation of Science Research Institute.

Shay, Ted. 1986. The stature of military conscripts: New evidence on the standard of living in Japan. Paper given at the 1986 Social Science History Association meetings, St. Louis.

Steckel, Richard H. 1983. Height and per capita income. *Historical Methods* 16:1–7.

———. 1986. A peculiar population: The nutrition, health, and mortality of American slaves from childhood to maturity. *Journal of Economic History* 46:721–41.

———. 1995. Stature and the standard of living. *Journal of Economic Literature* 33:1903–40.

Stigler, George J. 1945. The cost of subsistence. *Journal of Farm Economics* 27:303–14.

Sukhatme, P. V., ed. 1982. *Newer concepts in nutrition and their implications for policy.* Pune: Maharashtra Association for the Cultivation of Science Research Institute.

Tanner, J. M. 1966. Growth and physique in different populations of mankind. In *The biology of human adaptability,* ed. Paul T. Baker and J. S. Weiner, 45–66. Oxford: Oxford University Press.

———. 1978. *Fetus into man: Physical growth from conception to maturity.* Cambridge, Mass.: Harvard University Press.

———. 1981. *A history of the study of human growth.* Cambridge: Cambridge University Press.

Tanner, J. M., T. Hayashi, M. A. Preece, and N. Cameron. 1982. Increase in length of leg relative to trunk in Japanese children and adults from 1957 to 1977: Comparisons with British and with Japanese Americans. *Annals of Human Biology* 9:411–23.

Thaler, Richard, and Sherwin Rosen. 1976. The value of saving a life: Evidence from the labor market. In *Household production and consumption,* ed. Nestor E. Terleckyj, 265–98. New York: National Bureau of Economic Research.

United Nations. 1954. *Report on international definition and measurement of standards and levels of living.* New York: United Nations.

United Nations Development Programme (UNDP). 1990. *Human development report.* New York: United Nations Development Programme.

———. 1993. *Human development report.* New York: United Nations Development Programme.

———. 1994. *Human development report.* New York: United Nations Development Programme.

Usher, Dan. 1973. An imputation to the measure of economic growth for changes in life expectancy. In *The measurement of economic and social performance,* ed. Milton Moss. New York: Columbia University Press.

———. 1980. *The measurement of economic growth.* New York: Columbia University Press.

Viscusi, W. Kip. 1978. Wealth effects and earnings premiums for job hazards. *Review of Economics and Statistics* 60:408–16.

Waaler, Hans Th. 1984. Height, weight, and mortality: The Norwegian experience. *Acta Medica Scandinavica,* Suppl. 679.

Wachter, Kenneth W., and James Trussell. 1982. Estimating historical heights. *Journal of the American Statistical Association* 77:279–93.

Waterlow, J. C., and B. Schürch. 1994. Causes and mechanisms of linear growth retardation. *European Journal of Clinical Nutrition* 48 (Suppl. 1):1–216.

World Bank. 1993. *World development report.* Washington, D.C.: World Bank.

1   The Standard of Living Debate in International Perspective: Measures and Indicators

Stanley L. Engerman

1.1   Determining the Standard of Living

Probably the most famous debate on economic change has been that known as "the standard of living debate," about the impact of the British industrial revolution.[1] This debate began among individuals living in those times, continues today, and will go on, no doubt, tomorrow. The debate's vehemence has several distinct sources—the politics of the British class struggle, comparisons of British growth with the pattern of communist economic growth in the twentieth century, and more general questions of the attitudes toward society and culture that emerged in modern times.

Given the broad and emotion-laden sweep of the issues in the British case, it is perhaps surprising that no such prolonged debate has arisen for most of the other nations that developed subsequently. It is not that such debates could not have been generated elsewhere, for periods in which dramatic structural changes in the economy took place, with the expansion of urbanization and industrialization. Surely one might anticipate such concerns for late-nineteenth-century Germany or Japan. Perhaps it has been the earlier dating of the "First Industrial Revolution" in Britain, or maybe it was the focus of Marx and Engels on this case in their general discussions of the rise of capitalism, that made the British case so important a historical issue. For whatever reason, the concern with the changing standard of living has produced an extensive literature, with frequent appeals to various quantitative measures to represent economic growth and welfare. While what could be numerically measured was

Stanley L. Engerman is the John H. Munro Professor of Economics and professor of history at the University of Rochester and a research associate of the National Bureau of Economic Research.

The author wishes to thank Robert Gallman, David Eltis, David Galenson, Sherwin Rosen, and the attendees of the conference for useful suggestions and comments.

1. For recent examinations of this debate, see Lindert (1994) and Engerman (1994).

not the exclusive focus of the debate, numbers came to play a critical part in the analysis and rhetoric of the issues.

Other issues related to economic matters have arisen in some cases—for example, debates on the causes of out-migration in Scandinavia and Eastern Europe and on the economic and demographic effects of this immigration on those already resident in areas such as the United States, Canada, and Australia. These, however, seem to focus on narrower issues than does the British debate. There have recently been some signs of a debate emerging concerning the standard of living among the free population in the United States in colonial times and in the years before the Civil War, but at present it has not generated as much heat as has the British debate.[2] This may be because such a controversy would have seemed rather more surprising to residents of early-nineteenth-century New York than to residents of London at that same time.

The British debate poses two major questions, questions that have also been asked in regard to other issues. First, what can be said about changes pertaining to the entire national population, normally approached by considering per capita income, aggregate national income divided by the entire population? In answering such a question, collections of data by earlier scholars have presented much contemporary information, although later scholars have often been able to expand on these sources and to construct or reconstruct basic estimates of economic and demographic variables. Second, what has happened to the distribution of rewards (relatively or absolutely) among specific groups or individuals within the population? While some depiction of such patterns had been possible earlier, mainly by using measures that apply to specific parts of the population, such as real wages, answers to these questions have recently been facilitated by the application of the computer to the masses of individual-level data available in various public and private archives.

Many different types of measures have featured in the economic aspect of the standard of living debate—national income and wealth, per capita consumption, population, per capita income and wealth, consumption of various items, real wages, hours of work, mortality rates, heights, and so forth. Arguments relate to which measure, if any, deserves prominence, or else how best to aggregate the diverse constructs to come up with one simple summary number. In addition to these material issues, a range of concepts, each difficult to quantify, are debated, including relative changes in the rights of men, women, and children; expansion or contraction of political freedoms; changes in high-brow, middle-brow, and low-brow culture; and advantages and disadvantages of living in urban as contrasted with rural areas. All of these present major difficulties in evaluation, either separately or in combination with other material and nonmaterial components of the quality of life.[3]

2. See the discussions in Gallman and Wallis (1992).
3. The many debates on "progress," long a staple for historians and philosophers, will not be entered into, but they do illustrate that difficulty in agreeing on concepts and interpretations is not solely a characteristic of more quantitative and economically based debates. A recent examination

In this paper I shall not present a description of all the measures used to describe economic growth, nor an evaluation of the accuracy and interpretation of the broad set of measures that have been used in debates on economic change. Rather I shall attempt to place the discussion of some measures and indicators of economic change in perspective. In particular, I shall focus on two of the basic measures that have recently been used in examining economic progress, or its absence, national income estimates and physical measures of well-being, particularly heights of individuals.

1.2   Ideas of Progress

There have long been debates about the nature and existence of human progress over time, as well as about the comparative rankings of different nations and of different groups at particular times. These debates have referred to material progress, as well as political progress, cultural progress, and intellectual progress, and have been concerned both with the total population in a given area and with the behavior of specific groups within that population. Such comparisons, over time and place, have always been rather difficult to make, since it is often difficult to agree on the appropriate question, on the appropriate (conceptual) indicator, and on the best way to go from whatever information is available to the accurate measurement or description of that indicator. Moreover, given our customary desire to answer "yes" or "no," or "good" or "bad," to any question, difficulties may arise when more than one indicator can be used, or when they refer to quite different questions. This is particularly so when indicators present somewhat different patterns; this generates considerable dissatisfaction with the procedures and leads to a continuing search for the one single, unambiguous measure or concept for evaluation. That there may often be different concepts of progress and that any measurement or description must be severely limited by what information is available or can be applied to the past may, however, mean that for a number of distinct reasons any attempt to define one specific, all-purpose indicator is beyond our capacity.

Within the sphere of material changes the choice of measures to be used will depend on what information has been collected and made available by past agencies and individuals and how well it can be taken to represent what is desired. This need not mean that the measures we utilize are necessarily only those prepared in the past, as is shown by the importance of recent historical reconstructions of aggregate incomes and wealth and of their distributions. If we restricted ourselves to measures prepared in the past by official authorities, we would generally be confined to measures of population, foreign trade, government revenues and expenditures, and national debt. Population censuses on

of this set of issues can be found in Lasch (1991). For a broad discussion of "the idea of progress" by a leading economic historian, see Pollard (1968).

a continuing basis began in the nineteenth century, in 1790 for the United States. Despite the late-seventeenth-century emergence of a concept of national income, official governmental preparation of this measure did not begin until the 1930s. It is not usually true that contemporaries or earlier scholars prepared better estimates of economic variables than have subsequent scholars, as seen, for example, in the eighteenth-century debate on whether the population of England had increased or decreased, and also in the related debate between Hume and Wallace on the trend in population between the ancient and the modern worlds.[4] There are, of course, many fragments of incomplete data that have been used in examining changes in the past. These were often in the nature of partial indicators that are believed to be related to broader aggregates of interest, and which might serve as a proxy for the desired measure. Thus, for example, the earlier used measures of specie stocks and flows, of imports and exports, of urbanization, of nonagricultural workers, and so forth, were intended to serve as indexes of broader income measures, based either on theoretical arguments about economic relationships or else on some currently advocated empirical relationship with economic growth.

1.3 Early Measures of Economic Progress

It is perhaps not surprising, given the paucity of early data on aggregate economic variables, that most early measures of growth were based on physical concepts. In the eighteenth century population was seen as the primary measure of economic and social progress. This was stated rather concisely by David Hume: "But, if every thing be equal, it seems natural to expect, that, wherever there are most happiness and virtue, and wisest institutions, there will be the most people."[5] "The principle that Hume states here . . . was widely held in the seventeenth and eighteenth century" (Eugene F. Miller in Hume 1985, 382). Hume's debate with Wallace concerning the relative size of populations in the ancient and the modern worlds was premised on the contention that larger populations were a sign of human betterment. Thus the debate on numbers reflected an analysis of the moral and philosophical question of whether mankind had or had not progressed. Hume had proposed some other physical indicators for determining whether this was a "flourishing age of the world," including "stature and force of body, length of life," but argued that they were "in all ages, pretty much the same." They would be expected to change too slowly in the period for which there was a historical record (Hume 1985, 387–88).

---

4. For the eighteenth-century debate on the trend in English population, see Price (1780), Howlett (1968), and Young (1967). Price based his argument on the use of excise tax collections, home building, house counts, and bills of mortality. The arguments for an eighteenth-century population decline did not convince, among others, Smith (1976, 344). For more recent discussions, see Glass (1973, 11–89), Bonar (1966), and Pearson (1978, 370–421).

5. See Hume's "Of the Populousness of Ancient Nations," in Hume (1985). The quotation is from p. 382.

While Hume discussed the relationship between economic growth and population, other writers in the seventeenth and eighteenth centuries used other physical measures to depict changes over time. In England, in the debate on progress versus decay ("moderns versus ancients"), advocates drew on indicators of height and life expectation, as well as population size, in making their arguments.[6] While little in the way of acceptable empirical evidence could be presented, one of the major participants in these debates, George Hakewill (1630, 198–99, 203–8), argued for the use of evidence from the sizes of, among other things, armor, beds, doors, altars, and seats and suggested the use of "bones dug up" to indicate changes in stature over time.[7]

The use of population as a proxy for economic progress was frequent in the mercantilist literature, where population growth was also seen as a way to achieve national power (Schumpeter 1954, 251; see also United Nations 1973, 1:35–37). Similarly, the early classical economists, including Adam Smith, argued that "what encourages the progress of population and improvement, encourages that of real wealth and greatness" (Smith 1976, 566). Even though Malthus pointed to the negative aspects of population growth, he notes that "favourable circumstances" in the English North American colonies, economically and politically, led to a population that had "a rapidity of increase probably without parallel in history" (Malthus 1970, 105). As long as the resources were there, population could increase without adding to human misery. Under different circumstances, however, a larger population would lead to difficulties. This set of differences made the use of population size as an index of progress more limited, even at a time when more reliable numbers on the sizes of populations were, for the first time, becoming available.

Although the size or rate of growth of population by itself is now seldom used as an indicator of economic progress, it has frequently been used as part of the definition used to determine the presence of economic growth. Kuznets's primary definition of economic growth, based on the observed pattern of modern economic growth, is that of a sustained rise in per capita output accompanied by a sustained rise in population (see, e.g., Kuznets 1966, 19–20).[8] Such a concern with population increase referred mainly to questions about the interpretation of the economic performance of Ireland, whose quite rapid post-famine growth in per capita income had been preceded, or perhaps caused, by

6. For summaries of these debates, see Jones (1961), Harris (1949), and Spadafora (1990, 21–84). The last book also includes much of interest for England and Scotland for the entire eighteenth century.

7. Hakewill's third book (1630, 154–286) in this work deals with "the pretended decay of mankinde in regard to age and duration, of strength and stature, of arts and wits." Various of the Greek and Roman historians did mention heights, life expectation, and relative population sizes, but these were not generally used as the basis for arguments about changes over time. The preparation of life tables by Halley (1942, 6) led him to argue that these tables "give a more just *Idea* of the *State* and *Condition* of *Mankind* than anything yet extant that I know of."

8. Kuznets (1965, 6, 10) also argued that since "a combination of secular stagnation or decline of population with a sustained rise in per capita product has been observed only rarely in the last two centuries," these nations lack the common experience of modern economic growth that would help in drawing meaningful generalizations. See also United Nations (1973, 1:505–19).

population decline due to high mortality, reduced fertility, and extensive out-migration (Kuznets 1959, 20–21).[9] There are, however, several historiographic antecedents that remain of relevance, where population changes may have meant that total income and per capita income moved in different directions. The debate on the economic circumstances of the Renaissance relates to its actual economic conditions in a time of apparent population decline, with the otherwise relatively limited economic data suggesting little increase in aggregate income.[10] R. A. Bridbury's depiction of the Black Death as the Marshall Plan of the Middle Ages may seem rather severe, but it does raise an important historical question—Were the deaths in the fourteenth century due to exogenously caused diseases or were they the endogenous economic outcome of prior rapid expansion of population beyond the capacity of England's resources?[11] Further, the interpretation of the settlement of the New World could look quite different if we begin with Native American GNP in 1491 and make explicit allowance for the overall population declines after the arrival of Columbus. The interpretation of this decline might vary depending on whether these demographic patterns were attributed primarily to disease, to warfare, or to other factors.[12]

In addition to population, other physical measures were used as indicators of past economic progress, both by contemporaries and by subsequent scholars. Macaulay, in his depiction of British economic growth written at the end of the industrial revolution, discusses population growth and notes several other favorable indicators, including decreased mortality and greater life expectation, and increased real wages (Macaulay 1849, chap. 3). Contemporaries often pointed to the comparative heights in different countries as indicators of differential welfare and living standards.[13] Some comparisons of military height standards over time, to indicate deterioration in living standards among the

9. See also Mokyr (1983) for a description and analysis of the causes and consequences of the Irish Famine.

10. See, e.g., the selections from Robert S. Lopez and Hans Baron in Dannenfeldt (1959); Lopez (in Dannenfeldt 1959, 50) commented in regard to interpretations linking artistic and economic flourishings that "the notion that wherever there was an economic peak we must also find an intellectual peak, and vice versa, has long enjoyed the unquestioned authority of mathematical postulate."

11. "For the survivors, the fourteenth-century famines were, no doubt, on personal grounds, inexpressibly grievous. But they unlocked a cornucopia. England was given a sort of Marshall Aid on a stupendous scale" (Bridbury 1962, 91). Postan (1966, 565–70) argued that increased real wages in England in the fourteenth century reflect the decline in labor supply and population due to increased mortality. The issue posed by endogeneity or exogeneity of population change remains central to many discussions of the welfare significance of changes in per capita incomes.

12. It probably took more than three centuries before the population of the Americas reachieved the pre-Columbian level. This also raises another issue concerning estimates where there may be explicit or implicit disagreement as to the specific groups whose welfare is considered to be appropriately evaluated. This arises also in the appropriate definition of national income in a society with slavery, and of how to balance free and slave height changes in such societies.

13. See, e.g., some of the descriptions regarding the Americas in Gerbi (1973, 5–6, 53–56, 82–86, 240–45, 508–11). This debate included evaluations not only of relative human heights but also the sizes of animals and plants.

lower classes in Europe in the nineteenth century, were presented by Karl Marx, quoting the work of J. von Liebig (Marx 1906, 264; see also pp. 221, 434).[14] Estimates of mortality and life expectation had been, as noted earlier, proposed quite early as central measures of human welfare. More recent discussions by Sen and others have suggested that mortality data can be used to analyze economic performance, and life expectation has become a key component in the composite indices of welfare and the quality of life prepared by Morris D. Morris and by the World Bank.[15]

1.4   Estimating National Income

The list of social and economic indicators that have been utilized as measures of, or proxies for, economic growth seems almost unlimited, constrained only by what numbers are available and the imagination of the investigator. It is often unclear exactly what these measures are intended to demonstrate and how to interpret them. In some cases, they seem to be meant as direct indicators of the concept (whether related only to a specific economic sector or as a useful indicator to be applied more generally). In other cases, they seem meant primarily as proxies related to the concept used because of the absence of an appropriate direct measure, while at still other times they are apparently part of some theory of either the causes or the consequences of economic change. Early discussions included, in addition to population estimates, exports (and their components), imports (and their components), shipping, public debt, specie supply, and urban population, while later the more frequently added variables included steel production, railroad miles, freight car loadings, percentage literate, and occupational structure.[16] Extrapolations were sometimes made on the basis of regional tax collections, particularly those on real estate, or from housing counts. Wealth in real and personal property was often made the basis

14. Von Liebig had noted that "in general and within certain limits, exceeding the medium size of their kind, is evidence of the prosperity of organic beings. As to man, his bodily height lessens if his due growth is interfered with, either by physical or social conditions."

15. See Sen (1993), Morris (1979), and United Nations Development Programme (1994). For discussions of the relation of mortality to per capita income, see, among others, Preston (1975) and Kunitz and Engerman (1992). For an interesting examination of "Expectation of Life as an Index of Social Progress," see Hart and Hertz (1944). Of course, not all additional years of life may yield positive utility, as suggested by the Greek myth of Aurora and Tithonus, in which Aurora requests "eternal life" but, unfortunately, not "eternal youth" for Tithonus. Or, as the Indian philosopher quoted in Plutarch's chapter on Alexander responded to the question "How long is it good for a man to live?"—"So long as he does not regard death as better than life."

16. Smithies (1946, 68) described an interesting sidelight to the Dawes negotiations regarding German reparations after World War I. It was argued that the burden should be proportional to national income, but since national income was regarded as an ambiguous number, they utilized a "prosperity index," based on "combining indexes of total exports and imports, revenues and expenditures of the federal and chief state governments, tonnage carried by the railroads, consumption of sugar, tobacco, beer, and liquor, population, and per capita consumption of coal." Writing in 1949, Smithies stated his belief that given the greater availability of "statistical material" (69), national income will now more frequently be used for such international arrangements.

of interregional comparisons, when such data were collected, as in the United States between 1850 and 1870. Various measures of outputs and inputs based on U.S. census collections of production data after 1840 were made central to contemporary discussions, particularly those comparing the North and South in the antebellum United States. This discussion led to several antebellum preparations of national income estimates, two of which have been deemed reasonably respectable (see Gallman 1961). A most imaginative measure was proposed by John Clapham, based on the quality of rags, but it is not clear that he ever systematically pursued this analysis.[17]

Most of us have been raised with the measure of national income per capita as the central concept for determining and measuring economic progress, and with the use of distributions of individual or family incomes as the basis for evaluating relative changes in economic well-being over time. These measures are derived, ultimately, from production and demographic data. The broader the extent of governmental and private data collection, the less the need for interpolation or extrapolation, and the more reliable will seem the resulting estimates. Nevertheless, many issues of inclusion and exclusion of items persist. Even with the attempts at standardization of definition and with its preparation by various governmental and international agencies, differences remain in what, precisely, is being measured as national income. Even if there could be agreement on the precise nature of the measure, the translation from specific amounts of goods and services to a belief in what this measure might represent for human welfare remains uncertain.

Standardized preparation by governments of national income accounts was in most cases a product of the depression of the 1930s, when the interest was in determining for policy purposes the magnitude of the economic problem, and of World War II, when the need for large-scale planning made knowledge of the scope and nature of the broad economy vital. Otherwise, it was a product of the post–World War II concern with aiding the growth of the then underdeveloped nations. The timing of national income preparation reflects also the dominance at the time of Keynesian approaches to macroeconomic policy and measurement. These various considerations, and their changing nature, have had a significant impact on the construction of national income accounts, influencing choices as to what to include and what to exclude, and the choice of what particular breakdowns of the national income total should be used. Prior to these governmental attempts, however, there had been numerous estimates of national income prepared by individual observers in several countries, and for various reasons, frequently to determine relative national power. Paul Studenski's (1958) study of the history of the income of nations presents a rela-

---

17. He claimed that "this is a sure test; for prosperous nations and classes throw away their clothes early" (Clapham 1961, 406–7). He did make some rough comparisons, claiming that "English specialists noted, in the ten years before the war [World War I], that German rags were not quite so good as they used to be," and "the best rags on the market are American and Canadian; the worst Italian and Greek."

tively full description of those pre-twentieth-century income estimates prepared by authors in England, France, Russia, the United States, Austria, Germany, Australia, Switzerland, Greece, India, Italy, and Norway, generally based on census and tax records, although several, particularly those before the nineteenth century, were based on imaginative constructions from quite limited partial data.[18]

The first estimate of national income, as opposed to national wealth, is generally attributed to William Petty, in 1665, although these estimates were not published until a quarter-century later (Petty 1899, 98–120).[19] More familiar to most, given their frequent appearance as a demographic and economic starting point for the study of modern British economic and social history, are the estimates of Gregory King for the year 1688. First published in 1696 and influenced, according to Studenski, by the writings of Petty, King's (1936) estimates rested primarily on information from various taxes, although other data sources were also employed.[20] Two innovations were made by King: (1) a comparison of years between 1688 and 1695 to see what the effects of England's wars had been and (2) a comparison of the per capita incomes of England, France, and Holland. There were several other calculations of a national income total for eighteenth- and nineteenth-century England (Studenski 1958, 101–19; Deane 1956, 1957). In addition to those by King, Studenski (1958, 140–41) also described two pre-1900 estimates of comparative per capita national incomes. Leone Levi's (1860) brief and unexplained comparison of Eng-

18. Studenski also provided a review of the various debates and disagreements on the concept of national income and how it is to be measured. Another rather complete discussion of issues and problems is to be found in the pioneering work of Simon Kuznets, most explicitly, in Kuznets (1941). Many of the volumes in the Conference on Research in Income and Wealth series contain important conceptual and practical discussions of the measurement of national income. Of particular interest are volume 20, *Problems in the International Comparison of Economic Accounts* (1957), particularly Kendrick's introduction and Kravis's essay, with comments by Jacob Viner, and volume 22, *A Critique of the United States Income and Product Accounts* (1958), particularly Jaszi's opening essay and Easterlin's comments. Also of interest are Clark (1957) and Rostow (1990, 209–22). Other surveys of the background of national income accounting are Kendrick (1972), Carson (1975), and Steckel (1992); the last also examined the use of heights as a measure of changing living standards.

19. The title of this essay is "Verbum Sapienti." See also "Political Arithmetick" (Petty 1899, 232–313), probably completed in 1676 but not published until 1690. Petty also computed "the value of the People," the capitalized value of the stock of human capital; made comparisons of the economic conditions of Holland, England, France, Scotland, and Ireland; and in "The Political Anatomy of Ireland," written in 1672 and published in 1691, noted that "for their Shape, Stature, Colour, and Complexion, I see nothing in them inferior to other People" (201). In describing policies for the Irish he argued that "their Lazing seems to me to proceed rather from want of Employment and Encouragement to Work" than from any natural factors. See Kiker (1968, 1–4) for a discussion of Petty's concept of human capital.

20. See Studenski (1958, 30–37) and Deane (1955). For another discussion of Petty and King (as well as of contemporaneous estimates of mortality and life expectation), see Pearson (1978). Pearson included a rather interesting 1796 calculation by the mathematician Lagrange, based on some material collected by the chemist Lavoisier, to attempt to determine whether France was self-sufficient in food during the wars (628–35). See also Studenski (1958, 68–75). For a broad view of the early development of "statistics as a social science," see Porter (1986, 17–39).

land, France, Russia, and Austria indicated that England had by far the highest income.[21] Michael Mulhall, in his 1899 *Dictionary of Statistics,* one of his very imaginative collections of data and calculations, presented, for 1885, per capita income estimates for 14 European countries, plus the United States, Canada, Australia, and Argentina.[22] In the United States, Ezra Seaman, in 1852, presented comparative data on per capita incomes in France, the Netherlands, and England and Wales, as well as the United States, with the English having the highest income.[23]

The concept of national income and its usefulness have thus long been recognized and discussed, but it was only with the basic work of Simon Kuznets that a more theoretical as well as empirical basis of estimation was applied to the measurement of national income. There were, of course, others working on these issues in the United States and elsewhere. Occasional early estimates had been conceptually more sophisticated than most customary estimates of the times, such as those by Seaman in the United States and by Timothy Coughlan in Australia.[24] No earlier estimates anywhere, however, were as detailed, systematic, and analytical as they were in the works of Kuznets, once he turned to the estimation of national income in the United States during the interwar period.[25]

The basic question of what should or should not be included in national income poses many problems, and it is often extremely difficult to be consistent, particularly if one wishes to relate national income to welfare.[26] Some activities that occur in the market are generally excluded, if they are illegal and if legality is considered among the criteria for inclusion in national income.

---

21. Such calculations do not seem to appear in some of his subsequent work, such as Levi (1880). Levi (1885, 25–27), drawing on the British Academy of Social Sciences studies of height, suggested the use of such measures for determining changes in well-being but commented that "there is no reliable evidence of the physique of the people at any distinct period." He pointed to the 1882 report of the British Association for the Advancement of Science, "which will afford a useful standard whereby to compare their future progress," but since "no such observations were made before" there are no "reliable data" for current comparisons.

22. Mulhall (1899, 320). The United Kingdom had the highest European income but lagged behind the United States and Australia. Mulhall briefly described the underlying basis of his calculations, based on census data for the various countries.

23. Seaman (1852, 418–68). In addition to contemporary data drawn from "official valuations made by government officers in detail . . . for purposes of taxation" (439), Seaman gives estimates for the three European countries going back to 1200, "taking into consideration the present condition and productive industry of Mexico and South America" (438–39).

24. On Seaman, see Gallman (1961). On Coughlan, see Studenski (1958, 135–37) and Snooks (1993, 143–50; 1994, 152–54). While both provided some brief explanations of the specifics of measurement and understood the distinction between gross output and value-added, neither went into much detail on either concepts or measurement.

25. For some background on the political aspects of the U.S. government's adoption of national income accounts, see Perlman (1987).

26. For some, among many, useful discussions of the relation between measured income and welfare, in addition to those by Kuznets, see Abramovitz (1959, 1989), Denison (1971), Usher (1968, 1980), and Pigou (1929). For some broad economic discussions of the meaning of welfare, see also Scitovsky (1976), Hirsch (1978), and Zolotas (1981). An important extension of conventional national income accounts is Eisner (1989). See also Kendrick (1976) for the measurement of a broader definition of capital, and the discussion by Engerman and Rosen (1980).

The debate on the Smithian conception, adopted by marxists, of restricting consideration to material production is quite familiar but can probably now be considered resolved (see Studenski 1958, 181–88). Restriction to market transactions, however it might be considered desirable, is difficult, particularly since changes in economic structure will affect the extent to which various activities are performed in the market.[27] Those variations in the locus of family and individual activity that have taken place, whether related to the process of economic change or due to other factors, have long been the source of controversy in using national income accounts. Some of these problems could be solved by imputations of value, based on actual or hypothetical market transactions, but a large area of disagreement will no doubt remain.

Among the major disputes about national income accounting is that concerning the value of the spouse's time in the household, and the contribution of cooking, cleaning, child care, and so forth, to measured output.[28] At present this work time is not included in national income, reflecting in part the development of systematic national income accounting in the depression of the 1930s, although the argument for its inclusion has long been known and earlier calculations made (Kuznets 1941, 432–33; Studenski 1958, 177–78).[29] A. C. Pigou's 1920 remark that "if a man marries his housekeeper or his cook, the national dividend is diminished," presents a frequently discussed "paradox" (Pigou 1929, 32–33).[30] Ten years earlier, Philip Wicksteed posed a related problem, combined with what he regarded as the difficulties posed by "inherently vicious activities":

> The "services" for which the wages of shame are paid constitute a part of the national revenue as much as any other; but if Portia is Brutus's wife and not his harlot her companionship ceases to count in the national revenue. And, moreover, any changes in the tastes, habits, or morals of the community which enabled them to derive increased enjoyment from their own personal activities or their mutual intercourse would tell for nothing in the estimates of national wealth. (1910, 651)

27. See the discussion in Kuznets (1953, 192–252).

28. See, e.g., Folbre and Abel (1989) and Folbre and Wagman (1993), and the works cited therein, as well as Snooks (1994). This debate goes back to quite early in the preparation of national income accounts, as seen in the writings of Seaman (1846) and W. I. King (1969). King (1969, 133–35) noted the role of value-added by housewives, which when shifted to the factory raised income as measured, in addition to the problems due to the "disappearance" of free goods. Solomon Fabricant's introduction to this volume is quite useful.

29. Kuznets's estimate for 1929 was that housewives' services were about one-fourth of total national income, in reasonable approximation to the estimates made by Snooks for Australia and Folbre and Wagman for the United States. Ezra Seaman (1846, 305) spoke of adding various services, including "ordinary domestic labour" to estimated income, and this treatment of all services raised income by about one-third. In 1852, however, he excluded from the "rank of productive industry, housekeeping, the labor of domestic servants," and other services, on the basis that they are not material products.

30. Similarly, Pigou notes that if a woman leaves "factory work or paid home-work to unpaid home-work," the national dividend also, paradoxically, falls.

Various estimates of the value of a housewife's time using wages in domestic service and other measures had been made by those preparing earlier national income accounts, including Kuznets, but these were made primarily for illustrative purposes and were not included in the basic estimates of national income, which were generally restricted to transactions in the market.[31] Since the national accounts do not impose any breakdown of consumption within the home and the family unit itself, no division relating to the importance of changes between spouses is estimated. The present treatment of household production is not intended to answer questions concerning changes in the relative benefits and costs to the different spouses. Not all of the gross output in the household is omitted from national income, however, only the amount of value-added by the labor within the household. As Robert Gallman (1966) pointed out, the basic raw materials going to household production of food, clothing, and so forth, are already included as part of national income.[32]

In considering the family unit there are other issues of imputations that might be raised. If children are regarded as the outcome of a choice that could have led to more leisure or more parental consumption, is it appropriate to ignore the utility provided to parents in excess of the costs of a child's consumption of market goods? If children are desired, should the more appropriate denominator of the national income calculation be per family rather than per capita? Can we attribute an effect on imputed income of the fertility decline in the demographic transition, due either to changed demand for numbers of children or for "quality-adjusted" children, whether or not these are regarded as reflecting a change in tastes? And how will such an adjustment influence the measure of economic growth in recent times?

Some types of imputations for nonmarket consumption are considerably less controversial and are conceptually and empirically easier to make, as they can be based on market prices for closely related items that are subject to frequent transactions. These include imputations for food grown and consumed on a farm, without entering the market, and for owner-occupied housing, which does not involve a market transaction for its periodic rental.

Other forms of imputations, since they are not strictly based on market exchange, present more complex problems. Among the concomitants of modern

31. Indeed, the first set of national income accounts that also provided an estimate for the value of housewife services, by Mitchell et al. (1921, 57–60, 67), placed it at equal to about 25–31 percent of measured national income. A detailed worldwide survey of the estimated value of housewife services, by Goldschmidt-Clermont (1982), has almost all values falling within the range of 20–40 percent of national income or GNP.

For an analysis of the 1890 census adjusting female labor force participation for boarding housekeepers, unpaid agricultural family farm workers, and some manufacturing workers, see Goldin (1990, 42–55, 219–27). She estimated that "the inclusion of these activities increases the participation rate of married women across the entire economy by about 10 percentage points."

For a different approach to the evaluation of housewife's services, based on nineteenth-century legal cases, see Segal (1994).

32. There may, of course, be some disagreement about how to value this labor time, depending on whether alternative uses of labor were available.

economic growth has been a reduction in the time worked per surviving capita, with fewer hours per day, days per year, and years per lifetime worked. There have been several attempts to value this leisure, on the presumption that its increase has been voluntary and not involuntary. At the margin, the value of voluntary leisure would be evaluated at the wage rate, while the value to be placed on involuntary leisure is less obvious. A similar outcome for the measure of growth could be obtained by shifting from output per capita to output per man-hour. Familiar estimates of the value of increased leisure, by Kuznets (1952) for 1869–1948 and by Nordhaus and Tobin (1972) for 1929–65, demonstrate the great impact this adjustment has on measured consumption.[33] Similarly influential, but with somewhat more complexity, is the consumption value of increased life expectation, first proposed by Dan Usher and estimated by Usher for Canada and several other countries and by Jeffrey Williamson for Britain (Usher 1980, 223–57; Williamson 1984). These provide, in effect, composite measures of goods and services output and life expectation, with their own particular set of weights, at least to the extent that increased life expectation was not attributed to increases in measured consumption. (Presumably, if utility or market gain could be applied to height, the same procedure could be tried.)

Another set of suggested imputations requires the use of hedonic price regressions to obtain appropriate "prices," since no adequate direct analogue can be provided in the market. Noteworthy here is the analysis of the costs of the "dark satanic mills" of England conducted by Williamson (1981) on the basis of a regression of the argued for disutility-causing aspects of urban life—mortality and density.[34] Possible offsetting gains from urban residence (privacy, entertainment, and culture) are, however, not fully examined and evaluated. Since the historical debates have frequently regarded movement to an urban residence as a negative factor, Williamson's test of the factors in the urban-rural wage differential does point to procedures useful to those who wish to adjust national income estimates rather than keep various components of welfare separate for discussions.[35]

In addition to the complexities of estimating measured income, the interpretation of changes in measured income as demonstrating changes in welfare has a number of other important problems. While prices can be a measure of relative marginal scarcity, they need not reflect the full benefits of a priced good or the value of an unpriced one to consumers. The Smithian evaluation prob-

33. See, e.g., the calculation by Kuznets (1952, 63–69) and Nordhaus and Tobin (1973), who discuss some of the complexities involved in these imputations. See also Usher (1980, 135–47).

34. The subsequent exchange between Pollard and Williamson points to some of the problems in trying to evaluate these issues, such as the various problems in determining causes of death and in getting better measures of what influences worker decisions.

35. Other measures of the cost of "disamenities of urbanization" are based on regressions including population density in trying to explain differentials in income. See Nordhaus and Tobin (1973) and, for a later discussion of this set of issues, Roback (1982). Kuznets (1952, 60–62) used estimated price differentials by city size to adjust for costs of increased urbanization.

lem posed by the diamond-water paradox and also Lord Lauderdale's distinction of public wealth and individual riches, based on property ownership, reflect complications in the use of market prices.[36] The use of market prices based on transactions with some specific distribution of income was questioned by Wicksteed (1910, 649–59), who argued that redistribution of income could change market evaluations, a point that was central to the discussion of welfare economics criteria in the 1940s and 1950s. The discussion of prices and their meaning thus raises issues as to whether these prices contain all desired welfare information and also, more simply, as to what might be regarded as the appropriate set of weights to be applied when aggregating individual outputs into national income totals.

A related problem, one early noted as a paradox by Pigou, was that "the frequent desecration of natural beauty through the hunt for coal or gold, or through the more blatant forms of commercial advertisement, must, on our definition, leave the national dividend intact" (1929, 33). Important issues about the most appropriate treatment of the depletion of natural resources and of pollution have recently been raised. Unpriced pollution and other disamenities serve to raise questions about the precise meaning of current income measures, as based on estimates of their costs by Roback (1982) and Nordhaus and Tobin (1973). Such resource depletion and pollution can both influence our beliefs regarding current levels of income (welfare) and affect prospects for future economic growth. Further, whether differences in current levels of income provide the best forecast of differences in future levels of income, even when allowing for differential levels of investment, public and private, is not easy to evaluate, particularly given the uncertainty of exogenous changes in the economic environment and of the economy's ability to respond to them.[37]

Working in a direction opposite to these costs of growth are some benefits of growth that are either unpriced or priced at an inappropriate level. Benefits such as clean water, a healthier atmosphere, and safer transportation are often not priced, while the nature of quality changes in existing goods or the introduction of new goods (which are at times functionally equivalent to existing products) means that there are benefits that are usually undervalued when entered into the national income accounts. Given the magnitude of such new and improved goods in the process of economic growth, it is expected that this factor will cause some understatement of long-term economic growth and its contribution to welfare.[38]

---

36. Smith (1976, 44–45) made a distinction between "value in use" and "value in exchange" and claimed that "the things which have the greatest value in use have little or no value in exchange," and vice versa. Lauderdale (1819, 39–110) commented, "the wealth of the nation, and the mass of individual riches, cannot be regarded in every respect the same" (45).

37. Such difficulties in linking present and future measures exist, of course, for any particular measure chosen. This can be seen, e.g., by the comparisons of Irish and English heights before the Irish Famine, and by the discussion of the effects of wars on various economies.

38. For a recent discussion of this issue, applied mainly to producer and consumer durables, see Gordon (1990).

The distinction between final goods and intermediate goods has also long presented difficulties of both theory and measurement. The conceptual distinction between final output in a slave and that in a free society, noted by Seaman, has been further discussed recently. More generally, however, as Kuznets pointed out, the costs to a free individual of earning his or her living, including the necessary food input and clothing costs, could be considered intermediate inputs into the economic system in redefining final outputs, although Kuznets concluded by rejecting this because he regarded human wants as the basic end of the system (Kuznets 1941, 36–45; Studenski 1958, 188–94).[39] More recently, John Wallis and Douglass North (1986) estimated the magnitude of the increased transactions costs of doing business in a modern economy, arguing that much of the output of the service sector should more reasonably be regarded as intermediate not final outputs.[40] Variations on this problem were investigated in detail by Kuznets in a comparison of national incomes in China and in the United States, as well as in his examination of the role of the government sector in the economy (Kuznets 1941, 31–36; 1953, 145–91; Studenski 1958, 194–204).

The philosophical complexities of treating what have been called "regrettable necessities" in national income comparisons have also long been discussed. Some of these reflect, in part, the impact of climatic and other forces on needs and relative evaluations.[41] There are also items of expenditure, such as for war or defense, that do not directly provide welfare as usually argued but do play a crucial role (as do what we call intermediate goods) in offsetting what might otherwise have been more difficult individual or societal circumstances.

1.5   Alternative Concepts of Welfare

Because of these many different problems, as well as others not mentioned, such as the general index number (and quality difference) problems in making international comparisons and comparisons over time, some dissatisfaction with measures of national income has emerged. This has led to the search for alternative indicators to be used to evaluate economic change. Such measures are generally based on some available social and economic indicators that, it is argued, are related somewhat more directly to economic welfare, as either cause or consequence, than a single national income estimate. The League of Nations and its International Labor Office focused on studies of the importance

---

39. Various other measured consumption components, such as education, health care, and migration, may also be regarded as forms of investment, with additions for their opportunity costs, including time.

40. See also the discussion of this paper by Lance Davis.

41. Usher (1968) provided a detailed recomputation of national income differentials between Thailand and the United Kingdom based primarily on price differences in the two economies. As is well known, for international comparisons of income it can make a considerable difference depending upon which price indexes are used for the examination.

of nutrition in the 1930s.[42] In the 1940s and 1950s the search for nonmonetary measures was pursued by various economists in the United States and elsewhere, as well as by several United Nations commissions.[43] Bennett (1951), for example, used 16 nonmonetary measures of relative consumption to compare nations, achieving a single index by an arbitrary weighting scheme applied to relative data. The UN study listed considerably more items, rejecting the usefulness of national income for welfare measures since "no type of monetary index as a general international measure of levels of living could be recommended" (United Nations 1954, vi). They did not, however, provide any theoretical resolution of what measures to include, or of how to weight items in order to obtain a single index to be used for comparative purposes. Such listings of items have long been used, often to supplement income comparisons, and to indicate what economic growth has meant, without necessarily being seen as a replacement for income estimates. As presented by Stanley Lebergott (1976, 1993), for example, their principal purpose has been to bring out the dramatic changes meant by economic growth, which are highlighted by giving attention to the creation and diffusion of some specific items (see also U.S. Department of Labor, n.d.).

One of the major characteristics of economic growth has been constant change in the structure of the economy, due to shifting patterns of consumption and production. Changes in consumption patterns are best described by Engel's law, which gives the expected variation in expenditure patterns with changes in income, whether over time or in a cross section (see, e.g., Kuznets 1966, 262–84). Perhaps the most firmly supported part of Engel's law is that as income rises, the share of consumption expenditures on food declines, even as the absolute amount expended continues to rise. Applied to nations this would mean that estimates of growth based only on food consumption will understate the rate of economic growth, at least as compared with the rate estimated from conventional national income accounts. Since it is expected that height will increase with increased food consumption, not increased total consumption, it is anticipated that as income and consumption increase height should increase less than proportionately. If income elasticities for food consumption are known, however, growth in income can be estimated from growth in food consumption. It would seem, then, that income is the preferred index, with food

42. See, e.g., League of Nations (1937) and International Labor Office (1936). The League of Nations report used conscription data for northern and Western Europe to argue that "there was undoubtedly an increase in stature" (25–26). These increases were Sweden (1840–1926) 8 cm, Denmark (1840–1913) 8 cm, Norway (1800–1900) 10 cm, and the Netherlands (1850–1907) about 5 inches. It mentioned that similar results were observed for "male and female students at American universities." They attributed some of this to increased outputs, particularly of food. They then tried to disentangle the effects of "the economic and medical" factors in this change in health and concluded, based on comparisons of timing, that it was the economic forces that played a "perhaps dominant role."

43. See, e.g., Bennett (1937, 1951), Davis (1945), and United Nations (1954). Some earlier discussions of the issue of standards and their measurement can be found in Zimmerman (1936), Eliot (1931), and works cited in Lamale (1958).

consumption used primarily as a proxy for the desired measure, not itself being the welfare concept.

1.6   New Indexes of Welfare

More recently, several attempts at simpler composite measures with fewer, but hopefully more essential, categories have been made. One such index, presented by Morris D. Morris in 1979, the Physical Quality of Life Index, is based on three measures: infant mortality, life expectancy at age one, and literacy rates. These variables all have reasonable, but not perfect, correlations with levels of national income. Morris detailed his procedures of calculation and weighting, but the weighting is, as it must be, somewhat arbitrary. Starting with its 1990 *Human Development Report,* the United Nations has prepared a Human Development Index (HDI) as a "contribution" to the search "for a better, more comprehensive socio-economic measure" (United Nations Development Programme 1994). It is described as "an alternative to GNP for measuring the relative socio-economic progress of nations. It enables people and their governments to evaluate progress over time—and to determine priorities for policy intervention. It also permits instructive comparisons of the experiences in different countries." As the authors indicate, both the contents and the methods of calculating the HDI have been adjusted, and estimates for various subgroups as well as for the nation have been introduced. The basic variables that went into HDI estimates in 1994 were life expectancy, adult literacy, mean years of schooling, and real GDP per capita. The principle underlying the combination of these different concepts is to provide a common measuring rod for "the socio-economic distance travelled," based on "a minimum and a maximum for each dimension." The concept of the HDI was extended in a study by Partha Dasgupta (1993, 108–16) to include measures of both political rights and civil rights, in order to provide an "inter-country comparison of the quality of life." Unlike the United Nations, however, Dasgupta presented his summary rankings in ordinal, not cardinal, form. For all listed countries, the correlation of rankings between this index and per capita income are reasonable but not perfect, but the breakdown into developed nations in contrast with developing nations is basically the same. What additional guides this measure provides for the planning of policy that are not also given by GNP (and its related indexes) is not clear, except perhaps that it encourages a focus on making improvements primarily in regard to the specific variables that go into the index.

The discussion thus far has focused on the measurement of aggregate national income averaged over the population and on various indexes of the quality of life. Such measures say nothing about the distribution of income among members of society, nor about how the distribution of income changed over time with the process of economic growth. Kuznets suggested a U-shaped relation between income equality and economic growth, with inequality increasing in the early stage of economic expansion and then declining as growth proceeds.[44] While others have found this pattern to be widespread, the overall shape of the income distribution as well as the actual changes for each particular individual or family seem to follow no obvious pattern. As the debates on welfare criteria have shown, comparisons of two situations are difficult when it cannot be argued that each and every individual has been made better off absolutely (here putting aside those issues arising when there are interdependent utilities and when utilities are based on relative positions), and when no real-world compensation of losers by gainers can be undertaken. Presumably, however, this type of distributional problem exists for any attempt at a single index, unless we believe with certainty that the underlying distribution around that average number is known and can be related to changes in the mean.

1.7   Heights as a Welfare Measure

In the past two decades there has been considerable work, as this volume demonstrates, using another index of economic change to describe the historical past—heights of individuals at specified ages.[45] This approach to social and economic change has long been known and utilized, as James Tanner has amply demonstrated, and the use of height as a measure of well-being, with information about heights frequently coming from military data, has been undertaken in many Continental countries. Height is an attractive measure since it was used as a primary source for the identification and recognition of individuals. Moreover, in the case of the military, reported height was the result of direct measurement under quite specific conditions. A wide variety of sources going back for long periods—farther back than the data required to prepare systematic estimates of national income—have been found that contain data on heights, such as military records, shipping records for convicts, slaves, and indentured servants, criminal records, runaway slave advertisements, slave registrations, school records, and records of public and private agencies. While military records have been almost exclusively for males of adult or near adult age, other sources have permitted estimation of heights for women and children. In addition to achieved adult heights, it has been possible to measure rates of change in heights at preadult ages, and to make comparisons not only for one country over time but also for different nations. Further, this has led to

44. On trends in income distribution, see also Williamson (1991) and Adelman and Morris (1973). At issue is not only the distribution at any moment of time but also the changes in the relative and absolute positions of various individuals and generations over time, the question of social mobility. For an examination of some early measures in the United States of the distribution of wealth and income by size, see Merwin (1939), and the discussion by Kuznets.

45. Because of the focus of this volume, I will not provide a more complete set of citations but will restrict myself mainly to general observations. For discussions of the study of heights in history and by economic historians, see Tanner (1981), Harris (1994), Fogel (1986, 1993), Komlos (1994, 1995), Floud, Wachter, and Gregory (1990), and Steckel (1992); see also Kunitz (1987).

some expansion in the use of physical measures to describe well-being, including data on birthweights, reflecting maternal conditions, and the body mass index (BMI), a composite measure of the present height and weight of individuals.[46]

Given the widely discussed and often believed expected relationship between height and nutrition, and the relationship between nutritional input and per capita income, and given that usable height data exist for times and places where reliable national income estimates are not available, it was initially thought that heights could serve as a useful proxy for income in those cases where no estimates of the latter had been presented. The initial studies of heights suggested a quite reasonable correlation between heights and income, both when dealing with growth in one country and when comparing different countries during similar time periods. These early studies had to deal with two major problems, one statistical, one conceptual. Because of the importance of military data, and the facts that the military did not accept everyone who was examined, for health and other reasons, and that its standards of acceptable height and health varied over time (often in response to greater manpower needs in wartime), means of determining statistical truncation points and the number of applicants who were eliminated because of truncation were needed. Clearly, the measured heights of those entering the army could present a misleading picture of the heights of the overall population of adult men, and this led to some difficulties in interpretation in the past. Two procedures, both premised on there being a normal distribution of the relevant group (however this group is defined), were devised and discussed in a study by James Trussell and Kenneth Wachter (Wachter and Trussell 1982). These adjustments compensated for the effects of various minimum and maximum height requirements and of their change over time. These improved measures were, nevertheless, subject to discussions and controversies about their relevance and accuracy.

Second, since there are calls on nutritional input for work and other activities, and thus nutritional requirements vary with work effort and intensity of input, the relevant concept to describe the expected impact of nutrition on height is not gross nutrition, the input of foodstuffs, but rather net nutrition— net of work and other requirements. Height measures, unlike measures of national income, can thus allow for the disutility of increased work intensity. Further, in going from gross nutrition to net nutrition the role of disease is of obvious importance, both in causing an increase in the nutritional input needed to maintain health and also as an element determining the efficiency in converting energy from food input into physical growth.

46. For studies of birthweights, see Goldin and Margo (1989) and Ward (1993). Studies of BMI by economic historians are discussed in Fogel (1993). While these can supplement the information provided by heights, many of the issues discussed below also apply to them.

Since the earlier studies seemed to demonstrate a high correlation between height and income, and their change, as well as between height and mortality, measures of height and of income were seen to be complementary rather than competitive. It was, however, with subsequent studies that provided height estimates for periods in which national income estimates existed that some important and interesting differences arose. In many different places, there were seen to be cycles, with expansions and downturns, in the patterns of height change, not the basically upward linear trend found for incomes and expected to have occurred for heights as well. While expectations regarding heights seem to be better met for cross-sectional comparisons both within and across countries, with the expected class differences within nations generally to be found, it was in the measurement of economic growth over time that problems arose and the nature of interpretation became more difficult. Given the desire for a unique answer to a question, initial responses in dealing with these different measures were more often to argue a preference for one or the other of the measures as dealing with the most important welfare concept, rather than to aim at resolving the apparent paradox by reconciling what were possibly measures of different concepts. In some cases there seemed to be a possible reconciliation of measures going in different directions. Possibly, for example, there was some reduced food input in agricultural regions newly opened to trade as part of the economic growth process, or increased income may have meant that food consumption shifted to varieties of food that were more processed and had, per dollar of expenditure, less nutrient value. These possibilities have been mentioned as different means of reconciling increased incomes and decreased heights, even if it leaves open the welfare implications. Similarly, it has been claimed that new disease environments, whether exogenous or endogenous, imposed costs on society that were not reflected in national incomes, a situation that again could lead to increased incomes and decreased heights. On the other hand, as the example of public health measures suggests, it is possible that gains (or losses) in mortality experience occur without any major, direct changes in individual incomes. Thus reconciliations have been suggested between changes in heights and in incomes in different directions or of different orders of magnitude, although disagreement persists on how best to answer the question of whether people were better or worse off.

The difficulties in measuring national income are well known and have long been discussed and debated, as pointed out above. The concept of national income has survived much of this criticism and is still in general use, pitfalls and all. What I want to do now is to raise certain conceptual issues about the use of height measures, which deal with the interpretation of findings from empirical studies, leaving aside the various issues of appropriate measurement and of correction for known biases. While it is clear that studies of changing heights have made and will continue to make a major contribution to the study of economic history, to take full advantage of their promise certain pieces of information would be useful for detailed analysis.

1.8   Factors in Human Physical Growth

One problem whose importance for the study of heights has become clear only relatively recently concerns the precise nature of diseases, their causes and their consequences. It is obvious that certain diseases can influence physical growth patterns of individuals. Since these diseases may influence individuals at different ages, with generally the greatest impact at ages from birth to age two, it may be necessary to consider the full sequence of the growth path in order to determine the conditions that permit "catch-up" growth to occur or to see whether the losses suffered are permanent. Interacting with disease in influencing infant growth could be changes in breast-feeding practices, with some direct effects on nutrition as well as on disease susceptibility.

Diseases can result from human behavior (e.g., from migration or from health and cleanliness habits), as well as being generated by the natural environment (e.g., climatic changes, hurricanes, earthquakes, and insect and animal population changes). Disease may be the outcome of the process of economic change, or it can be independent of the economic situation. More plausibly, perhaps, there is some degree of interaction between the two. Since disease will influence the relation between food input and achieved height, changes in the disease environment that affect stature can mean that height changes are not to be regarded as the direct result of changes in nutrition. The worsening of the disease environment, for any reason, can reduce the achieved height consistent with any level of national income, although the interpretation of the welfare significance of such a height reduction will vary depending on whether the cause of the disease change is endogenous or exogenous to the economic growth process. Thus more information on the nature and causes of diseases, and on their influence on the relationship of foodstuffs to height, will help us to better understand the process and evaluation of economic change.

Comparisons between changes in national income and changes in height are often difficult because there remains uncertainty as to the precise period of time to which to attribute the causes of height variations, while the specific year for which national income is measured is clearly known. Explanations of the nature and timing of some specific events leading to height changes often suggest the existence of a long and varying lag, so that contemporaneous comparisons of heights and incomes will be misleading. The relative role of birthweight (and maternal influences) and of various ages prior to, during, and after growth spurts have been frequently discussed but, as noted, with little apparent certainty at present as to critical periods of impact. Physiological impacts may vary with individual age and with time of changes, so that the value of indicators will vary depending on whether our primary interest is in long-term trends or in shorter periods, including business cycles. Short-term movements, including famines, may not be as sensitively or as accurately measured by heights as by national incomes, nor may height data show up rapidly enough to serve as a useful guide to economic and social policy.

Related to this issue of physical growth patterns is the question of what is precisely known about the relationship between food input and height: Is it linear or nonlinear? Are there threshold levels at either the short or the tall end? The conversion of income into height may also depend on level of education, which can influence the efficiency of the individual's diet selection and food preparation. These pieces of information will be useful for several questions, including that of the expected relationship between income and height at different levels of food input, and the relationship between the distribution of heights and the distribution of incomes and food inputs. Further, it may be important to distinguish among the impacts of different foodstuffs in adding to physical growth potential, a distinction that suggests that the relation of income, food input, and height may be considerably more varied than earlier anticipated. Given the impact of Engel's law over time and across income levels at a moment of time, the translation between relative heights and relative incomes is frequently not obvious.

The persistence of the pattern of higher mortality for those of smaller heights can also present certain problems in the interpretation of changes over time. There will be some measured increase in average height over time since in general those who die tend to have been shorter than the average (see, e.g., Friedman 1982). And as overall mortality declines over time there could be a small tendency for average heights to fall since there will now be more survivors of below average height. Whether these points are of any quantitative significance awaits more data on patterns of mortality and mortality change attributable to factors related to height.

1.9   Concluding Reflections

It remains difficult to find any one measure or index that can provide us with all we wish to know about the magnitude of welfare and its distribution, as well as their changes over time. None of the indicators seem to always provide the expected answers, either over time or across countries. We have a number of imperfect indicators, and while there are often adjustments that can be made to better approximate our goal, these will often leave many issues open. Disagreements on interpretations exist for numerous reasons, including a failure to agree on the proper set of weights for calculating indexes based on more than one component, and in the desire to go beyond ordinal rankings to get cardinal differences, attempted so that we can discuss orders-of-magnitude differentials across classes and nations. And for each possible indicator it is necessary to determine the proportionality between the index and the welfare we are attempting to measure, and to determine if the components of the index rise equally with what we regard as welfare over time.

Some attempts to go beyond the basic economic indicators have led to interest in so-called social indicators, which include various measures of social ills and social betterment.[47] As with other nonmonetary indicators, however, there are no schemes of weighting to provide an unambiguous single-number index. Some scholars have utilized questionnaires, asking people about their perceived happiness and well-being. In an analysis of such questionnaires by Richard Easterlin, it appears that the results do suggest that individuals, in any nation, with above average income feel better than those whose incomes fall below average, but there seem to be no major increases in happiness with growth of income over time (Easterlin 1974; see also Campbell, Converse, and Rodgers, 1976). However interesting these surveys, they present many basic difficulties—some peculiar to the method, including understanding what makes for individual evaluations, as well as some similar to those of other measures.

The difficulty in choosing among indicators or in somehow combining them reflects two different types of problems. One concerns the possibility and the costs of obtaining the data necessary to appropriately measure the desired concept. Do the data exist, presumably as a result of some other functions within society, and are they easily translatable into the concept of interest, either directly or with some suitable adjustments? Or if new data are required, can they be obtained at low enough cost? Second, how can we relate any of the measures to some basic underlying economic model? Which measures can be argued to be the direct outcome of maximizing behavior, and which are more the by-products of individual behavior that had sought other goals? Such issues are difficult to argue about since, while we might believe that individuals maximize utility, not measured income, life expectation, food consumption, or height, it is not clear how to determine what enters into different individual utility functions. Given the difficulties in finding an answer to any basic question of differential welfare, perhaps our best strategy is to accept the specific value of particular indicators for answering particular questions but also remain aware of the complexity of the multitude of factors that makes these examinations so difficult and generalization so uncertain.

References

Abramovitz, Moses. 1959. "The welfare interpretation of secular changes in national income and product." In *The allocation of economic resources: Essays in honor of Bernard Francis Haley,* ed. Moses Abramovitz et al., 1–22. Stanford, Calif.: Stanford University Press.

47. This was a concern of various governmental agencies in the United States in the 1960s and 1970s, but this effort did not seem prolonged. See, e.g., U.S. Department of Health, Education, and Welfare (1969) and U.S. Department of Commerce (1977)—the first such publication was in 1973; this was the second. More generally on this approach, see Bauer (1966).

————. 1989. *Thinking about growth: And other essays on economic growth and welfare.* Cambridge: Cambridge University Press.

Adelman, Irma, and Cynthia Taft Morris. 1973. *Economic growth and social equity in developing countries.* Stanford, Calif.: Stanford University Press.

Bauer, Raymond A., ed. 1966. *Social indicators.* Cambridge, Mass.: MIT Press.

Bennett, M. K. 1937. On measurement of relative national standards of living. *Quarterly Journal of Economics* 51 (February): 317–35.

————. 1951. International disparities in consumption levels. *American Economic Review* 41 (September): 632–49.

Bonar, James. 1966. *Theories of population from Raleigh to Arthur Young.* New York: Augustus Kelley (first published 1931).

Bridbury, A. R. 1962. *Economic growth: England in the later Middle Ages.* London: Allen and Unwin.

Campbell, Angus, Philip E. Converse, and Willard L. Rodgers. 1976. *The quality of American life: Perceptions, evaluations, and satisfactions.* New York: Russell Sage Foundation.

Carson, Carol S. 1975. The history of the United States national income and product accounts: The development of an analytical tool. *Review of Income and Wealth* 21 (June): 153–81.

Clapham, J. H. 1961. *The economic development of France and Germany, 1815–1914,* 4th ed. Cambridge: Cambridge University Press.

Clark, Colin. 1957. *The conditions of economic progress,* 3d ed. London: Macmillan.

Dannenfeldt, Karl H., ed. 1959. *The Renaissance: Medieval or modern?* Boston: Heath.

Dasgupta, Partha. 1993. *An inquiry into well-being and destitution.* Oxford: Clarendon.

Davis, Joseph S. 1945. Standards and content of living. *American Economic Review* 35 (March): 1–15.

Deane, Phyllis. 1955. The implications of early national income estimates for the measurement of long-term economic growth in the United Kingdom. *Economic Development and Cultural Change* 4 (October): 3–38.

————. 1956. Contemporary estimates of national income in the first half of the nineteenth century. *Economic History Review* 8 (April): 339–54.

————. 1957. Contemporary estimates of national income in the second half of the nineteenth century. *Economic History Review* 9 (April): 451–61.

Denison, Edward F. 1971. Welfare measurement and the GNP. *Survey of Current Business* 51 (January): 13–16, 39.

Easterlin, Richard A. 1974. Does economic growth improve the human lot? Some empirical evidence. In *Nations and households in economic growth: Essays in honor of Moses Abramovitz,* ed. Paul A. David and Melvin W. Reder, 89–125. New York: Academic Press.

Eisner, Robert. 1989. *The total incomes system of accounts.* Chicago: University of Chicago Press.

Eliot, Thomas D., ed. 1931. *American standards and planes of living: Readings in the social economics of consumption.* Boston: Ginn.

Engerman, Stanley L. 1994. Reflections on "the standard of living debate": New arguments and new evidence. In *Capitalism in context: Essays on economic development and cultural change in honor of R. M. Hartwell,* ed. John A. James and Mark Thomas, 50–79. Chicago: University of Chicago Press.

Engerman, Stanley, and Sherwin Rosen. 1980. New books on the measurement of capital. In *The measurement of capital,* ed. Dan Usher, 153–70. Chicago: University of Chicago Press.

Eversley, D. E. C. 1959. *Social theories of fertility and the Malthusian debate.* Oxford: Clarendon.

Floud, Roderick, Kenneth Wachter, and Annabel Gregory. 1990. *Height, health and history: Nutritional status in the United Kingdom, 1750–1980.* Cambridge: Cambridge University Press.

Fogel, Robert W. 1986. Nutrition and the decline in mortality since 1700: Some preliminary findings. In *Long-term trends in American economic growth,* ed. Stanley L. Engerman and Robert E. Gallman, 439–555 (includes comment by Peter Lindert). Chicago: University of Chicago Press.

———. 1993. New sources and new techniques for the study of secular trends in nutritional status, health, mortality, and the process of aging. *Historical Methods* 26 (Winter): 1–44.

Folbre, Nancy, and Marjorie Abel. 1989. Women's work and women's households: Gender bias in the U.S. census. *Social Research* 56 (Autumn): 545–69.

Folbre, Nancy, and Barnet Wagman. 1993. Counting housework: New estimates of real product in the United States, 1800–1860. *Journal of Economic History* 53 (June): 275–88.

Friedman, Gerald C. 1982. The heights of slaves in Trinidad. *Social Science History* 6 (Fall): 482–515.

Gallman, Robert E. 1961. Estimates of American national product made before the Civil War. *Economic Development and Cultural Change* 9 (April): 397–412.

———. 1966. Gross national product in the United States, 1834–1909. In *Output, employment and productivity in the United States after 1800,* ed. Conference on Research in Income and Wealth, 3–76. New York: Columbia University Press.

Gallman, Robert E., and John Joseph Wallis, eds. 1992. *American growth and standards of living before the Civil War.* Chicago: University of Chicago Press.

Gerbi, Antello. 1973. *The dispute of the new world: The history of a polemic, 1750–1900.* Pittsburgh: University of Pittsburgh Press.

Glass, D. V. 1973. *Numbering the people: The eighteenth-century population controversy and the development of census and vital statistics in Britain.* London: Gordon and Cremonesi.

Goldin, Claudia. 1990. *Understanding the gender gap: An economic history of American women.* New York: Oxford University Press.

Goldin, Claudia, and Robert A. Margo. 1989. The poor at birth: Birth weights and infant mortality at Philadelphia's Almshouse Hospital. *Explorations in Economic History* 26 (July): 360–79.

Goldschmidt-Clermont, Luisella. 1982. *Unpaid work in the household: A review of economic evaluation methods.* Geneva: International Labour Office.

Gordon, Robert J. 1990. *The measurement of durable goods prices.* Chicago: University of Chicago Press.

Hakewill, George. 1630. *An apologie or declaration of the power and providence of god in the government of the world,* 2d ed. Oxford: William Turner (first published 1627).

Halley, Edmund. 1942. *Degrees of mortality of mankind.* Baltimore: Johns Hopkins University Press (first published 1693).

Harris, Bernard. 1994. Health, height, and history: An overview of recent developments in anthropometric history. *Social History of Medicine* 7:297–329.

Harris, Victor. 1949. *All coherence gone.* Chicago: University of Chicago Press.

Hart, Hornell, and Hilda Hertz. 1944. Expectation of life as an index of social progress. *American Sociological Review* 9 (December): 609–21.

Hirsch, Fred. 1978. *Social limits to growth.* Cambridge, Mass.: Harvard University Press.

Howlett, John. 1968. *An examination of Dr. Price's essay on the population of England and Wales.* New York: Augustus M. Kelley (first published 1781).

Hume, David. 1985. *Essays: Moral, political, and literary,* ed. Eugene F. Miller. Indianapolis: Liberty Fund (first published 1777).

International Labour Office. Studies and Reports. 1936. *Workers' nutrition and social policy.* Geneva: League of Nations.

Jones, Richard Foster. 1961. *Ancients and moderns: A study of the rise of the scientific movement in seventeenth-century England.* St. Louis: Washington University Studies.

Kendrick, John W. 1972. *Economic accounts and their uses.* New York: McGraw-Hill.

———. 1976. *The formation and stocks of total capital.* New York: Columbia University Press.

Kiker, B. F. 1968. *Human capital: In retrospect.* Columbia: University of South Carolina, Bureau of Business and Economic Research.

King, Gregory. 1936. *Two tracts,* ed. George E. Barnett. Baltimore: Johns Hopkins University Press.

King, Willford Isbell. 1969. *The wealth and income of the people of the United States.* New York: Johnson Reprints (first published 1915).

Komlos, John, ed. 1994. *Stature, living standards, and economic development: Essays in anthropometric history.* Chicago: University of Chicago Press.

———. 1995. *The biological standard of living on three continents: Further explorations in anthropometric history.* Boulder, Colo.: Westview.

Kunitz, Stephen J. 1987. Making a long story short: A note on men's height and mortality in England from the first through the nineteenth century. *Medical History* 31 (July): 269–80.

Kunitz, Stephen J., and Stanley L. Engerman. 1992. The ranks of death: Secular trends in income and mortality. *Health Transition Review* 2 (Suppl.): 29–46.

Kuznets, Simon. 1941. *National income and its composition, 1919–1938.* New York: National Bureau of Economic Research.

———. 1952. Long-term changes in national income of the United States since 1870. In *Income and wealth of the United States: Trends and structure,* ed. Simon Kuznets, 2ᶜ -241. Cambridge: Bowes and Bowes.

— ———. 1953. *Economic change: Selected essays in business cycles, national income, and economic growth.* New York: Norton.

———. 1959. *Six lectures on economic growth.* Glencoe, Ill.: Free Press.

———. 1965. *Economic growth and structure: Selected essays.* New York: Norton.

———. 1966. *Modern economic growth: Rate, structure, and spread.* New Haven, Conn.: Yale University Press.

Lamale, Helen H. 1958. Changes in concepts of income adequacy over the last century. *American Economic Review* 48 (May): 291–99.

Lasch, Christopher. 1991. *The true and only heaven: Progress and its critics.* New York: Norton.

Lauderdale, Earl of. 1819. *An inquiry into the nature and origin of public wealth and into the means and causes of its increase,* 2d ed. Edinburgh: Archibald Constable (first published 1804).

League of Nations. Mixed Committee for the Study of Problems of Nutrition. 1937. *Nutrition: Final report of the Mixed Committee of the League of Nations on the relation of nutrition to health, agriculture and economic policy.* Geneva: League of Nations.

Lebergott, Stanley L. 1976. *The American economy: Income, wealth, and want.* Princeton, N.J.: Princeton University Press.

———. 1993. *Pursuing happiness: American consumers in the twentieth century.* Princeton, N.J.: Princeton University Press.

Levi, Leone. 1860. On the distribution and productiveness of taxes with reference to the prospective ameliorations in the public revenue of the United Kingdom. *Journal of the Royal Statistical Society* 23 (March): 37–65.

———. 1880. *The history of British commerce and of the economic progress of the British nation, 1763–1878,* 2d ed. London: John Murray.

———. 1885. *Wages and earnings of the working classes.* London: John Murray.

Lindert, Peter. 1994. Unequal living standards. In *The economic history of Britain since 1700,* 2d ed. vol. 1, *1700–1860,* ed. Roderick Floud and D. N. McCloskey, 357–86. Cambridge: Cambridge University Press.

Macaulay, Thomas Babington. 1849. *The history of England from the accession of James II,* vol. 1. New York: Harper (first published 1848).

Malthus, Thomas Robert. 1970. *An essay on the principle of population and a summary view of the principle of population,* ed. Anthony Flew. Harmondsworth: Penguin (first published 1798 and 1830).

Marx, Karl. 1906. *Capital: A critique of political economy.* Chicago: Charles H. Kerr (first published 1867).

Merwin, C. L., Jr. 1939. American studies of the distribution of wealth and income by size. In *Studies in income and wealth,* vol. 3, ed. Conference on Research in Income and Wealth, 1–93. New York: National Bureau of Economic Research.

Mitchell, Wesley C., et al. 1921. *Income in the United States: Its amount and distribution, 1909–1919.* New York: Harcourt, Brace.

Mokyr, Joel. 1983. *Why Ireland starved: A quantitative and analytical history of the Irish economy, 1800–1850.* London: Allen and Unwin.

Morris, Morris David. 1979. *Measuring the condition of the world's poor: The physical quality of life index.* New York: Pergamon.

Mulhall, Michael G. 1899. *The dictionary of statistics,* 4th ed., rev. ed. London: George Routledge and Sons.

Nordhaus, William D., and James Tobin. 1973. Is growth obsolete? In *The measurement of economic and social performance,* ed. Milton Moss, 509–32. New York: Columbia University Press (also published, with appendixes, in *Economic growth,* Fiftieth Anniversary Colloquium 5. New York: Columbia University Press, 1972).

Pearson, Karl. 1978. *The history of statistics in the 17th and 18th centuries against the changing background of intellectual, scientific and religious thought: Lectures by Karl Pearson given at University College London during the academic sessions, 1921–1933,* ed. E. S. Pearson. New York: Macmillan.

Perlman, Mark. 1987. Political purpose and the national accounts. In *The politics of numbers,* ed. William Alonso and Paul Starr, 133–51. New York: Russell Sage Foundation.

Petty, William. 1899. *The economic writings of William Petty,* ed. Charles Henry Hull. Cambridge: Cambridge University Press.

Pigou, A. C. 1929. *The economics of welfare,* 3d ed. London: Macmillan (first published 1920).

Pollard, Sidney. 1968. *The idea of progress: History and society.* New York: Basic Books.

Porter, Theodore M. 1986. *The rise of statistical thinking, 1820–1900.* Princeton, N.J.: Princeton University Press.

Postan, M. M. 1966. Medieval agrarian society in its prime: England. In *The Cambridge economic history of europe.* vol. 1, *The agrarian life of the Middle Ages,* 2d ed., ed. M. M. Postan, 549–632. Cambridge: Cambridge University Press.

Preston, Samuel H. 1975. The changing relation between mortality and level of economic development. *Population Studies* 29 (July): 231–48.

Price, Richard. 1780. *An essay on the population of England, from the Revolution to the present time,* 2d ed. London: T. Cadell (first published 1779).

Roback, Jennifer. 1982. Wages, rents, and the quality of life. *Journal of Political Economy* 90 (December): 1257–78.

Rostow, W. W. 1990. *Theorists of economic growth from David Hume to the present: With a perspective on the next century.* New York: Oxford University Press.

Schumpeter, Joseph A. 1954. *History of economic analysis.* New York: Oxford University Press.

Scitovsky, Tibor. 1976. *The joyless economy: An inquiry into human satisfaction and consumer dissatisfaction.* Oxford: Oxford University Press.

Seaman, Ezra C. 1846. *Essays on the progress of nations, in productive industry, civilization, population, and wealth.* Detroit: M. Geiger.

———. 1852. *Essays on the progress of nations, in civilization, productive industry, wealth and population.* New York: Charles Scribner.

Segal, Reva B. 1994. Home as work: The first woman's rights claims concerning wives' household labor, 1850–1880. *Yale Law Journal* 103 (March): 1073–1217.

Sen, Amartya. 1993. The economics of life and death. *Scientific American* 268 (May): 40–47.

Smith, Adam. 1976. *An inquiry into the nature and causes of the wealth of nations,* 2 vols. Oxford: Oxford University Press (first published 1776).

Smithies, Arthur. 1946. National income as a determinant of international policy. In *Studies in income and wealth,* vol. 8, ed. Conference on Research in Income and Wealth, 47–67. New York: National Bureau of Economic Research.

Snooks, Graeme Donald. 1993. *Economics without time: A science blind to the sources of historical change.* London: Macmillan.

———. 1994. *Portrait of the family within the total economy: A study in longrun dynamics, Australia, 1788–1990.* Cambridge: Cambridge University Press.

Spadafora, David. 1990. *The idea of progress in eighteenth-century Britain.* New Haven, Conn.: Yale University Press.

Steckel, Richard H. 1992. Stature and living standards in the United States. In *American economic growth and standards of living before the Civil War,* ed. Robert E. Gallman and John Joseph Wallis, 265–308. Chicago: University of Chicago Press.

Studenski, Paul. 1958. *The income of nations: Theory, measurement, and analysis: Past and present.* New York: New York University Press.

Tanner, J. M. 1981. *A history of the study of human growth.* Cambridge: Cambridge University Press.

United Nations. Committee of Experts on International Definition and Measurement of Standards of Living. 1954. *Report on international definition of measurement of standards and levels of living.* New York: United Nations.

United Nations. Department of Economic and Social Affairs. 1973. *The determinants and consequences of population trends: New summary of findings on interaction of demographic, economic and social factors,* 2 vols. New York: United Nations.

United Nations Development Programme. 1994. *Human development report, 1994.* New York: Oxford University Press.

U.S. Department of Commerce. 1977. *Social indicators 1976: Selected data on social conditions and trends in the United States.* Washington, D.C.: Government Printing Office.

U.S. Department of Health, Education, and Welfare. 1969. *Toward a social report.* Washington, D.C.: Government Printing Office.

U.S. Department of Labor. n.d. *How American buying habits change.* Washington, D.C.: Government Printing Office.

Usher, Dan. 1968. *The price mechanism and the meaning of national income statistics.* Oxford: Clarendon.

———. 1980. *The measurement of economic growth.* New York: Columbia University Press.

Wachter, Kenneth W., and James Trussell. 1982. Estimating historical heights. *Journal of the American Statistical Association* 77 (June): 279–93.

Wallace, Robert. 1969. *A dissertation on the numbers of mankind in ancient and modern times.* New York: Augustus M. Kelly (second edition 1809; first edition 1753).

Wallis, John Joseph, and Douglass C. North. 1986. Measuring the transaction sector in the American economy, 1870–1970. In *Long-term factors in American economic growth,* ed. Stanley L. Engerman and Robert E. Gallman, 95–161 (including a comment by Lance E. Davis). Chicago: University of Chicago Press.

Ward, W. Peter. 1993. *Birth weight and economic growth: Women's living standards in the industrializing West.* Chicago: University of Chicago Press.

Wicksteed, Philip H. 1910. *The common sense of political economy: Including a study of the human basis of economic law.* London: Macmillan.

Williamson, Jeffrey G. 1981. Urban amenities, dark satanic mills, and the British standard of living debate. *Journal of Economic History* 41 (March): 75–83.

———. 1984. British mortality and the value of a life. *Population Studies* 38 (March): 157–72.

———. 1991. *Inequality, poverty, and history: The Kuznets Memorial Lectures of the Economic Growth Center, Yale University.* Cambridge, Mass.: Blackwell.

Young, Arthur. 1967. *Political arithmetic: Containing observations on the present state of Great Britain.* New York: Augustus M. Kelley (first published 1774).

Zimmerman, Carle C. 1936. *Consumption and standard of living.* New York: Van Nostrand.

Zolotas, Xenophon. 1981. *Economic growth and declining social welfare.* Athens: Bank of Greece.

2   Long-Term Trends in Health, Welfare, and Economic Growth in the United States

Dora L. Costa and Richard H. Steckel

2.1 Introduction

Economists and historians have long been intrigued by the connection between health and economic growth. Because health is an input to economic growth, long-run increases in living standards may be sped by the improving health of a population. People in better health are able to increase their productivity and output. At the same time, economic growth enables people to purchase the nutrition, sanitation, shelter, and medical care that are so necessary to health.

Economic growth is not always benign, however. Industrialization was generally associated with increased urbanization, crowded factories and tenements, and the pacing of workers by machines. Economic growth might therefore lead to a deterioration in health. Examining the interrelationship between industrialization and health will help us understand how adverse effects associated with economic growth can be mitigated.

Establishing the secular trend in health and understanding its causes is also important for understanding the present. The past is still with us both because older generations are still with us and because physiological processes have an intergenerational reach. The oldest generation alive today was born when life expectancy at birth was only 50 years. A growing body of evidence indicates

Dora L. Costa is professor of economics at the Massachusetts Institute of Technology and a faculty research fellow of the National Bureau of Economic Research. Richard H. Steckel is professor of economics at Ohio State University and a research associate of the National Bureau of Economic Research.

The authors have benefited from the comments of the conference participants and of two referees. Dora Costa gratefully acknowledges the support of an NIA Aging Fellowship at the National Bureau of Economic Research and of NIH grants AG12651-01A1 and AG10120-05. Richard Steckel gratefully acknowledges the support of a fellowship at Harvard University's Charles Warren Center and of Ohio State University.

47

that chronic diseases at older ages and premature older age mortality are, to a considerable degree, the result of exposure to infectious diseases, malnutrition, and other types of biomedical and socioeconomic stress early in life (see the papers collected in Barker 1992). The health of this generation matters for understanding the health of succeeding generations. Recent studies suggest that a mother's ability to nourish her baby is established during her own life, including the fetal stage (see Barker 1994).

Past trends in health are also important for predicting morbidity and mortality. Recent forecasts have, for the most part, been based on information derived from surveys that began to be collected only in the late 1960s. These may not provide a long enough period of observation to differentiate adequately between short-term fluctuations and the underlying long-term trends over the entire twentieth century. They are also based on empirical extrapolations and do not directly reflect physiological processes.

This paper reviews the evidence on economic growth and health as measured by stature and mortality rates in the nineteenth and twentieth centuries. We also present new evidence on body mass index, lean body mass, waist-hip ratio, and the prevalence of chronic conditions. These anthropometric variables are useful predictors of both overall and disease-specific mortality and morbidity at later ages and provide us with a more complete picture of past health than stature and mortality rates alone. The twentieth century has witnessed a dramatic improvement in both health and economic indicators. The improving trend in health indicators remained unbroken even by the Great Depression. In the nineteenth century the opposite situation prevailed—health status began to decline in about 1830 while income continued to rise. Examining the interaction between environmental variables and anthropometric variables in both the nineteenth and the twentieth centuries will enable us to understand the factors underlying the twentieth-century improvement in health and to improve our predictions of future trends. It will also tell us whether a decline in health was a necessary cost of industrialization. We also consider implications of changes in health for human welfare. One of the central questions of this paper is whether the bundle of evidence on health and economic performance leaves us with little more than intuitive notions of the net change in human welfare or whether it is possible to quantify the dimensions of welfare change.

2.2 Trends in Economic Indicators

Numerous indicators establish that the nineteenth and twentieth centuries were a period of long-term improvement in living standards as conventionally measured. Although scholars have speculated about the course of economic development in the late eighteenth and early nineteenth centuries, the first reasonably comprehensive evidence on performance was not collected until the federal census of 1840. Gallman's estimates of output from this and later censuses combined with prices and imputations for omitted categories, such as services, indicate that real net national product grew at nearly 4 percent per annum from 1840 to 1900, a phenomenon fueled by a transportation revolution, technological change, improved capital markets, capital accumulation, and other factors (see tables from Davis et al. 1972). Although the rate of growth slowed to slightly more than 3 percent in the period from 1900 to 1960, the growth of factor inputs also fell. Output per worker grew at approximately 1.4 percent per year from 1840 to 1960, a performance similar to that achieved by other early industrializers.

Despite macroeconomic fluctuations that caused significant variation in real wage growth, real wages increased during the nineteenth and twentieth centuries. In the first half of the nineteenth century, the real wages of men hired by army quartermasters increased substantially across all regions of the country and within a moderately broad base of occupations. Hefty gains occurred in the 1820s and early 1830s, but the trend was broken by the economic distress of the late 1830s. Although the experiences of artisans and unskilled laborers differed somewhat across regions, the overall gains were in the range of 30–60 percent from the early 1820s to the mid-1850s (Goldin and Margo 1992). Wages continued to rise in the second half of the nineteenth century, increasing by one-third between 1860 and 1900 (Margo in press). In the twentieth century, real annual wages increased by 1.43 percent per annum on average from 1900 to 1929, by 2.35 percent from 1948 to 1973, and by 0.46 percent after 1973. Benefits as a fraction of compensation continued to rise (Goldin in press).

Changes in the composition of the labor force signaled the rise of an industrial economy. At the beginning of the century, farming dominated economic activity. According to Weiss (1992) agriculture absorbed 72 percent of the labor force in 1810 but by 1840 had slipped to 67 percent and by 1860 to 56 percent. A majority of those employed worked outside agriculture by 1890, but farm sector employment continued to grow in absolute numbers, reaching a peak in 1910. The transformation to an industrial service economy was completed in this century, and by 1950 only 12 percent of the labor force was in agriculture.

The economic transformation of the nineteenth century registered gradually in the shift of population from rural to urban areas (see U.S. Bureau of the Census 1975, Series A, 52–72). Reflecting the country's agricultural orientation, less than 8 percent of the population lived in urban areas (places of 2,500 or more population). However, the transition to urban living was less rapid than changes in the labor force, indicating that an important share of early industrial activity took place in rural or semirural areas. Between 1810 and 1840 the labor force involved in agriculture declined by approximately 22 percentage points, but the population living in urban areas grew from 8 to only 11 percent. As late as 1860 less than 20 percent of the population lived in cities or towns of more than 2,500 residents and only 10 percent lived in cities with a population of 50,000 or more. The surge in city growth awaited large-scale immigration from Europe following the Civil War, and by 1900 nearly 40 percent of the population lived in urban areas.

2.3 Trends in Health

2.3.1 Heights

The most abundant evidence on long-term trends in health was recorded by military organizations. From the mid-1700s heights were often recorded as part of the mustering process to help identify deserters, to assess fighting strength, and to ensure that soldiers received their proper pay. Figure 2.1 presents trends in the heights of native-born soldiers from the eighteenth through the twentieth centuries and of native-born men in the last decades of this century.[1] The data, which are arranged by birth cohort, show that troops who fought in the French and Indian War of the 1750s and 1760s or who fought in the American Revolution of the 1770s nearly attained 1930s heights of 175 cm. Cohorts born from the early 1700s to 1830 achieved a gradual increase in average stature of approximately 1 cm. Average heights fell by approximately 4 cm in the ensuing half-century, reaching a trough among births in the 1880s.[2] Thereafter, American men experienced the familiar secular increase in stature of recent times, gaining approximately 6 cm by the mid-twentieth century. The secular increase in heights continues in recent decades, although at a much slower pace.

The nineteenth-century decline in heights was initially viewed with caution or skepticism since it clashed with well-established views on the economic prosperity of the era. Steckel and Haurin discovered the mid-nineteenth-century downturn among the Ohio National Guard in 1981 but delayed publication until confirmation of a downturn in health was available and some reasonable explanations could be provided. Corroborating evidence was obtained from various sources including stature, weights, and mortality rates. West Point cadets lost approximately 1.4 cm in height between cohorts of the 1820s and those of the 1860s, then recovered in the 1870s, a pattern of change that existed across regions and occupational groups (Komlos 1987). Their loss in height was less than that experienced by regular troops, possibly because the cadets came from a higher socioeconomic stratum.

Life expectancy at age 10 follows a pattern similar to that of heights. After rising for most of the eighteenth century, life expectancy began to decline dur-

1. Since the sample sizes are substantial, particularly for those periods before the large wars, the major movements in the series are unlikely to represent sampling variation. In fact, the difference in average height between rejectees and those who served in the Union Army was 0.25 inches. The averages have been corrected for minimum height standards.
2. No national height series is available for the end of the nineteenth century. Interpolation was based on the assumption that the time pattern for the country followed that for Ohio.

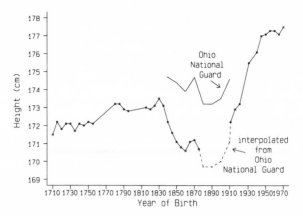

Fig. 2.1   Mean heights of white, native-born males by birth cohort, 1710–1970

Note: Compiled from Steckel (1992), Ohio National Guard recruits, 1959–62 NHES, 1971 NHANES, and 1991 NHIS. The data used in Steckel (1992) come from Fogel (1986), Steckel and Haurin (1982), and from several of the data sets listed in the appendix (Union Army Recruits in White Regiments in the United States, 1861–1865; French and Indian War Army Recruits; American Revolution Army Recruits; United States Army Recruits, 1815–1820; and United States Army Recruits, 1850–1855). Year of birth is centered at the marks. The interpolation is from the Ohio National Guard. Estimates for 1955–70 were adjusted to account for biases resulting from self-reporting in the 1991 and 1981 NHIS.

ing the 1790s and continued to do so for the first half of the nineteenth century (Fogel 1986). Mortality rates for native-born adults calculated from genealogies also identify a loss in health during the first half of the nineteenth century. Life expectation for men at age 20 declined from approximately 47 years at the beginning of the century to slightly less than 41 years in the 1850s. Among women the decline was steeper: from nearly 48 years in 1800–1809 to 37.1 years in the 1840s. Recovery to levels of the early 1800s was not attained until the end of the century (Pope 1992).

Evidence for the South suggests that the cycle in heights may have been a national phenomenon. Among slaves, the heights of children born after approximately 1830 declined by 2.5 to 7.5 cm in the two decades following (Steckel 1979a). The heights of slave women measured as adults declined by more than 1 cm over two decades for those born after 1810. In contrast, the heights of adult men rose by more than 1 cm over the same time period. Consistent with the trend for women and children, the infant mortality rate calculated from plantation records approximately doubled during the early 1800s, reached a peak in the 1830s, and then declined to its former level in the late 1850s (Steckel 1979b). Data on the heights of Southern white men who signed amnesty oaths in the 1860s suggest that the loss in stature extended beyond slaves. The average stature of these men born before 1820 was approximately 1 cm above those born in the 1820s (Margo and Steckel 1992).

The implications of changes in height for mortality have been studied only

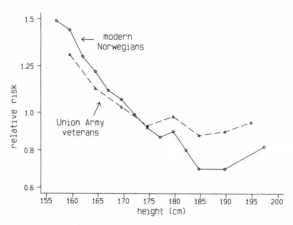

Fig. 2.2   Comparison of relative mortality risk by height among modern Norwegian males and Union Army veterans circa 1900
Note: Height for 309,554 modern Norwegians was measured at ages 40–59, and the period of risk was seven years. Height of 322 Union Army veterans aged 23–49 was measured at enlistment, and the period of risk was from ages 55 to 75. Calculated from data in Waaler (1984) and Early Indicators of Later Work Levels, Disease, and Death.

recently.[3] Costa (1993b) found that the functional relation between height and subsequent mortality is similar among a sample of 322 Union Army recruits measured at ages 23–49 who lived to age 55 and were observed over a 20-year period and among modern, Norwegian males aged 40–59 observed over a 7-year period.[4] Both the Norwegian curve and the U.S. curve show that mortality first declines with height to reach a minimum at heights close to 185 cm and then starts to rise (see fig. 2.2). A similar relationship is found between height and self-reported health status (Fogel, Costa, and Kim 1994). Height appears to be inversely related to heart and respiratory diseases and positively related to hormonal cancers (Barker 1992). The relationship between height and mortality remains unchanged controlling for socioeconomic covariates, such as occupation, nativity, and urbanization. The Norwegian height curve suggests that had the distribution of heights in the Union Army sample been the same as in the 1991 National Health Interview Survey (NHIS), older age mortality rates would have fallen by 9 percent.

Data from developing countries suggest that the impact of height on productivity is substantial. Using data for rural south India, Deolalikar (1988) found that the elasticity of wage rates with respect to height is in the range of 0.28–0.66. Haddad and Bouis (1991) reported that wages in the rural Philippines are strongly influenced by height. In an extension, Foster and Rosenzweig (1992)

---

3. The relationship between height and mortality for slaves was studied earlier (e.g., Friedman 1982).
4. The Norwegian population is used for comparison because this population provides the largest available data set.

found that height and calories have particularly large effects on piece rate wages. Data from the antebellum American South show that height and weight were positively associated with value, suggesting that better fed, healthier slaves were more productive (Margo and Steckel 1982).

2.3.2   Body Mass Index

The body mass index (BMI), defined as weight in kilograms divided by the square of height in meters, may be an even stronger predictor of productivity, morbidity, and mortality than height. The relation between weight and mortality among Union Army veterans measured at ages 50–64 and observed from age 50 until 75 resembles that seen among modern Norwegian males (Costa 1993b). Mortality risk first declines rapidly at low weights as BMI increases, stays relatively flat over BMI levels from the low to high 20s, then starts to rise again, but less steeply than at very low BMIs (see fig. 2.3). Among modern American males aged 50–64 the relationship between BMI and self-reported health status, number of bed days, number of doctors' visits, and number of hospitalizations follows a similar U-shaped pattern (Costa 1996). Costa (1993b) argued that the low weights of Union Army veterans can partially explain why mortality for their cohort was higher than for cohorts today. Had it been possible to shift the BMI distribution of Union Army veterans one standard deviation to the right so that the mean would be equivalent to that prevailing in modern Norway, the implied 14 percent reduction in the mortality rate would explain roughly 20 percent of the total decline in mortality above age 50 from 1900 to 1986, a percentage greater than that explained by changes in height.[5]

A U-shape similar to that observed between mortality and BMI is also observed between labor force nonparticipation and BMI. Costa (1996) found that among Union Army veterans measured at ages 50–64, the relative risk of labor force nonparticipation increases sharply at both high and low levels of BMI, but height and labor force nonparticipation are not related. She found a similar U-shaped relation between BMI and labor force nonparticipation in a sample of white men aged 50–64 in 1985–91. However, the relative risk at high BMI levels is much lower. In both samples, the BMI that maximized labor force participation was around 25—statistically indistinguishable from the BMI that minimizes relative mortality risk. Had the distribution of BMI in the Union Army sample been the same as that observed today, the probability of nonparticipation would have fallen by 10 percent. Assuming that the probability of nonparticipation among all men would have fallen by 10 percent, the total output of male workers would have increased by 1.7 percent (Costa 1996).

Evidence from developing countries also demonstrates the importance of

---

5. When height and weight are jointly related to subsequent mortality, the predicted decline explains 15 percent of the total decline in mortality. When height and weight are jointly related to subsequent morbidity, the predicted decline explains 35 percent of the total decline in morbidity (Fogel et al. 1994).

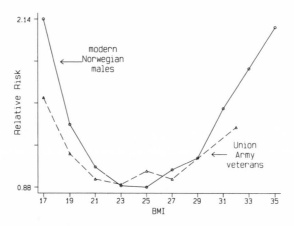

Fig. 2.3   Comparison of relative mortality risk by BMI level among men 50 years of age, Union Army veterans circa 1900, and modern Norwegians
Note: In the Norwegian data, BMI for 79,084 men was measured at ages 45–49, and the period of risk was seven years. BMI of 550 Union Army veterans was measured at ages 45–64, and the observation period was 25 years. Calculated from data in Waaler (1984) and Early Indicators of Later Work Levels, Disease, and Death.

BMI. Deolalikar (1988) found that the elasticity of farm output with respect to BMI is as large as 2. As previously noted, the elasticity of wage rates with respect to height was only in the range of 0.28–0.66. Behrman and Deolalikar (1989) found that market productivity in India is heavily influenced by BMI during the off-peak season but is not influenced by height in either the peak or off-peak season.[6]

Evidence on BMI trends is sparse. BMI of Citadel cadets aged 18 declined from 20.2 in the 1870s to 19.4 in the 1890s and rose to 21.4 by 1920. BMI of cadets aged 20 rose from 20 in the 1890s to 23.0 in the 1920s (Coclanis and Komlos 1995). This time pattern agrees with that of stature. Cuff (1994) found a similarly low BMI of 19.8 at age 18 and of 20.8 at age 21 among West Point cadets from 1874 to 1994. Evidence from military sources, however, indicates that average BMI for a more representative sample of the population may have been higher. One of us has collected a sample of the detailed anthropometric measurements on Union Army soldiers carried out by the U.S. Sanitary Commission from 1863 to 1865 (see Costa 1994). These show that average BMI among recruits aged 18–19 was 21.7 and that among recruits aged 20–21 was 22.5. Among native white army recruits aged 20–24 in 1892–97, average BMI was 22.0 (Hathaway and Foard 1960).

Figure 2.4 uses military sources, data on Union Army veterans collecting

---

6. These relations are derived from instrumental variables estimates and thus account for potential endogeneity between BMI and wage rates.

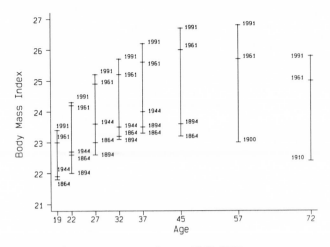

Fig. 2.4   Mean BMI by age group and year, 1863–1991

Note: The age groups are centered at the marks and are ages 18–19, 20–24, 25–29, 30–34, 35–39, 40–49, 50–64, and 65–79. For some years BMI is not available for a specific age group. Calculated from Anthropometric Statistics of Union Army Recruits, Early Indicators of Later Work Levels, Disease, and Death, Hathaway and Foard (1960), Karpinos (1958), 1959–62 NHES, and 1991 NHIS. See the appendix for a description of these data sets.

pensions, and recent surveys to estimate mean BMI by year of measurement and by age group.[7] BMI among men aged 20–24, 25–29, and 30–34 declined between 1864 and 1894, consistent with the decline in heights. But, at ages 35–39 and 40–49 the pattern is reversed. One possible explanation may be the time of measurement. Men in 1892–97 were measured at induction into the army. Men in 1863–65 were measured while in the army, and their experience

7. The age groups are ages 18–19, 20–24, 25–29, 30–34, 35–39, 40–49, 50–64, and 65–79. The years are 1863–64, 1892–97, 1900, 1910, 1943–44, 1959–62, and 1991. Anthropometric measurements carried out by the Sanitary Commission on Union Army soldiers aged 18–49 were used for 1863–65, native-born white army recruits aged 20–39 were used for 1892–97, and Union Army veterans aged 50–64 for 1900 and aged 65–79 for 1910, as well as the 1959–62 NHES and the 1991 NHIS.

The results for 1892–97 are roughly consistent with medicoactuarial data for 1885–1908 after adjusting for indoor clothing by subtracting 1 inch from height to account for heels and 5 pounds from weight to account for clothes (Hathaway and Foard 1960, table 3). Medicoactuarial data for older ages yields a greater BMI. Among men aged 40–49 mean BMI is approximately 24.4, and among men 50–64 approximately 24.7. Studies of New York in the 1920s and Illinois in 1927–29 in which men were measured without clothes also indicate that mean BMI was about 24.3 at ages 40–49, and 24.9 at ages 50–59. However, a study of New York in 1934 yields a mean of 23.1 for men aged 40–49 and 50–59 (Hathaway and Foard 1960, table 6). It is not surprising that BMI is higher among men in the medicoactuarial data than among Union Army veterans. The medicoactuarial data contain a high proportion of professional men, and among Union Army veterans aged 50–64 collecting pensions, men who were either current or retired professionals or proprietors had a mean BMI of 24.3 while men who were either current or retired laborers had one of 22.5. Differences in BMI by occupational class at young ages among Union Army recruits in 1863–65 were not as pronounced as differences at older ages among veterans.

while in the army may have affected the relationship between BMI and age. However, when men who stated that they were either more or less vigorous than before joining the army are deleted from the sample, mean BMI remains unchanged. Although there are differences in BMI between 1863–65 and 1892–97, these are marginal compared to those observed between the nineteenth century and the post–World War II era. The differences in BMI between the nineteenth and the late twentieth century are especially pronounced at older ages.

Why the difference in BMI between the nineteenth and twentieth centuries should be especially pronounced at older ages and why differences in BMI by occupational class were small at young ages and large at old ages can be explained by a wide array of factors. These include the accumulated effects of work intensity and of working conditions, early life conditions that led to chronic conditions that only became evident at older ages, and accumulated effects of differences in nutritional intakes and physical activity. Socioeconomic factors have been found to affect the rate of deterioration in health with age. A recent study of musculoskeletal capacity over a three-and-a-half-year period finds that not only was musculoskeletal capacity lower among men in physical rather than mental or mixed work, but the rate of deterioration in musculoskeletal capacity among men in physical work was greater, perhaps because of the increasing prevalence of musculoskeletal diseases (Nygård, Luopajärvi, and Illmarinen 1988).

It is not enough to consider BMI alone in comparing health across a century. BMI consists of both fat and lean body mass. Lean body mass in turn consists of skeletal, muscle, and visceral mass. A lower lean BMI among Union Army soldiers compared to men today would be an indicator that Union Army soldiers were at greater mortality and morbidity risk. A reduction in skeletal, but not in visceral mass, can arise from mild to moderate undernourishment (Soares and Shetty 1991). Severe undernourishment affects visceral mass as well (Shetty 1984). Table 2.1 shows that for all age groups the estimated percentage of body fat was lower among Union Army soldiers compared to men in the 1959–62 National Health Examination Survey (NHES). However, estimated lean BMI (calculated from total weight minus fat mass in kilograms) among Union Army soldiers was also lower.[8]

---

8. Because the data on Union Army soldiers collected by the U.S. Sanitary Commission contains not only information on height and weight, but also information on a wide array of anthropometric measures, including waist and hip girth and shoulder breadth, these can be used to estimate the percentage of body fat of Union Army veterans. Using the NHES of 1959–62, the percentage of body fat was estimated from the sum of biceps and subscapular skin folds using the method of Durnin and Womersley (1974). The percentage of body fat was then related to BMI, waist girth, and waist girth divided by shoulder breadth entered up to a cubic term by means of ordinary least squares regressions for the age groups 18–19, 20–29, 30–39, and 40–49. These anthropometric measures were able to explain 60–70 percent of the variation in body fat. The percentage of body fat among Union Army soldiers was then predicted from these regression equations.

Table 2.1   **BMI, Percentage of Body Fat, and Lean BMI among Union Army Soldiers and White American Men in 1959–62 in the National Health Examination Survey (NHES)**

	Union Army				NHES			
Age	BMI	(%) Body Fat	Lean BMI	N	BMI	(%) Body Fat	Lean BMI	N
18–19	21.7	18.4	17.6	689	22.9	19.5	18.3	121
20–29	22.8	18.4	18.6	2,869	24.5	20.8	19.1	568
30–39	23.3	21.9	18.1	680	25.5	22.9	19.5	693
40–49	23.3	23.4	17.8	204	27.0	27.4	18.7	636

Note: The numbers for Union Army soldiers were estimated after deleting men whose vigor had been either reduced or improved by the war. Including these men does not change the results.

2.3.3   Central Body Fat

Although height and weight are the most readily available anthropometric measures, studies of recent populations have suggested that measures of central or abdominal body fat are better markers than BMI of risk of death, especially risk of fatal heart disease (e.g., Folsom et al. 1993). Abdominal fat distribution is associated with antecedents of cardiovascular disease such as hypertension, non-insulin-dependent diabetes, high plasma concentrations of atherogenic lipids, and low concentrations of high-density lipoprotein cholesterol (Ohlson et al. 1985; Hartz, Rupley, and Rimm 1984; Vague 1956; Blair et al. 1984; Folsom et al. 1989; Soler et al. 1988; Noord et al. 1990).[9] A 23-year follow-up study of World War II soldiers whose waist-hip ratio was measured at ages 16–35 found that the relative risk of ischemic heart disease mortality of a 0.10 increase in the waist-hip ratio was 1.13 (Terry, Page, and Haskell 1992).

Table 2.2 compares waist-hip ratio and BMI among Union Army soldiers and among World War II soldiers. The comparison is striking. While BMI is greater among World War II recruits, waist-hip ratio is greater among Union recruits. These results suggest that the prevalence of heart disease at older ages among Union Army recruits should have been higher than among World War II veterans, a prediction consistent with the findings of Fogel et al. (1994), who reported that cardiovascular disease was 2.9 times as common among Civil War veterans as among World War II veterans. In fact, if World War II soldiers had had the waist-hip ratio of Union Army soldiers, their risk of death from

---

9. Atherogenic lipids such as chylomicrons, very low density lipoproteins, and low-density lipoproteins accelerate the deposition of lipids in the intima of the arteries. This deposition of lipids is associated with atherosclerosis. High levels of high-density lipoproteins may protect against risk of atherosclerosis, perhaps because these lipoproteins may be scavengers for excess cholesterol present in arterial walls.

Table 2.2   Waist-Hip Ratio (WHR) and BMI among Union Army Soldiers and U.S. World War II Soldiers

	Union Army			World War II		
Age	N	WHR	BMI	N	WHR	BMI
16–20	992	0.843	21.8	33,305	0.820**	22.7**
21–25	1,540	0.854	22.9	20,869	0.833**	23.2**
26–30	709	0.864	23.2	21,121	0.850**	23.8**
31–35	347	0.867	23.3	8,053	0.862	24.0*

Sources: Data on Union Army soldiers are from Anthropometric Statistics of Union Army Recruits described in the appendix. Data on World War II soldiers are from Terry et al. (1992).

*Significant at the 5 percent level.

**Significant at the 1 percent level.

ischemic heart disease 23 years after follow-up would have been 1.04 times greater for men measured at ages 16–20, 1.09 times greater for men measured at ages 21–25, and 1.07 times greater for men measured at ages 26–30. Their risk of death from cerebrovascular disease would have been 1.09 times greater for men measured at ages 16–20, 1.07 times greater for men measured at ages 21–25, and 1.05 times greater for men measured at ages 26–30.

Although a high waist-hip ratio, like all measures of body fat, is commonly regarded as a problem of affluent societies, evidence from a series of studies by Barker and his colleagues (collected in Barker 1992) suggests that a high waist-hip ratio reflects maternal or fetal undernutrition. They find that waist-hip ratio falls with increasing birthweight and rises as the ratio of placental weight to birthweight rises. Both low birthweights and high ratios of placental weight to birthweight may be markers of maternal and fetal undernutrition. One possible explanation for the relationship between waist-hip ratio and maternal and fetal undernutrition is that sustained adrenal overactivity, initiated by early growth restraint, increases abdominal fat depositions. The available evidence on nineteenth-century birthweights suggests that in mid-nineteenth-century Philadelphia the poor had high birthweights by mid-twentieth-century standards (Goldin and Margo 1989), but that the Boston poor at the end of the nineteenth century did not (Ward 1993). Nothing is known about the ratio of placental weight to birthweight in the nineteenth century. However, the low lean BMI of Union Army soldiers may be an indicator of fetal malnutrition. It is known that some low-birthweight babies have disproportionate retardation of the abdominal viscera, especially the liver (Gruenwald 1963).[10] An examination of Union Army recruits suggests that socioeconomic factors do play a role in explaining differences in waist-hip ratios. Controlling for age, BMI, and other characteristics, laborers had a greater waist-hip ratio than farmers, artisans, professionals and proprietors, and farm laborers and the waist-hip ratio

10. It is not known whether this retardation persists into adult ages.

of the foreign-born was greater than that of the native-born. Both laborers and the foreign-born faced more severe environmental stresses compared to the native-born or men in other occupational classes.

2.3.4   Chronic Conditions

The evidence that has been presented on anthropometric measures suggests that in the past men should have been at much greater risk of chronic disease than men today, especially for heart and respiratory diseases since these are associated with shorter heights and higher waist-hip ratios. This is borne out by the research of Fogel et al. (1994), who found that heart disease was 2.9 times as prevalent, musculoskeletal and respiratory diseases were 1.6 times as prevalent, and digestive diseases were 4.7 times as prevalent among Union Army veterans aged 65 or over in 1910 as among World War II veterans of the same ages in 1985–88. In fact, because nineteenth-century physicians did not have the technological capability to diagnose certain conditions, relative prevalence rates may be underestimated. These rates suggest that the prevalence rate of heart disease among the elderly has declined at a rate of 12.8 percent per decade since 1910, while musculoskeletal and respiratory diseases each have declined at a rate of 5.9 percent per decade. Furthermore, chronic conditions began at much earlier ages among the cohorts that reached age 65 between 1900 and 1915 than among the cohorts that reached the same age in the 1980s. Within the earlier cohort, over 7 percent of those between ages 30 and 35 had circulatory diseases, and another 5 percent had incapacitating musculoskeletal diseases.

Examining the data used in Fogel et al. (1994) by cohort suggests that prevalence rates for chronic conditions among cohorts who were born in 1840–49 were higher than those for cohorts who were born in 1830–39 and in 1820–29 (see table 2.3). Among men aged 65–74, those who were born in 1820–29 were significantly less likely to suffer from rheumatism, hemorrhoids, respiratory disorders, hernias, and stomach disorders compared to men born in 1840–49. Those born in 1830–39 were less likely to suffer from hemorrhoids than were those born in 1840–49. Among men aged 55–64, those who were born in 1830–39 were significantly less likely to have varicose veins, rheumatism, heart disease, hemorrhoids, respiratory disorders, stomach disorders, and genitourinary conditions. It is suggestive that there were no differences by cohort in conditions that could not possibly be related to early life environmental factors, such as injury and gunshot wounds.

Although no evidence is yet available on the impact of specific chronic conditions on labor supply in the nineteenth century, recent U.S. data suggest that chronic conditions such as heart disease, arthritis and other musculoskeletal conditions, and respiratory disorders substantially reduce hours worked and the probability of labor force participation, and this reduction in labor supply accounts for up to 45 percent of the decline in earnings observed among middle-aged men (Bartel and Taubman 1979; Yelin and Katz 1991; Burkhauser

Table 2.3   **Prevalence of Chronic Conditions by Cohort and Age (percentages) among Union Army Veterans**

	Year of Birth and Age				
	1820–29	1830–39		1840–49	
Condition	65–74	55–64	65–74	55–64	65–74
Rheumatism	62.4[a]	54.5[b]	71.9	65.2	77.2
Heart	67.3	54.5[b]	72.0	69.3	75.7
Varicose veins	29.7	23.4[b]	36.7	34.1	35.1
Hemorrhoids	33.7[a]	33.4[b]	40.1[b]	41.6	53.6
Hernia	27.7[c]	27.4	38.5	36.6	30.6
Respiratory	26.7[a,c]	27.1[b]	41.2	36.6	42.6
Genito-urinary	19.8	10.4[b]	23.6	18.7	28.3
Stomach	34.7[a,c]	43.8[b]	56.1	49.7	46.0
Diarrhea	26.7	26.8	32.1	28.3	28.3

Note: Prevalence rates for men aged 65–74 in 1830–39 and in 1840–49 were calculated by re-weighting the age distribution to reflect that for men born in 1820–29. Prevalence rates for men aged 55–64 in 1840–49 were calculated by reweighting the age distribution to reflect that for men born in 1830–39.

[a]Prevalence rates for men born in 1820–29 significantly different at the 10 percent level from those for men born in 1840–49.

[b]Prevalence rates for men born in 1830–39 significantly different at the 10 percent level from those for men born in 1840–49.

[c]Prevalence rates for men born in 1820–29 significantly different at the 10 percent level from those for men born in 1830–39.

et al. 1986). The high prevalence of chronic conditions among men aged 65 and over in 1910 suggests that the impact of disease on labor productivity may have been substantial.

2.3.5   Trends in the Distribution of Health

The evidence that we have presented indicates that, by all measures of health, those born in the nineteenth century fared much worse than those born in the twentieth and those born in the latter half of the nineteenth century were worse off than those born in the first half. Yet it is not enough to examine aggregate health. Although the impact of inequalities in health on aggregate production and output has not yet been incorporated in computable general equilibrium models, the intuition of economists has long been that long-run economic growth may be slowed if the health of a large fraction of the population is so poor that this fraction of the population is too unhealthy to increase its productivity and output. High mortality rates might also affect incentives to invest in human capital.

One way to establish changes in the distribution of health is to examine health differentials by occupational class. The data on heights provides the longest series on the distribution of health by occupational class. Figure 2.5

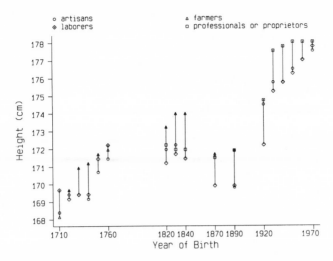

**Fig. 2.5   Mean height differentials by occupational class and birth cohort,
1710–1970**

Note: Year of birth is centered at the marks. Estimates for 1950–70 were adjusted to account for
biases resulting from self-reporting in the 1991 and 1981 NHIS. See note to fig. 2.1 for sources.

illustrates height differentials by occupational class for 10-year cohort intervals
among white, native-born males aged 25–49. Height differentials by occupational class narrowed from the cohort that was born in 1705–14 to those born
in 1745–54 and 1755–64 and then rose again to reach relatively high levels for
the cohort that served in the Civil War.[11] Height differentials by occupational
class did not substantially narrow until the cohort born in 1935–45. Evidence
from the Ohio National Guard suggests that the range in heights was over 2
cm in the latter half of the nineteenth century (Steckel and Haurin 1982). Similarly, BMI differentials were greater during the Civil War and at the turn of the
century than in more recent years (see fig. 2.6).

Another way to examine the distribution of health is by looking at height and
BMI differentials by race. Height differentials by race appear to have increased
sharply from the cohorts born in 1815–24 and 1825–34 to those born in 1835–
45. Differentials among cohorts born in 1935–45 and later were smaller than
those among cohorts born in the two earlier decades (see fig. 2.7). Less is
known about BMI. Fogel (1992) reported that the mean BMI of runaway adult
male slaves treated as contraband of war by a Mississippi field commander was
24.3, far greater than the mean BMI of 22.2 of Union Army soldiers. However
by World War II differences in BMI by race among men were insignificant and
have remained so to this day.

11. Sokoloff and Villaflor (1982) noted this widening of height differentials by occupational
class from the cohort that served in the American Revolutionary War to the cohort that served from
1815 to 1820.

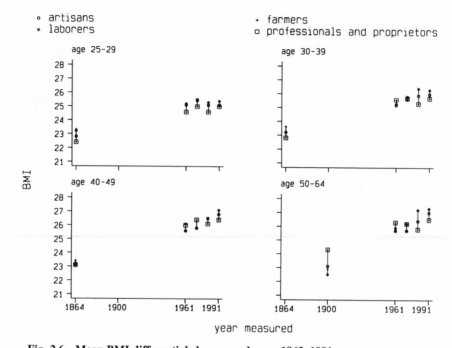

Fig. 2.6 Mean BMI differentials by age and year, 1863–1991

Note: Year of birth is centered at the marks. The means for 1950–70 were adjusted to account for biases in self-reported heights in the NHIS. See note to fig. 2.4 for sources.

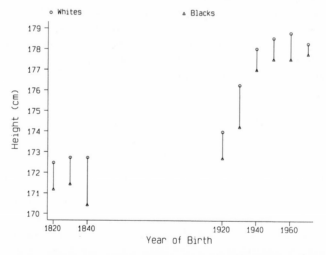

Fig. 2.7 Mean adult height differentials by race and birth cohort, 1820–1970

Note: The data have not been adjusted to reflect self-reporting biases in height in the 1981 and 1991 NHIS. Data come from Union Army Recruits in White Regiments in the United States, 1861–1865, Union Army Recruits in Black Regiments in the United States, 1862–1865, Karpinos (1958), 1959–62 NHES, 1971 NHANES, and 1991 NHIS.

Differences in rural and urban areas deserve mention as well. Most of the nineteenth-century height decline occurred within the rural population. Soldiers who were born in urban areas of 10,000 or more people were approximately 3.3 cm shorter than farmers (Margo and Steckel 1983). Since the share of the U.S. population living in places with 10,000 or more residents increased from 6 percent in 1830 to 14.8 percent in 1860, urbanization could explain only 0.29 (= 0.088 × 3.3) cm of the height decline that was approximately 2.5 cm between 1830 and 1860. We note, however, that urbanization may have played a supporting role in the continuing height decline since evidence from the Ohio National Guard shows a modest height decline in large cities later in the century. Compared with those born before 1880, the heights of those Ohio National Guard troops born from 1880 to 1896 were 2.3 cm less among residents in cities of 50,000 or more. The share of the population living in cities of 50,000 or more residents increased from 12.7 percent in 1870 to 22.3 percent in 1900. There are still some differences in average heights today by extent of urbanization of place of residence among white, native-born men aged 18–19, but the differences are much smaller than in the past. In the 1991 NHIS, men in central-city metropolitan statistical areas were about 1 cm shorter than their counterparts in non-central-city metropolitan statistical areas and in nonfarm areas that were not metropolitan statistical areas.

2.4 Explaining Trends in Health

What is striking about the trend in health is both the dramatic improvement witnessed in the twentieth century and the decline in health during the middle of the nineteenth century at a time of rising incomes. The twentieth-century trends suggest that health and income should be positively associated. Numerous studies on modern data have shown a positive association between health and socioeconomic status. In the absence of evidence to the contrary, economic historians tend to assume that relationships established on modern evidence also hold for the past. Indeed, an important thrust of the profession has been to elucidate the continuity of economic behavior and to demonstrate the relevance of the past for understanding the present.

We begin by noting that low or negative time-series correlation between income or real wages and mortality rates have been reported for historical data in countries such as England and Italy (Livi-Bacci 1991; Kunitz and Engerman 1992). Among groups that in the United States have been studied at the individual level, the relationship between wealth and survival rates suggests a more egalitarian pattern of death. Wealth conveyed no systematic advantage for survival of women and children in households matched in the 1850 and 1860 censuses (Steckel 1988; Davin 1993). Preston and Haines (1991) reported that place of residence and race were the most important correlates of child survival in the late nineteenth century. Although Costa (1993a) found that gains in height from wealth were significant in the East, they were negligible in the

West. The work of Lee (1997) provided an explanation. He found that among recruits inducted into the Union Army, the probability of dying of illness while in the service was not related to wealth, but the probability of dying from a disease with a nutritional basis was strongly and significantly related to wealth. What his findings suggest is that it is hard to identify the effect of wealth under a very severe disease environment in which acute infectious diseases are common. The effects of other factors, such as the difference in immunity status or rates of exposure to disease, may dominate the effect of wealth.

Support for this view is provided by the seemingly weak association in the Union States between individual heights and access to resources. Support for a strong relationship comes from the finding that occupational differences in stature among Europeans amounted to several centimeters (Komlos 1990; Floud, Wachter, and Gregory 1990). On the streets the nobility were easily distinguishable from the poor by their greater height, bulk, and fine clothing. Yet, the variation in average heights across the range of occupations in America was much smaller, usually less than 2 or 3 cm in the middle of the nineteenth century and nearly nonexistent in the eighteenth, which suggests that class differences in health were small; even the poor may have been well fed in the United States, and place of residence appears to have been more important than wealth (Sokoloff and Villaflor 1982; Margo and Steckel 1983).

One of the plausible explanations for the nineteenth-century decline and twentieth-century improvement in health therefore emphasizes the consequences of greater exposure to infectious diseases. Infections such as rubella, hepatitis, cytomegalovirus, and toxoplasmosis in the mother can lead to damage in developing fetal organs and tissues including the myocardium, skeletal muscle, the inner ear, the optical lens and nerve, the teeth, the liver, and the brain. Damage to fetal organs also may arise from the ingestion of toxic substances by the mother and maternal chronic conditions, such as rheumatic heart disease. During early infancy, when growth and expansion of the alveoli are still being completed, a respiratory infection will retard infant growth and lead to worsened lung capacity at late adult ages, a condition associated with both respiratory disorders and heart disease. In fact, the geographical distribution of ischemic heart disease in Great Britain correlates more closely with past infant respiratory mortality than with other leading causes of neonatal disease (Barker 1992).

At later childhood ages, repeated exposure to infectious disease will lead to growth retardation. Whitehead (1977) concluded from work in developing countries that although children are capable of very rapid growth rates when they are not suffering from disease and when they have sufficient food to support catch-up growth, high rates of infection lead to low average growth rates. Many studies find a significant relationship between growth retardation and the incidence of diarrhea, but not of respiratory infections (Martorell and Habicht 1986). At adult ages repeated exposure to infectious disease will lead to wasting. The high levels of chronic diarrhea reported in table 2.3 among Union

Army veterans are likely to have resulted in low BMIs. Other chronic diseases may well play a role. Chronic respiratory disorders show a U-shaped relation to BMI (Roman Diaz 1992; Makela et al. 1991; Negri et al. 1988). The incidence of pulmonary tuberculosis is greater at lower BMI levels (Tverdal 1988).

The nineteenth-century decline in health may be explained by the greater exposure to infectious disease brought on by higher rates of interregional trade, migration, and immigration, and by the push of midwestern farming into marshy and river-bottom lands that hosted malaria. Migration and trade may increase morbidity and mortality by spreading communicable diseases and by exposing newcomers to different disease environments (Smillie 1955; May 1958; Curtin 1989). These adverse consequences could have been substantial before public health measures became effective. Indeed, prior to the late nineteenth century isolated, preindustrial populations in sparsely settled regions were often relatively tall, as discovered in Ireland, the interior of the American South, Austria-Hungary, Sweden, and Japan (Sandberg and Steckel 1988; Shay 1986; Komlos 1989; Nicholas and Steckel 1992; Margo and Steckel 1983, 1992).

In the twentieth century, exposure to infectious disease may have been lessened by the investments in public health made between 1870 and 1930, such as the cleaning of the water supply, the establishment of sewage facilities, the development of effective systems of quarantine, the cleaning of the milk supply, and the clearing of slums. Condran and Cheney (1982) found that in Philadelphia during 1870–1930 the spread of knowledge about the environmental sources of disease and the isolation of carriers of disease were extremely effective in reducing mortality rates. The importance of improvements in sanitation is suggested by the finding of Preston and Haines (1991) that by 1900 the largest cities were not the most lethal. However, with the exception of the top 10 cities, mortality did rise with city size. The importance of exposure to infectious disease is also suggested by Higgs's (1979) finding that in large cities toward the end of the nineteenth century, the death rate varied positively with immigration rates into the city.

A second line of research aimed at explaining the nineteenth-century decline in heights emphasizes the sensitivity of average heights to the distribution of income or wealth. Based on regressions on height from twentieth-century data, a rise of 0.17 in the Gini coefficient would have offset the rise in per capita income and account for a 4 cm decline in average stature (Steckel 1995). The modest evidence on inequality trends in the United States has evoked controversy, but it seems plausible that growth in inequality could have contributed significantly to the secular decline in stature. The Gini coefficient on taxable wealth in Massachusetts increased from 0.734 in 1820 to 0.907 in 1900, and in Ohio it rose from 0.806 in 1830 to 0.864 in 1900 (Steckel 1994).

Yet another explanation for the height decline is provided by Komlos (1987), who argues that the height decline may have been caused by a deterioration in the diet created by the sectoral shift in production that occurred during industrialization. According to this view, urbanization and the expansion of the industrial labor force increased the demand for food while productivity per worker and the agricultural labor force grew slowly, causing a decline in food production (especially meat) per capita. A decline in per capita meat consumption could lead to maternal malnutrition and anemia and therefore to fetal malnutrition.

Changes in labor organization that led to greater exposure to disease in the workplace in the nineteenth century also deserve attention in a list of potential explanations for the mid-nineteenth-century decline in health. The home manufacturing typical of the eighteenth century diffused geographic patterns of work and insulated the population from contagious disease. In contrast, factories and artisan establishments that emerged in the 1820s and 1830s concentrated employees in the workplace under conditions that increased the risk of exposure to infectious diseases. The crowding of numerous people in dusty or humid environments, typical of textile mills, led to the spread of tuberculosis and pulmonary illnesses. These conditions are important for understanding the secular decline in stature of the mid-nineteenth century because children comprised a substantial share of the labor force during America's industrial revolution (Goldin and Sokoloff 1982). The geographic spread of industrialization to the Midwest widened the scope of this claim on nutrition.

Despite improvements in working conditions at the beginning of the twentieth century such as the decline in hours of work, especially those of women and children, occupational health hazards remained high in the first third of the century in part because few safety precautions were taken. The adverse health consequences of employment in most manufacturing, extractive, and agricultural occupations were well recognized by insurance companies, industrial physicians, directors of compensation boards, factory inspectors, and general practitioners of medicine, and lists of hazardous occupations were compiled (e.g., Britten and Thompson 1926). Among the hazards were extreme dry heat such as that found in foundry work, sudden variations in temperature, dampness, organic and inorganic dust, infections from the handling of animal products, and exposure to infected soil and to poisons used in the manufacturing process. Increased safety precautions in manufacturing, the shift of women into the clerical sector, and the more recent shift of male employment into the service sector have reduced exposure to hazardous working conditions.

Advances in medical technology must also be credited with improving quality of life in the latter half of the twentieth century. Table 2.3 shows an extremely high prevalence of hernias at the beginning of the century when they were still untreatable. Among Union Army veterans age 65 and over in 1910, the prevalence of hernias was 35 percent, but it was only 7 percent among World War II veterans of the same age in 1985–88. However, 27 percent of veterans of the same age in 1983 had ever had a hernia, suggesting that most of the improvement in prevalence rates for hernias has come from medical advances (Fogel et al. 1994).

A major therapeutic advance has been the introduction of antibiotics. Infectious diseases in infancy and early childhood can now be cured before they lead to large reductions in the rate of growth and damage to developing organs. In fact, the introduction of antibiotics between 1930 and 1950 coincides with a rapid increase in height.[12] The cohorts that were born in the age of antibiotics have not yet reached age 65. They will not reach age 90 for another quarter of a century. As pointed out by Preston (1993), those who are now 90 were born in 1905 when life expectancy at birth was only 50 years, 12 out of 100 children did not survive infancy, and the burden of infectious diseases was exceptionally heavy. Nonetheless, they were born at a time when life expectancy at birth had improved. In fact, improvements in the disease environment that resulted in the development of better physiques and less scarring by the sequelae of infectious disease may explain the increase in the size of the "old-old" population since the 1970s. Continued improvements in the disease environment are likely to lead to further increases in the size of the "old-old" population. Kim (1995) argued that the rapid increase in the final height of birth cohorts between 1910 and 1945 explains a large part of the improvement in elderly health that started in the late 1970s to early 1980s. Social Security Administration projections of the size of the elderly population are based on the percentage decline in mortality over the last 10 to 15 years. Past projections have failed to anticipate improvements in mortality (Crimmins 1984). The marked improvement in stature between 1930 and 1950 suggests that elderly health will improve rapidly at least 10 to 20 years in the future. Projections based on recent mortality declines are therefore likely to be off the mark once more.

2.5   Welfare

Since health is a major component of human welfare, it is important to know whether traditional measures of the standard of living, such as per capita income, adequately incorporate the value of health status. The measurement problem is diminished to the extent that measured incomes are spent to improve health. For example, if households spend additional income on a better diet, the health benefits of these expenditures are reflected in a higher GNP. Similarly, outlays on medical equipment are incorporated in the same way as purchases of other consumer products that increase satisfaction. The issue is whether traditional measures of the standard of living, such as per capita income, are overshadowed by the consumer surplus of these expenditures.

The decline in health of the mid-nineteenth century occurred despite income growth. Although it is conceivable that this happened by shifting income away from health-producing products such as diet and housing, the explanations discussed earlier suggest that the decline in health was largely independent of

---

12. The increase in heights also coincides with the first period in which public health investments were fully in place.

consumer expenditures. Of course, the same cannot be said of the connection between income growth and improvement in health that took place late in the century.

If changes in income per capita inadequately reflect changes in welfare, it is important to consider methodologies for appraising welfare change. Although it is possible to show that for any social well-being function, there is a corresponding formulation of real national income that, if used, would reflect what is claimed of it (Dasgupta 1993), in practice such a formulation cannot be computed. The prices that would be used for computing an ideal national income index are shadow prices, not market prices. Furthermore, a number of the components of an ideal index remain unrecorded, such as the social worth of commodities that enhance health.

Below we compare the results of alternative methodologies for appraising welfare change based on techniques used in the economics literature. Because each method in use has shortcomings, here we are unable to provide quantitative estimates of welfare change that are definitive or convincing. Nevertheless, the pattern of results establishes the importance of including health in our conceptual apparatus for the standard of living and suggests that the course of welfare in the middle of the nineteenth century diverged importantly from that indicated by per capita income alone.

An early exploration of computable ways of improving on estimates of real national income as measures of well-being is represented by the work of Usher (1973, 1980). Usher used age-specific mortality rates and their shadow prices to calculate willingness to pay for an improvement in the chances of survival. The fairly strong assumptions that he needed to make about utility functions were (1) that utility, U_t, is a function of consumption, C_t, in each time period, t; (2) that utility is separable in C_t; (3) that all utility functions take the special form $U_t = \sum_{i=0}^{t-1} C_i^\beta/(1 + r)^i$, where β is the elasticity of annual utility with respect to consumption and r is the subjective rate of discount; and (4) that consumption is constant across all ages. He then calculated willingness to pay for an improvement in the chances of survival as

(1)
$$\frac{1}{\beta} C_0 \sum_{j=0}^{n} \frac{S_j}{(1 + r)^j},$$

where S_t is the probability of surviving to year t and is equal to $\Pi_{j=0}^{t-1}(1 - D_j)$, where D_t is the mortality rate t years from the individual's current age. Usher then defines $\hat{C}(t)$ to be the level of consumption at which one would be as well off with the mortality rates of some base year, T, as one was with the actual consumption level, $C(t)$, and mortality rates of that year. That is,

(2)
$$\hat{C}(t) = C(t)[L(t)/L(T)]^{1/\beta},$$

where $L(t)$ is an index of mortality (or survival) rates capturing life expectancy effects and is defined as $L(t) = \sum_{j=0}^{n} S_{j+1}(t)/(1 + r)^j$. The impact of improvements in mortality over time is then measured by the difference between the growth of $\hat{C}(t)$ and $C(t)$, or

(3) $$G_{\hat{c}} = G_c + \frac{1}{\beta}G_L.$$

Usher's approach can therefore be implemented from a time series of real net national income per head and age-specific mortality rates.

Age-specific mortality rates at 10-year age intervals are available for 1850 onward (Haines 1994; Preston, Keyfitz, and Schoen 1972). These indicate that from 1850 to 1860 and from 1860 to 1870 mortality decreased; it then increased in 1880, almost reaching the level prevailing in 1850. After 1880 there was a sustained decrease in mortality rates. What this mortality pattern suggests is that real per capita GNP will overestimate the increase in well-being from 1870 to 1880 and underestimate the increase in well-being after 1880. Table 2.4 shows actual real per capita GNP and revised GNP estimates under various assumptions about the interest rate, r, and the elasticity of annual utility with respect to consumption, β. The base year is 1940. The parameters were chosen solely to give an indication of the variation in the resulting estimates. Actual and revised decadal growth rates of real per capita GNP are given in table 2.5. These indicate that conventional estimates of the growth rates of per capita GNP overestimate well-being by 30–75 percent during the increases in mortality from the 1870s to the 1880s and underestimate increases during other time periods. The underestimates are up to 530 percent (1910–20).

The extent of variation seen in the revised GNP estimates under different assumptions about the interest rate and the elasticity of annual utility with respect to consumption suggests that assessments of the exact dollar value of improvements in longevity can easily be disputed. Another potential problem is the treatment of longevity gains as exogenous. If measured consumption

Table 2.4   **Measured and Revised Real Per Capita GNP in 1958 Dollars**

Year	Actual	$r = 0.05$		$r = 0.10$	
		$\beta = 0.25$	$\beta = 0.45$	$\beta = 0.25$	$\beta = 0.45$
1849	254	62	116	96	148
1859	300	90	154	132	190
1869–78	531	187	298	258	356
1879–88	774	209	374	313	468
1890	836	292	466	411	564
1900	1,011	387	593	537	711
1910	1,299	634	872	776	975
1920	1,315	683	914	819	1,011
1930	1,490	1,079	1,245	1,198	1,320
1940	1,720	1,720	1,720	1,720	1,720
1950	2,342	3,150	2,761	2,771	2,572
1960	2,699	4,007	3,362	3,356	3,046

Sources: Decadal averages were used for the years 1869–78 and 1879–88 (Gallman 1966; U.S. Bureau of the Census 1975, Series F-4). Life tables for 1870 and 1880, respectively, were used for these years (Haines 1994).

Table 2.5   Measured and Revised Decadal Growth Rates (percentage) of Per
                   Capita GNP

Years	Actual	$r = 0.05$		$r = 0.10$	
		$\beta = 0.25$	$\beta = 0.45$	$\beta = 0.25$	$\beta = 0.45$
1849 to 1859	18.1	45.2	32.8	37.5	28.4
1859 to 1869–78	77.8	107.8	93.5	95.5	87.4
1869–78 to 1879–88	46.0	11.8	25.5	21.3	31.5
1879–88 to 1890	8.0	83.0	24.6	31.3	20.5
1890 to 1900	20.9	32.3	27.3	30.7	26.1
1900 to 1910	28.5	63.8	47.0	44.5	37.1
1910 to 1920	1.2	7.7	4.8	5.5	3.7
1920 to 1930	13.3	58.0	36.2	46.3	30.6
1930 to 1940	15.4	59.0	38.2	43.6	30.3
1940 to 1950	36.2	83.1	60.5	61.1	49.5
1950 to 1960	15.2	27.2	21.8	21.1	18.4

Sources: See the note to table 2.4.

includes investments in health that influenced longevity, then there will be double counting (Williamson 1984). This is especially likely to be a problem during the latter half of the twentieth century when medical technology advanced to a level high enough to allow effective cures.

Another problem is that Usher's calculation only accounts for the impact of longevity and not that of health. Consider the following calculation. A way to estimate willingness to pay to achieve modern BMIs is to estimate the present value of lost income as a result of lowered participation. A lower bound estimate of the present value of lost income is simply discounted earnings times the probability of nonparticipation. An increase in mean BMI from 23.0 to 26.4 among Union Army veterans suggests that the probability of labor force nonparticipation should fall by 6 percent. Then, accounting for the decreased mortality risk, assuming an interest rate of 5 percent, and assuming that life ends at age 80, a man aged 50 in 1900 should be willing to pay about 9 percent of the average annual earnings of a manufacturing worker to increase his BMI from the mean in 1900 to the mean in 1990. Note that although in this calculation the present value of lost income is interpreted as the morbidity cost of a low BMI, we could also interpret the present value of lost income as willingness to pay for a reduction in mortality under the assumption that utility is strictly equal to income. The much lower estimate of the value of life that results from this interpretation suggests that equating utility with income provides an extreme lower bound of willingness to pay for a reduction in mortality.[13]

13. Rosen (1988) pointed out that using the present value of lost income as an estimate of the value of life is unjustifiable from the viewpoint of utility theory.

An alternative approach to the direct valuation of improvements in longevity was that taken by Morris (1979), who used a weighted sum of life expectancy at birth, the infant survival rate, and the adult literacy rate. The United Nations Development Programme's (1990) Human Development Index (HDI) builds on the work of Morris. The HDI is simply the sum of normalized indices of per capita national income, life expectancy at birth, and adult literacy rate. Comparisons can be made across a set of countries by determining maximum and minimum values for each of the indicators: life expectancy (X_1), literacy (X_2), and logarithm of real GDP per capita (X_3). A deprivation measure places a country on a scale of zero to one as specified by the difference between the maximum and minimum values. Specifically, I_{ij} is the deprivation indicator for country j with respect to indicator i, where $I_{ij} = (\max X_{ij} - X_{ij})/(\max X_{ij} - \min X_{ij})$, and the average level of deprivation for country j is given by $I_j = (I_1 + I_2 + I_3)/3$. The HDI for country j is defined as one minus the average deprivation index: $(HDI)_j = 1 - I_j$.

The index immediately attracted attention and scrutiny; a recent survey addresses several concerns including the number of dimensions, choice of indicators, weights, and selection of minimum and maximum values (United Nations Development Programme 1993, 104–14). The HDI measures relative progress on a scale of basic or minimal measures, and as the quality of life in a country improves, additional attributes or dimensions become important in distinguishing levels of welfare. Of particular concern for work in economic history is the choice of indicators and the selection of maximum and minimum values. Lack of data may constrain the choice of indicators, and the maximum and minimum values should be wide enough to encompass a broad range of historical experience.

Since a consistent series on life expectancy is unavailable for the United States in the early nineteenth century, we chose stature as our basic measure of health.[14] Indeed, as a measure of net nutrition, height is a good alternative since it is sensitive to the consumption of basic necessities and to disease that absorbs or diverts nutritional intake. We are aware that use of stature as a health indicator gives a somewhat different meaning to the HDI since height emphasizes conditions in childhood as opposed to the entire life span captured by life expectancy at birth. Moreover, life expectancy at birth is a cross-sectional measure of health, whereas the data on stature are arranged by birth cohort.[15]

In order to place our HDI in a broad historical context, we chose zero and 100 percent as the minimum and maximum for literacy rates, and our range

14. Our estimates of stature are derived from fig. 2.1, using linear interpolation where necessary. Where gaps appear in the national height series in the late nineteenth century, we used interpolation based on the Ohio National Guard under the assumption that the national time pattern followed that in Ohio (see data reported in Steckel 1992, 288).

15. Specifically, our HDI mixes cross-sectional and cohort indicators whereas the United Nations' HDI uses cross-sectional measures only. In principle, one could place stature on a cross-sectional basis by calculating the average height of those who were alive in a particular year, an approach complicated by lack of information on deaths.

Table 2.6   **Human Development Index (HDI) and Components, 1800–1970**

Year	HDI	Income/N	Literacy	Height (cm)
1800	0.580	302	0.724	172.9
1810	0.588	318	0.725	173.0
1820	0.603	326	0.737	172.9
1830	0.624	349	0.745	173.5
1840	0.617	391	0.761	172.2
1850	0.632	430	0.780	171.1
1860	0.661	523	0.803	170.6
1870	0.702	659	0.800	171.2
1880	0.735	909	0.830	169.5
1890	0.750	1,113	0.867	169.1
1900	0.802	1,395	0.893	170.0
1910	0.865	1,747	0.923	172.1
1920	0.884	1,743	0.940	173.1
1930	0.894	2,025	0.957	173.4
1940	0.936	2,370	0.971	176.1
1950	0.951	3,133	0.974	177.1
1960	0.955	3,623	0.978	177.3
1970	0.962	4,774	0.990	177.5

Sources: Compiled from the sources cited in the notes to fig. 2.1, Weiss (1992), U.S. Bureau of the Census (1975), and the Public Use Sample of the 1850 census. See footnotes 16 and 17 for more details.

for stature of adult men adopts the height of the Bundi of New Guinea as the minimum (156 cm) and the upper end is defined by the current tallest national population, which is approximately 180 cm (Eveleth and Tanner 1990). The price of a subsistence diet, $140 in 1970 dollars, is our minimum for per capita income, and we take the United Nations' upper bound of $4,861 (in 1987 dollars, or $1,660 in 1970 dollars) as our maximum (see the introduction to this volume).

The results displayed in table 2.6 give perspective to welfare during industrialization. We first note that the level of the index is quite high on the eve of industrialization despite the poverty (as measured by per capita income) of the era. Americans were reasonably well off as measured by the HDI—certainly much better off than the residents of poor developing countries of the late twentieth century.[16] Despite low incomes, stature was relatively high and a sub-

16. The 10 worst countries on the scale of "human development" had an average HDI of 0.172 in 1987 (United Nations Development Programme 1990, 128–29). The index we tabulated for the United States is not quite comparable, however, because the measure of health is different and the minima and maxima for the other indicators also differ. If we adopt the minima and maxima for literacy (12.3 percent to 100 percent) and income ($220 to $4,861) used by the United Nations in 1987, and if we adjust the income reported for the United States in 1970 prices to 1987 levels ($884), the HDI for the United States in 1800 was 0.615. We note that the high HDI ranking in 1800 exists in part because the United States had a lower deprivation ranking using stature as opposed to life expectancy. If we use life expectancy in place of health, invoking a reasonable

stantial majority of the population was literate (note that the literacy rate includes slaves, who we assume were illiterate).[17]

Second, the years after 1830 are often glorified by economic historians as signifying the onset of industrialization and improving living standards, yet our measure of HDI indicates that welfare essentially stagnated during the early phase of industrialization. The stagnation occurred because modest increases in per capita income and literacy were offset by declines in stature. Although stature declined after 1860, reaching a low point in 1890, the HDI increased substantially in the closing decades of the nineteenth century because literacy improved moderately (largely through education of blacks) and there were large absolute increases in per capita income.

It may seem difficult to reconcile welfare declines with early industrialization, but an important point often overlooked is that the base from which gains were made was very low in the early industrial period. Put another way, the HDI increased more in the last three decades than it did in the first 70 years of the century. Growth rates at newly high (modern or near modern levels) were impressive, but though they deserve our study as a significant departure from the past, the consequences initially took the population only a small way toward modern welfare levels because the absolute gains from these higher growth rates were small enough to be offset by health losses associated with industrialization.

Economic historians must understand that the HDI is a retrospective index of welfare; it asks how and when modern levels of welfare were attained. The early period of industrialization contributed only a tiny absolute portion to the welfare levels we now enjoy, but the percentage changes in per capita income that it involved were still important for contemporaries. Annual income gains on the order of 1.5 percent, experienced in the second quarter of the nineteenth century, were significant, particularly at base levels that were only moderately above subsistence. Thus, in terms of measuring progress, there is no inconsistency or contradiction between the HDI and income growth rates, only a difference in perspective. The growth rate is a velocity measure, and the HDI is a

---

guess of 45 years, the HDI in 1800 falls to 0.412, which would achieve a rank of 35th among the list of 130 countries in 1987.

17. Literacy rates from 1850 onward were taken from the federal censuses as reported in *Historical Statistics of the United States*. We estimated literacy rates for the free population from 1800 to 1840 using reports of literacy by age contained in the 1850 Public Use Micro Sample (PUMS). We used the literacy of those aged 30 and above in 1850 to estimate literacy in 1840, the literacy of those aged 40 and above in 1850 to estimate literacy in 1830, and so on. We understand this procedure may contain biases to the extent that survival rates varied with literacy. In defense of the procedure, we note that literacy was an impotent predictor of survival of married women from 1850 to 1860 (see Steckel 1988). The procedure also neglects cohort trends in literacy that may have existed among older generations alive in the early 1800s who did not survive to 1850, a defect we cannot remedy. An alternative is to estimate literacy from signature lists available from marriage registers, wills, and other sources, an approach that involves questions of selectivity, representation by age and region, and so forth.

distance measure; both are relevant for understanding the past. Growth rates stress changes witnessed by contemporaries, while the HDI measures how far an economy has come along the path to modern living standards. Put differently, the income gains of the first generation of industrial workers, however important to them, amounted to only a pittance compared with income growth experienced by typical modern workers.

A third approach to measuring welfare ranks numerous indicators of the quality of life. Dasgupta (1993) proposed the construction of a ranking based on six indexes—national income, life expectancy at birth, infant mortality rates, adult literacy rates, and two indexes of political and civil liberties. Comparisons are then based on ordinal measures derived from a "Borda" rule. According to the Borda rule each time period is awarded a point equal to its rank within each index (with one representing the lowest rank). The ordinal distance between two time periods depends on how many time periods squeeze themselves in between for each index that is studied. The rankings are then summed across all indexes to construct a Borda rank. The use of this methodology for comparing developing countries in the 1980s yields reasonable results (Dasgupta 1993).

We have calculated two indexes based on the Borda rule. The first one is by decade from 1849 to 1970 and has as its component indexes real per capita GNP, infant mortality rates, life expectancy at birth (e_0), school enrollment rates, and average heights for white, native-born men (see table 2.7). The second index has as its component indexes only real per capita GNP, literacy, and

Table 2.7   Rankings of Living Standards Data by Year, 1849–1970

Year	Borda Rank	GNP/N	Infant Mortality	e_0	School Enrollment	Height
1849	1	1	1	1	1	5
1859	2	2	3	3	3	4
1869–78	3	3	4	4	2	6
1879–88	2	4	2	2	6	1
1890	4	5	5	5	5	2
1900	5	6	6	6	4	3
1910	6	7	7	7	7	7
1920	7	8	8	8	8	8
1930	8	9	9	9	9	9
1940	9	10	10	10	10	10
1950	10	11	11	11	11	12
1960	11	12	12	12	12	11
1970	12	13	13	13	13	13

Sources: Decadal averages were used for the years 1869–78 and 1879–88 (Gallman 1966; U.S. Bureau of the Census 1975, Series F-4). Life tables for 1870 and 1880, respectively, were used for these years. Life tables for 1850–1900 are from Haines (1994) and for 1910–60 from Preston et al. (1972). School enrollment is from U.S. Bureau of the Census (1975). Heights are from Fogel (1986) and Steckel and Haurin (1982).

Table 2.8   **Rankings of Living Standards Data by Year, 1800–1970**

Year	Borda Rank	GNP/N	Literacy	Height
1800	1	1	1	10
1810	2	2	2	11
1820	3	3	3	10
1830	6	4	4	13
1839	4	5	5	9
1844	5	6	6	8
1849	5	7	7	6
1854	6	8	8	5
1859	7	9	9	4
1869–78	10	10	10	7
1879–88	8	11	11	1
1893	9	12	12	2
1898	11	13	13	3
1903	12	14	14	3
1907	13	15	15	8
1911	14	17	16	9
1916	15	16	17	10
1921	16	18	18	12
1931	17	19	19	14
1940	18	22	21	15
1945	19	21	22	17
1950	20	21	22	18
1955	21	23	23	19
1960	21	24	24	17
1965	23	25	25	16
1970	24	26	26	20

Sources: Decadal averages were used for the years 1869–78 and 1879–88. See notes to tables 2.6 and 2.7 for details on construction.

average heights of white, native-born men but extends back to 1800 (see table 2.8). The average height that is used is that for the cohort born near the specified year.

The Borda rankings in table 2.7 indicate that well-being fell from 1869–78 to 1879–88 to reach a level comparable to that prevailing in 1859. After 1888 well-being rose steadily. According to the Borda rankings in table 2.8 net welfare was stagnating in the antebellum period. Rankings are high at the end of the nineteenth century because of steady improvements in literacy. When a Borda index constructed only with height and per capita GNP is used, the nadir of well-being is reached in 1879–88 after a pronounced decline from the levels prevailing in 1839 and 1844, and despite a doubling of per capita GNP from 1830 to 1898, net welfare does not improve.

An alternative methodology for appraising welfare changes is to apply the model of Thaler and Rosen (1976) to measure the value of life. In a life cycle model the value of eliminating risk to life at a specific age is the expected value of additional consumer surplus it generates. The value of a current-age-independent risk can be estimated from equalizing wage differentials on risky jobs. Thaler and Rosen (1976) found that workers in 1967 were willing to pay from 2 to 4 percent of their annual income to reduce death risk from 0.001 per year to zero. Viscusi (1978) estimated that the risk premium to jobs perceived as dangerous in 1969 was approximately 5 percent of average annual earnings. Although no comparable work has been done for the past, using the *Thirteenth Annual Report of the Kansas Bureau of Labor and Industry* for 1897 we find that the risk premium for dangerous jobs was about 7 percent.[18] Assuming that, as a percentage of annual earnings, the risk premium has remained constant over time, we can use Thaler and Rosen's and Viscusi's estimates to derive willingness to pay for a reduction in mortality in the nineteenth century.

In 1850 the probability of a 25-year-old man living to age 65 was .45 (Haines 1994), and his average height was 171 cm. Had a man in 1850 had the average height of one in 1830 (174 cm) he would have experienced a 3 percent fall in mortality.[19] Had he had the average height of a man in 1890 (169 cm) he would have experienced a 6 percent increase in mortality. Assuming that the risk premium is 2–5 percent of average annual earnings, a man in 1850 would have been willing to pay 27–68 percent of his annual income to have the height of a man in 1830. He would have been willing to give up 54–135 percent of his annual income not to have the height of a man in 1890. Since per capita income increased by 23 percent between 1830 and 1850 and by 159 percent between 1850 and 1890, the increase in per capita income does not outweigh the mortality increase between 1830 and 1850, but it does outweigh the mortality increase between 1850 and 1890. A man in 1850 would thus have been willing to sacrifice increases in mortality for gains in income for the postbellum but not the antebellum period.

2.6 Concluding Remarks

We have presented evidence showing that the course of health and economic growth diverged in the nineteenth century and converged in the twentieth, findings that hold regardless of whether health is measured by stature, BMI, mortality rates, or prevalence of chronic conditions. In view of the questions posed by these patterns for the adequacy of national accounts as a welfare measure, we quantified the monetary value of changes in life expectancy. Employing several approaches to analyze welfare changes, we estimated a Human Development Index and a Borda ranking, and we calculated Usher-adjusted incomes and the willingness to pay for a reduction in mortality risk. We found that in the antebellum period the increase in income was insufficient to com-

18. The risk premium is estimated from a regression of the wage on worker characteristics and a dummy equal to one if the worker reported being in a dangerous occupation.
19. Calculated from Waaler's (1984) height-mortality relationship.

pensate for the decline in health. The absolute gain in income achieved by modern economic growth in the early industrial period, though important to those alive at the time, was simply too low to offset declines in health. In contrast, improvements in health outpaced economic growth in the twentieth century. Our estimates indicated that whereas real per capita GNP more than doubled between 1900 and 1960, the "true" increase in GNP was six- to tenfold.

We argue that changes in the disease environment, among other factors, can partially account for the decrease in well-being in the nineteenth century and the increase in well-being in the twentieth. In the nineteenth century, higher rates of interregional trade, migration, and immigration exposed a previously isolated population to disease. Other contributing factors included the rise of public schools, which spread diseases among children; hardships caused by the Civil War; urbanization; growing inequality; and dietary deterioration associated with relatively higher food prices. In the twentieth century, higher incomes combined with growing awareness of expenditures and practices that improved health led to the prevention of disease, while advances in medicine, such as antibiotics and vaccinations, lessened the consequences of exposure to infectious disease. Nutritional status improved in part because public health investments reduced the population's exposure to infectious disease. The full impact of the public health investments made from 1870 to 1930, such as the establishment of sewage systems and clean water supplies and the cleaning of the milk supply, may not have been manifest for up to 50 or 60 years. Quantification of the impact of changes in the disease environment must await the creation of longitudinal data sets that link ecological and environmental variables in early life to subsequent morbidity and mortality.[20]

Our findings suggest that the adverse health consequences noted for the United States in the nineteenth century were significantly a matter of timing. The changes associated with industrialization and modernization occurred before substantial knowledge of effective mechanisms of disease prevention or cure were available. Consequently, the cohorts born before the late nineteenth century bore the scars of infectious disease for the rest of their lives. Later cohorts were more fortunate. By reducing the transmission of disease, public health measures alleviated the effects of urban congestion and of mass migrations. But the failure of the United States to implement public health measures earlier cannot be blamed on poor policy decisions.

The new evidence that we presented on trends in health, such as waist-hip ratio, BMI, and the prevalence of chronic conditions at older ages suggested that early life conditions may exert an impact on mortality and morbidity that is not manifest until older ages. The improvement in BMI and the decline in

---

20. A data set that does this for the cohort born in the 1830s is currently being created by Fogel et al. A brief description of Early Indicators of Later Work Levels, Disease, and Death is provided in the data appendix.

the prevalence of chronic conditions at older ages were especially striking features of the trend in health. The evidence indicates that a symbiotic relationship existed between disease and BMI: disease increased nutritional status and therefore lowered BMI while a low BMI increased susceptibility to disease. Chronic conditions, and therefore low BMIs, may be linked to malnourishment and exposure to infectious diseases during the fetal and neonatal states, infancy, and early childhood. The waist-hip ratio seen among Union Army soldiers reinforces this hypothesis. A high waist-hip ratio is associated with an increased risk of heart disease and diabetes and is related to markers of maternal and fetal malnutrition. Thus, early life conditions may well affect the entire future experience of a cohort.

The rapid increase in stature from the 1930s to the 1950s suggests that the cohorts now approaching their sixties will experience a much greater rate of increase in health and longevity than past generations. Because most recent predictions of the size of the elderly population are based on the percentage decline in mortality over the last 10 to 15 years, current forecasts are likely to be off the mark. The sensitivity of long-term Social Security balances to uncertainty about the future course of mortality suggests that we can only ignore the evidence from the long-term trend at our peril.

Data Appendix

The available data sources on height, weight, and other anthropometric measures and on chronic conditions for the United States include publicly available machine-readable data sets, machine-readable data sets that were not yet publicly available at the time of writing, and published sources. The sources that we used in the paper or that were used in papers referred to in the text are described in detail, by category, below. The detailed descriptions give some indication of available variables, manuscript sources, and how to obtain the data. First, though, we present the reader with a brief chronological guide to the data sources.

Information on the cohorts born in the early colonial period and in the early republic comes from military sources. The anthropometric information that is in these sources is limited to height. Although not yet publicly available, these sources are in machine-readable form and are

- French and Indian War Army Recruits
- American Revolution Army Recruits
- United States Army Recruits, 1815–1820

The information on nineteenth-century cohorts is more extensive and includes not only information on height but also information on weight and other anthropometric measures and on chronic conditions. Some published information for slaves is available from Richard Steckel's 1979 article listed below. The bulk of the information comes from Civil War records, particularly those of the Union Army. These records include information on blacks, as well as whites. Information from pre–Civil War records comes from the machine-readable data sets

- Height and Weight of West Point Cadets, 1843–1894
- United States Army Recruits, 1850–1855

The first data set is publicly available. The second is not.

The publicly available, machine-readable Civil War records are

- Union Army Recruits in White Regiments in the United States, 1861–1865
- Union Army Recruits in Black Regiments in the United States, 1862–1865
- Confederate Amnesty Records for the United States Civil War, 1863–1866
- Union Army Slave Appraisal Records from Mississippi, 1863–1865, ICPSR 9427
- Early Indicators of Later Work Levels, Disease, and Death

All of the data sets contain information on height measured at the time of the Civil War. Union Army Slave Appraisal Records contains information on weight as well. Early Indicators contains information on illnesses incurred while in the service. Although the data in Early Indicators are limited to the Civil War cohort, the sampled Civil War cohort is followed until death and therefore is an excellent source of information on the height, weight, and chronic conditions of the elderly in the first three decades of the twentieth century.

The machine-readable Civil War data sets that are not yet publicly available are

- Union Army Rejects
- Anthropometric Statistics of Union Army Recruits

Both data sets contain information on height. The first data set includes causes of rejection as well, and the second detailed anthropometric measurements such as weight, waist circumference, hip circumference, shoulder breadth, and dynamometer. Published Civil War sources are

- Gould 1869
- Baxter 1875

Relatively few machine-readable sources are available for nineteenth-century postbellum cohorts. With the exception of the already mentioned Height and Weight of West Point Cadets, 1843–1894, the only other source is

• Ohio National Guard

and the anthropometric information in this source is limited to height. Information can, however, be gathered from published sources such as

• U.S. Army, Surgeon General, various years
• Hathaway and Foard 1960
• Davenport and Love 1920, 1921

Information on the twentieth century comes from World War II publications and from the large, machine-readable surveys of the entire U.S. population whose collection began in the late 1950s and early 1960s and continues to the present day. These surveys contain information on height, weight, and chronic conditions and are all publicly available. They include

• National Health Examination Survey (NHES), Cycle I, 1959–1962
• National Health Interview Survey (NHIS), 1970 to present
• Health and Nutrition Examination Survey (NHANES) I, 1971–1975
• Health and Nutrition Examination Survey (NHANES) II, 1976–1980

The published World War II sources are

• Karpinos 1958
• U.S. Selective Service System 1944

A detailed description of the data sources is given below. The data sources are in alphabetical order within the three categories (1) machine readable and publicly available, (2) machine readable but not yet publicly available, and (3) published.
    1. Publicly available machine-readable data sets used in the paper or in papers referred to in text:

• *Confederate Amnesty Records for the United States Civil War, 1863–1866, ICPSR 9429*. Principal investigator: Richard Steckel. Available from: Inter-University Consortium for Political and Social Research, Ann Arbor, MI. Cases: 6,762. Variables: Date of amnesty, county and state of amnesty, age, occupation, and height. Original data source: All amnesty oaths signed by persons in the Confederacy and kept in the Diplomacy Branch, Record Group #59, Entries 466 and 467 in the National Archives.
• *Early Indicators of Later Work Levels, Disease, and Death*. Principal investigators: Robert W. Fogel et al. A subsample of this data set had been released to Inter-University Consortium for Political and Social Research, Ann Arbor, MI, as The Aging of Veterans of the Union Army. Additional data will be released as it becomes available. Cases: 39,616. Longitudinal data set of

Union Army recruits linked to 1850, 1860, 1900, and 1910 censuses and military, medical, and pension records, including detailed examinations by examining surgeons. Information is available on morbidity, mortality, height, weight, stresses endured while in service, and socioeconomic and demographic variables, including labor force participation and pension recipiency.

- *Health and Nutrition Examination Survey (NHANES) I, 1971–1975.* Principal investigator: U.S. Department of Health and Human Services, National Center for Health Statistics. Available from: Inter-University Consortium for Political and Social Research, Ann Arbor, MI. Detailed information on specific conditions obtained from clinical exams as well as past medical history. Contains also socioeconomic and demographic variables and information on diet. Information on height, weight, and skinfold measurements is also available. Epidemiological follow-ups are available. Universe: Civilian noninstitutionalized population aged 1–74 of the United States.
- *Health and Nutrition Examination Survey (NHANES) II, 1976–1980.* Principal investigator: U.S. Department of Health and Human Services, National Center for Health Statistics. Available from: Inter-University Consortium for Political and Social Research, Ann Arbor, MI. Similar to NHANES I, with the exception that no epidemiological follow-up is available.
- *Height and Weight of West Point Cadets, 1843–1894, ICPSR 9468.* Principal investigator: John Komlos. Available from: Inter-University Consortium for Political and Social Research, Ann Arbor, MI. Cases: 4,178. Variables: Age, height, weight, state of birth, state of appointment, date of physical exam, father's occupation and income, and parents' residency.
- *National Health Examination Survey (NHES), Cycle I, 1959–1962, ICPSR 9203, 9206, 9208, 9209, 9201, 9204, 9207, 9202.* Principal investigator: U.S. Department of Health and Human Services, National Center for Health Statistics. Available from: Inter-University Consortium for Political and Social Research, Ann Arbor, MI. Cases: 6,672. Variables: Physical measurements (including right arm girth, chest girth, waist girth, right arm skinfold, right infrascapular skinfold, height, weight, sitting normal height, sitting erect height, knee height), physician examination and medical history for cardiovascular, diabetes, osteoarthritis and rheumatoid arthritis, and vision, and socioeconomic and demographic characteristics. Universe: Civilian noninstitutionalized population aged 18–79 of the coterminous United States.
- *National Health Interview Survey (NHIS), 1970 to present.* Principal investigator: U.S. Department of Health and Human Services, National Center for Health Statistics. Available from: Inter-University Consortium for Political and Social Research, Ann Arbor, MI, and 1988 to present on CD-ROM from Data Dissemination Branch, National Center for Health Statistics, Centers for Disease Control and Prevention. Yearly survey with questions on chronic impairments, medical care utilization, height, weight, and socioeconomic and demographic variables. Each year special supplements include questions on specific topics such as diabetes, smoking, health insurance, exercise, and

so forth. Universe: Civilian noninstitutionalized population of the United States.

- *Union Army Recruits in Black Regiments in the United States, 1862–1865, ICPSR 9426.* Principal investigators: Jacob Metzer and Robert A. Margo. Available from: Inter-University Consortium for Political and Social Research, Ann Arbor, MI. Cases: 8,592. Variables: Height, age, birthplace, occupation before enlistment, enlistment date, and changes in rank.
- *Union Army Recruits in White Regiments in the United States, 1861–1865, ICPSR 9425.* Principal investigators: Robert W. Fogel and Stanley L. Engerman et al. Available from: Inter-University Consortium for Political and Social Research, Ann Arbor, MI. Cases: 39,616. Variables: Date, place, and term of enlistment, place of birth, occupation before enlistment, age at enlistment, height, and county and town latitude and longitude and population figures. Original data source: Union Army muster rolls.
- *Union Army Slave Appraisal Records from Mississippi, 1863–1865, ICPSR 9427.* Principal investigator: Robert A. Margo. Available from: Inter-University Consortium for Political and Social Research, Ann Arbor, MI. Cases: 1,213. Variables: Age, weight, height, sex, appraised value of slave, and date of appraisal. Original data source: All slaves who appeared in a set of appraisal records for Civil War Mississippi.

2. Machine-readable data sets that were not publicly available at time of writing:

- *American Revolution Army Recruits.* Principal investigators: Kenneth Sokoloff and Georgia Villaflor. Obtained from: Center for Population Economics, Graduate School of Business, University of Chicago. Cases: 5,609. Variables: Age, occupation, height, place and date of enlistment, place of birth. Original data source: Army and militia muster rolls.
- *Anthropometric Statistics of Union Army Recruits.* Principal investigator: Dora L. Costa. The release date to Inter-University Consortium for Political and Social Research, Ann Arbor, MI is expected to be the year 2001. Cases: 22,818 (projected). Variables: Age, race, occupation, ethnicity, marital status, place of birth, place of enlistment, date of examination, date of enlistment, height, height to lower part neck, height to knee, height to perineum, waist circumference, hip circumference, chest circumference, breadth neck, breadth shoulders, breadth pelvis, arm length, foot length, weight, chest capacity, condition teeth, condition muscles, pulse rate, respiration rate, dynamometer, whether vaccinated for smallpox, whether athletic before war. Original data source: Records of the U.S. Sanitary Commission, New York Public Library.
- *French and Indian War Army Recruits.* Principal investigators: Kenneth Sokoloff and Georgia Villaflor. Obtained from: Center for Population Econom-

ics, Graduate School of Business, University of Chicago. Cases: 9,016. Variables: Age, occupation, height, place and date of enlistment, place of birth. Original data source: Army and militia muster rolls.
- *Ohio National Guard.* Principal investigators: Richard Steckel and Donald Haurin. Obtained from: Richard Steckel. Cases: 5,035 aged 23–49. Variables: Name, regiment, company, age, occupation, stature, birthplace, residence, and marital status. Original data source: Ohio National Guard Muster rolls housed in the Ohio Historical Society and the Beightler Armory in Columbus, Ohio.
- *Union Army Rejects.* Principal investigator: Richard Steckel. Obtained from: Center for Population Economics, Graduate School of Business, University of Chicago. Cases: 2,015. Variables: Age, place and date of enlistment, occupation, height, and reason for rejection. Original data source: Union Army rejection records.
- *United States Army Recruits, 1815–1820.* Principal investigators: Kenneth Sokoloff and Georgia Villaflor. Obtained from: Center for Population Economics, Graduate School of Business, University of Chicago. Cases: 15,169. Variables: Age, height, place and date of enlistment, place of birth. Original data source: Army and militia muster rolls.
- *United States Army Recruits, 1850–1855.* Principal investigators: Kenneth Sokoloff and Georgia Villaflor. Obtained from: Center for Population Economics, Graduate School of Business, University of Chicago. Cases: 2,497. Variables: Age, height, place and date of enlistment, place of birth. Original data source: Army muster rolls.

   3. Published sources used in the paper or related to data sets and series used in the paper:

- Baxter, J. H. 1875. Statistics, medical and anthropological, of the provost-marshal-general's bureau, derived from records of the examination for military service in the armies of the United States during the late war for the rebellion of over a million recruits of drafted men, substitutes, and enrolled men. Washington, D.C.
- Davenport, Charles B., and Albert G. Love. 1920. *Defects found in drafted men.* Prepared for War Department. Washington, D.C.: Government Printing Office.
- Davenport, Charles B., and Albert G. Love. 1921. *Army anthropology.* Prepared for Medical Department of the U.S. Army in the World War. Washington, D.C.: Government Printing Office.
- Gould, Benjamin Apthorp. 1869. *Investigations in the military and anthropological statistics of American soldiers.* Published for the U.S. Sanitary Commission. New York: Hurd and Houghton.
- Hathaway, Millicent L., and Elsie D. Foard. 1960. *Heights and weights of*

adults in the United States. U.S. Department of Agriculture, Agricultural Research Service, Human Nutrition Research Division, Home Economics Research Report no. 10. Washington, D.C.: Government Printing Office.
- Karpinos, Bernard D. 1958. Height and weight of Selective Service registrants processed for military service during World War II. *Human Biology* 30:292–321.
- Steckel, Richard H. 1979. Slave height profiles from coastwise manifests. *Explorations in Economic History* 16:363–80.
- U.S. Army. Surgeon General. Various years. *Report of the surgeon general U.S. Army to the secretary of war.* Washington, D.C.: Government Printing Office.
- U.S. Selective Service System. 1944. *Physical examinations of Selective Service registrants during wartime.* Medical Statistics Bulletin no. 3. Washington, D.C.: Government Printing Office.

References

Barker, D. J. P., ed. 1992. *Fetal and infant origins of adult disease.* London: British Medical Journal.
———. 1994. *Mothers, babies, and disease in later life.* London: British Medical Journal.
Bartel, A., and P. Taubman. 1979. Health and labor market success: The role of various diseases. *Review of Economics and Statistics* 61(1): 1–8.
Behrman, Jere R., and Anil B. Deolalikar. 1989. Agricultural wages in India: The role of health, nutrition, and seasonality. In *Seasonal variability in Third World agriculture,* ed. D. Sahn. Baltimore: Johns Hopkins University Press.
Blair, D., J. P. Habicht, E. A. H. Sims, et al. 1984. Evidence for an increased risk of hypertension with centrally located body fat and the effect of race and sex on this risk. *American Journal of Epidemiology* 119(4): 526–40.
Britten, Rollo H., and L. R. Thompson. 1926. A health study of ten thousand male industrial workers. U.S. Public Health Bulletin no. 162. Washington, D.C.: Government Printing Office.
Burkhauser, Richard V., J. S. Butler, Jean M. Mitchell, and Theodore Pincus. 1986. Effects of arthritis on wage earnings. *Journal of Gerontology* 41(2): 277–81.
Coclanis, Peter, and John Komlos. 1995. Nutrition and economic development in post-Reconstruction South Carolina: An anthropometric history. *Social Science History* 19(1): 91–116.
Condran, G. A., and R. A. Cheney. 1982. Mortality trends in Philadelphia: Age-specific and cause-specific death rates 1870–1930. *Demography* 19(11): 97–123.
Costa, Dora L. 1993a. Height, wealth, and disease among the native-born in the rural, antebellum North. *Social Science History* 17(3): 355–83.
———. 1993b. Height, weight, wartime stress, and older age mortality: Evidence from the Union Army records. *Explorations in Economic History* 30(4): 424–49.
———. 1994. Health of young adults: Evidence, causes, and outcomes. Grant proposal submitted to the National Institutes of Health.

————. 1995. Pensions and unemployment: Evidence from Union Army veterans. *Quarterly Journal of Economics* 110(2): 297–320.

————. 1996. Health and labor force participation of older men, 1900–1991. *Journal of Economic History* 56(1): 62–89.

Crimmins, E. M. 1984. Life expectancy and the older population: Demographic implications of recent and prospective trends in old age mortality. *Research on Aging* 6(4): 490–514.

Cuff, Timothy. 1994. The body mass index values of mid-nineteenth-century West Point cadets: A theoretical application of Waaler's curves to a historical population. *Historical Methods* 26(4): 171–82.

Curtin, Philip D. 1989. *Death by migration.* Cambridge: Cambridge University Press.

Dasgupta, Partha. 1993. *An inquiry into well-being and destitution.* Oxford: Clarendon; New York: Oxford University Press.

Davin, Eric Leif. 1993. The era of the common child: Egalitarian death in antebellum America. *Mid-America: An Historical Review* 75(2): 135–63.

Davis, Lance E., et al. 1972. *American economic growth.* New York: Harper and Row.

Deolalikar, Anil B. 1988. Do health and nutrition influence labor productivity in agriculture? Econometric estimates for rural South India. *Review of Economics and Statistics* 70(2): 406–13.

Durnin, J. V. G. A., and J. Womersley. 1974. Body fat assessed from total body density and its estimation from skinfold thickness: Measurements on 481 men and women aged from 16 to 72 years. *British Journal of Nutrition* 32(1): 77–97.

Eveleth, Phyllis B., and James M. Tanner. 1990. *Worldwide variation in human growth.* Cambridge: Cambridge University Press.

Floud, Roderick, Kenneth W. Wachter, and Annabel S. Gregory. 1990. *Height, health, and history: Nutritional status in the United Kingdom, 1750–1980.* Cambridge: Cambridge University Press.

Fogel, Robert W. 1986. Nutrition and the decline in mortality since 1700: Some preliminary findings. In *Long-term factors in American economic growth,* ed. S. L. Engerman and R. E. Gallman. Chicago: University of Chicago Press.

————. 1992. The body mass index of adult male slaves in the United States circa 1863 and its bearing on mortality rates. In *Without consent or contract: The rise and fall of American slavery: Evidence and methods,* ed. R. W. Fogel, Ralph A. Galantine, and Richard L. Manning. New York: Norton.

Fogel, Robert W., Dora L. Costa, and John M. Kim. 1994. Secular trends in the distribution of chronic conditions and disabilities at young adult and late ages, 1860–1988: Some preliminary findings. University of Chicago. Unpublished manuscript.

Folsom, A. R., S. A. Kaye, T. A. Sellers, C. P. Hong, J. R. Cerhan, J. D. Potter, and R. J. Prineas. 1993. Body fat distribution and 5-year risk of death in older women. *Journal of the American Medical Association* 269(4): 483–87.

Folsom, A. R., R. J. Prineas, S. A. Kaye, et al. 1989. Body fat distribution and self-reported prevalence of hypertension, heart attack, and heart disease in older women. *International Journal of Epidemiology* 18(2): 361–67.

Foster, Andrew D., and Mark R. Rosenzweig. 1992. Information flows and discrimination in rural areas in developing countries. *Proceedings of the World Bank annual conference on development economics,* 173–203. Washington, D.C.: World Bank.

Friedman, Gerald C. 1982. The heights of slaves in Trinidad. *Social Science History* 6(4): 482–515.

Gallman, Robert E. 1966. Gross national product in the United States, 1834–1909. In *Output, employment, and productivity,* ed. D. S. Brady. Studies in Income and Wealth no. 30. New York: National Bureau of Economic Research.

Goldin, Claudia. In press. Labor markets in the twentieth century. In *Cambridge economic history of the United States,* ed. Stanley Engerman and Robert Gallman. New York: Cambridge University Press.

Goldin, Claudia, and Robert A. Margo. 1989. The poor at birth: Birth weights and infant mortality at Philadelphia's Almshouse Hospital, 1848–1873. *Explorations in Economic History* 26(3): 360–79.

———. 1992. Wages, prices, and labor markets before the Civil War. In *Strategic factors in nineteenth century American economic history: A volume to honor Robert W. Fogel,* ed. C. Goldin and H. Rockoff, 67–104. Chicago: University of Chicago Press.

Goldin, Claudia, and Kenneth Sokoloff. 1982. Women, children, and industrialization in the early Republic: Evidence from the manufacturing censuses. *Journal of Economic History* 42(4): 741–74.

Gruenwald, P. 1963. Chronic fetal distress and placental insufficiency. *Biology of the Neonate* 5:216–65.

Haddad, Lawrence J., and Howarth E. Bouis. 1991. The impact of nutritional status on agricultural productivity: Wage evidence from the Philippines. *Oxford Bulletin of Economics and Statistics* 53(1): 46–68.

Haines, Michael R. 1994. Estimated life tables for the United States, 1850–1900. NBER Working Paper Series on Historical Factors in Long Run Growth, Historical Paper no. 59. Cambridge, Mass.: National Bureau of Economic Research.

Hartz, A. J., D. C. Rupley, and A. A. Rimm. 1984. The association of girth measurements with disease in 32,856 women. *American Journal of Epidemiology* 119(1): 71–80.

Hathaway, Millicent L., and Elsie D. Foard. 1960. *Heights and weights of adults in the United States.* U.S. Department of Agriculture, Agricultural Research Service, Human Nutrition Research Division, Home Economics Research Report no. 10. Washington, D.C.: Government Printing Office.

Higgs, Robert. 1979. Cycles and trends of mortality in 18 large American cities, 1871–1900. *Explorations in Economic History* 16(4): 381–408.

Kansas Bureau of Labor and Industry. 1,204 wage-earners in Kansas, 1897. *Thirteenth Annual Report of the Kansas Bureau of Labor and Industry.* Machine-readable data available from University of California, Berkeley, Institute of Business and Economic Research, Historical Labor Statistics Project.

Karpinos, Bernard D. 1958. Height and weight of Selective Service registrants processed for military service during World War II. *Human Biology* 30:292–321.

Kim, John M. 1995. The health of the elderly, 1990–2035: An alternative forecasting approach based on changes in human physiology, with implications for health care costs and policy. University of Chicago, Center for Population Economics. Unpublished manuscript.

Komlos, John. 1987. The height and weight of West Point cadets: Dietary change in antebellum America. *Journal of Economic History* 47(4): 897–927.

———. 1989. *Nutrition and economic development in the eighteenth-century Habsburg monarchy.* Princeton, N.J.: Princeton University Press.

———. 1990. Height and social status in eighteenth-century Germany. *Journal of Interdisciplinary History* 20(4): 607–21.

Kunitz, Stephen J., and Stanley L. Engerman. 1992. The ranks of death: Secular trends in income and mortality. *Health Transition Review* 2 (Suppl.): 29–46.

Lee, Chulhee. 1997. Socioeconomic background, disease, and mortality among Union Army recruits: Implications for economic and demographic history. *Explorations in Economic History* 34 (1): 27–55.

Livi-Bacci, Massimo. 1991. *Population and nutrition: An essay on European demographic history.* Cambridge: Cambridge University Press.

Makela, M., M. Heliovaara, K. Sievers, O. Impivaara, P. Knekt, and A. Aromaa. 1991. Prevalence, determinants, and consequences of chronic neck pain in Finland. *American Journal of Epidemiology* 134(11): 1356–67.

Margo, Robert A. In press. The labor force in the nineteenth century. In *Cambridge economic history of the United States,* ed. Stanley Engerman and Robert Gallman. New York: Cambridge University Press.

Margo, Robert A., and Richard H. Steckel. 1982. The heights of American slaves: New evidence on slave nutrition and health. *Social Science History* 6(4): 516–38.

———. 1983. Heights of native-born whites during the antebellum period. *Journal of Economic History* 43(1): 167–74.

———. 1992. The nutrition and health of slaves and antebellum Southern whites. In *Without consent or contract: Conditions of slave life and the transition to freedom,* ed. R. W. Fogel and S. L. Engerman, 508–21. New York: Norton.

Martorell, Reynaldo, and Jean-Pierre Habicht. 1986. Growth in early childhood in developing countries. In *Human growth: A comprehensive treatise,* vol. 3, ed. F. Falkner and J. M. Tanner. New York: Plenum.

May, Jacques M. 1958. *The ecology of human disease.* New York: MD Publications.

Morris, Morris David. 1979. *Measuring the condition of the world's poor: The physical quality of life index.* New York: Pergamon.

Negri, E., R. Pagano, A. Decarli, and C. La Vecchia. 1988. Body weight and the prevalence of chronic diseases. *Journal of Epidemiology and Community Health* 42(1): 24–29.

Nicholas, Stephen, and Richard H. Steckel. 1992. Tall but poor: Nutrition, health, and living standards in pre-famine Ireland. NBER Working Paper Series on Historical Factors in Long Run Growth, Historical Paper no. 39. Cambridge, Mass.: National Bureau of Economic Research.

Noord, P. A. H. Van, J. C. Seidell, I. Den Tronkelaar, E. A. Baabders-Van Halewijn, and I. J. Ouwehand. 1990. The relationship between fat distribution and some chronic diseases in 11,825 women participating in the DOM-Project. *International Journal of Epidemiology* 19(3): 564–70.

Nygård, C.-H., T. Luopajärvi, and J. Illmarinen. 1988. Musculoskeletal capacity of middle-aged women and men in physical, mental and mixed occupations. *European Journal of Applied Physiology* 57(2): 181–88.

Ohlson, L. O., B. Larsson, K. Svardsudd, et al. 1985. The influence of body fat distribution on the incidence of diabetes mellitus: 13.5 Years of follow-up of the participants in the study of men born in 1913. *Diabetes* 34(10): 1055–58.

Pope, Clayne L. 1992. Adult mortality in America before 1900: A view from family histories. In *Strategic factors in nineteenth century American economic history: A volume to honor Robert W. Fogel,* ed. C. Goldin and H. Rockoff, 267–96. Chicago: University of Chicago Press.

Preston, Samuel H. 1993. Demographic change in the United States, 1970–2050. In *Forecasting the health of elderly populations,* ed. K. G. Manton, B. H. Singer, and R. M. Suzman, 51–78. New York: Springer.

Preston, Samuel H., and Michael R. Haines. 1991. *Fatal years: Child mortality in late nineteenth century America.* Princeton, N.J.: Princeton University Press.

Preston, Samuel H., Nathan Keyfitz, and Robert Schoen. 1972. *Causes of death: Life tables for national population.* New York: Seminar.

Roman Diaz, M. 1992. Prevalencia de Obesidad y Condiciones Asociades en un Centro de Medicina de Familia. *Boletin-Asociacion Medica de Puerto Rico* 84(11): 302–4.

Rosen, Sherwin. 1988. The value of changes in life expectancy. *Journal of Risk and Uncertainty* 1:285–304.

Sandberg, Lars G., and Richard H. Steckel. 1988. Overpopulation and malnutrition rediscovered: Hard times in nineteenth century Sweden. *Explorations in Economic History* 25(1): 1–19.

Shay, Ted. 1986. The stature of military conscripts: New evidence on the standard of living in Japan. Paper given at the 1986 Social Science History Association meetings, St. Louis.

Shetty, P. S. 1984. Adaptive change in basal metabolic rate and lean body mass in chronic undernutrition. *Human Nutrition–Clinical Nutrition* 38(6): 443–51.

Smillie, Wilson G. 1955. *Public health: Its promise for the future.* New York: Macmillan.

Soares, M. J., and P. S. Shetty. 1991. Basal metabolic rate, body composition and whole-body protein turnover in Indian men with differing nutritional status. *Clinical Science* 81(3): 419–25.

Sokoloff, Kenneth L., and Georgia C. Villaflor. 1982. The early achievement of modern stature in America. *Social Science History* 6(4): 453–81.

Soler, J. T., A. R. Folsom, L. H. Kushi, et al. 1988. Association of body fat distribution with plasma lipids, lipoproteins, apolipoproteins AI and B in postmenopausal women. *Journal of Clinical Epidemiology* 41(11): 1075–81.

Steckel, Richard H. 1979a. Slave height profiles from coastwise manifests. *Explorations in Economic History* 16(4): 363–80.

———. 1979b. Slave mortality: Analysis of evidence from plantation records. *Social Science History* 3(3,4): 86–114.

———. 1988. The health and mortality of women and children, 1850–1860. *Journal of Economic History* 48: 333–45.

———. 1992. Stature and living standards in the United States. In *American economic growth and standards of living before the Civil War,* ed. R. E. Gallman and J. J. Wallis. Chicago: University of Chicago Press.

———. 1994. Census manuscript schedules matched with property tax lists: A source of information on long-term trends in wealth inequality. *Historical Methods* 27(2): 71–85.

———. 1995. Stature and the standard of living. *Journal of Economic Literature* 33(4): 1903–40.

Steckel, Richard H., and Donald R. Haurin. 1982. Height, nutrition, and mortality in Ohio, 1870–1900. Columbus, Ohio. Mimeograph.

Terry, R. B., W. F. Page, and W. L. Haskell. 1992. Waist/hip ratio, body mass index and premature cardiovascular disease mortality in U.S. Army veterans during a twenty-three year follow-up study. *International Journal of Obesity* 16(6): 417–23.

Thaler, Richard, and Sherwin Rosen. 1976. The value of saving a life: Evidence from the labor market. In *Household production and consumption,* ed. N. E. Terleckyj, 265–98. New York: National Bureau of Economic Research.

Tverdal, A. 1988. Height, weight, and incidence of tuberculosis. *Bulletin of the International Union against Tuberculosis and Lung Disease* 63(2): 16–18.

United Nations Development Programme. 1990. *Human development report 1990.* New York: Oxford University Press.

———. 1993. *Human development report 1993.* New York: Oxford University Press.

U.S. Bureau of the Census. 1975. *Historical statistics of the United States, colonial times to 1970.* Washington, D.C.: Government Printing Office.

Usher, Dan. 1973. An imputation to the measurement of economic growth for changes in life expectancy. In *The measurement of economic and social performance,* ed. M. Moss, 193–226. New York: Columbia University Press.

———. 1980. *The measurement of economic growth.* New York: Columbia University Press.

Vague, J. 1956. The degree of masculine differentiation of obesities: A factor determining predisposition to diabetes, atherosclerosis, gout, and uric calculous disease. *American Journal of Clinical Nutrition* 4:20–34.

Viscusi, W. Kip. 1978. Wealth effects and earnings premiums for job hazards. *Review of Economics and Statistics* 60(3): 408–16.

Waaler, H. T. 1984. Height, weight, and mortality: The Norwegian experience. *Acta Medica Scandinavica [Suppl.]* 679(Suppl.): 1–56.

Ward, Peter W. 1993. *Birth weight and economic growth: Women's living standards in the industrializing West.* Chicago: University of Chicago Press.

Weiss, Thomas. 1992. U.S. labor force estimates and economic growth, 1800–1860. In *American economic growth and standards of living before the Civil War,* ed. R. E. Gallman and J. J. Wallis, 19–78. Chicago: University of Chicago Press.

Whitehead, R. G. 1977. Protein and energy requirements of young children living in the developing countries to allow for catch-up growth after infections. *American Journal of Clinical Nutrition* 30(9): 1545–57.

Williamson, J. G. 1984. British mortality and the value of life, 1781–1931. *Population Studies* 38(1): 157–72.

Yelin, E. H., and P. Katz. 1991. Labor force participation among persons with musculoskeletal conditions, 1970–1987. *Arthritis and Rheumatism* 34(11): 1361–70.

3 Health, Height, and Welfare: Britain, 1700–1980

Roderick Floud and Bernard Harris

In recent years, an increasing number of historians have combed the records of military recruiting officers, convict ships, prison officers, and local education authorities to examine the impact of economic and social change on the height of the British population during the last three centuries. Although this work was originally inspired by an investigation into the causes of mortality decline in North America, it soon became apparent that the historical analysis of human height could offer new insights into the long-running controversy over the standard of living during the industrial revolution, and the techniques developed during these investigations were also applied to debates over the demographic impact of the First World War and the impact of the interwar recession (Fogel et al. 1978; Floud, Wachter, and Gregory 1990; Harris 1988, 1993). The most comprehensive account of long-term trends in the height of the British population was provided by Roderick Floud, Kenneth Wachter, and Annabel Gregory, but their work has since been challenged and extended by a long list of other authors (see, e.g., Komlos 1993a, 1993b, 1993c; Mokyr and Ó Gráda 1994; Nicholas and Steckel 1991; Nicholas and Oxley 1993; Riggs 1994). As a result, it is probably fair to say that more attention has been devoted to changes in the height of the British population than to those of any other population group.

The aim of this paper is to synthesize some of this evidence against the background of the history of British industrialization and its impact on the health and welfare of the mass of the population since circa 1750. Sections 3.1

Roderick Floud is provost of London Guildhall University and a research associate of the National Bureau of Economic Research. Bernard Harris is lecturer in social policy in the Department of Sociology and Social Policy, University of Southampton.

Bernard Harris's attendance at the NBER conference was facilitated by a grant from the British Academy. The authors wish to thank Rick Steckel, John Komlos, and Ralph Shlomowitz for their helpful comments.

and 3.2 are concerned with the pace and timing of the "industrial revolution" and with its effects on real wage rates, mortality, and literacy. Section 3.3 summarizes the current literature on changes in human stature during the eighteenth and nineteenth centuries, while section 3.4 extends this analysis into the twentieth century. Section 3.5 seeks to combine a range of "human development indicators" into a composite index of changes in human welfare in Britain between 1839 and 1914. The final section summarizes the main conclusions of the paper and suggests some lines for further research.

3.1   The Origins of British Industrialization

Although this paper is primarily concerned with the impact of industrialization on welfare since the mid-eighteenth century, it is appropriate to begin with a brief account of the origins and nature of Britain's industrial revolution. For many years, historians used the term "industrial revolution" to describe a rapid and fundamental transformation in the development of the British economy between, say, 1760 and 1840 (see, e.g., Toynbee 1884). However, in recent years, historians have questioned the traditional image of "an industrial revolution, tied directly to radical changes in methods of production, having their decisive consequences over a relatively short period of time" (Lee 1986, 18). The "new economic historians" in particular have argued that the roots of Britain's industrial growth must be sought in the seventeenth and early eighteenth centuries, and that their impact was slower and more patchy than previously thought (Crafts 1994, 47).

This transformation in our understanding of the origins of the industrial revolution has led to a renewed interest in the pattern of economic growth throughout the eighteenth century. In contrast to many earlier accounts, it is now argued that the eighteenth-century economy was rather more buoyant than historians once believed. This was particularly true of British agriculture, where—according to the latest estimates—agricultural productivity increased by between 0.1 and 0.6 percent per annum between 1700 and 1800 (Allen 1994, 111). The eighteenth century also witnessed a significant increase in per capita incomes, although the effects of this may have been at least partially offset by a parallel increase in income inequality (McKendrick 1982; Porter 1982, 230–31; Lindert 1994, 378–81). Crafts has estimated that per capita incomes rose by 0.31 percent per annum between 1700 and 1760, by 0.01 percent per annum between 1760 and 1780, and by 0.35 percent per annum between 1780 and 1801 (Crafts 1985a, 45). However, this optimistic assessment has recently been challenged by Komlos, who argued that the British economy experienced an "incipient Malthusian crisis" during the eighteenth century, from which it only emerged at the end of the Napoleonic Wars (Komlos 1989, 1993a, 1993c).

The growing tendency to "backdate" the onset of the industrial revolution has led some historians to question the validity of the concept altogether, but it is clear that the British economy and society did undergo a number of fundamental changes between 1700 and 1850 (Cameron 1978; Fores 1981). The most obvious and unequivocal change was in the number of people who inhabited the British Isles during this period. The statistics for England alone show that the population increased from 5.06 million in 1701 to 8.66 million in 1801 and 16.74 million in 1851. The population of Scotland increased from 1.1 million in 1700 to 2.1 million in 1821, and the population of Ireland increased from approximately 2 million to approximately 7 million over the same period (Wrigley and Schofield 1981, 208–9; Schofield 1994, 93). The eighteenth and nineteenth centuries also witnessed a profound change in the occupations pursued by the majority of the employed population. In 1700, 61.2 percent of male workers were employed in agriculture and 18.5 percent were employed in industry. By 1840, these figures had changed to 28.6 and 47.3 percent, respectively (Crafts 1994, 45).

The increase in the overall size of the population was reflected in the pace of urbanization. E. A. Wrigley has calculated that the proportion of the population that lived in towns containing more than 5,000 inhabitants increased from 17 percent in 1700 to 27.5 percent in 1801, while the proportion of the population living in towns containing more than 2,500 inhabitants increased from 34 percent to 54 percent between 1801 and 1851 (Wrigley 1987, 170; Thompson 1990, 8). The increase in the proportion of the population who lived in towns was accompanied by a dramatic increase in the size of the towns in which they lived. In 1801 only London had a population of more than 100,000, but this situation changed rapidly as the nineteenth century progressed. By 1851 there were 10 towns with populations over 100,000, and the population of London itself had grown to 2.5 million (Waller 1983, 25; Wohl 1983, 4).

3.2   Industrialization and the Standard of Living

The controversy surrounding the interpretation of changing living standards during the period of the "classic" industrial revolution has been described as "the most sustained single controversy in British economic history" and as "the most contentious issue in economic history" (Mathias 1975, vii; Horrell and Humphries 1995, 90). For much of the twentieth century, the debate has tended to be polarized between conflicting groups of "optimists" and "pessimists," who have often appeared to be divided as much by politics and methodology as by the conclusions they reached (Taylor 1975, xi–xviii). During the 1950s and 1960s the debate was dominated by Max Hartwell and Eric Hobsbawm (Hobsbawm 1957; Hartwell 1961), but in recent years a new generation of historians has entered the fray. During the first half of the 1980s Peter Lindert and Jeffrey Williamson published a series of articles that attempted to combine traditional economic indicators, such as real wages, with more "qualitative" factors, such as health and mortality, but their efforts have failed to win universal acclaim (Williamson 1982; Lindert and Williamson 1983, 1985a, 1985b; Crafts 1985b; Mokyr 1988).

The controversies that have surrounded this debate are of more than historical interest. Although the debate is primarily concerned with the relationship between economic change and human welfare at a particular point in time, it also raises much broader questions about the way in which we define and measure the "standard of living" (Floud 1984). In this section, we attempt to summarize three of the most important components of the "standard of living" in the form of real wages, mortality, and access to educational opportunities. We shall then be in a better position to present the results of our own investigations into the relationship between industrialization and stature.

3.2.1 The Real Wage Debate

The most obvious starting point for discussions about the impact of industrialization on workers' living standards is provided by information on real wages. During the past 40 years, a great deal of scholarly energy has been devoted to the calculation and refinement of different local series in the hope of constructing a composite picture of national trends (Botham and Hunt 1987; Crafts 1985a, 1985b, 1989; Flinn 1974; Lindert and Williamson 1983, 1985a, 1985b; Phelps Brown and Hopkins 1956; Schwarz 1985, 1990; von Tunzelmann 1979). The task has been complicated by the fact that we still know relatively little about the movement of wages and prices or the precise details of individual consumption patterns (Floud et al. 1990, 281–82).

Nevertheless, there is now a general consensus that the real wages of the majority of manual workers increased during the first half of the eighteenth century, either stagnated or declined during the second half of the eighteenth century, and then began to rise once more at some point between 1800 and 1820 (Lindert 1994, 369–71).

Two of the most important recent attempts to investigate trends in real wages are those made by Lindert and Williamson in 1983 and Schwarz in 1985. Lindert and Williamson calculated wage rates for a range of workers at various periods between 1755 and 1851. They found that there was little evidence of any significant change in real wage rates for blue- or white-collar workers in the period between 1755 and 1819 but that real wages rose substantially between 1819 and 1851 (Lindert and Williamson 1983, 12–13). Schwarz calculated trends in the real wages of London bricklayers from 1700 to 1860 (see fig. 3.1). His findings suggested that real wages rose between 1700 and 1720 and leveled off between 1720 and 1750. They fell sharply between 1750 and 1800 and rose between 1800 and 1860 (Schwarz 1985, 28).

One of the biggest difficulties associated with the interpretation of real wage statistics is the difficulty of making sufficient adjustments for variations in unemployment and in female labor force participation rates. However, in 1983 Lindert and Williamson calculated that the national unemployment rate would

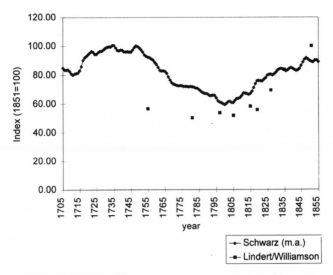

Fig. 3.1   Real wages, 1705–1855
Sources: Lindert and Williamson (1983) and Schwarz (1985).
Notes: Schwarz (m.a.): 11-year moving average of London bricklayers' nominal wages deflated by the Phelps Brown and Hopkins price index.

have had to rise from zero percent to 50 percent, or from 10 percent to 55 percent, to obliterate the increased value of real wages between 1819 and 1851 (Lindert and Williamson 1983, 13). In a more recent publication, Peter Lindert has argued that unemployment would have needed to rise from zero percent to 34 percent to cancel out the effects of increased real wages (Lindert 1994, 373). However, although the margin of error appears to be narrowing, it is still difficult to believe that employment opportunities could have deteriorated by a sufficient amount to overturn the authors' basic contention (Burnett 1994).

So far as women's employment is concerned, Lindert suggested that women's wages either stagnated or declined as a percentage of male wages between 1750 and 1820, and that they rose less rapidly than male wage rates between 1820 and 1850 (Lindert 1994, 375). However, Lindert made relatively little effort to consider the impact of changes in the female labor force participation ratio or in the population's age structure (see also Joyce 1990, 139; Bythell 1993, 49; Horrell and Humphries 1995, 89–90). In 1995 Horrell and Humphries calculated that the percentage of married women who were active in the labor force declined from 61.7 percent between 1821 and 1840 to 45.3 percent between 1846 and 1865, while in 1981 Wrigley and Schofield estimated that the dependency ratio (the ratio of people of nonworking age to people of working age) rose from 699:1,000 in 1751 to 744:1,000 in 1851 (Horrell and Humphries 1995, 98; Wrigley and Schofield 1981, 216–19, 528–29; see also Anderson 1990, 38). Taken together, these statistics suggest that the impact of increases in the real value of male wages may have been at least partially offset by the increased number of nonearners who depended on each breadwinner.

3.2.2 Industrialization and Mortality

Critics of Britain's industrialization have often argued that such increases in incomes as did occur were bought at the cost of reductions in health and longevity (Lindert 1994, 361–64). In 1833 one of the factory commissioners, Dr. Bisset Hawkins, claimed that "most travellers are struck by the lowness of stature, the leanness and paleness which present themselves so commonly to the eye at Manchester, and above all, among the factory classes," while an investigation into the physical condition of the handloom weavers in 1840 concluded that "they are decayed in their bodies; the whole race of them is rapidly descending to the size of Lilliputians" (Flinn 1965, 247, 251–52). In 1845 Friedrich Engels alleged that English society "daily and hourly commits what the workingmen's organs, with perfect correctness, characterise as social murder" because "it has placed the workers under conditions in which they can neither retain health nor live long" (Engels 1969, 127).

The essential starting point for any discussion of demographic trends in the eighteenth and nineteenth centuries is Wrigley and Schofield's *Population History of England* (1981). Wrigley and Schofield showed that the crude mortality rate for the population as a whole fluctuated sharply during the first half of the eighteenth century (though less sharply than in the preceding centuries), before falling between circa 1780 and 1830. However, the aggregate mortality rate leveled off during the middle years of the nineteenth century and only resumed its downward path during the 1870s (Wrigley and Schofield 1981, 228–36). This interpretation is supported by the statistics collected by the registrar-general for the whole of England and Wales from 1838 onward. The registrar-general's calculations suggest that aggregate mortality rates averaged about 21–23 deaths per 1,000 living between the 1840s and 1860s, before falling to 14 per 1,000 in 1914 (fig. 3.2).

It is usual for demographers to measure mortality in terms of the number of people dying from a particular cause at a particular point in time, but it is also possible to compare the mortality experience of different birth cohorts. In 1934, Kermack, McKendrick, and McKinley examined the pattern of mortality decline among different age groups during each decade from 1841–50 to 1921–30, finding that each generation or cohort carried with it the same relative mortality throughout life (Kermack, McKendrick, and McKinley 1934; Kuh and Davey Smith 1993, 108–9). This argument derives considerable support from table 3.1, which shows that the process of mortality decline began with those aged 5–24, before spreading to those aged 0–4, then to those aged 25–64, and finally to those aged 65 and over. The largest reductions in mortality, in percentage terms, occurred among those aged 5–24. According to Wohl, the general death rate declined between 1841–50 and 1891–1900 by over 12 percent among those aged 0–4, by over 50 percent among those aged 5–24, by

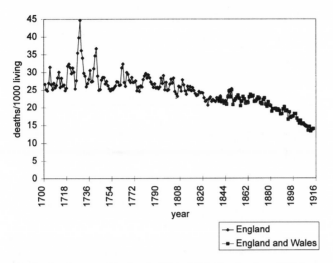

Fig. 3.2   Crude death rates: England, 1701–1871; England and Wales, 1838–1914
Sources: Wrigley and Schofield (1981, table A3.3) and Mitchell (1988, 57–59).

almost 38 percent among those aged 25–34, and by almost 19 percent among those aged 35–44 (Wohl 1983, 329).

The aggregate mortality rate concealed important regional variations. It is well known that urban mortality rates were generally higher than rural mortality rates, and that an increasing proportion of the British population was living under urban conditions. However, there is evidence that mortality rates *within* urban areas may actually have been improving. In 1983 Lindert and Williamson claimed that mortality rates declined within both urban and rural areas from about 1800 onward, with the possible exception of mortality rates in Liverpool and Manchester (Lindert and Williamson 1983, 21). This impression was reinforced by Robert Woods's investigations into the trends in both urban and rural mortality rates during the whole of the nineteenth century. Woods found that life expectancy improved in both urban and rural areas from the early nineteenth century onward, but that the improvement in life expectancy in the most populous areas was much more marked after 1860 (Woods 1985, 650).

The analysis of trends in mortality rates has a number of implications for the earlier discussion of trends in real wage rates. The fact that the decline of mortality was arrested between circa 1830 and circa 1870 provides strong evidence in support of the view that any wage increases that did occur were bought at a high price in terms of health and mortality. At the same time, the fact that mortality rates continued to decline *within* urban areas suggests that even though urban areas were less healthy than rural areas, there was no absolute decline in the living standards of those who already lived in these areas.

Table 3.1 England and Wales: Age-Specific Mortality Rates (Males), 1838–42 to 1908–12

Years	Ages												
	0–4	5–9	10–14	15–19	20–24	25–34	35–44	45–54	55–64	65–74	75–84	85+
1838–42	71.34	9.52	5.18	7.24	9.34	9.92	12.58	17.88	31.60	65.56	144.12	304.60
1843–47	71.68	8.70	4.94	7.02	9.54	9.80	12.78	17.92	31.52	68.36	151.00	323.22
1848–52	72.66	9.50	5.32	7.04	9.46	10.16	13.10	18.70	31.86	66.06	144.82	297.34
1853–57	72.24	8.22	4.96	6.80	9.02	9.78	12.68	18.22	31.20	66.08	149.38	312.76
1858–62	72.02	8.18	4.52	6.38	8.36	9.18	12.34	17.80	31.08	65.28	144.96	309.94
1863–67	74.56	8.50	4.64	6.36	8.88	10.24	13.92	19.76	33.96	68.00	149.14	325.12
1868–72	71.92	8.06	4.30	5.98	8.36	10.22	13.78	19.44	33.10	66.96	145.16	303.36
1873–77	68.32	6.54	3.68	5.28	7.38	9.44	14.08	20.36	35.32	70.48	150.72	327.80
1878–82	64.76	6.28	3.32	4.64	6.26	8.36	13.00	19.56	34.68	69.10	150.68	322.18
1883–87	62.70	5.40	3.02	4.40	5.82	7.84	12.46	19.26	34.54	70.92	149.12	311.74
1888–92	61.88	4.76	2.66	4.08	5.40	7.42	12.34	20.24	36.80	74.48	151.84	310.46
1893–97	62.28	4.34	2.46	3.80	5.00	6.60	11.14	18.14	33.28	66.86	138.90	269.30
1898–1902	60.30	4.00	2.26	3.52	4.84	6.42	11.00	18.50	34.52	69.42	144.52	287.10
1903–7	51.64	3.48	2.04	3.08	4.16	5.62	9.18	16.28	32.02	64.32	137.16	283.26
1908–12	42.38	3.26	1.96	2.92	3.80	5.00	8.20	15.00	30.18	63.92	138.02	272.30

Source: Mitchell (1988, 60–62).

The main reason for the arrest of progress in the decline of mortality was not a deterioration in the living standards of those who lived in towns, but the disproportionate increase in the size of the urban population. This meant that even though the average level of real wages was increasing, a growing proportion of the population was being subjected to the unhealthy conditions of town life.

3.2.3   Education and Literacy

A third issue that has attracted considerable attention in debates about the standard of living is the question of educational opportunity and literacy. Many nineteenth-century commentators argued that public provision of educational services was necessary either as a means of enforcing "social control" or as a means of improving economic efficiency, but access to education is also an important component of the standard of living (Sanderson 1991; Sutherland 1990). It is often the key to social mobility. It broadens horizons, encourages the communication of ideas, and facilitates political activity.

Historians who have studied changes in educational standards have tended to concentrate on two sets of statistics: school attendance and literacy. E. G. West (1970) examined the number of schools built, and the number of scholars in attendance, in a number of early-nineteenth-century towns, but his conclusions have not been widely accepted (Sutherland 1990, 121). The majority of educational historians believe that formal educational opportunities expanded during the first two-thirds of the eighteenth century because the growth in the number of schools outstripped that of the population as a whole, but this situation was reversed during the years of more rapid population growth between 1780 and 1830. The expansion of educational opportunities was also halted by the increase in child labor, particularly in the industrial areas of northwest England. According to Michael Sanderson, children's access to education was limited by the need to contribute to the family's income and because the changing nature of child employment provided fewer opportunities for educational advancement (Sanderson 1991, 13).

The divergence of opinions over school provision is also reflected in debates about adult literacy. It is generally accepted that literacy rates rose during the first two-thirds of the eighteenth century, but opinions differ about the period between 1780 and 1850. In 1969 Lawrence Stone argued that the majority of areas witnessed an increase in literacy levels over the whole of the period, but Michael Sanderson has argued that many industrial areas experienced a decline in general literacy between circa 1750 and 1810. The most comprehensive national survey of changing literacy rates was conducted by Roger Schofield in 1973. Schofield found that literacy levels rose very slowly between 1750 and 1840, and that more than half the population was still functionally illiterate in the middle of the nineteenth century. Schofield also found that literacy levels were higher in rural areas than in industrial areas, but he rejected the view that this reflected a collapse in educational opportunities in industrial areas. He

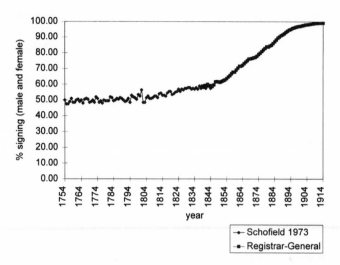

Fig. 3.3   Percentage of marriage partners signing their names, 1754–1914
Sources: Data for 1754–1844 are based on Schofield (1973, 445); data for 1839–1914 are derived from the *Annual Reports of the Registrar-General for England and Wales, 1839–1914.* The authors are grateful to Roger Schofield for supplying the original data on which his calculations were based.

argued that literacy rates in industrial towns were often low because illiterate workers moved from agricultural areas to industrial areas in search of jobs that did not require literacy skills (Schofield 1973).

One of the biggest problems associated with this debate concerns the nature of the evidence on which it is based. The majority of historians have based their conclusions on the numbers of men and women who signed their names on marriage registers (cf. Nicholas 1990). As Gillian Sutherland has pointed out, this may be a misleading guide to the level of literacy in the population as a whole (or, at least, in that section of the population that is getting married) because many people may have been able to read even though they were unable to sign their own names (Sutherland 1990, 124–25). We cannot rule out the possibility that the earlier figures underestimate the real level of literacy in preindustrial and industrializing England, and that the dramatic improvement in the number of men and women who were able to sign their own names between 1850 and 1914 reflects a change in attitudes to the acquisition of *writing* skills as well as an improvement in literacy as a whole (fig. 3.3).

3.3   Industrialization and Stature

The continuing debates about the movement of real wages, mortality rates, and literacy trends illustrate the depth of interest that continues to be aroused by the debate over the standard of living during the industrial revolution, but they also provide a further illustration of the difficulties raised by this debate (Floud 1984). It is in this context that a number of historians have begun to focus on changes in human stature during this period. It is well known that the heights of both adults and children are responsive to a wide range of environmental and nutritional influences, including both dietary inputs and environmental and epidemiological demands (Eveleth and Tanner 1991, 1; Komlos 1994, x–xi). However, it is also clear that the delineation and interpretation of trends in average height is itself becoming increasingly controversial. We shall therefore begin by reviewing some of the latest evidence on trends in average stature during the eighteenth and nineteenth centuries.

The most obvious starting point for this analysis is Floud et al's (1990) study *Height, Health and History*. This work was based on an analysis of changes in the heights of poor boys recruited by the Marine Society of London between 1770 and 1870, and of men who were recruited by the Royal Marines and the British Army between 1740 and 1914. These data were supplemented by information about the heights of upper-class recruits attending the Royal Military Academy at Sandhurst from 1806 onward (Floud and Wachter 1982; Floud et al. 1990, 128–33).

The results of Floud et al.'s analysis of the military recruiting data are shown in figure 3.4. These graphs suggest that the average heights of successive birth cohorts of British males increased between the 1740s and 1760s and fell back between the 1760s and the 1780s. The average heights of successive birth cohorts also increased between the late 1780s and the 1820s and declined between the 1820s and 1840s. The average heights of successive birth cohorts of British men only began to increase consistently from the 1840s onward (fig. 3.4). Floud et al. also expressed concern about the size of the samples at the beginning of their period, and this led them to "smooth" the data with the aid of Cleveland's "locally weighted scatterplot smoother." The application of this procedure led them to conclude that, on average, the heights of successive birth cohorts of British males rose between 1740 and 1840, fell between 1840 and 1850, and rose once more from 1850 onward (Floud et al. 1990, 136–54, 325).

Floud et al. supplemented their analysis of trends in aggregate heights by examining changes in the pattern of regional and socioeconomic height differentials. One of their most striking findings was the discovery that, in the early part of the nineteenth century, men who lived in Scotland and the north of England were between 1.0 and 1.5 cm taller than men who lived in London and the southeast, a pattern that has been almost entirely reversed over the last 150 years (Floud et al. 1990, 200–206; Knight and Eldridge 1984). Floud et al. also showed that men who grew up in urban areas were shorter than men who grew up in rural areas, and that there were significant differences in the heights of men and boys from different socioeconomic backgrounds. At the beginning of the nineteenth century, 14-year-old boys attending the Royal Military Academy at Sandhurst were nearly six inches taller than their counterparts in the Marine Society, and there were still considerable differences in the

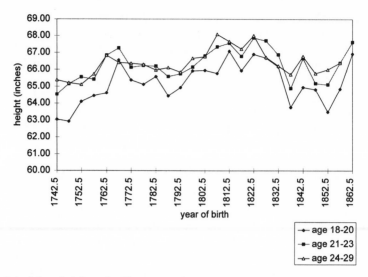

Fig. 3.4   Mean heights of military recruits aged 18–29, by year of birth
Source: Harris (1994a, 311).

heights of children from different social backgrounds a hundred years later (Floud et al. 1990, 196–200).

The most controversial aspect of Floud et al.'s work concerned their delineation of trends in the average height of British males in the eighteenth and early nineteenth centuries. They argued that "the early part of the industrial revolution led to an absolute as well as relative increase in the welfare and nutritional status of the working class, but . . . the impact of urban growth eroded that increase and even led to decreases in average height as large proportions of the working class were subjected to town life" (Floud et al. 1990, 326). However, these conclusions have been subjected to a variety of criticisms. In 1993 John Komlos criticized the statistical procedures followed by Floud et al. and reworked their data to show that the average height of British males deteriorated throughout the second half of the eighteenth century (Komlos 1993c). His account of changes in the average height of the British population was supported in different ways by the work of Nicholas and Steckel (1991), Nicholas and Oxley (1993), and Riggs (1994).

In their reply to Komlos, Floud et al. identified four key areas of disagreement. Komlos argued that Britain experienced an "incipient Malthusian crisis" during the second half of the eighteenth century, and that Floud et al. were wrong to "pool" the data derived from the army recruiting records and the Royal Marines. He also criticized their use of the Lowess smoothing procedure and reworked their original data using a procedure developed by Komlos and Kim three years earlier (Floud, Wachter, and Gregory 1993; Komlos and Kim 1990). We agree that the application of the Lowess smoothing procedure may have been overcautious, and that the average height of British men decreased as well as increased during the course of the eighteenth century, but we still believe that the overall trend was upward rather than downward. We also believe that the decision to pool the data from the army and marine records was justified because the two organizations derived their recruits from the same population even though they operated different height standards. Finally, even though we believe that the estimating procedure developed by Komlos and Kim is a valuable addition to the literature of anthropometric history, we do not think that it is capable of supporting the conclusions that have been derived from it in this instance.

The conclusions presented by Floud et al. have also been challenged by Stephen Nicholas and Richard Steckel. Nicholas and Steckel contrasted Floud et al.'s analysis of the military data with new data derived from the heights of English and Irish convicts who were transported to Australia between 1817 and 1840 (Nicholas and Steckel 1991). Their results are clearly important, and they are reproduced, together with Komlos's estimates, in table 3.2. However, although the numbers in this table suggest that the average height of English workers may have declined after 1780, we believe that more work needs to be done to establish the representativeness of the convict data (see also Shlomowitz 1990, 1991; Nicholas 1991a, 1991b). We also feel that more work is needed to explain the discrepancies between Nicholas and Steckel's analysis of changes in the average heights of male convicts and Nicholas and Oxley's analysis of changes in the heights of female convicts who were drawn from a similar sample (Nicholas and Oxley 1993).

Floud et al.'s second major finding was that there was a decline in the average heights of men born during the second quarter of the nineteenth century. The findings themselves have been challenged by Riley (1994), and the conclusions drawn from them have been criticized by Crafts (1992). In 1994, Riley argued on the basis of a contemporary anthropological survey that there was no evidence of any trend in the average heights of men born between 1817 and 1841 (Riley 1994, 477). However, his findings were based on a comparatively small sample, and they did not all point in the same direction. It is particularly interesting to note that when Riley reallocated his subjects into subgroups of English, Scots, and Welsh, "only the English . . . exhibited a strong change in height with age" (Riley 1994, 481). There is also a mounting volume of evidence from other studies that suggests that average heights did decline during the second quarter of the nineteenth century. Paul Riggs has shown that there was a decline in the average heights of Scottish men and women who were born between 1800 and 1840, and Paul Johnson and Stephen Nicholas have found evidence of a decline in the heights of "habitual criminals" who were born between 1812 and 1857 (Riggs 1994, 70–73; Johnson and Nicholas 1995).

Crafts's objections raise a more fundamental challenge to the practice of anthropometric history. He accepted that there was a decline in the average

Table 3.2   Estimated Trends in Heights of Different Groups of English-Born Workers, 1710–1815 (height in inches)

Period of Birth	Convicts (1)	Indentured Servants (2)	13-Year-Old Boys (3)	14-Year-Old Boys (4)	Urban Convicts (male) (5)	Rural Convicts (male) (6)	Urban Convicts (female) (7)	Rural Convicts (female) (8)
1710–19		67.40						
1720–29	67.90	67.40						
1730–39	67.83	66.70						
1740–49	67.58	66.75						
1750–59	67.79	66.88	51.57	54.41				
1760–69			50.67	53.46				
1770–79			51.54	53.39				
1780–84					66.40	66.42		
1785–89					66.11	65.83		
1780–89			51.38	53.27				
1790–94					65.94	65.78		
1795–99					65.94	65.72	60.72	61.38
1790–99			51.54	52.40				
1800–1804					66.12	65.41	60.59	61.55
1805–9					65.81	65.43	60.76	61.65
1800–1809			51.50	51.97				
1810–14					66.48	65.87	60.39	61.08
1815+					65.46	65.40	60.44	61.72

Sources: Cols. (1) and (2), Komlos (1993b, 775); cols. (3) and (4), Komlos (1993c, 128); cols. (5) and (6), Nicholas and Steckel (1991, 952); cols. (7) and (8), Nicholas and Oxley (1993, 742).

height of the British population but challenged the conclusions that Floud et al. derived from it. He argued that there was "no justification at all" for the claim that average heights deteriorated as a result of environmental demands "as no way of measuring the exchange rate of height for real income has yet been devised" (Crafts 1992, 428). However, although we agree that the "exchange rate of height for real income" remains uncertain, we do not believe that this invalidates our research. The claim that the average height of British men declined as a result of urban conditions is based on the clearly observed fact that urban-born men were shorter than rural-born men, and that an increasing proportion of the national population was being born in urban areas. Floud et al. also showed that the bulk of the decline in average heights was concentrated in urban areas between circa 1820 and circa 1860 (Floud et al. 1990, 206–7). Under these circumstances, it does not seem unreasonable to suggest that the unhealthy disease environment of Britain's cities was primarily responsible for the decline in the average height of men who were born during this period.[1]

3.4   Height and Social Change in the Twentieth Century

Most of the research that has been undertaken into the height of British people during the eighteenth and nineteenth centuries has focused on the heights of adults, but there have also been a number of investigations into the heights of children. The authors of *Height, Health and History* examined changes in the heights of poor boys who were recruited by the Marine Society of London and compared their heights with those of upper-class boys at the Royal Military Academy (Floud and Wachter 1982; Floud et al. 1990, 163–75). Jordan has collected data from a number of contemporary studies to depict changes in the heights of both working-class and non-working-class children of both sexes between 1807 and 1913 (Jordan 1993). In general, these studies confirm the pattern of change that Floud et al. found among military recruits. The average heights of successive birth cohorts fell during the second quarter of the nineteenth century and increased slowly from the 1850s onward (Floud et al. 1990, 165–71; Jordan 1993, 137).

In contrast to the eighteenth and nineteenth centuries, the study of children's heights has loomed much larger in the anthropometric history of the twentieth century. In 1936 Karn discussed changes in the heights of children who were born between 1820 and 1920, and in 1952 Weir examined trends in the heights of children who were measured between 1906 and 1949 (Karn 1936; Weir 1952). These studies were followed by Clements's account of changes in the heights of children between 1880 and 1947, and by Boyne, Aitken, and Leitch's

---

1. It is difficult to make more precise statements about the differences between urban and rural areas because of the size of the samples needed to make such statements (see Floud et al. 1990, 201–2). For an alternative explanation of "urban disamenities," see Clark, Huberman, and Lindert (1995).

much larger survey of the heights of children between 1911 and 1953 (Clements 1953; Boyne, Aitken, and Leitch 1957; see also Leitch and Boyne 1960). The most comprehensive study of changes in the average heights of children was conducted by Harris in 1989. Harris used the records of individual school medical officers to assemble data on the heights of children in over 50 areas and examined a number of different issues, including the impact of the First World War between 1914 and 1918, and the impact of unemployment between 1918 and 1939 (Harris 1988, 1989, 1993, 1994b, 1995).

The basic results of Harris's survey are shown in table 3.3. The table shows the average height of five-year-old boys in different parts of Great Britain between 1908 and 1950. The figures show that every area witnessed an increase in the average value of children's heights during the course of the period, although the pace and timing of these changes varied from area to area. The average heights of five-year-old boys in Cambridge, Croydon, Leeds, Rhondda, and Warrington increased by between 2.0 and 2.9 inches between 1908 and 1950. The average heights of boys in Bradford increased by 1.9 inches between 1908 and 1938, while the average heights of boys in Huddersfield increased by 1.8 inches between 1918 and 1949. Similar increases were also recorded in Glasgow between 1921 and 1949, in Reading between 1921 and 1937, and in Wakefield between 1932 and 1949 (table 3.3).

The data on the heights of schoolchildren can also be used to shed light on the question of gender differences in height, or "sexual dimorphism in stature." In recent years a number of writers have examined long-term trends in the heights of boys and girls to establish whether girls are more resistant to adverse influences than boys, and to see whether there is any systematic evidence of female neglect (Kuh, Power, and Rodgers 1991; Nicholas and Oxley 1993). Our findings suggest that there was very little difference between the general trends in the heights of boys and girls in either prosperous or depressed areas; this tends to contradict the view that female children experienced systematic neglect in poor families (figs. 3.5 and 3.6). The figures also suggest that past generations of girls may have been slightly taller, in comparison with past generations of boys, when their heights are compared with those of children of the same age and sex today. This tends to support the view that past generations of girls were more resistant to adverse influences than their male siblings (Tanner 1962, 127–28; see also Brennan, McDonald, and Shlomowitz 1994, 166).

In addition to these general trends, it is also possible to conduct a much more detailed examination of changes in the average height of different groups of schoolchildren during particular periods. In 1993 Harris examined the heights of children in 24 areas to see whether the First World War had any systematic impact on the heights of children who were measured between 1914 and 1918. Winter had claimed in 1986 that the war led to the most dramatic improvements in the standard of public health in the first 30 years of the twentieth century, but Harris's analysis of both the height data and the statistics of infant mortality suggested that this conclusion was somewhat overoptimistic

Table 3.3   **Changes in Average Height of Five-Year-Old Boys, 1908–50**

Area	Year	Average Age	Height (inches)	Height[a] (centiles)
Bradford	1908	5.50	40.31	3.21
	1922	5.50	41.34	9.35
	1938	5.50	42.24	19.61
Cambridge	1908	5.50	40.44	3.73
	1921	5.50	41.21	8.28
	1938	5.50	43.35	38.84
	1949	5.50	43.29	37.66
Croydon	1908	5.50	41.00	6.75
	1922[b]	5.50	42.40	21.97
	1938	5.50	43.10	34.00
	1950	5.50	43.40	39.83
Glasgow	1921	5.25	40.20	6.21
	1938	5.33	41.70	18.81
	1949	5.33	42.39	29.44
Huddersfield	1918	5.50	41.49	10.71
	1938	5.50	43.06	33.25
	1949	5.50	43.31	38.05
Leeds	1909	5.50	40.20	2.82
	1921	5.50	41.00	6.75
	1939	5.50	42.10	17.67
	1946	5.50	42.30	20.48
Reading	1921	5.00	40.75	15.61
	1937	5.00	41.75	31.71
Rhondda	1912	5.50	40.20	2.82
	1922	5.50	40.75	3.38
	1938	5.50	41.91	15.25
	1945	5.50	42.20	19.04
Wakefield	1932	5.25	40.75	10.42
	1938	5.25	41.25	15.73
	1949	5.25	41.75	22.65
Warrington	1911	5.00	39.00	2.58
	1939	5.00	41.40	25.36
	1944	5.00	41.20	22.06

Source: Harris (1989, 218–48).

[a]The numbers in this column show the average value of the heights of five-year-old boys expressed as centiles of the distribution of the heights of five-year-old boys in London in 1965.

[b]The figures for Croydon in 1922 are based on the heights of an unknown number of children attending 10 unnamed schools in the area.

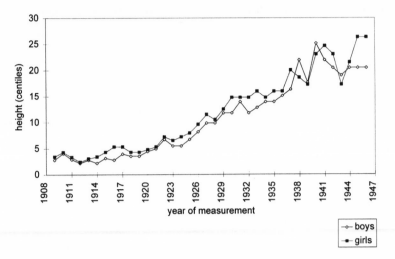

Fig. 3.5   Average heights (in centiles) of five-year-olds in Leeds, 1909–46
Source: See appendix table 3A.2.

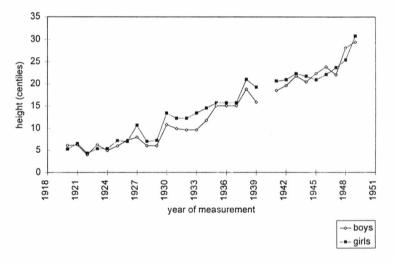

Fig. 3.6   Average heights (in centiles) of five-year-olds in Glasgow, 1920–49
Source: See appendix table 3A.2.

(Winter 1986; Harris 1993). Harris concluded that the average value of children's heights increased in some areas and decreased in others, but that the overall impact of these changes was not very great (Harris 1993, 359–64).

The second major focus of research concerned the impact of unemployment on children's heights during the interwar recession. In 1988 Harris divided the data for 11 areas into three different groups and found that changes in the average rate of adult male unemployment were related to changes in the aver-

Table 3.4   **Effect of Changes in Average Rate of Adult Male Unemployment (ΔU) on Changes in Average Value of Children's Heights (ΔH) in Individual Areas, 1927–37**

Area	Period	Constant	ΔU_{-1}	R^2	d^*	Sig. F
Blackburn	1928–37	1.18	−0.32	0.28	1.66	0.02
Bradford	1927–37	0.74	−1.45	0.70	0.75	0.00
Cambridge	1926–37	1.64	−4.54	0.40	0.77	0.03
Croydon	1930–37	0.74	−0.14	0.00	3.46	0.92
Glasgow	1926–37	0.71	−0.05	0.01	1.59	0.72
Huddersfield	1926–37	1.00	−1.28	0.72	1.45	0.00
Leeds	1926–37	0.78	−0.55	0.57	2.04	0.00
Reading	1926–37	1.08	0.41	0.02	2.79	0.67
Rhondda	1926–37	0.77	−0.17	0.26	1.85	0.09
Wakefield	1931–37	0.64	−0.31	0.55	2.15	0.06
Warrington	1926–37	1.34	−0.07	0.01	1.54	0.80

Area	Period	Constant	ΔU_{-2}	R^2	d^*	Sig. F
Blackburn	1928–37	1.11	−0.06	0.01	1.20	0.78
Bradford	1927–37	0.77	−0.98	0.29	0.59	0.09
Cambridge	1927–37	1.66	−5.09	0.50	0.90	0.02
Croydon	1930–37	0.81	−0.84	0.07	3.59	0.54
Glasgow	1927–37	0.72	−0.11	0.06	1.44	0.47
Huddersfield	1927–37	1.10	−1.35	0.75	2.25	0.00
Leeds	1927–37	0.80	−0.61	0.64	2.36	0.00
Reading	1927–37	1.12	0.47	0.03	2.72	0.64
Rhondda	1927–37	0.80	−0.12	0.11	1.60	0.33
Wakefield	1931–37	0.86	−0.47	0.92	1.72	0.00
Warrington	1927–37	1.32	−0.47	0.35	1.77	0.05

Source: Harris (1994b, 37).
Note: Method was ordinary least squares.

age value of children's heights in some of these areas, but not in others (see table 3.4; Harris 1988; 1989, 271). In 1994 Harris sought to extend this analysis by looking at the relationship between unemployment and stature in each area individually. He found that changes in the average rate of adult male unemployment were related to changes in the average value of children's heights in about half the areas studied, but the size of this relationship was not very great (Harris 1994b, 35–38). His overall conclusion was that unemployment played an important role in exacerbating the hardship that many unemployed people and their families already faced, but that the extent of this relationship varied from area to area. His results also demonstrated the importance of the local context within which unemployment occurred, and the difficulties of disentangling the effects of unemployment from those of poverty and bad housing generally (Harris 1995, 141–42).

In addition to examining changes in the average value of children's heights during the first 40 years of this century, Harris has also examined the changing pattern of children's heights during and after the Second World War. His analysis of changes in the average height of children in 10 areas between 1939 and 1945 confirms the view that there was a definite improvement in the average standard of child health during this period (Harris 1995, 165–71). His findings show that seven areas witnessed consistent improvements in the average height of both boys and girls at all ages, while two areas witnessed a period of deterioration followed by improvement. Only one area failed to produce evidence of an improvement in height, and the data for this area were limited to the period 1939–44 (table 3.5).

Although there was a considerable revival of interest in anthropometric measuring during the late 1930s and early 1940s, very few Local Education Authorities continued to publish tables of average heights and weights after circa 1950. One of the exceptions was Sheffield, which published details of the average heights and weights of all children between 1936 and 1968, and the average heights and weights of children attending schools in different types of district between 1951 and 1968. The second set of figures provides a clear demonstration of the increase in average heights as well as the persistence of health inequalities during the era of the "classic" welfare state (Lowe 1993, 63). This period witnessed an increase in the proportion of children attending schools in "good" and "medium" districts and a decline in the proportion of children attending schools in "poor" districts, but the average height of children attending good and medium schools was greater than the average height of children attending poor schools throughout the period (fig. 3.7).

3.5 Height and Human Development

The preceding sections have examined some of the ways in which studies of adults' and children's heights can be used to shed new light on the history of human welfare in Britain since 1700. However, although there is now a much wider degree of acceptance of the basic principles of anthropometric history, a number of commentators have continued to express reservations about the interpretation of these trends (Tilly, Tilly, and Tilly 1991; Crafts 1992). One of the most important issues concerns the relationship between trends in average height and trends in other welfare measures. In order to try to address this problem, we have attempted to compare our results with those obtained from an analysis of changes in human welfare using a modified version of the UN Human Development Index (United Nations Development Programme 1990–95).

The Human Development Index (HDI) is a composite index that seeks to rank individual countries on the basis of literacy, the logarithm of their GDP per capita, and life expectancy at birth.[2] In order to construct the index, the

---

2. The HDI uses literacy as a proxy for educational achievement. Strictly speaking, the literacy indicator should be combined with an estimate of mean years of schooling to provide a composite value for this variable. See United Nations Development Programme (1991, 15, 90).

Table 3.5 **Changes in Average Heights of Boys and Girls at Different Ages, 1939–45**

Area	Sex	Age Group	Height (inches)						
			1939	1940	1941	1942	1943	1944	1945
Cambridge	Male	Entrants	43.19	42.85	43.11	43.10	43.26	43.23	43.27
		Intermediates	50.04	49.57	49.85	49.78	49.77	50.02	50.08
		Leavers	56.99	57.09	57.44	57.25	57.94	57.79	57.61
	Female	Entrants	43.10	43.03	42.69	42.75	42.63	42.69	43.26
		Intermediates	49.55	49.34	49.58	49.54	50.71	50.09	49.80
		Leavers	57.97	58.10	58.17	58.18	57.89	58.23	58.20
Croydon	Male	Entrants	41.80	n.a.	n.a.	n.a.	43.20	n.a.	43.30
		Intermediates	49.00	n.a.	n.a.	n.a.	51.10	n.a.	51.30
		Leavers	58.40	n.a.	n.a.	n.a.	58.00	n.a.	58.00
	Female	Entrants	41.20	n.a.	n.a.	n.a.	42.90	n.a.	43.30
		Intermediates	50.90	n.a.	n.a.	n.a.	49.40	n.a.	50.70
		Leavers	58.80	n.a.	n.a.	n.a.	58.90	n.a.	59.00
Dumbartonshire	Male	Entrants	42.43	42.18	42.71	42.71	42.67	42.63	42.66
		Intermediates	49.64	n.a.	49.87	48.63	49.91	49.80	49.81
		Leavers[a]	59.44	59.51	59.02	58.87	58.87	57.99	58.82
	Female	Entrants	42.13	42.68	42.03	42.32	42.40	42.19	42.39
		Intermediates	49.34	49.61	49.61	48.33	49.42	49.23	49.38
		Leavers[a]	60.48	59.68	59.50	59.25	59.20	59.61	59.61
Glasgow	Male	Entrants	41.70	n.a.	42.16	41.99	41.91	41.82	41.95
		Intermediates	50.20	n.a.	50.59	50.88	50.69	50.71	50.93
		Leavers	57.60	n.a.	58.33	58.35	58.39	58.54	58.62
	Female	Entrants	41.50	n.a.	41.84	41.62	41.49	41.45	41.62
		Intermediates	49.80	n.a.	50.66	50.46	50.33	50.26	50.48
		Leavers	58.50	n.a.	58.90	58.89	59.17	59.10	59.30

(continued)

Table 3.5 (continued)

Area	Sex	Age Group	Height (inches)						
			1939	1940	1941	1942	1943	1944	1945
Huddersfield	Male	Entrants	43.00	43.45	43.42	43.38	43.54	44.11	44.00
		Intermediates	49.17	49.26	49.14	49.37	49.65	50.72	50.00
		Leavers	56.52	56.24	56.52	56.79	56.03	57.00	57.91
	Female	Entrants	42.43	42.66	42.16	42.53	41.34	42.00	41.97
		Intermediates	48.86	49.10	48.96	48.76	48.62	49.59	49.21
		Leavers	57.29	57.22	57.01	57.72	57.95	56.52	57.50
Leeds	Male	Entrants	42.10	42.60	42.40	42.30	42.20	42.30	42.30
		Intermediates	48.60	48.90	48.80	48.60	48.60	48.60	49.50
		Leavers	55.60	56.10	56.00	55.90	56.00	56.00	56.20
	Female	Entrants	41.60	42.00	42.10	42.00	41.60	41.90	42.20
		Intermediates	48.20	48.60	48.40	48.60	48.30	48.20	48.60
		Leavers	56.50	56.90	56.70	56.30	56.70	56.50	56.50
Rhondda	Male	Entrants[b]	40.96	40.93	39.97	40.64	40.66	41.36	41.10
		Intermediates	48.34	48.02	48.62	47.66	47.07	48.68	49.12
		Leavers	55.99	56.16	56.00	58.20	56.06	55.92	55.91
	Female	Entrants[b]	40.53	38.69	40.45	40.11	40.25	41.01	40.50
		Intermediates	47.88	48.34	48.39	48.82	48.38	47.58	48.59
		Leavers	56.31	56.81	56.31	55.94	56.22	56.77	56.42
Sheffield	Male	Entrants	42.56	42.68	42.87	42.53	43.14	42.76	42.93
		Intermediates	49.29	49.41	49.45	n.a.	n.a.	n.a.	n.a.
		Leavers[c]	57.80	58.19	58.54	58.27	59.02	58.85	59.10

Place	Sex	Category							
	Female	Entrants	42.20	42.44	42.60	42.25	42.86	42.46	42.64
		Intermediates	49.17	49.17	49.13	n.a.	n.a.	n.a.	n.a.
		Leavers^c	58.74	59.33	59.76	59.26	59.96	59.90	60.02
Wakefield	Male	Entrants	41.25	41.75	41.50	41.50	41.25	41.50	41.50
		Intermediates	48.75	49.00	48.50	48.75	48.50	48.75	n.a.
		Leavers	54.00	54.50	54.75	54.25	54.75	54.50	54.75
	Female	Entrants	40.75	41.00	41.25	41.50	41.25	41.25	41.75
		Intermediates	48.50	48.50	48.75	49.00	48.75	49.00	n.a.
		Leavers	54.50	54.75	54.50	54.75	54.75	54.75	55.00
Warrington	Male	Entrants	41.40	41.20	41.30	40.50	41.20	41.20	n.a.
		Intermediates	48.60	48.50	50.20	49.00	48.50	48.60	n.a.
		Leavers	55.50	55.30	56.20	55.90	55.80	56.20	n.a.
	Female	Entrants	41.20	41.10	41.10	41.60	40.90	41.10	n.a.
		Intermediates	48.50	48.30	48.30	48.20	48.10	48.34	n.a.
		Leavers	56.50	56.20	56.30	55.50	56.60	56.60	n.a.

Source: Harris (1995, 167–68).

aThe apparent decline in the heights of school leavers in Dumbartonshire is probably attributable to a change in the age at which the children were measured.

bThe figures for "entrants" in Rhondda are based on the average heights of children aged 4–6.

cThe figures for school leavers in Sheffield are based on the heights of children aged 13–14. The number of children measured in this age group in 1939 was comparatively small.

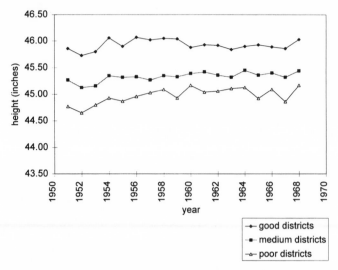

Fig. 3.7   Average heights of six-year-olds in Sheffield, 1951–68
Source: Annual Reports of the School Medical Officer for Sheffield 1951–68.

value of each variable is plotted on a scale of zero to one, where zero is the minimum value of each variable and one the maximum. The HDI itself is equal to the average of the three component variables. In 1990, the United Nations specified minimum values of 42 for life expectancy at birth, zero percent for adult literacy, and U.S.$220 (in 1987 prices) for GDP per capita. The maximum values were 78 years for life expectancy, 100 percent for adult literacy, and U.S.$4,861 for GDP per capita (United Nations Development Programme 1990, 13). In 1994 the United Nations proposed an alternative set of maximum and minimum values that were designed to encompass the broadest possible range of human experience and thus to facilitate comparisons across time. The revised figures are reproduced in table 3.6.

Since its introduction, the concept of a human development index has attracted a great deal of critical attention (see United Nations Development Programme 1993, 104–14). Some of the most important criticisms relate to the choice of dimensions (i.e., health, education, and access to resources) and indicators (expectation of life at birth, adult literacy, and log GDP per capita). The HDI has also been criticized on the grounds that it is based on inaccurate or incomplete statistics, and that its results are overdependent on the choice of maximum and minimum values. Some commentators have also attacked the decision to give each component of the index the same weighting. However, it is clear that there is widespread support for the concept of a human development index, and the United Nations' own investigations do not suggest that any of the proposed modifications would produce a radically different set of outcomes. In view of this, there is a strong case for using the latest formulation of the HDI to investigate the level of human welfare in the past. Such an inves-

Table 3.6   **Maximum and Minimum Values for Variables in the Human Development Index**

Variable	Minimum	Maximum
Expectation of life at birth (years)	25	85
Adult literacy (%)	0	100
GDP per capita (1990 U.S.$)	200	40,000

Source: United Nations Development Programme (1994, 92).

tigation may well shed light on the welfare of past generations and facilitate further debate over the measurement of human development in the present.

In order to apply the concept of the human development index to the welfare of British people over the last 250 years, we have utilized information from a range of sources. Our estimates of life expectancy at birth are based on figures provided by Wrigley and Schofield for England (excluding Monmouth) between 1756 and 1871, and by the registrar-general (for England and Wales) between 1871 and 1980. Our estimates of adult literacy are based on Schofield's figures for 274 English parishes between 1756 and 1838, and on the figures provided by the registrar-general for the whole of England and Wales between 1839 and 1914. It is important to note again that these figures are based on a minimal measure of functional literacy—namely, the ability to sign one's name in a marriage register—and that they represent a very inadequate measure of educational achievement. Our estimates of GDP are based on Crafts's estimates of the growth of Britain's GNP between 1700 and 1831, and on Mitchell's estimates of the United Kingdom's GDP (at market prices) between 1830 and 1980. Our figures have been converted into 1990 U.S. dollars using data provided by the Central Statistical Office, but—unlike the United Nations—we have been unable to make any further adjustments for variations in purchasing power parity (see United Nations Development Programme 1990, 12).[3]

The basic results of our analysis are set out in table 3.7 and are represented graphically in figure 3.8. The results show that there were significant variations in the level and fluctuations of the different series over time. There was little change in the relative value of the different components of the index between the mid-eighteenth and the mid-nineteenth centuries, when the literacy variable was consistently higher than the GDP variable and the GDP variable was consistently higher than the life expectancy variable, but the three series began to show divergent trends from the 1830s onward. The literacy variable began to increase rapidly during the mid-1830s, while the life expectancy variable

3. Full details of the sources used in the construction of the HDI are given in table 3.7. Our original estimates of GDP per capita (in 1990 U.S. dollars) are given in appendix table 3A.3. These estimates are based on an exchange rate of 0.560 pounds to the dollar. Maddison, whose figures are adjusted for variations in purchasing power parity, suggests an exchange rate of 0.587 pounds to the dollar. It is unlikely that these variations would make a significant difference to our overall results. See Maddison (1995, 172, table C-6).

Table 3.7   **Changes in the Human Development Index, 1756 to 1978–80**

Year	E_0	Original Values Literacy (%)	Log GDP per Capita	E_0	Index Values Literacy (%)	Log GDP per Capita	HDI
1756	37.29	47.50	3.19	0.20	0.48	0.39	0.36
1761	34.23	50.00	3.19	0.15	0.50	0.39	0.35
1766	35.04	50.50	3.20	0.17	0.51	0.39	0.35
1771	35.60	50.00	3.20	0.18	0.50	0.39	0.36
1776	38.17	49.50	3.20	0.22	0.50	0.39	0.37
1781	34.72	49.50	3.20	0.16	0.50	0.39	0.35
1786	35.93	51.00	3.21	0.18	0.51	0.40	0.36
1791	37.33	49.00	3.21	0.21	0.49	0.40	0.36
1796	36.76	52.00	3.22	0.20	0.52	0.40	0.37
1801	35.89	56.50	3.22	0.18	0.57	0.40	0.38
1806	38.70	51.00	3.24	0.23	0.51	0.41	0.38
1811	37.59	51.50	3.25	0.21	0.52	0.41	0.38
1816	37.86	52.50	3.26	0.21	0.53	0.42	0.39
1821	39.24	54.00	3.27	0.24	0.54	0.42	0.40
1826	39.92	57.00	3.28	0.25	0.57	0.43	0.41
1831	40.80	58.00	3.30	0.26	0.58	0.44	0.43
1836	40.15	57.00	3.33	0.25	0.57	0.45	0.42
1841	40.28	59.20	3.32	0.25	0.59	0.44	0.43
1846	39.56	59.60	3.38	0.24	0.60	0.47	0.44
1851	39.54	61.90	3.41	0.24	0.62	0.48	0.45
1856	40.39	65.50	3.45	0.26	0.66	0.50	0.47
1861	41.19	70.30	3.48	0.27	0.70	0.51	0.50
1866	40.32	74.20	3.52	0.26	0.74	0.53	0.51
1871	41.31	76.90	3.56	0.27	0.77	0.55	0.53
1871–80	43.00	80.38	3.57	0.30	0.80	0.55	0.55
1881–90	45.50	88.49	3.60	0.34	0.88	0.56	0.60
1891–1900	46.00	95.52	3.64	0.35	0.96	0.58	0.63
1901–10	50.50	98.20	3.68	0.43	0.98	0.60	0.67
1910–12	53.50	98.92	3.69	0.48	0.99	0.60	0.69
1920–22	57.60	100.00	3.65	0.54	1.00	0.59	0.71
1930–32	60.80	100.00	3.70	0.60	1.00	0.61	0.73
1950–52	69.00	100.00	3.85	0.73	1.00	0.67	0.80
1960–62	71.10	100.00	3.95	0.77	1.00	0.72	0.83
1970–72	72.20	100.00	4.07	0.79	1.00	0.77	0.85
1978–80	73.50	100.00	4.13	0.81	1.00	0.79	0.87

Sources: Expectation of life at birth (E_0): 1756–1871, Wrigley and Schofield (1981, table A3.1); 1871–80 to 1978–80, Office of Population Censuses and Surveys (1987, table 22). Adult literacy: 1756–1838, Schofield (1973); 1839, *Second Annual Report of the Registrar-General of Birth, Deaths and Marriages in England* (PP 1840 [263] xvii: 13); 1840, *Third Annual Report of the Registrar-General of Birth, Deaths and Marriages in England* (PP 1841 [11] [345] vi: 15); 1841–64, *Forty-fifth Annual Report of the Registrar-General of Birth, Deaths and Marriages in England* (PP 1884 C. 4009 xx: table 7); 1865–1914, *Seventy-seventh Annual Report of the Registrar-General of Birth, Deaths and Marriages in England and Wales* (PP 1916 Cd. 8206 v: table 10). GDP: 1756–1829, Crafts (1985a, 45); 1830–1980, Mitchell (1988, 531–41). U.K. population: 1756–1800, Wrigley and Schofield (1981, table A3.3); 1801–1980, Mitchell (1988, 11–44).

Notes: Expectation of life at birth (E_0): data for 1756–1871 are for England only (excluding Mon-

Table 3.7   (continued)

mouth); data for 1871–80 to 1978–80 cover the whole of England and Wales. Adult literacy: data for 1756–1838 are for 274 English parishes; data for 1839–1914 cover the whole of England and Wales. GDP per capita: Mitchell (1988, 531–41) provided estimates of U.K. GDP at market prices for 1830–1980. These figures were extrapolated backward using Crafts's (1985a, 45) estimates for the growth of Britain's GNP between 1701 and 1831. Mitchell's data were standardized at 1980 prices and then converted into 1990 prices using the price index in Central Statistical Office (1995b, 20–21). The revised data were converted into U.S. dollars using the exchange rate in Central Statistical Office (1995a, T62). Wrigley and Schofield (1981, table A3.3) provided estimates of English population totals for 1756–1801, and Mitchell (1988, 11–14) provided estimates for the whole of the United Kingdom from 1801 onward. The ratio of Mitchell's 1801 figures to Wrigley and Schofield's 1801 figures was used to convert Wrigley and Schofield's earlier estimates into figures for the United Kingdom as a whole.

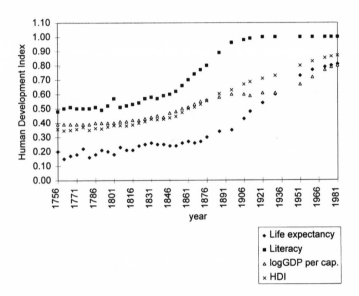

Fig. 3.8   Human development index (England and Wales/United Kingdom), 1756–1981
Source: See table 3.7.

increased from the early 1870s, and the literacy variable reached its maximum possible value on the eve of the First World War. The GDP variable remained relatively static during the second quarter of the twentieth century and only resumed its upward path after the end of the Second World War.

If we concentrate on the value of the index as a whole, a number of points stand out. In the first place, there is little evidence of any decline in the level of human welfare during the second half of the eighteenth century. The figures appear to show a very slow rate of improvement, which is broadly consistent with our interpretation of the changes in human height over the same period. The increase in the level of human development accelerated at the end of the

Napoleonic Wars, but there is some evidence of a decline in the rate of progress during the 1830s and early 1840s. The decline is less marked than the apparent decline in the average value of soldiers' heights, but it provides further evidence in support of the view that improvements in human welfare were arrested during the second quarter of the nineteenth century. The index reinforces the view that there has been a dramatic improvement in the standard of human welfare since the 1850s. The rate of improvement in the twentieth century is particularly remarkable, given the overall stability of the literacy indicator, and shows the overwhelming importance of increases in life expectancy.

3.6   Conclusions

This paper has had two main aims. Its first was to summarize the existing evidence of changes in the average height of the British population since the mid-eighteenth century. We believe that the history of human height in this period can be divided into three broad phases. During the first phase, which lasted from the middle of the eighteenth century to the end of the first quarter of the nineteenth century, the average height of British men increased very slowly, but there was a decline in the average heights of men born during the second quarter of the nineteenth century, followed by a sustained increase in average heights from the 1850s onward. We have also presented the results of some additional research into the heights of schoolchildren during the twentieth century. This research shows that the average height of British schoolchildren increased throughout the present century, but that there were still significant disparities in the heights of children from different social backgrounds at the end of the 1960s. Height continues to provide a powerful index of social and economic disadvantage.[4]

The second aim of the paper was to develop a modified version of the UN Human Development Index for use in historical analysis. We have shown that the average standard of "human development" increased very slowly during the second half of the eighteenth century, and that there is some evidence of an increase in the rate of progress during the early part of the nineteenth century. The rate of progress slowed down during the 1830s and early 1840s, and may even have been reversed, but the graph of human development resumed its upward path from the 1850s onward. It is important to recognize that the principles that underlie the calculation of the human development index are still under dispute, and that many of the figures that have been included in our calculations are subject to a wide margin of error. However, it is reassuring to note that there is a broad similarity between the results that have emerged from our analysis of the human development index and from our investigations into the history of human height during the course of this period.

---

4. For studies of the height of the British population since the 1960s, see Goldstein (1971), Rona, Swan, and Altman (1978), Knight and Eldridge (1984), and Gregory et al. (1990).

Appendix

Table 3A.1　　Average Age, Height, and Height in Centiles of Children in Leeds, 1909–46

	Boys				Girls			
Year	Estimated Age	Number	Height (inches)	Centile (1965 = 50)	Estimated Age	Number	Height (inches)	Centile (1965 = 50)
1909	5.50	1,922	40.20	2.82	5.50	1,916	39.90	3.44
1910	5.25	1,618	39.80	4.09	5.25	1,618	39.40	4.31
1911	5.25	1,650	39.50	2.92	5.25	1,685	39.30	3.36
1912	5.50	2,441	40.00	2.22	5.50	2,414	39.60	2.42
1913	5.50	2,540	40.20	2.82	5.50	2,576	39.80	3.07
1914	5.50	2,116	40.00	2.22	5.50	2,181	39.90	3.44
1915	5.50	2,764	40.30	3.18	5.50	2,621	40.10	4.30
1916	5.50	2,745	40.20	2.82	5.50	2,720	40.30	5.33
1917	5.50	2,070	40.50	3.98	5.25	1,990	39.60	5.32
1918	5.50	1,443	40.40	3.56	5.50	1,319	40.10	4.30
1919	5.75	2,200	40.80	3.56	5.50	2,099	40.10	4.30
1920	5.50	2,872	40.60	4.45	5.50	2,953	40.20	4.80
1921	5.50	2,361	40.70	4.95	5.50	2,194	40.30	5.33
1922	5.50	1,784	41.00	6.75	5.50	1,922	40.60	7.23
1923	5.50	1,747	40.80	5.50	5.50	1,767	40.50	6.55
1924	5.50	1,747	40.80	5.50	5.50	1,776	40.60	7.23
1925	5.50	2,695	41.00	6.75	5.50	2,697	40.70	7.97
1926	5.50	2,263	41.20	8.20	5.50	2,347	40.90	9.61
1927	5.50	2,074	41.40	9.88	5.50	2,146	41.10	11.49
1928	5.50	1,896	41.40	9.88	5.50	1,915	41.00	10.52
1929	5.50	1,649	41.60	11.79	5.50	1,669	41.20	12.52
1930	5.50	1,647	41.60	11.79	5.50	1,682	41.40	14.77
1931	5.50	1,440	41.80	13.95	5.50	1,539	41.40	14.77
1932	5.50	1,599	41.60	11.79	5.50	1,553	41.40	14.77
1933	5.50	1,376	41.70	12.84	5.50	1,478	41.50	15.99
1934	5.50	1,392	41.80	13.95	5.50	1,393	41.40	14.77
1935	5.50	1,445	41.80	13.95	5.50	1,515	41.50	15.99
1936	5.50	1,365	41.90	15.13	5.50	1,394	41.50	15.99
1937	5.50	1,479	42.00	16.37	5.50	1,403	41.80	20.04
1938	5.50	1,290	42.40	21.97	5.50	1,309	41.70	18.63
1939	5.50	833	42.10	17.67	5.50	816	41.60	17.28
1940	5.50	1,010	42.60	25.14	5.50	871	42.00	23.05
1941	5.50	1,839	42.40	21.97	5.50	1,711	42.10	24.65
1942	5.50	2,264	42.30	20.48	5.50	2,145	42.00	23.05
1943	5.50	1,942	42.20	19.04	5.50	1,922	41.60	17.28
1944	5.50	1,324	42.30	20.48	5.50	1,450	41.90	21.52
1945	5.50	1,479	42.30	20.40	5.50	1,476	42.20	26.30
1946	5.50	1,888	42.30	20.48	5.50	1,781	42.20	26.30

Source: Harris (1989, 234–37).

Table 3A.2   **Average Age, Height, and Height in Centiles of Children in Glasgow, 1920–49**

Year	Boys				Girls			
	Estimated Age	Number	Height (inches)	Centile (1965 = 50)	Estimated Age	Number	Height (inches)	Centile (1965 = 50)
1920	5.50	7,296	40.90	6.10	5.75	6,932	40.70	5.25
1921	5.25	7,849	40.20	6.21	5.25	7,800	39.80	6.52
1922	5.50	7,845	40.50	3.98	5.50	7,550	40.10	4.30
1923	5.25	6,910	40.20	6.21	5.25	6,666	39.60	5.32
1924	5.50	5,899	40.70	4.95	5.50	5,892	40.30	5.33
1925	5.75	8,586	41.30	5.97	5.25	8,350	39.90	7.19
1926	5.42	10,209	40.80	7.29	5.42	10,250	40.30	7.02
1927	5.42	9,718	40.90	8.02	5.42	9,635	40.70	10.68
1928	5.42	10,331	40.60	6.00	5.42	10,086	40.30	7.02
1929	5.42	9,494	40.60	6.00	5.42	9,461	40.40	7.24
1930	5.33	9,133	41.00	10.84	5.33	9,059	40.80	13.41
1931	5.33	9,371	40.90	9.94	5.33	9,257	40.70	12.25
1932	5.33	8,827	41.10	9.63	5.33	8,661	40.70	12.25
1933	5.33	8,147	41.10	9.63	5.33	8,055	40.80	13.41
1934	5.33	9,060	41.20	11.82	5.33	8,811	40.90	14.52
1935	5.33	8,536	41.40	15.04	5.33	8,217	41.10	15.68
1936	5.33	8,793	41.40	15.04	5.33	8,921	41.10	15.68
1937	5.33	8,468	41.40	15.04	5.33	8,257	41.10	15.68
1938	5.33	8,375	41.70	18.81	5.33	8,181	41.40	20.99
1939	5.42	9,252	41.70	15.83	5.42	9,170	41.50	19.23
1940	n.a.	n.a.	n.a.	n.a.	n.a.	n.a.	n.a.	n.a.
1941	5.50	7,697	42.16	18.49	5.50	7,615	41.84	20.62
1942	5.42	8,158	41.99	19.62	5.42	8,031	41.62	20.92
1943	5.33	8,284	41.91	21.77	5.33	7,936	41.49	22.32
1944	5.33	7,961	41.82	20.47	5.33	8,046	41.45	21.72
1945	5.33	8,260	41.95	22.36	5.33	8,072	41.62	20.92
1946	5.33	8,024	42.05	23.88	5.42	8,115	41.70	22.10
1947	5.33	7,496	41.93	22.06	5.33	7,218	41.58	23.68
1948	5.25	7,592	42.10	28.16	5.33	7,451	41.69	25.41
1949	5.33	8,601	42.39	29.44	5.50	8,036	42.02	30.79

Source: Harris (1989, 228–31).

Table 3A.3   U.K. GDP per Capita (in 1990 U.S. dollars), 1756 to 1978–80

Year	GDP per Capita (1990 U.S. $)	Year	GDP per Capita (1990 U.S. $)
1756	1,544.28	1846	2,405.27
1761	1,558.55	1851	2,574.45
1766	1,580.39	1856	2,839.43
1771	1,593.15	1861	3,025.17
1776	1,578.10	1866	3,285.38
1781	1,573.71	1871	3,666.11
1786	1,623.44	1871–80	3,702.37
1791	1,632.48	1881–90	3,957.18
1796	1,645.61	1891–1900	4,354.28
1801	1,662.61	1901–10	4,777.70
1806	1,719.43	1910–12	4,875.51
1811	1,775.17	1920–22	4,488.87
1816	1,814.88	1930–32	5,016.94
1821	1,859.11	1950–52	7,044.67
1826	1,907.24	1960–62	8,979.07
1831	2,015.02	1970–72	11,877.80
1836	2,136.43	1978–80	13,470.45
1841	2,077.15		

Sources: See table 3.7.

References

Allen, R. 1994. Agriculture during the industrial revolution. In *The economic history of Britain since 1700,* ed. R. Floud and D. McCloskey, 1:96–122. Cambridge: Cambridge University Press.

Anderson, M. 1990. The social implications of demographic change. In *The Cambridge social history of Britain 1750–1950,* ed. F. M. L. Thompson, 2:1–70. Cambridge: Cambridge University Press.

Botham, F. W., and E. H. Hunt. 1987. Wages in Britain during the industrial revolution. *Economic History Review* 40:380–99.

Boyne, A. W., F. C. Aitken, and I. Leitch. 1957. Secular change in height and weight of British children, including an analysis of measurements of English children in primary schools 1911–53. *Nutrition Abstracts and Reviews* 27:1–17.

Brennan, L., J. McDonald, and R. Shlomowitz. 1994. Secular changes in the height of Fijians and Indo-Fijians. *Journal of the Australian Population Association* 11:159–69.

Burnett, J. 1994. *Idle hands: The experience of unemployment 1790–1990.* London: Routledge.

Bythell, D. 1993. Women in the workforce. In *The industrial revolution and British society,* ed. P. O'Brien and R. Quinault, 31–53. Cambridge: Cambridge University Press.

Cameron, R. 1978. The industrial revolution: A misnomer. In *Wirtschaftskräfte und Wirtschaftswege: Festschrift für Hermann Kellenbenz,* ed. J. Schneider. Stuttgart: Klett Cotta.

Central Statistical Office. 1995a. *Economic Trends,* 500, T62.

————. 1995b. *United Kingdom national accounts 1995.* London: HMSO.

Clark, G., M. Huberman, and P. H. Lindert. 1995. A British food puzzle. *Economic History Review* 48:215–37.

Clements, E. M. B. 1953. Changes in the mean stature and weight of British children over the past seventy years. *British Medical Journal* 2:897–902.

Crafts, N. 1985a. *British economic growth during the industrial revolution.* Oxford: Oxford University Press.

————. 1985b. English workers' living standards during the industrial revolution: Some remaining problems. *Journal of Economic History* 45:139–44.

————. 1989. Real wages, inequality and economic growth in Britain 1750–1850: A review of recent research. In *Real wages in nineteenth and twentieth century Europe: Historical and comparative perspectives,* ed. P. Scholliers. Oxford: Berg.

————. 1992. Review of R. Floud, K. Wachter, and A. Gregory, *Height, health and history: Nutritional status in the United Kingdom 1750–1980. Economic History Review* 45:427–28.

————. 1994. The industrial revolution. In *The economic history of Britain since 1700,* ed. R. Floud and D. McCloskey, 1:44–59. Cambridge: Cambridge University Press.

Engels, F. 1969. *The condition of the working class in England from personal observation and authentic sources.* London: Granada (first published 1845).

Eveleth, P. B., and J. M. Tanner. 1991. *Worldwide variation in human growth.* Cambridge: Cambridge University Press.

Feinstein, C. H. 1972. *National income, expenditure and output of the United Kingdom 1855–1965.* Cambridge: Cambridge University Press.

Flinn, M. W., ed. 1965. *Report on the sanitary condition of the labouring population of Great Britain.* Edinburgh: Edinburgh University Press.

————. 1974. Trends in real wages 1750–1850. *Economic History Review* 27:395–411.

Floud, R. 1984. Measuring the transformation of the European economies: Income, health and welfare. CEPR Discussion Papers, no. 33. London: Centre for Economic Policy Research.

Floud, R., and K. Wachter. 1982. Poverty and physical stature. Social Science History, 6, 422–52.

Floud, R., K. Wachter, and A. Gregory. 1990. *Height, health and history: Nutritional status in the United Kingdom 1750–1980.* Cambridge: Cambridge University Press.

————. 1993. Measuring historical heights: Short cuts or the long way round: A reply to Komlos. *Economic History Review* 46:145–54.

Fogel, R., S. Engerman, J. Trussell, R. Floud, C. Pope, and L. Wimmer. 1978. The economics of mortality in North America, 1650–1910. *Historical Methods* 11:75–108.

Fores, M. 1981. The myth of the industrial revolution. *History* 66:181–98.

Goldstein, H. 1971. Factors affecting the height of seven-year-old children: Results from the National Child Development Study. *Human Biology* 43:92–111.

Greenwood, A. 1913. *The health and physique of schoolchildren.* London: P. S. King and Son.

Gregory, J., K. Foster, H. Tyler, and M. Wiseman. 1990. *The dietary and nutritional survey of British adults: A survey carried out by the Social Survey Division of OPCS with dietary and nutritional evaluations by the Ministry of Agriculture, Fisheries and Food, and the Department of Health.* London: HMSO.

Harris, B. 1988. Unemployment, insurance and health in interwar Britain. In *Interwar unemployment in international perspective,* ed. B. Eichengreen and T. Hatton, 149–83. Dordrecht: Kluwer.

————. 1989. Medical inspection and the nutrition of schoolchildren in Britain 1900–50. Ph.D. thesis, University of London.

———. 1993. The demographic impact of the First World War: An anthropometric perspective. *Social History of Medicine* 6:343–66.

———. 1994a. Health, height and history: An overview of recent developments in anthropometric history. *Social History of Medicine* 7:297–320.

———. 1994b. The height of schoolchildren in Britain 1900–50. In *Stature, living standards and economic development: Essays in anthropometric history,* ed. J. Komlos, 25–38. Chicago: University of Chicago Press.

———. 1995. *The health of the schoolchild: A history of the school medical service in England and Wales.* Buckingham: Open University Press.

Hartwell, R. M. 1961. The rising standard of living in England, 1800–50. *Economic History Review* 13:397–416.

Hobsbawm, E. J. 1957. The British standard of living, 1790–1850. *Economic History Review* 10:46–68.

———. 1975. The standard of living debate. In *The standard of living in Britain in the industrial revolution,* ed. A. J. Taylor, 179–88. London: Methuen.

Horrell, S., and J. Humphries. 1995. Women's labour force participation and the transition to the male-breadwinner family, 1790–1865. *Economic History Review* 48:89–117.

Johnson, P., and S. Nicholas. 1995. Male and female living standards in England and Wales, 1812–57: Evidence from criminal height records. *Economic History Review* 48:470–81.

Jordan, T. 1993. *The degeneracy crisis and Victorian youth.* Albany: State University of New York Press.

Joyce, P. 1990. Work. In *The Cambridge social history of Britain 1750–1950,* ed. F. M. L. Thompson, 2:131–94. Cambridge: Cambridge University Press.

Karn, M. 1936. Summary of results of investigations into the height and weight of the children of the British working classes during the last hundred years. *Annals of Eugenics* 7:376–98.

Kermack, W. O., A. G. McKendrick, and P. L. McKinley. 1934. Death rates in Great Britain and Sweden: Some general regularities and their significance. *Lancet* 1:698–703.

Knight, I., and J. Eldridge. 1984. *The heights and weights of adults in Great Britain: Report of a survey carried out on behalf of the Department of Health and Social Security among adults aged 16–64.* London: HMSO.

Komlos, J. 1989. *Nutrition and economic development in the eighteenth-century Habsburg monarchy: An anthropometric history.* Princeton, N.J.: Princeton University Press.

———. 1993a. Further thoughts on the nutritional status of the British population. *Economic History Review* 46:363–66.

———. 1993b. A Malthusian episode revisited: The height of British and Irish servants in colonial America. *Economic History Review* 46:768–82.

———. 1993c. The secular trend in the biological standard of living in the United Kingdom, 1730–1860. *Economic History Review* 46:115–44.

———. 1994. Preface. In *Stature, living standards and economic development: Essays in anthropometric history,* ed. J. Komlos, ix–xv. Chicago: University of Chicago Press.

Komlos, J., and J. Kim. 1990. Estimating trends in historical heights. *Historical Methods* 23:116–20.

Kuh, D., and G. Davey Smith. 1993. When is mortality risk determined? Historical insights into a current debate. *Social History of Medicine* 6:101–23.

Kuh, D., C. Power, and B. Rodgers. 1991. Secular trends in social class and sex differences in adult height. *International Journal of Epidemiology* 20:1001–9.

Lee, C. 1986. *The British economy since 1700: A macroeconomic perspective.* Cambridge: Cambridge University Press.

Leitch, I., and A. W. Boyne. 1960. Recent change in the height and weight of adolescents. *Nutrition Abstracts and Reviews* 30:1173–86.

Lindert, P. 1994. Unequal living standards. In *The economic history of Britain since 1700,* ed. R. Floud and D. McCloskey, 1:357–86. Cambridge: Cambridge University Press.

Lindert, P., and J. Williamson. 1983. English workers' living standards during the industrial revolution: A new look. *Economic History Review* 36:1–25.

———. 1985a. English workers' living standards during the industrial revolution: A new look. In *The economics of the industrial revolution,* ed. J. Mokyr, 177–205. Totowa, N.J.: Rowan and Allanheld.

———. 1985b. English workers' real wages: A reply to Crafts. *Journal of Economic History* 45:145–53.

Lowe, R. 1993. *The welfare state in Britain since 1945.* London: Macmillan.

Maddison, A. 1995. *Monitoring the world economy 1820–1992.* Paris: Organisation for Economic Co-operation and Development.

Mathias, P. 1975. Preface. In *The standard of living in Britain in the industrial revolution,* ed. A. J. Taylor, vii–x. London: Methuen.

McKendrick, N. 1982. The consumer revolution of eighteenth-century England. In *The birth of a consumer society: The commercialisation of eighteenth-century England,* N. McKendrick, J. Brewer, and J. Plumb, 9–33. London: Europa.

Mitchell, B. R. 1988. *British historical statistics.* Cambridge: Cambridge University Press.

Mokyr, J. 1988. Is there still life in the pessimist case? Consumption during the industrial revolution 1790–1850. *Journal of Economic History* 48:69–92.

Mokyr, J., and C. Ó Gráda. 1994. The heights of the British and Irish circa 1800–15: Evidence from recruits to the East India Company's Army. In *Stature, living standards and economic development: Essays in anthropometric history,* ed. J. Komlos, 39–59. Chicago: University of Chicago Press.

Nicholas, S. 1990. Literacy and the industrial revolution. In *Education and economic development since the industrial revolution,* ed. G. Tortella. Valencia: Generalitat Valenciana.

———. 1991a. Matters of fact: Convict transportees were not members of the criminal class. *Australian Economic History Review* 31:109.

———. 1991b. Understanding convict workers. *Australian Economic History Review* 31:95–105.

Nicholas, S., and D. Oxley. 1993. The living standards of women during the industrial revolution. *Economic History Review* 46:723–49.

Nicholas, S., and R. Steckel. 1991. Heights and living standards of English workers during the early years of industrialisation. *Journal of Economic History* 51:937–57.

Office of Population Censuses and Surveys. 1987. *Mortality statistics: Review of the registrar-general on deaths in England and Wales, 1985.* London: HMSO.

Phelps Brown, E. H., and S. V. Hopkins. 1956. Seven centuries of the prices of consumables, compared with builders' wage rates. *Economica,* n.s., 23:296–314.

Porter, R. 1982. *English society in the eighteenth century.* Harmondsworth: Penguin.

Riggs, P. 1994. The standard of living in Scotland 1800–50. In *Stature, living standards and economic development: Essays in anthropometric history,* ed. J. Komlos, 60–75. Chicago: University of Chicago Press.

Riley, J. 1994. Height, nutrition and mortality risk reconsidered. *Journal of Interdisciplinary History* 24:465–92.

Rona, R. J., A. V. Swan, and D. G. Altman. 1978. Social factors and height of primary schoolchildren in England and Scotland. *Journal of Epidemiology and Community Health* 32:147–54.

Sanderson, M. 1991. *Education, economic change and society in England 1780–1870.* London: Macmillan.

Schofield, R. S. 1973. Dimensions of illiteracy. *Explorations in Economic History* 10:437–54.

———. 1994. British population change 1700–1871. In *The economic history of Britain since 1700,* ed. R. Floud and D. McCloskey, 1:60–95. Cambridge: Cambridge University Press.

Schwarz, L. D. 1985. The standard of living in the long run: London, 1700–1860. *Economic History Review* 38:26–41.

———. 1990. Trends in real wages 1750–90: A reply to Botham and Hunt. *Economic History Review* 40:90–98.

Shlomowitz, R. 1990. Convict workers: A review article. *Australian Economic History Review* 30:67–88.

———. 1991. Convict transportees: Casual or professional criminals? *Australian Economic History Review* 31:106–8.

Sutherland, G. 1990. Education. In *The Cambridge social history of Britain 1750–1950,* ed. F. M. L. Thompson, 3:119–70. Cambridge: Cambridge University Press.

Tanner, J. M. 1962. *Growth at adolescence, with a general consideration of the effects of hereditary and environmental factors upon growth and maturation from birth to maturity,* 2d ed. Oxford: Blackwell.

Taylor, A. J. 1975. Introduction. In *The standard of living in Britain in the industrial revolution,* ed. A. J. Taylor, xi–lv. London: Methuen.

Thompson, F. M. L. 1990. Town and city. In *The Cambridge social history of Britain 1750–1950,* ed. F. M. L. Thompson, 1:1–86. Cambridge: Cambridge University Press.

Tilly, C., L. Tilly, and R. Tilly. 1991. European economic and social history in the 1990s. *Journal of European Economic History* 20:645–71.

Toynbee, A. 1884. *Lectures on the industrial revolution of the eighteenth century in England.* London: Rivington.

Tunzelmann, N. von. 1979. Trends in real wages, 1750–1850, revisited. *Economic History Review* 32:33–49.

Tuxford, A. W., and R. A. Glegg. 1911. The average height and weight of English schoolchildren. *British Medical Journal* 1:1423–24.

United Nations Development Programme. 1990. *Human development report 1990.* New York: Oxford University Press.

———. 1991. *Human development report 1991.* New York: Oxford University Press.

———. 1992. *Human development report 1992.* New York: Oxford University Press.

———. 1993. *Human development report 1993.* New York: Oxford University Press.

———. 1994. *Human development report 1994.* New York: Oxford University Press.

———. 1995. *Human development report 1995.* New York: Oxford University Press.

Waller, P. J. 1983. *Town, city and nation: England 1850–1914.* Oxford: Oxford University Press.

Weir, J. B. de V. 1952. The assessment of the growth of schoolchildren with special reference to secular changes. *British Journal of Nutrition* 6:19–33.

West, E. G. 1970. Resource allocation and growth in early-nineteenth-century British education. *Economic History Review* 23:68–95.

Williamson, J. G. 1982. Was the industrial revolution worth it? Disamenities and death in nineteenth-century British towns. *Explorations in Economic History* 19:221–45.

Winter, J. 1986. *The Great War and the British people.* London: Macmillan.

Wohl, A. S. 1983. *Endangered lives: Public health in Victorian Britain.* London: Methuen.

Woods, R. 1985. The effects of population redistribution on the level of mortality in nineteenth-century England and Wales. *Journal of Economic History* 45:645–51.

Wrigley, E. A. 1987. Urban growth and agricultural change: England and the Continent in the early-modern period. In *People, cities and wealth: The transformation of traditional society,* by E. A. Wrigley, 157–93. Oxford: Blackwell.

Wrigley, E. A., and R. S. Schofield. 1981. *The population history of England 1541–1871: A reconstruction.* Cambridge: Cambridge University Press.

4   Was Industrialization Hazardous to Your Health? Not in Sweden!

Lars G. Sandberg and Richard H. Steckel

4.1   Introduction

The consequences of industrialization and associated urbanization for the health and well-being of the mass of the population have been a topic of study and intensive debate in Britain at least since the days of Toynbee and Marx. Two sides quickly crystallized: the "optimists," who argued that most British workers experienced some modest increase in their standard of living even before 1840, and the "pessimists," who painted a far grimmer picture of impoverishment and degradation. In terms of traditional measures of the standard of living, the consumption of goods and services, the optimists seem to have largely won, although they admit that the pre-1840 gain to the workers was very modest and involved an increasingly unequal distribution of income (the first leg of the "Kuznets curve"). The attempt by the pessimists to counter, by stressing deteriorating living and working conditions (from "sweet Auburn" to the "satanic mills"), was cleverly repulsed by Williamson, who pointed out that the workers accepted increased squalor and risk of disease in return for modest wage premiums (Williamson 1981, 1982). It might be noted, however, that the most striking consequence of an unhealthy environment—namely, increased infant and child mortality—only affected the wage earner–decision maker indirectly. While parents, and would-be parents, no doubt found the prospect of high child death rates distressing (and indeed the result was somewhat higher wage rates in particularly unhealthy areas), still, the principal losers were the dead children themselves. They, however, had no say in the family's location decision.

Lars G. Sandberg is professor emeritus of economics at Ohio State University and adjunct professor of economic history at Uppsala University, Sweden. Richard H. Steckel is professor of economics at Ohio State University and a research associate of the National Bureau of Economic Research.

127

More recent work on the health status of the population, in the United States as well as in Great Britain, indicates a deterioration during periods of rapid industrialization and urbanization around the middle 50 years of the nineteenth century (see, e.g., Komlos 1987). This deplorable development is discernible not just in mortality and morbidity, but also, and perhaps most strikingly, in height and weight measures. Despite some apparent increase in the standard of living as conventionally measured, the population was physically deteriorating. Nutrition, net of the demands of growth, work, and struggle against disease and infection, seems to have been tending downward for a majority of the population.

These results raise a number of interesting historical questions. One rather obvious question is whether the "welfare" of the population was in fact improving, even if per capita real income and consumption (as traditionally measured) were tending upward. Another equally important question is what specific aspects of the British and American experience were responsible for the observed deterioration in health. Was it a more or less inevitable consequence of industrialization or urbanization or was it specific to some particular aspect of these processes in those particular countries? Hopefully, this second question can be answered with the help of studies, interesting in their own right, of the health consequences of industrialization and urbanization in other countries and therefore in other settings and time periods.

One interesting alternative case is Sweden. By Western European standards it experienced a rather late but, by any standard, extremely rapid industrialization. Thus the country was in relatively short order transformed from one of the poorest to one of the richest countries in Europe. Today Sweden also has one of the healthiest and, not coincidentally, one of the tallest populations of any country. The fact that Swedish industrialization had distinct rural, or at least semirural, aspects also makes it an interesting contrast to the United States and, particularly, to Great Britain. Finally, the plenitude of (believable) economic, social, and demographic data makes Sweden a prime candidate for study.

4.2 Economic and Demographic Trends: 1800–1995

4.2.1 1800–1870

The important characteristic required of this initial period is that it predate the onset of rapid industrialization and economic growth. The key problem, therefore, is the choice of end point. Although some economic historians have opted for 1850 or 1860 as the most useful break point between traditional and modernizing Sweden, the consensus clearly leans toward (circa) 1870. The best available national income data indicate that per capita GDP increased by approximately 0.25 percent per annum between 1820 and 1850, approximately 1 percent per annum between 1850 and 1870, and approximately 2 percent per

Table 4.1   **Raw Data for the Human Development Indexes**

Year	Life Expectancy	Stature	Infant Mortality	Literacy	Index of Per Capita Income	Per Capita Income (1970 U.S. $)
1820	39.16	167.0	17.06	82.50	6.87	294.8
1825	44.18	167.6	15.79	83.75	6.81	292.2
1830	39.02	167.9	18.18	85.00	6.75	289.5
1835	42.46	168.2	16.46	86.25	6.91	296.4
1840	42.09	167.6	16.13	87.50	7.07	303.3
1845	42.99	168.1	15.70	88.75	7.24	310.5
1850	43.91	168.2	14.87	90.00	7.41	317.6
1855	40.67	168.4	14.84	91.25	7.98	342.1
1860	44.81	169.5	13.72	92.50	8.55	366.6
1865	45.26	169.0	13.43	93.75	8.42	361.0
1870	44.99	170.2	13.76	95.00	9.33	399.9
1875	45.43	170.3	13.80	96.25	10.86	465.5
1880	48.05	170.9	12.07	97.50	11.32	485.6
1885	49.61	171.5	11.15	98.75	12.09	518.4
1890	51.11	172.3	10.55	100	12.92	554.0
1895	52.80	172.4	9.97	100	14.65	628.2
1900	52.89	172.5	9.83	100	16.12	691.4
1905	55.52	173.0	8.47	100	18.46	791.8
1910	57.65	172.9	7.51	100	20.91	896.8
1915	58.28	173.4	7.05	100	17.87	766.4
1920	57.33	174.1	6.48	100	22.55	966.9
1925	62.61	174.8	5.76	100	27.77	1,190.9
1930	63.07	175.2	5.59	100	32.47	1,392.4
1935	64.95	175.8	4.62	100	35.58	1,525.5
1940	67.02	176.1	3.75	100	39.38	1,688.7
1945	68.89	177.4	2.84	100	42.85	1,837.3
1950	71.40	177.9	2.18	100	49.64	2,128.5
1955	72.56	178.6	1.80	100	54.97	2,357.2
1960	73.38	179.1	1.61	100	63.59	2,726.7
1965	73.94	179.3	1.37	100	77.23	3,311.7

Sources: Keyfitz and Fleiger (1968), Krantz and Nilsson (1980), Maddison (1991), and Cipolla (1968). See text for discussion of height data. The literacy numbers are based on Cipolla's conclusion that Swedish literacy in 1850 was 90 percent and virtually all youths were literate. We concluded that a reasonable rate of increase of literacy in this period was 0.25 percent per year, which implies that literacy reached 100 percent around 1890. The real per capita GDP figures for the period 1820–60 are taken from Maddison (1991). They are then connected to estimates from Krantz and Nilsson until 1970. This procedure was recommended by Krantz, who is the ultimate source of both series. Swedish kronor were converted into 1970 U.S. dollars assuming an exchange rate of 5.18 Skr per dollar.

annum in the following decades (see table 4.1). While these numbers lend some credibility to using either 1850 or 1870 as the break point, other factors point especially to 1870. For example, the fact that Sweden experienced its last non-war-induced subsistence crisis in the late 1860s, together with the extremely rapid industrialization spurt of the early 1870s, certainly argues for making 1870 the year of choice. More generally, after 1870, numerous economic and demographic indicators started to rise or, when appropriate, to fall rapidly compared with previous rates. More important, even if they on occasion later slowed down, or even reversed slightly, nothing even close to pre-1870 levels were ever to be seen again (Sandberg 1978).

The choice of starting date for the period is less obvious and less important. Whether it is 1720, 1750, 1800, or even 1820 matters relatively little. Whatever the starting date, the period before 1870 presents a basically agrarian country with periods of relative prosperity interspersed with war- or crop-failure-induced periods of famine and unspeakable suffering. The cycle was not of business but of harvests (Carlsson 1961, 33–49).

This is not to deny that things were changing. A distinct upward trend can be discerned in population, and organizational and technological change was beginning to affect the economy, definitely including agriculture. Still, as one of us once wrote with only slight exaggeration, "About the best thing that can be said for the country's economic performance between 1720 (or 1800) and 1850 (or 1870) is that Sweden proper was supporting more than twice as large a population in 1850 as in 1720" (Sandberg 1978, 651). Between 1800 and 1870, the Swedish population increased from 2.3 to 4.2 million. Since a virtually unchanged 75–80 percent of the population was dependent on agriculture for its living in both years, it is hardly surprising that the share of the population categorized as belonging to the "rural proletariat" was increasing. It had grown from about 25 percent of the agricultural population and 20 percent of the entire population in 1750 to close to 50 percent and 40 percent, respectively, during the period between 1850 and 1870. Despite the fact that substantially more land was being cultivated in 1870 than in 1750 or 1800, it was also the case that the average holding of those fortunate enough to be land-owning peasants had clearly shrunk (Gårdlund 1942, 268; Heckscher 1954, 171–72; Samuelsson 1963, 10–13; Hildebrand 1978, 597).

On a slightly more optimistic note, it does seem likely (as confirmed by the per capita GDP figures mentioned above) that output per worker in Swedish agriculture was starting to increase, albeit slowly, after circa 1830. In view of rapidly rising (real) land prices, however, it seems unlikely that per capita income among the agricultural proletariat was improving, and it certainly was declining during the crisis years of the "hungry forties" and the late 1860s. Data on the real wages of day labor tend to support this conclusion. They shows no discernible trend before circa 1870, and there are distinct downturns in the 1845–54 and 1865–69 periods. In view of the positive relationship between rural wages and work opportunities, the wage rate downturns probably fail fully to reflect the true level of distress (Sandberg and Steckel 1988, 12–14).

With regard to other sectors of the economy, there were stirrings in the pre-1870 period. Ironworking began to make a noticeable comeback around the middle of the nineteenth century, and there was progress in mechanical industry. Even more important, the growing demand for timber products, especially in Great Britain, led to a major expansion of the timber industry starting around 1850. It was not before 1870, however, that modernization got up a real head of steam. The very modest level of industrialization before 1870, together with the rural, or at most semiurban, nature of that industrialization is reflected in the data on urban population. Even though it must be kept in mind that Swedish cities were defined in legal rather than economic or demographic terms, it is still apparent that at least until 1870 urban Sweden was stagnating. Indeed, a recent demographic and economic history of Stockholm during this period is entitled *A Stagnating Metropolis* (Soderberg, Jonsson, and Persson 1991). The share of the total population classified as urban had increased only from around 10 percent in 1800 to around 13 percent in 1870. Even more striking, Stockholm's share of the entire population declined between 1800 and 1850 and had barely recovered to its 1800 level by 1870 (Montgomery 1939, 108; Statistiska Centralbyrån 1969, table 6).

4.2.2   1870–1914

By any standard, this period witnessed extremely rapid industrialization and economic growth. Scholarly debate deals with questions of how fast it was— for example, did Sweden grow faster than any other country in Europe? About the basic trend, there is no disagreement. The same can be said about the late 1890s, which was the most remarkable subperiod within this longer period (Sandberg 1978). It might also be noted that the reason for ending in 1914 is strictly related to World War I (Sweden was neutral) and has no particular economic significance.

During these decades, Sweden's population increased from approximately 4.2 to approximately 5.7 million inhabitants (Statistiska Centralbyrån 1969, 46–47). This reflects a rate of growth somewhat below that experienced during the previous period. It was the net result of falling birth and death rates combined with a very high rate of emigration, overwhelmingly to the United States (see Hofsten and Lundström 1976). Close to a million Swedes departed their homeland, and since virtually all of them were young adults, the long-term effect on the Swedish population was even greater than that number implies (Carlsson 1961, 454–62; Hildebrand 1978, 599). Absent this emigration, the rate of population growth clearly would have been outpacing that of the previous period. While the great mass of the emigrants no doubt improved their economic condition, whether those staying behind gained or lost is less clear and depends, among other things, on the rate of remittances from the emigrants. As for the age structure of the population, the net effect was a very modest change in the size of the working-age (15–64) population from 60.5 percent in 1870 to 59.9 percent in 1910 (Statistiska Centralbyrån 1969, 68).

Our economic data, which are admittedly imperfect, indicate that Swedish national income grew at an average annual rate of approximately 2.8 percent between 1870 and 1910. In per capita terms, this amounts to an equally impressive rate of 2.0 percent (Krantz and Nilsson 1980, table 3.1; Maddison 1991, table B1). Not surprisingly, statistical measures of rising living standards show similar growth. Real hourly wages and annual incomes more than doubled (Hildebrand 1978, 609). This growth, of course, was also reflected in a rapid change in the sectoral distribution of the population. The share of the population dependent on agriculture dropped from approximately three-quarters to less than one-half, while the share dependent on manufacturing rose from less than one-sixth to approximately one-third (Cole and Deane 1968, 27; Jörberg 1994, 452–53).

From an international perspective, a striking aspect of Swedish industrialization, especially during this period, was its predominately nonurban location. The percentage of all industrial workers employed in noncity locations reached its peak only around the turn of the century. At that time, something in the vicinity of 65 percent of all industrial workers were employed outside the cities (Gårdlund 1942, 296). While it is true that these distinctions are based on legal rather than strictly economic definitions of cities and that the "rural" industrial "agglomerations" were not salubrious garden spots, still, there is, and especially was, a big difference between them and large industrial cities (Swedish or not). Naturally, this rural-dominated location of industry is also reflected in the general urbanization statistics. Between 1870 and 1913, the percentage of the population living in cities had roughly doubled from 13 to 26 percent (Statistiska Centralbyrån 1969, 46). Of course, the figures, especially the latter, would be somewhat higher if the "rural industrial agglomerations" are included. While this rate of growth was far from trivial, it still does not compare with urbanization in the major industrial countries. Furthermore, Swedish cities were overwhelmingly small. In 1910, the population of Stockholm was still less than 350,000, and of the others, only Gothenburg exceeded 100,000 (Milward and Saul 1973, 497–98; Heckscher 1954, 145). The fact of the matter is that almost all Swedish "cities," in 1914 containing a clear majority of all city dwellers, would by contemporary American or British standards best be described as "towns" or, in some cases, as "small towns."

4.2.3   1914–1950

The road Sweden traveled to get from 1914 to midcentury was, in many respects, a rocky one. At the same, however, it clearly was less painful than that of most, or even all, other industrialized countries. Sweden's big advantage, of course, was the ability to remain neutral in both world wars.

Though war is never a good thing, World War I only became a source of suffering in Sweden with the introduction of unlimited submarine warfare and tight blockades in 1917. The food shortage of the winter of 1917–18 was sufficiently serious, however, to set off food riots and to earn Prime Minister Hammarskjöld the less than complimentary nickname "Hungerskjöld." Thus, although Sweden did not endure anything like the hardships of the combatants, the peace was certainly welcome. Unfortunately, there, as elsewhere, it was accompanied by the arrival of the Spanish flu pandemic.

The interwar period began rather inauspiciously with a deliberately created deflation crisis. Once the prewar position of the krona had been reestablished in 1922, however, the 1920s evolved into a period of growth and prosperity. As in the rest of the industrial world, the good times ran out with the onset of the Great Depression. Despite the distinctly Swedish nature of the so-called Krueger crash of 1932, Sweden weathered the 1930s a lot better than most other countries. The principal reasons for this relatively favorable experience were (1) a prompt devaluation of the krona, (2) the generally favorable development of Swedish export markets, (3) a more expansionary—or at least less contractionary—economic policy than that pursued in most other industrial countries, and (4) good luck. While international political developments were obviously worrisome, not to say downright scary, Swedes had little reason to complain about economic conditions during the late 1930s.

World War II was certainly unpleasant in Sweden. Fuel in particular was in short supply—lots of shivering, not many baths, and virtually no driving. Food was rationed, but unlike the latter part of World War I, nothing resembling starvation or malnutrition threatened. For most people, the biggest irritation was probably the lack of coffee and tobacco. None of this, of course, even deserves to be mentioned in the same breath as the unspeakable suffering that occurred in many other countries.

At the end of the war, Sweden's Keynesian economic establishment shared the general fear of renewed worldwide depression. In fact, of course, a lack of effective demand was the least of Europe's, or the world's, problems. Physically unscathed by the war, Sweden was in almost as good a position as the United States (although obviously on a much smaller scale) to take advantage of the postwar reconstruction boom. Thus, good, if inflationary, times started almost immediately with the war's end, and they were far from over in 1950. Over the entire period 1914–50 the Swedish population grew, but only modestly. The total population increased from approximately 5.7 million in 1914 to approximately 7.0 million in 1950. This slowing rate of growth was the joint result of rapidly falling birth and death rates (Hofsten and Lundström 1976, 12–17). As for migration, after a modest final burst in the 1920s, Swedish emigration fell to very low levels. Instead, a rising level of immigration, much of it consisting of political refugees, took over. Migration was now a net contributor to population growth. It also had the effect of slowing the percentage shrinkage of the economically active age groups (Statistiska Centralbyrån 1969, 124, 130–31). Despite the fluctuations of the period, the general economic trend was clearly upward. Real per capita domestic product increased by an average of 2.5 percent per year (Krantz and Nilsson 1980, table 3.1; Maddison 1991, table B1). Similar gains were recorded in per capita income and other measures of living standards. Between 1913 and 1939, real hourly wages in industry increased by 88 percent, with annual real earnings increasing by 52 percent. The difference was due to a sharp decrease in the workweek. Between 1939 and 1949, these percentage increases were 25.5 and 27 percent, respectively (Heckscher 1954, 280–81).

The continuing rapid industrialization of Sweden can be seen in the figures for the sectoral distribution of the labor force. By 1950, the share of the population dependent on agriculture had declined to 25 percent. Meanwhile, the share of manufacturing had increased to 43 percent while that of the service sector had risen to an impressive 22 percent. As for the urban-rural division, the cities maintained a fairly steady rate of relative growth. By 1937, the population of the cities had reached the 36 percent level, and by 1950 their share stood at 48 percent (Statistiska Centralbyrån 1969, 46). Once again, these percentages would have been larger if the "industrial agglomerations" were included. In addition, on a world scale, Stockholm was now beginning to approach the size of at least a midsized metropolitan area. Still, the lack of crowding and the availability of space, both within the cities, and certainly in rural areas, continued to be a principal characteristic of Sweden.

4.2.4   1950–1995

The period since 1950 can best be divided into two periods, the split occurring around 1975. The first half, especially the 1960s, was a period of truly spectacular economic growth and prosperity. During the whole quarter of a century between 1950 and 1975 real per capita GDP increased at an annual rate of approximately 2.5 percent. During the period 1960–75, it did so by over 3 percent per annum. Starting around the middle of the 1970s, however, developments in Sweden, as in most of Western Europe, became much more mixed. Between 1975 and 1989, real GDP per capita increased at an annual rate of approximately 1.5 percent. Since then growth has been even slower and more uncertain.

These years, of course, also witnessed the emergence of a so-called service economy. At least in the Swedish case it was, and continues to be, dominated by government services. The share of government expenditures in GNP, as well as the share of taxes in income, reached levels (well above 50 percent) unprecedented in Sweden or elsewhere. Indeed, although apologists for the exploding public sector like, or at least liked, to blame the "oil shocks" for Sweden's recent economic, and especially its productivity, retardation, most informed observers tend principally to blame the bloated government services sector together with the incentive-destroying features of the income redistribution policies being followed.

Sweden's population continued to grow at a modest rate during this period. Increasingly, however, such growth came to depend on continued large-scale immigration. This dependence is seen to be even greater when it is noticed that the immigrant groups have much higher birthrates than do native-born Swedes.

Sweden's urbanization also has continued apace, despite government policies favoring rural areas and small towns. In particular, there has been a striking concentration of population in the three major urban areas centered around Stockholm, Gothenburg, and Malmo. Even these metropolitan areas, however, are characterized by an availability of space not typical of the European continent. In the rest of the country, the forests and their denizens are making a spectacular comeback. Wolves and bears are reappearing in areas where they have not been seen since the late eighteenth century. Indeed one of the currently popular political justifications for agricultural subsidies is that they help prevent Sweden from losing its open landscape and becoming a single great big forest.

4.3   Mortality, Health, and Heights

4.3.1   1800–1870

One of the most striking features of this period overall is the clear downward trend in mortality and the associated increase in life expectancy (see table 4.1 and figs. 4.1–4.6). This development is made even more intriguing by the absence of any pronounced trend in per capita incomes at least until 1850. Indeed, even if there was some modest increase in average incomes, that trend, as far as health and mortality is concerned (once again, at the very least until 1850), tended to be offset by the increasingly unequal distribution of income and wealth. It thus seems clear that the improvement in health and life expectancy was not principally, or at all, the result of higher incomes and living standards (as normally defined). It is, of course, possible that the opposite effect, from health to income, was at work. That, however, would imply that without the improvement in health, incomes would have been falling.

It is also interesting to look at the trend in heights. Our principal source of height data for this paper comes from measurements of conscripted militia.[1] These records cover cohorts of virtually the entire male population, but unfortunately they only go back to cohorts born in 1819. For earlier periods we have to rely on measurements of the settled (*indelta*) army. The trend in military heights was clearly upward for cohorts born in the 1790s until the 1840s. After that point, average adult heights declined either a lot (based on the settled army) or a little (based on the militia). Growth then resumed, especially for those young men who reached puberty after the subsistence crisis of the late 1860s (Sandberg and Steckel 1988).

We suppose it is possible to argue that the fact that adult heights for cohorts born around 1840, and reaching maturity in the 1860s, were similar to those born in the 1800–1810 period indicates the absence of any overall trend in heights during the whole 1800–1870 period. From such a conclusion, it would then follow that there was little or no connection between trends in mortality

---

1. Three qualifications about this data source are fully described in the data appendix. First, the age at measurement, originally 21 years, gradually decreased until it reached 18 years after World War II. Since the age was reduced in line with the decline in age at maturation, however, these changes have very little effect on the trend in final adult heights. Second, data are missing for a few scattered years, which required us to interpolate. Third, the military imposed nontrivial minimum height standards on cohorts born between 1819 and 1839. We adjusted for the resulting shortfall using the Quantile Bend Estimator.

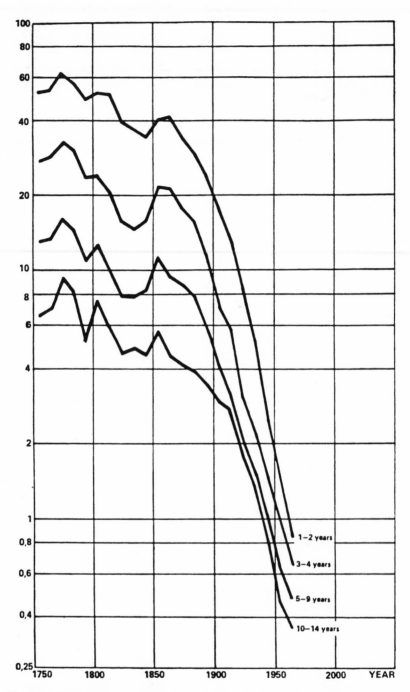

Fig. 4.1 Age-specific mortality rates for men aged 1–14, 1751–1970 (deaths per 1,000)
Source: Hofsten and Lundström (1976).

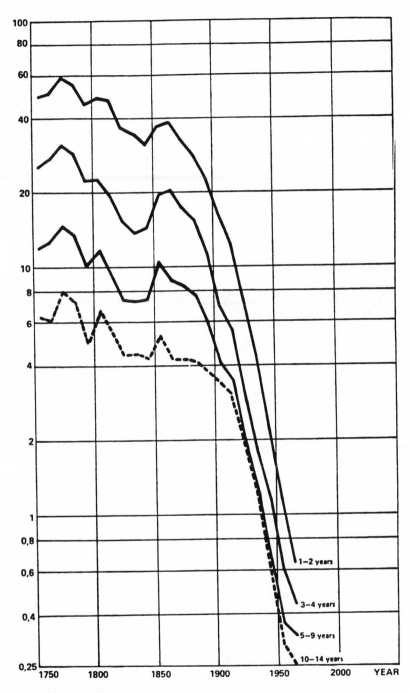

Fig. 4.2 Age-specific mortality rates for women aged 1–14, 1751–1970 (deaths per 1,000)

Source: Hofsten and Lundström (1976).

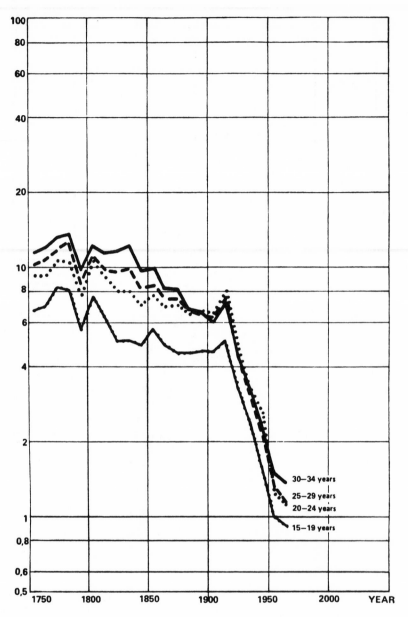

**Fig. 4.3 Age-specific mortality rates for men aged 15–34, 1751–1970
(deaths per 1,000)**
Source: Hofsten and Lundström (1976).

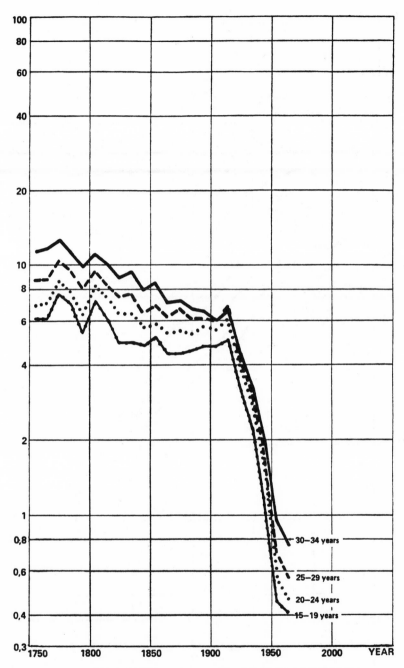

Fig. 4.4   Age-specific mortality rates for women aged 15–34, 1751–1970 (deaths per 1,000)

Source: Hofsten and Lundström (1976).

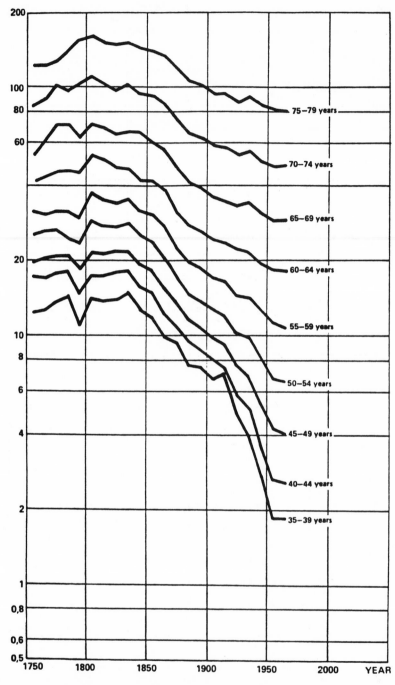

**Fig. 4.5   Age-specific mortality rates for men aged 35–79, 1751–1970
(deaths per 1,000)**
Source: Hofsten and Lundström (1976).

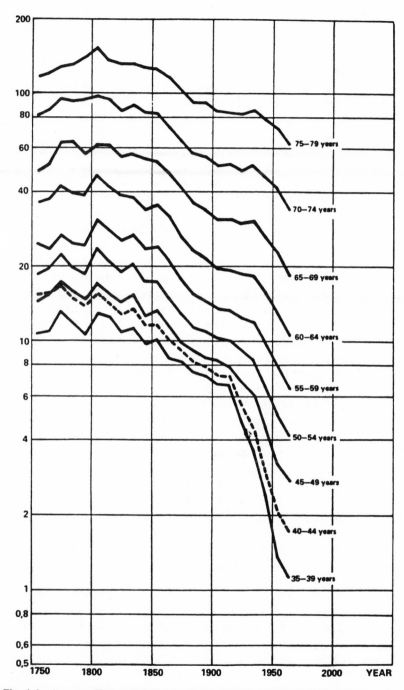

Fig. 4.6 Age-specific mortality rates for women aged 35–79, 1751–1970 (deaths per 1,000)

Source: Hofsten and Lundström (1976).

and trends in average adult heights. That would be a rather startling result. From an even longer perspective, however, it seems clear that the decline in heights for cohorts of the 1840s was quickly reversed and constituted no more than a temporary dip in an upward trend. The levels reached by the cohorts of the 1830s were soon reestablished and surpassed after 1870. Furthermore, while there was no large increase in mortality rates for adults during the late 1840s and early 1850s, there was a sharp increase for children, especially young children. Since average adult heights are not materially affected by the income and nutrition levels of adults, it seems clear that the drop in recorded heights was the result of the particularly, and indeed atypically, harsh conditions endured by young children during those years (Sandberg and Steckel 1988). An additional explanation of this rising child mortality would stress factors that spread disease, such as the substantial increase in internal migration as well as growing school attendance around the middle of the century.[2]

Accepting that argument leads to the conclusion that the trend in heights during the 1800–1870 period was clearly upward. Thus, the larger conclusion is that during those decades life expectancy and average adult heights tended upward, while income or the standard of living fluctuated without trend at least until 1850. After 1850, the increase in per capita GDP may or may not have been offset by an increasingly unequal distribution of income. Obviously then, the apparent trend toward improving health, while perhaps contributing to income growth, cannot have been a product of such growth until, at the very earliest, 1850. One possible boost to improving health probably came from the general lack of urbanization. As noted above, there was very little growth in urbanization during this period, and Stockholm especially stagnated. In view of the unhealthy condition of Swedish cities, and especially of Stockholm, this lack of urbanization certainly must have been beneficial to health.

The absence of both income growth (a supposed plus for health) and urbanization (a supposed minus for health) prior to at least 1850, however, can hardly constitute an explanation for improved health. Clearly, some other forces must have been at work. The standard explanations offered by historians are the potato, peace, and smallpox vaccinations (e.g., Carlsson 1961, 37).

This was the period during which the extremely high yielding potato became a field crop in Sweden. This in turn led to a considerable increase both in direct human consumption and to the replacement of grain in distilling. Since potatoes are more nutritious than bread and bread is more nutritious than alcohol, it is not surprising that this development tended to raise both life expectancy and average heights. The low price of potatoes, however, meant that increases in its consumption had little impact on measured incomes. It seems apparent that the population preferred to eat bread, but low incomes, or the

---

2. The Elementary Education Act of 1842 promoted schooling of young children, and the Poor Law Act of 1847 eliminated restrictions on personal movement. For a discussion of these points, see Carlsson (1961, 377, 380).

attraction of low potato prices, induced them to eat potatoes instead. The resulting improvement in nutrition, and consequently in health, thus becomes ultimately a matter of serendipity. Consumers simply may not have anticipated the health benefits of the potato. If, on the other hand, those benefits were recognized, thus making potato consumption more attractive, then what we have is a case of massive, unrecognized (and unrecorded) consumer surplus.

Peace, or the absence of war, was certainly a blessing. The disastrous consequences of war on health and mortality in Sweden can easily be seen from data on the eighteenth and very early nineteenth centuries. On the other hand, it is clear that nineteenth-century health was considerably better even than that of the peaceful years of the eighteenth century, once again without there being any great difference in measured incomes.

We are choosing to expand "vaccination" beyond its, certainly very important, literal meaning to include public and, to a lesser extent, private health measures. In addition to vaccinations (especially against smallpox) per se, there were marked improvements in sanitation, hygiene, and child care. Much of this was accomplished through government propaganda in favor of breast-feeding and general improvements in sanitation (Lithell 1981, 183). The church and, even more so, the system of compulsory schools were effectively used to spread official views on these subjects. The fact that Sweden was a highly literate country with a long tradition of bureaucratic and church control over the individual's private life meant that these campaigns were a good deal more successful than would have been the case in countries, such as England or the United States, where much more emphasis was put on individual freedom and autonomy.

More concrete measures were also undertaken. The system of training midwives, first controlled by the government as early as 1711, was improved and expanded following the issuance of new regulations in 1819 and again in 1840 (Lundquist 1963, 645–48). During the same period, the system of state district physicians that dated back to 1773 was similarly expanded and improved markedly (Bergstrand 1963, 127, 156–57). Even more important, the 1857 statute on epidemics, which put great emphasis on improved sanitation, was quickly followed by improvements in water and sewage systems. The major improvements in Stockholm's access to clean water and efficient sewers during the 1860s had immediately observable effects on the city's death rate from typhus (Bergman 1963, 379–80).

Some interesting facts concerning the human capital aspects of low Swedish, and other Scandinavian, infant and child mortality rates can be gleaned from data on various ethnic groups in the United States in 1900. The infant mortality rate for children of Swedish-born women in America was very low, both relative to other groups of immigrants and relative to the children of native-born white American women, but it was somewhat higher than contemporaneous Swedish levels. It is also noteworthy that the superior mortality performance of the Swedes et al. in America, just as in Scandinavia itself, was greatest for young children (Sandberg 1979, 234). A final alternative, or supplementary, explanation for the improving health trend is an improving epidemiological environment. That is certainly possible, although at least one major new disease, cholera, appeared in Sweden during this period. Once again, however, although it was a terrible killer in the major cities, especially Stockholm, the basically rural nature of the country strictly limited the effect even of this new killer disease.

Although no long-run connection can be established between rising income and improving health during this period, there seems to be a clear connection between downturns in income, almost invariably the result of poor harvests, and downturns, or at least stagnation, in health. This connection can be seen especially in the late 1840s and early 1850s. Similar, although perhaps not so powerful, effects can be seen resulting from income declines in roughly the late 1810s, the early 1830s, and the late 1860s. The apparent connection between income and health during these periods at least raises the possibility that the effects of rising income and nonincome trend effects on improving health can be separated. Such a separation would also be very useful in interpreting the experience of later periods when income and health were trending upward together.

4.3.2   1870–1914

The time after 1870 is in some sense less interesting than the preceding period. This is so because, starting around 1870, all Swedish indicators of health and income have rapidly trended upward together. Nonetheless, there are some differences in rate and composition that throw light on the interrelationship among the variables being studied. If the increase in child mortality that occurred around the middle of the century is impressive, the even greater drop that followed after circa 1870 is truly startling. Ultimately, all that can be said is that child mortality in Sweden nosedived after the onset of rapid industrialization and income growth. Clearly, the conditions, presumably a shortage of food, that had caused the crisis in child health were totally reversed.

Not only was the crop failure of 1868–69 never repeated but increasing domestic production was augmented by a rising flood of basic foodstuffs from America. To the distress of Swedish commercial agriculture, but to the benefit of consumers, the result was a clear fall in the relative price of food (see Carlsson 1961, 558). Thus even the rapid growth of real incomes fails fully to reflect the increased access to food. The commencement of major public health projects, especially the construction of water and sewer facilities, in urban areas also was a major plus for life expectancy.

For other age groups, there were also benefits, but they were less spectacular than those for the children. Interestingly enough, by far the smallest gains were achieved by young adults. Since these groups, generally speaking, were the survivors of the young child cohorts that had experienced such high rates of mortality during the previous decades, there is an implication here that the hungry forties and fifties were still claiming victims a decade or two later. Put somewhat differently, it implies that any selectivity effect from the earlier high child death rates was more than offset by the damage to the long-run health of the survivors.

Height data are consistent with such an observation. The cohorts that reached maturity before circa 1870 were clearly shorter than those who matured later. It should not be surprising if these height-impaired cohorts showed evidence of poor health and high mortality throughout their lives.

It is also interesting to note that the special position of Stockholm, shorter than the national average, and of the north, taller than the national average, began to erode during this period. The health disadvantage of urban living, especially big city living, was beginning to disappear. By the same token, the advantage of low-density, relatively high protein (mostly from game) living in the north also was coming to an end. Today Stockholm is no different from the rest of the country, and the north, possibly due to ethnic genetic differences, is on the short side.

These trends in health and heights, of course, are perfectly compatible with the rapid growth of income. On the other hand, greater urbanization does not seem to have been a major health problem. As already noted, Swedish urban areas generally had never been as bad as in many other countries. More important, the pre-1870 public health measures described above were accelerating during this period. Stockholm, in particular, was rapidly losing its previously well-deserved reputation as a pesthole.

4.3.3   1914–1950

Rising incomes allowed greater access to food, decent housing, and ever improving medical care. The government helped things along with greater expenditures on water and sanitation facilities, as well as an expansion and improvement of the system of publicly provided district medical facilities and personnel. Once again, during this period health, heights, and incomes steadily advanced together. The only noticeable exception to this experience occurred in the period right around the end of World War I. The food shortage of 1917–18 was closely followed by the Spanish flu pandemic. The net effect was serious enough to lower, albeit very briefly, life expectancies at birth. The reversal in mortality rates, however, was heavily concentrated among young adults. These groups were then the first to benefit spectacularly once the pandemic had passed. In this case, there might have been some selectivity effect—the survivors were on average healthier than the whole cohort, and the Spanish flu had left no serious permanent ill effects on those who recovered from it.

Over the entire period, it is clear that all age groups, with the possible exception of the elderly, benefited from a spectacular decrease in all mortality rates. For the elderly, the improvement was merely impressive. For some older groups, there was also a slight, but certainly perceptible, upturn in mortality during the 1930s.

Throughout the period, average heights continued their upward trend. Similarly, the special position of the large cities, on the short side, and the north, on the tall side, vanished entirely before the period was over. Another interesting development was the shrinkage of the height difference between social classes (by now it has disappeared entirely). This was probably a combined effect of a more equal distribution of income and the sharp general increase in income and, therefore, in nutrition. Virtually all children were at least, and at last, well fed.

4.3.4   1950–1995

This most recent period continues to show improvements in the health of the Swedish population. An ever rising standard of living has included improvements in diet, housing, and medical care. The government has chipped in with increased expenditures on public health measures, while the advance of medical science, especially in the form of new vaccines and antibiotics, has played a major role. Average life expectancy at birth has continued to increase as have average adult heights. It seems clear, however, that, particularly for the most recent decades, the increase in heights has slowed to at most a crawl. Apparently, genetic limits are being approached. The fact that social class differences in heights no longer seem to be detectable tends to confirm the belief that better nutritional status can yield little in the way of greater stature. By the same token, the great reduction in infectious diseases that has already occurred leaves little room for improvement in that regard.

There may be greater room for increases in average life expectancy. Once again, however, better access to food is not likely to be the key. Rather a combination of increasingly sophisticated medical knowledge and procedures together with some helpful "lifestyle" changes are the most likely remaining possible sources of greater life expectancies.

4.4   Trends in Human Welfare

As was noted in the introduction, the interrelationship in various countries among industrialization, urbanization, income growth, and health is a complex and contentious matter. While the Swedish experience might be said to be similar to that of the United States and Great Britain in that signs of declining health, that is, a reduction in heights and an increase in mortality rates, occurred around the middle of the nineteenth century, the comparison is misleading. The Swedish problems were the result of population growth and poor harvests, not of industrialization and urbanization. While it is certainly possible that industrial work and city living per se might have had bad effects on health even in Sweden, rapid industrialization and urbanization were in fact accompanied by clear net improvements in health. Whatever negative effects there may have been were clearly more than offset by favorable developments, no doubt including, but not limited to, income growth.

There is no doubt that the level of health is a major component of human welfare and, therefore, of any reasonable definition of the standard of living. A serious question thus arises as to whether our standard measures of per capita income, particularly those for earlier periods, take adequate account of the level, and changes in the level, of health. To the extent that part of measured incomes are spent for the express purpose of attaining improved health and increased life expectancy, there is probably no great measurement problem. Thus, the vast amounts currently expended on health care in all industrial countries can be considered purchases of improved health and extended life. To the extent that we eat to live longer, part of the health benefits of a better diet might be said to be reflected in our level of measured income and expenditures. By the same token, expenditures on medical research create improvements in the production of better health and longer life pretty much the same way as other research produces more enjoyable consumer products. All such improvements raise questions of adequate accounting for consumer surplus.

It is difficult to believe, however, that past improvements in health are adequately accounted for in income statistics. Changes in health have often occurred in the form of externalities that have no noticeable effect on income figures. For example, the Swedish experience in 1800–1850 of a noticeable upward trend in health during a period of stagnating incomes can hardly have been included in those income figures. Such an inclusion would imply that the Swedish population was shifting substantial amounts of its income away from other goods and services and toward health-producing goods and services. This simply did not happen. The role of the potato was serendipitous, and the expenditures on public health (e.g., smallpox vaccines and improved sanitation and hygiene) were tiny compared to the resulting health benefits. In short, major improvements in welfare in the form of better health were occurring that were barely, if at all, recorded in the income data.

Even for the later period, it seems clear that health and life expectancy were largely being improved by factors that were not adequately accounted for in income data. Thus, a case can be made for trying explicitly to account for changes in health status when constructing historical income (or welfare) series.

One approach recently developed by the United Nations for dealing with this problem has been to calculate a so-called Human Development Index (HDI; United Nations Development Programme 1990).[3] The HDI is calculated by subtracting the average of three "deprivation" indexes from 1.00. The deprivations used are lack of life expectancy, lack of literacy, and lack of income. These indexes are based on a country's position on a scale between minimum and maximum values for life expectancy, literacy, and income, respectively. In order to incorporate a wide range of historical human experience, we have chosen scales between 30 and 80 years for life expectancy, from zero to 100

---

3. For a summary of critiques of this approach, see United Nations Development Programme (1993, 104–14).

Table 4.2   **Deprivation Indexes**

Year	Life Expectancy	Stature	Infant Mortality	Literacy	Per Capita Income
1820	0.817	0.542	0.487	0.175	0.699
1825	0.716	0.517	0.451	0.163	0.702
1830	0.820	0.504	0.519	0.150	0.706
1835	0.751	0.492	0.470	0.138	0.697
1840	0.758	0.517	0.461	0.125	0.687
1845	0.740	0.496	0.449	0.113	0.678
1850	0.722	0.492	0.425	0.100	0.669
1855	0.787	0.483	0.424	0.088	0.639
1860	0.704	0.438	0.392	0.075	0.611
1865	0.695	0.458	0.384	0.063	0.617
1870	0.700	0.408	0.393	0.050	0.575
1875	0.691	0.404	0.394	0.038	0.514
1880	0.639	0.379	0.345	0.025	0.497
1885	0.608	0.354	0.319	0.013	0.471
1890	0.578	0.321	0.301	0.000	0.444
1895	0.544	0.317	0.285	0.000	0.393
1900	0.542	0.313	0.281	0.000	0.354
1905	0.490	0.292	0.242	0.000	0.299
1910	0.447	0.296	0.215	0.000	0.249
1915	0.434	0.275	0.201	0.000	0.312
1920	0.453	0.246	0.185	0.000	0.218
1925	0.348	0.217	0.165	0.000	0.134
1930	0.339	0.200	0.160	0.000	0.071
1935	0.301	0.175	0.132	0.000	0.034
1940	0.260	0.163	0.107	0.000	0.000
1945	0.222	0.108	0.081	0.000	0.000
1950	0.172	0.088	0.062	0.000	0.000
1955	0.149	0.058	0.051	0.000	0.000
1960	0.132	0.038	0.046	0.000	0.000
1965	0.121	0.029	0.039	0.000	0.000

Source: Calculated from table 4.1.

percent for literacy, and from the cost of a subsistence diet ($140 in 1970 U.S. prices) to the upper bound on the per capita income component recommended by the United Nations ($4,861 in 1987 U.S. dollars, or $1,660 in 1970 U.S. dollars; see the discussion of the HDI in the introduction of this volume). The index is linear for life expectancy and for literacy (implying constant marginal utility) and logarithmic for income (implying declining marginal utility of income).

We have calculated this index and its components for Sweden at five-year intervals between 1820 and 1965 (see tables 4.2 and 4.3 and figs. 4.7–4.9). In order to determine the sensitivity of the index to alternative measures of health, we have made the same calculation substituting adult male heights (by birth

Table 4.3   **Human Development Indexes**

Year	Life Expectancy	Stature	Infant Mortality
1820	0.436	0.528	0.546
1825	0.473	0.539	0.561
1830	0.441	0.547	0.542
1835	0.472	0.558	0.565
1840	0.476	0.557	0.576
1845	0.490	0.571	0.587
1850	0.503	0.580	0.602
1855	0.496	0.597	0.617
1860	0.537	0.626	0.641
1865	0.542	0.621	0.646
1870	0.558	0.655	0.660
1875	0.586	0.681	0.685
1880	0.613	0.700	0.711
1885	0.636	0.721	0.733
1890	0.660	0.745	0.752
1895	0.688	0.764	0.774
1900	0.701	0.778	0.788
1905	0.737	0.803	0.820
1910	0.768	0.818	0.846
1915	0.751	0.804	0.829
1920	0.776	0.845	0.865
1925	0.839	0.883	0.900
1930	0.863	0.910	0.923
1935	0.888	0.930	0.945
1940	0.913	0.946	0.964
1945	0.926	0.964	0.973
1950	0.943	0.971	0.979
1955	0.950	0.981	0.983
1960	0.956	0.988	0.985
1965	0.960	0.990	0.987

Source: Calculated from table 4.2.

cohort) and infant mortality respectively for life expectancy.[4] We are also planning to utilize alternative measures of education for literacy. The problem with using literacy in the Swedish case is that it had reached a level around 90 percent by 1850 and was close to 100 percent before the turn of the twentieth century. Thus, despite the clear benefits accruing through increasing levels of schooling, education ends up playing very little role in the growth of the HDI for Sweden. The results of our calculations are presented in table 4.3 and figure

4. Our range for stature was defined at the low end by possibly the smallest population ever measured—the Bundi of New Guinea (156 cm)—and at the upper end by 180 cm, which approximately corresponds to the tallest population today (Eveleth and Tanner 1976, 1990). Our range for infant mortality extends from zero percent to 35 percent, which is approximately the highest found for large historical populations.

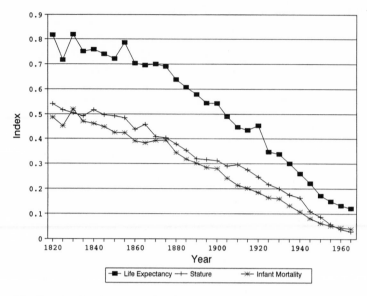

Fig. 4.7   Deprivation indexes of health
Source: Table 4.2.

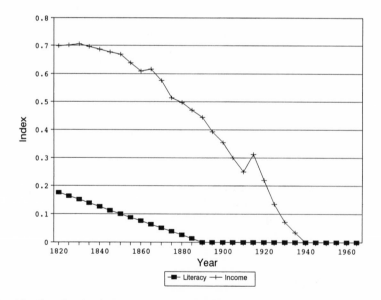

Fig. 4.8   Deprivation indexes of income and literacy
Source: Table 4.2.

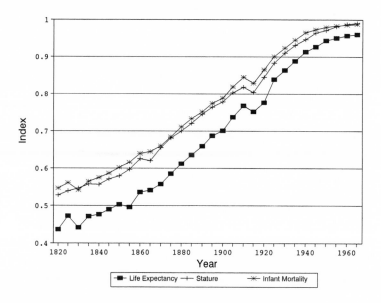

Fig. 4.9   Human development indexes
Source: Table 4.3.

4.9. A number of interesting aspects of these indexes are apparent even from casual observation. First of all, all three alternative HDIs show very similar growth patterns. Indeed, the HDIs based on infant mortality and human stature are virtually identical. This result tends to confirm our view that final adult height in Sweden was very heavily influenced by conditions during the first year of life. Furthermore, while the level, although not the growth pattern, of the life-expectancy-based HDI differs from its siblings, that difference reflects substantially the choice of the life expectancy minimum. If 25 years, rather than 30 years, were used as the minimum, all three series would be nearly identical.

Another striking feature of these HDIs, particularly compared to those for some other industrialized countries, is their persistent upward trend. There are virtually no reversals. Even if annual data had created a few more such instances, at least in the preindustrial period, the result is still remarkable. The only post-1870 reversal is recorded for 1915 (i.e., 1913–17) and, of course, is the result of the serious economic problems caused by World War I. The food supply problems and the Spanish flu epidemic included in the 1920 (1918–22) index numbers are not enough to prevent a modest increase between 1915 and 1920. The fact that the indexes continued to grow during the 1930s (at least on a five-year average basis) confirms the view that the Great Depression was both relatively mild and short lived in Sweden. Yet another interesting aspect of these indexes is their growth rate by periods. Clearly, they all accelerate after roughly 1870—that is, with the onset of rapid industrialization. While there was improvement before industrialization, it has been much more rapid since. This more rapid growth has occurred despite the fact that literacy, having reached 100 percent by 1890 (at least according to our measure), stopped contributing to the HDIs at that point. As to the relative contributions of income growth and health improvement, it is clear that health improvement was the dominant factor up to circa 1850. Income growth then began to play a greater role, especially after 1870. This situation was then reversed during the twentieth century, largely because of the assumption that the marginal utility of income is declining.

It is also interesting to compare the HDIs we have computed for Sweden with the results reached for other countries. One such comparison can be made with the HDI (stature based) that Costa and Steckel have computed for the United States. In 1820 the American HDI (including slaves) was 0.580 while the comparable result for Sweden was 0.528. Since Swedes then were clearly more literate than Americans, the difference is the result of American advantages in income and especially health (height). By the time of the great Swedish migration to the United States (circa 1870), the indexes stood at 0.702 for America (including African Americans) and 0.655 for Sweden. Since Swedes were still considerably more literate and almost as healthy (tall), the American advantage was unquestionably in income. Thus, emigration, particularly of landless (literate and healthy) Swedish farm youths made good sense. By 1960, however, improvements in Swedish health (height) had reached the point that the Swedish HDI nosed out that for the United States despite higher U.S. incomes.

Finally, a comparison can be made between the Swedish HDI and those of various less developed countries today. Overall, the Swedish HDI (this time based on life expectancy) just before the onset of rapid industrialization around 1870 was at a level similar to that of countries currently classified as being at the lower level of "medium human development" (e.g., Egypt). The components of the index, however, were drastically different. In the case of Egypt in 1987, per capita incomes are roughly similar (Sweden, $1,224; Egypt, $1,357) but life expectancy and literacy differ greatly. In 1870, Swedish life expectancy at birth was 44.99 years, compared to 62 years for Egypt in 1987. Clearly, Egyptian life expectancy has benefited greatly from developments in public health that have occurred during the past 120 years. On the other hand, the Swedish literacy rate in 1870 was in the vicinity of 95 percent compared to 45 percent for Egypt in 1985. For the individual, a long life expectancy may well be more important than being literate, but it seems likely that Sweden's prospects for rapid future economic growth in 1870 were a good deal better than Egypt's prospects today.

As an alternative to the HDI calculations, we have also applied Daniel Usher's well-known work assigning dollar values to increases in survival probabilities (Usher 1973, 1980). Usher's work rests on the following set of, admittedly rather strong, assumptions: (1) utility (U) is a function of consumption (C) in each time period (t); (2) utility is separable in C_i; (3) all utility functions are of the form $U_t = \sum_{i=0}^{t-1} C_i^\beta / (1 + r)^i$, where β is the elasticity of utility with respect to C and r is the individual's subjective rate of discount; and (4) consumption is constant across age groups. On this basis, he is able to calculate the change in consumption that a person would be willing to forgo in return for a given increase in survival rates as a function of C, β, and r. The presence of a discount factor means that the further into the future a person's reduced age-specific mortality decrease lies, the less it will be worth. Thus, reductions in infant and child mortality rates will have an especially great effect on the Usher-adjusted well-being of the population.

Table 4.4 presents actual Swedish five-year interval GDP growth in addition to Usher-adjusted (actual GDP plus or minus the value of changes in survival rates) well-being rates using four different, reasonable, assumptions about β and r for the period 1820–1965. Table 4.5 presents numerical values for per capita Swedish GDP, both Usher adjusted and unadjusted, in terms of 1970 U.S. dollars, with 1820 being the base. In effect, survival rates in 1820 are given zero value while the value of post-1820 changes in those survival rates is added (or subtracted) from actual per capita GDP. The same information for the period 1870–1965 is presented in table 4.6, but this time per capita GDP in 1870 is taken as the base where survival rates have zero value.

All these tables tend to confirm the general pattern of Swedish HDI development, that is, a steady upward trend with setbacks only on a few occasions in the first half of the nineteenth century and once around World War I. The Usher-adjusted numbers, however, fluctuate much more drastically than does the HDI. The reason for this is that survival rates, especially infant and child mortality rates, which weigh very heavily in the Usher-adjusted calculation, fluctuated much more than the other components of the HDI. These results, especially for the pre-1850 period, strongly support the conclusions concerning welfare, especially child welfare, that we presented in an earlier paper (see Sandberg and Steckel 1988).

The overall result for the 1820–50 period is that it was a time of very modest, preindustrial, growth in both per capita GDP and in Usher-adjusted welfare. What is worse, there were extremely wide swings in dollar-evaluated survival rates. Clearly, this represents a preindustrial regime where agricultural growth was low and subject to wide swings in harvest outcomes, which resulted in even wider welfare swings. In addition, the epidemiological environment was highly variable. Improvements in welfare were slow and uncertain.

We do not, however, accept the possible implication of the 1820–50 line in table 4.7, which shows no clear-cut gain in welfare from the Usher adjustment, that there was no improvement in health whatsoever during that period. The apparent lack of health improvement is entirely the result of a temporary upward blip in young child, but not infant, mortality during the period around 1850. In view of the temporary nature of this unfortunate development, as well

Table 4.4   **Measured and Revised Per Capita GDP Five-Year Growth Rates**
                   (in percentages)

Years	Measured	$r = 0.05$		$r = 0.10$	
		$\beta = 0.25$	$\beta = 0.45$	$\beta = 0.25$	$\beta = 0.45$
1820–25	−0.88	44.81	24.50	41.88	22.88
1825–30	−0.92	−41.55	−23.49	−37.70	−21.36
1830–35	2.38	32.52	19.13	29.56	17.48
1835–40	2.33	−0.79	0.60	−0.52	0.75
1840–45	2.34	9.47	6.30	8.39	5.70
1845–50	2.32	−17.44	−8.66	−10.07	−4.57
1850–55	7.71	7.42	7.55	1.43	4.22
1855–60	7.16	41.84	26.43	37.48	24.01
1860–65	−1.53	2.38	0.64	2.07	0.47
1865–70	10.80	9.13	9.87	9.48	10.07
1870–75	16.38	18.45	17.53	17.44	16.97
1875–80	4.32	23.62	15.04	21.44	13.83
1880–85	6.75	18.43	13.24	17.76	12.87
1885–90	6.87	18.27	13.20	17.90	12.99
1890–95	13.39	24.47	19.54	23.31	18.90
1895–1900	10.06	10.98	10.57	11.16	10.67
1900–1905	14.52	32.24	24.36	31.17	23.77
1905–10	13.26	27.33	21.08	26.64	20.70
1910–15	−14.54	−10.13	−12.09	−9.96	−12.00
1915–20	26.16	20.20	22.85	21.32	23.47
1920–25	23.17	55.76	41.27	51.73	39.04
1925–30	16.92	19.88	18.56	19.74	18.49
1930–35	9.56	20.31	15.53	19.28	14.96
1935–40	10.70	22.17	17.07	20.97	16.40
1940–45	8.80	18.33	14.09	17.25	13.49
1945–50	15.85	28.44	22.84	26.89	21.98
1950–55	10.74	16.13	13.73	15.25	13.25
1955–60	15.68	19.10	17.58	18.47	17.23
1960–65	21.45	23.42	22.54	23.18	22.41

Source: See text.

as the fact that heights, infant mortality, and overall life expectancy all improved, we are sticking to our view that there was a modest general trend toward better health during the 1820–50 period.

After 1850, the situation improved markedly. Indeed for the period 1850–70, the rate of growth of per capita GDP was approximately 1.1 percent per annum, with the Usher-adjusted welfare index growing at approximately twice that rate. Thus, increased survival rates added as much to welfare as did the, not inconsiderable, growth of per capita GDP. After 1870, the rate of growth of per capita GDP accelerated while the growth in the value of rising survival rates appears to, at least, have continued at the 1850–70 rate. Over the entire period, 1870–1950 per capita GDP grew at a rate of about 2.1 percent per

Table 4.5   **Measured and Revised Real Per Capita GDP (in 1970 U.S. dollars), 1820–70**

| Year | Measured | r = 0.05 | | r = 0.10 | |
		β = 0.25	β = 0.45	β = 0.25	β = 0.45
1820	295	295	295	295	295
1850	318	297	327	328	335
1870	400	506	491	510	486

Source: See text.

Table 4.6   **Measured and Revised Real Per Capita GDP (in 1970 U.S. dollars), 1870–1965**

| Year | Measured | r = 0.05 | | r = 0.10 | |
		β = 0.25	β = 0.45	β = 0.25	β = 0.45
1870	400	400	400	400	400
1890	554	820	693	792	679
1910	897	1,908	1,380	1,803	1,335
1950	2,128	8,598	4,731	7,684	4,428
1965	3,311	14,677	7,752	12,923	7,196

Source: See text.

Table 4.7   **Measured and Revised Real Per Capita GDP Annual Growth Rates (in percentages), 1820–1965**

| Year | Measured | r = 0.05 | | r = 0.10 | |
		β = 0.25	β = 0.45	β = 0.25	β = 0.45
1820–50	0.3	0.0	0.3	0.4	0.5
1850–70	1.1	2.7	2.1	2.3	1.8
1820–70	0.6	1.1	1.0	1.1	1.0
1870–1950	2.1	3.9	3.1	3.8	3.1
1950–65	3.0	3.6	3.4	3.5	3.3
1870–1965	2.3	3.9	3.2	3.6	3.1

Source: See text.

annum, while increasing survival rates added at the very least another percentage point to the annual growth of Usher-adjusted welfare.

What is perhaps most striking, however, is that after circa 1950 (and up to the end of our data in 1965), increasing survival rates have added very little, perhaps a third of a percentage point, to the annual growth of Usher-adjusted welfare. This is less than for any substantial number of years since approximately 1850. Equally intriguing, a similar result can be observed for the United States.

This clear recent slowdown in the contribution of reduced mortality to increasing well-being is made no less interesting by the fact that, during this same period, expenditures on medical care in Sweden, and the United States and elsewhere, have been increasing at an extraordinary and, indeed, a frightening rate. Today, of course, controlling the "monstrous" level and rate of growth of medical expenditures is a major economic and political problem in all high-income countries. It is no doubt this relatively recent experience with huge and exploding medical costs that has made the criticism of double counting levied, especially by Jeffrey Williamson, at the Usher welfare adjustment seem so compelling. That is, the charge that the decrease in mortality rates has to a very substantial degree been the direct result of the deliberate expenditure of resources already counted in per capita GDP.

Our data, however, seem to indicate that the really impressive contribution of mortality decrease to welfare, at least in Sweden, occurred during a period when the share of national product devoted to public health and medical care was still quite modest. During that period, it seems likely that the very impressive drops in mortality were largely (1) the by-product of income-induced improvements in nutrition and housing, (2) the result of disembodied advances in knowledge concerning sanitation and health, and (3) the result of public health and medical expenditures (e.g., sanitation infrastructure and vaccinations) that yielded huge amounts of consumer surplus in the form of improved health. More recently, these cheap sources of reduced mortality and improved health have been largely exhausted. For the past 40 or 50 years, further improvements have come in return for great expenditures on medical research, equipment, and personnel. Thus, it may well be that in the relatively recent past there should not be any Usher adjustment of welfare growth. The modest increases recorded in the value of survival probably have been fully paid for by expenditures recorded in GDP.

4.5 Conclusions

The principal conclusion of this paper is stated in the title. In Sweden rapid industrialization certainly accompanied, and almost certainly was responsible for, major improvements in health and welfare. The general state of health of the population was improving, albeit at a modest and uncertain rate, even during the pre-1850 period when average incomes were stagnating and the distribution of that income was deteriorating. After 1850, and especially after the onset of rapid industrialization around 1870, the improvement in health accelerated. It took the events of World War I and the Spanish flu to create one (hopefully) final downward blip in Swedish health statistics.

The fact that health conditions, and the level of human welfare, were trending upward even while average incomes were stagnating, income distribution was becoming less equal, and the earnings of the mass of the population was probably declining clearly indicates that other developments (composition of diet, public health measures, improved child care, and epidemiological conditions) favored improved health. The very rapid, and continuing, improvements in health conditions following 1870 indicate that the income gains that industrialization generated more than offset any deleterious effects of industrialization and, rather limited, urbanization. More and better food, housing, medical care, and (government financed) public health measures carried the day. Compared to most other nationalities, Swedes had, and continue to have, no right to be dour. Skoal!

Data Appendix

In this paper we have relied on four basic types of historical data.

Real Per Capita Income

All of our real per capita income (strictly, per capita GDP) figures for the period 1820–1965 ultimately are based on the work of Olle Krantz and Carl-Axel Nilsson. On the recommendation of Krantz, we used the figures published in Maddison (1991) for the period 1820–60. This series was then connected to the series for the period 1860–1965 contained in Krantz and Nilsson (1980). These original numbers were reported in 1970 Swedish kronor, which we converted to U.S. dollars at the 1970 exchange rate of 5.18 Skr per U.S. dollar.

Life Expectancy at Birth

Our life expectancy at birth figures come from Keyfitz and Fleiger (1968). It is their five-year intervals that dictated our use of the same interval for calculating the HDI.

Literacy Rates of the Adult Population

The literacy numbers are based on the conclusion reported by, although by no means unique to, Cipolla (1969) that Swedish literacy had reached 90 percent by 1850 and that virtually all Swedish youths were then literate. The compulsory education act of 1842 was unquestionably having an effect, although schools were certainly commonplace even before that year. Given a flow of virtually 100 percent literate cohorts reaching adulthood after 1850, a 0.25 annual rate of increase in literacy up to 100 percent in 1890 seems highly reasonable. Similarly, a 0.25 percent rate before 1850 also yields a reasonable result of 82.5 percent in 1820.

Adult Male Heights

Estimates of Swedish heights come from two different military sources. The data for cohorts born starting in 1820, and used in our numerical calculations, come from the heights of the conscripted militia. These nationwide average data cover the great majority of young men measured in the year they turned age 21 (born 1820–97), age 20 (born 1898–1929), age 19 (born 1930–35), and finally age 18 (born 1936–present). Since these age reductions occurred in line with the decline in the age of maturation, however, these changes have very little effect on the trend in final adult heights. More worrisome was the fact that the military imposed nontrivial height standards on cohorts born between 1819 and 1839. We corrected for the resulting shortfall using the Quantile Bend Estimator (Wachter and Trussell 1982). The fact that data are missing for a few scattered years forced us to interpolate for those years.

Our second source of height data, the trend results of which we discuss for cohorts born before 1820 but which are *not* included in any of our indexes, is based on a sample of approximately 40,000 soldiers of various ages who served in the "settled" (*indelta*) army between roughly 1730 and 1980. In social and economic terms, the soldiers were approximately on a par with crofters. Below them were all the various categories of landless rural residents. We sampled the data by selecting regiments scattered around the country (including the city of Stockholm) and then drew a sample of soldiers from each regiment. In view of the inevitable shortfall in these data, the average heights were then corrected using the Quantile Bend Estimator. See Sandberg and Steckel (1988) for a more extensive discussion of these data.

References

Bergman, R. 1963. Det Epidemiska Sjukdomarna Och Deras Bekämpande. In *Medicenalväsendet i Sverige, 1813–1962,* ed. W. Kock. Stockholm: Medicinalstyrelsen.

Bergstrand, H. 1963. Läkarkåren och Provinsalläkarväsendet. In *Medicenalväsendet i Sverige, 1813–1962,* ed. W. Kock. Stockholm: Medicinalstyrelsen.

Carlsson, S. 1961. *Svensk Historia II.* Stockholm: Bonniers.

Cipolla, C. 1969. *Literacy and development in the West.* Baltimore: Johns Hopkins University Press.

Cole, W., and P. Deane. 1968. The growth of national income. In *Cambridge economic history of Europe,* vol. 6, ed. M. Postan and H. Habakkuk. Cambridge: Cambridge University Press.

Eveleth, P. B., and J. M. Tanner. 1976. *Worldwide variation in human growth.* Cambridge: Cambridge University Press.

———. 1990. *Worldwide variation in human growth,* 2d ed. Cambridge: Cambridge University Press.

Gårdlund, T. 1942. *Industrialismens Samhälle.* Stockholm: Pettersons.

Heckscher, E. 1954. *An economic history of Sweden.* Cambridge, Mass.: Harvard University Press.

Hildebrand, K.-G. 1978. Labor and capital in the Scandinavian countries in the 19th and 20th centuries. In *Cambridge economic history of Europe,* vol. 7, ed. P. Mathias and M. Postan. Cambridge: Cambridge University Press.

Hofsten, E., and H. Lundström. 1976. Swedish population history: Main trends from 1750 to 1970. *Urval,* no. 8:3–186.

Jörberg, L. 1994. Structural change and economic growth: Sweden in the 19th century. In *The industrial revolution in Europe,* vol. 2, ed. P. O'Brien. Oxford: Oxford University Press.

Keyfitz, N., and W. Fleiger. 1968. *World population: An analysis of vital data.* Chicago: University of Chicago Press.

Komlos, J. 1987. The height and weight of the West Point cadets: Dietary change in antebellum America. *Journal of Economic History* 47:897–928.

Krantz, O., and C.-A. Nilsson. 1980. *Swedish national product, 1861–1970: New aspects on methods and measurement.* Copenhagen: Gleerup.

Lithell, U.-B. 1981. Breast-feeding habits and their relation to infant mortality and marital fertility. *Social Science History* 6:182–94.

Lundquist, B. 1963. Barnmorskeväsendet. In *Medicenalväsendet i Sverige, 1813–1962,* ed. W. Kock. Stockholm: Medicinalstyrelsen.

Maddison, A. 1991. *Dynamic forces in capitalist development: A long-run comparative view.* New York: Oxford University Press.

Milward, A., and S. Saul. 1973. *The economic development of continental Europe.* London: Allen and Unwin.

Mitchell, B. R. 1978. *European historical statistics, 1750–1970.* Cambridge: Cambridge University Press.

Montgomery, G. 1939. *The rise of modern industry in Sweden.* London: King.

Moore, M. J., and W. K. Viscusi. 1988. Doubling the estimated value of life: Results using new occupational fatality data. *Journal of Policy Analysis and Management* 7:476–90.

Samuelsson, K. 1963. *Hur vår moderna industri vuxit fram.* Stockholm: Prisma.

Sandberg, L. G. 1978. Banking and economic growth in Sweden before World War I. *Journal of Economic History* 38:650–80.

———. 1979. The case of the impoverished sophisticate: Human capital and Swedish economic growth before World War I. *Journal of Economic History* 39:225–42.

Sandberg, L. G., and R. H. Steckel. 1988. Overpopulation and malnutrition rediscovered: Hard times in 19th century Sweden. *Explorations in Economic History* 25:1–18.

Soderberg, J., U. Jonsson, and C. Persson. 1991. *A stagnating metropolis: The economy and demography of Stockholm, 1750–1850.* Cambridge: Cambridge University Press.

Statistiska Centralbyrån. 1969. *Historisk statistik for Sverige,* Del. 1. Befolkning. Stockholm: Statistiska Centralbyrån.

United Nations Development Programme. 1990. *Human development report, 1990.* New York: Oxford University Press.

———. 1993. *Human development report, 1993.* New York: Oxford University Press.

Usher, D. 1980. *The measurement of economic growth.* New York: Columbia University Press.

Wachter, K. W., and J. Trussell. 1982. Estimating historical heights. *Journal of the American Statistical Association* 77:279–93.

Williamson, J. 1981. Urban disamenities, dark satanic mills and the British standard of living debate. *Journal of Economic History* 41:75–84.

———. 1982. Was the industrial revolution worth it? Disamenities and death in 19th century British towns. *Explorations in Economic History* 19:221–45.

———. 1984. British mortality and the value of life, 1781–1931. *Population Studies* 38:157–72.

5 Economic Welfare and Physical Well-Being in France, 1750–1990

David R. Weir

Economic growth is desirable to the extent that it improves the human condition. Because of that intimate connection, economic history has always tempered studies of the process of economic growth with a concern for its consequences for human welfare. A familiar example is England, where the "standard of living" debate over the consequences of early industrialization has raged since the dawn of the industrial revolution (Engerman 1994). The controversy over English living standards has produced considerable empirical knowledge as well as a store of critical insights into the limits and problems of specific sources and methods of measurement.

In France there has been no comparable debate, not because of any well-established empirical consensus but rather because of a lack of comparable empirical attention. Quantitative economic history has not been as important in France as elsewhere, and that has been compounded by the well-known historiographical divide at the French Revolution, which has partitioned historians into two independent groups: one working on the eighteenth century and preoccupied with the origins of the French Revolution and another working on the nineteenth century. The economic history of the revolutionary era itself has drawn attention mainly to macro/financial issues and not to "real" issues like national output or living standards. As a result there are very few studies of the long-term evolution of the economy that span the Revolution.

This paper seeks to review the French experience of economic growth and its welfare consequences. The English standard of living debate serves as a standard of reference and a primer on how to use (and not to use) sources. The introduction outlines the theoretical basis for concerns that economic growth might have had negative consequences, sets out the main types of empirical

David R. Weir is visiting associate professor of economics and research associate in public policy at the University of Chicago.

evidence needed to address those concerns, and describes some crucial differences between France and other European countries that may have influenced the welfare consequences of economic growth.

5.1   Introduction: Economic Growth and Human Welfare

Two traditional theories link the historical realities of economic growth to possible deteriorations in the welfare of the general population. The first is based on the notion of "primitive accumulation." Economic growth is driven by increases in capital stock per worker and by improvements in technology; the latter are themselves generally introduced in the form of new capital investment. The accumulation of capital necessarily requires savings that must come at the expense of current consumption, hence the hypothesis that the initial stages of industrialization "squeeze" consumption. Consumption would be reduced even more if the primitive accumulation resulted from a concentration of wealth in the hands of a capitalist class at the expense of peasants or artisans who would have utilized nonlabor income for their own consumption, and further still if industrialization coincided with rapid population growth, either exogenously driven or due to a surge in marriage and household formation following the breakdown of traditional restraints under proletarianization. It then follows that income per capita is not necessarily a good indicator of the economic welfare of the general population when savings rates or income distribution change rapidly.

Gershenkron (1966) went to considerable lengths to show that primitive accumulation was not a necessary "prerequisite" of economic development. In the case of England, where the facts about consumption remain in dispute, the "optimists" offer three main arguments to explain how the consumption squeeze was avoided: (1) disembodied technical progress that raised productivity enough without new capital to provide enough income to maintain consumption levels and finance higher investment, (2) capital imports, notably from Holland, and (3) improvements in domestic capital markets that funneled existing savings into more productive investments.

The second traditional theme centers on "negative externalities." Economic development alters the spatial organization of production and consumption. Industrialization in the West created crowded urban-industrial areas. In addition to the (potentially) measurable effects on the cost of housing and food supply and distribution, high population densities contributed to the spread of epidemic and other contagious diseases. Therefore, even if we measure adequately the material economic well-being of the population, conventional measures will not take account of important systematic consequences of industrialization.

An examination of the standard of living issue requires four kinds of evidence, two direct and two indirect. First, we need general measures of output, savings, and structural change to identify the timing of economic growth and particularly the periods when a consumption squeeze was most likely to occur. Second, we should examine direct and comprehensive economic measures of living standards such as real wages. Because direct measures of material welfare are often limited to specific occupational groups and specific localities, there is also a place for the study of indirect or partial economic measures like the consumption of particular commodities that are likely to bear a stable relationship to the general level of well-being.

The final category is demographic or anthropometric evidence. Such data can be interpreted in several ways. To the extent that health or life expectancy contributes to individual utility independent of material consumption, it can in principle be considered a component, along with real wages, of a broader standard of living index. Assigning appropriate weights will be a difficult matter because we do not observe prices (Williamson 1981). The weighting problem is not so important when consumption of all the "goods" moves in the same direction, but it is crucial when the components move in opposite directions. Heights and mortality are also "produced" by material consumption, although the extent of that influence remains highly controversial. Some authors, chastened by the criticisms of real wage indexes, have proposed anthropometric measures as a more comprehensive and reliable indicator of the well-being of the population. When both sorts of indicators can be reliably measured, as I believe they can for France, it seems more informative to consider them separately as reflecting different aspects of living standards rather than as competing proxies for some single underlying truth. Material consumption was not the sole determinant of heights or mortality, so anthropometric data will also reflect conditions of public health and private hygiene that are not captured in economic measures or purchased with family income.

Two crucial characteristics set France apart from other European countries in the nineteenth century: slow population growth due to deliberately restrained marital fertility and a wider distribution of property ownership. These underlying factors contributed to make economic growth a slow and gradual transformation not marked by sudden discontinuous changes. That is of course a statement about national aggregates. Economic change was more rapid in some regions, disruptive to some villages or cities, and at times profoundly destructive to some families. The hypothesis we wish to explore here is that low demographic pressure and less concentration of income and wealth took the steam out of the forces that would otherwise have produced a consumption squeeze and negative externalities.

5.2 The Evidence

The data sources and methods underlying the following discussion and the accompanying figures are discussed in appendix A.

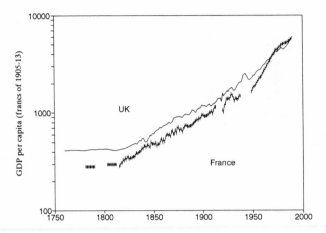

Fig. 5.1   Real GDP per capita in France and the United Kingdom, 1750–1990

5.2.1   Output per Capita

Figure 5.1 shows real output per person in France and the United Kingdom from 1750 to 1990. The period 1750–1913 is remarkable in that the two paths were largely parallel, with the United Kingdom's eighteenth-century advantage declining rather little in the long run. Both countries saw slow growth or stagnation from 1750 to 1820, followed by more rapid "modern" economic growth from 1820 to 1913. In France, growth rates of per capita income were on the order of 0.3 percent per year in the first phase and 1.3 percent per year in the second.

The twentieth-century experience is offered here for perspective. Growth rates in the United Kingdom seldom exceeded the rates established during earlier periods, but in France the post–World War II "miracle" saw growth rates of 4 percent per year. The comparability of levels between the two countries is more difficult in this period. Fixed exchange rates and stable international relative prices under the gold standard prior to 1913 make the conversion of U.K. figures into francs at par of exchange a relatively safe procedure compared with later years. The relative level of real output in the United Kingdom after 1920 was set by using Maddison's (1991) purchasing-power-parity exchange rate for 1985 to fix the relative levels in 1985. An extension based on the pre-1913 relative levels would show the United Kingdom at a much lower level. The use of Maddison's data to study convergence runs the risk of serious distortion if changes over time in purchasing power parity are not carefully considered.

We can be confident that sustained economic growth in France had begun by 1820 (Lévy-Leboyer's estimates of real per capita output begin in 1820 and are virtually identical in levels and trend to those shown here). We are hindered in identifying the starting point of rapid growth by the uncertainty of the evi-

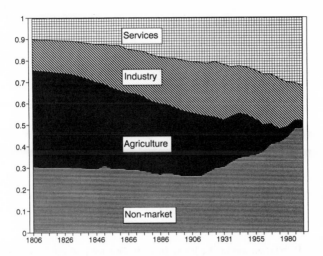

Fig. 5.2   Activity distribution of the potential adult labor force in France, 1806–1990

dence prior to 1820. The 0.3 percent per year growth rate from 1750 to 1780 is merely an assumption based on a review of existing estimates (see Riley 1986, chap. 1). The Institut de Science Economiques Appliquées' estimates for 1781–90 and 1803–12 leave the impression that the Revolution held growth somewhat below even the low level of the eighteenth century. If growth rates were higher during the Revolution, that would also imply a lower level of real output in the eighteenth century.

5.2.2   Labor Force Reallocation

A perspective on the timing of industrialization comes from the structural changes in labor force activity and location (urbanization). Figure 5.2 gives a long perspective on the activities of French adults. It shows the allocation of the "potential" adult labor force, defined simply as men over age 15 plus 62 percent of women over age 15 (62 percent being the ratio of female to male wages). Those who pursue nonmarket activities, usually classified as out of the labor force, include housewives, students, and retirees. Their share declined very slowly in the nineteenth century and then rose rapidly in the twentieth, reflecting primarily the rise of advanced schooling and retirement. The "modern" sectors of industry and services gained at the expense of agriculture throughout the period.

Figure 5.3 shows a more narrow measure of the industrialization of the labor force—the share of industrial workers in the market labor force. Here again France and the United Kingdom moved roughly in parallel, with the United Kingdom always substantially more industrial. The most rapid growth apparently came before 1860, coinciding with a period of slightly more rapid output

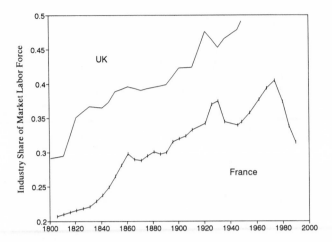

Fig. 5.3   Industrialization of the labor force in France and the United Kingdom, 1806–1990

growth in France. The slowdown after 1860 corresponds to the "deceleration" of the French economy that has been emphasized by Lévy-Leboyer.

Urbanization is not precisely coterminous with industrialization because of the wide extent of rural industry early and its decline later. Nevertheless, urbanization is the more relevant measure for some of the negative externality issues, and in the face of uncertainty over the labor force activities of the rural population it may be a useful proxy for other aspects of structural change. Table 5.1 shows the timing of urban growth in France.

Urban growth was never as rapid in France as it was elsewhere in Europe. This is entirely attributable to low fertility and low natural increase in France and not to any shortcomings of rural-urban migration. French cities grew fastest at midcentury, from 1831 to 1881. That is later than the peak rate of net investment or the peak rate of change of the industrial labor force. Paradoxically, it includes the period of deceleration identified by Lévy-Leboyer. The paradox is at least partially resolved by the fact that rural industry was declining rapidly after 1860.

5.2.3   Consumption

Can we find evidence of a "consumption squeeze" in the early years of industrialization? The most direct approach is to identify the personal consumption component of GDP using the familiar national income accounting identity:

$$Y = C + I + G + (X - M).$$

Given the nature of historical data, consumption is generally found as a residual after deducting gross domestic investment (I), net foreign investment

Table 5.1   **Urban Growth in France**

Years	Urban Growth Rate (%)	Percentage Urban (period average)
1756–81	.66	17
1781–1806	.28	19
1806–31	.54	20
1831–56	1.11	24
1856–81	1.06	31
1881–1906	.79	38

Source: See Weir (1994b).

Notes: Urban growth in percent per year is the growth rate of communes classified as urban at the beginning of the period; i.e., it excludes the additions to urban population due to the reclassification of communes from rural to urban during the period. By definition, urban communes are those with at least 2,000 population in an agglomerated area.

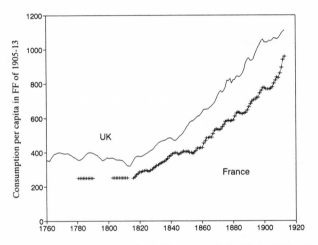

Fig. 5.4   Real consumption per capita in France and the United Kingdom, 1750–1913

($X - M$), and government spending on goods and services (G). The work of Feinstein for the United Kingdom and Lévy-Leboyer for France provides the crucial estimates of investment, yielding the real consumption per capita estimates shown in figure 5.4.

Personal consumption declined slightly in the United Kingdom during its early industrialization phase from 1750 to 1815. A detailed look at the expenditure components reveals that the crucial variable was government (military) spending (which increased) rather than investment (which remained fairly steady). There is an ongoing debate about whether government spending crowded out private investment in Britain during the Napoleonic Wars, but it appears clear that personal consumption was "crowded out" by the two in combination. French expenditure data are lacking for this period, so the consumption figures are built on a crude guess about the shares of each.

With the return of peace in 1815 personal consumption rose in both countries. The 1840s saw a short, sharp setback in Britain (even before the Irish Famine) and ushered in a longer phase of no growth in France. From the mid-1850s personal consumption increased fairly steadily in both countries.

The evidence for a consumption squeeze in the United Kingdom is ambiguous: there was a very slight decline in consumption during early industrialization, but it appears to have been caused by the burden of war and not by "primitive accumulation." We have less evidence about the effects of the same wars on France. It is clear, however, that there was no consumption squeeze during its early industrialization in the first half of the nineteenth century.

5.2.4 Real Wages

Real wages are the traditional measure of living standards and have remained at the center of the English standard of living debate. Index numbers of real wages are typically constructed by dividing indexes of nominal wages for some specified group by indexes of the prices of the commodities they consume. Unlike some other measures of living standards, there is a specific microeconomic foundation for real wage indexes that is worth setting out.

We assume that income equals expenditure, so that the index of nominal wages in year t relative to nominal wages in the base year 0 is also equal to the ratio of expenditures:

$$\frac{W_t}{W_0} = \frac{\sum_i p_{it} \times q_{it}}{\sum_i p_{i0} \times q_{i0}}.$$

A Laspeyres cost-of-living index relates the cost of purchasing a fixed bundle of commodities in year t to the cost of purchasing the same fixed bundle in the base year:

$$\frac{P_t}{P_0} = \frac{\sum_i p_{it} \times q_{i0}}{\sum_i p_{i0} \times q_{i0}}.$$

A real wage index formed by dividing the nominal wage index by the cost-of-living index therefore compares expenditures in year t to the cost in year t of purchasing the same bundle of consumption as was attainable in the base year:

$$\frac{RW_t}{RW_0} = \frac{W_t/W_0}{P_t/P_0} = \frac{\sum_i p_{it} \times q_{it}}{\sum_i p_{it} \times q_{i0}}.$$

When the real wage index for year t is greater than 1 (or greater than 100 if set to 100 in the base year), we can infer that the worker-consumer could purchase the exact base year consumption bundle plus some more, that is, that he is better off in year *t*.

The most common practice, and the one followed here, is to use the wages of unskilled labor. Part of the improvement in economic welfare during development is due to the shift in labor force composition toward higher skilled and higher paid occupations. By holding constant the labor force composition, wage indexes will trace a more pessimistic path than would indexes of average earnings that included the compositional change.

Despite, or perhaps because of, heated controversies over technical issues in the construction of real wages for England, there is a general consensus emerging, at least within the narrow confines of the New Economic History between such participants as Crafts and Lindert and Williamson (Lindert and Williamson 1983, 1985; Crafts 1985; Williamson 1985; Crafts and Mills 1994). That consensus comprises both methodological issues and substantive findings. On substance, there is wide agreement that English real wages were largely stagnant from 1750 to sometime around 1815, after which time they began to rise slowly. On methods, all sides now recognize that the major source of divergent findings is in the cost-of-living indexes rather than in nominal wages. By that I mean that cost-of-living indexes are sensitive to the component price series chosen and the budget weights applied. The question of whether nominal prices "cause" real wages is a separate matter not considered here.

At the present time, Paris is the only city for which we have long runs of consistent nominal wages and prices from which real wage indexes can be constructed in a careful manner from the early eighteenth century. The wage index is based on unskilled construction workers. Its overall movement from 1820 to 1914 is not much different from the more sketchy data on similar workers in the rest of France. Agricultural wages, on the other hand, rose much less after 1870 than urban or Parisian wages. The cost-of-living index is taken from Singer-Kérel after 1840, but the index constructed for the earlier years shows very similar movement from 1840 to 1913. The earlier index combines price indexes for bread and related products, meat, dairy products, drink, house rent, textiles, and fuel and is of the usual Laspeyres form, using a single fixed set of weights for the entire period (Weir 1991). One rationale for a fixed-weight Laspeyres index is that it reflects the cost of "subsistence." Certainly, the weights given by budget studies for nineteenth-century France give dominance to essential foods. The close similarity of this index to Singer-Kérel's index of 213 articles using twentieth-century weights suggests that the precise weightings are not critical in the post-1840 period.

Figure 5.5 shows real wages in France and Britain, with the relative levels fixed by a direct comparison in 1905 (Williamson 1995). Parisian real wages fluctuated around a stable level in the eighteenth century while the higher British real wages declined very slowly. Influenced to some extent by war-induced labor shortages, French real wages under Napoleon were generally above their previous levels. Fighting Napoleon was hard on British consumers, and the

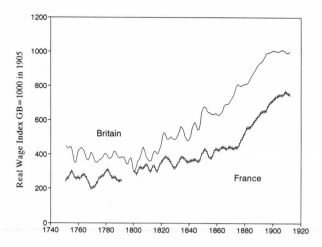

Fig. 5.5   Real wages in France and the United Kingdom, 1750–1913

"hot" war years around 1801 and 1812–15 marked the nadir of British real wages during industrialization.

From 1820 to 1860 real wages advanced sharply in Britain and more slowly in France, creating a wider gap than had existed before 1790. Recall from figure 5.3 that it was in this period that France reached the levels of industrialization that Britain had achieved in the late eighteenth century. Despite the later start, France industrialized at lower levels of real wages and per capita incomes. Perhaps because of greater opportunities for technological imitation France was able to grow more rapidly and sustain better real wage growth than Britain at a comparable phase of development. Population growth was also modest, which makes the discrepancy between real wages and per capita income or consumption all the more striking. Apparently, the distribution of income was shifting away from manual labor in this period.

The rapid fall in international food prices after 1870 led to rapid gains in both countries. Britain's stronger commitment to free trade in this period did not have a noticeable impact on real wages as compared with France, where the protection of agriculture was increased.

5.2.5   Meat Consumption: Indirect Evidence of Living Standards

In a famous article, Eric Hobsbawm, a leading pessimist in the English standard of living debate, proposed to use indirect evidence to assess living standards (Hobsbawm 1957). There are many reasons to question the direct evidence of real wages: doubts about the underlying evidence on prices and budgets, limited scope, failure to account for unemployment, narrow focus on male workers to the exclusion of other family members, and so on. If one could trace the per capita consumption of some commodity that bore a stable

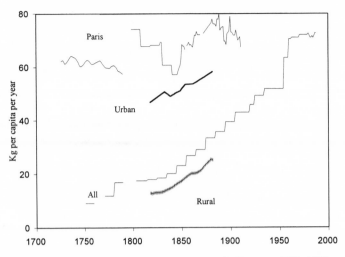

Fig. 5.6   Meat consumption by place of residence in France, 1750–1980

relationship to full family income, then its trends would mirror overall living standards. Hobsbawm reasoned that meat was such a commodity and presented evidence from the Smithfield meat markets outside London that indicated a decline in per capita consumption. His conclusions have largely been rejected because he failed to take account of a rising slaughter weight of animals brought to market, because he neglected pork (the consumption of which was rising), and because secondary sources of supply increased around the Smithfield markets (Hartwell 1961). The reasoning, however, still stands. Joel Mokyr recently applied it to the consumption of "luxuries" like tea and sugar and found weak support for the pessimist case (Mokyr 1988). English data problems may favor the use of tea and sugar, but common sense would suggest that the consumption of such items could more easily be influenced by taste, fashion, and the development of retail delivery systems than would be the case for meat, which is a central element of family budgets. For France the problems faced by Hobsbawm's study of London are resolved, and we can learn something from the data on meat consumption.

Figure 5.6 shows per capita meat consumption in Paris and in France as a whole, with shorter series for urban areas other than Paris and for rural areas. The most striking aspect is the enormous urban-rural differential. Urban-rural wage gaps were relatively small in France, so there were clearly other factors at work driving relative demand. The most important factor must have been nonwage income spent in cities. In addition to the obvious urban advantage in human capital and industrial wealth, a sizable proportion of the returns to agricultural land must have been spent in cities by absentee landowners or their family members. Given the rapid rate of spoilage of meat, there may have been economies of scale in urban consumption where entire animals could be consumed quickly as compared with dispersed rural areas where it might have been difficult to ensure a continuous supply at low levels of consumption without waste.

Paris consumed more than other cities and had already attained by the mid-eighteenth century a level of per capita meat consumption not reached by the national average until after World War II. Parisian consumption apparently increased under Napoleon and then fell until the 1850s, returning to its eighteenth-century levels. The second half of the nineteenth century saw renewed growth, pushed mainly by sources of supply that bypassed the main Paris slaughter markets. The declining Parisian meat consumption of the early nineteenth century is the first evidence we have seen of declining living standards, and it conflicts with the evidence of real wages, at least after 1820. Given the obvious influence of nonlabor income in urban consumption, the most likely explanation is that Parisian meat consumption was influenced by the social composition of the capital. The labor market served to constrain the differentials in workers' living standards between Paris and the rest of the country, but no such force determined where the wealthy would live or consume their meat. A rapid influx of working-class population could well have driven down the average consumption of meat without any deterioration in occupation or class-specific living standards.

Clearly, indirect inferences about living standards based on consumption statistics in a particular locality are subject to more spurious influences than are direct real wage measures, so we will focus instead on national patterns. Inferring the course of general material welfare from meat consumption entails knowledge of three things: the income elasticity of meat demand, the course of relative meat prices, and the price elasticity of demand. Several sorts of evidence suggest an income elasticity of demand for meat in the range of 0.7. That is what we get from a crude time-series regression of aggregate national meat consumption on per capita output. Postel-Vinay and Robin (1992) estimated a demand system on a cross section of districts in 1852 and found that the elasticity of meat consumption with respect to total food expenditure was about 1.5. They do not report the elasticity of food expenditure with respect to total income, but it was on the order of 0.5 in the aggregate data, which yields an income elasticity for meat demand around 0.75. Holding quality constant, we would expect income elasticities to decline as the absolute level of meat consumption increased toward some satiation point. Price elasticities are less easily pinned down. Postel-Vinay and Robin estimated (and worried over) a very small price elasticity found also in regressions on time-series aggregates. Department cross sections tend to find a positive price elasticity, that is, that quantity and price move together. That suggests that we are identifying a supply curve rather than a demand curve because we have not fully accounted for the determinants of demand. In the end, these econometric difficulties are not terribly worrisome for basic inferences because the trend of meat prices relative to other prices was very simple: no trend prior to 1840 or so, and a rising

Table 5.2   **Determinants of Meat Consumption by Department, 1840–1911**

Independent Variable	(1)	(2)	(3)
Constant	1.565***	−6.13***	−5.44***
	(.057)	(1.22)	(1.08)
Log real wage	.756***	.519***	.420***
	(.025)	(.045)	(.041)
Year		.0044***	.0040***
		(0.0007)	(.0006)
Urbanization			.910***
			(.065)
R^2	.55	.57	.66

Notes: The dependent variable is the log of per capita meat consumption in a department in a year. The total sample size is 81 departments in nine cohorts, or 729 observations. Regressions were ordinary least squares; standard errors are in parentheses. Asterisks following coefficients indicate statistical significance of a *t*-test of the null hypothesis that the true coefficient is zero.

*$p < .05$.

**$p < .01$.

***$p < .001$.

trend after about 1860 (as international relative price movements dictated). Thus, whatever the true price elasticity of demand, relative prices would not have much affected meat consumption prior to the middle of the nineteenth century and should only have held it back after that time.

Returning to figure 5.6, we see that the available estimates suggest that national meat consumption grew very little from 1780 to 1840, despite the estimated increase in per capita income and real wages. From 1840 to 1913 meat consumption grew at just about exactly seven-tenths the rate of real per capita output, as the elasticity estimates would predict. The rapid gains in meat consumption after World War II were nevertheless at a rate slower than 0.7 times real output growth, indicating that the income elasticity was declining as the whole population approached high average levels of consumption.

Table 5.2 shows the results of a pooled cross-section time-series regression of meat consumption per capita by department over time. When real wages are used alone, they indicate an elasticity of 0.75, consistent with other estimates of income elasticities. When time trends and urbanization are included as predictors, the estimated effect of real wage declines and urbanization emerges as an important predictor of meat consumption independent of the level of real wages. The large urban-rural differential in meat consumption is therefore not entirely explicable by urban-rural differences in real wages. It seems reasonable to suppose that unmeasured nonwage income sources (including human capital) were greater in cities and that they account for the greater meat consumption.

Meat consumption is of interest not only as a good indicator of average income but also because it was the primary source of protein, an important

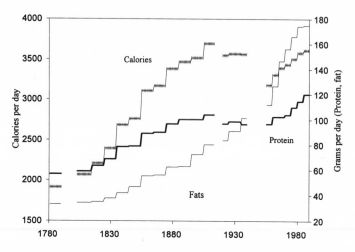

Fig. 5.7   Nutrient consumption per capita in France, 1780–1980

nutrient. Figure 5.7 shows the course of average availability for human consumption of total calories, protein, and fats. In the nineteenth century total calories rose faster than proteins as the population augmented previously inadequate diets with cheap grain-based calories. Over the twentieth century protein consumption rose faster than total calories as the generally adequately nourished population shifted into more expensive and protein-rich sources of calories. The decline of energy-consuming manual labor may also have been a factor in the retreat from the high levels of total calories reached at the end of the nineteenth century.

5.2.6   Heights

France provides the best data for the study of long-term changes in male heights of any European country. The main source of height data after 1800 are the records of conscripts into the French armies. Prior to the Revolution of 1789, French armies were volunteer armies, like those of the rest of Europe. Conscription began with the first revolutionary wars, but the data only become regular and reliable in the years after 1815. For constructing representative samples, conscription records have distinct advantages over the records of volunteer services. French conscripts were selected by lottery from all the 20-year-olds in the district. In volunteer services there are two selection processes at work, neither of which can be considered random: the demand of the recruiting services for men of certain heights (or other characteristics correlated with height) and the supply of potential recruits. If the estimation methods do not fully eliminate the influence of selection, then changes over time in the strength of selection can appear as changes in the estimated height.

The statistical methods that have been developed to cope with selection problems depend crucially on the assumption that there is a range of heights

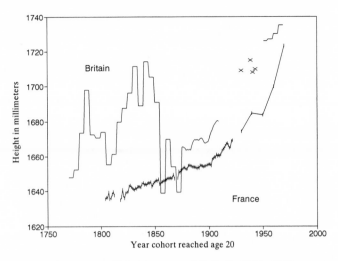

Fig. 5.8   **Male height at age 20 in France and Britain, 1770–1980**

(typically the upper tail of the distribution) in which selection effects do not operate. The shape of the observed distribution over this selection-free range provides enough information to identify the mean and variance of the underlying population distribution. This works well when the recruiter's selection excludes persons below some minimum height. But if selection is continuous, in the sense that the probability of inclusion increases with height throughout the entire observed range, then the available estimators break down. Moreover, it is possible for the selected sample to closely resemble a Gaussian distribution with a mean well above the mean of the whole population (and, typically, a smaller standard deviation). An extreme example is the distribution of heights of players in the National Basketball Association (Fogel et al. 1983, 459–62). That distribution appears roughly normal in shape and yet comparison with the true population distribution reveals that the probability of playing in the NBA rises exponentially with each inch of added height. No one would suggest that historical military height preferences were as extreme as those of modern professional basketball, but neither would we expect a bias of 20 cm or more in the estimated mean. Errors of 5 cm (2 inches) would be quite large relative to historical variations over time or between countries.

Figure 5.8 displays my estimates of the median height of 20-year-olds in France from 1803 to 1970, compared with estimates of British heights. The French data, which differ slightly from those of van Meerten (1990), are described in appendix B; data for later years come from Chamla (1964) and Olivier et al. (1977). The British data are derived from Floud, Wachter, and Gregory (1990) as described in appendix A.

In France, heights confirm the general patterns found in economic data. The overall impression is one of slow but steady increase in height from 1820 to

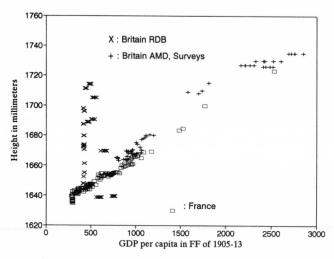

Fig. 5.9   Male height by real GDP per capita in France and Britain, 1770–1980
Note: RDB, recruit description books; AMD, Army Medical Department.

1913 (birth cohorts of 1800 to 1893), with a total gain of about 1 inch or 2.5 cm from 164 cm to 166.5 cm. On closer inspection one might detect slightly faster growth at the beginning and the end of the period, with a period of near stability from 1880 to 1900. The rate of growth was substantially faster in the twentieth century, with a gain of 4 cm by 1970 (cohort of 1950), despite severe setbacks in the two world wars. The data before 1815 are less reliable because I needed to make corrections for incomplete regional coverage and for changes in the age at recruitment. It seems fairly clear, however, that the heights of the classes of 1804–5 and 1810–11 were on a par with those of the early years of the Restoration and thus that there was probably little trend in heights over the first 20 years of the nineteenth century. No reliable estimates can be made prior to 1800.

British men were generally taller than French, but the patterns were quite unstable, at least in the years before 1860 for which the estimates are based on recruit description books. Heights in Britain climbed rapidly in the early years of the nineteenth century, when real wages and per capita incomes were stagnant, and then fell dramatically after 1840 (cohorts born 1820), when the economic evidence suggests that living standards were improving.

Another perspective on heights and living standards is given by figure 5.9, which sets the mean height of a birth cohort against the level of per capita GDP prevailing around its tenth birthday. In France, the scatter of observations traces a very regular and nearly linear relationship between per capita income and height. From the British data after 1860 it appears that the British height advantage at any given date was only partially due to higher British per capita incomes. Other additional factors, including possibly genetic differences, con-

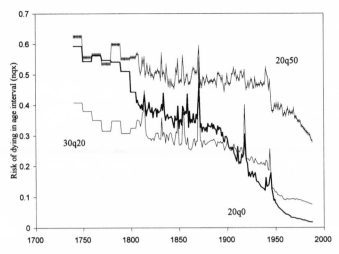

Fig. 5.10   Life table mortality rates by age in France, 1740–1990

tributed to the gap. Heights in northern France were systematically higher than in the south, so the British-French difference may be an extension of the same phenomenon. Figure 5.9 also illustrates the magnitude of the puzzle raised by the pre-1860 British height estimates. Based on the crude height-GDP profile, the heights attained in the pre-1840 peak would have been consistent with per capita incomes three to four times higher than the actual levels. That is far beyond any plausible range of measurement error in GDP and suggests that there must have been other very powerful forces driving the heights of British volunteer forces.

5.2.7   Mortality Decline

The pace of mortality decline in France is shown in figure 5.10. It displays rates for three broad age groups. Infant and child mortality (20q0) declined much more than that of other ages, and young adults (30q20) progressed slightly faster than older adults (20q50). This is a typical pattern and not unique to France. The long trend of mortality decline can be divided into three phases: rapid declines from the late eighteenth to the early nineteenth centuries, slow decline during most of the nineteenth century, and rapid declines beginning toward the end of the nineteenth century for children. Real progress for older adults did not occur until after World War II.

It is the early period of rapid decline that merits most attention. Per capita incomes grew relatively slowly between the 1780s and 1820s, while real wages appear to have risen more substantially. It is certainly possible that the Revolution did have egalitarian consequences for income distribution, with working people and their children benefiting most. We should note, however, that the early phase of decline in infant and child mortality brought French rates down to the general range of European rates from what had been comparatively high levels. It may have been a "catching-up" phase in which France adopted the better child-care "technologies" already in place elsewhere. For example, there is evidence that maternal breast-feeding became more widespread at this time (Mroz and Weir 1990). Although infant feeding is well established as a determinant of infant mortality, its effects on mortality after age one or two are not so clear, so there must have been other complementary changes.

I am not generally inclined to credit the Enlightenment for everything that happened in French society at the end of the eighteenth century, but it is worth noting that the same Rousseau, who advocated maternal nursing, also advocated improved hygiene, calling hygiene "the only useful part of medicine." The same viewpoint was reflected in the *Encyclopédie,* which urged each individual to be "his own doctor." Even if the scientific basis for connecting hygiene to mortality was not yet established, it is certainly possible that changes in hygienic practice within families and households, adopted for other reasons, contributed to the mortality decline during the Revolution that brought French infant health in line with European norms.

The scientific breakthroughs of Louis Pasteur had their greatest impact in mobilizing public health efforts (including hospital practice) rather than in changing family behavior. The effects on mortality began to be felt at the end of the nineteenth century and can be seen in infancy through early adulthood, where epidemic disease was most important. Older adults, who were after all survivors of earlier exposures to infectious disease, benefited less from reductions in the extent of exposure.

Figure 5.11 shows crude death rates in Paris, all other French cities, and rural areas. Crude rates understate the magnitude of urban excess mortality because cities had a "favorable" age structure dominated by young adults with lower mortality rates, and because many infants were sent out of cities to be wet-nursed where their deaths were counted in rural totals. In 1876, urban crude death rates were perhaps 2 per 1,000 lower (and rural 1 per 1,000 higher) than corrected age-standardized rates would show (see Weir 1994b).

Much of the limited mortality decline that did occur between 1820 and 1880 occurred in the cities. Paris and the other cities differed little, and the gap between them and rural areas closed considerably. Paris suffered more than the average city during the epidemics prior to 1860, as it did in the fighting of the Franco-Prussian War. It also gained more in the more rapid mortality declines after 1880, dropping well below the urban average and reaching the rural level by the end of the nineteenth century (though an age-adjusted Paris rate would be higher). Public health investments have commonly been cited in explaining the different pace of change in different urban areas (Preston and van de Walle 1978). The capital led the more provincial cities in modernizing its water and sewage systems.

The big urban-rural mortality differential in the early nineteenth century suggests that there were large potential negative externalities from rapid indus-

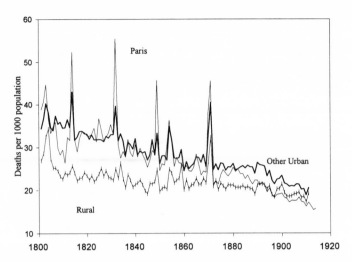

Fig. 5.11   Crude death rates by place of residence in France, 1806–1913

trialization. The low level and slow rate of urbanization in France compared with other countries therefore had beneficial public health consequences.

5.2.8   The Impact of Economic Welfare on Physical Well-Being

The relationship between the narrowly defined material standard of living (as captured by real wages or per capita consumption) and physical health is extremely complex. We do not know the full extent of how food and other consumption might have influenced health and mortality, and there is the very real possibility that improved health contributed to higher productivity and living standards. Here I present a few descriptive analyses that provide some empirical input to the speculations. By using a cross-section time-series "panel" data set of 81 French departments at 10-year intervals in the nineteenth century we can explore these relationships in more depth than would be possible from aggregate time-series data alone.

Tables 5.3–5.6 report various specifications of the determinants of height at age 20. Unless otherwise indicated, the right-hand-side variables are measured at about the 10th birthday of the cohort whose height is the dependent variable. Most of the variables are not measured frequently enough to attempt any more finely distributed lag structure. Within each table there are four models corresponding to different treatments of time and region effects. The tables differ slightly in the specification of the basic equation. A good case could be made for the exogeneity of the (log) real wage, proportion urban, and literacy of the parent's generation as in table 5.3. Table 5.4 includes the crude death rate (around the cohort's 10th birthday) as an independent variable. Tables 5.5 and 5.6 repeat 5.3 and 5.4 but use logarithms of the urbanization, literacy, and death

Table 5.3   Determinants of Heights by Department, 1840–1911

Variable	(1a)	(1b)	(1c)	(1d)
Constant	1,607.8***	2,018.6***	1,641.4***	1,629.6***
	(3.27)	(48.11)	(60.75)	(14.97)
Log real wage	7.71***	18.21***	15.34***	9.93*
	(1.79)	(2.10)	(2.01)	(4.54)
Proportion urban	13.08***	14.47***	11.18***	−8.82
	(2.95)	(2.81)	(2.68)	(10.47)
Female literacy	8.87*	14.95***	−4.35	−5.43
	(4.55)	(4.40)	(4.55)	(5.57)
Male literacy	24.45***	20.34***	25.87***	18.61**
	(5.27)	(5.05)	(4.81)	(6.08)
Crude death rate				
Year		−0.232***	−0.061	
		(0.027)	(0.031)	
Northeast			1.451***	
			(.155)	
Fixed effects	No	No	No	Yes
R^2	.53	.58	.62	.80

Notes: The dependent variable is the median height of the cohort of 20-year-old men in a given department in a given year (s.d. = 15). Independent variables are measured at approximately the 10th birthday of the cohort, except for literacy, which is measured at marriage for marriages in the five years prior to the birth of the recruitment cohort and thus corresponds to the parents of the cohort. The fixed effects in model d are (80) dummy variables for the departments and (8) dummy variables for cohorts. The total sample size is 81 departments in nine cohorts, or 729 observations. Regressions were ordinary least squares; standard errors are in parentheses. Asterisks following coefficients indicate statistical significance of a *t*-test of the null hypothesis that the true coefficient is zero.
*$p < .05$.
**$p < .01$.
***$p < .001$.

rate variables. Within each table the model is run in four variants corresponding to different treatments of possible time and region effects: (a) with no controls, (b) with a continuous time trend, (c) with a continuous time trend and a continuous regional variable (northeast = latitude + longitude), and (d) with dummy fixed effects for year and department.

Consider first the impact of the different controls for time and region effects. The fixed effects explain a lot of variance in all four tables. Compared with model c, the fixed-effect model d tends to have smaller coefficients and larger standard errors, but the general pattern of results is the same. That is not surprising, given the much higher ratio of measurement error to "signal" variance when we take out the regional means. The one exception is urbanization (and to a lesser extent female literacy), where the inclusion of fixed effects has a big effect on the results in tables 5.3 and 5.4, using levels, but not in tables 5.5 and 5.6, using logs. Tables 5.5 and 5.6, using logs of the independent variables,

Table 5.4   **Determinants of Heights by Department, 1840–1911**

Variable	(2a)	(2b)	(2c)	(2d)
Constant	1,622.4***	2,115.6***	1,709.8***	1,650.9***
	(5.67)	(49.99)	(58.68)	(15.88)
Log real wage	5.94**	16.88***	13.06***	9.97*
	(1.79)	(2.07)	(1.94)	(4.49)
Proportion urban	16.09***	20.08***	18.23***	−13.00
	(3.08)	(2.92)	(2.70)	(10.42)
Female literacy	8.59	15.51***	−6.80	−3.52
	(4.52)	(4.30)	(4.44)	(5.54)
Male literacy	23.63***	18.17***	23.87***	9.87
	(5.25)	(4.96)	(4.60)	(6.45)
Crude death rate	−0.467***	−0.831***	−1.126***	−0.620***
	(0.149)	(0.144)	(0.136)	(0.165)
Year		−0.272***	−0.086**	
		(0.027)	(0.030)	
Northeast			1.692***	
			(.151)	
Fixed effects	No	No	No	Yes
R^2	.54	.59	.65	.81

Note: See notes to table 5.3.
*$p < .05$.
**$p < .01$.
***$p < .001$.

have very slightly higher R^2 values, but one can hardly claim that as sufficient reason to prefer them.

Real wages have a significant positive effect on heights in all models. In the fixed-effect model (d) the wage effect is smaller than in models using continuous time, but larger than in the model (a) with no time or region controls. Its effect is pretty much the same between tables.

The literacy results give little support to the idea that mother's literacy was particularly important for children's health in nineteenth-century France, in contrast to what is often found in developing countries today. Male literacy was much more strongly related to heights in all the models and specifications. In the models without regional controls (a and b), female literacy has a barely significant positive effect. Adding either type of regional control generally reverses its sign, although in the log version (tables 5.5 and 5.6) it is very weakly positive with fixed effects. It may be that in the economy of the nineteenth century women's literacy did not translate readily into higher potential wages or domestic bargaining power. Because male literacy was always higher than female (and because literate women almost always married literate men), it may be that male literacy was sufficient for the family to acquire whatever knowledge was available about hygiene and the like, rendering female literacy superfluous.

Table 5.5   Determinants of Heights by Department, 1840–1911

Variable	(3a)	(3b)	(3c)	(3d)
Constant	1,648.5***	2,064.8***	1,694.1***	1,642.3***
	(4.63)	(47.40)	(59.18)	(13.03)
Log real wage	7.86***	18.86***	14.86***	8.90*
	(1.66)	(2.01)	(1.94)	(4.45)
Log proportion urban	4.21***	4.64***	3.86***	7.41**
	(0.80)	(0.76)	(0.72)	(3.03)
Log female literacy	5.92**	7.95***	−0.42	2.57
	(4.55)	(1.79)	(1.90)	(2.25)
Log male literacy	11.52***	9.99***	13.89***	9.45**
	(2.77)	(2.64)	(2.53)	(3.24)
Log crude death rate				
Year		−0.234***	−0.071*	
		(0.027)	(0.030)	
Northeast			1.418***	
			(0.148)	
Fixed effects	No	No	No	Yes
R^2	.54	.59	.64	.81

Note: See notes to table 5.3.
*$p < .05$.
**$p < .01$.
***$p < .001$.

Urbanization is the most perplexing. Its effect is clearly positive in all the models except some of the fixed-effect models. In tables 5.3 and 5.4, using levels, the inclusion of fixed effects causes a huge change and sign reversal. In tables 5.5 and 5.6, using logs, the effect remains positive and statistically significant even when fixed effects are used. Adding the (potentially endogenous) crude death rate adds very little to R^2 but is itself highly significant and negative in its effect on height. A plausible interpretation would be that local health conditions were correlated with urbanization, literacy, and real wages but nevertheless operated independently to improve heights and mortality. On the one hand, these results suggest that the real wages of unskilled workers are a narrow measure even of economic welfare. Both urbanization and literacy, which were certainly correlated with the income of other factors of production, including especially human capital, had independent beneficial effects on the development of children. On the other hand, urbanization had negative consequences for mortality. This suggests that heights and mortality are not simply interchangeable measures of some general notion of "health." They responded differently to economic progress. For mortality, the most plausible explanation is that urbanization increased the incidence of exposure to disease and this effect overwhelmed the beneficial effects of higher consumption at improving resistance, as suggested for Japan by Johansson and Mosk (1987; Mosk and Johansson 1986). Economic progress unambiguously raised heights because

Table 5.6   **Determinants of Heights by Department, 1840–1911**

Variable	(4a)	(4b)	(4c)	(4d)
Constant	1,675.0***	2,181.7***	1,801.4***	1,672.5***
	(12.72)	(52.48)	(58.44)	(17.63)
Log real wage	6.71***	18.05***	12.84***	9.24*
	(1.73)	(1.99)	(1.88)	(4.43)
Log proportion urban	4.72***	5.78***	5.46***	7.06*
	(0.83)	(0.78)	(0.72)	(3.02)
Log female literacy	5.61***	7.59***	−2.60	2.28
	(1.86)	(1.76)	(1.84)	(2.25)
Log male literacy	11.36***	9.43***	13.80***	6.86*
	(2.77)	(2.61)	(2.42)	(3.39)
Log crude death rate	−7.54***	−15.95***	−24.41***	−9.95*
	(3.37)	(3.73)	(3.10)	(3.94)
Year		−0.268***	−0.092**	
		(0.027)	(0.029)	
Northeast			1.692***	
			(.147)	
Fixed effects	No	No	No	Yes
R^2	.55	.60	.66	.81

Note: See notes to table 5.3.
*$p < .05$.
**$p < .01$.
***$p < .001$.

the higher level of nutritional intake was more than enough to offset the negative effects of increased morbidity from exposure to disease.

5.3   Conclusions

In contrast to some other countries for which physical well-being and material economic indicators apparently moved in contrary directions (Fogel 1986; Sandberg and Steckel 1988; Komlos 1989; Floud et al. 1990), none of the indicators reviewed here suggested that the standard of living declined in France during the early stages of industrialization. For the period after 1820, when the data sources are better, we found that steady advance in economic measures was accompanied by slow but steady advance in heights and life expectancy. In the twentieth century, all the indicators showed accelerated progress.

Low fertility and the resulting slow population growth contributed to this distinctive French pattern of slow but steady improvement in physical well-being during industrialization. Given the higher mortality in urban areas, the urbanization that accompanied economic growth in the nineteenth century did generate negative externalities, but slow population growth led to a slow pace of urbanization that did not outstrip the pace of mortality decline. Moreover, urbanization was associated with improvements in real incomes and in consumption that contributed to male heights. Finally, the decline of marital fertility itself may have been related to increased familial investments in the health of children (Weir 1993).

Doubts about the early stages of economic development in France will focus, as they now do in the English standard of living debate, on the period 1780–1820. The disruptive effects of the Napoleonic Wars on Britain's economy have complicated the picture there, but that is nothing compared to the complexity of the French case. Sorting out the effects of economic growth from those of the Revolution, legal reform, war, the Continental Blockade, and the other tumultuous events is made still more difficult by the shortage of sources and of scholarly work on the economic history of the period.

Because the various economic and noneconomic indicators of living standards tended to move in the same direction in France, we did not need to specify their interrelationships in order to draw an unambiguous conclusion that the welfare of the population improved during industrialization. The cross-sectional time-series analysis suggested, however, that the different economic indicators measured different aspects of economic welfare just as the different demographic indicators measured different dimensions of physical well-being. We can, therefore, still learn more about the interaction of economic welfare and physical health during French development.

Appendix A
Data Sources and Methods

Nominal GDP at Market Prices

France: 1781–1938, Toutain (1987, V41); 1948–89, *Annuaire Statistique*.

United Kingdom: 1949–80, *National Accounts* expenditure-side estimates, as reported in Mitchell (1988, 834–35); 1855–1948, Feinstein's (1972) "compromise" estimate at factor cost, reported in Mitchell (1988, 836), plus Feinstein's factor cost adjustment reported in Mitchell (1988, 831–35); 1830–54, Feinstein's expenditure-side estimate at market prices from Mitchell (1988, 837), ratio-spliced in 1855 to the "compromise" estimate; 1760–1829, new estimates and conjectures about GDP at factor cost in Great Britain and Ireland, converted to GDP at market prices by ratio splicing in 1831 to the estimates based on Feinstein's compromise series for the United Kingdom. The main benchmarks for Great Britain are from Deane and Cole (1962, 166) for 1801, 1811, 1821, and 1831, and from Crafts (1985) based on Lindert and Williamson (1983) for 1760. Annual variation between the benchmarks is based on smooth trends in real growth and annual fluctuations in prices.

Real GDP

France: Real GDP in constant francs of 1905–13 formed by creating an index of real GDP base 1905–13 = 100 and reflating to the level of nominal GDP in 1905–13. The index is formed by: 1781–1960, Toutain (1987, V40); 1960–70, INSEE estimates of GDP in constant prices of 1970 from *Annuaire Statistique*, spliced to index at 1960; 1970–89, INSEE estimates of GDP in constant prices of 1980 from *Annuaire Statistique* spliced to index at 1970.

United Kingdom: Real GDP in constant pounds of 1913 formed by creating an index base 1913 = 100 and reflating to the level of nominal GDP in 1913. The index is formed by: 1965–80, real GDP at 1980 market prices (Mitchell 1988, 841), spliced to index at 1965; 1948–65, real GDP at 1958 market prices (Mitchell 1988, 841), spliced to index at 1948; 1913–48, Feinstein's compromise GDP at factor cost in 1913 prices (index 1913 = 100 and nominal GDP from Mitchell 1988, 836), plus factor cost adjustment in constant prices (Mitchell 1988, 839–40, gives figures in 1938 prices, which I converted to 1913 prices by the ratio of the 1913 estimate in nominal 1913 prices [Mitchell 1988, 833] to the 1913 estimate in 1938 prices); 1855–1913, Feinstein's compromise GDP at factor cost in 1913 prices (index 1913 = 100 and nominal GDP from Mitchell 1988, 836), plus factor cost adjustment in constant prices (Mitchell 1988, 837–39, gives figures in 1900 prices, which I converted to 1913 prices by the ratio of the 1913 estimate in nominal 1913 prices [Mitchell 1988, 833] to the 1913 estimate in 1900 prices); 1830–55, as for 1855–1913, with compromise GDP at factor cost in 1913 prices estimated by splicing Feinstein's expenditure-side estimate of GDP at factor cost in constant 1913 prices to this 1855 compromise GDP estimate at factor cost in 1913 prices; 1760–1829, nominal GDP at market prices for the United Kingdom as described above, deflated by my implicit price deflator for Great Britain based on Crafts (1985). The overall trend rate of growth in real GDP for Great Britain is that of Crafts for 1760–80, 1780–1801, and 1801–31. Growth rates within the period 1801–31 have been allowed to vary to match the nominal GDP benchmarks. Irish real GDP per capita was assumed constant.

Exchange Rates

The general approach taken was to obtain real output series using domestic prices as deflators and then convert the level of the U.K. series to its equivalent in French francs of 1905–13. In principle, the conversion could be done for any year in which nominal output and the exchange rate were known for both countries. In practice, the choice of year and exchange rate basis can have a large influence on the relative levels of the converted real output series (U.K. expressed as constant francs). Under the stable gold standard regime prior to 1913 there is ample evidence that the fixed exchange rate imposed by free convertibility exercised a strong influence on international relative prices and that purchasing-power-parity (PPP) exchange rates did not stray far from the par exchange rate. I have therefore used the par rate of exchange up to 1913.

In the years since World War I the deviations of PPP from market exchange rates have been substantial. A serious effort at making internationally comparable real output estimates after World War I would require detailed attention to the evolution of international relative prices. For simplicity, I have followed Maddison (1991, 187) and used the 1985 PPP exchange rate for the period 1914–90, even though it creates an inconsistency with the pre–World War I years. In 1905–13, British GDP per capita in 1905–13 pounds was £48.1. Converted at the prewar par of exchange it was 1,214 francs of 1905–13; Maddison's conversions would place it at 1,598 francs of 1905–13. French real GDP per capita in 1905–13 was 1,030 francs of 1905–13.

U.K. real GDP in francs of 1905–13: 1750–1919, the series in pounds of 1913 converted to a 1905–13 pounds base and then converted to francs at the par exchange rate of 25.22 francs per pound; 1920–89, conversion via the PPP exchange rate for 1985. According to Maddison (1991, 187), the PPP exchange rate in 1985 was 12.681 francs per pound, which, using nominal output and population data, implies that U.K. real GDP per capita was 93.11 percent of French in 1985. French real GDP per capita in 1985, expressed in constant francs of 1905–13, was 5,308.1, implying U.K. GDP per capita was 4,942.2 francs of 1905–13. Expressed in constant pounds of 1905–13, U.K. GDP per capita in 1985 was £148.85. The ratio (4,942.2/148.85) was used to convert the series in constant pounds of 1905–13 to constant francs of 1905–13.

Population (Variable Borders)

France: For 1740–1860, Henry and Blayo (1975, 92–93) give quinquennial estimates based on population reconstruction for the territory of 1861 (present-day territory). I made annual interpolations using annual births and deaths (corrected for underregistration) and assuming constant migration rates between quinquennial estimates. These were converted to the territory of 1815 by dividing by 1.0182, and midyear population estimates made by averaging adjacent 1 January estimates. For 1861–1911, Bourgeois-Pichat's (1952, 320–21) similar population reconstruction estimates were used and interpolations made. For consistency with GDP data the territories of Alsace and Lorraine were included through 1870 and excluded beginning 1871. From 1912–90, the official census and *Statistique Générale de la France* estimates were used, with Alsace and Lorraine restored beginning 1919.

United Kingdom: For 1921–80, Mitchell (1988, 11–14) gives midyear population estimates for England and Wales, Scotland, and southern Ireland; for 1801–1920, Mitchell (1988, 11–14) gives midyear population estimates for England and Wales, Scotland, and Ireland. Wrigley and Schofield (1981) noted some underregistration in censuses of England and Wales, especially before 1841. The data reported in Mitchell apparently contain some correction vis-à-vis the census. To determine the remaining extent of correction needed, I compared the figures for England and Wales in Mitchell with the estimates of Wrigley and Schofield (multiplied by 1.073 to account for their exclusion of Monmouth). The Wrigley and Schofield estimates were 2.6 percent higher in 1801 and 1811, and 1.86 percent higher in 1821 and 1831, with the differences essentially eliminated by 1851. I interpolated between census years to get annual correction factors and applied the same correction factor to the population of Great Britain and the United Kingdom. For 1760 to 1801, I assumed that the populations of Ireland and Scotland grew at the same rate as the population of England and Wales estimated by Wrigley and Schofield and extrapolated the 1801 U.K. total back on the English growth rate.

Consumption

Consumption was estimated as a residual from the national income accounting identity:

$$C = Y - G - I - (X - M).$$

The estimates of nominal income (Y) are the nominal GDP estimates described above. The other elements are taken from the following.

France: 1820–1913, government spending excluding transfer payments (G) given by Toutain (1987, V25), gross domestic investment (I) from Lévy-Leboyer and Bourguignon (1985, table A-III, col. 4 + col. 6 + col. 8), net foreign investment ($X - M$) from Lévy-Leboyer and Bourguignon (1985, table A-III, col. 5 minus col. 7); 1803–20, consumption share assumed at 85 percent of GDP; 1781–90, consumption share assumed at 89 percent of GDP.

United Kingdom: For 1830–1913, I estimated the share of nominal GDP at market prices going to consumption from Feinstein's expenditure-side data (Mitchell 1988, 831–33) and applied that ratio to the nominal GDP series described above to obtain nominal consumption, and to the real GDP in 1913 prices to obtain real consumption; 1760–1831, aggregation of separate series for Great Britain and for Ireland. For Britain, Feinstein's (1978) estimates of domestic and foreign investment have been slightly revised and are reported in Feinstein and Pollard (1988, 462) in current prices. They are reported as decade averages, and it was necessary to assume the same value for each year within decades up to 1830. For 1831 it was possible to use his annual estimates of investment in the United Kingdom to determine the ratio of 1831 to its decade average. Government expenditures are reported in Mitchell (1988, 578–89). I deducted total debt charges from total net expenditure to arrive at an estimate of government purchases of goods and services. The bulk of remaining expenditure was on the military. Data are for Great Britain up to 1801 and the United Kingdom thereafter. It then remains to estimate investment in Ireland and government spending in Ireland prior to 1801. I assumed investment and government combined to be 5 percent of Irish GDP at factor cost from 1760 to 1801, and investment at 3 percent of GDP from 1801 to 1831.

Labor Force Distribution by Sector

France: Marchand and Thélot (1991, 170). Women were weighted at 62 percent of men.

United Kingdom: Deane and Cole (1962) for Great Britain 1801–1951 (p. 142) and United Kingdom 1851–1911 (p. 147). Prior to 1846, the data for Britain were converted to the United Kingdom on the assumption that the Irish labor force was 32 percent of the U.K. total and that 20 percent of the Irish labor force was in industry. From 1921 on, the Irish share of labor force was sufficiently small that British figures were used without modification.

Nutrient Consumption

Coefficients representing average nutritional content were applied to estimates of the availability for human consumption of foods of various kinds (including wine). Food availability estimates: 1781–1938, Toutain (1971) decade averages; 1950–89, Organisation for Economic Co-operation and Development (1975).

Nominal Wages

France: The index is of unskilled construction labor in Paris.

Britain: Several nominal wage indexes (fixed-weight labor force composition) were spliced together at adjoining years. 1881–1913, Feinstein (1990, 612), index of changes *within* sectors; 1851–81, Wood (1909, 102–3), index for workman of unchanged grade; 1750–1851, Crafts and Mills (1994), the general movement of which is governed by benchmark-year estimates for blue-collar workers from Lindert and Williamson (1983).

Cost-of-Living Indexes

France: The index is for Paris. 1840–1913, Singer-Kérel (1961, 452–53), index of 213 articles; 1726–1840, data underlying Weir (1991), subindexes based 1851 = 100 for comparability with British index.

Britain: 1870–1913, Feinstein (1991, table 6.4); 1851–70, Bowley's index given in Mitchell (1988, 738); 1781–1851, Lindert and Williamson's (revised) "southern urban" index based 1851 = 100 given in Mitchell (1988, 737); 1750–81, Crafts and Mills (1994, 179–82).

Purchasing Power Parity

To compare the levels of real wages in France and England it is necessary to compare directly the nominal wages and the prices of a fixed consumption bundle for some year. This was done for circa 1905 in a study published by the (British) Board of Trade (1909), which has recently been reworked by Williamson (1995). Because the cost of living includes substantial nontradables (notably house rent), it could deviate substantially from the par exchange rate even under the gold standard. Nevertheless, Williamson finds that the French cost of his standard consumption bundle was only 2 percent higher at market exchange rates than the British cost. Nominal wages of French workers were about 76 percent of the wages of similar British workers, implying that French real wages were 75 percent of the British level in 1905.

Meat Consumption

National averages for France are given by Toutain (1971) for 1781–1939 and by the Organisation for Economic Co-operation and Development (1975) for the postwar years. Toutain's estimates derive mainly from the agricultural surveys of 1840, 1852, 1862, 1882, 1892, and 1929, which also provide the data by departments used in the cross-sectional regressions in this paper.

Urban consumption data were also reported in some of the agricultural surveys, derived from records of the *octroi,* the urban consumption tax system. Retrospective data for 1816–33 are reported in *Archives Statistiques* (France 1837) and for 1839–62 in the agricultural survey of 1862. Per capita urban consumption was calculated by dividing the reported consumption by the population of the cities included in the report. Rural meat consumption and population were then calculated by deducting the urban totals from the national total. The residual rural sector therefore includes some cities not included in the urban consumption reports (about 10 percent of the total "rural" population), and its per capita consumption may be slightly overstated as a result.

Parisians consumed meat from three sources: by far the largest was the slaughter at the city's main slaughterhouses of "butcher's meat," that is, beef, veal, mutton, and lamb. Pork was accounted for separately, and over the course of the nineteenth century external sources of prepared meat became increasingly important. For the eighteenth century the number of animals and their average weights are reported by Lachiver (1984). Similar data for 1799 to 1854 are reported by Husson (1856), along with data on external supplies. For the later nineteenth century, Parisian meat consumption was the subject of annual reports in the *Statistique Agricole.*

Heights of Men at Age 20

France: See appendix B.

Britain: For men born before 1890, Floud et al. (1990, table 4.1). The data are estimated mean heights by year of birth and age at measurement from two different sources: recruit description books (RDB) and the Army Medical Department (AMD). I separated the estimates by source. The RDB estimates are for five-year birth cohorts 1740–44 to 1855–59. To reduce variability due to the small sample sizes measured at single year of age 20, I converted other age groups to an age-20 basis by the average ratio of height at age 20 to height at age x for all birth cohorts and then averaged the single-year-of-age series by birth cohort. A check against the age-20-only series shows that the main movements and levels are indeed similar. A similar age-20 index was constructed from the AMD estimates by single-year birth cohorts. The quinquennial RDB estimates are used for cohorts 1740–1854 (recruitment years 1760–1874) and a five-year centered moving average of the annual AMD estimates for birth cohorts 1855–1889 (recruitment years 1875–1909). Data for subsequent years are based on numerous studies discussed by Floud et al. (1990, 153–62).

Life Table Mortality Rates

Life tables for 1740–1829 were produced by Blayo (1975). For the twentieth century life tables have been published by Vallin (1973) and in annual volumes of the *Annuaire Statistique*. For the years 1830–1900 it was necessary to calculate life table values from estimated age-specific mortality rates. Deaths by age and births were reported annually by the Statistique Générale de la France. The age distribution of the population was taken from the population reconstructions of Bourgeois-Pichat (1951, 1952) and Henry and Blayo (1975). For further discussion of data sources and reconstruction methods see Weir (1994a).

Crude Death Rates by Urban-Rural Residence

Total deaths were reported separately for urban and rural communes beginning in 1854, with the classification of urban updated at each quinquennial census using the official definition of urban (population of 2,000 or more in an agglomerated area). Prior to that date records were kept for cities of over 10,000 population and the capitals of the arrondissements, which together accounted for over 70 percent of the urban population. A total of urban deaths was estimated by multiplying the crude death rate in the covered cities by the total urban population according to the census definition. Rural deaths were then calculated by subtracting the urban total from the national total. Deaths in Paris were reported retrospectively in the *Annuaire Statistique de la Ville de Paris*. They were deducted from the total of urban deaths to obtain the category of "other urban."

Appendix B
Heights of French Men Born 1784–1902: Sources and Methods

Time Periods Covered

For the purpose of estimating the median heights shown in table 5B.1, there are four distinct periods with different methodological challenges. The problems are relatively simple in the two periods after 1871. The simplest of all is the recruitment period 1872–1912, for which my estimates are identical to those of van Meerten (1990). After 1886, everyone was measured and the complete distribution of heights was reported. This is about 300,000 individuals in total each year, or an average of about 3,400 in each department. From 1872

Table 5B.1   **Estimated Median Height at Age 20–21, by** *Classe*
                        (year cohort reached age 20)

Year	Height (mm)	Year	Height (mm)	Year	Height (mm)
1804	1,635.4	1844	1,644.7	1884	1,654.3
1805	1,636.2	1845	1,644.6	1885	1,653.7
1806	1,636.3	1846	1,645.1	1886	1,653.9
1807	1,639.4	1847	1,642.5	1887	1,653.6
1808	1,635.5	1848	1,643.5	1888	1,653.7
1809	1,636.1	1849	1,644.8	1889	1,652.9
1810	1,638.3	1850	1,645.4	1890	1,653.7
1811	1,639.6	1851	1,646.1	1891	1,653.2
1812	1,637.6	1852	1,645.8	1892	1,654.8
1813		1853	1,646.7	1893	1,654.7
1814		1854	1,643.9	1894	1,654.4
1815		1855	1,644.3	1895	1,654.1
1816		1856	1,645.2	1896	1,654.1
1817	1,632.2	1857	1,645.4	1897	1,654.4
1818	1,634.9	1858	1,645.9	1898	1,654.9
1819	1,636.7	1859	1,645.9	1899	1,655.1
1820	1,640.8	1860	1,646.5	1900	1,655.4
1821	1,637.5	1861	1,647.1	1901	1,655.4
1822	1,636.0	1862	1,647.4	1902	1,654.7
1823	1,638.8	1863	1,647.2	1903	1,658.3
1824	1,639.5	1864	1,647.7	1904	1,659.0
1825	1,639.8	1865	1,647.3	1905	1,659.8
1826	1,642.7	1866	1,647.7	1906	1,659.5
1827	1,643.3	1867	1,649.4	1907	1,661.1
1828	1,642.2	1868	1,647.0	1908	1,660.2
1829	1,641.6	1869		1909	1,660.8
1830	1,641.2	1870		1910	1,660.5
1831	1,640.7	1871	1,647.5	1911	1,661.1
1832	1,641.7	1872	1,651.3	1912	1,663.3
1833	1,641.2	1873	1,650.4	1913	
1834	1,642.5	1874	1,651.6	1914	1,664.7
1835	1,642.5	1875	1,652.5	1915	
1836	1,642.5	1876	1,652.9	1916	1,667.1
1837	1,642.1	1877	1,653.6	1917	1,667.5
1838	1,644.1	1878	1,653.3	1918	1,666.5
1839	1,644.8	1879	1,652.5	1919	1,664.9
1840	1,643.4	1880	1,652.7	1920	1,665.6
1841	1,643.9	1881	1,654.5	1921	1,668.9
1842	1,643.4	1882	1,654.7	1922	1,669.2
1843	1,644.3	1883	1,654.7		

to 1885 only about half of each cohort was measured. Lotteries determined who was called in for examination, so the selection was random, and a full distribution of heights was reported, including the heights of men exempted from service. For the years after 1872 it is therefore a simple matter to calculate conventional medians from the reported height distributions, which were published in centimeters. The years 1913–22 were affected by the war, and especially by early call-up of some cohorts, which resulted in mean ages at recruitment as much as two years younger than usual. The medians require adjustment in those years.

Prior to 1871, height data were kept only on men actually recruited into the army, which requires us to assess the number exempted below the minimum height requirements. Here my methods differ slightly from van Meerten's. There was also apparently a problem associated with conversions between metric units and the older traditional units of measure prior to 1867. Beginning in 1867 the data are reported in pure metric units. Between 1866 and 1867 uncorrected medians such as estimated by van Meerten leap up by 8 mm: a larger increase than had occurred over the entire preceding 40 years! An alternative estimation procedure described below can overcome the problem. For the period of the First Empire there are two additional problems: we have data only on a regionally biased subset of departments, and the ages at recruitment varied. We must address four issues before advancing an estimation method: recruitment procedures, minimum height standards, replacement, and units of measure.

Recruitment Procedures

Local officials maintained a *tableau de recensement,* keeping track of men by birth cohort. The *classe* of a given year, say 1831, consisted of all men born 20 years prior, in this case 1811. They would be examined early in the next year (1832), when the men were aged approximately 20 years, 8 months (plus or minus 6 months depending on birthdate within the year). On average, about 61 percent of the male births survived to be counted in the *classe,* and the average year's *classe* consisted of just over 300,000 men. The selection of conscripts from the *classe* varied over time, as did the role of height measurement.

From 1816 to 1871 heights are reported only for those actually recruited into the *contingent.* The total size of the *contingent* was set each year by the army according to its manpower needs and was then allocated across departments roughly in proportion to the size of *classe.* The *contingent* increased from 40,000 in 1816–23 to 60,000 in 1824–29 to 80,000 in 1830–52 to 100,000 from 1853 to 1870, with a few years of higher demands. After 1870 the numbers were somewhat more variable around 170,000 per year. All the members of the *classe* were assigned numbers in a lottery (*tirage au sort*). In theory, local recruiters examined the men in the order determined by lottery until they had found enough eligible men to fill out the required *contingent.* The total number of men examined (*examinés*) therefore depended on the rate of exemptions (*exemptés*). On average, just under half the *examinés* made it into the *contingent,* so the number of *examinés* was about half the *classe* up to 1852, and nearly two-thirds thereafter. About 19 percent of the *examinés* were exempted for physical deformities, 17 percent for legal reasons, 9 percent for constitutional weakness (*faiblesse de constitution*), and 7 percent for insufficient height (*défaut de taille*).

Minimum Height Standards

There was a minimum height standard of 1.57 meters before 1830, 1.54 in 1830, 1.56 from 1831 to 1867, 1.56 to 1871, and finally 1.54 from 1872 until its abolition in 1886. Prior to 1871, the reported height distributions refer only to the *contingent,* that is, the men actually conscripted, all of whom were above the minimum height. They are thus truncated distributions, and the mean heights of recruits will be greater than the true mean of the population. There are two ways to make use of such data: estimate the population mean from the truncated distribution using maximum likelihood techniques, or obtain separately an estimate of the proportion of men below the minimum standard.

The first strategy could be applied quite easily in France. The minimum height standard is known precisely. By contrast, in the English data the minimum standard was variable and so the truncation point itself had to be estimated. The Quantile Bend Estimator is an iterative procedure designed to estimate simultaneously the maximum truncation point and the parameters of the population distribution. With a known minimum standard, estimation is much easier. Moreover, the minimum was sufficiently low in France that the reported "upper" tail was probably in the vicinity of 90 percent of the whole distribution. By contrast, some recent estimates for Sweden relied on data for which only that part of the distribution above the mean could be considered reliably recorded (Sandberg and Steckel 1988).

For reasons given below, complete reliance on reported heights above the minimum standard presents other problems. It is preferable to make use of the available information about the number of persons below the minimum. Insufficient height was one of several possible reasons for exemption from service, and the number of exemptions for *défaut de taille* was usually reported, along with those for other reasons. Each individual was only counted once, no matter how many exemptions he may have been eligible for. We thus have a numerator: a count of men below the minimum height standard. We need a denominator; that is, we need to know the number of men who were "at risk" of being found below the minimum. The upper limit is the total number of men who were examined. From this we should deduct men who were dismissed prior to height measurement, or for reasons that were unrelated to their height.

Obviously, the men taken into the *contingent* were at risk, including those whose heights were listed as unknown. The problem is classifying the other exemption categories. If a particular exemption was granted before height measurement took place, then we may assume that the men who were granted that exemption were not at risk for a finding of insufficient height and so should not be included in the denominator. This was certainly the case for exemptions on legal grounds, primarily for the only sons of widows and other special family situations. Ambiguities arise when dealing with exemptions for other physical problems. In principle, other physical exemptions were supposed to take precedence over *défaut de taille;* for example, someone who was both short and missing a few fingers (*perte des doigts*) would be classified as missing a few fingers. Since many of the exemptions for deformities carried some advantages to the family, it seems likely that the precedence rule would be followed. The large and vague category of *faiblesse de constitution* (constitutional weakness) poses a different case. There were no advantages to the family from this exemption, and it was the most subjective of all the possible reasons, raising the specter of challenge. It therefore seems reasonable that a young man of insufficient height would be classified by the absolute standard, and that *faiblesse de constitution* would be reserved for men of adequate height and no obvious deformities but who nevertheless presented an unappealing prospect to the local recruiter.

The most sensible procedure, therefore, is to construct the denominator as the sum of the number in the *contingent,* including unknown heights, plus the number exempted for *défaut de taille,* plus the number exempted for *faiblesse de constitution.* One arrives at the same total by deducting from the total number of men called for examination (*examinés*) the number of legal exemptions and the number of exemptions for physical deformities other than *faiblesse.* This is the procedure used from 1831 forward. Using the same procedure before 1830 creates a big discontinuity in the estimated share of the population under 1.57 meters, which is a key parameter in the estimation method described below. It is possible that the exemption for insufficient height took precedence over other infirmities in the years before 1830. If we include all exemptions for infirmities in the denominator used to calculate the share below the minimum height standard before 1830 we obtain a series that appears more consistent with the later years.

Replacement

Prior to 1872, service in the army could be avoided by hiring a "replacement." On average, about 23 percent of draftees hired replacements, but the rate varied considerably by region (Schnapper 1968). The price was typically around 1,000 francs at a time when the average yearly earnings of an agricultural laborer probably did not exceed 500 francs. The result would be a substitution of a poor (and, therefore, perhaps shorter) man for a wealthier one. Men ultimately replaced were examined and measured. It seems that the reported distributions were based on the original cohort of draftees *prior* to replacement. Obviously, there was no reason for the family to pay a replacement if the son could obtain exemption on other grounds, so he would go through the examination. Moreover, we do not observe any discontinuity in the trend of heights when replacement was abolished.

Units of Measure

The other problem that must be corrected is not one that has ever been discussed in the literature. It becomes apparent only when looking at the height distributions. Prior to 1867 the data were grouped in old-style *pieds* and *pouces*

Table 5B.2   **Exact Millimeter Ranges Corresponding to Round Units of Measure**

Round *Pouces* (1)	Millimeter Range (2)	Round Centimeters inside Range (3)	Millimeter Range of Round Centimeter Scale (4)
<58	1,560–1,569	156	1,560–1,569
58	1,570–1,597	157, 158, 159	1,570–1,599
59	1,598–1,624	160, 161, 162	1,600–1,629
60	1,625–1,651	163, 164, 165	1,630–1,659
61	1,652–1,678	166, 167	1,660–1,679
62	1,679–1,705	168, 169, 170	1,680–1,709
63, 64	1,706–1,760	171, 172, 173, 174, 175, 176	1,710–1,769
65, 66	1,761–1,814	177, 178, 179, 180, 181	1,770–1,819
67+	1,815–	182, . . .	1,820–

(French feet and inches, one inch being approximately 27.07 mm). Each range was also labeled with approximate metric equivalents in millimeters. We know, however, that in many cases conscripts were measured in centimeters. Imagine a nineteenth-century French bureaucrat asked to put a distribution by round centimeters into a distribution by *pouces*. Table 5B.2 shows how it must have been done. Column (2) shows the millimeter ranges published by the army, and column (1) shows the (unpublished) old-style *pouces* to which they correspond. The round centimeter values would be placed within the appropriate millimeter ranges given by the army, as shown in column (3). These round centimeter values correspond to the millimeter ranges shown in column (4) if we assume that height measures were rounded down; for example, anyone of at least 160 cm but less than 161 cm in height would be recorded at 160 cm.

There are two notable features of this regrouping. The millimeter ranges corresponding to the round centimeter measurements are slightly higher than the millimeter ranges corresponding to the old units, and some *pouce* ranges have three and others only two exact-centimeter groups. If recruits were measured in round *pouces,* or in exact millimeters, we should use the millimeter ranges of column (2) to calculate median heights. If, on the other hand, they were measured in round centimeters and simply regrouped we should use the millimeter ranges of column (4), which would produce higher medians.

Unfortunately, neither assumption is completely accurate for all years. By the late 1860s the evidence suggests that nearly everyone must have been measured in centimeters and regrouped. The published data switched from *pouces* to centimeter ranges beginning in 1867. The (conditional) mean height of men over the minimum estimated from the metric data for 1867–68 was higher than a similar conditional mean calculated from the millimeter ranges of column (2) and virtually identical to the mean calculated from the ranges of column (4). Another indicator that the reported distributions were really a clumsy regrouping of centimeter data is the relative size of the range corresponding to

61 *pouces*. Since it corresponds to only two exact-centimeter groups it would have fewer observations than "expected" given the mean and standard deviation. That was certainly the case in the 1860s. Data in the 1830s appear to have had a less severe form of the same regrouping problem, suggesting that the use of the metric system at the individual level diffused over time.

One possible solution would be to estimate two versions, one metric and one old-style and then weight them according to the probable extent of metric usage. This is feasible for the national averages, but highly questionable for the departments. We need a procedure to estimate the median that is not affected by the regrouping problem.

The reported height data can be collapsed into groups for which the ranges in old-style inches correspond to whole-centimeter ranges. Unfortunately, the first such range is from 1,570 to 1,679 mm (roughly the 12th to the 70th percentile of the height distribution). The usual procedure of estimating a median by linear approximation within a range can create large errors when the range is so wide. Instead, I estimate the median by a nonlinear procedure using two observed parameters: the proportion of all men below 1,570 mm, and the share of the above 1,570 group who are under 1,680 mm. These two parameters are based on largely independent sources: the lower tail is based primarily on the estimated proportion exempted for insufficient height, while the other is based on the distribution of reported heights only.

The approximation formula for the median was obtained from simulations of normal distributions of height with means from 1,620 to 1,675 mm and a coefficient of variation equal to 0.035 in all cases. It is quite precise within that range (and thus for the samples studied in this paper), but better approximations could be obtained for samples with very different characteristics. The median is calculated by

$$h = 1745.78 - 92.3864 * s1 - 132.698 * s2,$$

where $s1$ is the proportion of all men in the population under 1,570 mm (58 *pouces*), and $s2$ is the proportion of men 1,570 mm or taller who were between 1,570 and 1,679 mm (at least 58 but less than 62 *pouces*).

Heights in the First Empire, 1803–12

The data were reported in the same nonmetric ranges as were used in the Restoration. It is not completely clear what rules governed who was included in the reported height distributions, and they may have varied from one region to another. The large number of men in the category of under 4 *pieds*, 9 *pouces* (154 cm) suggests that there was no effective minimum (or that all men were measured). There was no separate listing of exemptions. I therefore assume that lower truncation is not a problem with this data and calculate medians (using the nonlinear approximation formula) without further correction for missing observations below the minimum.

Villermé (1829) reports the ages at which men were called in each of these classes. I adjusted the mean height for those years in which the recruitment age fell below the norm of 20.5 years. Based on Floud et al.'s (1990) English data on heights by age, it appears that a fall of one year in the average age of recruitment lowered mean heights by about 0.7 percent. The correction formula was therefore $H = h * [1 + (20.5 - a) * .007]$, where h is the observed median height of recruits and a is their average age.

The regional composition of the sample was not representative of France as a whole. In the years 1820–40 the departments in the sample had a median height about 4 mm below the national average. I therefore augmented the estimated medians for 1803–12 by a further 4 mm to correct for regional composition.

World War I

The examination dates of cohorts mustered during and immediately after World War I (1913–22) varied considerably. At the extremes, the *classe* of 1912 was measured in the usual way in February and March 1913, while the *classe* of 1917 (born five years later) was called in and measured in summer 1915 (only two years later). Cohorts measured at younger ages had systematically lower heights. However, the correction formula used for 1803–12 and derived from the English data resulted in very obvious overcorrection of the data from 1913–22. Quite possibly the better nourished cohorts born at the end of the nineteenth century reached final adult height at younger ages. I used instead

$$H = h * [1 + (20.67 - a)*.0025].$$

No detail on height distributions was published for the *classes* of 1913 and 1915. Estimates were obtained by simple linear interpolation between adjacent single-year cohorts.

Sources

The army produced an annual report, the *Compte-rendu sur le recrutement de l'armée,* providing data for each department on the number of men in different height ranges, and the number of exemptions granted for different reasons. The *Comptes-rendus* were used for the department-level estimates of 1840, 1846, 1856, and 1866. Beginning with the recruitment class of 1873, the *Annuaire Statistique* published department-level data on an annual basis. For the years 1873–85 the *Annuaire Statistique* is the preferred source, because the *Compte-rendu* gives data by military district rather than department. After 1905 the *Compte-rendu* provides a more detailed distribution of heights than the summary in the *Annuaire Statistique* and was used for the department cross sections of 1905 and 1911. The *Annuaire Statistique* also published frequent retrospective tables of the national height distribution from 1836 forward. Although they were not used in this paper, department-level data for 1819–26 combined can be found in Aron, Dumont, and LeRoy Ladurie (1972).

National-level totals of the number of *examinés* and exemptions for various causes from 1816 to 1871 were found in Tschouriloff (1876, 636–47) and confirmed by other official sources. The *Compte-rendu* of 1835 gave height distributions for 1834 and 1835. Annual data on the heights of conscripts prior to 1834 were obtained from Villermé (1929, 399), Boudin (1863, 177–201), and Hargenvilliers (1817).

The height distributions for 1803–12 were found in France, Archives Nationales F20 439 and F20 440[1]. The cartons include reports from some occupied non-French departments as well.

References

Aron, Jean-Paul, Paul Dumont, and Emmanuel LeRoy Ladurie. 1972. *Anthropologie du conscrit français d'après les comptes numériques et sommaires du recrutement de l'armée (1819–1826)*. Paris: Mouton.
Blayo, Yves. 1975. La mortalité en France de 1740 à 1829. *Population* 30(5): 123–42.
Boudin, Jean C. M. 1863. De l'accroissement de la taille et l'aptitude militaire en France. *Journal de la Société de Statistique de Paris* 4(7–10): 177–201, 231–41, 259–70.
Bourgeois-Pichat, Jean. 1951. Evolution générale de la population française depuis le XVIIIe siècle. *Population* 6(4): 635–60.
———. 1952. Note sur l'evolution générale de la population française depuis le XVIIIe siècle. *Population* 7(2): 319–29.
Chamla, Marie-Claude. 1964. L'accroissement de la stature en France de 1880 à 1960; comparaison avec les pays d'Europe occidentale. *Bulletins et Mémoires de la Société d'Anthropologie de Paris,* 11th ser., 6(2): 201–78.
Crafts, N. F. R. 1985. *British economic growth during the industrial revolution*. Oxford: Clarendon.
Crafts, N. F. R., and Terence C. Mills. 1994. Trends in real wages in Britain, 1750–1913. *Explorations in Economic History* 31(2): 176–94.
Deane, Phyllis, and W. A. Cole. 1962. *British economic growth, 1688–1959*. Cambridge: Cambridge University Press.
Engerman, Stanley L. 1994. Reflections on the standard of living debate: New arguments and new evidence. In *Capitalism in context: Essays on economic development and cultural change in honor of R. Max Hartwell,* ed. John James and Mark Thomas. Chicago: University of Chicago Press.
Feinstein, Charles H. 1972. *National income, expenditure and output of the United Kingdom, 1855–1965*. Cambridge: Cambridge University Press.
———. 1978. Capital formation in Great Britain. In *Cambridge economic history of Europe,* vol. 7, ed. Peter Mathias and M. M. Postan, 28–96. Cambridge: Cambridge University Press.
———. 1990. New estimates of average earnings in the United Kingdom, 1880–1913. *Economic History Review* 43(4): 595–632.
———. 1991. A new look at the cost of living, 1870–1914. In *New perspectives on the late Victorian economy,* ed. James Foreman-Peck, 151–79. Cambridge: Cambridge University Press.
Feinstein, Charles H., and Sidney Pollard, eds. 1988. *Studies in capital formation in the United Kingdom, 1750–1920*. Oxford: Clarendon.

Floud, Roderick, Kenneth Wachter, and Annabel Gregory. 1990. *Height, health and history: Nutritional status in the United Kingdom, 1750–1980.* Cambridge: Cambridge University Press.

Fogel, Robert W. 1986. Nutrition and the decline in mortality since 1700: Some preliminary findings. In *Long-term factors in American economic growth,* ed. Stanley L. Engerman and Robert E. Gallman, 439–556. Chicago: University of Chicago Press.

Fogel, Robert W., Stanley Engerman, Roderick Floud, Gerald Friedman, Robert Margo, Kenneth Sokoloff, Richard Steckel, James Trussell, Georgia Villaflor, and Kenneth Wachter. 1983. Secular changes in American and British stature and nutrition. *Journal of Interdisciplinary History* 14(2): 445–81.

France. 1837. *Archives statistiques du ministère des travaux publics.*

Gerschenkron, Alexander. 1966. Reflections on the concept of prerequisites of modern industrialization. In *Economic backwardness in historical perspective,* ed. Alexander Gerschenkron. Cambridge, Mass.: Belknap.

Hargenvilliers, Antoine Audet. 1817. *Recherches et considerations sur la formation et le recrutement de l'armée en France.* Paris: Didot.

Hartwell, R. M. 1961. The rising standard of living in England, 1800–1850. *Economic History Review* 13(3): 397–416.

Henry, Louis, and Yves Blayo. 1975. La population de la France de 1740 à 1829. *Population* 30(5): 71–122.

Hobsbawm, Eric J. 1957. The British standard of living, 1790–1850. *Economic History Review* 10(1): 46–68.

Husson, Armand. 1856. *Les consommations de Paris.* Paris: Guillaumin.

Johansson, Sheila Ryan, and Carl Mosk. 1987. Exposure, resistance and life expectancy: Disease and death during the economic development of Japan, 1900–1960. *Population Studies* 41(1): 207–35.

Komlos, John. 1989. *Nutrition and economic development in the eighteenth-century Habsburg monarchy: An anthropometric history.* Princeton, N.J.: Princeton University Press.

Lachiver, Marcel. 1984. L'approvisionnement de Paris en viande au XVIIIe siècle. In *La France d'Ancien Régime: Etudes réunies en l'honneur de Pierre Goubert,* 345–54. Paris: Privat.

Lévy-Leboyer, Maurice, and François Bourguignon. 1985. *L'économie française au XIXe siècle: Analyse macro-économique.* Paris: Economica.

Lindert, Peter H., and Jeffrey G. Williamson. 1983. English workers' living standards during the industrial revolution: A new look. *Economic History Review* 36(1): 1–25.

———. 1985. English workers' real wages: A reply to crafts. *Journal of Economic History* 45(1): 145–53.

Maddison, Angus. 1991. *Dynamic forces in capitalist development: A long-run comparative view.* Oxford: Oxford University Press.

Marchand, Olivier, and Claude Thélot. 1991. *Deux siècles de travail en France.* Paris: INSEE.

Mitchell, B. R. 1988. *British historical statistics.* Cambridge: Cambridge University Press.

Mokyr, Joel. 1988. Is there still life in the pessimist case? Consumption during the industrial revolution, 1790–1850. *Journal of Economic History* 48(1): 69–92.

Mosk, Carl, and Sheila Ryan Johansson. 1986. Income and mortality: Evidence from modern Japan. *Population and Development Review* 12(3): 415–40.

Mroz, Thomas A., and David R. Weir. 1990. Structural change in life cycle fertility during the fertility transition: France before and after the Revolution of 1789. *Population Studies* 44(1): 61–87.

Olivier, G., Marie-Claude Chamla, G. Devigne, and A. Jacquard. 1977. L'accroissement de la stature en France. *Bulletins et Mémoires de la Société d'Anthropologie de Paris,* 13th ser., 4(2): 197–214.

Organisation for Economic Co-operation and Development. 1975. *Food consumption statistics, 1955–1973.* Paris: Organisation for Economic Co-operation and Development.

Postel-Vinay, Gilles, and Jean-Marc Robin. 1992. Eating, working, and saving in an unstable world: Consumers in nineteenth-century France. *Economic History Review* 45(3): 494–513.

Preston, Samuel H., and Etienne van de Walle. 1978. Urban French mortality in the nineteenth century. *Population Studies* 32(2): 275–97.

Riley, James C. 1986. *The Seven Years War and the Old Regime in France: The economic and financial toll.* Princeton, N.J.: Princeton University Press.

Sandberg, Lars, and Richard Steckel. 1988. Overpopulation and malnutrition rediscovered: Hard times in nineteenth-century Sweden. *Explorations in Economic History* 25(1): 1–19.

Schnapper, Bernard. 1968. *Le remplacement militaire en France: quelques aspects politiques, économiques et sociaux du recrutement au XIXe siècle.* Paris: SEVPEN.

Singer-Kérel, Jeanne. 1961. *Le coût de la vie à Paris de 1840 à 1954.* Paris: Armand Colin.

Toutain, J.-C. 1971. La consommation alimentaire en France de 1789 à 1964. *Économies et Sociétés. Cahiers de l'Institut de Science Économique Appliquée* 5(11): 1909–2049.

———. 1987. Le produit intérieur brut de la France de 1789 à 1982. *Économies et Sociétés, Série AF: Histoire quantitative de l'économie française* 21(5): 49–237.

Tschouriloff, Michel. 1876. Étude sur la dégénérescence physiologique des peuples civilisés. *Revue d'anthropologie* 5:605–64.

Vallin, Jacques. 1973. *La mortalité par génération en France depuis 1899.* INED Travaux et Documents Cahier no. 63. Paris: Presses Universitaires de France.

van Meerten, Michiel Alexander. 1990. Développement économique et stature en France, XIXe–XXe siècles. *Annales ESC* 45(3): 755–77.

Villermé, Louis R. 1829. Mémoire sur la taille de l'homme en France. *Annales d'hygiène publique* 1(1): 551–59.

Weir, David R. 1991. Les crises économiques et les origines de la Révolution française. *Annales ESC* 46(4): 917–47.

———. 1993. Parental consumption decisions and child health during the early French fertility decline, 1790–1914. *Journal of Economic History* 53(2): 259–74.

———. 1994a. New estimates of nuptiality and marital fertility in France, 1740–1911. *Population Studies* 48(3): 307–31.

———. 1994b. Urbanization, cities, and fertility decline in France, 1700–1911. University of Chicago, Population Research Center. Mimeograph.

Williamson, Jeffrey G. 1981. Urban disamenities, dark satanic mills, and the British standard of living debate. *Journal of Economic History* 41(1): 75–83.

———. 1985. *Did British capitalism breed inequality?* Boston: Allen and Unwin.

———. 1995. The evolution of global labor markets since 1830: Background evidence and hypotheses. *Explorations in Economic History* 32(2): 141–96.

Wood, George H. 1909. Real wages and the standard of comfort since 1850. *Journal of the Royal Statistical Society* 72(1): 91–103.

Wrigley, E. A., and Roger Schofield. 1981. *The population history of England, 1541–1871: A reconstruction.* Cambridge: Cambridge University Press.

6 Health and Welfare of Women in the United Kingdom, 1785–1920

Paul Johnson and Stephen Nicholas

6.1 Introduction

Women's status within the family and economy was transformed by industrialization. Whether the change worsened or improved the living standards and position of women remains one of the most important and contentious issues in economic history. This paper uses new data on the heights of women and men born in Britain and Ireland between the 1780s and the 1850s, and information on mortality, to assess the changing fortune of women's welfare during early and late industrialization.

It is well established in biomedical studies that changes in average height within a population reflect changes in net nutritional status, and this finding has been widely applied in anthropometric history to draw inferences from heights to living standards and other measures of welfare. Two significant problems have been identified with this procedure, one methodological and the other inferential. First, the use of military records in the majority of historical studies of height can be problematic because of minimum height standards for recruits, which erode the left-hand side of the military height distributions, biasing the average height estimates. There has been debate over how best to adjust for such biases (Floud, Wachter, and Gregory 1990, 1993; Komlos 1993). Second, the exact nature of the relationship between height and other measures of living standards, such as real income per capita, is unclear. This means that it has not been possible to map directly from heights to economic indicators of welfare.

Paul Johnson is reader in economic history at the London School of Economics. Stephen Nicholas is professor and head of the Department of Business Development and Corporate History, University of Melbourne.

The authors wish to acknowledge financial support from the Suntory-Toyota International Centre for Economics and Related Disciplines (STICERD) and from the Nuffield Foundation for the collection of data on Newgate prisoners and habitual criminals. They also wish to thank Sue Kimberley (Melbourne) and Ahmet Akarli (LSE) for their able research assistance.

Our data on heights are derived solely from convict and criminal records and no minimum or maximum height restrictions apply, which avoids the truncation problem that infects the military recruitment data. We partially circumvent the second problem of mapping from heights to alternative measures of living standards by comparing the height movements of women relative to men. Changes in the height gap between men and women is a powerful test of the relative changes in female and male living standards during industrialization.

The paper begins with a survey of the historical literature on industrialization and female living standards. Section 6.3 discusses the three separate sources of data on female criminal heights that we use in this paper, and section 6.4 reviews the existing literature on the relationship between height and industrialization in a number of countries. Section 6.5 presents our analysis and interpretation of female heights and living standards in the United Kingdom during early and late industrialization, and this is followed by a more detailed analysis of occupational and regional influences on heights. The final section compares the height data with information on the female mortality experience in Victorian Britain.

6.2   Historiography

The issue of whether industrialization worsened or improved the living standards and socioeconomic position of women has a long history. Marx and Engels (1977; Marx 1977) forecast the disintegration of oppressive family obligations, and John Stuart Mill (1988) argued that industrialization opened up more economic opportunities for women than it did for men. In contrast, Mary Wollstonecraft (1792) and William Thompson (1983) believed that an unequal sharing of unpaid family responsibilities prevented women from competing equally with men, intensifying female oppression in an era of individual competition.

Arguments by historians have split along similar lines. Alice Clark (1919) dated the rise of capitalism, and the demise of women, from the seventeenth century. Prior to capitalism, production in its numerous forms (textile, mining, agriculture) had been based on the family labor system. Employment contracts either explicitly or implicitly entailed that the male worker worked with his wife and children. Wages reflected this, being payment sufficient to cover the entire family; this conferred some, but not equitable, power to women. Patriarchy determined the degree of power that men exercised over the resources of the household, including the labor power of women within the family and the labor market. Within the preindustrial and protoindustrial household, men were the controlling members of the family labor system who employed various strategies, including access to intrahousehold resources and the organization of work, to maintain their unequal authority over women. However, the family labor and wage system, in operating subject to mutual rights and obligations between men and women and children, explicitly recognized the contribution of women to household income, which meant that the family wage was recognized as joint income (Seccombe 1986, 66).

The family wage system was not always inconsistent with capitalism. Many factory industries duplicated the household workshop where males dominated the labor power of women by subcontracting the labor of their wives. For example, in cotton textiles and coal mining, the patriarchal control over women's labor in the household was extended to the factory, where men determined the sexual division of labor in the workplace by allocating work tasks and dictating the process of work (Mark-Lawson and Witz 1988).

But, increasingly, emerging capitalist production became inconsistent with the family labor system. In many industries, such as hosiery and silk, there were not sufficient male workers in factories populated by unskilled female and child labor to operate a system of family subcontracting (Rose 1986; Lown 1990), and protective legislation, in mining for example, prohibited underground work by women, which destroyed the family subcontract system (Mark-Lawson and Witz 1988). More generally, men restricted women's work to unskilled and low-paid labor or forced women out of employment altogether, leaving them at home with the children. Concomitant with the shift from the family labor system to the individual worker, the family wage was converted to an individual wage. But the individual wage was higher for the "breadwinning" man, even if he was unmarried, since men were deemed to have a family to support while women workers only supported themselves. Working-class living standards suffered, but within the working class the onus of the suffering was deeply gendered.

Subsequent historians have challenged Clark's periodization, bringing the date of the rapid change from family to breadwinner wage to the early to mid-nineteenth century. Work has progressed from the study of waged employment in industry to include wage work in agriculture, the changing forms of the family, and increasingly, the continuing economic roles of women in the household or "nonmarket" sector. The parts played in the declining status of women by economic necessity, biology, ideology, and labor aristocrats have all been considered, as have the differences across industries, geographical area, and class, with a continuing debate over the relative significance of each (Tilly and Scott 1978; Berg 1985; McBride 1976; Davidoff and Hall 1987).

While Clark's tale was pessimistic, Pinchbeck (1930) had a positive story to tell. Pinchbeck focused on the opportunities that industrialization opened up for single urban women. Factories provided jobs with cash payment and a degree of freedom unknown to domestic and farm servants and girls used to working under the close scrutiny of parents. Optimistically, Pinchbeck declared that factories "meant higher wages, better food and clothing and an improved standard of living. This was especially so in the case of women" (Pinchbeck 1930, 311). The perils for women working in the factory were no more than "the experience of cottage and workshop industry writ large for all to see"

(McKendrick 1974, 161). Married women, too, benefited. Like Clark, Pinchbeck identified the changing wage form as highly significant for women, but her appraisal was favorable. The gradual movement toward a male breadwinner wage for the whole family meant financial recognition for women's reproductive labors, which freed women from the burden of paid work while acknowledging that "in the rearing of children and in home-making, the married woman makes an adequate economic contribution" (Pinchbeck 1930, 313).

Subsequent optimists have advanced a somewhat modified argument. Rather than liberating women from the burden of paid work, the benefit of industrialization was the opening up of the labor market to women. In the pre-industrial past, production was heavily dependent on strength, which disadvantaged women. This, plus domestic responsibilities, fostered a strong division of labor in which women did "women's work" and men did "men's work." Popular culture, religion, and the legal system provided evidence of the low status of women (Shorter 1976b, 1982; Thomas 1988, 537). Industrialization wrought change, to the advantage of women. Machinery reduced the need for physical strength, and medical advances reduced the number of pregnancies women needed to bear (Goode 1963; Fox-Genovese 1982, 21–22; Shorter 1982). Compared with agriculture and domestic service, industry offered women and children more jobs, and they were better paid (McKendrick 1974, 185). The logic of capitalism reduced inequalities. The demand for labor, particularly skilled labor, broke down gender barriers. Facing a more equitable labor market, women increased their bargaining power and status within the family; work and responsibilities were shared more equitably.

Williamson and Lindert (1983, 17) have used the ratio of women's hourly wage rates to those of unskilled men to argue that women's earning power relative to unskilled men did not decline between 1820 and 1850; it may have stayed the same or even advanced slightly. Critics of Williamson and Lindert argue that women's wages cannot be accurately measured, and one recent antagonist has suggested that a resolution to the Clark-Pinchbeck debate is impossible, given the lack of adequate data on female wages (Thomas 1988, 545). Further, critics have argued that declining participation rates for women in the formal labor market point to involuntary unemployment and falling living standards. Williamson and Lindert (1983, 19) thought such an argument "hard to sustain" because there was no institution that compelled employers to hire men in preference to women. But the patriarchal system of male headship in family households was exactly such an institution, forcing women involuntarily out of the paid workforce.

There is increasing qualitative evidence from parliamentary papers, the evidence of witnesses, detailed studies of household accounts, and newspapers that labor market segmentation increased and women's position in the paid labor market deteriorated, with the proportion of working-age females in the labor market falling rapidly between the 1820s and the 1890s (Humphries

1987, 1990; Richards 1974; Snell 1981). These changes held true for women in agriculture, handicraft, and the modern sector and are consistent with a patriarchal interpretation of job segmentation. This position has received support from Horrell and Humphries's (1992, 1995) statistical work on household budget data, which showed increased institutional and ideological obstacles to women working. There emerged both the patriarchal family where wives did not work and a sustaining ideology that women need not work. As need became a criterion in determining pay rates, the wage structure based on the individual earner bifurcated along gender lines, with a male breadwinning wage norm granted to men irrespective of conjugal status (Holley 1981; Land 1980; Seccombe 1986). Although the pattern was not uniform or continuous across occupational categories, by the mid-nineteenth century women's financial dependence on men had increased. Recently, Horrell and Humphries (1995) found an overall decline in the participation of married women in the labor force and a declining relative contribution of women's earnings to those of their husbands in family income between 1795 and the mid-nineteenth century.

Using data on female height, combined with information on mortality and life expectancy, we provide an evaluation of women's standard of living in the United Kingdom since 1780 that supplements and extends the existing literature.

6.3   The Data

Our data are derived from three separate sources, all of which relate to women either accused of or found guilty of criminal offences between 1817 and 1876. The sources are the indents of 2,926 English-born and 3,370 Irish-born female convicts transported between 1826 and 1840 from the United Kingdom to the penal colony of New South Wales ("convict data"), registers of 20,519 female prisoners admitted to Newgate prison in London between 1817 and 1860 ("Newgate prisoner data"), and a register containing details of 3,552 female habitual criminals compiled by Scotland Yard in 1877 ("criminal data"). These three sources contain information on the height of over 30,000 women, and this provides for women equivalent data sources to the Description Books of the army and Royal Marine recruits used by Floud et al. (1990) to assess the trend in male heights. It is unlikely that any other extant data set of this size is available for the study of the long-term trend in the height of women in Britain.

Detailed tests of the representativeness of our data are presented in the data appendix. Here we will outline the key points and identify important differences in the quality of data derived from the three sources. The minimum requirement for inclusion in our sample was that data exist on the age, height, and date of measurement of the female. The convict indents provide the richest set of data, with details of name, age, education, religion, marital status, number of children, place of birth, up to four occupations, crime, place of trial, date, sentence, and prior convictions, as well as height. The Newgate registers report information on name, age, height, place of birth, and marital status, together with crime and sentence, but do not give occupational information for females. The register of habitual criminals contains details of crime and sentence, place of imprisonment (but not place of birth), age, occupation, height, color of hair and eyes, complexion, and distinguishing features such as scars and tattoos.

All three sources displayed height distributions that were normally distributed and free of truncation bias, a problem that typically infects army records due to minimum height standards for recruits. All three sources were dominated by women aged 30 or below. This, however, allows us to estimate terminal height, since adult height was attained between 21 and 23 years of age. To avoid biases due to shrinkage in height of older women, all women older than 49 years were excluded from our analysis.

For the convict data, a comparison of occupational structure was made with the 1841 census, which showed that 78 percent of English female convicts and 83 percent of English women workers were in the skilled and semiskilled categories. The literacy of these English and Irish female convicts was very similar to that of the home populations. No occupations were recorded for female Newgate prisoners, but among the habitual criminals there appears to have been a bias toward unskilled occupations, with 60 percent of male habitual criminals and 80 percent of females recorded as semiskilled or unskilled, compared with 41 percent of males in the 1841 census. This suggests that female habitual criminals were drawn from the lower half of the occupational distribution.

There is no evidence, however, that the women in any of these three data sets represented a distinct "criminal class." Among the habitual criminals, only 8.7 percent of the women had more than two previous convictions, and the majority were for petty theft, resulting in prison sentences of just a few months. The majority of Newgate female prisoners were also awaiting trial for alleged crimes of petty theft, but over 40 percent had their cases dismissed or were found not guilty. Among the convicts, over 60 percent of females were first offenders, and their crimes were almost entirely against property, involving theft of money or items for immediate consumption—clothes, cloth, household goods (e.g., pots, candles, and pans), bedding, and foodstuffs accounted for nearly three-fifths of the items stolen.

The case for the convicts, prisoners, and criminals as ordinary working-class men and women also gains support from recent work by historians of British crime who reject the idea of a separate nineteenth-century criminal or dangerous class, born and bred to a life of crime and operating as organized gangs (Beattie 1975; Emsley 1987; Jones 1982; Philips 1977; Rudé 1985). While not "honest men and women," British and Irish criminals were mainly working people who supplemented their incomes by theft. We are confident, therefore, that there are no obvious selection biases that would make the heights of females included in our three data sets unrepresentative of the heights of the working-class female population in Britain and Ireland.

6.4   Height, Living Standards, and Industrialization

Height-by-age, change in height between successive ages (velocity or rate of growth), age at which final height is reached, and final adult height are reliable indexes of a country's health and nutrition (Eveleth and Tanner 1976, 1; Fogel et al. 1983). Anthropologists, biologists, and nutritionists have found each of these measures of stature to be sensitive indicators of nutritional inputs and environmental impacts during the growing years. The health and the average nutritional status of a country's citizens are a good guide to its standard of living. In a sample of developed and underdeveloped countries, average height was found to be highly correlated with the logarithm of per capita income, which suggests that factors correlated with poverty such as poor diet, hard work, and poor medical care are major sources of nutritional deprivation and slow growth (Steckel 1986, 1–7).

Height data, used in conjunction with information on wages, mortality, and morbidity, offer a new way of assessing U.K. living standards. Poor nutrition, revealed during wartime shortages, may slow growth, and disease may also retard growth by impeding the absorption of nutrients and diverting nutrition to combat infection. Malnutrition and illness may interact to produce an effect on height larger than the separate effects of each in isolation (Scrimshaw 1975, 22). Catch-up growth (where velocity exceeds the average rate for a given chronological age) may follow brief periods of malnutrition, but if environmental conditions are unsatisfactory, growth may resume at no more than the normal rate. Prolonged but moderate malnutrition tends to delay and diminish the adolescent growth spurt and postpone the age at which adult height is attained. Malnutrition that is severe and chronic may substantially erode the typical growth pattern and result in permanent stunting (Steckel 1986, 1992).

Height provides a net rather than a gross measure of nutrition and depends on the nutrition available for physical growth after claims made by body maintenance. Clearly, the economic historian must investigate work intensity, the disease environment, and the state of public health, as well as nutritional inputs, if the growth spurt and average heights are going to be used to proxy changes in female living standards in the past. This paper deals with the height of birth cohorts because access to food, environmental disadvantages, and work intensities affected women during their growing years from birth to attained final height at age 21. Unfortunately, it is not possible to determine precisely when, during their growing years, women were affected by changes in their living standards, but environmental factors predominate. While genes are important determinants of individual height, studies of genetically similar and dissimilar populations under various environmental conditions show that differences in average heights across most populations are due to environmental, not genetic, factors (Steckel 1992, 16).

In this paper, Ireland is treated as a control economy, largely unaffected by the industrial transformation taking place in England. Of course, Ireland was not simply England without an industrial revolution. There were strong interdependencies between the eastern counties of Ireland and Britain, and Belfast's industrialization was as "dramatic and thoroughgoing as anything happening in Preston or Middlesborough" (Ó Gráda 1988, 25–27). Yet the differences between the two economies overshadow the similarities, leading Mokyr and Ó Gráda (1988, 216) to declare that Ireland experienced nothing like an industrial revolution. The distribution of resources in the preindustrial Irish family resulted in an unusually tall population. From a sample of Irish recruits into the East India Company army, Mokyr and Ó Gráda (1988, 227–28; 1990, 11) discovered that Irish recruits born around 1810 were taller than their counterparts in England, although England was a much richer economy.

The height advantage of the poor preindustrial Irish over the richer industrializing English is confirmed by data on the height of army recruits in other preindustrial economies. Komlos (1989, 1993) was the first to argue that the positive correlation between height and per capita income for market economies was not always true for preindustrial economies. He found that the populations of Lower Austria and Bohemia, the most economically developed regions of the Habsburg empire, were generally the shortest, while those of Hungary and Galicia, the least developed provinces, were taller (Komlos 1989, 96–97). In the American Civil War, Union troops from less developed Kentucky and Tennessee were the tallest (177.0 cm) followed by the other slave states and the Midwest (at approximately 174.5 cm), while troops from the more developed New England (173.5 cm) and the Middle Atlantic states (172.7 cm) were shortest (Gould 1869, 123). Among Southern whites who signed amnesty oaths during the 1860s, those from the interior states of Kentucky, Tennessee, Missouri, and Arkansas tended to be 0.75–1.8 cm taller than residents from the more densely settled lower coastal states. A similar but less pronounced regional pattern existed among ex-slave recruits (Margo and Steckel 1992). In Sweden in the mid-nineteenth century, soldiers from the less densely settled regions (north and east) were 3.0–5.0 cm taller than those from the more densely settled western areas (Sandberg and Steckel 1988). Japanese soldiers of the late nineteenth century born in the outlying prefectures such as Tottori and Iwate were 3.0–4.0 cm taller than recruits from the wealthier, more central and developed regions (Shay 1986). It is exactly in this connection between heights in preindustrial economies and heights in economies undergoing industrialization that our Irish-English height comparisons are particularly useful in measuring the changing living standards of women.

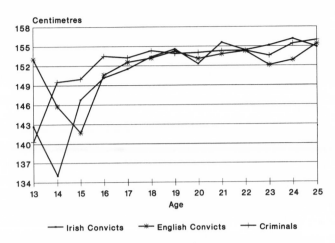

Fig. 6.1   Female convict and criminal growth spurts
Sources: Convict Indents and Alphabetical Register of Habitual Criminals.

6.5   Female Heights and Living Standards in Early and Late Industrialization

6.5.1   Growth Spurts of Early Industrial Revolution Women

Average height-by-age and the timing and extent of the adolescent growth spurt are sensitive both to nutritional factors and to the external environment, providing a good indicator of living standards experienced by women. While sample sizes were small before age 15, figures 6.1 and 6.2 indicate that English and Irish convict women, Newgate women, and English criminal women experienced a growth spurt that began around age 14 and lasted until age 16.5 or 17.5. The growth spurt for girls living through the industrial revolution period began later, and continued about four years longer, than that for well-nourished girls today, whose spurt begins about age 10.5 and continues until age 13 (Tanner 1962, 1). The delayed and much longer spurt experienced by the females was also typical of the Irish and English males, who spurted between ages 14 and 15 (one year later than well-nourished children today) and continued to grow until about age 23, nearly three years longer than boys born today. The later and longer spurt suggests that an "insult" due to insufficient food intake or increased work effort or adverse environmental conditions or some combination of all three was general, affecting males and females and Irish and English alike and extending over the whole 1785–1857 period.

Recently, Jackson (1996) has criticized Nicholas and Oxley's (1993) estimates of the growth profile of rural-born convict women, arguing that women continued to grow into their late 20s, not reaching their terminal height until age 26–30 years. Jackson's criticism misinterprets the evidence on the growth

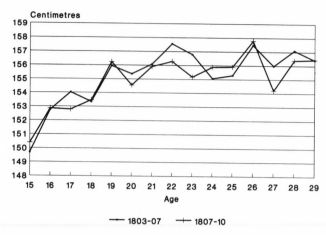

Fig. 6.2   Newgate female prisoner growth spurts, born 1803–7 and 1807–10
Source: Newgate Prison Registers.

spurt, confusing period effect and age effect (Nicholas and Oxley 1996). Unlike the military recruitment data, where soldiers were measured each year, 21-year-old women born in 1815 were measured in 1836 and 22-year-old women born in 1815 were measured in 1837. The organization of the female height data means that older women are overrepresented in the earlier periods and younger women are overrepresented in later years. Inclusion of women who were still growing would provide a downward bias to the average height, creating an artificial decline in heights. To overcome this problem, we estimate the height-by-age profiles for women born within a few years of each other to minimize any period effects. The shorter the time period in years, the less the period effect, but the fewer the number of observations. Figure 6.2 presents height-by-age profiles for urban and rural women born in the years 1803–7 and 1807–10 and shows that terminal height was attained by age 21, and certainly by age 23. The number of observations are usually more than 50 for each age, and over 80 observations for each age up to 23. A number of unreported height-by-age profiles for different time periods were constructed, all pointing to a terminal height attained by age 21–23.

6.5.2   Convict Women's Living Standards during Early Industrialization, 1790–1815

The delayed growth spurt affected women and men, English and Irish alike, but the effect was not equal. English-born women were shorter than Irish-born women, resulting in a statistically significant difference in terminal heights shown in table 6.1. Urban-born English females were over 1 cm shorter than rural-born English girls during their growth spurt and were over 2 cm shorter by age 23. There was, however, no significant difference in the heights of urban- and rural-born Irish women during their growth spurt or in their termi-

Table 6.1   **Terminal Height and *t*-Test Differences in Terminal Heights of English and Irish Workers**

Worker Type	English Rural	English Urban	Irish Rural	Irish Urban
Females				
Height (cm)	156.6	154.3	155.7	155.3
English rural		10.71*	5.71*	4.18*
English urban			8.44*	3.68*
Irish rural				0.73
Males				
Height (cm)	167.5	166.2	167.9	167.2
English rural		7.12*	1.94	1.39
English urban			8.16*	3.57*
Irish rural				1.09

Source: Convict Indents.
*Significant at the 5 percent level.

nal heights reported in table 6.1. All these women, however, were very short compared to modern "Western" standards—between the 6th and the 12th percentiles of a modern height standard (Steckel 1995, 10).

What are the causes of these height differentials between English rural-born and urban-born women? The English female urban-born height disadvantage also applies to English males in table 6.1. The English urban-rural height differential, and its absence in Ireland, is partly explained by environmental factors. Being born in a town implied different conditions depending on whether a woman or man was born in England or Ireland. Shielded from the full force of the urban transformation occurring in England, those born in Irish towns, except Dublin, escaped many of the worst features of overcrowding, poor housing, and inadequate public health typical of the burgeoning towns in industrializing England. The smaller size of Irish towns and their closer links to the countryside also meant that the urban Irish had better access to food supplies than women workers in London or Manchester.

But not all the urban-rural height differences in England are due to environmental factors. First, as shown below, female heights fall relative to male heights, and rural-born female heights fall relative to urban-born female heights. Second, the English urban-rural female height differential (2.3 cm) in table 6.1 was nearly twice that of the urban-rural male differential. These data focus attention on the access to food and nutrients by women in England.

Our evidence shows that the average height of rural-born English women fell further, and more rapidly, than the average height of urban-born women in the 25 years after 1795. Figure 6.3 shows that from a peak of 157.0 cm in 1800, the height of birth cohorts born in rural locations fell to just under 155 cm by 1815. Urban-born English women experienced a similar, if less dramatic, decline in height of about 1.3 cm over this same period. By contrast, the height

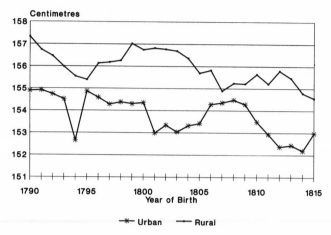

Fig. 6.3   English female convict heights, born 1790–1815, five-year moving averages
Source: Convict Indents.

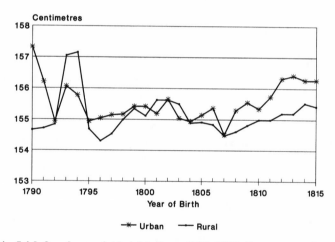

Fig. 6.4   Irish female convict heights, born 1790–1815, five-year moving averages
Source: Convict Indents.

of rural-born male cohorts fell by only 0.6 cm in the same period (Nicholas and Oxley 1993).

The deteriorating living standards of English women contrasted with the increasing heights of Irish women in figure 6.4. From the late 1790s the average height of Irish women increased, with the height of urban Irish women rising 1.3 cm, about twice the rate of that of rural Irish women. The English deterioration is evident in figure 6.5, which shows a widening gap between English rural-born women and Irish rural-born women.

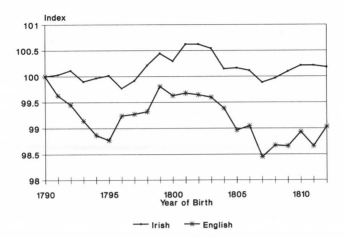

Fig. 6.5 English and Irish rural female heights, index based on five-year moving average: 1790 = 100
Source: Convict Indents.

6.5.3 The Family Economy

The family is an economic and social unit in which controlling family members determine the allocation of household resources vital to their children's future standard of living. Food and schooling are two resources allocated within families that are fundamental to the physical and human capital development of children. Well-fed men and women earn higher incomes than poorly fed workers since they can work longer hours at harder tasks and can better resist diseases that reduce work capacity. Parents allocate scarce nutrients and education between competing family members in order to maximize total household economic returns in the long run. The allocation of intrahousehold resources between children will, therefore, depend on gender differences in expected labor market outcomes.

Substantial empirical evidence from today's developing countries exists to support this model of intrahousehold resource allocation. Gender-specific differences in food allocation are linked to different labor market outcomes for women and men. We know that labor market returns to men and women diverge as developing economies shift from subsistence to market-based production. The higher economic value that families place on males vis-à-vis females is related to the greater ability of men to support parents in their old age, the higher labor force participation of boys and men, and the greater earning power of men (Sen and Sengupta 1983). This gender-based differential in expected labor market returns has led to a promale distribution of nutrients and education within the family in many developing countries (Behrman 1988).

The promale bias has been revealed in weight-by-age and height-by-age data, which show a systematic sex bias in malnutrition, with a higher nutrient deprivation for girls than boys (Sen and Sengupta 1983, 863). Survey and econometric estimation found that household members claimed extra food when their occupations required high levels of calories and paid work took place outside the home. During industrialization it was males who increasingly found outside work and males who were hired for labor-intensive tasks (Sen 1990, 62–64; Pitt, Rosenzweig, and Hassan 1990, 1139–41). Those households that enhanced the health endowment of males had higher incomes (Pitt et al. 1990, 1153). The promale discrimination in the allocation of food was greatest in a sample of Indian and Pakistani villages with the best overall nutritional record. It was in these better fed villages that market forces and land reform had proceeded furthest and that employment opportunities for women had declined most (Sen and Sengupta 1983, 863). This contemporary evidence confirms that height data provides a reliable measure of the changing status and living standards of women during industrialization.

6.5.4   Access to Intrahousehold Resources

There is considerable evidence of a promale allocation of food within industrial revolution families. Oddy (1976, 220) reported that women and children ate less meat than men, and that women acquiesced because "the husband wins the bread and must have the best food." In the nineteenth century, Charles Booth noted the same fact and Shorter (1976a, 54–55; 1982, 21) and Humphries (1981) argued that women got smaller proportions of everything because men worked harder. Oren (1974) reviewed later nineteenth-century sources to conclude that wives restricted their own and their children's nutrition in periods of economic want in order to maintain their husbands' standard of living. These decisions about the care and feeding of the family and the preferential allocation of food remained the wife's responsibility regardless of the degree of involvement or detachment of the husband (Ittmann 1995, 227). Ross (1993, 30–39) further suggested that this "breadwinner effect" in the distribution of food—especially meat—came to be a cultural norm that sanctioned an unequal distribution of resources to male heads of household and to fully employed elder sons even in households with adequate incomes. This allocative asymmetry did not apply just to food. In a systematic analysis of family budgets since the 1840s, Wall (1994, 328–30) showed that average expenditure on clothing for the male head of household exceeded that for his wife by between 12 and 15 percent, a bias that has been dramatically reversed since the midtwentieth century.

Different work requirements and unequal access to food underpin the economic model of the maximizing family household where "parents controlled resources vital to their children's future standard of living" (Anderson 1980, 51; Pahl 1985, 20–21). Allocation of nutrients was determined by expected differential labor market returns on parental investments in boys and girls. It was control over their children's inheritance and their immediate employment opportunities that consolidated parents' power over intrahousehold resources. Such power meant that working children frequently turned over their wages to parents who determined how the family used this additional income. Even where parents did not directly control employment, by distributing food inputs within the household they influenced their children's job prospects since strength determined opportunities for manual work (Anderson 1971).

Girls were likely to have been affected by discrimination in food allocation at the critical periods in their growth profile. A Bangladesh study showed a large and statistically significant difference in the average calories allocated to boys over age 12 and under age 6 compared to girls, while girls and boys between ages 7 and 12 received similar allocations of calories (Pitt et al. 1990, 1140). We hypothesize that a similar age effect operated in industrializing England. Children in the middle age group took on a multitude of largely home-based tasks, which offered employment to girls as much as to boys. After about age 12 or 13 boys took on different work than girls, increasingly participating in high-energy intensive activities outside the household. The timing of the unequal allocation of calories occurred during the two most sensitive growth periods for the human body, resulting in maximum negative impact on women's height and health.

All the historical evidence points to declining labor market opportunities for English girls in the older age group, reinforcing our household model of intergender resource allocation that disadvantaged women (see Richards 1974; Thomas 1988; Berg 1988; Rose 1986). In preindustrial and agricultural economies, gender inequalities were less pronounced than in modernizing societies (Ehrenreich and English 1979, 7; Smock 1977, 418; Sen 1990, 62–63). Women were partners with men, both at home (as managers of children and household financial resources) and in outside work and paid employment. Protoindustrialization and industrialization worsened the economic and social position of women and children, limiting their employment opportunities, restricting the range of jobs open to them, and segmenting them into unskilled work with low pay. These gender divisions occurred mainly in the agricultural sector, but also to a lesser extent in manufacturing, transforming the traditional role of women and children in the labor market and the household.

There is considerable qualitative evidence that work relations between men and women were changing during early industrialization in England. In agriculture, shifts from livestock to grain production intensified the gender specialization of agricultural work, restricting the participation of women in the agricultural workforce; they went into low-paid and unskilled summer and spring work, such as picking stones and clearing ground (Snell 1985, 51–62; 1981, 411–23). The shift to heavier technology associated with grain harvesting further restricted women to nonharvest work (Roberts 1979). The sexual division of labor in agriculture was partly a consequence of the expansion of grain production and new technology, but also a result of discrimination as male agricultural workers opposed the employment of females (Snell 1985, 61; 1981, 433). From 1780, at least in the east, restricted job opportunities for women and children saw female wage rates decline (Snell 1985, 59; Pahl 1984,

37). The gender division of labor had important implications for household income: while males may have experienced more stable employment in well-paid harvest work, the loss of female earnings impacted negatively on family income. At the same time, enclosures and the loss of common rights led to a change in the economic role of women and children, the primary exploiters of the commons. The elimination of sources of family income not deriving from wages, such as gleaning, gathering and scavenging, and tending pigs and cows, all traditionally "women's work," increased the household's dependency on wages and wage earners (Snell 1985, 62; Humphries 1990, 39–41). The loss of paid employment opportunities meant that women went into low-paid "female jobs" that devalued and undervalued the unpaid household work undertaken by them. Anderson argued that the newly emerging definition of men as the family wage earners legitimized the irregular employment and below subsistence wages for female agricultural workers (Anderson 1980, 83).

Loss of common rights made women and children more available for domestic, protoindustrial, and industrial work, but even here the range of opportunity for women was reduced, and they were obliged to take the lowest paid and worst of jobs in the "sweated" trades (Humphries 1990, 41). The textile factory, which did increase the job opportunities for women and children, was not the "typical" form of female employment (McKendrick 1974, 153). Most women worked as domestic servants, laundry workers, charwomen, and agricultural laborers, and those women and children employed in producing textiles, clothing, boots and shoes, nails, and metal goods usually worked in their own homes or in small workshops. Slop or sweated workers were disadvantaged by the industrial revolution, and those urban trades employing women involved irregular employment, long hours, and poor pay. Women now rarely entered into the "mysteries" of the trade and were only infrequently employed in trades that required formal apprenticeship. The industrial revolution limited the employment chances of women and children, creating a secondary labor market segmented by gender both in agriculture and in manufacture. This qualitative evidence on market exclusion, segmentation, and discrimination against women suggests that families adopted the promale allocation of household nutrients in an attempt to maximize long-run income.

Might not families have invested in their daughters' potential as marriage partners, offsetting or attenuating the labor market effects that discriminated against women? It is not clear that tall and healthy girls found marriage partners more easily than other women since selection depended mainly on other qualitative factors. Even if healthier and more productive girls found marriage partners more easily, the gains from having a healthier and stronger female worker were captured by the husband or the husband's family, at least in the absence of a dowry paid by the prospective husband to the woman's family. Dowries were not normally paid in the British working classes.

Did the distribution of other intrahousehold resources also discriminate against English women and girls? Education is an investment in human capital,

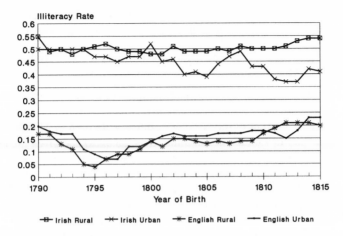

Fig. 6.6   Female education
Source: Convict Indents.

budgeted by households between family members, and relative to other inputs such as food, clothing, and housing. According to Burnett (1966, 22), what the English laboring family spent on bacon, beer, and white bread was spent by its Scottish counterpart on the education of its children. From a listing of the inhabitants of Cardington (Bedfordshire) in 1792, Schofield (1970, 265–66) found that boys typically attended school until age 11 while girls had only a one in three chance of schooling (Nicholas and Nicholas 1992; Mokyr and Ó Gráda 1988, 222–27). Illiterate societies are likely to be poor and slow growing, less able to adjust to structural change than literate ones. Literacy, of course, is valued in its own right: it releases people from ignorance and prejudice and also enhances their ability to find work and attain occupational and social advancement.

The convict indents contained information on whether each transportee could read and write, read only, or neither read nor write, allowing us to define literate individuals as those claiming the ability to read or to read and write. In figure 6.6, both rural- and urban-born English females experienced rising illiteracy from 1797 to 1814, while urban-born Irish females had declining illiteracy and rural Irish women experienced no significant change. This pattern of rising illiteracy among English female convicts is consistent with Schofield's parish register data. Although he discovered a declining trend in illiteracy for the whole period 1750–1840, for women born between 1803 and 1813 and marrying between 1828 and 1838, illiteracy rates, based on ability to sign parish marriage registers, rose (Schofield 1973, 445). The tendency for height and literacy to move together suggests that when households reduced their expenditure on food intake they also invested less in expensive schooling. Male illiteracy also rose after 1800, which provides additional evidence that declining English male and female stature may have been caused by financial stress on families, which also registered in lower investments in schooling.

6.5.5   Newgate Women's Living Standards during Early Industrialization, 1785–1815

The heights of Newgate women provide an alternative data source to the convict records for assessing women's living standards during the 1785–1815 period. Since 61 percent of the Newgate women were born in Middlesex (effectively that part of London north of the River Thames) and given the urban-rural height differential for convict women, the Newgate sample was divided into urban-born and rural-born women using Hunt's (1973) classification of urban and rural counties. There was an urban-rural height differential among 21–49-year-old Newgate prisoners, with urban-born prisoners (155.8 cm) 1.6 cm shorter than rural-born prisoners. This urban-rural height differential persisted when a higher terminal age (23 years) was used (155.9 vs. 157.3 cm) and when a subperiod (1803–13) was selected (156.2 vs. 157.0 cm). These urban-rural height differentials are consistent with the convict data above. However, the prisoners from the Newgate sample were taller than the convict women, particularly the urban born. Using Hunt's urban-rural classification, urban-born convict women were only 154.5 cm tall, over 1.3 cm shorter than Newgate prisoners. The height differential between rural convict (156.6 cm) and Newgate women (157.4 cm) was less than for urban born, 0.8 cm. The differences between the convict and Newgate women are probably due to different sample characteristics of the women, but the absence of information on occupations for the Newgate women precludes a direct test of this speculation. Nevertheless, compared with the convict men in table 6.1, Newgate women were about 10 cm shorter than their male counterparts.

The five-year moving average height profiles of the Newgate prisoners in figure 6.7 show that rural heights fell over 1 cm from about 157.7 cm in the 1785–97 period to a low point of 156.5 cm in 1810 before recovering in the last years of the Napoleonic Wars. This is unambiguous evidence of declining living standards during the early industrial revolution. Urban heights followed a different path. Falling between 1785 and 1797, urban heights rose about 1.4 cm from about 155 cm in 1797 to a peak of 156.4 cm in 1802 before stabilizing near their late 1780s level. The fall in the average height of women was confirmed by simple regression results of height against year of birth. Table 6.2 reports these results and shows that all the coefficients on the time variable are statistically significant. These Newgate height profiles confirm the convict evidence that rural living standards fell before 1815, providing additional support for women's unequal access to intrahousehold food resources.

The differences between the timing in the profiles of the urban-born convicts (fig. 6.3) and Newgate women (fig. 6.7) are principally due to the different definitions of urban and rural birthplace and the high proportion of Newgate prisoners from Middlesex. Figure 6.8 displays the profile of the Newgate

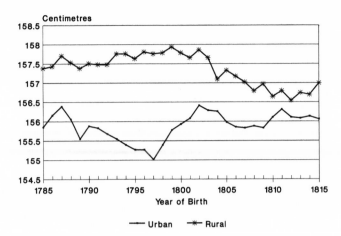

Fig. 6.7   Urban and rural Newgate female prisoner heights, 1785–1815, ages 23–49
Source: Newgate Prison Registers.

Table 6.2   **Regression Results on Heights of Rural-Born Newgate Female Prisoners, 1788–1815**

Variable	Age 21–49	Age 23–49	Age 26–49
Constant	88.17	91.73	87.86
	(7.30)*	(6.24)*	(13.71)*
Birth year	−0.02	−0.02	−0.01
	(−2.17)*	(−2.03)*	(−1.89)*
Adjusted R^2	0.0024	0.0022	0.0020
N	1,567	1,394	1,270

Source: Newgate Prison Registers.
Note: Numbers in parentheses are *t*-statistics.
*Significant at the 5 percent level.

women born in Middlesex, whose height fell until 1797 (154.2 cm), before rising to a peak of 155.9 cm in 1812. Also in figure 6.8 is the profile of urban-born Newgate women, excluding those born in Middlesex, which shows a different five-year moving average. After an improvement in height before 1803, women's heights fell over 2 cm from a peak of 158.7 cm in 1802 to a low of 156.6 cm in 1812. Non-Middlesex urban-born Newgate women suffered declining living standards after 1802, which is consistent with the experience of rural-born women.

6.5.6   Women's Living Standards 1815–57

Height data from the habitual criminal records and the Newgate prison records were joined to create a new data series on female heights in the 1815–57

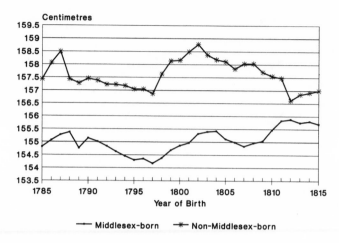

Fig. 6.8   Middlesex-born and urban non-Middlesex-born Newgate female prisoner heights, ages 23–49
Source: Newgate Prison Registers.

period. Since the criminal data only contain information on place of imprisonment, we have had to assume that county of imprisonment was county of birth in order to determine location for the pooled data. In the convict data, in which both place of birth and place of trial were recorded, 66 percent of convicts were tried in their county of birth (Nicholas and Shergold 1987a, 1987b), and in the Newgate data, 62 percent of female prisoners were born in and around London. We have no reason to believe that female habitual criminals exhibited a significantly different level of intercounty mobility. In figure 6.9, rural-born female heights rose in the immediate post–Napoleonic War period to a peak of 158.1 cm in 1823 before falling to a trough of 153.9 cm in 1853, with brief comebacks in 1832–35 and 1843–48. Urban-born heights followed a different profile, with heights stable at about 156 cm before declining in the 1840s. These profiles were repeated for women reaching terminal height at age 21. Most of the improvement in the rural heights of women in the 1820s in figure 6.9 was due to the Newgate women, whose height rose from 156.8 cm in 1816 to 158.8 cm in 1825.

Given the high proportion of women from London and the Home Counties (the counties closest to London, being Middlesex, Surrey, Sussex, Kent, and Essex) in the Newgate sample, we present profiles for women born in the Home Counties and the rest of England in figure 6.10. For Home County women, heights rose from a low of 155.6 cm in 1820 to a peak of 157.9 cm in 1838 then declined to their 1820s level by the early 1840s before falling rapidly after 1848. For women born outside the Home Counties, heights rose from 156.8 cm to 157.6 cm in the years before 1824, before these women experi-

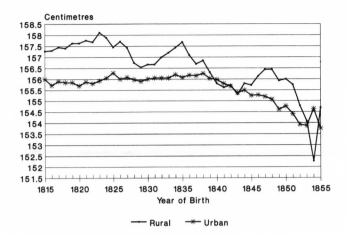

Fig. 6.9   Urban and rural female heights, 1815–55, ages 23–49
Sources: Newgate Prison Registers and *Alphabetical Register of Habitual Criminals.*

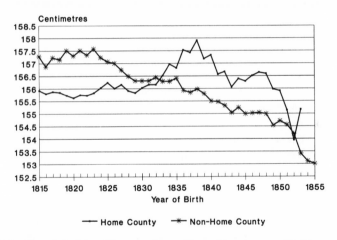

Fig. 6.10   Female heights, Home and non-Home County, ages 23–49
Sources: Newgate Prison Registers and *Alphabetical Register of Habitual Criminals.*

enced a continuous fall in living standards, with their heights falling to 155 cm in the late 1840s.

However, the locational information in this pooled data may contain biases because, as noted above, we suspect that in around one-third of the habitual criminal cases the county of birth does not correspond with the county of incarceration. Therefore, the criminal data are presented on their own in figure 6.11, simply in terms of male and female profiles. Between 1825 and 1835 female and male heights both rose, before falling together over the period 1834–55.

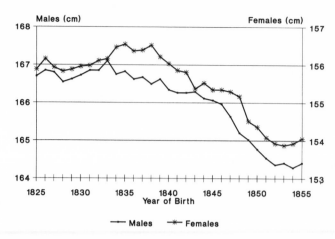

Fig. 6.11   Rural and urban male and female criminal heights, ages 19–49
Source: Alphabetical Register of Habitual Criminals.

From 1834 female heights declined 2.5 cm to a low point of 153.9 cm in 1853, with male heights falling almost 3 cm from 167.1 cm in 1833 to only 164.3 cm in 1856. There is no evidence that women's living standards suffered more than those of men in the post-1825 period. This is confirmed by an analysis of female and male criminal data grouped by urban and rural place of incarceration; in both cases the declining height trajectories for females closely follow those for males.

The evidence that female heights moved roughly in unison with male heights produces a very different reading of the course of women's living standards from that suggested in the early industrial revolution period. After 1825 working-class women experienced a substantial deterioration in nutritional status, although the fall began earlier and was greater for rural-born than for urban-born women. It is, however, a deterioration that is almost exactly matched by that found in the male criminal data. This decline begins roughly at the same time as that identified in the military recruit data by Floud et al. (1990). We now consider the occupational and regional composition of our samples.

6.6   Heights and Occupations

Heights may vary by occupation. This happens when women are apprenticed or encouraged to work in the same trades as their mothers and when strength is important for the job, channeling tall women into certain occupations. To the extent that intergenerational correlations exist for occupations of mother and daughters, then income, wealth, housing, and work conditions of parents impact directly on the height of children.

Table 6.3   **Regression Model for Composition Effects by Occupation for English Female Convicts**

Variable	Rural Age 21+ Years	Urban Age 21+ Years
Unskilled rural	0.63	0.62
	(1.81)	(1.00)
Manufacturing and transport	−0.16	0.24
	(−6.43)	(0.79)
Domestic service	0.16	0.04
	(0.58)	(0.19)
Birth 1795–99	−0.17	0.03
	(−0.51)	(0.08)
Birth 1800–1804	−0.004	−0.10
	(−0.14)	(−0.34)
Birth 1805–9	0.10	0.07
	(0.36)	(0.24)
Birth 1810–14	−0.47	−0.30
	(−1.83)	(−1.08)
Birth 1815+	0.17	−0.25
	(0.53)	(−0.75)
Constant	61.55	60.69
	(200.33)	(219.59)
R^2	0.02	0.01
D-W	2.04	1.89
N	767	747

Source: Convict Indents.
Note: Numbers in parentheses are *t*-statistics.

To test this hypothesis, regressions were run on height allowing for occupation and birth by quinquennia. For convict women occupational dummy variables were constructed for four broad occupational groups: rural unskilled, manufacturing and transport, domestic service, and the excluded category of all other occupations (unskilled urban, professional and dealing, construction and building, and public service). To test for period effects, we created dummy variables for quinquennia, excluding the pre-1795 period. Since the height profiles in figures 6.3 and 6.4 showed different trends for the same quinquennium in the heights of rural and urban women, separate regressions were run for the rural and urban born. The regressions in tables 6.3 and 6.4 show that composition effects by occupations were important only for rural Irish women. Irish females who worked in rural unskilled and domestic service jobs were 0.8 cm (0.32 inches) taller than the excluded group. These jobs required extra strength and endurance, and there is evidence of some self-selection in terms of stature by Irish rural women who sought unskilled and domestic employment. Since employment in domestic service (especially as general servant, chambermaid, laundress, and kitchenhand) and rural unskilled jobs (dairyhand and farm servant) accounted for the overwhelming number of opportunities open to rural Irish females, there is little evidence that there were significant shifts across

Table 6.4   Regression Model for Composition Effects by Occupation for Irish Female Convicts

Variable	Rural Age 21+ Years	Urban Age 21+ Years
Unskilled rural	0.32	0.03
	(2.24)	(0.06)
Manufacturing and transport	−0.07	−0.69
	(−0.34)	(−1.11)
Domestic service	0.31	−0.21
	(2.53)	(−0.50)
Birth 1795−99	−0.004	0.48
	(−0.28)	(0.89)
Birth 1800–1804	−0.14	0.49
	(−0.94)	(0.95)
Birth 1805–9	0.05	0.59
	(0.03)	(1.18)
Birth 1810–14	0.11	1.02
	(0.74)	(2.22)
Birth 1815+	−0.17	0.24
	(−1.05)	(0.51)
Constant	61.02	60.73
	(425.13)	(113.22)
R^2	0.002	0.03
D-W	1.88	1.99
N	2,528	249

Source: Convict Indents.
Note: Numbers in parentheses are *t*-statistics.

occupational categories. Therefore, the height profiles of Irish rural females in figure 6.4 were not artifacts of changes in the occupational structure of the convict sample.

The regressions in table 6.3 also display the period effects that are evident in the quinquennial moving averages in figure 6.3. The fall in the average height of English cohorts after 1800 is clearly evident in the negative coefficients on the 1800–1804 and 1815+ dummies for urban-born women and the negative coefficients for the 1795–99, 1800–1804, and 1810–14 birth periods for rural English females. For example, English women born in rural locations in 1810–14 were 1.2 cm (0.47 inches) shorter than rural cohorts born before 1795. Further, the results in table 6.3 for each quinquennium are consistent with the movements in heights in figure 6.3. These regression results confirm falling heights and living standards for women born in England. The Irish quinquennial dummies in table 6.4 reflect the increasing heights of Irish females, both rural and urban born, which are also evident in figure 6.4.

For the criminal data, there exists information only on place of trial, but one partial test for urban-rural effects is to regress height on county of trial using Hunt's (1973) wage data to classify counties as rural or urban. Regression analysis in table 6.5 shows that urban conditions affected women tried in urban counties, who were shorter than those tried in rural counties, but not signifi-

Table 6.5   **Regression Model for Composition Effects by Location and Occupation for Female Habitual Criminals**

Variable	Coefficient
Semiskilled	0.033
	(0.16)
Unskilled	−0.389
	(−2.66)
Manufacturing	−0.653
	(−4.71)
Dealing	−0.290
	(−1.60)
Domestic service	−0.195
	(−1.41)
Location (1 = urban; 0 = rural)	−0.126
	(−1.24)
Born 1825–29	−0.252
	(−1.21)
Born 1830–34	−0.192
	(−1.01)
Born 1835–39	−0.070
	(−0.38)
Born 1840–44	−0.302
	(−1.71)
Born 1845–49	−0.511
	(−2.85)
Born 1850+	−0.918
	(−4.70)
Constant	62.27
	(274.73)
R^2	0.026
D-W	1.95
N	2,723

Source: Alphabetical Register of Habitual Criminals.
Note: Numbers in parentheses are *t*-statistics.

cantly so. The occupational dummies in table 6.5 show that unskilled workers and women working in manufacturing are significantly shorter than our reference group of skilled women born before 1825 working in all other industries except manufacturing, dealing, and domestic service. The year-of-birth dummies are negative for each five-year period, although significant only for the 1845–49 and 1850–55 birth periods. There is conclusive evidence that the height and well-being of women born after 1825 declined.

6.7   Heights and Regions

Historians agree that living standards varied by region, and that English and Irish diets differed in their nutritional input by geographical area. Regressing the final attained height by county, region, and urban-rural location provides a

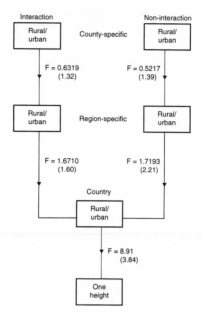

Fig. 6.12   Regional regression model of English female convicts

Source: Convict Indents.

Note: The critical value of the $F_{0.5}$ test is given in parentheses. When the F-value is less than the critical value the model is rejected. See text for further explanation and for a breakdown of the regions. Number of observations: English = 1,522.

powerful new test for uncovering regional patterns in female living standards. Figures 6.12 and 6.13 present a set of nested hypotheses regarding attained height and location. In the most general model, at the top of figure 6.12, final attained height depends on whether a woman was born in an urban or rural part of a specific English county, while the model at the bottom predicts one height for all of England. Formally, the figure tests whether the coefficients on the additional variables in the more general models (but excluded from the less general models directly below) are significantly different from zero. If the coefficients in the more general model are not significant (i.e., the F-value is less than the critical value in brackets immediately beneath), the reader should proceed to the next, less general, model. When the F-value is greater than the critical value in brackets immediately beneath, the coefficients in the more general model are significant and should be accepted. The most general inter-action model on the left in figure 6.12, which predicts that female English heights depended on whether a woman was born in a rural or urban part of a particular English county, should be rejected. Similarly, the noninteraction model, which tests whether height depended on the county of birth and the urban-rural location of birth, can also be rejected. This is also true of the Irish models in figure 6.13. The absence of significant differences in height by indi-

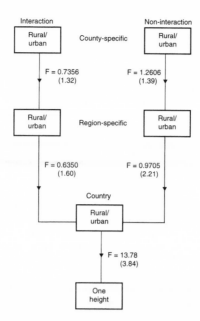

Fig. 6.13   Regional regression model of Irish female convicts
Source: Convict Indents.
Note: See note to fig. 6.12. Number of observations: Irish = 2,790.

vidual counties is not surprising since employment, industrial, and wage and cost regimes spanned county boundaries.

Counties were grouped together into specific regions based on Hunt's agricultural wage areas of England: London and the Home Counties, the south, midlands, the north and the fringe (including Cornwall, Devon, Cumberland, Westmoreland, and Northumberland), and regions used by Mokyr and Ó Gráda for Ireland (Dublin and east Ulster; west Ulster; Connacht, Kerry, and Clare; Munster excluding Kerry and Clare; and Leinster excluding Dublin; Hunt 1973; Mokyr and Ó Gráda 1990, 28). The preferred model for England (fig. 6.12) is the noninteraction regional model, where height depended on whether a woman was born in a particular region and whether the location was rural or urban. For Ireland (fig. 6.13), the regional models were not significant. Irish female heights depended on whether a woman was born in a rural or urban location.

The regression models uncovered regional patterns in English women's living standards. Rural-born women in the north and south were the tallest in our sample, while those born in the Home Counties were the shortest. The urban pattern was slightly different. Those born in the south, midlands, and fringe were the tallest, with the towns and cities of the north and London producing the shortest women. This general pattern, particularly the disadvantageous position of Londoners, is similar to that found by Floud et al. (1990, 200–202) for male military recruits. These data support the view that urban disamenities (poor housing and disease environment), together with regional differences in diet and workloads in the industrializing and urbanizing regions, reduced the living standards and quality of life for women. The absence of regional height differences for Irish women is consistent with Mokyr's dual economy hypothesis that the cash and the subsistence economy were intertwined and mutually dependent rather than being two geographically separate sectors (Mokyr 1983, 20). If the subsistence and cash economies were continuous, living alongside each other, then urban-rural differences, not regional differences, would have had the most important effect on Irish women's stature.

6.8   Heights and Mortality

The substantial decline in both female and male heights in the 1840s revealed by the criminal data indicates that workers in this period were subjected to a substantial nutritional insult. This finding is consistent with a similar decline in the military height data of Floud et al. (1990) and with historical interpretations of the "hungry forties." This decade saw a surge in working-class political organization in the Chartist movement, which was in part a response to economic distress. Yet the most recent assessment of trends in real wages indicates that this was a period of increasing prosperity. Crafts and Mills (1994) estimated a trend rate of growth in real wages of 1.2 percent per annum between 1813 and 1903 and found that the cost-of-living real wage rose over the decade of the 1840s as a whole, with only 1847 exhibiting substantial real wage reductions as a result of short-run price changes.

One way to resolve or reconcile these different findings is to examine a further indicator of well-being—mortality experience. Mortality data is available in detail only from 1841 (vital registration in England and Wales began in 1837), so it is not possible to compare mortality and height trends for the early nineteenth century. For the period from 1841, however, the mortality data are instructive. Floud et al. (1990, 314) argued from the heights of male recruits that "the fall in mortality in late nineteenth century England and Wales follows almost exactly the pattern that we would expect from the evidence of nutritional status."

Figure 6.14 presents mortality rates for age ranges up to 19 years for males and females separately. Three points should be noted. First, the rise and decline in mortality rates for all three age groups (5–9, 10–14, and 15–19) and for both males and females over the period 1841–55 corresponds with the decline and slight recovery in both male and female criminal heights for individuals born in this period. The coincidence of the mortality peak in 1846–50 for all three age groups together with the negative and significant coefficients for females born in 1845–49 shown in table 6.5 suggests that the dominant influence is a period rather than a cohort effect. However, the absence of mortality data for

Deaths per 1000

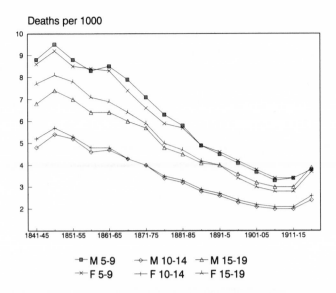

-■- M 5-9   -◇- M 10-14   -△- M 15-19
-✕- F 5-9   -+- F 10-14   -▲- F 15-19

Fig. 6.14   Child and juvenile death rates, England 1841–1920
Source: Case et al. (1962).

the pre-1841 period means that we cannot determine whether the child mortality peak in 1845–49 is a short-run deviation from a downward trend or a significant break in trend.

Second, this decline in child mortality is quite different from the pattern of infant mortality, which remained high to the end of the century. This divergence between infant and child mortality rates is important and may give an insight into the determinants of nineteenth-century height profiles. Szreter (1988) has challenged McKeown's (1976) argument that the major reason for the pre-1901 mortality decline is the reduction in incidence of airborne disease, and that the only generic explanation for this must be a general rise in resistance to infection due to improved nutrition and living standards.

Szreter suggests that the decline in death rates from the major food- and water-borne disease categories (typhoid/typhus and cholera/diarrhea) "would between them be responsible for at least half as much again, and perhaps almost twice the absolute quantity of mortality reduction during the nineteenth century as that attributable to the airborne combination of t.b. and the bronchitis group." Infants were particularly susceptible to food-borne diarrheal diseases, while children were proportionately more at risk from water-borne enteric diseases. An improvement in the urban environment from midcentury, and particularly the construction of water supply and sewerage systems during the "sanitary revival" from the mid-1860s, would have reduced the incidence of enteric diseases among children. A decline in infant diseases, on the other hand, required a more specific improvement in the working-class domestic environment, which itself required a reduction in overcrowding brought about by family limitation and by the implementation of minimum housing regulations from the 1890s.

If Szreter's interpretation of the mortality data is correct (and it has not gone unchallenged—see Guha 1994), it suggests that a deterioration and subsequent improvement in environmental conditions, rather than a deterioration and then improvement in nutrition, is the primary explanation for the nineteenth-century child mortality trends. Since we know that repeated infections retard growth, we would expect this environmental pattern to produce lower final adult heights in the population that experienced the worst childhood environmental conditions, and we would expect males and females to be affected equally. If, on the other hand, the decline in criminal heights was a result of an economically determined reduction in nutritional intake (i.e., reduced real wage), then we would expect to see a bias against females because of their lower earning potential. The lower adult heights achieved by both male and female criminals born in the 1840s and early 1850s is consistent with the environmental interpretation of the mortality decline.

There is, however, a third point of interest in these mortality data. Although the male and female age-specific mortality rates in figure 6.14 track each other fairly closely, there is an important change over time in the male-female mortality gap. Females aged 10–14 have slightly higher age-specific death rates than males over the period 1841–65, and females aged 15–19 have substantially higher death rates than males aged 15–19 in the period 1841–65, an excess mortality that is not eliminated until 1891–95. This is of some significance since in modern developed societies females are found to have a "natural" mortality advantage over males in each and every age group. However, this "natural" advantage is not universal; in some developing countries where women have limited autonomy and restricted access to economic opportunity, they also experience excess mortality, at least up to their mid-30s (Johansson 1991).

The proximate cause of the excess mortality of young females in early Victorian Britain was tuberculosis, and this was to a large degree a disease of poverty (Johansson 1977). The elimination of the female excess mortality gap from the 1860s does, therefore, suggest that females enjoyed greater benefits from increases in real incomes and economic opportunity in the mid-Victorian period, while the similar downward trend for both males and females indicates that they benefited equally from environmental improvements.

Humphries (1991) further investigated excess female mortality by both county and town in England in the 1840s and concluded that it was affected by the economic environment, but in a complex way. She found that predominantly agricultural counties were hostile to female life chances, as were many towns that were organized around centralized factory production, but the underlying economic rationale was different. In rural areas it was the absence of productive opportunities for women in increasingly capitalist agriculture that adversely affected their life chances, whereas in the factory towns it was the excessive physical demands and harsh environment of the workplace that took its toll. This analysis of excess female mortality is fully consistent with the height data reported in section 6.5, which sees a decline in rural female heights relative to urban heights up to 1840 (figs. 6.7 and 6.9), and a decline in non–Home County heights (which include northern industrial birthplaces) relative to Home County heights (fig. 6.10).

6.9 Conclusion

This analysis of convict and criminal height data for birthdates 1790 to 1857, and of mortality data from 1841 to 1920, has allowed a detailed examination of female living standards in England. We have been able to look at three separate elements of the height data—the *gap* between male and female heights, the *level* of female heights for women born in different places, and the *trend* in female heights over time. The gap between male and female heights in Britain appears to widen over the period up to the end of the Napoleonic Wars, but thereafter the height trajectories move in parallel (fig. 6.11). This suggests that up to 1815 female height profiles are strongly influenced by factors endogenous to the household economy. The very low overall level of household income made it essential to distribute resources in a way that maximized household utility, and this implied a bias against female infants and children.

There are important intrasample variations in the level of female height that are related to location and occupation. Rural-born women in England are consistently taller than urban-born women up to 1840 (figs. 6.3, 6.7, and 6.9), and the absence of this urban-rural height gap in Ireland (fig. 6.4) is broadly indicative of urban disamenities in England. Within the urban- and rural-born groups, there were significant regional effects, with rural-born women in the Home Counties and urban-born women in London and in northern industrial towns being the shortest groups. Employment in manufacturing had a significant negative impact on the height of English women, but not on Irish women (tables 6.3–6.5).

These locational and occupational differences change over the medium to long term. Female rural heights decline relative to urban up to 1840, and non–Home County heights decline whereas Middlesex/Home County heights rise from 1797 to 1835 (figs. 6.8 and 6.10). All heights fall in the 1840s, and by 1850 regional differences have largely disappeared. These differences in levels and trends indicate that rural-born women experienced declining relative living standards in the first half of the nineteenth century, but that Middlesex/Home County women enjoyed improvements in relative welfare despite living in a crowded urban environment. When supplemented by evidence on excess female mortality, these findings are indicative of declining economic opportunities for women in English agriculture after the Napoleonic War enclosures, and of increasing economic opportunities in urban areas, particularly in the metropolitan economy, which had very little large-scale factory employment.

However, the similarity between male and female height trends and the greater uniformity of the male-female height gap in the post-1825 period (fig. 6.11), even for people living in rural areas, is consistent with an increase in real wages from the second decade of the nineteenth century that permitted a more equitable distribution of resources between male and female children. Aggregate male and female height profiles come to follow similar trajectories, with the rate of deterioration in the 1840s and 1850s determined largely by environmental factors exogenous to the domestic economy.

Data Appendix

This appendix presents information on the content and representativeness of the three separate sources of data on female heights used in this paper.

Convict Data

Convict Women

Our first set of data, on the heights of women born between 1790 and 1815, is derived from the indents of 2,926 English-born and 3,370 Irish-born females transported from the United Kingdom to the penal colony of New South Wales between 1826 and 1840 (State Archives of New South Wales, *Convict Indents of Transported Prisoners,* 4/4003–4019; *Convict Indents of Transported Irish Prisoners,* 4/7076–7078).[1] The distributions of the heights of the female convicts were free of truncation bias. The absence of truncation in the lower tail and of overloading in the upper tail of the female height distributions indicates the absence of any twisting or distortion of the distributions. Jarque-Bera tests reported in table 6A.1 found that the female distributions were normal, or Gaussian, when measured to the half-inch or full inch. The Jarque-Bera (Jarque and Bera 1980) statistic tests whether the first four moments of the sample distribution are consistent with the normal distribution. There was evidence of heaping, the concentration of measurements at the whole or half-inch for the English females and rural Irish women. The height of females was measured to the quarter-inch, and the heaping was largely symmetrical around the half-inch. Heaping affects many studies of height, including modern ones, and while not a desirable quality is not uncommon (Fogel et al. 1983). Simulations suggest that heaping on the half-inch is a relatively minor adverse effect in the estimation of mean heights because the biases tend to cancel out one another (Steckel 1992).

---

1. This section on convict women draws from joint work with D. Oxley. See Nicholas and Oxley (1993, 1994, 1996).

Table 6A.1   **Jarque-Bera Tests for Normality of Convict Height**
(critical value at 95 percent confidence is 5.99)

Convict Type	Statistic
English urban females	5.87[a]
English rural females	2.37[b]
Irish urban females	3.82[c]
Irish rural females	1.38[a]
English males	3.48[c]
English urban males	2.21[c]
English rural males	2.24[c]
Irish males	2.01[c]
Irish urban males	1.88[c]
Irish rural males	1.99[c]

Source: Convict Indents.
[a]Half-inch.
[b]Full inch.
[c]Quarter-inch.

The convict indents that accompanied each shipload of transportees docu-mented name, age, education, religion, marital status, number of children, place of birth, up to four occupations, crime, place of trial, date, sentence, and prior convictions, as well as height, for each individual. These data allow the representativeness of the convicts to be assessed. The occupational structure of the female convict sample was compared with the female occupations in the 1841 English and Irish censuses. Employing Armstrong's social skill classifi-cation as a common "yardstick," 78 percent of English female convicts and 83 percent of English women workers were in the skilled and semiskilled catego-ries (Armstrong 1972). Similarly, almost three-quarters both of Irish women workers in the census and of convict women transported from Ireland were skilled or semiskilled.

The predominance of skilled and semiskilled women among the convicts is not surprising since most women convicts were employed in domestic service, classified mainly as a skilled or semiskilled occupation according to the Arm-strong scheme. Unfortunately, the aggregation of the skilled and semiskilled occupations disguises the complex distribution of female skills and trades. The problem lies with the 1841 English and Irish censuses, which lump together one-half of all working women into one amorphous "domestic servant" cate-gory. In contrast, the convict indents provide a fine detail of women's occupa-tions, including over 160 distinct jobs. In order to make comparisons with the 1841 census, we were forced to collapse most of these carefully listed trades of the English and Irish convict women into one aggregate "domestic servant" category, which combined skilled and semiskilled jobs. While this aggregation showed that the convict data were broadly coincident with the 1841 census,

Table 6A.2   **Occupations of Female Convicts, 1817–40**

Occupation	Sample[a] (%)	Stock of Skills[b] (%)
Housemaid	28.4	20.2
Allworker[c]	25.4	18.1
Kitchenhand	11.0	7.8
Nursemaid	9.7	6.9
Cook	8.7	6.2
Laundress	8.3	5.9
Dairyhand	7.5	5.4
Needlewoman	6.9	4.9
Country servant	5.6	4.0
Laundrymaid	3.9	2.8
Washerwoman	3.3	2.3
Children's maid	2.9	2.0
Country allworker[c]	2.2	1.6
Dressmaker	1.8	1.3
Nurse	1.3	0.9
General house servant	1.0	0.7
Barmaid	1.0	0.7
Farm laborer	0.8	0.6
Housekeeper	0.5	0.4
Thorough servant[c]	0.5	0.4
Other	10.5	6.9

Source: Convict Indents.

[a]Percentage of sample engaged in given occupation. Due to the listing of multiple occupations, the total exceeds 100 percent.

[b]Percentage of stock of skills (combined multiple job listings) accounted for by given occupation.

[c]Allworkers, also known as maids of all work, and thorough servants were workers who, because they were employed in single-servant households, had to perform all of the duties divided among specialist servants in larger households.

the occupational variety of female convict employment was investigated, in order to assess further the representativeness of our data.

For many women in our sample, two or more skills, such as housemaid and kitchenhand or country allworker and dairyhand, were listed in the indents. As table 6A.2 shows, Irish and English female convict employment fell into roughly a dozen major categories. Two-thirds of the convict women had held jobs as housemaid, allworkers, or kitchenhands, and 86 percent were employed in the first 12 occupations in table 6A.2. In table 6A.3 the skill composition of English female convicts was similar to that for the male convicts, and the male convict skill distribution was broadly in line with that for the working-class population in the 1841 census. The overrepresentation of domestic servants arose from the age distribution of the convict women, who were disproportionately young (with 75 percent of the English and 79 percent of the Irish convict women below 31 years of age) and single (59 percent of the English and 65 percent of the Irish). Our data show that the number of women employed in domestic service declined from 82.4 percent for English convict women under age 20 to 68 percent of women over age 20. Employment in resident domestic service required women to be single, and the high percentage of single women among the transportees also explains the high percentage of domestic servants in our sample. The underrepresentation of textile workers probably reflects some overrepresentation of southern and London workers.

Details of Irish female convict occupations in the 1841 census and the convict sample were grouped into laborers, textile workers, farmers, other artisans, white-collar workers, and others as used by Mokyr and Ó Gráda (1982, 379). There were many more women in the farm servant category and far fewer in the textile worker categories in the indents than in the 1841 census. These differences can be explained by the fact that female textile workers identified in the census worked at home as domestic workers with many classified as female farm servants (laborers) in the Mokyr and Ó Gráda scheme.

Our data on occupations suggest that women were representative of the English and Irish working classes, although they were not representative of the age distribution of the population. Our sample contains sufficient observations to estimate accurately terminal height in each year. The concentration of female convicts in the under 31 age group is not a problem since terminal height was attained at the time by women at age 21, which marked the end of their growing years. Height did not change between ages 21 and 49, at which time shrinkage occurred, which led us to exclude all women older than age 49 from our analysis.

Convict Men

For comparative purposes, the heights of 12,528 English-born and 7,358 Irish-born males transported between 1817 and 1840 are also analyzed. Male height was typically recorded to the nearest inch, and the frequency distribution shows little sign of heaping. The Jarque-Bera tests shown in table 6A.1 indicated that the distribution of male English and Irish height is normal, or Gaussian.

One test of the accuracy of the data was to compare the indents with the court records. In a survey of Old Bailey court records of 593 male convicts sentenced between 1816 and 1834, all the occupations listed in the court records agreed with those in the convict sample, although only 3.5 percent of the court records reported occupations. Table 6A.3 shows that the male convict sample was representative of the men in the English working classes using Armstrong's classification scheme. The major difference between the 1841 English census and the male sample of convicts was that over three times as many English men as convicts were in Armstrong's professional and middling categories. However, the proportions of skilled and semiskilled convicts corresponded very closely to those in the English population. A Spearman's rank correlation between 83 occupations with over 50,000 workers in the 1841 cen-

Table 6A.3   Skill Classification of English Workforce (1841) and Convicts (1817–40)

Armstrong Classification	Convict Females (%)	Convict Males (%)	English 1841 Census Males (%)
Professional	0	0.3	1.7
Intermediate	0.3	3.1	9.2
Skilled	49.8	45.6	45.2
Semiskilled	27.9	26.3	25.7
Unskilled	22.0	24.7	15.5

Sources: Convict Indents and *Census of Great Britain* (PP 1841, xiv).

sus and the convict indents was 0.714, suggesting a close match between the sample occupations and those of the English workforce. These tests give us confidence that the male convicts were representative of the English working class.

For the Irish male convicts, the indents and the census differed in terms of laborers (71 percent in the indents and 55 percent in the census) and farmers (1.1 percent in the indents and 20.7 percent in the census). A similar discrepancy was found by Mokyr and Ó Gráda in their comparison of occupations in the census with those in the shipping lists for Irish emigrants to the United States. The differences are not as great as they might first appear. In preindustrial Ireland, the border line between farmer, cottier, and farm laborer was not well defined (Mokyr 1983). Combining laborers and farmers, 72 percent of the Irish convicts and 76 percent of the 1841 Irish male population fell into this aggregate group, giving us confidence that the Irish convicts were broadly representative of the Irish working class at home.

Convict Literacy

The representativeness of our convict data can be assessed further by utilizing the indent information on literacy. The convicts in the indents and the population at home had similar levels of literacy. While less than half of women marrying between 1825 and 1840 could sign the marriage register, 45 percent of convict women tried in England could read and a further 34.6 percent could write also (Laquer 1974, 98). Of course, the tests are not identical, since the indent information is questionnaire data while the marriage registers provide a test of practical literacy. But other questionnaire-style data exist for paupers and migrants. Compared with the literacy rate of only 50 percent for adult paupers in 1838, 80 percent of the female convicts were literate (*Report from the Select Committee on Education of the Poorer Classes in England and Wales* [PP 1838, vii: 42]). Only 11 percent of paupers could read and write, while one-third of the convict women could do both. English convict literacy (80 percent could read, write, or both) was also very similar to the literacy rate of free female migrants to Australia in 1838 (79 percent; Penglase 1983, 43–49)

England's convict women seem less like paupers, and more like workers generally.

Male English convict literacy was 74 percent, significantly higher than the registrar-general's average of 58 percent able to sign the marriage registers, and Schofield's average of a little over 60 percent able to sign the registers in a random sample of 274 English parish registers between 1790 and 1820 (Schofield 1970, 445). In a sample of politically conscious prisoners involved in a rising in the manufacturing districts of Lancashire, Cheshire, and Staffordshire, Webb (1950, 335) found that 73 percent were literate, virtually the same rate (74 percent) as that for English male transportees for these counties. A rank correlation of 0.92 between Sanderson's (1983) sample of occupations by literacy for Lancashire in the 1830s and the convict sample provides additional evidence for the robustness and representativeness of our data. From the 1841 Irish census, where literacy was measured in the same way as in the indents, 54 percent of the Irish male population was literate while 67 percent of the male transportees could read, write, or both. Irish female convicts and Irish women were much alike with less than half of both groups literate: 48 percent of convicts compared with 45 percent of adult Irish women could read, write, or both. The Irish transportees were at least as literate as the Irish left at home.

The Criminal Class

There has been considerable debate among Australian historians on the class origins of the convicts. Wood's (1922) nationalist interpretation of the convicts as "innocent and manly" unfortunates fighting for freedom and social justice was attacked by Clark (1956) for "grossly distorting Australia's past." Clark argued that the transportees were persistent thieves engaged in a life of crime; they were by choice and training members of a professional criminal class. This view of the convicts as a criminal class, separate and distinct from the working class, dominated Australian convict historiography until the 1980s. Using the information on occupations presented above, Nicholas (1988) and Oxley (1988) showed that the transportees to New South Wales were not members of a criminal class, but were working-class men and women who stole. While this new interpretation is not without its critics, it has attracted considerable support (Shlomowitz 1990; Nicholas 1991; Garton 1991).

The majority of transportees had no previous convictions (over 60 percent of the women were first offenders), all reported workplace skills, and most stole to satisfy immediate consumption needs. Overwhelmingly, female convicts committed crimes against property—96.2 percent of all reported crimes. In order to assess whether the female criminals were professional criminals or casual pilferers, Oxley (1988) categorized the crimes of women transportees into 11 basic categories. Most women stole clothes (33 percent) or money (22 percent) or cloth and yarn (10 percent), which were used for basic consumption. Theft of clothes, cloth and household goods (e.g., pots, candles, and pans), bedding, and foodstuffs accounted for nearly three-fifths of the items stolen. Valuable items, jewelry (6 percent), and metals (0.9 percent), which were not for immediate consumption, required resale, and were more likely to be targeted by a professional criminal, accounted for less than 10 percent of the crimes.

An attempt was made to assess whether crime was work related. For men in each occupational category with more than 30 observations, work-related crimes were defined as stealing tools, stealing goods, and stealing from an employer. Theft of tools included tools that were specific to the job, for example, a sawyer stealing a saw, and all thefts that were listed as "tools" on the indents. Theft of goods involved stealing movable property and foodstuffs related to the job, such as iron by a blacksmith, sheep by a butcher, or livestock and small farm animals by farm servants and farm laborers. Stealing from one's master included all thefts where the indents specified master, mistress, or employer and all thefts by nursemaids, general servants, housemaids, and kitchenhands that were listed as theft from inside the house. On this basis about 10 percent of the thefts were work related, ranging from 0.7 percent for general servants to 40 percent for butchers and farm servants.

These are lower bound estimates because most thefts were listed in the indents simply as stealing money or stealing clothing without any indication of whether they were work related. While some work-related thefts were easily identified, such as horses or saddles stolen by grooms, the indents rarely tell one if the money, clothes, trunks, spoons, watches, food, and handkerchiefs were taken from employers. Upper bound estimates were then calculated. Upper bound estimates of work-related theft for each occupation assumed that all theft that could be work related was work related. If the lower bound underestimates work-related crime, then our upper limit percentages, which show about 95 percent of thefts as work related, are overestimates. What is clear from our calculation of lower and upper bounds on work-related crime is that a significant proportion of crime was related to male workers' employment. Convicts were working-class men and women who normally held jobs, frequently stealing from their employers for immediate consumption needs.

The case for the transportees as ordinary working-class men and women also gains support from recent work by historians of British crime. For Black Country criminals, Philips (1977, 287) found that the great majority of crimes were committed by ordinary men and women, who worked at jobs normally, but also stole on occasion. Beattie (1975, 102–3), Emsley (1987), and others (Gatrell and Hadden 1972, 382; Jones 1982, 13) have related the late-eighteenth- and early-nineteenth-century crime rates to economic distress, arguing that most criminals were people in employment pushed into crime by hard economic times. There can be little doubt that the transportees were typical of such British criminals. Compared with offenders in the Black Country, transported convict workers had a similar occupational breakdown: 59 and 53 percent, respectively, were unskilled and semiskilled, 38 and 44 percent skilled, and 3 percent middle and upper class. They had committed the same types of offenses, less than 3 percent against persons and the rest property offenses, mainly larceny (Philips 1977). The rank correlations between the occupations of the transported male convicts and the male prisoners held in Pentonville Gaol was 0.908. (Unfortunately, similar comparative statistics were not available for women or the Irish, but no one has suggested a criminal class consisting of women and the Irish.) On the basis of all these tests, it seems fair to argue that the female and male convicts transported to Australia were broadly coincident with the skill composition of the English and Irish working classes.

Newgate Prisoner Data

Our second, and largest, data set is drawn from 24 manuscript registers of prisoners admitted to Newgate Prison in London between 1817 and 1860 (Public Records Office [PRO], *Newgate Prison Registers,* PCOM2/191–214). This source provides information on 20,519 female prisoners (16,325 English, 3,199 Irish, 248 Welsh, 27 Scottish, and 720 foreign-born) and, using the lower and upper age thresholds of 21 and 49, provides us with height data for women born between 1768 and 1839. (The registers also contain information on approximately 100,000 male prisoners, but these male data have not been collected.) In this period Newgate served primarily as a prison for accused persons awaiting trial at the Old Bailey. The Old Bailey served both as a City of London court and as the assize court for the county of Middlesex, and it was from Middlesex that most of the prisoners came. The magistracy in Middlesex, unlike that in the rest of the kingdom, did not hear cases of grand larceny at the quarter sessions, but instead always forwarded these for trial at the Old Bailey. Since the monetary threshold between simple larceny and grand larceny in the early nineteenth century was just one shilling, the majority of Old Bailey cases related to what were effectively alleged crimes of petty theft (Select Committee on the State of Gaols [PP 1819, vii: 283]).

In 1819 the governor of Newgate reckoned that almost 2,000 of the 2,396 prisoners admitted in the previous year had been Middlesex assize cases (Select Committee on the State of Gaols [PP 1819, vii: 263]). By 1835 the remit of the Old Bailey (and so the catchment area for Newgate) had been extended to cover Kent, Surrey, and Essex as well as Middlesex (Select Committee of the House of Lords on Gaols and Houses of Correction [PP 1835, xi: 77]). The great majority of Newgate prisoners, therefore, were people from London and surrounding districts who were accused of low-value theft. When female prisoners were found guilty of theft, they typically received short sentences of between one and six months in a House of Correction. There is little indication that Newgate inmates were dominated by professional criminals.

Information on the crime, sentence, occupation, age, place of birth, and height was also recorded. Data on the place of birth of prisoners listed in the registers confirm the very heavy London and southeast bias of the female prisoners—62 percent were born in the south, with an underrepresentation of women from the north, shown in table 6A.4. The Newgate registers gave information about each prisoner's height, usually measured to the full inch though sometimes to the half or quarter. Jarque-Bera tests for normality indicate that English and Welsh (0.910) and English (0.901) women's heights measured to the half-inch were normally distributed, with no signs of truncation or other distortions to the distributions.

There was little information collected on female occupations, in contrast to male prisoners, where occupation was nearly always stated. In place of occupation, women's marital status—single/spinster, married, or widowed—was given in 99.5 percent of the cases. Table 6A.5 shows the marital and age status of the Newgate prisoners. The women were predominantly young, displaying an age distribution similar to that of the female convicts. Young women under age 21 were predominantly single, with the proportion of single women falling from 93 percent of the sample for those under age 21 years to 57 percent aged 21–30 years, 22 percent aged 31–40 years, and 10 percent aged 41–50 years. Generally, the age distribution fits the young female offender category—a woman who stole articles of small value for immediate use. The gross underrecording of female occupations means that we cannot construct any statistical tests of the socioeconomic representativeness of these female prisoners, but the unexceptional nature of their crimes suggests that they were not significantly different from either female convicts or female habitual criminals.

Criminal Data

Habitual Criminals

Our final set of data on heights of women born between 1812 and 1857 is taken from a register of habitual criminals compiled by Scotland Yard and circulated in printed form in 1877 to local police forces (PRO, *Alphabetical Register of Habitual Criminals,* PCOM2/404). The register contains information on 8,612 males and 3,552 females who had been designated "habitual criminals" under the Habitual Criminals Act of 1869 and the Prevention of Crimes Act of 1871. These were people who had been convicted on indictment of a crime and against whom a previous conviction could be proved. The purpose of the register was to enable police forces to identify and take action against repeat offenders. In addition to details of crime and sentence, the register recorded age, occupation, height (measured to the half-inch), color of hair and eyes, complexion, and distinguishing features such as scars and tattoos. As an instrument of criminal identification the central criminal register proved to be inadequate and haphazard, but it was the best that could be done before the development of Bertillon's system of body measurement and Galton's "finger mark" system (Radzinowicz and Hood 1986, 263).

Habitual criminals will not be representative of the entire population if there

Table 6A.4   County Distribution of Newgate Female Prisoners

| County | Newgate Prisoners | | Non-Middlesex Percent | Female Percentage of Population |
	Number	Percent		
Bedfordshire	61	0.3	1.0	0.7
Berkshire	234	1.4	3.8	1.2
Buckinghamshire	127	0.8	2.1	1.2
Cambridgeshire	131	0.8	2.1	1.1
Cheshire	39	0.2	0.6	2.4
Cornwall	69	0.4	1.1	2.3
Cumberland	19	0.1	0.3	1.4
Derbyshire	43	0.3	0.7	1.9
Devonshire	280	1.7	4.6	3.9
Dorsetshire	67	0.4	1.1	1.3
Durham	80	0.5	1.3	1.7
Essex	421	2.6	6.8	2.6
Gloucester	363	2.2	5.9	3.0
Hampshire	305	1.9	5.0	2.5
Herefordshire	81	0.5	1.3	0.9
Hertfordshire	224	1.4	3.6	1.2
Huntingdonshire	21	0.1	0.3	0.4
Kent	527	3.2	8.6	3.1
Lancashire	354	2.2	5.8	9.3
Leicestershire	49	0.3	0.8	1.5
Lincolnshire	89	0.5	1.4	2.5
Middlesex	10,175	62.3	–	13.1
Norfolk	195	1.2	3.2	3.0
Northampton	44	0.3	0.7	1.4
Northumberland	113	0.7	1.8	1.9
Nottinghamshire	49	0.3	0.8	1.7
Oxfordshire	178	1.1	2.9	1.2
Rutland	2	0.0	0.0	0.2
Shropshire	127	0.8	2.1	1.8
Somerset	240	1.5	3.9	3.2
Staffordshire	98	0.6	1.6	3.1
Suffolk	203	1.2	3.3	2.4
Surrey	370	2.3	6.0	1.2
Sussex	206	1.3	3.4	2.1
Warwickshire	196	1.2	3.2	2.4
Westmorland	3	0.0	0.0	0.5
Wiltshire	188	1.2	3.1	1.9
Worcester	102	0.6	1.7	1.7
Yorkshire	252	1.5	4.1	10.4
Total	16,573	100.0		

Source: Newgate Prison Registers.

Table 6A.5   Age and Marital Status of Newgate Female Prisoners

Age Category	Single	Married	Widow	Total
Up to 20	5,185	337	30	5,552
(%)	(93.4)	(6.1)	(0.5)	(100.0)
21–30	3,465	2,227	384	6,076
(%)	(57.0)	(36.7)	(6.3)	(100.0)
31–40	559	1,439	558	2,556
(%)	(21.9)	(56.3)	(21.8)	(100.0)
41–50	141	793	515	1,449
(%)	(9.7)	(54.7)	(35.5)	(100.0)
51–60	40	259	272	571
(%)	(7.0)	(45.4)	(47.6)	(100.0)
61–70	12	55	115	182
(%)	(6.6)	(30.2)	(63.2)	(100.0)
71+	1	1	18	20
(%)	(5.0)	(5.0)	(90.0)	(100.0)

Source: Newgate Prisoner Registers.

are regional and occupational biases in the data. Analysis of the working of the Habitual Criminals Act over the period 1869–90 by Stevenson (1986) demonstrated that registration was pursued more vigorously north of a line from the Severn to the Wash than elsewhere, and in towns with populations between 20,000 and 100,000. He found no clear relationship between the registration rate for habitual criminals and other indicators of crime and concluded that local variation in the density of policing and the sentencing policies of magistrates and judges were the most important determining factors. We find little general evidence of regional overrepresentation in our sample, with the correlation between county shares of habitual criminals and population in 1871 standing at 0.94. The only significant outlier is Lancashire, which accounted for 12.4 percent of the population of England and Wales in 1871 but 21.8 percent of habitual criminals.

However, we do find evidence of occupational bias in our sample of criminals. The occupations were coded using Armstrong's occupational-social class scheme. As shown in table 6A.6, the major difference between the female and male criminals and the 1841 English census was the small proportion of criminals that came from Armstrong's first two occupational-social classes, repeating the same pattern found in the convict data. There were also fewer skilled workers among the criminals than in the population as a whole, with an overrepresentation of unskilled workers.

We ran several tests on the internal accuracy of the data using 1,046 individuals who were identified in the records more than once. In 58 percent of the cases the occupations of criminals who appear twice in the records were exactly the same. This is a lower bound estimate since the computer match of

Table 6A.6   **Skill Classification of English Workforce and English Habitual Criminals**

Armstrong Classification	Criminal Total (%)	Criminal Males (%)	Criminal Females (%)	English 1841 Census (%)	English 1841 Census Males (%)
Professional	<1	<1	0	1.2	1.7
Intermediate	1.6	2.1	<1	8.7	9.2
Skilled	32.9	38.5	19.5	53.1	47.9
Semiskilled	14.6	13.5	17.3	21.2	25.7
Unskilled	50.8	45.8	63.0	15.9	15.5

Sources: *Alphabetical Register of Habitual Criminals* and *Census of Great Britain* (PP 1841, xiv).

occupations did not allow for slight variations in occupations, so bootmaker and shoemaker were treated as a mismatch, although the two occupations were the same. In 70 percent of the repeat cases the same place of trial was listed, and in 90 percent of the cases the ages agreed (allowing for a higher age when the two occurrences in the records were separated by a number of years). The heights of the criminals who occurred more than once in the records agreed to the nearest 0.5 inch in 70 percent of cases, which rose to 75 percent for criminals over age 23, who had reached their terminal height. These various tests give us confidence in the accuracy of the criminal data.

In the crucial variable of height we find that the female and male height distributions were free of truncation bias, and the Jarque-Bera tests found that the female (5.23) and male (5.51) distributions were normal, or Gaussian. Female height was measured at the half-inch since there was some evidence of heaping on the quarter-inch.

Crimes and the Working-Class Victorian Criminal

How representative were these criminals of the population as a whole? The concept of a "habitual criminal," which was given legal standing in 1869, derived from a deep-seated Victorian belief in the existence of a "criminal class," but it had more proximate origins. The virtual cessation of transportation to Australia in 1853 removed the option of expulsion, which had hitherto been the lot of many repeat offenders, and an outbreak of garrotting in London in 1862 created a moral panic that saw an increase in the number of violent crimes reported and a call for tougher policing and tougher sentencing (Davis 1980). The Habitual Criminals Act introduced a system of police supervision for repeat offenders after their release from prison and allowed them to be summarily imprisoned if they were found to be acting suspiciously.

This does not mean, however, that these repeat offenders were social outcasts who gained a living through crime. Summary statistics presented in the register, and reproduced in tables 6A.7 and 6A.8, show that the majority of

Table 6A.7   **Marital and Occupational Status of Female Habitual Criminals by Age Group**

Age	Married	Single	Stated Occupation	Prostitute	No Occupation
Up to 20	40	604	478	31	135
21–30	559	590	689	77	383
31–40	722	169	561	19	311
41–50	473	62	338	11	186
51–60	228	18	155	1	90
61–70	62	9	45	–	26
71+	16	–	11	–	5
Total	2,100	1,452	2,277	139	1,136

Source: Alphabetical Register of Habitual Criminals.

Table 6A.8   **Marital and Occupational Status of Male Habitual Criminals by Age Group**

Age	Married	Single	Professional, Trades, etc.	Artisans	Unskilled
Up to 20	19	2,079	46	641	1,411
21–30	829	2,490	160	1,051	2,108
31–40	900	769	128	518	1,023
41–50	549	275	52	253	519
51–60	349	129	40	142	296
61–70	151	40	19	57	115
71+	27	6	4	8	21
Total	2,824	5,788	449	2,670	5,493

Source: Alphabetical Register of Habitual Criminals.

habitual criminals were unmarried young adults, predominantly from unskilled occupations, although one-third of the males were listed as artisans or as having a trade or profession. These were clearly not just the economically inferior residuum assumed in contemporary discussion of the habitual criminal class. Nor were they the physically defective, a description that was applied (according to unknown criteria) to only 7.4 percent of males and 4.3 percent of females on the register. Only 616 males (7.2 percent) and 310 females (8.7 percent) had more than two previous convictions, and the majority of convictions were for petty theft (larceny simple), resulting in prison sentences of 3 to 12 months. The majority of these repeat offenders were not, therefore, hardened professional criminals. Their appearance on the register fits with mainstream historical interpretation, which sees the great majority of crime as being committed by ordinary people who worked at jobs and lived in generally law-abiding communities, but who stole on occasion (Rudé 1985; Jones 1982; Philips 1977).

References

Anderson, M. 1971. *Family structure in nineteenth century Lancashire.* Cambridge: Cambridge University Press.
————. 1980. *Approaches to the history of the Western family, 1500–1914.* London: Macmillan.
Armstrong, W. A. 1972. The use of information about occupations. In *Nineteenth century society: Essays in the use of quantitative methods for the study of social data,* ed. E. A. Wrigley, 191–310. Cambridge: Cambridge University Press.
Beattie, J. M. 1975. Criminality of women in eighteenth-century England. *Journal of Social History* 8:80–116.
Behrman, J. 1988. Intrahousehold allocation of nutrients in rural India: Are boys favoured? *Oxford Economic Papers* 40:32–54.
Berg, M. 1985. *The age of manufacturers: Industry, innovation and work in Britain, 1700–1820.* Oxford: Blackwell.
————. 1988. Women's work, mechanization and the early phases of industrialisation in England. In *On work: Historical, comparative and theoretical approaches,* ed. R. E. Pahl, 61–93. Oxford: Blackwell.
Burnett, J. 1966. *Plenty and want: A social history of diet in England.* London: Nelson.
Case, R. A. M., C. Coghill, J. Harley, and J. Pearson. 1962. *Serial abridged life tables: England and Wales, 1841–1960.* London: Chester Beatty Research Institute.
Clark, A. 1919. *Working life of women in the seventeenth century.* London: Routledge and Kegan Paul.
Clark, C. M. H. 1956. The origins of the convicts transported to eastern Australia, 1787–1852. *Historical Studies, Australia and New Zealand* 7:121–35, 314–27.
Crafts, N. F. R., and T. C. Mills. 1994. Trends in real wages in Britain, 1750–1913. *Explorations in Economic History* 31:176–94.
Davidoff, L., and C. Hall. 1987. *Family fortunes: Men and women of the English middle class, 1780–1850.* London: Hutchinson.
Davis, J. 1980. The London garrotting panic of 1862: A moral panic and the creation of a criminal class in mid-Victorian England. In *Crime and the law: The social history of crime in Western Europe since 1500,* ed. V. A. C. Gatrell, B. Lenman and G. Parker. London: Europa.
Ehrenreich, B., and D. English. 1979. *For her own good.* London: Pluto.
Emsley, C. 1987. *Crime and society in England, 1750–1900.* London: Longman.
Eveleth, P. B., and J. M. Tanner. 1976. *Worldwide variation in human growth.* Cambridge: Cambridge University Press.
Floud, R., K. Wachter, and A. S. Gregory. 1990. *Height, health and history: Nutritional status in the United Kingdom.* Cambridge: Cambridge University Press.
————. 1993. Measuring historical heights—short cuts or the long way round: A reply to Komlos. *Economic History Review* 46(1): 145–54.
Fogel, R., S. Engerman, R. Floud, R. Steckel, J. Trussell, K. Wachter, R. Margo, K. Sokoloff, and G. Villaflor. 1983. Secular changes in American and British stature and nutrition. *Journal of Interdisciplinary History* 14:445–81.
Fox-Genovese, E. 1982. Placing women's history in history. *New Left Review* 133:5–29.
Garton, S. 1991. The convict origins debate: Historians and the problem of the "criminal class." *Australian and New Zealand Journal of Criminology* 24:66–82.
Gatrell, V. A. C., and T. B. Hadden. 1972. Criminal statistics and their interpretation. In *Nineteenth-century society: Essays in the use of quantitative methods for the study of social data,* ed. E. A. Wrigley, 336–96. Cambridge: Cambridge University Press.
Goode, W. 1963. *World revolution and family patterns.* New York: Free Press.

Gould, B. A. 1869. *Investigations in the military and anthropological statistics of American soldiers.* Cambridge: Riverside.

Guha, S. 1994. The importance of social intervention in England's mortality decline: The evidence reviewed. *Social History of Medicine* 7:89–113.

Holley, J. C. 1981. The two family economies of industrialism: Factory workers in Victorian Scotland. *Journal of Family History* 6:57–69.

Horrell, S., and J. Humphries. 1992. Old questions, new data and alternative perspectives: Families' living standards in the industrial revolution. *Journal of Economic History* 45:849–80.

———. 1995. Women's labour force participation and the transition to the male-breadwinner family, 1790–1865. *Economic History Review* 48:89–117.

Humphries, J. 1981. Protective legislation, the capitalist state, and working class men: The case of the 1842 Mines Regulation Act. *Feminist Review* 7:1–33.

———. 1987. "... The most free from objection ..." The sexual division of labour and women's work in nineteenth-century England. *Journal of Economic History* 47:929–49.

———. 1990. Enclosures, common rights and women: The proletarianization of families in the late eighteenth and early nineteenth centuries. *Journal of Economic History* 50:17–42.

———. 1991. "Bread and a pennyworth of treacle": Excess female mortality in England in the 1840s. *Cambridge Journal of Economics* 15:451–73.

Hunt, E. H. 1973. *Regional wage variation in Britain, 1850–1914.* Oxford: Clarendon Press.

Ittmann, K. 1995. *Work, gender and family in Victorian England.* New York: New York University Press.

Jackson, R. V. 1996. The heights of rural-born English female convicts transported to New South Wales. *Economic History Review* 49:584–90.

Jarque, C. M., and A. K. Bera. 1980. Efficiency tests for normality, homoscedasticity and serial independence of regression residuals. *Economic Letters* 6:255–59.

Johansson, S. R. 1977. Sex and death in Victorian England. In *A widening sphere: Changing roles of Victorian women,* ed. M. Vicinus, 163–81. Bloomington: Indiana University Press.

———. 1991. Welfare, mortality and gender: Continuity and change in explanations for male/female mortality differences over three centuries. *Continuity and Change* 6:135–77.

Jones, D. 1982. *Crime, protest, community and police in nineteenth-century Britain.* London: Routledge and Kegan Paul.

Komlos, J. 1989. *Nutrition and economic development in the eighteenth-century Habsburg monarchy: An anthropometric history.* Princeton, N.J.: Princeton University Press.

———. 1993. The secular trend in the biological standard of living in the United Kingdom, 1730–1860. *Economic History Review* 46:115–44.

Land, H. 1980. The family wage. *Feminist Review* 6:55–77.

Laquer, T. W. 1974. Literacy and social mobility in the industrial revolution in England. *Past and Present* 64:96–122.

Lown, J. 1990. *Women and industrialization: Gender at work in nineteenth-century England.* Cambridge: Polity.

Margo, R. A., and R. H. Steckel. 1992. The nutrition and health of slaves and antebellum Southern whites. In *Without consent or contract: The rise and fall of American slavery. Technical Papers,* ed. Robert William Fogel and Stanley L. Engerman, 508–21. New York: Norton.

Mark-Lawson, J., and A. Witz. 1988. From "family labour" to "family wage"? The case of women's labour in nineteenth-century coalmining. *Social History* 13(2): 151–74.

Marx, K. 1977. *Economic and philosophic manuscripts of 1844.* Moscow: Progress.

Marx, K., and F. Engels. 1977. *Manifesto of the Communist Party.* Moscow: Progress.

McBride, T. 1976. *The domestic revolution: The modernisation of household service in England and France 1820–1920.* London: Croom Helm.

McKendrick, N. 1974. Home demand and economic growth: A new view of the role of women and children in the industrial revolution. In *Historical perspectives: Studies in English thought and society,* ed. N. McKendrick, 152–210. London: Europa.

McKeown, T. 1976. *The modern rise of population.* London: Edward Arnold.

Mill, J. S. 1988. *The subjection of women.* Indianapolis: Hackett.

Mokyr, J. 1983. *Why Ireland starved: A quantitative and analytical history of the Irish economy 1801–51.* London: Allen and Unwin.

Mokyr, J., and C. Ó Gráda. 1982. Emigration and poverty in pre-Famine Ireland. *Explorations in Economic History* 19: 360–84.

———. 1988. Poor and getting poorer? Living standards in Ireland before the Famine. *Economic History Review* 41:209–35.

———. 1990. The heights of the British and the Irish c. 1800–1815: Evidence from recruits to the East India Company's army. Northwestern University, Evanston, Ill. Mimeograph.

Nicholas, S., ed. 1988. *Convict workers: Reinterpreting Australia's past.* Melbourne: Cambridge University Press.

———. 1991. Understanding *Convict workers. Australian Economic History Review* 31:95–105.

Nicholas, S., and J. Nicholas. 1992. Male illiteracy and workforce deskilling during the industrial revolution. *Journal of Interdisciplinary History* 22:1–18.

Nicholas, S., and D. Oxley. 1993. The living standards of women during the industrial revolution, 1795–1820. *Economic History Review* 46:723–49.

———. 1994. The industrial revolution and the genesis of the male breadwinner. In *Was the industrial revolution necessary?* ed. G. Snooks, 96–111. London: Routledge.

———. 1996. Living standards of women in England and Wales, 1785–1815: New evidence from Newgate Prison Records. *Economic History Review* 49:591–99.

Nicholas, S., and P. R. Shergold. 1987a. Intercounty labour mobility during the industrial revolution: Evidence from Australian transport records. *Oxford Economic Papers* 39:624–40.

———. 1987b. Internal migration in England, 1818–1839. *Journal of Historical Geography* 13: 155–68.

Oddy, D. 1976. The nutritional analysis of historical evidence: The working class diet. In *The making of the modern British diet,* ed. D. Oddy and D. Miller, 214–31. London: Croom Helm.

Ó Gráda, C. 1988. *Ireland before and after the Famine.* Manchester: Manchester University Press.

Oren, L. 1974. The welfare of women in labouring families: England, 1860–1950. In *Clio's consciousness raised,* ed. M. Hartman and L. Banner, 226–41. New York: Harper and Row.

Oxley, D. 1988. Female convicts. In *Convict workers,* ed. S. Nicholas, 85–97. Melbourne: Cambridge University Press.

Pahl, R. E. 1984. *Divisions of labour.* Oxford: Blackwell.

Penglase, B. M. 1983. An enquiry into literacy in early nineteenth century New South Wales. *Push from the bush* (Armidale, N.S.W.: University of New England, Department of History) 16:39–60.

Philips, D. 1977. *Crime and authority in Victorian England: The Black Country, 1835–1860.* London: Croom Helm.

Pinchbeck, I. 1930. *Women workers and the industrial revolution, 1750–1850.* London: Routledge.

Pitt, M. M., M. R. Rosenzweig, and M. N. Hassan. 1990. Productivity, health and inequality in the intrahousehold distribution of food in low-income countries. *American Economic Review* 80:1139–56.

Radzinowicz, L., and R. Hood. 1986. *A history of English criminal law.* Vol. 5, *The emergence of penal policy.* London: Stevens.

Richards, E. 1974. Women in the British economy since about 1700: An interpretation. *History* 59:337–57.

Roberts, M. 1979. Sickles and scythes: Women's work and men's work at harvest time. *History Workshop* 7:3–28.

Rose, S. O. 1986. Gender at work: Sex, class and industrial capitalism. *History Workshop* 21:113–31.

Ross, E. 1993. *Love and toil.* New York: Oxford University Press.

Rudé, G. 1985. *Criminal and victim: Crime and society in early nineteenth century England.* Oxford: Oxford University Press.

Sandberg, L. G., and R. H. Steckel. 1988. Overpopulation and malnutrition rediscovered: Hard times in nineteenth-century Sweden. *Explorations in Economic History* 25:1–9.

Sanderson, M. 1983. *Education, economic change and society in England, 1780–1870.* Basingstoke: Macmillan.

Schofield, R. S. 1970. Age-specific mobility in an eighteenth century rural English parish. In *Annales de Demographie Historique,* 260–74. Paris: Société de Demographie Historique.

———. 1973. Dimensions of illiteracy, 1750–1850. *Explorations in Economic History* 10:437–54.

Scrimshaw, N. S. 1975. Interactions of malnutrition and infection: Advances in understanding. In *Protein-calorie malnutrition,* ed. R. E. Olson, 353–67. New York: Academic Press.

Seccombe, W. 1986. Patriarchy stabilized: The construction of the male breadwinner wage norm in nineteenth-century Britain. *Social History* 2:53–76.

Sen, A. 1990. More than 100 million women are missing. *New York Review of Books* 37:61–66.

Sen, A., and S. Sengupta. 1983. Malnutrition of rural children and the sex bias. *Economic Political Weekly* 18:855–64.

Shammas, C. 1984. The eighteenth-century English diet and economic change. *Explorations in Economic History* 21:254–69.

Shay, T. 1986. The stature of military conscripts: New evidence on the standard of living in Japan. Paper presented at the Social Science History Association meetings, St. Louis.

Shlomowitz, R. 1990. *Convict workers:* A review article. *Australian Economic History Review* 30:67–88.

Shorter, E. 1976a. *The making of the modern family.* London: Collins.

———. 1976b. Women's work: What difference did capitalism make? *Theory and Society* 3:513–27.

———. 1982. *A history of women's bodies.* New York: Basic Books.

Smock, A. C. 1977. Conclusion: Determinants of women's roles and status. In *Women: Roles and status in eight countries,* ed. J. Z. Giele and A. C. Smock, 383–421. New York: Wiley.

Snell, K. D. M. 1981. Agricultural seasonal employment, the standard of living and women's work in the south and east, 1690–1810. *Economic History Review* 34:417–37.

————. 1985. *Annals of the labouring poor: Social change and agrarian England, 1660–1900.* Cambridge: Cambridge University Press.

Steckel, R. H. 1986. Height and per capita income. *Historical Methods: A Journal of Quantitative and Interdisciplinary History* 16:1–7.

————. 1992. Stature and living standards in the United States. In *American economic growth and standards of living before the Civil War,* ed. R. Gallman and J. Wallis, 265–308. Chicago: University of Chicago Press.

————. 1995. Percentiles of modern height standards for use in historical research. Ohio State University, Columbus. Mimeograph.

Stevenson, S. 1986. The "habitual criminal" in nineteenth-century England: Some observations on the figures. In *Urban History Yearbook,* 37–60. Leicester: Leicester University Press.

Szreter, S. 1988. The importance of social intervention in Britain's mortality decline circa 1850–1914: A reinterpretation of the role of public health. *Social History of Medicine* 1:1–37.

Tanner, J. M. 1962. *Growth at adolescence.* Oxford: Blackwell.

Thomas, J. 1988. Women and capitalism: Oppression or emancipation? A review article. *Comparative Studies Society and History* 30:534–49.

Thompson, W. 1983. *Appeal of one-half of the human race, women, against the pretensions of the other half, men, to retain them in political, and thence in civil and domestic slavery.* London: Virago.

Tilly, L. A., and J. W. Scott. 1978. *Women, work and family.* New York: Holt, Rinehart and Winston.

Wall, R. 1994. Some implications of the earnings, income and expenditure patterns of married women in populations in the past. In *Poor women and children in the European past,* ed. J. Henderson and R. Wall, 312–35. London: Routledge.

Webb, R. K. 1950. Working class readers in early Victorian England. *English Historical Review* 65:333–51.

Williamson, J. 1981. Urban disamenities, dark satanic mills, and the British standard of living debate. *Journal of Economic History* 41:75–83.

Williamson, J., and P. Lindert. 1983. English workers' living standards during the industrial revolution: A new look. *Economic History Review* 36:1–25.

Wollstonecraft, M. 1792. *A vindication of the rights of women.* Reproduced in *A vindication of the rights of women: An authoritative text, backgrounds, criticism,* ed. Carol H. Poslon, 1st ed. New York: Norton.

Wood, G. A. 1922. Convicts. *Journal and Proceedings: Royal Australian Historical Society* 8:177–208.

7   Differential Structure, Differential Health: Industrialization in Japan, 1868–1940

Gail Honda

7.1   Introduction

The most arresting characteristics of Japan's industrialization through the mid-twentieth century are its strongly military character and the development of a differential structure between traditional and modern sectors. The beginning of Japan's modern economic growth is often associated with the Meiji Ishin, a political, social, and economic upheaval that took place over several decades in the late nineteenth century. During this time, the *bakuhan* regime, which had been in power since 1600, was overthrown in numerous coups d'état. In its place, a government was created in 1868 that restored authority to the emperor.[1] In order to stave off the encroaching colonization they observed around them in Asia, the new leaders concentrated their efforts on building a "rich country and strong army" (*fukoku kyōhei*). To this end they promulgated a constitution in 1889 that granted power to the bureaucracy and military, established compulsory education and conscription, and promoted industry by importing technology and scientific knowledge from the West.

During the initial decades of the Meiji period (1868–1926) the government established a national banking system and standardized currency issued by the central Bank of Japan. The development of extensive sea transportation and railroad networks followed, which facilitated the integration of national markets. The financial and transportation infrastructure speeded the expansion of the mining and textile industries, as the government sold its initial interests in technology imported from Europe and the United States to private concerns.

Gail Honda is director of the Program in Applied Quantitative Research and a research associate of the Department of Sociology at the University of Chicago.

This paper is dedicated to the memory of Ted Shay, who was a Ph.D. candidate in the Department of Economics at Harvard University when he passed away in 1989.

1. Meiji is the name of the emperor at the time, hence the name Meiji Ishin, which can be translated as Meiji Restoration.

Then the boom of World War I ushered in a period of increased production, a rise in employment in secondary industries, and the development of heavy and chemical industries spurred by the harnessing and generation of electric power. Japan's industrial activities were largely concentrated in a narrow urban belt extending from Tōkyō on the eastern half of the main island of Honshū, through Nagoya and Ōsaka in western Honshū, to Fukuoka in the northern section of Kyūshū.

By 1940 Japan had built a colonial empire that included Taiwan, Korea, and Manchuria, and an economic infrastructure large enough to wage serious war with the Western allies and extend its control through north China, Burma, Indonesia, the Philippines, and the Solomon Islands. Japan's imperialist drive through Asia began in the Meiji period with the Taiwan expedition in 1874 and ended with the staggering blows that the United States dealt Japan finally to end the Pacific War. For all the excitement generated during the Meiji period over building a new state founded on principles of civilization, enlightenment, and human rights, for all the effort channeled into creating a new kind of emperor—a spiritual and timeless head of a divine people united by a pure and native soul—for all the capital, financial and human, invested in the drive to industrialize, Japan's modern economic growth led not to a liberal democratic society but to an unfree people governed by an expansionist military regime and ruled by an absolutist imperial system.

Closely linked to military expansion was the development of large-scale industry in communication, transportation, banking, trade, arms, chemicals, and metallurgy. Many of these industries were the cornerstones of enormous conglomerates (*zaibatsu*) such as Sumitomo (Bank, Metals, Rubber, Construction) and Mitsubishi (Bank, Heavy Industries, Motor, Petrochemical, and Trading). Because these industries served the needs of the state, powerful bureaucracies—Ministry of Posts and Telecommunications, Ministry of Munitions, Ministry of Transportation—were established to facilitate financing and manage output to meet national goals. Capital investment in plant and facilities, research and development, and rationalization of operations greatly boosted the productivity of these so-called modern industries relative to agriculture and traditional or small-scale industries. Real wage differentials between employees of the modern sector and those of the agricultural and traditional sectors reflected the productivity differentials. The industrial boom of World War I and the ensuing agricultural depression of the 1920s created a skilled labor shortage in the modern sector and excess labor in the traditional, which further widened productivity and real wage differentials. In addition, monopolistic positions held by the *zaibatsu* enabled them to take advantage of lower wages by subcontracting work to small-scale firms. By the mid-1930s the widening differentials in productivity and real wages between the modern and traditional sectors (hereafter referred to as the "differential structure") had become a pronounced characteristic of the Japanese economy, to the detriment of agriculture and the traditional sector.

The purpose of this paper is to examine the effects of militarization and formation of the differential structure on the health and well-being of the Japanese people during the period of industrialization from the *Meiji Ishin* through the Pacific War. The hypotheses driving the analysis are (1) investment in the military diverted funds that would otherwise have gone into improving the health of the people, such as investment in social welfare, public health technology, and sanitation, which resulted in poorer health, and (2) just as real wages reflected the gaps in technology between the modern and traditional sectors, so gaps in measures of health—nutritional status, mortality, and fertility—reflected gaps in real wages, leading to the formation of a differential structure in health.

The remainder of the paper proceeds as follows: section 7.2 discusses the health and welfare of the Japanese people before industrialization; section 7.3 introduces the foundation of modern economic growth and its attendant wars and epidemics; section 7.4 looks at the relationship between industrialization and nutritional status with respect to stature, diet and nutrition, and child growth; section 7.5 analyzes differential health; and section 7.6 concludes with a discussion of the results in the light of the proposed hypotheses.

7.2   Health and Welfare before Industrialization, 1600–1868

7.2.1   *Bakuhan* Political Economy

Though the first power looms that arrived from England in the 1880s might be interpreted as the seeds of Japan's industrial revolution, factors that eased the transition from an agricultural to an industrial society had long been developing during the Tokugawa period (1600–1868).[2] The *bakuhan* government in power during the Tokugawa period was characterized by a decentralized system of roughly 150 feudal lords (*daimyō*) who controlled their respective fiefs (*han*), collected taxes from the peasants residing in their domains, and paid them to the military seat of power (*bakufu*). In turn, to offset the autonomy granted to the *daimyō* and to minimize risk of collusion among them, the *bakufu* required them to reside for six months out of the year in the capital city of Edo (now Tōkyō) and often kept their families there as hostages. Accompanied by an entourage of servants, vassals, and flagbearers (the greater the entourage, the greater the perceived status), the *daimyō*, in their conspicuous consumption during the biannual treks to and from their *han*, contributed to the development of a mobile population and sophisticated commercial economy by the mid-nineteenth century.

Ogyū Sorai (1666–1728), counsel to the *bakufu* and arguably the most influential intellectual of the eighteenth century, caustically observed that the

---

2. This period is named after Tokugawa Ieyasu, the legendary warrior who subdued his rivals and unified the entire country in 1600.

constant transit of the *daimyō* was turning the entire samurai class into permanent hotel guests, so that "even a single chopstick had to be paid for."[3] The inns, restaurants, teahouses, and shops selling provisions that sprang up along the well-trodden routes leading to Edo were run or financed by the merchants, considered the lowest of all four classes (samurai-farmer-artisan-merchant) because of their association with money and profit. Moreover, since samurai lived on fixed stipends decreed by the *bakufu* they could afford their extravagant lifestyles only by incurring large debts with the merchant class. Thus, though merchants were ostensibly at the bottom of the social ladder, they in fact held the greatest economic power, fostered close ties with the *bakufu,* and were extremely sophisticated in their thinking on monetary and fiscal policy.[4]

7.2.2 Capital Formation

It was the Tokugawa peasants, however, who created the capital surplus that enabled the Meiji government to self-finance the initial steps of industrialization and infrastructure development.[5] Increased productivity and development of arable land led to a rise in agricultural output during this period, while periodic famine, increasing age at marriage, and decreasing marital fertility stemmed population growth.[6] This led to a rise in per capita agricultural output from around 1720 through the mid-nineteenth century. Changes in population growth, area of arable land, grain output, and corresponding per capita figures are given in table 7.1.

The numbers show rapid population growth from 1600 to 1720, then very little through 1850. Grain output, on the other hand, grew by 50 percent during the period of no population growth. This meant an increase of about 40 percent in per capita grain output during the latter half of the Tokugawa period. Due to the scattered nature of economic data from the Tokugawa period, no GDP figures exist. However, grain output serves as a reasonable proxy for demonstrating growth trends in GDP. This is because grain production accounted for at least two-thirds of agricultural production, which in turn occupied at least 80 percent of the labor force. Moreover, rice was the standard currency of exchange in which wages and taxes were paid.

If per capita grain output (GDP) was increasing, did this lead to an improved standard of living for the Tokugawa population? The evidence for the answer to this question is even sketchier, but the overall conclusion appears to be that

3. For more of Ogyū's incisive comments on Tokugawa economy and society, see Maruyama (1974).

4. For an exposition of the critical role Tokugawa merchants played in laying the intellectual foundations of the country's political economy, see Najita (1987).

5. For an international comparison of the "legacy of seclusion" that resulted in levels of capital adequate for self-financed industrialization, see Rosovsky (1961, 55–104).

6. For an analysis of age at marriage, see Hayami (1968, 1978). A synopsis of why marital fertility decreased can be found in Saitō (1992a). The discrepancy between agricultural output and population growth and its contribution to economic growth is discussed in Hanley and Yamamura (1977).

Table 7.1 **Changes in Various Economic Measures, 1600–1872**

Period	Population (N)	Arable Land (R)	Grain Output (Y)	R/N	Y/N	Y/R
1600	12,000	2,065	19,731	0.1721	1.644	9.55
1650	17,180	2,354	23,133	0.1370	1.346	9.83
1700	27,690	2,841	30,630	0.1026	1.106	10.78
1720	31,280	2,927	32,034	0.0936	1.024	10.94
1730	32,080	2,971	32,736	0.0926	1.020	11.02
1750	31,100	2,991	34,140	0.0962	1.098	11.41
1800	30,650	3,032	37,650	0.0989	1.228	12.42
1850	32,280	3,170	41,160	0.0982	1.275	12.98
1872	33,110	3,234	46,812	0.0977	1.414	14.47

Source: Hayami and Miyamoto (1988).
Note: Units are N in 1,000; R in 1,000 *chō* (1 *chō* = 2.45 acres); Y in 1,000 *koku* (1 *koku* = 180 liters).

if one "survived" abortion, infanticide, epidemics, and famine, one could enjoy a reasonably favorable standard of living. Stories of abortion and infanticide are legion, though quantitative evidence indicates that these forms of birth control were not used primarily to reduce family size in times of poverty, but were practiced by rich and poor alike as a form of family planning.[7] Also, while per capita grain output was increasing on a countrywide level, these numbers do not take into account regional and intervillage differences in yield and climate. Occasional crop failures and cold, wet climatic conditions led to periodic famines and outbreaks of infectious diseases that razed certain village populations and held the country's population growth in check (see Jannetta 1992).

7.2.3 Self-Help and Community Aid as Social Welfare

Periodic surges in mortality due to subsistence crises, when per capita surpluses in grain were increasing, suggest that the *bakuhan* government failed to effect an efficient countrywide food distribution system and adequate welfare measures for those in need. In keeping with Confucian ethics, which emphasize diligence and thrift, relief for the destitute took the form of assisting only victims of disaster and those physically unable to work. Also, the Confucian hierarchy of human relationships stressed the benevolent rule of the *daimyō* over his subjects and called for a more personal rather than institutional form of aid. In the farm villages in times of crop failure, richer neighbors and relatives were called upon to help their poorer counterparts. In the cities, poor-

---

7. This was the startling finding in Smith (1977). Smith writes, "Large landholders practiced it as well as small, and registered births were as numerous in bad as in good growing years. Also, infanticide seems to have been used to control the sex sequence and spacing of births and the sexual composition and final size of families. In short, it gives the impression of a kind of family planning" (147).

houses and workhouses were established to feed and shelter vagrants, but their main purpose was to get able-bodied vagabonds back to work again through training programs and moral suasion. This is in contrast to England and Germany, which had more institutionalized and ongoing forms of welfare.[8]

In theory, the purpose of government should be the economic well-being of society, according to Dazai Shundai (1680–1747), a leading figure in Tokugawa intellectual and political circles. Specifically, he defined political economy as *keisei saimin,* which means "gauging actual economic conditions and rendering aid to the people for general social order and well-being." Economic well-being and the accumulation of wealth would be effected through trade among various sectors and at all levels of society. The role of government, then, would be to manage (*keiei*) from above in order to ensure optimal conditions for trade and wealth accumulation. The enduring legacy of Dazai's theories can be observed in Japanese political economy today: its "managed economy," trade surpluses, and the modern Japanese word for economics, *keizai,* an elision of *keisei saimin.*[9]

Government aid in Dazai's sense could thus be described as encouraging self-sufficiency and intersocietal trade. Most commoners organized themselves into communal associations called *kō* that arranged loans, mutual assistance in times of emergency, and life and health insurance among other forms of aid for its members. The ubiquitous nature of *kō* and the degree to which people relied on them rather than the state are evident in the observation that every single village in Japan has at least one *kō.* One government survey in the late nineteenth century put the number of *kō* in Japan at around 350,000.[10] Thus, in the absence of statewide provisions for social welfare, commoners created their own forms of insurance and credit at the local level. The existence of periodic famines and epidemics does not mean that *kō* and stopgap forms of assistance were ineffectual; only that they had their limits in reducing mortality in times of disaster.

7.2.4 Longevity and Nutritional Status

Nevertheless, those who survived enjoyed relatively long and healthy lives. Life expectancy at birth as shown in table 7.2 varied widely over place and time but was comparable to, if not better than, life expectancy in England and Wales during the same period. This evidence refutes the long-held view of preindustrial Japan as a backward, impoverished society of starving people dying early and killing their newborn to limit family size. Life expectancy in Tokugawa Japan was bolstered by the absence of war and relative lack of pestilence. Whereas much of preindustrial Europe was ravaged by bloody military campaigns, there were no wars in Japan from 1600 through the mid-nineteenth

8. This discussion of Japanese and Western welfare measures is from an exposition by Garon (1994).

9. For the theoretical underpinnings of Japan's political economy in the thought of Dazai Shundai, see Najita (1972).

10. For the intellectual origins and various manifestations of *kō,* see Najita (1988).

Table 7.2   Life Expectancy at Birth in Japan and in England and Wales, 1700–1854

	Japan			England and Wales	
Period	Region	Male	Female	Period	Both Sexes
1700–1824	Chikuzen	44.7	43.3	1700–1725	35.1
1716–1872	Iwashiro	37.8	38.6		
1717–1830	Mino	43.2	43.2		
1720–1870	Iwashiro	37.7	36.4	1725–50	33.8
1773–1830	Mino	38.6	39.1		
1776–1875	Hida	32.3	32.0	1750–75	36.3
1782–96	Mikawa	34.9	55.0		
1800–1835	Bizen	41.1	44.9	1775–1800	37.0
1812–15	Shinano	36.8	36.5		
1819–54	Echizen	26.3	24.1		

Sources: Japan, Saitō (1992b); England and Wales, Fogel (1986).
Note: For England and Wales, life expectancy is for both sexes by birth cohort.

century. Also, although almost everyone in Tokugawa Japan contracted small-pox and some succumbed to measles and dysentery, the major killer diseases in premodern Europe—plague and typhus—did not appear in Japan before industrialization.[11]

When major famines did strike, the famine mortality rates were higher for males than they were for females. This phenomenon in which females exhibit greater resistance than males under conditions of environmental stress has been observed and documented in many studies from Bengal to Greece, during famines and during wartime. It may be attributable to the larger stores of body fat in women (see Jannetta 1992, 437; Eveleth and Tanner 1990, 200). Of the three major famines in the Tokugawa period—the Kyōhō famine (1722–33), the Tenmei famine (1783–87), and the Tenpō famine (1833–37)—the Tenmei famine was the most severe in terms of population loss and recovery time. The relatively short period of data available for the Mikawa sample in Japan shown in table 7.2, and the coincidence of the data years with the Tenmei famine, may account for most of the large difference in life expectancy between males and females. To a lesser extent the Bizen sample also exhibits a sex difference, which may be attributed to the effect of the Tenpō famine. Differences in estimated life expectancy among samples in table 7.2 may arise not only from actual regional differences but also from differences in the kinds of data sources.[12]

11. This is probably due to Japan's geographic isolation and very limited contact with foreign cultures. Trade was restricted to a single port at the southern tip of the island of Kyūshū for 250 years. See Jannetta (1987).

12. Buddhist temple registers (*kakochō*), from which the Chikuzen and Hida data are taken, record all deaths, infant as well as adult. Population registers (*shūmon aratame chō*), from which all other data in table 7.2 were retrieved, record only those who survived from birth to the subsequent compilation. See Jannetta and Preston (1991, 419–20) and Cornell and Hayami (1986, 321).

Table 7.3   Estimation of Height Based on Length of Right Femur 600 B.C. to A.D. 1900

Period		Female		Male	
Name	Years	N	Mean (m)	N	Mean (m)
Jōmon	600–200 B.C.	9	1.480	11	1.591
Yayoi	200 B.C. to A.D. 250	14	1.505	12	1.614
Kofun/Nara/Heian	250–1185	9	1.515	22	1.631
Kamakura	1185–1333	5	1.449	17	1.590
Muromachi/Momoyama	1333–1600	17	1.466	26	1.568
Tokugawa	1600–1868	45	1.456	95	1.571
Early Meiji	1868–1900	43	1.448	43	1.553

Source: Hiramoto (1972).

The nutritional status of Tokugawa society also appears to have been fairly high and above subsistence level. Engel's coefficient for food has been estimated at 0.6–0.8, but income elasticity for food was in the 0.3–0.4 range as additional income was spent not on more or better food, but on entertainment, travel, and capital investments.[13] Diet seems to have been nutritious though low in animal protein and showed little variation across income levels and over time. It consisted primarily of rice—usually mixed with other grains like barley, millet, and buckwheat—which was served at every meal. Supplementing the grains would be soybean products like tofu or miso (soybean paste), greens and root vegetables, pickled condiments, and dried seafood products. One of the standard measures of nutritional status, height, has been estimated for the Tokugawa period based on measurements of the maximum length of the right femur. These estimates are given in table 7.3 along with those for the other major periods in Japanese history dating back to 600 B.C.

The Tokugawa bone samples were dug up at a construction site in Tōkyō proper and are thought to be from commoners' graves. Bone samples from the early Meiji period were also unearthed from within Tōkyō proper and are thought to be those of common laborers who died from illness or execution. Thus, the two samples may be considered comparable with respect to socioeconomic class. Since anyone in Japan who could afford a proper funeral and burial would have been cremated, it is safe to assume that both samples are from the remains of the poor or indigent. Although the sample sizes are small, these estimates show that the average Tokugawa female was almost 1 cm taller than her early Meiji counterpart; the Tokugawa male nearly 2 cm taller than his. With 95 percent confidence intervals of 4 cm, these numbers must be used with caution. Nevertheless, they suggest at least that, among the lower socio-

---

13. This is based on an analysis of budgets for a Tokugawa carpenter, farmer, and samurai in Hanley (1983).

economic classes, Japanese nutritional status during the Tokugawa period was no worse than that during the period of early industrialization.

7.2.5 Summary: Tokugawa Health and Welfare

The health and welfare of the Japanese people during the 250 years prior to industrialization were good relative to that of the population of contemporary Europe and early industrial Japan. Population size held steady from 1720 to 1872 at about 32 million due to a combination of increasing age at marriage, lower marital fertility rates, use of birth control, occasional crises of subsistence, and outbreaks of infectious diseases. Improved agricultural technology and better land development resulted in rising per capita grain output. A proxy for per capita GDP, it increased 40 percent over the same period, which suggests an increasing standard of living.

The effect of government policy that had as its goal the economic well-being of the people and of a welfare system that stressed self-help and communal assistance over institutional forms of aid is more difficult to measure. During times of the most severe famine, there were significant crises of subsistence and surges in mortality. This is evidence of a flawed distribution system and a sign that perhaps more institutional forms of welfare were needed. Nevertheless, Tokugawa commoners managed to provide insurance and loans and other forms of aid to one another through communal *kō*, in times both good and bad.

There were no epidemics on the scale witnessed in premodern Europe and in Japan during the later period of industrialization. In addition, there were no wars in Japan from 1600 until the mid-nineteenth century. This relative absence of calamitous events resulted in a life expectancy at birth that varied widely with time and place but was comparable to, if not better than, life expectancy in eighteenth- and nineteenth-century England and Wales. The Japanese diet, virtually unchanged until the mid-twentieth century, was nutritious. The low income elasticity for food suggests that more income did not mean people bought more or better food. Estimates of the average height of Tokugawa commoners show that their nutritional status was no worse, and perhaps better, than that of commoners in the early period of industrialization that followed.

7.3 Foundations of Modern Economic Growth

7.3.1 Building a Rich Country and Strong Army

Meiji Ishin is the name given to the political, economic, and social revolution waged by self-proclaimed emperor loyalists (*shishi*) who overthrew military (*shōgun*) rule in the name of Emperor Meiji. The new government officials opened Japan's ports to foreign trade and engaged in cultural exchange after more than 250 years of seclusion from the rest of the world. Those who embarked on diplomatic missions to the West were amazed by the scientific and industrial achievements of Great Britain, Germany, and the United States. Using Western models gleaned from abroad, Meiji state architects instituted national conscription, compulsory elementary education, and land tax reform. Japan was set on a rapid course of industrialization and economic expansion in a quest to build a "rich country and strong army" (*fukoku kyōhei*) and maintain national independence.

The four pillars of the *shokusan kōgyō* ("increase production, promote enterprise") policy set forth in the 1870s were (1) establishment of a national banking system, (2) development of transportation and communication networks, (3) creation and subsequent sale of public sector factories, and (4) loans to private firms. The *han* system of *daimyō* rule was dismantled and the prefectural system established. Many reforms were enacted which liberalized social relationships and economic transactions. The class system (samurai-farmer-artisan-merchant) was abolished, and restrictions on occupational mobility and buying and selling of land were lifted. Japan became, by all appearances, a modern state.

Beneath the facade of a budding liberal democratic society, however, lay the foundations of an absolutist military regime unwilling to relinquish power to the people. The parliament (Diet), which opened in 1890, was originally voted in only by those who could afford the high price of a ballot, that is, wealthy industrialists and landlords. The military character of and impetus to economic growth remained a constant force from its well-intentioned origins to the insidious takeover of the economy in the 1930s. With state-run arms production a major industry, one of the greatest stimulants to economic growth during the early period of industrialization was war: the Sino-Japanese War (1894–95) and the Russo-Japanese War (1904–5). Though Japan was not a direct participant, World War I (1914–18) was a boon to exports as Japan supplied markets normally served by European countries then occupied with the war. Indeed, growth rates of GNP rose to 4–7 percent in the late 1890s, 11 percent in 1904, and 6–9 percent during World War I (calculated from Ohkawa et al. 1974).

Overall, the Japanese growth rate from 1868 to 1940 is estimated at somewhere between 3 and 4 percent. During the Meiji period (1868–1912), new monetary and national banking systems were developed, and the foundations of modern industry established. Once sea and rail transportation networks were in place, coal and metal mining developed to the extent that copper was Japan's fifth most important export in 1900. The textile industries, notably silk reeling and cotton spinning, followed mining to become a leading component of Japan's exports. World War I ushered in the boom age of heavy industries such as chemicals, metals, and machinery, fueled by newly harnessed electric power. Then the economy suffered a number of blows: namely, the panic of 1920, the agricultural depression of the 1920s, the great Kantō earthquake of 1923, the financial panic of 1927, and the downturn of the 1930s due to the worldwide depression. By 1940, the War with China had broken out, and the Japanese were on the verge of war with the United States. The final decade of

Table 7.4   **Employed Population by Sector, 1872–1940**

Year	Primary	Secondary	Tertiary	Unclassified	Total
1872	15,525	n.a.	5,846	n.a.	21,371
	(72.6)		(27.4)		(100)
1885	15,654	n.a.	6,685	n.a.	22,339
	(70.1)		(29.9)		(100)
1890	15,637	n.a.	7,405	n.a.	23,042
	(67.8)		(32.2)		(100)
1895	15,482	n.a.	8,242	n.a.	23,724
	(65.3)		(34.7)		(100)
1900	15,853	n.a.	8,525	n.a.	24,378
	(65.0)		(35.0)		(100)
1905	16,707	3,729	3,618	1,007	25,061
	(69.5)	(15.5)	(15.0)	(0)	(100)
1910	16,383	4,089	3,943	1,060	25,475
	(67.1)	(16.8)	(16.1)	(0)	(100)
1915	14,615	4,884	4,501	1,305	26,305
	(62.5)	(19.5)	(18.0)	(0)	(100)
1920	14,388	6,274	5,355	1,243	27,260
	(55.3)	(24.1)	(20.6)	(0)	(100)
1925	14,056	6,324	6,432	1,293	28,105
	(52.4)	(23.6)	(24.0)	(0)	(100)
1930	14,648	6,151	7,331	1,488	29,619
	(52.1)	(21.0)	(26.1)	(0)	(100)
1935	14,450	6,811	8,410	1,540	31,211
	(48.7)	(23.0)	(28.3)	(0)	(100)
1940	14,523	8,212	7,728	2,037	32,500
	(47.7)	(27.0)	(25.3)	(0)	(100)

Source: Nakamura (1983, 21).

Note: Population in thousands (by percentage in parentheses). Primary sector = agriculture, forestry, and fisheries. Secondary sector = mining, manufacturing, and construction. Tertiary sector = transportation, communication, utilities, commerce, services, and public administration.

the period was characterized by heavy industrialization to support the military.[14]

The changing composition of the economy as indicated by labor force participation in various sectors is shown in table 7.4. The percentage engaged in the primary sector declined by one-third, from 73 percent to 48 percent. Losses in the primary sector beginning in the early twentieth century fed directly into the other two sectors, both of which showed steady increases until 1940. The percentage of the total population attributed to the secondary sector nearly doubled from 15 percent to 27 percent between 1905 and 1940. Most of the increase occurred in manufacturing. Commercial activities, followed by com-

14. For more detailed analyses of the Japanese prewar economy, see Nakamura (1983) or Ohkawa and Rosovsky (1973).

Table 7.5   Growth of Japanese Urban Population, 1891–1940

Year	Urban Population (thousands)	Total Population (thousands)	Percentage Urban[a]
1891	3,812	40,719	9.36
1898	5,518	43,764	12.61
1903	6,748	46,732	14.44
1908	8,227	49,589	16.60
1913	8,920	53,363	16.71
1920	10,020	55,963	17.90
1925	12,823	59,737	21.47
1930	15,363	64,450	23.84
1935	22,582	69,254	32.61
1940	27,494	73,114	37.60

Source: Wilkinson (1965, 45).
[a]Urban = population in incorporated cities (*shi*).

munications and transportation, accounted for most of the increase in the tertiary sector. The initial high percentage of tertiary workers in the nineteenth century is attributed to the large portion of the population engaged in traditional services such as domestic servitude, entertainment, retail trade, and small commercial proprietorships.

The transition of Japan from a largely agricultural society to one in which over half of the population was engaged in nonagricultural activities was accompanied by a redistribution of the labor force from rural to urban areas. The absolute and proportionate growth of the population in incorporated cities (*shi*) from 1891 to 1940 is shown in table 7.5. From 1891 to 1940, the percentage of Japan's total population living in cities of 20,000 or more jumped from 9.4 percent to 37.6 percent. In other words, in 50 years, the proportion of the population living in cities of 20,000 or more went from less than one-tenth to over one-third. Comparable increases in the percentages of urban population took 80 years (1780–1860) in England and Wales and 75 years (1850–1925) in the United States (Wilkinson 1965, 37).

The rapid urbanization witnessed in Japan was initially spurred by the sudden opening of the country to the rest of the world in the late nineteenth century and the expansion of international trade. Though there were well over 400 incorporated cities by 1920, six great metropolitan centers accounted for one-half to two-thirds of the urban population of the prewar period. Of these six—Tōkyō, Yokohama, Nagoya, Ōsaka, Kōbe, and Kyōtō—only Kyōtō, the ancient capital and cultural center of Japan, was not a major port city or closely associated with an export center. The later wave of urbanization in the 1930s resulted from the agricultural depression of the 1920s and the collapse of the silk market due to the worldwide depression in the 1930s. Displaced laborers flocked

Table 7.6   Estimated Literacy Rates for Various Groups, 1897–1941

Year	Sample Population	Estimated Percentage Literate
1897	Ōsaka factory workers	21.5
1902	Ōsaka conscripts	53.1
1907	Ōsaka conscripts	66.1
1912	Ōsaka conscripts	74.8
1925	All conscripts	88.7
1933	All conscripts	95.8
1941	All conscripts	98.5

Source: Taira (1971, 378–81).

Note: Percentage of sample with at least a lower elementary school education (four years of school, six years from 1907 on) used as proxy for literacy. The 1897 sample = factory workers in Ōsaka; 1902–12 sample = conscripts in Ōsaka; 1925–41 sample = conscripts in all of Japan.

to the major industrial centers for jobs in the burgeoning military industries of chemicals, oil, shipbuilding, and munitions (Wilkinson 1965, 44–50).

The use of increasingly sophisticated technology in Japan's science-based industries and the growth of white-collar service industries in the early twentieth century required a trained, disciplined, and literate workforce. National compulsory education of four years (increased to six years in 1907) was promulgated in 1872, though several decades elapsed before virtual universal education was achieved. In 1873 the elementary school enrollment rate for both boys and girls was reported to be 28.1 percent. By 1883 it was 51.0 percent, and not until 1910 was 98 percent enrollment reported. Precise figures on literacy can at best be roughly estimated for the prewar period because of the difficulty in defining literacy for the Japanese population. While the ability to sign one's name is often interpreted as an indication of literacy in Western countries, knowledge of at least 2,000 Chinese characters in addition to two 50-character alphabets is required for functional literacy in the Japanese language.[15] Moreover, enrollment in elementary school is not equivalent to completion and certainly not to literacy. For example, the 98 percent enrollment rate in 1910 disguises the estimated elementary school completion rate among those in employable age brackets at the time: 40.6 percent of males and 22.6 percent of females (Ohkawa 1968, 136).

Table 7.6 is a compilation of some of the best estimates of literacy rates for the prewar period. Rates of completion of elementary school were used as a proxy because it was assumed that four to five years of schooling were necessary for minimum literacy, and six for functional literacy, "the ability to read,

15. Excellent analyses and discussions of this topic can be found in Taira (1971) and Japan National Commission for UNESCO (1966).

write, and reckon intelligently for one's own practical needs" (Taira 1971, 376–77). The 1897 estimate is from a study of Ōsaka factory workers in cotton spinning; weaving; manufacture of glass, tiles, matches, brushes, blinds, or machinery; shipbuilding; clock and watchmaking, chemical and drug production, and printing. Although the overall percentage of graduates is 21.5, there was much variation among the groups. For example, only 9.8 percent of male workers in glass and tile manufacturing completed elementary education, as compared to 78.7 percent of male workers in printing. The figures for 1902, 1907, and 1912 were taken from military conscript records from the prefecture of Ōsaka, which might be expected to be higher than the national average because of the prefecture's high urban concentration. Indeed, urban conscripts of Ōsaka had a literacy rate of 87 percent; rural conscripts 70 percent (Taira 1971, 379). It was not until the 1920s that near universal literacy as envisioned by nineteenth-century architects of the Japanese modern state was attained.[16]

Thus, in labor force composition, urbanization, and literacy, Japan had by 1940 attained levels characteristic of a modern state. The composition of the labor force was significantly altered as the percentage of the population in agriculture dropped from 75 to 50. The modern industries of the secondary sector included mining and textiles initially, followed by the heavy industries of machinery, metal, oil, and chemicals. The modern industries of the tertiary sector, which accounted for 25 percent of the labor force in 1940, were primarily banking and finance, transportation, and commercial trade. To accommodate the growing nonagricultural workforce, the urban population of Japan went from less than 10 percent of the total population in the late nineteenth century to nearly 40 percent in 50 years, a phenomenon that required 80 years in England and Wales and 75 in the United States at comparables stages of industrialization. The increasing sophistication of modern industries in manufacturing and services required a disciplined and literate workforce. Literacy rates, estimated by rates of completion of four to six years of elementary school, suggest that by the eve of the Pacific War near universal literacy in Japan had been achieved. Industrialization, however, also ushered in a new era of health and welfare for the Japanese population, one that introduced new diseases and stratified society into various levels of physical well-being.

7.3.2   The Age of Epidemics

As discussed in section 7.2, no wars were fought during the Tokugawa period until the mid-nineteenth century, when the *bakufu* government was first attacked by disgruntled *han* armies from the southern island of Kyūshū. Life expectancy during the Tokugawa period was also bolstered relative to preindustrial Europe by the absence of plague and typhus, and by the limited spread

16. The 88.7 percent rate for all male conscripts reported for Japan in 1925 surpasses estimated literacy rates in 1990 for China, India, and Indonesia. The rate for Japan when females are included would be less than 88.7 percent.

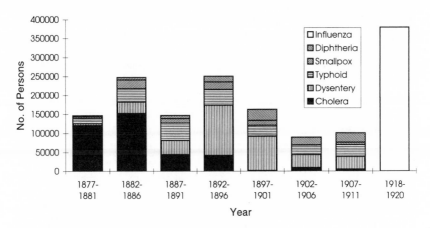

Fig. 7.1   Deaths by infectious diseases, 1877–1920
Sources: 1877–1911 calculated from Itō (1991); 1918–20 from Kōseishō imu kyoku hen (1976).

of measles, dysentery, and cholera. In contrast, once ports were opened to trade, early industrializing Japan was swept by wave after wave of cholera, smallpox, dysentery, and Spanish influenza. Figure 7.1 depicts the enormity of epidemic mortality figures of acute infectious diseases.

The worst of the cholera epidemics took place just after Japan opened its ports to foreign trade in the years of turmoil just preceding and during the Meiji Ishin. Many hundreds of thousands died in these initial outbreaks until the Central Sanitary Bureau was able to curb the spread of cholera through isolation of the ill, public education, and sanitation measures. While smallpox was the major killer disease of the Tokugawa period, by the Meiji period smallpox deaths were reduced to several tens of thousands as the result of widespread efforts to vaccinate all children. The influenza epidemic of 1918–20 in Japan killed twice as many people as the great Kantō earthquake of 1923 and was part of the worldwide influenza pandemic that claimed 25–30 million lives.[17]

Tuberculosis, while not listed as an epidemic disease, was claiming mortality rates of about 0.16 percent of the population around the turn of the century. This rate was comparable to that of Western Europe. Rates in Western industrial countries declined over the first half of the mid-twentieth century, dropping to well below 0.10 percent by 1940. Japan's tuberculosis mortality rate, however, remained high, fluctuating between a low of 0.18 percent in 1932 and a high of 0.28 percent in 1945 (see Hunter 1993). It was a well-documented killer of young women in textile factories in early industrializing Japan, and one of the leading causes of death throughout the prewar period along with pneumonia and gastrointestinal diseases.

17. For a detailed exposé of the Japanese influenza pandemic, see Rice and Palmer (1993).

War and epidemics have been discussed at some length to delineate prominent exogenous factors that distinguish Japan's preindustrial from its early industrial period. They also have significant bearing on the economy and serve to illustrate the quality and magnitude of the welfare policy that the government enacted to maintain or improve the health of its people. Despite major reforms in economic policy and development instituted by the Meiji government, welfare and health care during this period became only slightly more institutionalized. There was still a heavy reliance on ad hoc measures typical of the Tokugawa period of "mutual fellowship among the people," that is, dependence on the family and community for assistance. The people responded by drawing on the firmly established institution of communal *kō* from the Tokugawa period. Commoners in industrializing Japan—in villages and cities alike—organized themselves into larger insurance and medical co-ops. These were called *mujin kaisha,* literally "unlimited resource companies," and provided loans and other forms of assistance. Unable to rely on the state for health care and welfare, the Japanese people pooled resources among themselves to construct enduring institutions that continue today as important sources of credit in the form of *sōgō ginkō,* or "mutual trust bank."[18]

New forms of poverty created by industrialization and urbanization, however, prompted the passage of the Relief Regulations (Jukkyū Kisoku) in 1874, the only institutionalized poor law for 55 years. Though the Relief Regulations were passed in emulation of German social policy and English poor laws, government expenditures in reality were minimal and inconsistent. Medical care for the poor was offered and retracted at will. Moreover, it was largely financed by contributions solicited from the private sector and donated by the imperial household. For all the Home Ministry's rhetoric to promote the health and welfare of the people, it failed to support its words with the necessary capital.[19]

7.3.3   Military Expansion at the Expense of Social Welfare

Welfare, health care, epidemics, and war intersect in peculiar ways in early industrializing Japan. First, there appears to be a trade-off between government investment in the military and in social welfare. Following Japan's victory in the Russo-Japanese War, the government in 1908 cut the poor relief budget to finance military expansion. This act was part of an effort to increase Japan's world power by "creating a people who worked selflessly for national prosperity while making few demands on the state." Minimizing relief to the poor fitted in well with the centuries-old exhortation to encourage self-reliance and to use moral suasion to get people back into the productive labor force (Garon 1994, 82). Seen from the government's point of view, to build a "wealthy coun-

18. Najita (1993) brings to light these forms of insurance, health care, and credit in a discussion of commoner participation in and contribution to the industrial revolution.

19. This attitude toward poor relief was not unique to Japan. For a broader discussion of Japanese welfare in historical perspective, see Garon (1994).

try and strong army" the return on investment was far greater in the military sector than in social welfare.

Second, the government invested very little in public health technology so that it could instead boost its burgeoning military-industrial complex. For example, widespread measures were taken to bring cholera epidemics of the late nineteenth century under control, but these measures consisted primarily of vaccination and promoting sanitation through education and propaganda, rather than more capital-intensive efforts such as hospital and sanatorium construction, modern sewer systems, and piped water. Channeling of funds into the military and away from public health may have been a major factor in the failure of Japanese life expectancy to keep up with that of contemporary Western Europe in the first half of the twentieth century (Mosk and Johansson 1986, 430–32).

Finally, with heavy investment in the military, it is not surprising that Japan's major contribution to public health was in the field of military medicine. In the Sino-Japanese War Japan lost four times as many men to infectious diseases spread in camps as it did to battlefield wounds, a classic historical ratio of causes of death in war. By the Russo-Japanese War a decade later, it had managed to reduce mortality by infectious diseases in the war to one-fourth of all war deaths. This was accomplished through major investments in field hospitals and laboratories, the latest medicine and equipment, first aid handbooks for all soldiers, and a healthy military diet (Johansson and Mosk 1987, 221–22). Japan's advances in military medicine have been called "the real triumph of Japan" by an American officer, though the praise rings hollow when the diversion of funds from public health and the ensuing costs are considered.

7.4   Industrialization and Nutritional Status

7.4.1   Income and Height

The positive relationship between income and height as a proxy for nutritional status has been documented in many studies. These include both analyses of secular trends and comparisons among socioeconomic groups (see Fogel 1993; Floud, Wachter, and Gregory 1990; Eveleth and Tanner 1990; Steckel 1983). Thus it comes as no surprise that average heights of 20-year-old recruits in Japan increased during industrialization along with per capita GDP. Figure 7.2 captures these trends. From 1892 to 1937 there was a fairly steady increase in height, from 156.1 cm to 160.3 cm, or an average of 0.91 cm per decade.[20] As a point of comparison, the average height of 160.3 cm for Japanese recruits attained in the mid-twentieth century was still a good 3–8 cm shorter than

---

20. Because 20-year-old men in the nineteenth century had several more years of growing left, the increase in heights shown in fig. 7.2 is probably overstated. If adjusted for estimated further growth in nineteenth-century recruits, the increase in height over the period would be 3.3 cm, or an average of 0.7 cm per decade (Shay 1986).

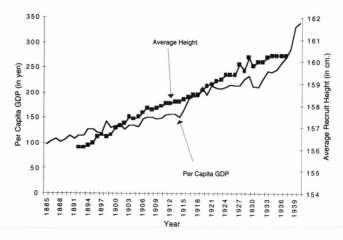

Fig. 7.2   Per capita GDP and average height of 20-year-old military recruits, 1886–1940

Sources: Per capita GDP in 1934–36 prices calculated from Ohkawa et al. (1974, 227) for GDP and Umemura et al. (1988, 169–71) for population. Average recruit height from Shay (1986, appendix).

Note: Year is year of measurement for recruits.

full-grown men in Great Britain, Norway, Sweden, and Hungary in the mid-*eighteenth* century.[21]

This difference has been largely attributed to the genetic pool, but rapid increases in heights of Japanese men and women born after World War II have narrowed the gap. Interestingly, nearly all of the secular trend is due to an increase in leg length. Thus, although Japanese adult height is still one standard deviation below that of North Europeans, their trunk-leg proportions are more similar (see Tanner et al. 1982). Reasons for the postwar secular increase include better nutrition and greater consumption of animal protein and dairy products, though one study emphasizes urbanization and a decreasing Engel's coefficient over nutrition (Matsumoto 1982).

Increases in height during industrialization through 1937 were uneven, with higher rates of growth (0.4 percent) in 1892–97 and 1917–27, and lower rates of growth (0.1–0.2 percent) in 1907–12 and 1927–37.[22] This leveling off of

21. For European comparisons, see Fogel (1994). Body mass index, or BMI = weight/height^2 (in kg/m^2), is another predictor of health but is difficult to obtain unless one has individual height and weight data. These are not available for Japan on a national scale, but another study shows that average BMI for recruits in an agricultural village in Shizuoka prefecture increased from 20 in 1913 to 21.5 in the mid-1930s, then became erratic in wartime with a downward trend from 1937 to 1943. It never rose above 21.5, however, which suggests that early-twentieth-century Japanese recruits were slightly more wasted than American men in 1910, who had an average BMI of 22.6. See Honda (1996) for Japanese recruits, Kim (1993) for American men.

22. This change in height trends in the 1930s has also been observed in microlevel studies of rural Japan, where average height of 20-year-old recruits tended to decrease in the 1930s (see Honda 1995).

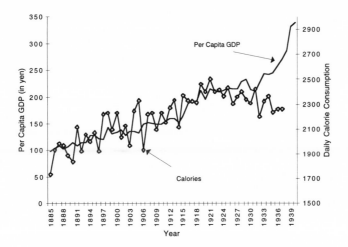

Fig. 7.3   Per capita GDP and daily caloric intake, 1886–1940
Sources: Per capita GDP in 1934–36 prices, as in fig. 7.2. Daily caloric intake from Mosk (1978, 279).

increases in the 1930s might reflect the decline in daily calorie consumption beginning in the early 1920s shown in figure 7.3. The decline is particularly pronounced against the backdrop of rising per capita GDP in the late 1930s due to military expansion. Why this drop occurred is unclear, though, based on the calculations from which the numbers are derived, it may have been due to a change in consumption patterns, a decrease in the total food supply of a particular food used in the calculations, or an increase in the population.[23]

7.4.2   Income, Diet, and Nutrition

A closer look at diet composition in table 7.7 reveals that most of the calories lost in the 1930s were from starchy staple consumption.[24] These declines were only partially offset by increases in animal protein consumption. Still, grains, noodles, and potatoes accounted for 83.3 percent of the Japanese diet through the mid-twentieth century. An estimated 72 calories per day in animal protein is scant; most of it probably came from fish and other marine products, which have long been a mainstay of the Japanese diet.

With estimated average caloric intake between 2,000 and 2,100 (or according to the graph's estimates, between 2,200 and 2,500) and declining from the 1920s, and with estimated caloric intake for various occupational categories as shown in table 7.8, it is remarkable that heights increased at all during

23. Caloric intake in fig. 7.3 was derived by calculating total nutrients consumed by food type and then dividing through by estimates of total population. Twenty-two food types were used. See the appendix in Mosk (1978).
24. These calorie estimates by Shinohara were derived differently from those shown in fig. 7.3, which were from Mosk (1978). See Kaneda (1970) for an explanation of Shinohara's estimates.

Table 7.7   Daily Calories per Capita by Major Food Group, 1911–35

Years	Starchy Staples (kcal)	Animal Proteins (kcal)	Other (kcal)	Total (kcal)
1911–15	1,765	40	232	2,037
	(86.6)	(2.0)	(11.4)	(100.0)
1921–25	1,807	47	269	2,123
	(85.1)	(2.2)	(12.7)	(100.0)
1931–35	1,711	72	272	2,055
	(83.3)	(3.5)	(13.2)	(100.0)

Source: Kaneda (1970, 409).

Note: Starchy staples include rice, barley, naked barley, other cereals, sweet potatoes, white potatoes, wheat flour, starch, and noodles. Animal proteins include meat, milk, eggs, fish, shellfish,
and other marine products. Estimates exclude canned and bottled foods and beverages. Figures in
parentheses are percentages of total calories.

Table 7.8   Caloric Intake by Occupational Class, 1926–36

Occupational Class	Caloric Intake (kcal)
Nonfarm household	2,578
Salaried worker	2,506
Laborer	2,614
Farm household	3,265
Owner or owner-tenant	3,279
Tenant	3,233

Source: Saitō (1989, 349).

this period. Small wonder that the final adult height for males in the mid-
twentieth century was far below that of Western industrialized countries. Furthermore, it seems that those who required the most energy (farmers) were
also the most economically disadvantaged. As will be shown in section 7.5.2,
evidence indicates that the combination of lower income and higher energy
requirements gave rise to one of the shortest occupational classes in industrializing Japan.

Until the 1920s, however, caloric intake rose along with per capita GDP.
This does not mean that Japanese spent more on food as their incomes rose. In
fact, income elasticities for food have been estimated at 0.3 or 0.4 from 1878
to 1940, which suggests that despite increasing exposure to Western lifestyles
during the first half of the twentieth century, people's food consumption patterns changed very slowly during the prewar period. This also means that as
incomes rose, most people still preferred the less expensive starch-based traditional Japanese meals to the more expensive Western-style meat-based fare,
though there was certainly some increase in consumption of animal proteins.

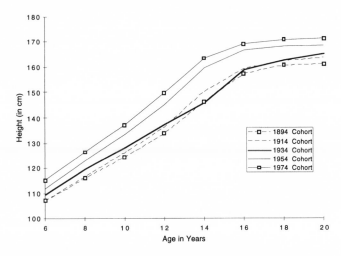

Fig. 7.4   Growth of schoolboys by birth cohort, 1894–1974
Sources: Calculated from Monbushō (1990, 270–71) and Umemura (1988, 14–15).

Another dietary switch that occurred as incomes rose was that from "inferior" starches, such as barley and naked barley, to the highly prized polished white rice (see Kaneda 1970). Consistently low levels of animal protein in the diet may have prevented greater increases in height such as those observed in the postwar period: spurts only came once the dietary habits of the Japanese incorporated greater proportions of meats and dairy products.

7.4.3   Nutritional Status and Growth of Schoolchildren

While final adult height represents one's nutritional status from birth through age at final height, the tempo of human growth measures one's physiological maturity at given ages. Two people may have the same final height, but they may mature at different times, depending on genetics, nutrition, and infection. Japanese children tend to mature earlier than European children, though they are on average shorter at full maturity. Acute, episodic malnutrition may temporarily stunt a child's growth, but full recovery can be expected if malnutrition is not protracted. Infectious diseases can prevent the body from absorbing vital nutrients even though nutrition is adequate, which can also stunt a child's development.[25]

The tempo of growth of Japanese schoolboys and schoolgirls is depicted in figures 7.4 and 7.5. The data are taken from annual reports published by the Ministry of Education on the physique and exercise skills of schoolchildren from 1900 through the year of publication. Mandatory education during the prewar years was six years. Thus heights recorded after age 12 are probably

25. This discussion of tempo of growth is from Tanner (1990, chaps. 6 and 9).

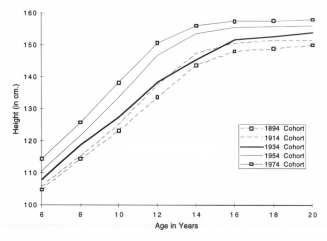

Fig. 7.5   Growth of schoolgirls by birth cohort, 1894–1974
Sources: As in fig. 7.4.

overstating the national average, as those children who could afford to remain in school were more likely to come from higher socioeconomic levels and thus be taller. Enrollment rates for mandatory elementary school were very high, even at the turn of the century. For 1901–5 they were 96.2 percent for boys and 88.6 percent for girls. By 1911–15 they were about 98 percent for each (*Nihon chōki tōkei sōran* 1978, 5:212–31).

The most useful information to be extracted from these graphs comes from comparisons between birth cohorts separated by 20-year intervals. For boys, between 1894 and 1914, the early phase of industrialization, differences in height do not appear until age 9, and they are then maintained at about 2–3 cm from age 12 until full maturity. Between 1914 and 1934, the later phase of industrialization, differences are quite discernible from age 6. Then the advantage of the later born begins to decline at around age 9 (with the onset of the Pacific War), and average height drops precipitously until 15-year-olds born in 1934 were no taller than 15-year-olds born in 1894. This reflects severe wartime and immediate postwar deprivation and malnutrition. By age 18, the 1934 cohort has begun to recover from the stunting, and by age 20 it has almost attained its expected height.

The 1954 and 1974 cohorts are used as a point of comparison for all prewar cohorts. Tempo of growth was much greater beginning at age 6 but was most prominent during the ages of puberty, between 12 and 15. The rate of increase in height is noticeably greater in the postwar cohorts beginning as early as age 10; it peaks at around age 13. Little growth is observed after age 16. Early maturation in the postwar period in comparison with the prewar period has been attributed to several reasons. Nutritional reasons include a doubling of animal protein intake in the six years following the end of the Pacific War (Mitchell 1962), an increase in milk consumption (Takahashi 1966), and changes in intake of fat, vitamin B2, and eggs (Matsumoto 1982). Socioeconomic reasons such as increasing urbanization, decreasing family size, and a decreasing Engel's coefficient have also been suggested (Matsumoto 1982).

Growth of schoolgirls presents a different picture of physiological maturity. While final height is a good 7–10 cm shorter than that of boys, this is due to genetic differences rather than nutritional disadvantages.[26] The difference between the 1894 and 1914 cohorts is apparent at age 6 and is much more pronounced than that of boys. This is consistent with the observation that girls experienced a greater degree of change in average height and experienced it earlier than did boys during the first half of the twentieth century (Wall 1993, table 7). It is interesting to note, too, that the 1934 girl cohort appeared to have weathered the war deprivations much better than its boy counterpart, at least relative to growth of earlier cohorts. Stunting of growth was less severe and seems to have been corrected by age 16. In general, environmental effects are more marked in the growth of boys than in that of girls, as one study on the effects of the atomic bombing at Hiroshima has shown (Greulich, Giswan, and Turner 1953). The difference in rates of increase in height between the prewar and postwar cohorts is evident at age 8, two years earlier for girls than for boys. Also, girls of the postwar cohorts exhibit little increase in height after age 16, whereas boys continued to grow until age 18.

The differences in tempo of growth among same-sex birth cohorts and between girls and boys highlight one of the most interesting problems in the relationship between industrialization and health, that is, examining differences among subgroups of the population to see whether one group benefited more or less than the others in the overall process of economic growth. The following section traces out the development of the differential structure in the Japanese economy and probes the demographic impact of productivity and wage gaps between the modern and traditional sectors.

7.5   Formation of the Differential Structure

7.5.1   Gaps in Productivity and Real Income

As World War I fueled the growth of Japanese industries such as arms, chemicals, and metals, modern large-scale industry for the first time experienced a skilled labor shortage. As a result, manufacturing processes became rationalized for maximum efficiency, which greatly increased not only the pro-

---

26. A comparable height gap appears between British boys and girls in the 1960s in Tanner (1990). An analysis of nutritional status of Japanese boys and girls in the early twentieth century shows little evidence of a female disadvantage with respect to nutritional resources. See Wall (1993).

Table 7.9   Real Per Capita GDP by Sector, 1907–40

Year	Primary	Secondary	Tertiary	Year	Primary	Secondary	Tertiary
1907	154	425	568	1924	191	765	682
1908	156	419	565	1925	210	811	642
1909	158	436	544	1926	194	852	632
1910	150	457	559	1927	205	872	614
1911	159	469	591	1928	200	944	682
1912	158	490	616	1929	203	1,031	656
1913	160	517	597	1930	213	1,052	474
1914	174	545	483	1931	186	1,094	495
1915	178	545	555	1932	220	1,097	586
1916	195	578	685	1933	242	1,156	628
1917	189	577	743	1934	193	1,214	614
1918	190	574	703	1935	203	1,273	548
1919	205	607	807	1936	217	1,323	584
1920	203	587	676	1937	227	1,261	648
1921	182	696	795	1938	224	1,392	642
1922	188	740	712	1939	243	1,510	786
1923	191	681	690	1940	237	1,531	783

Sources: Calculated from Ohkawa et al. (1974, 227) and Umemura et al. (1988, 204–15).
Note: GDP in yen, 1934–36 prices.

ductivity of the modern industrial sector relative to the agricultural and traditional manufacturing sectors, but its real wages as well. The productivity and
wage gaps widened during the 1920s and 1930s, which led to what is commonly known as the formation of the differential structure.[27]

In table 7.9 it is clear that productivity by sector—as measured in real GDP
per gainful worker[28]—increased at varying rates. Only the secondary sector
witnessed large and steady gains over the first four decades of the twentieth
century. In the primary sector, which includes agriculture, forestry, fishing, and
salt making, per capita real income grew very slowly and stagnated during the
1920s, the period of agricultural recession. The tertiary sector, which includes
many small-scale traditional services, also experienced little growth during
this period. Thus the differences arose from both rapid growth in large-scale
manufacturing and little growth in agriculture and traditional industries.[29] As
will be shown in this section, these gaps extended to the health and welfare of
the people as well.

27. This gap between modern and traditional sectors is also referred to as the "dual structure"
or "dual economy," more literal translations of *nijū kōzō*. I prefer to use "differential structure,"
coined by Ohkawa and Rosovsky (1965), since it is more general and acknowledges more complexity than a simple modern-traditional dichotomy in economic growth.
    28. May include part-time workers. See Ohkawa (1957, 142).
    29. Analysis by sector serves only as a proxy for the true differential structure that emerges
between so-called modern and traditional industries. Modern industry comprises goods and services introduced after the Meiji Ishin and those dependent on foreign technology (e.g., banking,
communications, transportation, arms, and medicine). Traditional industry includes old traditional

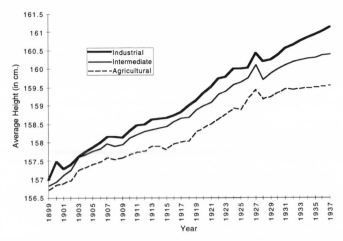

Fig. 7.6   Average height of 20-year-old recruits by prefectural type, 1899–1937
Source: Calculated from Shay (1986, appendix).

Note: Year is year of measurement. Industrial = less than 40 percent of labor force in agriculture in 1930; intermediate = 40–60 percent of labor force in agriculture in 1930; agricultural = more than 60 percent of labor force in agriculture in 1930. See Taeuber (1958, 88).

7.5.2   Differential Height

To determine whether the gaps in real wages between the traditional and modern sectors are manifested in the heights of those employed in the respective sectors, national recruit height data were divided into categories that would come closest to representing those sectors. Recruit height data were available by prefecture, so prefectures were divided into three categories: industrial, intermediate, and agricultural (according to Taeuber 1958, 88). Industrial prefectures had less than 40 percent of their labor force in agriculture; intermediate, between 40 and 60 percent; and agricultural, over 60 percent. The number of prefectures of different types totaled 7, 20, and 20, respectively.

The results are shown in figure 7.6. With clarity and consistency, recruits from industrial prefectures are tallest, those from agricultural prefectures shortest, and those from intermediate prefectures somewhere in between, but closer to those from industrial prefectures. Moreover, the gaps are increasing over time so that on the eve of the War with China, industrial recruits were on average close to 2 cm taller than agricultural recruits. At the turn of the century,

---

goods and services that existed before the Meiji Ishin (e.g., stonecutting, carpentry, food production, ricksha driving, and geisha) and new traditional goods and services that were originally introduced from the West but retained a traditional organizational structure (e.g., textile manufacture, tinsmithing, shoemaking, and painting). Modern and traditional industries can also be characterized by firm size. Though many exceptions exist, modern industry almost always refers to large-scale firms, while traditional industry, both old and new, has a strong association with small-scale, especially "midget" (one to three worker) enterprises. See Nakamura (1983, 27–28) and Ohkawa and Rosovsky (1973, 37–39).

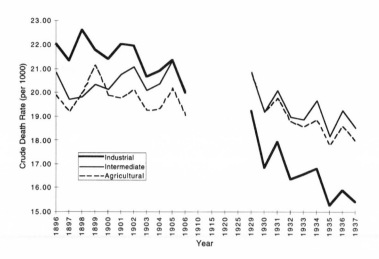

Fig. 7.7   Crude death rate by prefectural type, 1896–1937

Source: Calculated from *Nihon teikoku tōkei nenkan* (1899–1906, 1929–37).

Note: Number of deaths per 1,000 population. Definitions of industrial, intermediate, and agricultural prefectures as in fig. 7.6.

40 years earlier, there was virtually no difference between any of the heights. Thus total gains in average height over the period of industrialization for industrial, intermediate, and agricultural recruits were 4.1, 3.6, and 2.8 cm. Since recruitment physical examinations took place in the village, town, or city of birth, heights would be fairly accurate in measuring one's nutritional status and environmental effects from birth through recruitment in one's hometown. There may have been some migration in the later teen years as young men sought employment, but they would return to their place of birth for recruitment registration, so migration effects are minimized.

7.5.3   Differential Mortality

The same process of dividing prefectures into industrial, intermediate, and agricultural categories was performed on national statistics from the Cabinet Statistical Bureau, which covers the entire population, not just recruits. These are the so-called official statistics, which many have cautioned against using since they tend to underreport certain measurements. Since this analysis is more concerned with relative intersectoral differences than with absolute changes over time, using the official statistics may not be problematic. Figure 7.7 depicts crude death rates for each prefectural type (statistics for the years 1907–28 were unavailable). It appears that industrialization had a positive effect on mortality, as crude death rates for industrial prefectures were reduced from a high of 23 per 1,000 at the turn of the century to 15 by the late 1930s. Crude death rates in agricultural and intermediate prefectures showed only

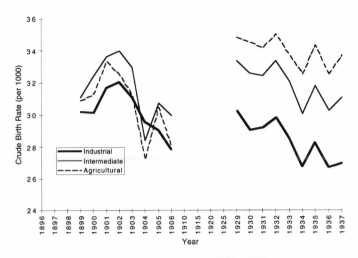

Fig. 7.8   Crude birthrate by prefectural type, 1899–1937
Source: Calculated from *Nihon teikoku tōkei nenkan* (1899–1906, 1929–37).
Note: Number of recorded births per 1,000 population. Definitions of industrial, intermediate, and agricultural prefectures as in fig. 7.6.

slight declines so that the high-to-low gradient from industrial to agricultural mortality was virtually reversed by the late 1920s. The reasons for this reversal include better medical care and public health measures in the cities in the later stages of industrialization, which mitigate the overcrowding and spread of infectious diseases characteristic of urban areas in the early stages of industrialization (see Mosk and Johansson 1986).

7.5.4   Differential Fertility

In crude birthrate, as shown in figure 7.8, there is little difference among the three prefectural types in the early stages of industrialization. By the late 1920s, the differences are pronounced and consistent. Agricultural birthrates are the highest, fluctuating between 32 and 35 per 1,000 population; intermediate, next highest, between 30 and 34; and urban, the lowest, between 26 and 30. Decline in birthrates is a much noted phenomenon of the so-called demographic transition from a traditional, agriculture-based society to a modern, industrial society. Urbanization and its attendant crowded living conditions in particular tend to reduce the number of children that people feel they can comfortably have, both financially and with regard to living space. Better education, which generally accompanies modern, industrial life, leads people to prefer "quality" of children over quantity. They prefer to invest available resources in more human capital for fewer children. In Japan birthrates on average do not appear to have declined very much over time, but the cross-sectional differences among sectors are significant.

In stillbirth rate per live births, shown in figure 7.9, agricultural prefectures

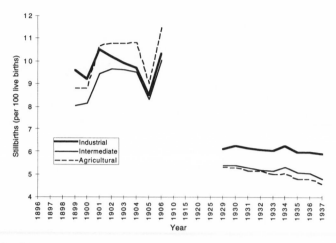

Fig. 7.9   Stillbirth rate by prefectural type, 1899–1937
Source: Calculated from *Nihon teikoku tōkei nenkan* (1899–1906, 1929–37).
Note: Number of recorded stillbirths per 100 live births. Definitions of industrial, intermediate, and agricultural prefectures as in fig. 7.6.

seem to be at a slight disadvantage in the early phases of industrialization. The situation is reversed by the late 1920s, with industrial prefectures showing on average one more stillbirth than the other prefectural types. This is consistent with another study, which showed that there was a high-to-low gradient in stillbirth rate from coastal to valley to mountain villages (representing decreasing levels of industrialization) in Shizuoka prefecture (Honda 1995). While causes of natural stillbirth are still largely unexplained, ones commonly cited are hypertension, antepartum hemorrhage and small-for-gestational-age fetuses (Herschel et al. 1994). Since these causes relate to prenatal care and maternal health, the reversal in figure 7.9 suggests that prenatal stress was higher for women in industrial prefectures. Intersectoral differences aside, the large drop in all sectors of the stillbirth rate indicate an overall improvement in the lives of women in their childbearing years.

While improved prenatal care and maternal health can account for some of the decline in natural stillbirths, they cannot account for the dramatic drop in stillbirth rates for all types of prefectures between 1910 and 1930. There appears to have been a change in reporting methods or a large decline in the rate of unnatural stillbirths. The precise definition of stillbirth used in this data set is unclear, since abortion, infanticide, natural losses, and deaths of infants up to one month old were often combined in a single category. Since no change in reporting methods has been documented, it might be hypothesized that much of the decline occurred among unnatural stillbirths, that is, abortion and infanticide. When stillbirths are divided into legitimate and illegitimate categories, the stillbirth rate for illegitimate births was on the order of 5 to 10 times higher than that for legitimate births from the 1920s through the 1940s. For example, in 1930 the stillbirth rate in large cities was 53 per 1,000 live births for legitimate children and 558 per 1,000 live births for illegitimate children. Outside the cities, the respective rates were 48 and 314 (Taeuber 1958, 270–71).

Also, stillbirth rates were higher among mothers of marginal childbearing ages (below 20 and over 40 years) in the prewar period. The high stillbirth rate among mothers below 20 years of age is undoubtedly linked to the high stillbirth rate among illegitimate births. There was also social stigma attached to older women giving birth, as though being old and pregnant was shameful or inappropriate.[30] Hence, if the larger part of the decline occurred among induced stillbirths, it must have occurred mostly among illegitimate births and births among women of marginal childbearing ages. In other words, there must have been a decline in abortion and infanticide among mothers to whose pregnancies some social stigma was attached. A possible explanation for this is the loosening of social ties and weakening of social mores that accompanied massive migration during industrialization. It was far easier for a woman to take her illegitimate pregnancy to term if she was living in a city away from the tight social nexus of her family and village.

7.6 Conclusion

The formation of the differential structure between modern and traditional sectors during industrialization was manifested in the health of the Japanese people. Average heights of 20-year-old recruits, when segregated into industrial, intermediate, and agricultural prefectures, displayed increasing differentials from 1899 to 1937. This is in accord with higher real income for nonagricultural workers in large-scale industries and lower real income for agricultural workers, which were characteristic of the differential structure. In addition, agricultural workers had much higher caloric requirements, which dealt a double blow to nutritional status: lower income and higher intake. The results are as expected: beginning with virtually no average height differences in 1899, industrial recruits grew an average of 4.1 cm, intermediate recruits 3.6 cm, and agricultural recruits 2.8 cm.

Mortality differentials, derived from national statistics for the entire population, were reversed over time. In the early phases of industrialization, industrial prefectures had the highest rates of mortality; agricultural, the lowest. By the late 1920s, the gradient was reversed, with the death rate of agricultural prefectures 2–4 points higher than that of industrial prefectures. Reasons for the reversal include better medical care and public health measures in the cities in

---

30. "In those days it was considered a great disgrace to have a baby after the age of forty—they were usually either aborted or killed at birth. A middle-aged woman only had to look tired or slack off from work and tongues would start wagging" (Saga 1987, 210).

the later stages of industrialization, which mitigated the effects of the over-crowding and spread of infectious diseases characteristic of urban areas in the early stages of industrialization.

Crude birthrates of different areas were virtually indistinguishable in the first decade of the twentieth century, but by the 1930s, patterns were clear and consistent. Agricultural birthrates were highest, fluctuating between 32 and 34 (per 1,000 population); intermediate, between 30 and 34; industrial, between 26 and 30. Industrialization and its attendant urbanization tend to reduce the number of children that people feel they can comfortably have. In addition, better education, which generally accompanies modern, industrial life, leads people to prefer "quality" of children over quantity. In stillbirth rates, which are inversely related to quality prenatal care and maternal health, industrial prefectures were at a slight disadvantage. Overall, however, the large drop in stillbirth rates for all sectors suggests a general improvement in the lives of women in their childbearing years.

Military expansion and war were major stimulants to the Japanese economy and contributed to the rise in per capita GDP during the period of industrialization. For example, although Japan was not a direct participant in it, World War I spurred the GNP to growth rates of 6–9 percent. Another positive effect was the breakthrough in military medicine and hygiene through research and education. This greatly reduced the number of deaths due to infectious diseases in battle camps between the Sino-Japanese War (1894–95) and the Russo-Japanese War (1904–5).

On the other hand, in the effort to meet the state objective of building a rich country and strong army (*fukoku kyōhei*), the government heavily favored amassing a formidable military-industrial complex over investing in social welfare, health care, public health technology, sanitation, and insurance.[31] The people's response was to draw on the centuries-old institution of communal associations (*kō*) and to form their own co-ops and companies that provided insurance, credit, and health care. Nevertheless, lack of major capital investments in public health on the part of the state may have delayed the control of epidemics in the early stages of industrialization and contributed to the stagnation of life expectancy throughout the period of industrialization.

Direct effects of war on the health of the people can be observed in the growth of schoolboys and schoolgirls. Birth cohorts of 1934, who would have reached puberty during the final years of the Pacific War and its devastating aftermath, showed significant stunting in both sexes. The effect on boys was more severe and protracted, as signs of stunting can be observed from ages 10 to 19, and 1934 birth cohorts at age 15 were no taller than their 1894 counterparts at age 15. Girls recovered more quickly, and the effects they suffered

31. See Honda (1995, table 6.1), in which it is shown that the Japanese government spent any-where from 10 to 1,000 times more on defense than on public welfare each year from 1868 to 1942.

were less severe. They showed signs of stunting from ages 10 to 16, and their heights did not drop to 1894 cohort levels.

While increases in per capita income can lead to some benefits for an industrializing society, per capita income is not well correlated with all measures of health. In the case of Japan, height as a proxy for nutritional status increased with per capita income, but leveled off in the 1930s even though per capita GDP rose rapidly. The leveling-off reflected a decrease in caloric intake, which in turn may have been due to the distribution of a limited amount of resources to a burgeoning population. Mortality rates and income are somewhat correlated over time and across occupational class, though reduction in mortality in higher income, industrial areas only occurred in the later stages of industrialization. Fertility rates and income are negatively correlated, but once again, only in the later stages of industrialization. In the early stages, industrial and agricultural birthrates are virtually indistinguishable. Thus, the relationship between industrialization and health is not a simple one: in addition to income, it is critical to consider the stage of industrialization and where the additional resources from higher income are being channeled.

References

Cornell, L. L., and Akira Hayami. 1986. The *shūmon aratame chō:* Japan's population registers. *Journal of Family History* 11:311–28.

Eveleth, Phyllis B., and James M. Tanner. 1990. *Worldwide variation in human growth,* 2d ed. Cambridge: Cambridge University Press.

Floud, Roderick, Kenneth Wachter, and Annabel Gregory. 1990. *Height, health and history.* Cambridge: Cambridge University Press.

Fogel, Robert W. 1986. Nutrition and the decline in mortality since 1700: Some preliminary findings. In *Long-term factors in American economic growth,* ed. Stanley L. Engerman and Robert E. Gallman. Chicago: University of Chicago Press.

———. 1993. New sources and new techniques for the study of secular trends in nutritional status, health, mortality, and the process of aging. Working paper. University of Chicago, Center for Population Economics.

———. 1994. Economic growth, population theory, and physiology: The bearing of long-term processes on the making of economic policy. Paper prepared for presentation as the Prize Lecture in Economic Sciences in Memory of Alfred Nobel. University of Chicago, Center for Population Economics. Typescript.

Garon, Sheldon. 1994. The evolution of "Japanese-style" welfare. Working paper. Princeton University, Department of History.

Greulich, W. W., C. S. Giswan, and M. L. Turner. 1953. The physical growth and development of children who survived the atomic bombing of Hiroshima or Nagasaki. *Journal of Pediatrics* 43:121–45.

Hanley, Susan B. 1983. A high standard of living in nineteenth-century Japan: Fact or fantasy? *Journal of Economic History* 43:183–92.

Hanley, Susan B., and Kozo Yamamura. 1977. *Economic and demographic change in preindustrial Japan, 1600–1868.* Princeton, N.J.: Princeton University Press.

Hayami, Akira. 1968. The demographic analysis of a village in Tokugawa Japan: Kando-shinden of Owari Province, 1778–1871. *Keiō Economic Studies* 5:50–88.

———. 1978. Nōbi chihō no rekishi jinkōgakuteki kenkyū josetsu (An introduction to the demographic history of Nōbi region). *Kenkyū Kiyō*, pp. 197–226.

Hayami, Akira, and Matao Miyamoto. 1988. Gaisetsu 17–18 seiki (An outline of the seventeenth and eighteenth centuries). In *Keizai shakai no seiritsu 17–18 seiki* (The development of seventeenth and eighteenth century economy and society), ed. Akira Hayami and Matao Miyamoto, 2–84. Tokyo: Iwanami shoten.

Herschel, Marguerite, et al. 1994. Fetal death in a population of black women. Working paper. University of Chicago, Departments of Pediatrics, Obstetrics, and Gynecology and the Harris School of Public Policy.

Hiramoto, Yoshisuke. 1972. Jōmon jidai kara kindai ni itaru Kantō chihōjin shinchō no jidaiteki henka (Periodic changes in the heights of Kantō region inhabitants from the Jōmon through the modern period). *Jinrui zasshi* (Journal of the Anthropological Society of Nippon) 80:221–36.

Honda, Gail. 1995. Social costs of Japan's industrial revolution 1868–1946. Ph.D. diss., University of Chicago.

———. 1996. Short tailors and sickly buddhist priests: Birth order and education effects on class and health in Japan 1893–1943. *Continuity and Change* 11:273–94.

Hunter, Janet. 1993. Quality of life in industrializing Japan. In *Japanese Women Working,* ed. Janet Hunter. London: Routledge.

Itō, Shigeru. 1991. An analysis of mortality in Meiji cities. Paper presented at the Hitotsubashi Conference on Demographic Change in Economic Development.

Jannetta, Ann. 1987. *Epidemics and mortality in early modern Japan.* Princeton, N.J.: Princeton University Press.

———. 1992. Famine mortality in nineteenth-century Japan: The evidence from a temple death register. *Population Studies* 46:427–43.

Jannetta, Ann, and Samuel H. Preston. 1991. Two centuries of mortality change in central Japan: The evidence from a temple death register. *Population Studies* 45:417–36.

Japan National Commission for UNESCO. 1966. *The role of education in the social and economic development of Japan.* Tokyo: UNESCO.

Johansson, S. Ryan, and Carl Mosk. 1987. Exposure, resistance and life expectancy: Disease and death during the economic development of Japan, 1900–1960. *Population Studies* 41:207–35.

Kaneda, Hiromitsu. 1970. Long-term changes in food consumption patterns in Japan. In *Agriculture and economic growth: Japan's experience,* ed. Kazushi Ohkawa, Bruce Johnston, and Hiromitsu Kaneda. Princeton and Tokyo: Princeton University Press and Tokyo University Press.

Kim, John M. 1993. Economic and biomedical implications of Waaler surfaces: A new perspective on height, weight, morbidity, and mortality. Working paper. University of Chicago, Department of Economics.

Kōseishō imu kyoku hen (Ministry of Welfare Bureau of Medical Affairs Compilation). 1976. *Eisei tōkei kara mita isei hyakunen no ayumi* (Hundred-year progress in the medical system as seen from health statistics). Tokyo: Gyōsei.

Maruyama, Masao. 1974. *Studies in the intellectual history of Tokugawa Japan,* trans. Mikiso Hane. Princeton, N.J.: Princeton University Press.

Matsumoto, K. 1982. Secular acceleration of growth in height in Japanese and its social background. *Annals of Human Biology* 9:399–410.

Mitchell, H. S. 1962. Nutrition in relation to stature. *Journal of the American Dietetic Association* 40:521–24.

Monbushō (Ministry of Education). 1990. *Tairyoku undō nōryoku chōsa hōsō sho* (Report on the study of physical strength and exercise ability). Tokyo: Ministry of Education.

Mosk, Carl. 1978. Fecundity, infanticide, and food consumption in Japan. *Explorations in Economic History* 15:269–89.

Mosk, Carl, and S. Ryan Johansson. 1986. Income and mortality: Evidence from modern Japan. *Population and Development Review* 12:415–40.

Najita, Tetsuo. 1972. Political economism in the thought of Dazai Shundai (1680–1747). *Journal of Asian Studies* 31:821–39.

———. 1987. *Visions of virtue in Tokugawa Japan: The Kaitokudō Merchant Academy of Osaka.* Chicago: University of Chicago Press.

———. 1988. Political economy in thought and practice among commoners in nineteenth-century Japan: Some preliminary comments. *Japan Foundation Newsletter* 16(3): 13–18.

———. 1993. Japan's industrial revolution in historical perspective. In *Japan in the world,* ed. Masao Miyoshi and H. D. Harootunian. Durham, N.C.: Duke University Press.

Nakamura, Takafusa. 1983. *Economic growth in prewar Japan,* trans. Robert A. Feldman. New Haven, Conn.: Yale University Press.

Nihon chōki tōkei sōran (Historical statistics of Japan). 1978. Tokyo: Sōmuchō tōkei kyoku (General Affairs Office Statistical Bureau).

Nihon teikoku tōkei nenkan (Imperial Japan statistical yearbook). 1899–1906, 1929–37. Tokyo: Cabinet Statistical Bureau.

Ohkawa, Kazushi. 1957. *The growth rate of the Japanese economy since 1878.* Tokyo: Kinokuniya.

———. 1968. Nihon keizai no seisan [to] bunpai, 1905–1963 (Production and distribution in the Japanese economy, 1905–1963). *Keizai Kenkyū* 19.

Ohkawa, Kazushi, et al. 1974. *Kokumin shotoku* (National income). Vol. 1 of *Chōki keizai tōkei* (Long-term economic statistics). Tokyo: Tōyō Keizai Shimpōsha.

Ohkawa, Kazushi, and Henry Rosovsky. 1965. A century of Japanese economic growth. In *The state and economic enterprise in Japan,* ed. William W. Lockwood. Princeton, N.J.: Princeton University Press.

———. 1973. *Japanese economic growth.* Stanford, Calif.: Stanford University Press.

Rice, Geoffrey W., and Edwina Palmer. 1993. Pandemic influenza in Japan, 1918–19: Mortality patterns and official responses. *Journal of Japanese Studies* 19:389–420.

Rosovsky, Henry. 1961. *Capital formation in Japan.* New York: Free Press.

Saga, Junichi. 1987. *Memories of silk and straw: A self-portrait of small-town Japan.* Tokyo: Kodansha.

Saitō, Osamu. 1989. Keizai hatten wa mortality teika wo motarashitaka (Did economic growth give rise to a decrease in mortality?). *Keizai kenkyū* 40:339–56.

———. 1992a. Infanticide, fertility and "population stagnation": The state of Tokugawa historical demography. *Japan Forum* 4:369–81.

———. 1992b. Jinkō tenkan izen no Nihon ni okeru mortality (Mortality in Japan before the demographic transition). *Keizai kenkyū* 43:248–67.

Shay, Ted. 1986. The level of living in Japan, 1885–1938: New evidence. Paper presented at the Social Science History Association meetings, St. Louis.

Smith, Thomas C. 1977. *Nakahara: Family farming and population in a Japanese village, 1717–1830.* Stanford, Calif.: Stanford University Press.

Steckel, Richard H. 1983. Height and per capita income. *Historical Methods* 16:1–7.

Taeuber, Irene B. 1958. *The population of Japan.* Princeton, N.J.: Princeton University Press.

Taira, Koji. 1971. Education and literacy in Meiji Japan: An interpretation. *Explorations in Economic History* 8:371–94.

Takahashi, E. 1966. Growth and environmental factors in Japan. *Human Biology* 38:112–30.

Tanner, J. M. 1990. *Fetus into man: Physical growth from conception to maturity.* Cambridge, Mass.: Harvard University Press.

Tanner, J. M., T. Hayashi, M. A. Preece, and N. Cameron. 1982. Increase in length of leg relative to trunk in Japanese children and adults from 1957 to 1977: Comparison with British and Japanese Americans. *Annals of Human Biology* 9:411–23.

Umemura, Mataji, et al. 1988. *Rōdō ryoku* (Manpower). Vol. 2 of *Chōki keizai tōkei* (Long-term economic statistics). Tokyo: Tōyō Keizai Shimpōsha.

Wall, Richard. 1993. Inequalities in the nutritional status of boys and girls in Britain, the United States and Japan in the early twentieth century. Working paper. University of Cambridge, Cambridge Group for the History of Population and Social Structure.

Wilkinson, Thomas O. 1965. *The urbanization of Japanese labor.* Amherst: University of Massachusetts Press.

8   Heights and Living Standards in Germany, 1850–1939: The Case of Württemberg

Sophia Twarog

8.1 Introduction

There is little doubt that, in the long run, industrialization generally benefits the population in the country in which it takes place. Yet, in the short run, optimist-pessimist debates concerning the social costs and benefits of industrialization exist for many countries. Optimists applaud rapidly rising per capita income and industrial output. Pessimists speak of rising income inequality and dismal living conditions of the urban working class.

In Germany, the optimist-pessimist debate usually focuses on the 1870s and 1880s—the beginning of the rapid industrialization period (1871–1914). Between 1871 and 1890, real per capita Net National Product (NNP) in 1913 prices rose at an average annual rate of 1.5 percent (calculated from table 8.3, below). Yet income inequality was rising (Dumke 1988), and there were other signs that all was not well with the German working class. According to Henderson (1975), "The poor-law authorities, the churches, and various charitable organizations were fighting an uphill battle against the effects of low wages, long hours, unemployment, sickness, and bad housing conditions." This distress prompted Bismarck to lay down the foundations of a social safety net. Several important pieces of social legislation were passed in the 1880s, including compulsory health and accident insurance for factory workers and others, as well as old age and disability pensions. Germany was the first large industrialized country to take such steps. It is possible that these measures helped

Sophia Twarog is an economic affairs officer with the United Nations Conference on Trade and Development (UNCTAD) in Geneva, Switzerland.

The opinions expressed in this paper are those of the author and do not necessarily reflect the views of UNCTAD. The designations and terminology employed are also those of the author.

This contribution is largely based on the author's dissertation, "Heights and Living Standards in Industrializing Germany: The Case of Württemberg," which was completed in 1993 at Ohio State University under the direction of Richard Steckel.

ameliorate some of the hardships that often seem to go hand-in-hand with industrialization's onset. After the 1880s, particularly after 1885, German living standards were generally improving.

The goal of this paper is to examine the changes in the health and well-being of the German population during and after industrialization. The strategy employed is to marshall evidence on a wide range of indicators of living standards in Germany. Special attention is given to average population height, which, as a measure of net nutrition, is of particular value. Other indicators include real per capita income, gross wages, infant mortality, mortality, life expectancy, emigration, working hours in industry, and Hoffmann's index of caloric balance. Finally, an attempt is made to construct for historical Germany a Human Development Index (HDI), which is a composite measure of longevity, knowledge, and command over resources (i.e., income).

In this paper, special attention is given to the kingdom of Württemberg. There are two main reasons for this. First, regional variations during German industrialization were so large that relying solely on national averages can distort the underlying processes. Württemberg can be considered as representative of the relatively late industrializing German regions. Second, trends in average population heights are a particularly valuable indicator of physical living standards. To the best of the author's knowledge, the only continuous data available on height trends in Germany during the second half of the nineteenth century are for Württemberg. The main goal of this study, however, is to depict changes in living standards in Germany as a whole. Thus, wherever possible, data on the various indicators will be presented for both Württemberg and for Germany.

This paper begins with a brief discussion of industrialization in Württemberg and how this region fit into the larger German context. Section 8.3 examines trends in a range of indicators of living standards in Germany and in Württemberg. Section 8.4 highlights the main findings of the study.

8.2   Industrialization in Germany and Württemberg

Germany's industrialization has been referred to as "the most remarkable economic achievement of the nineteenth century" (Dillard 1967). The most rapid period of industrialization (*Hochindustrialisierung*) took place between 1871 and 1914. But considerable progress was made prior to this. In the mid-1830s, the establishment of the German Customs Union (*Zoll Verein*) and the opening of the first railway line in German territory ushered in what has been called the "dawn of the industrial era," 1834–51 (Henderson 1975). After 1851, economic development accelerated. Real per capita NNP (in 1913 prices) rose from DM 312 in 1850, to DM 424 in 1871, and further to DM 783 in 1913 (calculated from Hoffman 1965; see table 8.3). This implies growth rates in real per capita income of 14.6 percent per decade! The percentage of the German labor force employed in agriculture dropped from 54.6 percent in 1849–

Table 8.1   **Commercial Sector Employment as a Percentage of the Population (*Gewerbesatz*) in Several German Regions, 1875–1939**

State or Province	1875	1882	1895	1907	1925	1933	1939
Saxony	22.91	26.33	30.38	34.25	42.95	28.91	44.76
Württemberg	15.31	14.72	18.86	22.08	31	26.86	38.38
Rhineprovince	19	20.57	22.97	26.25	32.85	23.28	35.62
Baden	15.82	15.51	20.94	25.42	30.22	23.02	34.95
Westphalia	18.5	18.37	21.24	24.43	31.66	22.14	33.8
German Empire	15.14	16.23	19.64	23.14	30.04	22.35	33.39
Prussia	14.09	15.43	18.45	21.81	29.11	21.29	32.47
Bavaria	14.09	13.01	17.25	20.38	25.08	20.89	31.57
Hesse	15.2	15.05	19.33	21.56	27.36	21.05	31.24

Source: Megerle (1982).

55, to 35.1 percent in 1910–13, and further to 21.6 percent in 1950–54 (Hoffmann 1965). Meanwhile, the index of industrial production rose from 9.5 in 1850, to 21 in 1871, and to 100 in 1913—an average growth rate of 37.4 percent per decade between 1850 and 1913. This rate far surpasses that of neighboring France (17.4 percent per decade) and the United Kingdom (20.2 percent per decade) during the same period.[1] In less than a century, Germany made the transition from a predominantly agrarian society to an industrial giant.[2]

What was Württemberg's place in this historic event? One could argue that Württemberg's industrialization was reasonably representative of the "average" German industrialization experience. In support of this statement, consider table 8.1 showing commercial sector employment as a percentage of the population (*Gewerbesatz*) in several German regions between 1875 and 1939.[3] Through 1925, the figures for Württemberg were always within 1.5 percentage points of the German Empire average, and the employment trends in Württemberg and the German Empire ran fairly parallel courses.

In reality, however, regional variations in industrialization were so large in Germany that no single region could be truly representative. The unification under the umbrella of the German Empire in 1871 took place relatively late. Thereafter, individual states still had a great deal of autonomy in most areas outside of trade, currency, and military duty. Differences in state industrial policies and in natural resource endowments contributed to the regional differences in German economic development.

Kiesewetter (1986) divided German regional industrialization processes into three categories. The first group included areas such as Saxony and the Ruhr, which industrialized relatively early with emphasis on heavy industry such as

1. These figures were calculated from Mitchell (1980).
2. Numerous books and articles have been written on German industrialization. See, e.g., Hoffmann (1965), Kiesewetter (1989), Stolper (1940), and Henderson (1975).
3. "Commercial sector" refers to traditional craftsmen, manufacturing, businessmen, etc. Expressed as a percentage of the labor force, the figures would be much higher, of course.

iron, coal, and capital equipment. The second group included Württemberg, Baden, and Hesse. The lack of large deposits of coal and iron ore in these areas delayed rapid industrialization until the late nineteenth century and led to a focus on light industry. The third group was further subdivided into two subcategories: In the deindustrializing areas (such as the Harz and the Erzgebirge), it was increasingly difficult for the traditional ironworks to compete with the huge factories in the Ruhr and elsewhere. In the agricultural regions such as Posen and lower Bavaria, industrialization was very slow.

Württemberg would be considered representative of the second category of German industrialization processes. Yet even here, there were certain factors such as agricultural structure, natural resource endowment, industrial policy, railway expansion, and population development that made its industrialization experience unique. For example, Württemberg was a land of small landholders, where many farmers were also craftsmen or worked in factories. The ties to the land prevented the formation of a "landless proletariat" and at the same time gave commercial sector employees a safety net. These ties to the land also led to the decentralized industrial structure still apparent today. Since Württemberg had no coal, it specialized in light industry—such as finished metal goods, textiles, instruments, and optics.

In a nutshell, Württemberg's economic development between 1852 and 1940 can be described as follows: A severe agricultural crisis began in 1846–47. The bad situation lasted until 1854–55. The following years were characterized by considerable growth in the commercial sector, particularly between 1852 and 1861. Growth then slowed, decreasing Württemberg's industrial position relative to other states. In the 1870s and 1880s, Württemberg was finally connected by rail to the rest of the German Empire. The large influx of cheap grain caused agricultural prices to fall dramatically, eroding the importance of the second job in agriculture. The increased willingness to work full time in factories opened the door to rapid industrialization after 1882 and especially after 1895. Although the two world wars and the Great Depression did not spare this region, Württemberg proved relatively resilient. Today it is one of the most industrial and richest parts of Germany.

Urbanization accompanied industrialization in both Germany as a whole and in Württemberg. Table 8.2 shows the percentage of the German population living in seven categories of community size between 1852 and 1961. The trends are clear: The percentage of the population living in communities of less than 2,000 residents fell from 67.3 percent in 1852 to 23.2 percent in 1961. Meanwhile, the percentage living in cities with over 100,000 residents rose from 2.6 percent in 1852 to 31.1 percent in 1961. In Württemberg between 1834 and 1910, although the number of people in communities with less than 5,000 residents was fairly stable over the period, it steadily declined as a percentage of Württemberg's growing population (from 86.2 percent in 1834 to 64.2 percent in 1910). Between 1871 and 1910, the percentage of the popula-

Table 8.2   **Percentage of German Population in Community Size Classes, 1852–1961**

Community Size Class (number of residents)	1852	1871	1880	1890	1900	1910	1925	1933	1939	1950	1961
Under 2,000	67.3	63.9	59.2	53.0	46.2	40.0	35.6	32.9	30.1	28.9	23.2
2,000–5,000	13.1	12.4	11.9	19.1	11.5	11.3	10.8	10.6	10.7	13.6	12.4
5,000–10,000	6.2	6.3	6.6	19.1	7.1	7.6	6.9	7.1	7.5	8.9	9.1
10,000–20,000	4.8	4.9	5.4	6.0	6.3	6.5	6.2	6.0	6.4	7.1	7.4
20,000–50,000	3.5	3.6	4.8	6.9	7.3	7.9	8.0	7.7	8.4	8.8	10.0
50,000–100,000	2.5	4.1	3.3	2.9	4.5	5.4	5.7	5.3	5.3	5.4	6.7
Over 100,000	2.6	4.8	8.8	12.1	17.1	21.3	26.8	30.4	31.6	27.3	31.1

Source: Hoffmann (1965).

tion living in communities of less than 2,000 residents fell from 68.9 percent to 49.8 percent. In contrast, the percentage of the population living in communities with over 20,000 residents more than tripled (from 6.4 percent in 1871 to 21.1 percent in 1910; Königliches Statistisches Landesamt 1913b).

It is clear that between 1850 and 1939 Germany made a major shift from a rural agricultural society to a more urban, industry-based economy. How did this momentous change affect the health and welfare of the average German? The following section addresses this question by presenting evidence on a wide range of living standard indicators.

8.3   Indicators of Living Standards in Germany and Württemberg

8.3.1   Real Per Capita Income and Real Gross Wages

Probably the most widely used indicator of living standards is real per capita income. Table 8.3 shows the development of real per capita NNP in 1913 prices for the period 1850–1950 in Germany.[4] The upward trend is unmistakable. Between 1850 and 1938, real per capita NNP nearly quadrupled! The average annual growth rate was 1.52 percent.

Between 1850 and 1873, real per capita NNP rose at an average annual rate of 1.84 percent. During the euphoric speculation boom in 1871–73, the average yearly rate was 5.78 percent. The financial crash came in May 1873, and numerous bankruptcies followed. This event ushered in the period often referred to as the great depression in Germany (1873–96), during which average annual growth rates of real per capita NNP dropped to 1.24 percent. Things started to pick up again after 1896, and particularly after the turn of the century. Between

---

4. I have not located a time series for real per capita income in the kingdom of Württemberg. Even if these data were available, standard income accounting would be somewhat inadequate since it is likely that home production accounted for much of the consumption of Württemberg's small landholders and craftsmen.

Table 8.3   **Real German Per Capita NNP in 1913 Prices, 1850–1950**

Year	NNP in 1913 Prices (million DM)	Average Population (thousands)	Real Per Capita NNP in 1913 Prices	Log Real Per Capita NNP
1850	10,534	33,746	312	2.49
1851	10,568	34,055	310	2.49
1852	11,121	34,290	324	2.51
1853	10,630	34,422	308	2.49
1854	10,961	34,531	317	2.50
1855	10,316	34,586	298	2.47
1856	11,553	34,715	333	2.52
1857	11,845	34,979	339	2.53
1858	12,053	35,278	342	2.53
1859	12,219	35,633	343	2.53
1860	13,604	36,049	377	2.58
1861	13,002	36,435	357	2.55
1862	13,731	36,788	373	2.57
1863	14,639	37,184	394	2.59
1864	14,667	37,602	390	2.59
1865	14,858	37,955	391	2.59
1866	15,106	38,193	396	2.60
1867	15,108	38,440	393	2.59
1868	16,621	38,637	430	2.63
1869	15,660	38,914	402	2.60
1870	16,706	39,231	426	2.63
1871	17,395	40,997	424	2.63
1872	19,133	41,230	464	2.67
1873	19,768	41,564	476	2.68
1874	21,316	42,004	507	2.70
1875	21,070	42,518	496	2.69
1876	20,890	43,059	485	2.69
1877	20,705	43,610	475	2.68
1878	21,803	44,129	494	2.69
1879	21,193	44,641	475	2.68
1880	19,874	45,095	441	2.64
1881	20,616	45,428	454	2.66
1882	20,444	45,719	447	2.65
1883	21,909	46,016	476	2.66
1884	22,712	46,396	490	2.69
1885	23,452	46,707	502	2.70
1886	24,142	47,134	512	2.71
1887	24,558	47,630	516	2.71
1888	25,840	48,168	536	2.73
1889	26,478	48,717	544	2.74
1890	27,754	49,241	564	2.75
1891	26,822	49,762	539	2.73
1892	28,390	50,266	565	2.75
1893	30,606	50,757	603	2.78

Table 8.3 (continued)

Year	NNP in 1913 Prices (million DM)	Average Population (thousands)	Real Per Capita NNP in 1913 Prices	Log Real Per Capita NNP
1894	30,190	51,339	588	2.77
1895	32,079	52,001	617	2.79
1896	33,377	52,753	633	2.80
1897	34,739	53,569	648	2.81
1898	36,813	54,406	677	2.83
1899	36,860	55,248	667	2.82
1900	36,466	56,046	651	2.81
1901	36,197	56,874	636	2.80
1902	36,918	57,767	639	2.80
1903	40,132	58,629	684	2.83
1904	42,263	59,475	711	2.85
1905	43,346	60,314	719	2.86
1906	44,299	61,153	724	2.86
1907	46,181	62,013	745	2.87
1908	46,410	62,863	738	2.87
1909	47,512	63,717	746	2.87
1910	47,457	64,568	735	2.87
1911	49,648	65,359	760	2.88
1912	51,914	66,149	785	2.89
1913	52,440	66,978	783	2.89
1925	46,897	62,410	751	2.88
1926	46,587	62,867	741	2.87
1927	53,108	63,253	840	2.92
1928	53,950	63,618	848	2.93
1929	51,694	63,958	808	2.91
1930	49,289	64,295	767	2.88
1931	43,913	64,631	679	2.83
1932	41,760	64,912	643	2.80
1933	47,375	65,225	726	2.86
1934	52,102	65,243	799	2.90
1935	58,658	66,871	877	2.94
1936	66,226	67,349	983	2.99
1937	73,167	67,831	1,079	3.03
1938	81,335	68,558	1,186	3.07
1950	44,904	47,060	954	2.98

Source: Hoffmann (1965)

Notes: The borders of Germany changed over the period in question. In this table, the data are for the following territories: 1850–70, German Empire, 1913 borders, without Alsace-Lorraine; 1871–1913, German Empire, 1913 borders, with Alsace-Lorraine; 1925–38, German Empire, 1935–37 borders (1925–34 without Saarland, which was French administered at this time); 1950, Federal Republic of Germany (without Saarland and Berlin).

Estimates of NNP in constant prices are incomplete through 1880 and 1936–38.

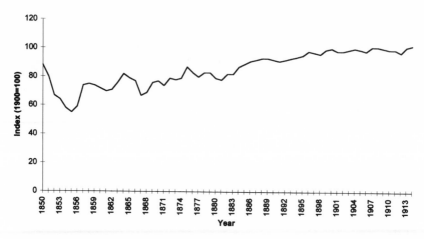

Fig. 8.1   Development of real gross wages in Germany, 1850–1914 (1900 = 100)
Source: Kuczynski (1947).

1900 and 1913, real per capita NNP increased at an average annual rate of 1.42 percent.

After 1913, the first available data in this time series are for 1925. Due to the First World War and the hyperinflation of 1921–23, real per capita NNP in 1913 prices fell from DM 783 in 1913 to DM 751 in 1925. The upswing that began in 1925 clipped along at an average annual rate of 1.83 percent until the Great Depression in 1929. Between 1929 and 1932, real per capita NNP fell from DM 808 to DM 643—an average annual decrease of 4.57 percent. After Hitler came to power in 1933, there was rapid economic recovery based on armaments and public works. Between 1934 and 1938, real per capita NNP rose from DM 799 to DM 1186—an average annual growth rate of 9.87 percent! After the Second World War, unlike most of its European neighbors, Germany had not yet attained its prewar real per capita income levels by 1950. This was due to heavy losses from fighting on German soil, low morale, reparations, monetary chaos through 1948, and military occupation. A rapid recovery began in 1949 and continued through the 1950s.

Figure 8.1 shows Kuczynski's index of real gross wages (1900 = 100) for German workers between 1850 and 1914. While the trend was generally positive, it was unevenly so, particularly before 1885. There was a large fall in real wages in the 1850s, and smaller ones in the late 1860s to early 1870s and in the early 1880s. These declines were largely driven by increases in the cost of living. Between 1885 and 1914, the cost of living continued to rise. However, nominal wages more than kept pace, leading to a steady gradual improvement in real gross wages. Also in Württemberg real wages were rising for many occupational categories during the second half of the nineteenth century (Losch 1898).

8.3.2   Average Population Heights

Württemberg Data and Methodology

When Germany was united in 1871, a universal draft law came into effect. All 20-year-old males were required to present themselves at the local recruiting depot to be measured and given a physical examination. For historical height studies, this is good news: there is no guesswork concerning the relationship between the observed population and the underlying population, as is the case with volunteer armies. The heights of all young German men were recorded. Unfortunately, the majority of these data were destroyed during World War II. To the best of my knowledge, only one data series has remained intact: the peacetime troop lists (*Friedenstammrollen*) of the army of Württemberg.

Luckily, this is a particularly rich source of information. Not only does it contain the soldier's height (recorded to the nearest half-centimeter), but also his occupation, often his father's occupation, his birthplace and birth date, his residence, his parents' residence, and his medical history during his term of duty. This enables some intriguing analysis of the covariates of historical heights.

Information was collected on approximately 15,000 soldiers serving between 1871 and 1913 (birth years 1851–93). Height trends were estimated using three statistical methods that correct for the lower tail erosion present in soldiers' height distribution due to minimum height and physical fitness standards. These methods are Reduced Sample Maximum Likelihood Estimation (RSMLE), which uses maximum likelihood estimation techniques on a truncated height distribution, Quantile Bend Estimation (QBE), which involves estimating the number of observations missing in the lower tail, and finally the simple mean of the reduced sample. Basic information on these methods and on the author's sampling procedure can be found in the appendix. For more detailed information, refer to Twarog (1993).

Height Trends in Württemberg for Birth Years 1852–93

Figure 8.2 shows QBE-estimated and unadjusted average heights, six-year moving averages, for the birth cohorts of 1852–57 to 1888–93. The QBE average height estimates for those born in the early 1850s were very low: the average stature for birth cohorts of 1852–57 was 164.1 cm.[5] When two-year moving averages were used, the QBE estimate for birth years 1852–53 was 161.2 cm. Average heights were rising for those born during this decade, reaching 167.4 cm for those born between 1856 and 1861. The early 1860s saw a short fall and recovery. A steeper fall in heights began with the late-1860s birth cohorts

---

5. When discussing historical height trends, it should be kept in mind that under suboptimal environmental conditions, growth can continue into the early 20s. It therefore seems likely that the height trends of 20-year-olds presented here slightly underestimate final adult male heights in Württemberg.

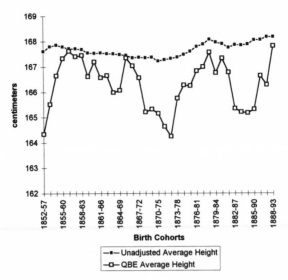

Fig. 8.2   Unadjusted and QBE average height estimates, six-year moving average, birth years 1852–57 to 1888–93
Source: Twarog (1993).

and reached its nadir in the mid-1870s (164 cm for birth years 1872–77). This was followed by a rise through the early 1880s (167.3 cm for those born between 1878 and 1883), a second dip in the late 1880s (nadir average height of 164.9 cm reached in birth years 1884–89), and an upward trend thereafter. The tallest six-year birth cohort was the last (1888–93), with a QBE-estimated average height of 167.6 cm.

For RSMLE, seven six-year phases were used. The reduced samples in each phase contained between 1,488 and 2,017 observations. Figure 8.3 shows the RSMLE average height estimates for the seven phases compared with the QBE estimates. Both methods indicated lowest stature in the earliest phase—birth years 1852–57. The RSMLE estimate of 163.1 cm was lower than the QBE estimate. Both estimators showed rising and then falling heights thereafter, with the RSMLE estimate reaching 165.2 cm for the birth cohorts of 1870–75. Then the stories diverged somewhat, with RSMLE showing steadily rising stature, and QBE showing the second dip in heights in the mid-1880s.

The results look much more similar, however, if one uses RSMLE truncated regression to estimate average height for two-year birth cohorts. Table 8.4 and figure 8.4 show that the RSMLE stature estimates were very low for those born in the early 1850s—160.56 for the 1852–53 cohort. Thereafter, they were rising. In the 1870s, there is a marked dip in heights, followed by a rise and then a second dip in the mid-1880s, followed by a recovery.

Figure 8.5 shows trends in the simple mean of the reduced sample using six-

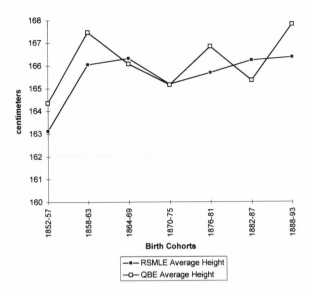

Fig. 8.3   RSMLE and QBE average height estimates, seven phases, birth years 1852–57 to 1888–93
Source: Twarog (1993).

year moving averages. One sees a similar pattern to that observed with the other methods, although the dip in heights in the 1870s was much shallower. However, if rising income inequality in the 1870s led to larger standard deviations in the population's height distribution, a small dip in the simple mean of the reduced sample would result from a steeper dip in the true average population height. Thus all three estimation methods yielded results that were reasonably consistent.

Interpreting average height trends in light of historical circumstances is complicated. The very feature that makes stature such a valuable indicator—that it is a net measure of a number of factors contributing to human well-being—also makes it hard to determine with absolute certainty what is driving a particular change in stature. This inherent difficulty is amplified by the lack of full historical information on all possible contributing factors (e.g., caloric and protein intake, illness, work effort, and breast-feeding practices). Moreover, since the use of stature in economic history is still fairly new, the exact equation mapping economic and environmental factors into average stature is still under study. Keeping these caveats in mind, one can still make educated guesses in light of the available information and continue to study the problem. This is what I have attempted to do for height trends in Württemberg.

Perhaps the most striking finding is that average heights were quite low in Württemberg throughout the second half of the nineteenth century. Average

Table 8.4   **RSMLE Average Height (AVHT) Estimates, Two-Year Birth Cohorts, Birth Years 1852–53 to 1892–93**

Phase	Coefficient	S.E.	t-Statistic	AVHT (cm)
Phase 1				
1852–53	160.56	1.196		160.56
1854–55	3.3892***	0.8749	3.874	163.95
1856–57	4.1063***	0.9199	4.464	164.67
Phase 2				
1858–59	165.87	0.5771		165.87
1860–61	0.0155	0.569	0.027	165.89
1862–63	0.5237	0.5693	0.092	166.39
Phase 3				
1864–65	165.89	0.5441		165.89
1866–67	0.7972	0.5475	1.456	166.69
1868–69	0.4578	0.5363	0.854	166.36
Phase 4				
1870–71	164.48	0.7042		164.48
1872–73	1.1975*	0.618	1.938	165.68
1874–75	0.90439	0.6334	1.428	165.38
Phase 5				
1876–77	164.86	0.6734		164.86
1878–79	0.8112	0.6171	1.315	165.67
1880–81	1.9174***	0.6184	3.101	166.78
Phase 6				
1882–83	166.85	0.5475		166.85
1884–85	−0.1928**	0.5918	−2.366	165.45
1886–87	−0.06263	0.5613	−1.116	166.22
Phase 7				
1888–89	166.24	0.5445		166.24
1890–91	−0.1928	0.5457	−0.353	166.05
1892–93	0.739	0.5369	1.376	166.98

Source: Twarog (1993).
*Significant at the 10 percent level.
**Significant at the 5 percent level.
***Significant at the 1 percent level.

stature never exceeded the 7th percentile of modern height standards.[6] The reasons for this included poor nutrition, hard work on family farms, poor health care (especially for children), and the practice of not breast-feeding infants.[7]

6. In the following discussion of height trends, the stature estimates referred to are RSMLE estimates for two-year birth cohorts. I prefer using the RSMLE results since they generally displayed less fluctuation than the QBE results, possibly due to the modest sample sizes.

The modern height percentiles used throughout this paper are those in Steckel (1996). They are based on data published by the National Center for Health Statistics (1977). These height standards are useful for most "Western" populations.

7. There was often a fatalistic attitude toward children's illnesses in Württemberg. Thus, many sick children died without ever having received medical attention (Königliches Statistisch-Topographisches Bureau 1875).

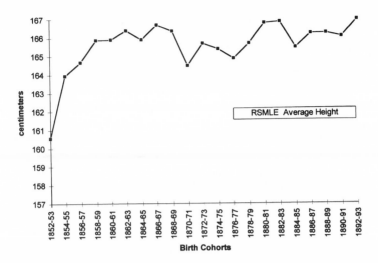

Fig. 8.4   RSMLE average height estimates, two-year birth cohorts, birth years 1852–53 to 1892–93
Source: Twarog (1993).

As will be discussed in section 8.3.3, these low average heights corresponded to extremely high infant mortality rates in Württemberg. As will be seen in section 8.3.5, the primary cause of death for infants was gastrointestinal illnesses. Even for those children who survived early childhood, it is likely that many of the nutrients they consumed were not absorbed properly into their bodies. Thus net nutrition—especially for children—was not very good throughout the period studied.

Some periods were, however, worse than others. Stature was extremely low for those born in the early 1850s. The RSMLE estimate of 160.56 cm for the birth cohorts of 1852 and 1853 was considerably below the first centile of modern height standards (161.7 cm). This corresponded to a time of severe agricultural crisis in Württemberg. Craftsmen who were farmers on the side shifted their labor into the handicraft sector. This, combined with decreased demand from the agricultural sector, caused the prices of manufactured goods to fall. Thus farmers and craftsmen were both hit hard by the crisis.

After the crisis ended, heights recovered unevenly, reaching the 6th percentile of modern height standards for birth years 1866–67. With the birth cohorts of the early 1870s, however, they plummeted once again, reaching the 3d modern height percentile. This height decline could be partially due to the Founder's Crisis. German unification in 1871 was followed by very high inflation in 1872 and 1873 and a speculation boom. The crash came in 1873. Industrial output, prices, and wages fell, while unemployment and bankruptcies rose.

Another factor that probably affected stature was the large surge in births owing in part to relaxed restrictions on marriage immediately following the

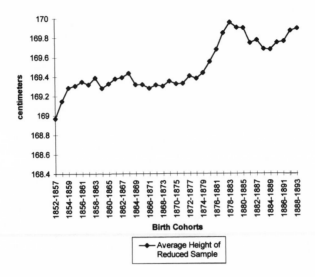

Fig. 8.5   Average height of reduced sample, six-year moving average, birth years 1852–57 to 1888–93
Source: Twarog (1993).

German unification. Birthrates between 1872 and 1877 ranged from 45.5 to 47.2 per 1,000 population—by far the highest levels of the century for Württemberg, which consistently had some of the highest birthrates in Europe (Königliches Statistisches Landesamt 1901). With so many children being born, it is probable that not all were cared for properly. In particular, such high birthrates could be reflecting lower breast-feeding rates, since breast-feeding acts as a natural contraceptive. The negative impact on infant health of not breast-feeding is discussed in the section on infant mortality. Other factors contributing to this dip in stature are under investigation.

In the 1870s and 1880s, Württemberg's railways were finally connected to the rest of Germany. Local industry and agriculture were suddenly confronted with an influx of cheaper grains and manufactured goods. Small farmers and traditional craftsmen suffered as their way of life was slowly being phased out.[8]

That the 1880s were rather difficult times is evidenced by the second dip in heights,[9] which coincided with a surge in emigration. There were stories of

8. While the changes brought on with Württemberg's rail connection initially led to some hardship for those forced to adapt, in the longer term the effect was beneficial. The railways could bring nutrients into Württemberg during local agricultural crises. They also eventually stimulated Württemberg's economy by providing an outlet for exportables. In fact, preliminary study indicates that toward the end of the period studied, stature was greater in those counties with railway connections (Twarog 1993).

9. Note that those belonging to the relatively short birth cohorts of the mid-1870s would have entered their adolescent growth spurt in the 1880s. Thus they were adversely affected during both of their rapid growth periods, which could help explain why the observed height dip of the 1870s was so deep.

social distress and increased numbers of people needing alms. These conditions in Germany prompted the passing of several important pieces of social legislation, including health and accident insurance laws. Perhaps these contributed to the upward trend in average heights seen after the mid-1880s. Certainly, rising incomes, better diet, improved public health, and possibly changes in breast-feeding practices also played a role. Between the birth cohorts of 1884–85 and 1892–93, average stature rose over 1.5 cm—from the 3d almost to the 7th percentile of modern height standards. This corresponded to a period of declining mortality and infant mortality rates in Württemberg and in Germany as a whole.

Occupational Differences

The Württemberg data always included the occupation of the soldier and often that of the soldier's father. This allowed analysis of height trends within occupation, a sample of which will be shown here. Occupations were classified into three broad categories: the upper class (consisting of white-collar workers), the working class (consisting of skilled, semiskilled, and unskilled workers), and those employed in agriculture.

Figures 8.6 and 8.7 show the QBE- and RSMLE-estimated height trends for these three occupational categories. The upper class was considerably taller than the agricultural class, which in turn was taller than the working class. The differentials between the upper and working classes widened considerably starting with the birth cohorts of the late 1860s, confirming Dumke's finding of increased income inequality during this period (Dumke 1988). The working

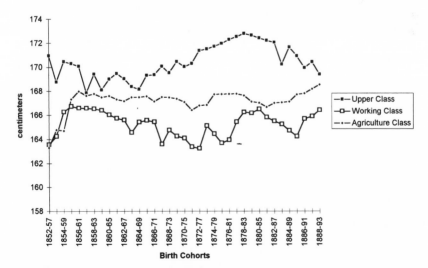

Fig. 8.6   QBE average height estimates by soldier's occupation, six-year moving average, birth years 1852–57 to 1888–93
Source: Twarog (1993).

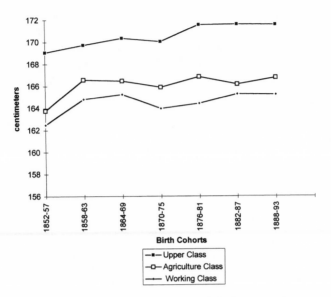

Fig. 8.7   RSMLE average height estimates by soldier's occupation, seven phases, birth years 1852–57 to 1888–93
Source: Twarog (1993).

Table 8.5   RSMLE Average Height Estimates (in centimeters) by Father's and Soldier's Occupation, Birth Years 1852–93

Father's Occupation	Soldier's Occupation		
	Upper	Working	N of R.S.[a]
Upper	170.42	165.53	1,129
Working	168.71	164.66	2,779

Source: Twarog (1993).

[a]*N* of R.S. refers to the number of observations in the reduced sample.

and agricultural classes were most severely hit by the agricultural crisis of the early 1850s. Those born into the working class appear to have seen a particular decline in their net nutrition in the 1870s.

Approximately half of the observations in the data set contained information on both the soldier's and the soldier's father's occupation. The analysis that this enabled indicated a clear positive correlation between stature and social mobility. Table 8.5 shows the results of running two RSMLE truncated regressions using the data subset where father and son were either upper or working class. Where the father and son were upper class, the average height was 170.42 cm. When, however, the father was upper class and the son was downwardly socially mobile (i.e., working class), the average height was 165.53 cm.

Table 8.6   Unadjusted Average Height (AVHT) by Father's and Soldier's Occupational Category

Father's Occupational Category	Soldier's Occupational Category																					Total
	1			2			3			4			5			6			7			
	N	%	AVHT	N	%	AVHT	N	%	AVHT	N	%	AVHT	N	%	AVHT	N	%	AVHT	N	%	AVHT	
1	286	50.8	172.68	90	16.0	170.13	24	4.3	168.46	2	0.4	167.5	0	0	–	151	26.8	171.29	10	1.8	168.5	563
2	73	28.7	172.42	82	32.3	170.53	34	13.4	169.90	8	3.1	167.44	1	0.4	164.5	38	15.0	171.26	18	7.1	168.33	254
3	44	1.7	171.58	67	2.6	170.41	1,735	68.0	166.49	285	11.2	165.99	52	2.0	166.37	83	3.3	168.12	284	11.1	166.05	2,550
4	3	0.4	167.5	25	3.5	167.22	298	42.3	165.74	228	32.3	166.82	16	2.3	167.53	15	2.1	170.90	120	17.0	166.29	705
5	0	0	–	2	0.4	171.00	182	36.8	165.94	91	18.4	166.00	35	7.1	166.06	1	0.2	168.50	184	37.2	165.57	495
6	58	15.2	170.80	40	10.5	169.88	58	15.2	166.78	25	6.5	165.04	5	1.3	168.00	176	46.1	169.72	20	5.2	167.63	382
7	40	1.5	171.71	31	1.2	169.95	613	23.1	166.14	208	7.8	166.62	34	1.3	167.49	27	1.0	170.54	1,699	64.1	167.69	2,652
Illegitimate	0	0	–	1	2.1	161.0	20	41.7	163.08	6	12.5	164.83	1	2.1	160.5	0	0	–	20	41.7	163.85	48

Source: Twarog (1993).

Notes: AVHT given in centimeters. The seven categories are (1) upper white collar, (2) lower white collar, (3) skilled, (4) semiskilled, (5) unskilled, (6) businessman, and (7) agriculture. There are also 48 illegitimately born soldiers whose father's occupation was not given.

Conversely, when both father and son were working class, the average height was 164.66 cm. When, however, the son was upwardly socially mobile, the average height was 168.71 cm. Both of these results were significant at the .000001 level.

Table 8.6 shows that similar patterns are observed if one divides occupations into seven categories. For example, where both the father's and son's occupations were upper white collar, the unadjusted average height was 172.68 cm. As the sons were increasingly downwardly socially mobile, the unadjusted average heights fell: 170.13 cm for lower white collar, 168.46 for skilled workers, and 167.5 for semiskilled workers.[10]

Urban-Rural Differences

In contrast to the findings in some other European countries, urbanization in Württemberg does not appear to be the main culprit in height declines seen during industrialization. In fact, as can be seen in figure 8.8, those born in urban areas (communities with over 2,000 residents) were significantly taller than those born in rural areas. This result remained significant even when occupational factors were included in the regression equation. This finding is likely due to relatively good public health infrastructure, regular inspections by public health authorities, higher incomes, and better medical attention in the cities. Moreover, urban dwellers probably listened more to government exhortations to breast-feed infants. The lower birthrates in the cities could be due to higher breast-feeding rates.[11]

It should be noted, however, that the cities in Württemberg were relatively small. Only Stuttgart had a population over 50,000 in the nineteenth century. In fact, when community size was further subdivided into six categories, one sees in figure 8.9 that the average height of those born in Stuttgart declined after the mid-1860s and was surpassed by those born in communities with 20,000–49,999 residents.[12] Thus it could be that urbanization's negative effects begin to show after a certain threshold is reached.

Heights in Württemberg for Birth Years before 1852

Information on stature before 1850 is limited.[13] Most published studies of military heights for the earlier period mention only the percentage of those called up that were under the minimum height or that were unfit for other reasons (Wurm 1990). There are, however, two studies that estimated the unadjusted average height of soldiers serving in Württemberg's army. In the first,

10. These differentials are probably underestimated since unadjusted average heights are used. However, the number of observations with information on father's occupation is too small to support accurate RSMLE estimates for all 49 occupational subsets.

11. More data and research on urban-rural breast-feeding practices are needed.

12. Community size classifications are based on population data for 1895.

13. John Komlos (University of Munich) has recorded height data contained in the *Musterungslisten* of the early nineteenth century in Württemberg. I look forward to the results of the data analysis.

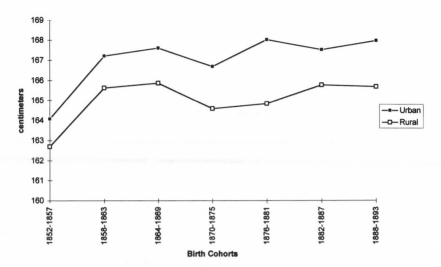

Fig. 8.8 RSMLE average height estimates for soldiers born in rural (less than 2,000 residents) and urban communities, seven phases, 1852–57 to 1888–93
Source: Twarog (1993).

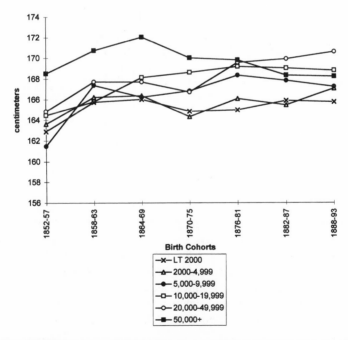

Fig. 8.9 RSMLE average height estimates by birth community size (in 1895), seven phases, birth years 1852–57 to 1888–93
Source: Twarog (1993).

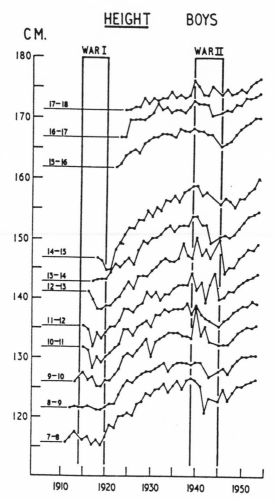

Fig. 8.10   Heights of Stuttgart schoolchildren, 1912–53
Sources: Tanner (1962), cited in Tanner (1978).

the soldiers' unadjusted average height for the years 1829–33 (mainly birth years 1809–13) was found to be 164.5 cm (Riedle 1834 in Wurm 1990). In the second, the unadjusted average height of soldiers in 1866 and 1867 (mainly birth years 1846–47) was calculated to be 166.1 cm (Retter 1869 in Wurm 1990). Both of these figures overestimate the true population mean since those who did not meet the minimum height or physical fitness standards were not included.[14] The figures do seem to indicate, however, that the net nutrition of

14. E.g., in 1866 and 1867, 10–11 percent of all those called up did not meet the minimum height requirement of 157.5 cm (Retter 1869 in Wurm 1990). For comparison purposes, in the author's sample of soldiers born in 1852 and 1853, the unadjusted average height was 166.8 cm; the QBE estimate was 161.2 cm, and the RSMLE estimate was 160.6 cm.

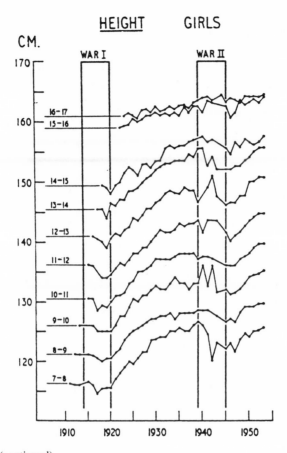

Fig. 8.10 (continued)

those born in Württemberg in the mid-1840s was better than that of those born 30 years earlier.

Heights in Württemberg for Birth Years after 1893

There are three pieces of evidence the author has thus far on height trends in Württemberg beyond 1893. One is figure 8.10—a graph of schoolchildren's heights in Stuttgart during the first half of the twentieth century.[15] In the mid-1920s, upper- and middle-class boys aged 17–18 years were approximately 171 cm tall. The average height of this group increased thereafter (except for declines during the World War II years) reaching approximately 175 cm by 1955.

15. The height data for children aged 15 and up are for children attending the *Oberschule* (upper school)—generally upper and middle-class children. The younger children were from the *Volksschule,* which all German children had to attend.

This represents an increase from approximately the 20th to the 40th percentile of modern height standards. During the same period, the stature of upper- and middle-class girls aged 16–17 increased from approximately 161 cm to 163 cm—from the 35th to the 50th percentile of modern standards for 17-year-olds. The height gains of children in age groups 7–8 through 14–15 (upper, middle, and lower classes together) during this period were even more dramatic—often more than 8 cm in 30 years. For example, the average stature of boys and girls aged 7–8 years increased 9–10 cm between 1911 and 1939—from approximately the 2d to the 30th percentile of modern height standards for 8-year-olds.[16] These figures clearly show that, despite setbacks during the war years, the net nutrition of children in Stuttgart increased substantially throughout the first half of the twentieth century.

Harbeck (1960) analyzed the heights of all 20-year-old German men called up and measured in 1957 (birth year 1937). The region of Baden-Württemberg (note, not just Württemberg) showed an average height of 171.8. This is more than 4.5 cm greater than the RSMLE estimate of average height for those born in 1892–93 (166.98 cm). It corresponds to a rise from approximately the 7th to the 22d percentile of modern height standards. Moreover, Jürgens (1971) found that the average stature of 1,142 draftable 20-year-olds born in Baden-Württemberg in 1948–49 was 176.8 cm. This equals the 50th percentile of modern height standards. These findings certainly strengthen the above evidence of an improvement in net nutrition in Württemberg during the first half of the twentieth century.

One other interesting fact emerges. For the birth cohorts of 1937, the average stature in Baden-Württemberg was 1.4 cm lower than the German average of 173.2 cm. This fits into the general pattern of historical heights in Germany, where stature decreased as one moved from north to south (Wurm 1982). For the birth cohorts of 1948–49, however, this pattern no longer held true. The average height in Baden-Württemberg was 0.5 cm greater than the German average of 176.3 (Jürgens 1971). Thus net nutrition of those born in Baden-Württemberg improved both absolutely and relative to the German average toward the middle of the twentieth century. It is likely that migration into Baden-Württemberg, increasing incomes and meat consumption, and possibly changes in infant feeding practices played a role in this outcome.

8.3.3 Infant Mortality Rates

Continuous data on infant mortality rates for all of Germany or for Württemberg in the nineteenth century are unavailable. There are, however, data for Prussia between 1816 and 1900. The average Prussian infant mortality rate was actually higher in the second half of the century than in the first half. Not until 1852 did more than 20 percent of Prussian infants die in the first year. Those

---

16. This is the equivalent of a shift from approximately the 10th to the 60th percentile of modern height standards for 7-year-olds.

born in the 1860s and 1870s had particularly high infant mortality rates (generally between 200 and 220 infant deaths per 1,000 births; Wiegand and Zapf 1982).

Infant mortality data are available for the territory of the German Empire (1881–1938) and the Federal Republic of Germany (after 1949). In the last two decades of the nineteenth century, between 230 and 280 infants died or were stillborn per 1,000 live births. After 1905, the trend was clearly downward, falling from 205/1,000 in 1905 to 105/1,000 in 1925—a nearly 50 percent drop in only 20 years. The fast decline continued through 1938, when the infant mortality rate reached 60/1,000. Thereafter, the rate of decrease slowed. Infant mortality rates finally went under 30/1,000 in 1963 and stayed there (Flora, Kraus, and Pfenning 1987).

For Württemberg, I have found data for some years between 1812 and 1897. Table 8.7 and figure 8.11 show these findings. One notices immediately that infant mortality rates in Württemberg were shockingly high—never falling below 200 per 1,000 live births, and even reaching 408/1,000 in 1865. The rates were generally rising through 1865. Data are missing for the years 1866–74. After 1875, the rates were clearly falling, albeit a bit unevenly. Württemberg had one of the highest infant mortality rates in Europe. For the period of the mid-1840s to mid-1850s, for example, Württemberg's rate was more than double that of Sweden, Denmark, Norway, Belgium, England, and France (Königliches Statistisch-Topographisches Bureau 1875). One reason for these high

Table 8.7   **Infant Mortality Rates per 1,000 Live Births in Württemberg, 1812–22 to 1897 (available years)**

Year	Infant Mortality	Year	Infant Mortality
1812–22	320.6	1882	273.2
1846–56	347.8	1883	275.4
1858–59	328	1884	291.8
1859–60	364	1885	276.1
1860–61	312	1886	282.6
1861–62	408	1887	234.9
1862–63	321	1888	254.4
1863–64	350	1889	265.1
1865	408	1890	246.1
1875	337.8	1891	256
1877	299	1892	256.3
1878	289	1893	249.8
1879	303	1896	207.7
1880	300.4	1897	248.8
1881	284.2		

Sources: Königliches Medizinal-Kollegium (1884, 1900), Königliches Statistisches Landesamt (1886, 1891, 1892, 1895, 1897), Königliches Statistisch-Topographisches Bureau (1875, 1877, 1878, 1880, 1885), and Württembergischer Ärztlicher Verein (1867).

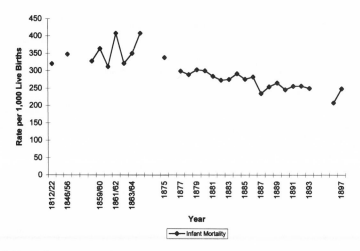

Fig. 8.11   Infant mortality rates per 1,000 live births in Württemberg, 1812–22 to 1897 (available years)
Source: Table 8.7.

infant mortality rates is that Württemberg was a land of small, relatively poor landowners. Farmers' wives generally had many children, were poorly nourished, and worked very hard in the house and the fields. Thus infants were often neglected and seldom received medical attention when ill.

An even more significant cause of the extreme infant mortality was the local custom of not breast-feeding infants.[17] Breast milk is beyond doubt the best food source for infants. It is designed especially for the human baby, with the ideal combination of proteins, carbohydrates, fats, vitamins, and so forth. Moreover, it contains antibodies that greatly increase an infant's resistance to infections. It is easily digestible and reduces the risk of food allergies. Breast-feeding significantly reduces infant morbidity and mortality rates (La Leche League International 1993).

In Württemberg, instead of breast milk, infants were often given an unsterilized mixture of flour and water.[18] Ironically, this custom was strongest in the Donaukreis, where landholdings tended to be larger and farmers' wives would have had the time and nourishment to tend their children properly.[19] Thus in

---

17. This lack of breast-feeding also contributed to Württemberg's exceptionally high birthrates, since breast-feeding is a natural contraceptive.

18. Wet-nursing was apparently not a widespread custom in Württemberg since I have found no mention of it in the course of my research.

19. How this local custom of not breast-feeding (*nicht stillen*) came about is still not obvious. It seems that land inheritance practices could have played a role. In the Donaukreis, all the land was generally inherited by the oldest surviving son. Thus, it was perhaps perceived to be less tragic if later sons died in infancy since they would have been second-class citizens in the agricultural hierarchy (Königliches Statistisch-Topographisches Bureau 1875).

Table 8.8   **Infant Mortality in Five Categories of Community Size in Württemberg, 1889–98 and 1899**

| Community Size Category (number of residents) | Infants Who Died in First Year of Life | | | |
| | 1889–98 Average | | 1899 | |
	Overall	Percentage of Live Births	Overall	Percentage of Live Births
Over 100,000	1,018	23.48	1,023	20.10
20,000–100,000	779	22.87	786	19.63
10,000–20,000	790	22.80	832	21.79
5,000–10,000	1,344	25.44	1,411	22.83
Under 5,000	13,481	25.07	11,885	21.72

Source: Königliches Statistisches Landesamt (1901).

1865, when 408 out of every 1,000 infants died in Württemberg, 470.4 out of every 1,000 born in the Donaukreis died in their first year. This is considerably higher than the rate in the poorest region (411 in Jaxtkreis) as well as the other two regions (383 in Schwarzwaldkreis and 381 in Neckarkreis; Württembergischer Ärztlicher Verein 1867).

Breast-feeding practices also appear to have a large impact on adult heights. The poor health conditions during the high-growth period of infancy can cause permanent stunting of heights if not followed by a period of excellent net nutrition—enough for catch-up growth. This could be a main reason for the relatively short stature in Württemberg during this period. Michael Haines (personal correspondence, 1993) examined this relationship in over 60 German regions in the early twentieth century. His findings clearly indicate that those areas with the highest percentage of infants breast-fed had the lowest infant mortality rates and the tallest young men. This correlation was seen in Württemberg as well: stature in the Donaukreis (discussed above) was lower than would be expected considering the relatively high incomes. This relationship needs to be studied further. Changes in women's work and breast-feeding practices linked with industrialization or urbanization could be a major avenue through which industrialization affects stature.

As table 8.8 shows, infant mortality rates in Württemberg tended to be lower in the cities. The above-mentioned two factors could be driving this result. Urban women did not have to work in the fields, and many could stay home to tend their less numerous offspring. Access to medical attention was much easier in the cities, and incomes tended to be higher. Furthermore, it is likely that urban women were more influenced by the health authorities' promotion of breast-feeding. The lower urban birthrates would support this proposition. The lower infant mortality rates correspond to the taller statures of those born in urban areas.

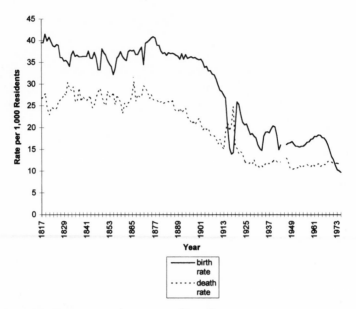

Fig. 8.12 Birth and death rates per 1,000 residents in Germany, 1817–1975
Source: Mitchell (1980).

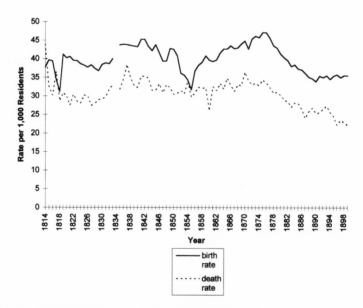

Fig. 8.13 Birth (including stillbirths) and death rates per 1,000 residents in Württemberg, 1814–99
Source: Königliches Statistisches Landesamt (1901).

8.3.4   Mortality Rates

Both Germany and Württemberg went through their demographic transitions in the time period under consideration. Figure 8.12 shows the demographic transition in Germany. Both birthrates and death rates peaked in the 1870s. Thereafter, the trend was downward. Birthrates fell particularly fast between 1895 and 1913, from 36.1 to 27.5 births per 1,000 population. Following the First World War, birthrates peaked for a few years and then remained below 21 births per 1,000 population. Between 1875 and 1934, mortality rates consistently declined (except during the war years), falling from 27.6 to 10.9 deaths per 1,000 population.

Figure 8.13 shows the birth and mortality rates in Württemberg between 1812 and 1897. In the 1820s, mortality rates were relatively low, averaging 29 deaths per 1,000 residents. From the 1830s through the late 1870s, mortality rates were higher, generally in the 31 to 35 deaths per 1,000 range. As in Germany as a whole, a downward trend began in the late 1870s and continued through the end of the century.

Birthrates dropped sharply during the agricultural crisis of the late 1840s and early 1850s but otherwise followed the same basic pattern as mortality rates. This similarity is not surprising when one looks at the information in table 8.9: in the second half of the nineteenth century, deaths of infants comprised 32–47 percent of all deaths in Württemberg. These percentages are ex-

Table 8.9   **Deaths of Infants under Age One as a Percentage of Total Deaths (including stillbirths) in Württemberg, 1846–56 to 1900 (available years)**

Year	Percentage of Total Births	Year	Percentage of Total Births
1846–56	40.1	1879	40.4
1858–59	43	1880	39.6
1859–60	44	1881	38.1
1860–61	41	1882	36.5
1861–62	45	1883	37.4
1862–63	39.5	1884	38.3
1863–64	42.3	1885	35.5
1865	47	1886	38.2
1875	43.6	1894	31.9
1876	42.9	1897	35.9
1877	40.6	1900	35.2
1878	39.4		

Sources: Königliches Medizinal-Kollegium (1896, 1900, 1902), Königliches Statistisches Landesamt (1889, 1901), Königliches Statistisch-Topographisches Bureau (1863a, 1877), and Württembergischer Ärztlicher Verein (1867).

Table 8.10   **Deaths by Age Category as a Percentage of Total Deaths (excluding stillbirths) in Württemberg, 1846–56, 1876–86, 1894, 1897, and 1900**

	Age Category and Percentage of Total Deaths in That Category						
Year	<1	1–6	7–13	14–19	20–44	45–69	>70
1846–56	42.2	10.0	2.4	1.9	10.8	20.7	12.0
		12.4			33.4		

	Age Category and Percentage of Total Deaths in That Category						
Year	<1	1–4	5–9	10–14	15–19	20–44	45–69	>70
1876–86	41.0	10.6	2.6	1.1	1.3	10.2	19.3	13.9
		14.3			30.8		

	Age Category and Percentage of Total Deaths in That Category		
Year	<1	1–15	15–60	>60
1894	33.4	17.4	22.9	26.3
1897	37.6	11.4	23.3	27.7
1900	36.9	10.1	23.0	30.0

Sources: Königliches Medizinal-Kollegium (1896, 1900, 1902), Königliches Statistisches Landesamt (1889), and Königliches Statistisch-Topographisches (1863b).

ceptionally high, often double that in other European countries during that time period (Königliches Statistisch-Topographisches Bureau 1875). Higher birth-rates combined with exceptionally high infant mortality rates drove up the overall mortality rates.

Table 8.10 shows deaths by age category as percentages of total deaths in Württemberg in 1846–56, 1876–86, 1894, 1897, and 1900. The age categories reported were unfortunately not constant across periods. Nevertheless, the trend toward a decreasing percentage of deaths under age 1 and an increasing percentage of deaths over age 60 or 70 is clear.

8.3.5   Causes of Death

According to Omran, there are three phases in a country's epidemiologic transition. Phase one could be termed the age of epidemics and famine. Mortality rates fluctuate a great deal, hindering population growth, and average life expectancy at birth varies from 20 to 40 years. The transitional phase two is the age of declining epidemics. Life expectancy at birth rises from around 30 years to 50 years. Declining mortality rates are followed by declining birth-rates. During phase three, mortality reaches even lower levels, and life expectancy at birth can surpass 70 years. The population becomes increasingly older, causing this age to be called the age of degenerative and man-made diseases (Omran 1971).

According to Reinhard Spree (1986), the transitional phase two began in

Germany around 1820 and lasted until the 1920s. This phase was characterized by the absence of great epidemics, the evolution of the so-called human crowd diseases into children's diseases, and a decline in deaths due to smallpox, typhoid fever, and tuberculosis. The period of study of this paper spans the last two-thirds of phase two and the beginning of phase three.

In the third quarter of the nineteenth century in Württemberg, deaths due to infectious diseases generally accounted for less than 8 percent of all deaths. Toward the end of the nineteenth century, deaths due to infectious diseases were decreasing, whereas deaths due to tuberculosis of the lungs, pneumonia, and other respiratory problems were on the rise and together accounted for 24.6 percent of all deaths in 1900. Approximately one-fifth of all deaths were due to gastroenteritis. Tumors, though accounting for less than 4.5 percent of all deaths, were also on the rise (Königliches Medizinal-Kollegium 1900; Königliches Statistisches Landesamt 1901).

More insight into Württemberg's mortality situation can be gained from table 8.11, which shows causes of death in four age categories in Württemberg in 1900. The victims of infectious diseases were overwhelmingly children. The

Table 8.11   Causes of Death in Four Age Categories in Württemberg, 1900

	Age Category				
Causes of Death	<1	1–15	15–60	>60	Total
Diphtheria	144	821	20	5	990
Whooping cough	768	325	4	7	1,104
Scarlet fever	34	155	16	–	205
Measles	158	204	–	–	362
Typhoid	–	6	136	12	154
Tuberculosis of lungs	198	374	3,338	712	4,622
Tuberculosis of other organs	85	222	234	59	600
Pneumonia	1,086	657	792	1,245	3,780
Other respiratory	753	416	908	1,963	4,040
Gastroenteritis	10,195	608	217	309	11,329
Puerperal fever	–	–	118	–	118
Other consequences of delivery or pregnancy	–	–	148	–	148
Tumor	7	19	911	1,097	2,034
Congenital weakness in first month of life	3,626	–	–	–	3,626
Infirmity (age 60+)	–	–	–	4,512	4,512
Accidents	24	209	457	190	880
Suicide	–	3	277	92	372
Other cited cause	1,588	1,103	4,058	4,972	11,720
Cause not stated	13	10	15	10	48
Total	18,679	5,132	11,649	15,185	50,645

Source: Königliches Medizinal-Kollegium (1902).

chief cause of death for infants under age 1 year was gastroenteritis, accounting for 54.6 percent of all infant deaths. This reflects the lack of breast-feeding in Württemberg and the substitution of nonhygienically prepared infant formulas. For infants, congenital weakness and pneumonia were also particularly lethal.

For children aged 1–15 years, infectious diseases, pneumonia, gastroenteritis, tuberculosis, and other respiratory problems were the main causes of death. For adults aged 15–60, tuberculosis of the lungs was the number one killer, accounting for nearly 29 percent of all deaths in that age category in all three years. This suggests inadequate nutrition and poor living conditions. Pneumonia, other respiratory problems, and tumors were also main causes of death for young and middle-aged adults. For those over age 60, the main cause was infirmity due to old age, followed by respiratory problems, pneumonia, tumors, and tuberculosis of the lungs.

The causes of death in Württemberg can be compared with those in German cities with over 15,000 residents for the years 1877, 1881, and 1884.[20] Infectious diseases accounted for over 10 percent of all deaths in German cities in the late 1870s to early 1880s. Tuberculosis of the lungs, the main cause of death cited, accounted for over 13 percent of all deaths in German cities. This is considerably higher than the 7.6–9.6 percent in Württemberg during the 1890s. However, in Württemberg, the mortality rate due to this illness in 1897 was considerably higher in the cities with populations over 10,000—22.85 lung tuberculosis deaths per 10,000 people as opposed to 18.81 in the rest of the kingdom.[21] Still it appears plausible that Württemberg's cities were healthier places to live than the average German city, perhaps because they were not huge agglomerates. On the other hand, the percentage of deaths caused by enteritis and diarrhea with vomiting was between 9 and 11 percent for German cities, whereas deaths due to gastroenteritis accounted for 18–23 percent of all deaths in Württemberg. This is due primarily to the lack of breast-feeding in Württemberg.

Data on the causes of death in Germany in 1949 clearly indicate that the country had entered phase three of the epidemiologic transition—the age of degenerative and man-made diseases. Deaths due to infectious diseases such as diphtheria, smallpox, and typhoid fever dropped dramatically compared to the previous century. The same was true for tuberculosis of the respiratory system (which now accounted for only 4.1 percent of all deaths) and for diarrhea and enteritis (1.3 percent of all deaths). These large declines point to much improved general health and hygiene conditions. Cancer and heart diseases had become the top two causes of death, causing 15.7 and 15.2 percent, respectively, of all deaths in 1949 (World Health Organization 1950).

---

20. The data on German cities are from Kaiserliches Statistisches Amt (1886).

21. In Württemberg's cities, however, the mortality rates due to infectious diseases and pneumonia were considerably lower than in the rest of the kingdom (Königliches Medizinal-Kollegium 1900).

8.3.6   Life Expectations

Data on life expectations are available from the founding of the German Empire in 1871 onward. Table 8.12 shows life expectancy at ages 0, 30, and 60 for males and females between 1871–80 and 1974–76 in the German Empire/Federal Republic of Germany. The trend was clearly upward, particularly for life expectancy at birth. Please note, however, that the figures for 1871–1910 are by decade and thus do not show yearly variations.

For Württemberg, table 8.13 summarizes what I was able to collect and compares life expectancies in the region with the German average. Württemberg's life expectancy trend was clearly positive between 1876–80 and 1900–10, for both males and females, and at all ages shown (0, 1, 2, 6, 30, and 60 years). Life expectancy at birth showed the greatest increase: for males this rose from 34.3 years in 1876–80 to 45.15 years in 1901–10. For females, it increased from 36.76 years to 48.08 years. This largely reflects declining infant mortality rates. Compared to the overall German average, females in Württemberg generally lived shorter lives throughout the periods studied. Württemberg's males generally improved their life expectancy relative to the German average.

Table 8.12   **Life Expectancy at Ages 0, 30, and 60 for Males and Females in the German Empire, 1871–80 to 1974–76**

Period	Age 0		Age 30		Age 60	
	Male (1)	Female (2)	Male (3)	Female (4)	Male (5)	Female (6)
1871–80	35.58	38.45	31.41	33.07	12.11	12.71
1881–90	37.17	40.25	32.11	34.21	12.43	13.14
1891–1900	40.56	43.97	33.46	35.62	12.82	13.60
1901–10	44.82	48.33	34.55	36.94	13.14	14.17
1910–11	47.41	50.68	35.29	37.30	13.18	14.17
1924–26	55.97	58.82	38.56	39.76	14.60	15.51
1932–34	59.86	62.81	39.47	41.05	15.11	16.07
1946–47	57.72	63.44	39.20	42.72	15.18	16.99
1949–51	64.56	68.46	41.32	43.89	16.20	17.46
1958–59	66.75	71.88	41.39	45.30	15.74	18.27
1959–60	66.69	71.94	41.21	45.27	15.53	18.22
1960–62	66.86	72.39	41.14	45.53	15.49	18.48
1962–63	67.10	72.77	41.02	45.64	15.33	18.55
1963–64	67.32	73.13	41.10	45.84	15.40	18.75
1964–66	67.58	73.48	41.17	46.03	15.46	18.92
1966–68	67.55	73.58	41.04	46.04	15.29	18.88
1968–70	67.24	73.44	40.75	45.90	15.02	18.77
1970–72	67.41	73.83	41.00	46.30	15.31	19.12
1972–74	67.87	74.36	41.24	46.70	15.52	19.46
1974–76	68.30	74.81	41.36	46.95	15.64	19.66

Source: See Wiegand and Zapf (1982).

Table 8.13   **Life Expectancy for Males and Females in Württemberg and Germany in the Late Nineteenth and Early Twentieth Centuries**

Age In Years	1876–80 Württemberg	1871–80 German Empire	1891–1900 Württemberg	1891–1900 German Empire	1901–10 Württemberg	1901–10 German Empire
Males						
At birth	34.3	35.58	39.74	40.56	45.15	44.82
Age 1	49.2	–	52.97	51.85	56.67	55.12
Age 2	51.5	–	54.25	53.67	57.53	56.39
Age 6	51.3	–	53.15	52.70	55.01	54.44
Age 30	32.8	31.41	33.95	33.46	34.94	34.55
Age 60	12.1	12.11	12.71	12.82	13.00	13.14
Females						
At birth	36.76	38.45	42.74	43.97	48.08	48.34
Age 1	49.8	–	53.87	53.78	57.62	57.20
Age 2	52.2	–	55.17	55.59	58.33	58.47
Age 6	52.0	–	54.16	54.66	56.04	56.57
Age 30	33.2	33.07	35.01	35.62	36.36	36.94
Age 60	12.2	12.71	12.98	13.60	13.69	14.17

Sources: Constructed from table 8.12 and Königliches Statistisches Landesamt (1913a).

8.3.7   Migration

Emigration from a region can be due to a number of factors, including high population density and growth and unfavorable economic conditions coupled with brighter prospects elsewhere. Thus, a surge in emigration could indicate a period of hardship in the home country. Table 8.14 shows the substantial net population loss due to migration for Württemberg during 12 phases between 1816 and 1900. The years 1847–55, the time of the agricultural crisis and economic downturn, had the highest emigration rates. Eighteen thousand people—approximately 1 percent of the population—left per year, many of whom headed for North America. Emigration in the early 1850s was so high that Württemberg's population actually declined from 1,733,263 in 1852 to 1,720,708 in 1861, despite high birthrates (Megerle 1982). The early 1880s had the second highest emigration rate; the late 1860s to early 1870s had the third highest. As can be seen in table 8.15, the emigration patterns for Germany as a whole are similar to those for Württemberg.

8.3.8   Average Workday and Workweek

Table 8.16 shows the trends in the average workday and workweek in German industry from 1800 (1830) to 1914. The average workday and workweek were highest in the 1830–60 period, when the average workday was 14–16 hours and the average workweek was 80–85 hours. Thereafter, the trend was

Table 8.14   **Loss of Population Due to Emigration from Württemberg, 12 Phases, 1816–1900**

Period	Migration Loss	
	Total	Per Year
1816–18	20,000	6,670
1819–28	16,500	1,650
1829–34	30,500	6,100
1835–46	36,000	3,000
1847–55	162,000	18,000
1856–64	45,000	5,000
1865–70	43,000	7,170
1871–73	14,913	4,970
1874–79	8,492	1,420
1880–84	47,707	9,540
1885–93	50,211	5,580
1894–1900	11,824	1,690
1816–1900	486,142	5,720

Source: Megerle (1982).

Table 8.15   **Overseas Emigration from Germany**

Period	Total
1821–30	8,500
1831–40	167,700
1841–50	469,300
1851–60	1,075,000
1861–70	832,700
1871–80	626,000
1881–90	1,342,400
1891–1900	529,900
1901–10	279,600
1911–20	91,000
1921–30	567,300
Total	5,989,400

Source: Stolper (1940).

downward. In the 1870s, the average workday was 12 hours. By 1911–14, on average 54–60 hours were worked per week, and 10 hours per day.

The story in Württemberg was similar. Although there was a fair amount of variation in working hours across different industrial branches, in the 1870s, the usual workday was 11–12 hours (without breaks). Many factory workers actually preferred working three 24-hour shifts since they lived in rural areas and traveled a relatively long way to get to work. By the turn of the century, roughly 10–11 hours were worked per day. In 1912, over 60 percent of Württemberg's workers worked 57 hours or less per week (Boelcke 1989).

Table 8.16   Development of Average Workday and Workweek in German Industry, 1800–1914

Period	Average Workday (hours)	Average Workweek (hours)
Around 1800	10–12	–
Around 1820	11–14	–
Around 1830–60	14–16	80–85
1861–70	12–14	75
1871–80	12	72
1881–90	11	66
1891–95	10.5–11	63–65
1896–1900	10.5	61–63
1901–5	10–10.5	59–61
1906–10	10–10.5	58–60
1911–14	10	54–60

Source: Wiegand and Zapf (1982).

8.3.9   Hoffmann's Index of Caloric Balance

Using aggregate data on German consumption of 26 categories of food and drink, Hoffmann (1965) calculated the estimated total number of calories consumed in Germany for each year between 1850 and 1959. He then figured out how many calories the population needed by age and sex,[22] adding additional calories for work (130 calories per hour worked in factories, agriculture, mining, and crafts; 500 calories per day in other kinds of work; 600 per day for housewives) and 150,000 calories per birth.

He then compared the calories consumed to those needed. Table 8.17 shows the results. In 1850–54, only 75 percent of calories needed were consumed. When one takes into account that food consumption was not evenly distributed, it is evident that many Germans were consuming considerably less than 75 percent of the calories they needed. The situation improved, reaching 100 percent (on average) in 1875–79. The ratio fell to 95 percent in 1880–84. Thereafter, it remained above 100 percent. Until 1900–1904, it rose steadily. Afterward, it declined and then steadied out in the 1930s at 111 percent.

The caloric deficits before the late 1880s almost certainly led to some stunting of stature in Germany. The period of most extreme caloric deficit (1850–54) corresponds to extremely short statures for those born in Württemberg during that period. The secular increase in heights did not begin prior to the mid-1890s, when Hoffmann's index of actual to needed calories rose to 119.

---

22. Hoffmann estimated, e.g., that children under six years of age normally need 1,000 (male) and 950 (female) calories per day. Adolescents (ages 14–19) need 2,800 (male) and 2,400 (female) calories per day. Adults (ages 20–44) need 2,400 (male) and 2,200 (female) calories per day. For more details, see Hoffmann (1965, 658).

Table 8.17   **Hoffmann's Index of Caloric Balance, 1850–1950**

Year	Actual (billion Kcal)	Needed (billion Kcal)	Actual/Needed (%)
1850–54	27,730	36,750	75
1855–59	30,240	37,650	80
1860–64	34,980	39,340	89
1865–69	36,710	40,860	90
1870–74	39,140	43,400	90
1875–79	46,530	46,440	100
1880–84	46,130	48,530	95
1885–89	52,850	50,610	104
1890–94	57,670	53,250	108
1895–99	67,410	56,860	119
1900–1904	74,620	60,820	124
1905–9	79,160	65,140	122
1910–13	81,530	69,100	118
1925–29	74,540	68,860	108
1930–34	76,440	68,650	111
1935–38	80,440	72,430	111
1950–54	56,490	50,800	111
1955–59	61,390	54,080	114

Source: Hoffmann (1965).

There is a good chance that in this period, despite some income and caloric inequality, the majority of the German population was eating enough to largely meet its caloric needs (although less can be said about its nutritional, particularly protein, needs). This, combined with rising incomes, improved hygiene and public health measures, and possibly better breast-feeding practices, is what most likely drove the secular increase in heights during the twentieth century.

8.3.10   Literacy Rates

Illiteracy was fairly rare in Germany and in Württemberg throughout the period studied. Table 8.18 shows the percentage of recruits in Germany and Württemberg who were illiterate in the period 1881–82 to 1912.[23] For the purposes of the German army, being literate meant being able to read "enough" and to write one's first and last name legibly. This is obviously a looser definition than would be used today, but it can still be indicative.

For Germany as a whole, there was a clear downward trend in the already low illiteracy rates. The percentage of illiterate soldiers fell from 1.54 percent in 1881–82, to 0.72 percent in 1886–87, to 0.22 percent in 1894, and to 0.07

23. I was unable to find hard data on literacy rates for all of Germany prior to the last quarter of the nineteenth century. Between 1875 and 1881, the literacy rate for German recruits was 98 percent. For earlier years, some data are available on literacy rates of Prussian recruits: 1841, 91 percent; 1851, 95 percent; 1865, 94 percent; and 1867–74, 96–98 percent (Cipolla 1969).

Table 8.18   **Illiteracy Rates (in percentages) of German and Württemberg
Recruits, 1881–82 to 1912 (available years)**

Year	Germany	Württemberg	Year	Germany	Württemberg
1881–82	1.54	0.00	1898	0.07	0.02
1882–83	1.32	0.00	1899	0.05	0.03
1883–84	1.27	0.02	1900	0.07	0.00
1884–85	1.21	0.03	1901	0.05	0.01
1885–86	1.08	0.00	1902	0.04	0.04
1886–87	0.72	0.00	1903	–	0.03
1887–88	0.71	0.01	1904	0.04	0.03
1888–89	0.60	0.03	1905	0.03	0.06
1889–90	0.51	0.01	1906	0.02	0.06
1890–91	0.54	0.04	1907	0.02	0.07
1892	–	–	1908	0.02	0.00
1893	0.24	0.01	1909	0.02	0.01
1894	0.22	0.03	1910	0.02	0.02
1895	0.15	0.03	1911	0.01	0.01
1896	0.11	0.03	1912	0.05	0.01
1897	0.08	0.02			

Sources: Königliches Statistisches Landesamt (1892, 1901, 1903, 1910a, 1912, 1913a).
Note: Literacy rate is defined as the percentage of recruits who could write their names and read sufficiently.

percent in 1900. From 1901 through 1912, it ranged from 0.01 to 0.05 percent. In Württemberg, the illiteracy rate in this period was never above 0.07 percent, and it generally ranged between zero and 0.03 percent. After 1912, it was generally believed that illiteracy had been virtually stamped out in Germany (Giese 1986).

8.3.11   The Human Development Index

Economic expansion is only a means to the end of human well-being. In recent years, the United Nations Development Programme (UNDP) has attempted to quantify human well-being or human development in a manner allowing comparisons between countries. According to the UNDP, "Human development is a process of enlarging people's choices. The most critical ones are to lead a long and healthy life, to be educated and to enjoy a decent standard of living. Additional choices include political freedom, guaranteed human rights and self-respect" (United Nations Development Programme 1990). Since quantifying all of the above factors can be difficult, UNDP decided to focus on the first three essential elements of human life in creating its Human Development Index (HDI).

The HDI has three components. For the first—longevity—life expectancy at birth is used as the indicator. For the second—education and knowledge—literacy rates are the chosen proxy. For the third—"command over resources needed for a decent living"—the logarithm of purchasing-power-adjusted real GDP per capita was chosen.

For each component, the minimum and maximum ranges must be defined. In 1990, the UNDP used the lowest 1987 national values for each indicator as the minimum. These were 42 years for life expectancy, 12 percent for literacy, and $220 for real per capita income. For the maximum, they used Japan's life expectancy in 1987 of 78 years, 100 percent literacy rate, and the average official poverty line in developed countries, $4,861. An index value was calculated for each component in each country. The HDI is a composite index, with each component given equal weight (United Nations Development Programme 1990).

To apply this method to historical data, some changes must be made in the minimum and maximum values used. For example, in many European countries in the nineteenth century, life expectancy was less than 42 years, so the minimum value must be lower. There is a need for economic historians to develop a common methodology for constructing historical HDIs to facilitate comparison between countries.

For historical Germany, the available data that have been presented earlier in this paper were used to construct the HDI index. Table 8.12 contains information on life expectancy at birth; table 8.18 contains information on literacy rates of German soldiers; table 8.3 contains data on real per capita NNP in 1913 prices, which is the historical time series available that is closest to purchasing-power-adjusted real GDP per capita.

The ranges used for the three component indices are for life expectancy, minimum = 30 years and maximum = 80 years; for literacy, minimum = zero percent and maximum = 100 percent; for real per capita income, minimum = DM 298 ($\log(298) = 2.474$) and maximum = DM 1,186 ($\log(1,186) = 3.074$)—the minimum and maximum real per capita NNP in 1913 prices during the period studied.[24]

Table 8.19 shows the indexes obtained for the three indicators, as well as the HDI for periods between 1871 and 1950. The HDI rose throughout the period, driven almost exclusively by increases in longevity and real per capita income, since literacy rates were very high throughout the period. The HDI's total increase was 37.47 points. This amounts to an average increase (using the midpoint of the first period as a starting point) of 0.5 points per annum.

Columns (6) and (7) show the changes in the HDI between periods. As can be seen in column (7), the average annual HDI increase between 1871–80 and 1881–90 was below the average for the period: the gains in life expectancy and real per capita income were relatively small. The HDI was increasing particu-

---

24. The choice of ranges for the three indexes comprising the HDI is not inherently obvious. This is particularly true for purchasing-power-adjusted real per capita income. Using the actual minimum and maximum values observed allows the tracking of a country's income development during the period of interest. It does not, however, greatly facilitate comparisons with other countries' income development. For this, a standard methodology needs to be adopted by all. The minimum value could be defined either as zero or the cost of a subsistence diet (also to be defined). The maximum value could be the highest per capita income level ever attained, the official poverty level in a specified country and year, or the cost of a certain bundle of goods and services. Defining an easily adoptable historical HDI is a rich area for future collaborative research.

Table 8.19   A Human Development Index (HDI) for Germany, 1871–80 to 1950

| | Indexes | | | | HDI Increase | |
Years (1)	Life Expectancy at Birth (2)	Literacy (3)	Real Per Capita Income (4)	HDI (5)	Total (6)	Per Year (7)
1871–80	14.03	97.4	33.50	48.31		
1881–90	17.42	99	38.17	51.53	3.22	.322
1891–1900	24.53	99.89	53.00	59.14	7.61	.761
1901–10	33.15	99.97	62.67	65.26	6.12	.612
1910–12	38.09	99.99	67.83	68.64	3.38	.615
1924–26	54.79	99.99	66.5	73.76	5.12	.366
1932–34	62.67	99.99	64.17	75.61	1.85	.231
1950	73.02	99.99	84.33	85.78	10.17	.598

Sources: Calculated from tables 8.3, 8.12, and 8.18 and Cipolla (1969).

Notes: The ranges used for the three single indexes are, for life expectancy, minimum = 30 years and maximum = 80; for literacy, minimum = zero percent and maximum = 100 percent; for real per capita income, minimum = DM 298 and maximum = DM 1,186—the minimum and maximum real per capita income over the period. The HDI is simply the average of the three single indexes. For life expectancy, data are for 1910–11 instead of 1910–12 and 1949–51 instead of 1950. The life expectancy used is the average of the rates for males and females. For real per capita income, data are for 1925–26 instead of 1924–26. For literacy, the 1910–12 value (99.99 percent) has been used for the later time periods.

larly fast between 1881–90 and 1891–1900, at an average annual rate of 0.76 points. Between 1910–12 and 1932–34, the rates were below average: the considerable increases in life expectancy were partially offset by declines in real per capita income during the global economic downturn. Despite World War II, Germany's HDI rose considerably between 1932–34 and 1950 (an average rate of 0.6 points per annum). The HDI's 10-point rise was driven by 10-point increases in both the life expectancy and real per capita income indexes.

Table 8.20 displays an alternative Human Development Index for periods between 1851 and 1950 using average population heights in the place of life expectancy. The height estimates used in constructing the table are from table 8.4 (RSMLE estimates for two-year birth cohorts of Württemberg recruits), Harbeck's (1960) recorded average height for draftees born in 1937 in Germany (173.2 cm) and in Baden-Württemberg (171.8 cm), and Jürgens's stature estimates for 20-year-old draftees born in 1948–49 in Germany (176.3 cm) and in Baden-Württemberg (176.8 cm). The range for the height index is 156 cm to 180 cm.[25]

Between 1851–60 and 1950, the alternative HDI rose by 44.2 points—an

25. The bottom of the height range, 156 cm, is the average height of the Bundi of New Guinea—one of the shortest populations ever measured. The top, 180 cm, is approximately the average height attained by the tallest populations today. The selection of this range implies that an increase in average stature of 0.24 cm increases the stature index by one point. Choosing a narrower range for stature would cause changes in stature to have a larger impact on the overall HDI.

Table 8.20   **An Alternative Human Development Index for Germany, 1851–60 to 1950**

Year	Average Height Index	Alternative HDI	HDI Increase	
			Total	Per Year
1851–60	34.12	45.43		
1861–70	41.46	52.32	6.89	.689
1871–80	39.48	56.79	4.47	.447
1881–90	42.77	59.98	3.19	.319
1891–1900	46.62	66.50	6.52	.652
1932–34	71.67	78.61	12.11	.323
	(65.83)	(76.66)	(10.16)	(.271)
1950	84.58	89.63	11.02	.648
	(86.67)	(90.33)	(13.67)	(.804)

Sources: Calculated from tables 8.3, 8.4, and 8.18, Cipolla (1969), Harbeck (1960), and Jürgens (1971).

Notes: The indexes for income and literacy are the same as in table 8.19, expanded by two decades. The income is 7.17 for 1851–60 and 20.5 for 1861–70. The literacy index for these two decades has been estimated from Prussian data to be 95. The time periods used for the height data (birth years 1852–61, 1860–71, 1870–81, 1880–91, 1890–1900, 1937, and 1948–49) are slightly different than those used for literacy and income. The height estimates for birth years 1851–93 are for the kingdom of Württemberg; for 1937 and 1948–49, they are for all of Germany, with the estimate for Baden-Württemberg in parentheses. The height index is based on a range from 156 to 180 cm.

average increase of 0.47 points per annum. The pattern is similar to that seen in the standard HDI. The rate of increase was lower than average between 1871–80 and 1881–90 (0.319), as well as between 1891–1900 and 1932–34 (0.323). The rate of increase was higher than average between 1881–90 and 1891–1900, as well as between 1932–34 and 1950.

For historical Germany, I prefer to use the standard HDI. The reason for this preference is that life expectancies from 1871 onward were calculated for all of Germany. The height data available before 1932 are simply for one part of Germany. However, it is reassuring that the two HDIs and their changes are rather similar. When data on one indicator are lacking, it seems plausible to substitute the other. Both HDIs indicate a rise in human development that was particularly rapid around the turn of the century.

8.4   Discussion and Conclusions

In the preceding pages, evidence on a range of indicators of health and well-being in Germany has been presented. From the middle of the nineteenth century to the middle of the twentieth, living standards in Germany undoubtedly improved. Real per capita NNP (in 1913 prices) more than tripled. The average workweek in German industry declined by more than 20 hours. Average male stature in Württemberg rose by over 15 cm—from the 0.7th to the 50th percentile of modern height standards. Hoffmann's index of caloric balance rose from

75 to 111. German mortality rates were cut in half. Between 1881 and 1937, infant mortality rates fell by over two-thirds. Between 1871–80 and 1949–51, life expectancy at birth increased by more than 29 years, and the Human Development Index rose by over 37 points.

Yet this upward trend was not always smooth. German living standards were increasing particularly fast in some periods and stagnating or even declining temporarily in others. Let us take a closer look at the trends between 1850 and 1939.

In the late 1840s to early 1850s, there was a severe agricultural crisis in Württemberg and an economic downturn throughout Germany. This corresponded to a period of very high emigration rates and extremely low average heights: the RSMLE height estimate of 160.56 cm[26] for 20-year-old males born in Württemberg in 1852 and 1853 is below the 1st percentile of modern height standards. Hoffmann's index of caloric balance indicated that the German population was consuming only 75 percent of the calories actually needed. Kuczynski's index of real wages showed a huge decline for the 1852–56 period. Clearly, these were not easy times for most Germans.

Recovery followed during the late 1850s and the 1860s. Once the agricultural crisis in Württemberg was over, average male heights increased by about 6 cm to 166.69 cm for the birth cohorts of 1866–67 (approximately the 6th percentile of modern height standards). This sizable improvement in net nutrition corresponded to a rise in Hoffmann's index of caloric balance from 75 to 90. German mortality rates fell during the 1850s but began to rise in the late 1860s, in part due to the Franco-Prussian War and perhaps to increasing urbanization.

In 1871, the German states were united under the umbrella of the German Empire. The early 1870s were boom years characterized by very high inflation rates (fueled by French reparation payments made ahead of schedule), an optimistic spirit, and massive speculation. The financial crash came in mid-1873 and ushered in the period known as the great depression (1873–96). Throughout Germany, there were many bankruptcies and economic growth slowed. Prices, profits, and wages fell while unemployment rose.

During this Founder's Crisis, real per capita NNP (in 1913 prices) fell from DM 507 in 1874 to DM 441 in 1880. This corresponded to a marked decline in average heights for those born in the 1870s (reaching the 3d percentile of modern height standards) and to high German mortality rates, which peaked in the mid-1870s. (In Württemberg, mortality rates peaked in 1870 and again in 1875.) On the other hand, emigration rates were not particularly high and Hoffmann's index of caloric balance rose from 90 in 1870–74 to 100 in 1875–79. Yet if income inequality was rising during the 1871–1914 period as Dumke (1988) claims and occupational height trends confirm, many of the additional calories could have gone to the better-off, leaving the net nutrition of the aver-

---

26. RSMLE estimate for two-year birth cohort.

age German the same as or even lower than before. Overall, the 1870s seem to have been a time of stagnation and possibly declines in the health and living standards of the average German. At the very least, pessimists' claims cannot be ruled out.

The 1880s is another period when the evidence is mixed but seems to point to a stagnation in the upward trend in German health and living standards. Optimists would point to rising real per capita NNP after 1882 (from 447 in 1882 to 564 in 1890), a small increase in literacy rates, and declining mortality rates (from 25.7/1,000 in 1882 to 24.4 in 1890). These factors drove an increase in the HDI of 3.22 points between 1871–80 and 1881–90. Pessimists would counter that the average annual rate of HDI change (0.322) was much lower than the average for the whole 1871–80 to 1950 period (0.5 per year). Indeed, the only period with a slower rate of HDI change was that ending with the Great Depression.

The pessimists have additional ammunition for their arguments. By 1880–81, average heights in Württemberg had recovered to reach their 1866–67 level. But then there was a second dip in stature, reaching its nadir with the birth cohorts of 1884–85. Some recovery followed, but stature did not regain its 1866–67 level again until 1892–93. So nearly 30 years passed with no significant improvement in net nutrition. The fall in heights in the 1880s corresponded to a decline in Hoffmann's index of caloric balance to 95 in 1880–84 and to huge increases in emigration, both from Germany and Württemberg.

For the period from 1890 until the First World War, both optimists and pessimists would have to agree that health and living standards in Germany were on the rise. Emigration rates dropped dramatically. Hoffmann's index of caloric balance rose from 108 in 1890–94 to 122 in 1905–9. The height data unfortunately ended with the birth cohort of 1893 but showed positive trends in the early 1890s. Life expectancy at birth rose by over 10 years—from 38.7 years in 1881–90 to 49 years in 1910–11. Between 1890 and 1913, German mortality rates fell from 24.4/1,000 to 15/1,000; infant mortality and stillborn rates fell from 255.5/1,000 live births to 181/1,000; real per capita NNP increased from DM 564 to DM 783. The HDI rose from 51.53 in 1881–90 to 68.64 in 1910–12. Clearly, the average German's standard of living and health improved considerably during this period.

During World War I, no data are available for most living standard indicators. We do know, however, that real per capita NNP dropped from DM 783 in 1913 to DM 751 in 1925 and German mortality rates jumped from 15/1,000 in 1913 to an average of 20.7/1,000 in 1914–18. Furthermore, the declines in stature of schoolchildren in Stuttgart indicate that the net nutrition of the civilian population declined during the war years. In addition, the psychological costs of war are always high albeit difficult to quantify. Clearly, the quality of life in Germany declined during the First World War.

Between the two world wars, Germans' health and welfare were generally improving. Real per capita NNP was rising from 1926 to 1928, declined during the 1929–32 Great Depression years, and rose rapidly during the armaments buildup of 1933–38. All health indicators showed positive trends throughout the interwar period, even during the Great Depression. Life expectancy rose by nearly four years between 1924–26 and 1932–34. This caused the HDI to rise by nearly two points, even though real per capita NNP had declined. Between 1919 and 1938, German mortality rates fell from 15.6/1,000 to 11.7/1,000; infant mortality and stillborn rates fell from 151.6 per 1,000 live births to 83.3. As figure 8.10 indicates, height trends and thus net nutrition were steadily positive (at least in Stuttgart). Hoffmann's index rose from 108 in 1925–29 to 111 in 1930–34 and 1935–38. Thus, despite the business cycle downturn during the Great Depression, the health and physical living standards of Germans clearly rose during the interwar period.

In summary, health and living standards in Germany improved considerably between 1850 and 1939. Yet progress was not always smooth. Particularly during the 1870s and 1880s, there are indications that the beginning of rapid industrialization was accompanied by some hardship for the German people. Thereafter, however, with the exception of the war years, most Germans experienced steady improvements in their health and living standards.

Appendix
Sampling Procedure and Methodology[27]

Information was collected on nearly 15,000 soldiers serving in the army of Württemberg between 1871 and 1913. For all observations, information was recorded on height, occupation (of the soldier and, where available, of his father), birthplace, and birth date. For approximately half of all observations, residence information was recorded. For approximately 20 percent, medical history was recorded.

The sample was drawn from the infantry, cavalry, and artillery in proportions reflecting the composition of the army. Most of the observations therefore came from the infantry. The infantry had eight (later ten) regiments, each drawn from different regions. To maintain geographical balance, records were drawn from each regiment for every two-year period. Each regiment had 12 companies, with noticeable sorting by height across companies. Thus it was necessary to draw observations randomly from each company.

Thanks to the universal draft law, the selectivity issues present with volunteer armies do not arise here. However, due to minimum height laws (157 cm until 1893; 154 cm thereafter) and physical examinations, the height distributions of the soldiers tend to be eroded at the lower tail. Thus, simple means

27. For more details on these topics, see Twarog (1993).

will overestimate true population means, and differences between groups will be underestimated. Three statistical methods were used in this study to deal with the above-mentioned scenario: Reduced Sample Maximum Likelihood Estimation (RSMLE), Quantile Bend Estimation (QBE), and the simple mean of the reduced sample.

The RSMLE approach truncates the lower tail of the distribution above the extent of erosion. Then standard maximum likelihood estimation is performed using the probability distribution of the truncated normal distribution. The RSMLE method can also be used for truncated regression aimed at estimating the covariates of heights.[28]

The QBE method plots the quantiles (i.e., centiles, etc.) of the observed distribution against those of the standard normal distribution. A straight line indicates the ranges where the distribution conforms to a normal distribution. At the lower eroded tail, the curve bends. The amount of observations missing from the observed distribution (i.e., the shortfall) is estimated by determining which quantity of shadow observations added to the lower tail generates the straightest quantile plot in the uncontaminated range. Once this is done, the population mean and standard deviation can be estimated from the slope and intercept of a robust regression line fitted to the uncontaminated range of the quantile plot.[29]

Komlos and Kim (1990) developed an alternative method of measuring height trends. Assuming a constant standard deviation and a given truncation point, the mean of the truncated normal distribution is an increasing function of the mean of the underlying distribution. Thus changes in the mean of the reduced sample reflect changes in the population mean. To deduce the actual average population height and standard deviation, they employ RSMLE or QBE methods for a base year.

For the height data collected, all three methods were used. For the RSMLE and Komlos and Kim methods, the reduced sample comprised those soldiers with heights greater or equal to 163 cm. This was chosen on the basis of a priori knowledge (i.e., minimum height standards of 157 and then 154 cm)[30] and limit testing (i.e., chopping off successive height cells to see at which point the mean estimates converge).

References

Boelcke, Willi A. 1989. *Sozialgeschichte Baden-Württembergs 1800–1989*. Stuttgart: Kohlhammer.

28. For details on this method, see Greene (1990) and Trussell and Wachter (1984).
29. For details and examples of the QBE method, see Wachter and Trussell (1982).
30. Although the minimum height standard until 1893 was 157 cm, those shorter than 162 cm had to be exceptionally healthy and strong to be accepted.

Cipolla, Carlo M. 1969. *Literacy and development in the West.* Baltimore: Penguin.

Dillard, Dudley. 1967. *Economic development of the North Atlantic community.* Englewood Cliffs, N.J.: Prentice-Hall.

Dumke, Rolf H. 1988. Income inequality and industrialization in Germany. In *Research in economic history,* ed. Paul J. Uselding. Greenwich, Conn.: JAI.

Eveleth, Phyllis B., and James M. Tanner. 1976. *Worldwide variations in human growth.* Cambridge: Cambridge University Press.

Flora, Peter, Franz Kraus, and Winifried Pfenning. 1987. *State, economy, and society in Western Europe 1815–1975: A data handbook in two volumes.* London: Macmillan.

Giese, Heinz W. 1986. Ursachen und Konsequenzen des Analphabetismus bei jungen Menschen in der Bundesrepublik Deutschland: Eine Studie für die UNESCO (Paris). University of Oldenburg, Germany. Unpublished paper.

Greene, William H. 1990. *Econometric analysis.* New York: Macmillan.

Harbeck, Rudolf. 1960. Die Körpergrössen 20jähriger Männer. In *Wehrdienst und Gesundheit: Abhandlungen aus Wehrmedizin, Wehrpharmazie und Wehrveterinärwesen,* vol. 1. Darmstadt: Wehr und Wissen.

Henderson, W. O. 1975. *The rise of German industrial power.* Berkeley: University of California Press.

Hoffmann, Walter G. 1965. *Das Wachstum der deutschen Wirtschaft seit der Mitte des 19. Jahrhunderts.* Berlin: Springer.

Jürgens, Hans W. 1971. Gruppenunterschiede des menschlichen Wachstums in zeitlicher und örtlicher Hinsicht. *Zeitschrift für Morphologie und Anthropologie* 63(1): 63–75.

Kaiserliches Statistisches Amt. 1886. *Statistisches Jahrbuch für das Deutsche Reich, Siebenter Jahrgang 1886.* Berlin: Puttkammer und Mühlbrecht.

Kiesewetter, Hubert. 1986. Regionale Industrialisierung in Deutschland zur Zeit der Reichsgründung. Ein vergleichend-quantitativer Versuch. *Vierteljahrschrift für Sozial- und Wirtschaftsgeschichte* (Stuttgart: Franz Steiner) 73(1): 38–60.

———. 1989. *Industrielle Revolution in Deutschland: 1815–1914.* Frankfurt am Main: Suhrkamp.

Komlos, John, and Joo Han Kim. 1990. Estimating trends in historical heights. *Historical Methods* 23(3): 116–20.

Königliches Medizinal-Kollegium. 1879. *Medizinal-Bericht von Württemberg für das Jahr 1876.* Stuttgart: Kohlhammer.

———. 1884. *Medizinal-Bericht von Württemberg für die Jahre 1882, 1883, und 1884.* Stuttgart: Kohlhammer.

———. 1896. *Medizinal-Bericht von Württemberg für das Jahr 1894.* Stuttgart: Kohlhammer.

———. 1900. *Medizinal-Bericht von Württemberg für das Jahr 1897.* Stuttgart: Kohlhammer.

———. 1902. *Medizinal-Bericht von Württemberg für das Jahr 1900.* Stuttgart: Kohlhammer.

Königliches Statistisches Landesamt. 1886. *Das Königreich Württemberg: Eine Beschreibung von Land, Volk und Staat.* Stuttgart: Kohlhammer.

———. 1889. *Württembergische Jahrbücher für Statistik und Landeskunde: Jahrgang 1887.* Stuttgart: Kohlhammer.

———. 1891. *Statistisches Jahrbuch für das Königreich Württemberg: Jahrgang 1889.* Stuttgart: Kohlhammer.

———. 1892. *Statistisches Jahrbuch für das Königreich Württemberg: Jahrgang 1890 und 1891.* Stuttgart: Kohlhammer.

———. 1895. *Württembergische Jahrbücher für Statistik und Landeskunde: Jahrgang 1894.* Stuttgart: Kohlhammer.

———. 1897. *Württembergische Jahrbücher für Statistik und Landeskunde: Jahrgang 1896.* Stuttgart: Kohlhammer.

————. 1901. *Statistisches Jahrbuch für das Königreich Württemberg: Jahrgang 1900.* Stuttgart: Kohlhammer.

————. 1903. *Statistisches Handbuch für das Königreich Württemberg: Jahrgang 1902 und 1903.* Stuttgart: Kohlhammer.

————. 1908. *Mitteilungen des Königlichen Statistischen Landesamts, 23. Juli 1908.* Stuttgart: Kohlhammer.

————. 1910a. *Statistisches Handbuch für das Königreich Württemberg: Jahrgang 1908 und 1909.* Stuttgart: Kohlhammer.

————. 1910b. *Württembergische Gemeindestatistik: Zweite Ausgabe nach dem Stand vom Jahre 1907.* Stuttgart: Kohlhammer.

————. 1912. *Statistisches Handbuch für das Königreich Württemberg: Jahrgang 1912.* Stuttgart: Kohlhammer.

————. 1913a. *Statistisches Handbuch für das Königreich Württemberg: Jahrgang 1913.* Stuttgart: Kohlhammer.

————. 1913b. *Volkszählung 1. Dezember 1910.* Stuttgart: Kohlhammer.

Königliches Statistisch-Topographisches Bureau. 1863a. *Das Königreich Württemberg: Eine Beschreibung von Land, Volk, und Staat.* Stuttgart: Nitzschke.

————. 1863b. *Württembergische Jahrbücher für vaterländische Geschichte, Geographie, Statistik und Topographie: Jahrgang 1862.* Stuttgart: Karl Aue.

————. 1870. *Württembergische Jahrbücher für Statistik und Landeskunde: Jahrgang 1869.* Stuttgart: Kohlhammer.

————. 1874. *Württembergische Jahrbücher für Statistik und Landeskunde: Jahrgang 1872.* Stuttgart: Kohlhammer.

————. 1875. *Württembergische Jahrbücher für Statistik und Landeskunde: Jahrgang 1874.* Stuttgart: Kohlhammer.

————. 1877. *Württembergische Jahrbücher für Statistik und Landeskunde: Jahrgang 1876.* Stuttgart: Lindemann.

————. 1878. *Württembergische Jahrbücher für Statistik und Landeskunde: Jahrgang 1877.* Stuttgart: Lindemann.

————. 1880. *Württembergische Jahrbücher für Statistik und Landeskunde: Jahrgang 1880.* Stuttgart: Kohlhammer.

————. 1885. *Württembergische Jahrbücher für Statistik und Landeskunde: Jahrgang 1884.* Stuttgart: Kohlhammer.

Kuczynski, Jürgen. 1947. *Die Geschichte der Lage der Arbeiter in Deutschland von 1800 bis in die Gegenwart.* Vol. 1, *1800 bis 1932,* 3d expanded ed. Berlin: Verlag die Freie Gewerkschaft.

La Leche League International. 1993. *The womanly art of breastfeeding,* 35th anniversary ed. New York: Plume.

Losch, Hermann. 1898. *Die Arbeitslöhne in Württemberg.* Stuttgart: Kohlhammer.

Megerle, Klaus. 1982. *Württemberg im Industrialisierungsprozess Deutschlands.* Stuttgart: Kett-Cotta.

Mitchell, B. R. 1980. *European historical statistics 1750–1975.* London: Macmillan.

National Center for Health Statistics. 1977. NCHS growth curves for children, birth–18 years, United States. DHEW Publication no. (PHS) 78–1650. Hyattsville, Md.: U.S. Department of Health, Education and Welfare.

Omran, A. R. 1971. The epidemiologic transition: A theory of the epidemiology of population change. *Milbank Memorial Fund Quarterly* 49–4:509–38.

Retter. 1869. Die Ergebnisse der Rekrutenaushebungen in Württemberg in den Jahren 1866 und 1867. In *Württembergische Jahrbücher für Statistik und Landeskunde: Jahrgang 1867.* Stuttgart: Kohlhammer.

Riedle, J. J. 1834. Ergebnisse der Militär-Conscriptionen in Beziehung auf körperliche Beschaffenheit der Conscriptionspflichtigen nach den verschiedenen Oberamts-Bezirken. In *Württembergische Jahrbücher für vaterländische Geschichte, Geographie, Statistik und Topographie: Jahrgang 1833.* Stuttgart: Karl Aue.

Spree, Reinhard. 1986. Veränderungen des Todesursachen-Panoramas und sozio-ökonomischer Wandel-Eine Fallstudie zum "Epidemiologischen Übergang." *Schriften des Vereins für Socialpolitik, Gesellschaft für Wirtschafts- und Sozialwissenschaften.* Neue Folge Band 159, *Ökonomie des Gesundheitswesens (Jahrestagung des Vereins für Socialpolitik in Saarbrücken 1985).* Berlin: Duncker und Humblot.

Steckel, Richard H. 1996. Percentiles of modern height standards for use in historical research. *Historical Methods* 29:157–66.

Stolper, Gustav. 1940. *German economy 1870–1940.* New York: Reynal and Hitchcock.

Tanner, J. M. 1962. *Growth at adolescence,* 2d ed. Oxford: Blackwell.

———. 1978. *Fetus into man: Physical growth from conception to maturity.* Cambridge, Mass.: Harvard University Press.

Tipton, Frank B., Jr. 1976. *Regional variations in the economic development of Germany during the nineteenth century.* Middletown, Conn.: Wesleyan University Press.

Trussell, James, and Kenneth Wachter. 1984. Estimating the covariates of historical heights. NBER Working Paper no. 1455. Cambridge, Mass.: National Bureau of Economic Research.

Twarog, Sophia. 1993. *Heights and living standards in industrializing Germany: The case of Württemberg.* Unpublished Ph.D. diss., Ohio State University, Columbus.

United Nations Development Programme. 1990. *Human development report 1990.* New York: Oxford University Press.

Wachter, Kenneth, and James Trussell. 1982. Estimating historical heights. *Journal of the American Statistical Association* 77:279–93.

Wiegand, Erich, and Wolfgang Zapf. 1982. *Wandel der Lebensbedingungen in Deutschland: Wohlfahrtsentwicklung seit der Industrialisierung.* Frankfurt: Campus.

World Health Organization. 1950. *Annual epidemiological and vital statistics 1947–1949.* Part I, *Vital statistics and causes of death.* Geneva: World Health Organization.

Wurm, H. 1982. Über die Schwankungen der durchschnittlichen Körperhöhe im Verlauf der deutschen Geschichte und die Einflüsse des Eiweißanteiles der Kost. *Homo* 33(1): 21–42.

———. 1990. Vorarbeiten zu einer interdisziplinären Untersuchung über die Körperhöhenverhältnisse der Deutschen im 19. Jahrhundert und der sie beeinflussenden Lebensverhältnisse. In *Gegenbaurs morphologisches Jahrbuch* 136(5):503–23.

Württembergischer Ärztlicher Verein. 1867. *Medicinisches Correspondenz-Blatt,* Vol. 37, no. 23. Stuttgart: Schweizerbart.

9   Paradoxes of Modernization and Material Well-Being in the Netherlands during the Nineteenth Century

J. W. Drukker and Vincent Tassenaar

9.1   Introduction

In the following chapter we will attempt to sketch the pattern of modernization in the Netherlands during the nineteenth and early twentieth century, with special emphasis on the questions of when and how the material conditions of the Dutch people were affected by modernization. We will focus on two points: First, we will try to establish a time pattern for the whole country showing when conditions improved or deteriorated. Second, we will look at regional differences within this time pattern. Now and then we will interrupt our story to speculate on possible explanations for the—in our opinion—rather surprising specific relative regional shifts in material well-being. Of course, these possible explanations are no more than very hypothetical attempts to relate

J. W. Drukker is professor of design history in the Faculty of Industrial Design Engineering of Delft University of Technology and associate professor of economic history in the Faculty of Arts of Groningen University, The Netherlands. Vincent Tassenaar is a researcher affiliated with the Dutch Stichting voor Economische, Sociaal-Culturele en Ruimtelijke Wetenschappen (ESR), which is part of the Dutch National Foundation for Scientific Research (Nederlandse Organisatie voor Wetenschappelijk Onderzoek NWO), working at the Faculty of Economics of Groningen University, The Netherlands.

Research for this article was supported by the Stichting voor Economische, Sociaal-Culturele en Ruimtelijke Wetenschappen (ESR), which is part of the Dutch National Foundation for Scientific Research, the Nederlandse Organisatie voor Onderzoek (NWO). The authors are indebted to Gerard Brefeld, Agnes Casemier, and Willem Tromp for their help in transforming hardly anthropo-readable, quantitative material into machine-readable form, and to Jan Luiten van Zanden for his generous supply of preliminary results of research, carried out by him, or under his supervision, that will be published in the near future. The authors, however, are exclusively responsible for any errors, omissions, and flaws in their arguments.

The authors are grateful for permission granted by E. Horlings to use data on the Dutch population first presented in Horlings (1993) and by E. Horlings, J. P. Smits, and J. L. van Zanden to use data on Dutch national income first presented in Horlings, Smits, and van Zanden (1995). The authors emphasize on behalf of Horlings et al. that these figures are very preliminary and are not the official results of the Historical National Accounts Project of the Posthumus Instituut.

our findings in some way to the more general "optimists versus pessimists" controversy on the early consequences of modernization for the standard of living (see, e.g., Mokyr 1988).

9.2 The Netherlands in the Nineteenth Century: A Retarded Late-Comer

Most foreign economic historians who have not given special attention to the economic and social history of the Netherlands after the so-called Golden Age (approximately 1600–1675) will probably have a distorted picture of the nation at the beginning of the nineteenth century. Of course, there is unanimous agreement that during the first three-quarters of the seventeenth century, the "Republic of the Seven United Provinces" was both the richest country in the world (measured in real income per capita) and a very "modern" country (characterized by high average labor productivity, a high rate of urbanization, a high stage of economic specialization, and a fair amount of large-scale, market-oriented agriculture; see, e.g., Maddison 1982, esp. 29–34). There is also no disagreement on the point that the Netherlands is today, in the last quarter of the twentieth century, again among the richest countries on earth. This is suggested not only from an orthodox economic point of view (real per capita income), but also by factors that a social biologist would probably prefer: average life expectancy is very high, child mortality belongs to the lowest known figures, and last but not least, the Dutch are among the tallest people in the world. For nonspecialists, therefore, it sometimes comes as a surprise that this "splendid position at the top" has not always been a characteristic feature of Dutch society in the period between the Golden Age and the present day. On the contrary, there are strong indications that in the early nineteenth century the Netherlands was a retarded nation, far more backward for instance than Belgium. So something must have gone wrong somewhere between the last quarter of the seventeenth century and the early nineteenth century. Although there is no dispute *that* something went wrong, *what, when, where,* and *why* things went wrong are still hotly debated issues in Dutch economic history. It is, for instance, not clear whether the Dutch economy underwent an absolute decline in the eighteenth century, or whether there was a long period of stagnation while other nations improved their lots substantially during the same years. This last view was put forward by de Vries in 1959, and it is still widely accepted (de Vries 1959). It is at least not contradicted by Maddison, who estimated that, although real income per capita around 1700 had been 50 percent higher in the Netherlands than in the United Kingdom, Dutch GDP showed a very slight decline (less than 1 percent) between 1700 and 1760 while the English figure almost doubled during the same years (Maddison 1982, appendix A, table A4). Although Dutch labor productivity was still roughly equal to the U.K. level as late as 1785 (Maddison, 1982, 30, graph 2.1), the United Kingdom was at that very moment on the verge of a soaring secular rise in productivity, while stagnation continued in the Netherlands for well into the nineteenth century, producing remarkable features of a retarded, aging "rentier society": "In 1790 . . . foreign investment was probably over three times the size of the domestic product. . . . As a result of this, the income distribution was disequalized, with pauperism and unemployment in the old industrial areas, and an increase in the share of the wealthy" (Maddison 1982, 33).

It was not before the second half of the nineteenth century that modernization took hold of the Dutch economy. When it finally did, it was not—as one might have expected—in the most urbanized region of the nation, the few large cities in the western provinces, Noord- en Zuid-Holland, that had been the core of the Republic in the seventeenth century. Industrialization started in the most traditional and rural areas of the nation: in the southern province of Noord-Brabant and an area called "Twente" in the eastern part of the province of Overijssel (Mokyr 1976). Serious modernization of the urbanized regions in the west started even later, at a time when the "infant industries" in Brabant and Twente were well on their way into puberty. A boom in infrastructural modernization, for instance, occurred between 1862 and 1885. Here the locus of investment activity was indeed first concentrated in the western parts of the nation, with central government playing a decisive role, aimed at improved connections with the sea for the main ports, Amsterdam and Rotterdam, an improved intraurban transport system, and efficient connections with the important industrialized German regions east of the border (Groote 1995). How this retarded process of modernization affected Dutch national income will become clear in the near future: a large-scale research project, intended to reconstruct on a yearly basis Dutch national accounts in the nineteenth century, was started some years ago in a cooperative effort by three teams of economic historians from the universities of Utrecht, Groningen, and Nijmegen under the guidance of the "Posthumus Instituut," the Dutch National Research Institute for Economic and Social History. Preliminary results of this project have been circulating among a limited number of interested scholars (Horlings, Smits, and van Zanden 1995).

What are the main reasons for the retarded modernization process of Dutch society in the nineteenth century? The answer to that question sounds like a classical paradox: the main reason is, it seems, that the Netherlands were already remarkably "modern" at a time when other European countries (like Belgium or Germany) were on the verge of a transformation process from a premodern society to a modern one, characterized (among other things) by rapid industrialization. By and large, this "premodern modernity" was the lasting result of Holland's Golden Age. De Vries, for instance, has argued that the delay in the construction of Dutch railways was mainly caused by the existence of a remarkably efficient "premodern" Dutch transport system: canals and barges (de Vries 1981). It is well documented that, while the Dutch agrarian sector had already been among the most productive in the world in the seventeenth century (de Vries 1974), Dutch farmers continued to improve on productivity during the years of decline and stagnation in the rest of the economy, with the result that "by the end of the eighteenth century, Dutch peasants had acquired a level of knowledge that could not be improved upon at the time" (van der Poel 1972, quoted by Mokyr 1975, 294, n. 4). There existed a very rich rentier class (another leftover of the Golden Age), which suggests that there was never a shortage of funds to finance a "timely" process of industrialization. The point was simply that these rentiers profited from modernization processes elsewhere in Europe by foreign investment. As Joel Mokyr has aptly put it: "The reason the Dutch industrialized so slowly was simply that they did not need the modern industry. After all, why should they have undertaken large investments in industry, not to mention all the unpleasant side-effects thereof, while they could make in general a good living out of agriculture and what was left over of the maritime sector" (Mokyr 1975, 298).

So, with the present state of affairs, we know now, more or less accurately, *when* modernization started in the Netherlands, *where* it started, and *how.* We will know in the near future, when the results of the Historical National Accounts Project are published, *what* quantitative effects modernization exactly had on the level of economic activity on a year-to-year basis. We know a lot less—in fact very little—about how the material circumstances of the Dutch people were affected by the retarded modernization process. It is here that we come across many problems and apparent contradictions, which we summarized above in the phrase "what, where, when, and why things went wrong."

As we have already stated, there is no controversy on the point that in the heyday of the Republic, not only rich merchants profited from the fact that Holland was the richest country in the world; laborers, craftsmen, and peasants were also well off compared with their colleagues in other countries at the time. The same holds for the 1960s, the period that was nicknamed by Maddison the "Golden Age of Managed Capitalism," when the Netherlands not only enjoyed high real income per capita, but was—together with the Scandinavian countries—also among the Western countries with the lowest inequality in income distribution, due to its very redistributive tax system. With the return to neoliberalism in the 1980s, and the preceding shift in the Netherlands from having traditionally been a net emigration country to becoming a net immigration country, the problem of poverty has returned as a serious issue on the Dutch political agenda, but no one denies that the problem of poverty in the nineteenth century was so completely different in nature from the present situation that it defies any reasonable comparison.

9.3   Paradoxes in the Dutch Standard of Living Debate

What, then, are the main problems and contradictions concerning the assessment of the pattern of changing material circumstances of the Dutch population in the nineteenth and early twentieth centuries, apart from the central issue that the Dutch people lived both in the seventeenth century (and probably also during a good part of the eighteenth) and in the 1960s apparently under—for the time—very favorable circumstances, while their fate is much less clear during the years in between? Let us try to summarize in the first place, two paradoxes in this field: the first is that the Netherlands was famous for its high level of wages not only during the golden years of the Republic (which is understandable, given the high level of productivity at that time), but also during the years of stagnation or decline. This was probably the result of an elaborate system of poor relief that was (it goes without saying: for the time) considered exceptionally generous: "[In the early 1820s] the average pauper in the Netherlands received *three times* the support of his Belgian counterpart" (Mokyr 1975, 293; emphasis added). Although, as Mokyr states, the high level of wages hampered early industrialization, it is also clear that high wages and generous relief in itself would have mitigated a deterioration of the standard of living, in spite of its detrimental effects on a rise in productivity in the long run.

But how, then, can we explain the fact that in the same period (say, from the end of the eighteenth century well up into the second half of the nineteenth) pauperism and a sharp decline in the material conditions of a great majority of the people were considered by a multitude of contemporary observers to be among the most pressing social problems of the time? What else than a deep concern for the public health situation could have inspired the Dutch government to create in 1818 a complete national health monitoring system, essentially consisting of Provinciale Commissies van Geneeskundig Toevoorzicht (Provincial Committees for Medical Control and Prevention), an integrated system of regional teams of medical doctors whose tasks were to supervise medical practice, to set professional exams for general practitioners entering the profession with a less than university background, to control the quality of poor relief, and to report on (and, if possible, control) the spread of epidemic diseases (Houwaert 1993, 19–45, esp. 19–25).

It would be a mistake to interpret the installation of these committees by the government as in itself evidence that common health care was of prime governmental importance. At least during the first years after the installation of these committees, their reports were never seriously analyzed at a central governmental level, nor is there anything known about a national health *policy,* coordinated by the different chairmen of these Provinciale Commissies and based on conclusions from their reports. The fact that the epidemic situation in the Netherlands was a rather stable one during the first two decades of the nineteenth century may serve as a partial explanation for this apparent neglect of health policy on the part of the government. However, things changed dramatically during the 1830s and 1840s. Because of consecutive crop failures and the following years of increasing misery and hunger, the incidence of smallpox suddenly increased, followed in the 1840s by an epidemic of typhoid fever. Together with the sudden appearance of cholera in the Netherlands in 1832 and 1848, its spread being completely enigmatic and erratic in light of generally accepted medical views at the time, the deteriorating situation caused panic among the population and laid bare the almost complete absence of adequate general health policy.

It was in these years of rapidly worsening health conditions that a group of young medical doctors, working mainly among poor people, and calling themselves "Hygienists," called for action and, in the course of time, gained influence. They asked for a radical reform of the public health system in which a general improvement of sanitary and dietary conditions was of central concern. Apart from that, they developed a completely new vision of the medical discipline: that it could be improved by elaborate statistical investigations into the living conditions of the people. It was the results of these investigations that indicate that material circumstances in general were indeed rapidly worsening in the Netherlands during the 1830s and 1840s, as we will show in the following sections.

Another apparent contradiction concerning the development of Dutch living standards applies to the circumstances of people living from agriculture. We have already pointed to the fact that, even during the era of stagnation or decline, it was not agriculture in the first place that suffered from worsening conditions: "During the French period, agriculture was the only sector that was not subject to a severe crisis, and appeared the most advanced in Europe with respect to technical knowledge. The period after 1813 is described as one of increasing prosperity for peasants, of technological progress and continuous investment in land improvement and augmentation" (Mokyr 1975, 294). We do not disagree with Mokyr's general picture, but the same picture is hiding some nasty problems concerning the development of the standard of living in the Dutch agricultural community.

In the first place, one should not forget that, according to contemporaries, the material situation of peasants in at least some of the agricultural provinces (Drenthe, Gelderland, and parts of Overijssel and Noord-Brabant are notorious in this respect) was so bad in the nineteenth and early twentieth centuries that it was commonly described as "inhuman." Until the present day, a well-known Dutch proverb states that the people of Drenthe have been "labouriously wrought from peat, gin, and suspicion," which sounds a bit less arcadian than Mokyr's description. But even if one is not willing to lend uncritical support to contemporary commentaries, abundant in number and congenial as they may be, one could point to the fact that even Mokyr needs some "Verelendung" (pauperization) among the peasants in order to get his explanation of the industrialization process in the Netherlands (Mokyr 1976) firmly rooted in the historical ground. At the core of Mokyr's view, after all, is the observation that Dutch industrialization—when it finally took off—started in Noord-Brabant and the Twente region of Overijssel: typical rural-traditional regions characterized by a relatively low wage level. Low wages were needed to ensure high profits, while high profits were needed to lure domestic capital out of foreign investment into domestic industry. However, what was true for the new entrepreneurs was in another sense also true for the workers. When Mokyr correctly observes the Dutch rentier or capitalist's reluctance to spend his money on domestic industry, the same must have been true for peasants: why should *they* have entered the low-wage labor market as industrial workers (for whom the side effects were even more unpleasant), if it was not for the one good reason that they could *not* make a living out of agriculture anymore? In other words, Mokyr's view of Dutch industrialization in itself implies that something must have gone wrong (in an absolute or relative sense) with the living conditions of the peasants in the area where and the years during which the new industries were born.

In the rest of this paper, we will try to shed some light on these issues. We do realize, however, that the limited scope of this paper, and the fact that there is at this very moment a wealth of undiscovered historical materials hidden in the archives, will ensure that much will remain shrouded in mist. Before we jump into the figures, however, it seems wise to interrupt our discourse for a moment to say something about the pattern of regional variation in the Netherlands. For regional differences are of core importance in an explanation of the Dutch pattern of changing living conditions in the nineteenth and early twentieth centuries.

9.4   The "Three" Netherlands: Regional Differentiation

There are two good reasons why the Netherlands is one of the very few countries that is written as a plural. The first is, of course, that the name is a historical reminder of the fact that the nation started as a union of different and, politically speaking, rather independent provinces, as is indicated in its first official name, "Republic of the Seven United Provinces." The second reason is that, small as the country is, there were—and, to a certain degree, still are—large regional differences in physical geography, economic structure, and social conditions (see map 9.1). And although the pattern of regional differentiation could be refined, no doubt without end, the crudest, but also most common regional division is threefold: urban, modern agricultural, and traditional rural. The urban region consists of the provinces of Noord-Holland and Zuid-Holland and is characterized by relatively large towns, some of which were known as centers of urban industry as early as the Middle Ages but declined substantially thereafter (like Delft or Leyden) while others gained their reputations as international ports during the Golden Age of the Republic (like Amsterdam or Rotterdam). Together with the province of Zeeland in the southwest, Noord- and Zuid-Holland constituted the core of the maritime empire in the seventeenth century. Of course, agriculture also existed in Holland and Zeeland in the days of the Republic, and it continued to do so when the waning of the Dutch empire set in: agriculture in these regions was dominated by horticulture and advanced dairy farming. With the decline of the seaports of Zeeland (e.g., Middelburg and Veere) after the seventeenth century, agriculture

Map 9.1   Urban, modern agricultural, and rural traditional regions in the Netherlands in the nineteenth century

grew in relative importance, so that at the beginning of the nineteenth century, Zeeland was generally considered to belong to the modern agricultural regions, of which the other part is to be found in the northern provinces of Groningen and Friesland. Large-scale, specialized, market-oriented, "capitalistic" agriculture, dairy farming, and animal husbandry dominated the picture in these regions as early as the seventeenth century and continued to do so in the following centuries, in fact up until the present day. Broadly speaking, the modern urban and modern agricultural provinces of the nation consisted of rich, alluvial soils, while the rest of the country, the traditional rural provinces of Drenthe, Overijssel, Gelderland, Utrecht, Noord-Brabant, and Limburg, located in the east and southeast, were characterized by poor, diluvial soils. It is important to realize that the famous "modernity" of the seventeenth-century Republic hardly applied to these so-called land provinces. In fact, these regions were more or less isolated from the rest of the country, except for the interregional export of peat, the main industrial fuel. A traditional rural economy dominated the picture on a smaller scale. Local and regional markets played a more important role than national—let alone international—markets, and the system in general was more geared to self-sufficiency, especially during times when market prices deteriorated. This traditional system persisted during the nineteenth and even during the first decades of the twentieth century. In the second half of the nineteenth century, it was in parts of this traditional rural economy that Dutch industrialization started, but it is important to realize that industrialization became dominant only in a tiny fraction of the eastern and southern provinces (the aforementioned areas of Twente and Noord-Brabant), while by far the largest parts of these regions were hardly touched by modern industry and urbanization. Indeed, even at the beginning of the twentieth century, the great majority of the counties in the traditional rural provinces of the Netherlands could not be characterized as "modern" by any standard.

This peculiar regional differentiation played an important part in the specific pattern of modernization of the Netherlands in the nineteenth century, as we will show. Let us look first, however, at the national picture.

9.5   The Dutch Pattern of Heights, 1817–1940

Although quantitative data for reconstruction of the development of the material circumstances of the Dutch population in general are rather limited and often of a scattered nature, this does not apply to data on the height of conscripts. Brinkman, Drukker, and Slot (1988) published the median heights of Dutch conscripts on a yearly basis from 1863 up to 1940, based on national height distributions. These data were revised (and for some years corrected) by Mandemakers and van Zanden (1990, 1993). Although earlier authors (e.g., de Meere 1982) were convinced that in these national data conscripts coming from the upper social echelons of society were underrepresented, Brinkman, Drukker, and Stuurop (1989) demonstrated that these figures reflected accurately the whole male population at the age of conscription.

Yearly figures on the median height of conscripts can, however, be extrapolated even further back in time by using fairly large samples collected by Oppers (1963). Oppers collected samples of the average height of boys at the age of conscription for consecutive conscription years between 1817 and 1896 from town archives in the cities of Groningen and Goes (modern agricultural regions), Assen, Nijmegen, and Roermond (traditional rural regions), and Rotterdam and Leyden (urban regions). Sample size differed from 312 observations in total for 1817 to more than 900 observations at the end of his research period. The overlapping period (1863–96) between Oppers's selected town samples and the national median heights was used to run a simple regression equation, and the results were used to estimate median height for the years 1817 up to 1892 (for details on calculations see the appendix). Some suspicion is warranted as far as the accuracy of the series of median heights estimated from Oppers's town samples is concerned: as we shall demonstrate, there are indications that health conditions in Dutch cities in the first half of the nineteenth century were generally worse than in the countryside, but that this contrast gradually faded away, and finally reversed during the second half of the century. This is, for instance, suggested by the changing pattern of regional differences in mortality (see fig. 9.9, below). This pattern is in itself no great surprise: Mokyr and Ó Gráda, for instance, found similar differences for Dublin and London (Mokyr 1988; Mokyr and Ó Gráda 1994). If it is true that conscripts coming from the countryside are absent from Oppers's samples, or at least severely underrepresented (this seems plausible from the text, but Oppers is not completely clear on this point), then one should expect the figures before 1863 to be somewhat downward biased. The high degree of covariability between the national median and the median estimated from Oppers's samples for the overlapping years 1863–96, however, strongly suggests that the pattern of rising heights from 1818 up to 1830, and rapidly declining heights thereafter, which is displayed by the estimated median heights for the years 1818–63, accurately reflects the national movement over time.

From figure 9.1, where the results of this analysis are summarized, a clear picture of growth, stagnation, and decline in national height can be deduced.

The first phase, 1817–30, is a bit surprising: This period falls definitely in the premodern era of the Dutch economy. Nevertheless, the data show a continuous and remarkably sharp rise in median height. Apparently, even during years of economic stagnation, substantial improvements in the material circumstances of the population could be realized. We will return to this curious phenomenon to speculate on a possible explanation.

From 1830 up to 1857, a sharp and continuing decline manifests itself. We should keep in mind, however, that the figures represent median height at the year of conscription, so that the data reflect some deterioration in the material circumstances *during the years before* actual measurement, rather than deterioration *in the year of* measurement: Conscripts did not suddenly "shrink" because circumstances worsened in the year they were measured. Nevertheless, if we are asking ourselves what, when, where, and why things went "wrong" with the Dutch living standard, the years between 1830 and somewhat before 1857 are apparently the years that we should concentrate on first.

In the years from 1857 up to 1887, steady improvement of the material conditions of the Dutch population can be inferred from the steep rise in median height. According to these figures, however, it was not before the end of this period that the stature of Dutch conscripts equaled that of their counterparts in 1830. There is a controversy among economic historians as to whether the

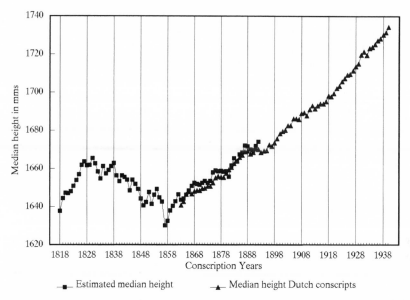

Fig. 9.1   Median heights of Dutch conscripts, 1818–1940
Note: See table 9A.1 for data.

Dutch economy experienced an absolute decline or merely a period of stagnation during the first half of the nineteenth century. The answer from the viewpoint of standard of living must be, it seems, that material circumstances deteriorated so badly (in an absolute sense) after the third decade of the nineteenth century, that it took only a little less than half a century to regain the level of the late 1820s.

A 10-year period of stagnation is visible from 1887 up to 1897. Finally, a seemingly endless period of steadily rising heights presents itself from 1897 to 1940, interrupted only by three years of more than marginal decline: 1910, 1913, and 1932.

Now that we have a clear periodization of increase, stagnation, and decline in stature, the question arises as to what this national pattern means in comparative perspective. Just because it is an undisputed fact that the Dutch at the moment are among the tallest people on earth—the average height of 20-year-old Dutch boys was well over 183 cm in 1992 (on the scale of fig. 9.1, well above the top of the page)—the question of whether this has always been the case becomes interesting: If it is true, the presumed retardation and backwardness of the Dutch economy in the first half of the nineteenth century can have had surprisingly little effect on the living conditions of the Dutch people. If it is not true, the contemporary concern of the Dutch government and the Dutch "Hygienists" (Coronel 1862a, 1862b, 1862c; *Rapport der Commissie* 1869;

Zeeman 1861) about the extremely poor physical state of the Dutch population in the middle of the nineteenth century seems to be supported by comparative empirical evidence.

9.6   Have Dutchmen Always Been Giants?

Even a superficial glance at figure 9.2 reveals that there is a clear answer to the question in the heading of this section: No. Compared with their Italian and French counterparts, Dutch male adolescents started to become exceptionally tall some 20 years after the Netherlands began its recovery from the long period of declining stature of 1830–57. Comparison of Dutch and French heights up to 1857 suggests that the Netherlands were indeed hit by a sort of subsistence crisis in the period between 1830 and 1857: Dutch conscripts were much taller (some 2 cm) than French ones in 1835, but during the years thereafter, French height remained more or less stable, while Dutch height fell rapidly, with the result that Dutch conscripts were markedly smaller than their French colleagues in 1857 and 1858. When the years of recovery set in, Dutch and French conscripts remained for years more or less of the same stature because French conscripts also started to grow in the late 1850s. It was only after 1877 that the French and the Dutch growth figures started to diverge.

Rough comparisons with height figures of other countries confirm the point that Dutch conscripts were exceptionally small in the third quarter of the nineteenth century: The 15-year moving average height of 20-year-old Swedish

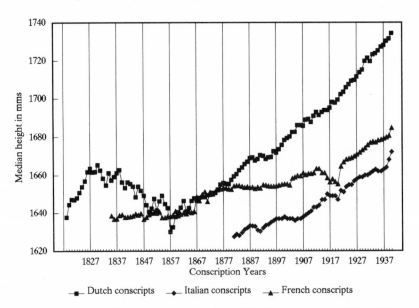

Fig. 9.2   Median heights of Dutch, French, and Italian conscripts, 1818–1940
Note: See table 9A.2 for data.

boys is well above 65 inches (i.e., 165.1 cm) for every conscription year between 1830 and 1870 (Sandberg and Steckel 1994), while the median height of 20-year-old Dutch boys is below the 165.0 cm level for each and every year between 1847 and 1873. In 1855 20-year-old Danish conscripts were on average 165.5 cm tall, while their Norwegian colleagues were even taller in the same year: 168.0 cm (Twarog 1994, 33, table 6), which means a difference of 1 and 3.5 cm, respectively, from the Dutch figure for that year.

The conclusion of this section is therefore straightforward: In the last quarter of the nineteenth century, the Dutch gradually became giants. In the preceding period, there had been times (e.g., around the end of the first quarter of the nineteenth century) when they were rather tall compared with other Europeans. During the intervening period (the second quarter of the nineteenth century), however, they were more or less dwarfed in comparative perspective, and it took them a long time (roughly, the third quarter) to recover from the apparently very poor living conditions that had prevailed during the foregoing years.

9.7 Population, Stature, Mortality, and the Price of Food

One should expect the pattern of changing material conditions suggested by the height data to be reflected in some way—at least in the premodern period—in the development of the Dutch population. Thanks to the work of Horlings (1993), rather accurate yearly data on population and crude birth and death rates, both nationally and by province, have been made available for the nineteenth century. Concentrating first on the national figures, it is clear that the periodization of good and bad times, as suggested by the fluctuations in the median height of conscripts, is indeed rather accurately reflected in periods of demographic growth and stagnation until the middle of the nineteenth century (see fig. 9.3).

Years of demographic stagnation or near stagnation are visible from 1805 until 1815, interrupted by a severe demographic crisis in 1808. Although we lack information on stature for this period, it would surprise us if this period were characterized by rising heights. The contrary seems more plausible.

The second phase, from 1815 up to 1860, has to be split into different subperiods. The first years (1815–24) were characterized by steady growth of the national population. The upward trend of the growth rate was reversed between 1825 and 1833, but increasing population growth returned thereafter (1834–45), until growth was suddenly halted by a serious subsistence crisis in the second half of the 1840s. The high rate of 1850 declined rapidly during the following years, as a result of which the 1850s overall must be seen as a decade in which population growth again gradually approached a near standstill in 1859.

The first phase of the Dutch demographic transition seems to have set in at the start of the 1860s, after which Dutch population seems to have grown at an ever increasing pace.

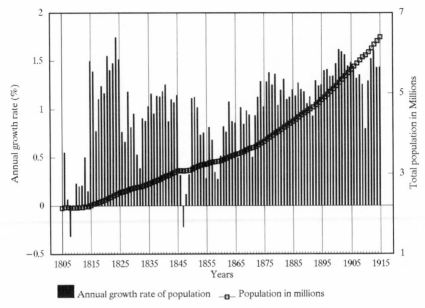

Fig. 9.3   Dutch population and population growth, 1805–1915
Note: See table 9A.3 for data.

There are some indications that the second phase of the demographic transition manifested itself somewhere around the end of the nineteenth century, but even as late as 1913, the growth rate was well above 1.5 percent per year, which seems surprisingly high in comparative perspective.

That the dawning of the demographic transition in the Netherlands started in the early 1860s is confirmed by the changing pattern of birth and death rates from 1860 onward (fig. 9.4). Before that year, both births and deaths displayed large and erratic fluctuations, although the deviations of the death rate around its trend are much greater (as expected) than those of the birthrate. It should be noted that both national rates for the whole period before the 1860s are typical for a premodern society in a demographic sense, including the recurrent demographic crises. After 1863, the birthrate stabilized quickly at the high level of around 35 births per 1,000 inhabitants per year, and around the same time the death rate started to decline, showing less erratic fluctuation from the last quarter of the nineteenth century onward. This is also the period during which the birthrate began to follow a slowly decreasing trend.

Should the demographic pattern of the Netherlands before 1860 indeed be seen as an important "sign of the times," in the sense that the Dutch economy should be regarded up to at least the middle of the nineteenth century as a backward, retarded, stagnating, in one word, as a traditional society? That remains to be seen. If it were true, one would expect at least three things: First, in the absence of substantial increases in labor productivity, real wages should

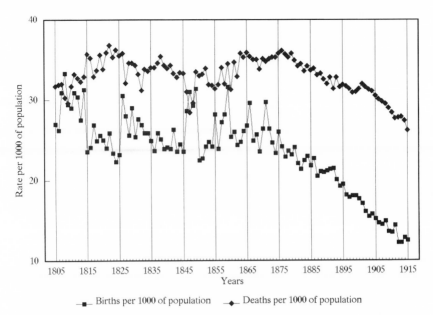

Fig. 9.4   **Crude death rates and birthrates, 1805–1915**
Note: See table 9A.4 for data.

fluctuate around some horizontal trend. Second, we should expect long-term fluctuations in population growth to at least roughly coincide with ups and downs in the standard of living, in the sense that some years of improving material conditions would be immediately reflected in an increase in the growth rate of the population and, vice versa, that a worsening of living conditions would mirror itself in a downturn in the growth rate of the population. In the third place, we should (following Pierre Goubert's dictum that in a premodern society the price of food is a precise demographic barometer) expect to find some evidence that demographic crises had indeed the character of subsistence crises, that is, that a rise in the long-term value of the price index for foodstuffs would be accompanied by an upward trend in the death rate.

It is not necessary to devote many new arguments here in defending the first point: It is a commonly accepted—and fairly well documented—fact that nominal wages remained remarkably stable from the middle of the seventeenth century onward up to the beginning of the 1860s (see, e.g., Noordegraaf 1980; Nusteling 1985). Recently, new national wage estimates for the period 1820–1913 (Vermaas 1995) were put forward, while Paping (1995) published new wage series for the northern, modern agricultural region of Groningen. Both series confirm the point mentioned above: nominal wages were fairly stable before 1860, and fluctuations in the real wage rate were therefore dominated by changes in the cost of living (cf. Horlings 1995, 197, graph 6.2).

If one is willing to accept yearly fluctuations of sex- and age-specific median height as a sensitive proxy for changes in the standard of living, then, from figure 9.5, it seems that the second point cannot be denied: between 1817 and 1857, Dutch population growth and lagged median height—the value in a given conscription year reflecting *past,* not present, conditions—moved broadly in the same direction. Up to 1823 improving material circumstances were accompanied by increasing population growth. Then a long period of worsening conditions set in and lasted at least until the late 1850s, only interrupted by a small, short-term improvement between 1847 and 1852. During the same years, population growth gradually and steadily declined, almost to a complete standstill at the middle of the century.

Was it indeed a rising long-term death rate that caused the decrease in the population growth rate, and were shifts in the trend of the death rate dominated by a shifting trend in food prices? Figure 9.6 suggests that this was indeed the case, at least up to the 1830s. The trend of both the death rate and the price index of agricultural products fall sharply between 1810 and 1820, and together they rise again between 1825 and 1831. The pattern suggested by figure 9.6 is, however, less clear than the relationship presented in the previous graph. This is hardly surprising; no one will deny that factors other than the trend value of the price of food are also influencing the death rate. It is worth mentioning in this respect that these other factors seem to become of increasing importance as we move ahead in time: after 1833, the death rate continues to fall up to 1840, while food prices remain more or less the same. From 1840

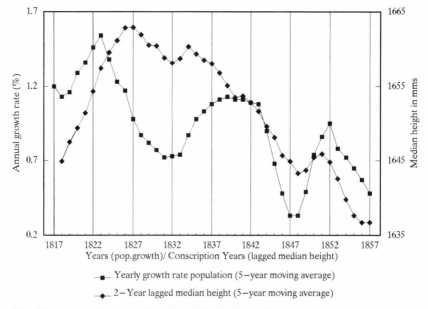

Fig. 9.5   Population growth and median heights, 1817–57
Note: See table 9A.5 for data.

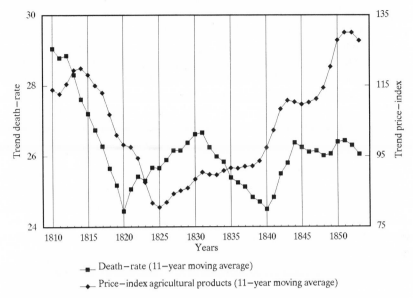

Fig. 9.6   Death rates and agricultural price indexes, 1810–53
Note: See table 9A.6 for data.

onward, rising food prices are again accompanied by rising death rates, but it is important to notice that the death rate in the meantime seems to have shifted to a substantially lower trend value: it does not return to its high level of the early 1830s, let alone its peak value of around 29 deaths per 1,000 in 1810.

Summarizing so far, we must conclude that Dutch society, seen from a national point of view concentrating for the moment on demographic aspects, and on sex- and age-specific height as a proxy for material conditions, presents itself, from the beginning of the nineteenth century up to 1860, in every aspect as a stagnant, retarded, and backward nation; it was a traditional society in the true sense of the word, showing for some subperiods serious signs (as seen from the sharply declining heights between 1830 and 1857) not only of stagnation, but of apparent decline. It is not inconceivable that some very small improvements in material conditions could be noticed during the 1840s (as seen from a marked fall in the trend of the death rate), but overall it seems safe to conclude that serious modernization did not start before the 1860s.

9.8   Real National Income and the Standard of Living: Two Paradoxes

Although it is, at the time this text is written, too early to make a detailed comparison between the development of real national income and the standard of living in the Netherlands for the whole of the nineteenth century, for the simple reason that accurate yearly estimates of Dutch national income will

only become available in the near future, with the results of the Dutch Historical National Accounts Project (cf. Horlings et al. 1995), it is too tempting not
to speculate a bit on this relationship on the basis of some preliminary results
of this project.

Recently, Horlings et al. (1995) published initial and—as the authors themselves stress—very preliminary yearly figures of Dutch GNP for the base year
1807 and the consecutive years 1850–1900. Given the recently published revised yearly population figures by Horlings (1993), the only thing missing in
order to be able to calculate preliminary estimates of real income per capita
for the same years is a proper GNP deflator. Although such a deflator has not
yet been put forward, we can rely on an index of wholesale prices based on
miscellaneous sources, published earlier by van Stuijvenberg and de Vrijer
(1980), as a rough proxy. It is true that the accuracy of this series has been
questioned, but a brand-new GNP deflator for the years 1800–50 published by
Horlings (1995) suggests at the least that the van Stuijvenberg–de Vrijer series
is probably more precise than most scholars would have guessed: Horlings's
deflator sets the price level of GNP in 1807 at 179, compared with his base
year 1850. Recalculating the van Stuijvenberg–de Vrijer index on an 1850 basis yields an average price level of 170 between 1805 and 1809 (cf. Horlings
1995; van Stuijvenberg and de Vrijer 1980, 9, col. 1).

A confrontation of these "guestimates" of real national income per capita,
based on the nominal GNP figures published by Horlings et al., with the national data on median height yields some surprising, and also rather paradoxi-
cal, results (fig. 9.7).

The growth pattern of real per capita income seems to confirm, from an
economic viewpoint, what we concluded on the basis of demographic changes
and height data: real per capita income clearly was stagnating from 1850 up to
1865. In the middle of the 1860s, it started to grow steadily until the middle of
the 1880s, when a downturn set in that lasted for almost a decade. Thereafter,
growth resumed its earlier pace.

That changes in height are indeed a sensitive indicator of changing material
circumstances is corroborated by the fact that this downturn of the growth rate
of real income is clearly reflected by a sudden stunting of the height figures
between 1888 and 1895. Even the much shorter and less pronounced slowdown
of real income growth in 1870 and 1873 is mirrored in stagnating height figures
between 1876 and 1879. In the period between 1850 and 1900, it seems, there
was a surprisingly precise relationship between the development of real per
capita income and the standard of living, as indicated by changes in the stature
of conscripts, as was suggested in 1988 by Brinkman et al. (1988). A three-
year moving average of their estimates for 1850–1913, purely derived from
median heights of conscripts for the second half of the nineteenth century,
related to income per capita by means of a polynomial-distributed, lagged
ALMON regression equation and the recent figures by Smits, Horlings, and
van Zanden, estimated by conventional methods, yields an R^2 of 0.90, which

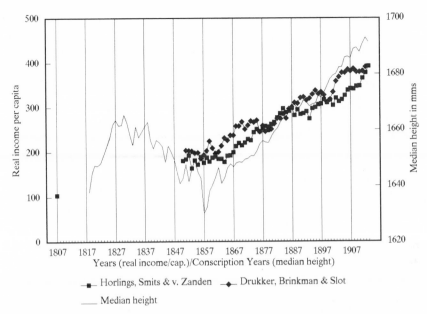

Fig. 9.7   Real per capita income and median heights, 1807–1913
Note: See table 9A.7 for data.

is for the time being probably the best (in any case, the shortest) reply to the severe criticism by Mandemakers and van Zanden (1990, 1993) of earlier estimates by Brinkman, Drukker and Slot.

There are, however, also two points to be mentioned that seem—in our opinion, at least—rather puzzling. Although real income per capita was stagnating for the years 1850–65, the standard of living over the same period apparently was not: a stagnation in median height is visible between 1850 and 1853, but then the figure drops sharply to its lowest value for the whole century (1857), as far as we have data, followed by a surprising sharp recovery from 1858 onward. Of course, the continuing sharp decline in heights between 1853 and 1857 could have been caused by years of dramatically falling real income figures *before* 1850, but that does not seem very likely: According to Horlings, value-added at constant prices for the whole service sector of the Dutch economy grew between 1840 and 1850 at an average rate of 1.6 percent per year (Horlings 1995, 476, table 16.1), while Groote estimated a yearly growth percentage of net capital formation in infrastructure between 1841 and 1850 of 1.1 percent (Groote 1995, 63, table 3.3). But even if it becomes evident with the publication of all final results of the Historical National Accounts Project that real income per capita had dramatically fallen during the 1840s, it would help us to explain the shrinking of conscripts up to 1857, but would make the next point only more mysterious.

The picture of a retarded, stagnating economy during the first half of the nineteenth century is clearly at odds with the estimate of real per capita income in 1807: If both the estimates for 1807 and 1850 are roughly correct, then real national income in the Netherlands increased during the first half of the nineteenth century at an average rate of approximately 2 percent per year, while real income per capita increased during the same period at more than 1 percent per year! Clearly, we have stumbled upon a typical phenomenon of Dutch economic development in the early nineteenth century that was aptly characterized by Richard Griffiths as "sneaky growth" (Griffiths 1979, 1980). The development was, however, not only sneaky in the sense that contemporary observers did not seem to notice it, it was also quite sneaky in the sense that material conditions for the great majority of the population apparently did not even remain more or less the same, but *worsened* very badly after 1830, as suggested by the continuously falling median height between 1830 and 1857 and the rising death rate between 1847 and 1865. As we have said, lack of adequate data at this moment prevents a detailed analysis of these two paradoxes, but with the newly available evidence, we can at least try a shot in the dark.

9.9   A Shot in the Dark

Thanks to the painstaking work of Horlings (1995) a yearly series of value-added at constant prices for the service sector is now at our disposal. Let us suppose for a moment that real national income between 1807 and 1850 grew at exactly the same pace as real value-added in the service sector. Given that real value-added in services grew on average 1.6 percent per year, and real national income on average 2.15 percent per year during the same period, it is clear that on the basis of this hypothesis, we will provide ourselves with an unrealistically *low* estimate of the development of real per capita income in the first half of the nineteenth century (fig. 9.8). It is nevertheless interesting to follow the pattern of income development stemming from this unrealistic assumption: Stagnation or even a slight decline from 1807 up to 1816; rapid growth between 1816 and 1823; a second period of stagnation between 1823 and 1831; a real growth spurt between 1831 and 1834; and finally, a long period of stagnation from 1834 onward. Over the same period, heights rose rapidly until 1830 and fell continuously thereafter. Now, knowing that sectors of the Dutch economy other than services must have been growing (per capita!) at a much faster pace than our "unrealistic" real income guesses to compensate for the huge difference between our "unrealistic" income estimate and the "real" real income estimate in 1850, it remains a mystery so far why heights did not at least remain the same after 1830. It seems wise, in trying to determine *why* things went wrong with the standard of living sometime during the late 1820s to concentrate first on the question of *where* things went wrong. In other words, let us see whether regional differences can shed some light on the

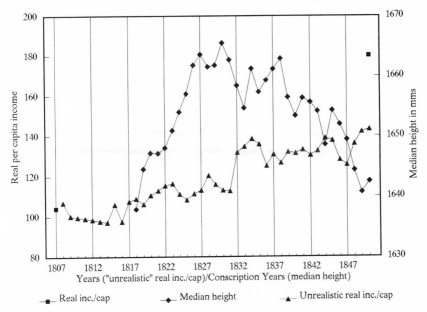

Fig. 9.8 **"Unrealistic" real income per capita and median heights, 1807–50**
Note: See table 9A.8 for data.

mystery of the shrinking conscripts during a period in which there must have been more than marginal growth in real per capita income.

9.10   Regional Differences in Mortality and Height

Figure 9.9, where regional differences in the death rate for the nineteenth century are presented, has some surprising features.

There were enormous differences in mortality between the modern urban, the modern agricultural, and the traditional rural regions in the Netherlands for the greater part of the nineteenth century; only in the last quarter of the century did regional death rates seem to converge.

Up to 1888, the death rate was highest in the modern urban region consisting of the provinces of Noord-Holland and Zuid-Holland, that is to say, in the core regions of the Golden Age of the Republic of the seventeenth century. After that year, mortality in the modern urban region dropped rapidly, with the result that the lowest death rates in the Netherlands at the beginning of the twentieth century were to be found in exactly the same region where life had apparently been extremely unhealthy for most of the nineteenth century.

Although life in the modern agricultural provinces of Groningen, Friesland, and Zeeland seems to have been much healthier than was that of city dwellers in the west of the country, it was, at least during the first half of the nineteenth

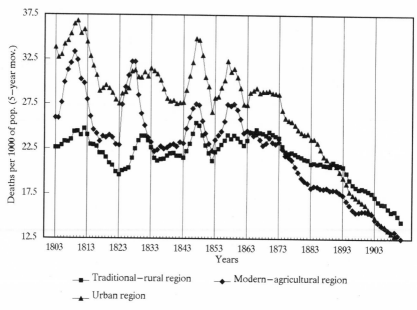

Fig. 9.9   Regional differences in mortality, 1803–1911
Note: See table 9A.9 for data.

century, and in fact up to 1863, not as merry and joyful as one might have expected from the much praised high level of agricultural technology that prevailed in these regions. The enormous up-swings of the death rate around 1810, 1828, 1848, and 1858 were felt not only in the modern urban regions but in the modern agricultural regions as well. In short, the national subsistence crises that we encountered in figure 9.5 were almost exclusively caused by severe increases in mortality in the modern "sea provinces" of the nation and not in the traditional rural "land-provinces."

The most surprising aspect of figure 9.9 is that the traditional rural regions of the Netherlands had by far, for each and every year, both the lowest death rates and the smallest fluctuations in mortality for the first 75 years of the nineteenth century. Then, for the last quarter of the century, the "traditional" death rate suddenly stagnated, while during the same years, the "modern" death rate fell, with the result that at the start of the twentieth century, mortality in the traditional rural regions was higher then anywhere else in the country.

Is this strange pattern corroborated by data on the height of conscripts? Although the data are a bit scattered, figure 9.10 strongly suggests that this is indeed the case.

Up to 1829, all regional heights moved sharply upward. After that year a sharp deterioration set in, and regional differences seem to have become increasingly dominant. What is striking is the pattern of regional differentiation in height up to 1833: all conscripts became smaller, but the situation was appar-

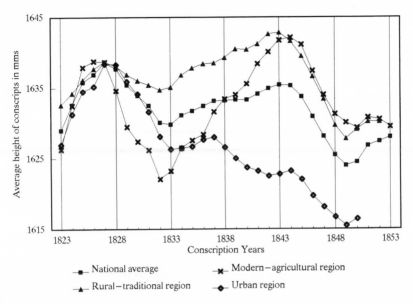

Fig. 9.10   Regional differences in height, 1823–53
Note: See table 9A.10 for data.

ently becoming much worse in both the modern urban and the modern agricultural regions, while the traditional rural regions seem to have been much less affected by the worsening circumstances.

During the next period, when things seem to have been improving again, the same pattern is—vice versa—again visible: All conscripts became a bit taller between 1833 and 1838, but in the modern urban region the height increase was hardly noticeable at all, and while heights increased fastest in the modern agricultural regions, this rapid increase was not enough to allow them to match the, relatively speaking, very tall conscripts in the traditional rural regions. Therefore, another five years are necessary.

From 1838 up to 1843 a slight improvement in the traditional rural regions was visible, while the standard of living in the modern agricultural provinces was still moving sharply upward. During the same years, life in the modern urban regions was worsening badly.

The years between 1843 and 1848 were characterized by a sharp deterioration of material conditions: seen also from the viewpoint of stature, these years are aptly called "the hungry forties." It is clear that the agricultural diseases of this period were affecting the standard of living in all regions more or less in the same degree. As a result, there was not much difference by the end of the 1840s in the height of conscripts between the modern and the traditional agricultural regions, but the difference between these two and the urbanized western provinces was striking.

9.11 Some Conclusions, More Speculations

Let us try to offer some very rough and speculative elements for an explanation of the paradox of worsening standard of living in the Netherlands during roughly the 1830s and 1840s, as suggested by the rising trend in the death rate and the continuing decline in the heights of conscripts, simultaneously with increasing real per capita income.

First, it should be noted that the national picture of worsening material conditions is dominated by the continuous deterioration of the standard of living in the most urbanized areas in the west: it was city life, rather than rural life, that was bad during the first half of the nineteenth century, and in some respects (heights) it became worse. An exception must be made for the disease-ridden years after 1843: during these years almost everyone was affected for the worse.

In the modern agricultural regions, material circumstances worsened during the years between 1827 and 1833 but improved substantially thereafter, until the "great overall potato crisis" of the second half of the 1840s. The drop in the standard of living before 1833 is easily explained: A sharp and continuous fall in agricultural prices between 1818 and 1829 (at the end of the period the price level was roughly 50 percent of what it had been at the beginning) caused a severe drop in real income per capita in the modern agricultural regions. This last point is confirmed by Paping (1995) in his recently published, brilliant analysis of the modern agrarian province of Groningen between 1770 and 1860. It is neatly reflected in the fact that between 1827 and 1833 heights fell more in the modern agrarian regions than in the urban regions (see fig. 9.10), where city dwellers could at least partly compensate for worsening circumstances by low food prices. The long-term drop in agricultural prices also accounts for the increase in national median height (see fig. 9.8) between 1818 and 1830. Finally, it is to be expected that the more self-sufficient peasants in the rural traditional regions were least affected by the price fall: they simply turned away from the market and increased their rate of self-sufficiency. This point is also reflected in figure 9.10.

From 1830 to 1848, conditions improved in the modern agrarian regions, not in the first place because agricultural prices were rising again, but mainly as the result of technologically induced productivity increases. This is reflected in a continuous and rapid rise in height in the modern agricultural provinces. It also helps to explain the presumed rise in per capita income: according to Paping, real national income per capita in the province of Groningen rose by 63 percent between 1830 and 1848, that is, an average yearly growth percentage of 1.85. A squeaky example of sneaky growth, as far as dairy farming was involved! The traditional rural regions also profited from the improvement in agricultural conditions but (probably because of the small-scale nature of their farms and lack of capital) to a far lesser degree than the modern agricultural regions. The urban regions, however, did not profit at all from these changes, simply because the locus of this early phase of modernization was in agriculture and hardly at all in industry or services (cf. fig. 9.8). As a consequence, modern urban heights continued to fall up to the "hungry forties," and then the grim years that followed did the rest to push the standard of living to its lowest level at the middle of the 1850s.

After the middle of the century, serious modernization of the urban regions finally started. During this phase, traditional rural regions could not catch up with the modernization process, being stuck, as it were, at a premodern ceiling as far as the standard of living is concerned. Their death rate started to stagnate at some 23 deaths per 1,000 per year and was finally passed by the falling rates of the two other regions. At the beginning of the twentieth century, conscripts in the rural—and now, indeed, backward—regions of Drenthe and Brabant were among the smallest in the whole of the nation, while they had been comparative "giants" for most of the nineteenth century.

Appendix

The tables in this appendix correspond to the consecutive numbered figures in the paper. So table 9A.1 contains the data for figure 9.1, and so forth. Missing data are indicated in the tables by "n.a."

Table 9A.1   Median Heights and Estimated Median Heights of Dutch Conscripts (conscription years; in millimeters), 1818–1940

Year (1)	Estimated Median Height (mm) (2)	Median Height (mm) (3)	Year (1)	Estimated Median Height (mm) (2)	Median Height (mm) (3)	Year (1)	Estimated Median Height (mm) (2)	Median Height (mm) (3)
1818	1,637.88	n.a.	1859	1,638.00	n.a.	1900	n.a.	1,678.21
1819	1,644.55	n.a.	1860	1,640.39	n.a.	1901	n.a.	1,679.46
1820	1,647.24	n.a.	1861	1,642.90	n.a.	1902	n.a.	1,680.02
1821	1,647.14	n.a.	1862	1,646.49	n.a.	1903	n.a.	1,682.46
1822	1,648.05	n.a.	1863	1,643.57	1,640.89	1904	n.a.	1,682.51
1823	1,650.94	n.a.	1864	1,644.27	1,642.70	1905	n.a.	1,686.09
1824	1,653.97	n.a.	1865	1,646.34	1,646.38	1906	n.a.	1,686.20
1825	1,656.96	n.a.	1866	1,648.48	1,647.85	1907	n.a.	1,685.68
1826	1,661.77	n.a.	1867	1,650.81	1,646.76	1908	n.a.	1,689.03
1827	1,663.54	n.a.	1868	1,652.55	1,648.09	1909	n.a.	1,689.45
1828	1,661.50	n.a.	1869	1,652.00	1,648.53	1910	n.a.	1,687.85
1829	1,661.76	n.a.	1870	1,651.44	1,648.40	1911	n.a.	1,690.92
1830	1,665.48	n.a.	1871	1,652.46	1,649.48	1912	n.a.	1,693.07
1831	1,662.63	n.a.	1872	1,653.55	1,649.75	1913	n.a.	1,691.38
1832	1,658.39	n.a.	1873	1,652.43	1,650.79	1914	n.a.	1,692.98
1833	1,654.63	n.a.	1874	1,653.46	1,650.75	1915	n.a.	1,694.06
1833	1,661.17	n.a.	1875	1,658.05	1,652.48	1916	n.a.	1,694.04
1835	1,657.32	n.a.	1876	1,658.90	1,655.07	1917	n.a.	1,695.27
1836	1,659.24	n.a.	1877	1,658.50	1,656.00	1918	n.a.	1,698.35
1837	1,661.14	n.a.	1878	1,658.80	1,655.52	1919	n.a.	1,697.93
1838	1,662.86	n.a.	1879	1,658.29	1,655.33	1920	n.a.	1,699.54
1839	1,656.41	n.a.	1880	1,658.55	1,657.56	1921	n.a.	1,702.34
1840	1,653.31	n.a.	1881	1,655.78	1,659.46	1922	n.a.	1,703.47
1841	1,656.30	n.a.	1882	1,661.49	1,660.58	1923	n.a.	1,705.83

Year	(2)	(3)	Year	(2)	Year	(2)	(3)	
1842	1,655.55	n.a.	1883	1,665.38	1924	1,662.68	n.a.	1,707.56
1843	1,654.07	n.a.	1884	1,663.55	1925	1,663.99	n.a.	1,709.29
1844	1,648.56	n.a.	1885	1,667.44	1926	1,665.82	n.a.	1,709.64
1845	1,654.20	n.a.	1886	1,668.50	1927	1,666.92	n.a.	1,711.60
1846	1,651.93	n.a.	1887	1,672.09	1928	1,668.79	n.a.	1,713.80
1847	1,649.38	n.a.	1888	1,671.60	1929	1,669.17	n.a.	1,715.18
1848	1,644.32	n.a.	1889	1,670.00	1930	1,667.54	n.a.	1,719.91
1849	1,640.70	n.a.	1890	1,669.60	1931	1,668.47	n.a.	1,721.47
1850	1,642.52	n.a.	1891	1,671.79	1932	1,670.50	n.a.	1,719.60
1851	1,647.72	n.a.	1892	1,674.01	1933	1,670.05	n.a.	1,723.33
1852	1,641.52	n.a.	1893	n.a.	1934	1,668.50	n.a.	1,723.82
1853	1,646.29	n.a.	1894	n.a.	1935	1,669.22	n.a.	1,725.16
1854	1,649.21	n.a.	1895	n.a.	1936	1,669.46	n.a.	1,727.21
1855	1,644.84	n.a.	1896	n.a.	1937	1,672.39	n.a.	1,728.18
1856	1,642.54	n.a.	1897	n.a.	1938	1,671.60	n.a.	1,730.19
1857	1,630.14	n.a.	1898	n.a.	1939	1,673.52	n.a.	1,731.53
1858	1,632.48	n.a.	1899	n.a.	1940	1,675.78	n.a.	1,734.31

Sources: Col. (2), Estimated median heights of 19-3/4-year-old Dutch conscripts in millimeters (conscription years): Weighted average heights of 19-year-old (conscription years 1818–61) and 20-year-old (conscription years 1862–92) conscripts were calculated from Oppers (1963, 55, table 12; 56–57, table 13; 57–58, table 14; 59–60, table 15; 61–62, table 16; 62–63, table 17; 64–65, table 18; 65–66, table 19), corrected for some apparent miscalculations in age, using the yearly fluctuating size of Oppers's different town samples as weights. Average heights of 19-year-old conscripts were standardized to estimated average heights of 20-year-old boys by adding 30 mm (according to Oppers 1963: graphical annexe, graph 18), using the graph for 1850, and shifting the resulting average height one year ahead. For the overlapping years (1863–92) with the data from col. (3) (median heights), a simple regression was run ($R^2 = 0.96$), and the result was used to estimate median heights of 20-year-old boys for the conscription years 1818–61.

Col. (3), Median heights of 19-3/4-year-old Dutch conscripts in millimeters (conscription years): Original median heights calculated in Brinkman et al. (1988, 72–74, bijlage: "Lengte en reëel inkomen per hoofd van de bevolking, 1845–1940" (Appendix: Height and real income per capita, 1845–1940), col. 1). Refined and corrected figures for some years from Mandemakers and van Zanden (1990, 19–21, bijlage "Verschillende berekeningen van de mediaan van de lengte van keurlingen, 1863–1940" (Different calculations of the median height of conscripts, 1863–1940), col. 3).

Table 9A.2 Median Heights of Dutch, Italian, and French Conscripts (conscription years; in millimeters), 1818–1940

Year (1)	Dutch (mm) (2)	Italian (mm) (3)	French (mm) (4)	Year (1)	Dutch (mm) (2)	Italian (mm) (3)	French (mm) (4)	Year (1)	Dutch (mm) (2)	Italian (mm) (3)	French (mm) (4)
1818	1,637.88	n.a.	n.a.	1859	1,638.00	n.a.	1,641.00	1900	1,678.21	1,638.00	1,655.40
1819	1,644.55	n.a.	n.a.	1860	1,640.39	n.a.	1,638.70	1901	1,679.40	1,637.00	1,655.40
1820	1,647.24	n.a.	n.a.	1861	1,642.90	n.a.	1,639.40	1902	1,680.02	1,637.00	1,654.70
1821	1,647.14	n.a.	n.a.	1862	1,646.49	n.a.	1,640.20	1903	1,682.46	1,637.00	1,658.30
1822	1,648.05	n.a.	n.a.	1863	1,640.89	n.a.	1,639.60	1904	1,682.51	1,636.00	1,659.00
1823	1,650.94	n.a.	n.a.	1864	1,642.7	n.a.	1,640.90	1905	1,686.09	1,637.00	1,659.80
1824	1,653.97	n.a.	n.a.	1865	1,646.38	n.a.	1,640.30	1906	1,686.20	1,637.00	1,659.50
1825	1,656.96	n.a.	n.a.	1866	1,647.85	n.a.	1,640.90	1907	1,685.68	1,638.00	1,661.10
1826	1,661.77	n.a.	n.a.	1867	1,646.76	n.a.	1,648.60	1908	1,689.03	1,639.00	1,660.20
1827	1,663.54	n.a.	n.a.	1868	1,648.09	n.a.	1,646.40	1909	1,689.45	1,640.00	1,660.80
1828	1,661.50	n.a.	n.a.	1869	1,648.53	n.a.	1,649.89	1910	1,687.85	1,641.00	1,660.70
1829	1,661.76	n.a.	n.a.	1870	1,648.40	n.a.	1,651.31	1911	1,690.92	1,643.00	1,661.10
1830	1,665.48	n.a.	n.a.	1871	1,649.48	n.a.	1,646.10	1912	1,693.07	1,643.00	1,663.30
1831	1,662.63	n.a.	n.a.	1872	1,649.75	n.a.	1,651.10	1913	1,691.38	1,644.00	1,663.30
1832	1,658.39	n.a.	n.a.	1873	1,650.79	n.a.	1,650.02	1914	1,692.98	1,647.00	1,661.10
1833	1,654.63	n.a.	n.a.	1874	1,650.75	n.a.	1,651.40	1915	1,694.06	1,647.00	1,661.10
1834	1,661.17	n.a.	n.a.	1875	1,652.48	n.a.	1,652.30	1916	1,694.04	1,650.00	1,658.50
1835	1,657.32	n.a.	1,638.67	1876	1,655.07	n.a.	1,652.70	1917	1,695.27	1,649.00	1,656.30
1836	1,659.24	n.a.	1,636.80	1877	1,656.00	n.a.	1,653.40	1918	1,698.35	1,649.00	1,657.90
1837	1,661.14	n.a.	1,637.00	1878	1,655.52	n.a.	1,653.10	1919	1,697.93	1,649.00	1,656.60
1838	1,662.86	n.a.	1,638.90	1879	1,655.33	n.a.	1,652.70	1920	1,699.54	1,647.00	1,655.40
1839	1,656.41	n.a.	1,639.20	1880	1,657.56	n.a.	1,652.60	1921	1,702.34	1,652.00	1,664.60
1840	1,653.31	n.a.	1,637.80	1881	1,659.46	1,627.50	1,654.40	1922	1,703.47	1,651.00	1,666.80
1841	1,656.30	n.a.	1,638.10	1882	1,660.58	1,629.00	1,654.60	1923	1,705.83	1,654.00	1,668.19
1842	1,655.55	n.a.	1,638.30	1883	1,662.68	1,628.20	1,654.60	1924	1,707.56	1,655.00	1,668.60
1843	1,654.07	n.a.	1,638.70	1884	1,663.99	1,629.80	1,654.20	1925	1,709.29	1,655.00	1,669.09

1844	1,648.56	n.a.			
1845	1,654.20	n.a.			
1846	1,651.93	n.a.			
1847	1,649.38	n.a.			
1848	1,644.32	n.a.			
1849	1,640.70	n.a.			
1850	1,642.52	n.a.			
1851	1,647.72	n.a.			
1852	1,641.52	n.a.			
1853	1,646.29	n.a.			
1854	1,649.21	n.a.			
1855	1,644.84	n.a.			
1856	1,642.54	n.a.			
1857	1,630.14	n.a.			
1858	1,632.48	n.a.			

Year		
1885	1,639.60	1,665.82
1886	1,639.10	1,666.92
1887	1,639.90	1,668.79
1888	1,636.80	1,669.17
1889	1,637.70	1,667.54
1890	1,639.30	1,668.47
1891	1,640.10	1,670.5
1892	1,640.50	1,670.05
1893	1,640.00	1,668.5
1894	1,640.70	1,669.22
1895	1,637.60	1,669.46
1896	1,637.60	1,672.39
1897	1,638.20	1,671.6
1898	1,638.30	1,673.52
1899	1,638.90	1,675.78

		Year			
1,631.30	1,653.60	1926	1,709.64	1,657.00	1,669.91
1,632.10	1,653.90	1927	1,711.60	1,658.00	1,670.88
1,633.40	1,653.60	1928	1,713.80	1,659.00	1,671.92
1,633.10	1,653.70	1929	1,715.18	1,659.00	1,673.06
1,632.90	1,652.90	1930	1,719.91	1,660.00	1,674.10
1,631.00	1,653.70	1931	1,721.47	1,660.00	1,675.78
1,630.40	1,653.20	1932	1,719.60	1,661.00	1,676.94
1,632.10	1,654.90	1933	1,723.33	1,662.00	1,677.43
1,633.60	1,654.70	1934	1,723.82	1,663.00	1,677.00
1,634.00	1,654.40	1935	1,725.16	1,662.00	1,678.08
1,635.20	1,654.10	1936	1,727.21	1,662.00	1,678.55
1,636.00	1,654.10	1937	1,728.10	1,663.00	1,679.06
1,637.00	1,654.40	1938	1,730.19	1,664.00	1,679.67
1,637.00	1,654.80	1939	1,731.53	1,668.00	1,680.55
1,637.00	1,655.10	1940	1,734.31	1,672.00	1,684.70

Sources: Col. (2), Median heights of Dutch conscripts in millimeters (conscription years): 1818–62, identical to data of table 9A.1 col. (2); 1863–1940: identical to data of table 9A.1 col. (3).

Col. (3), Median heights of Italian conscripts (standardized to 20-year-old) in millimeters (conscription years): For a summary of the data on height of Italian conscripts, see ISTAT (Instituto Nazionale di Statistica), *Sommario di Statistiche Storiche 1926–1985* (Roma, 1986); and ISTAT, *Sommario di Statistiche Storiche Italiane 1861–1955* (Roma, 1958). For the underlying work on these data see M. Cappieri, "La statura degli Italiani durante il secolo," *Rivista di Antropologia* 47 (1960): 295–300; A. Costanzo, "La statura degli Italiani ventenni nati dal 1845 al 1920," *Annali di Statistica* 8, no. 2 (1948): 63–123; R. Livi, "Sulla statura degli Italiani," *Archivio per l'Antropologia e l'Etnologia* 13 (1883): 243–90, 317–77; R. Livi, *Antropometria militare*, 3 vol. (Roma: Presso il Giornale medico del Regio Esercito, 1896–1905); C. Lombroso, "Sulla statura degli Italiani in rapporto all'antropologia ed all'igiene," *Archivio per l'Antropologia e l'Etnologia* 3 (1873): 373–429; G. de Rossi, "La statura degli Italiani e l'incremento in essa verificatosi nel periodo 1874–1898," *Archivio per l'Antropologia e l'Etnologia* 33 (1903): 18–533.

From 1875 onward, all Italian male citizens were liable to be conscripted, which meant they had to appear at a medical examination. The mean height of Italian conscripts therefore refers to all conscripts, whether declared unfit for military service or not. However, not all Italian boys did appear at the medical examination. These cases of absenteeism can be divided into three categories: those whch were canceled from the drafts (because of decease, errors, and so on); those which were

(continued)

Table 9A.2   (continued)

abroad, or legally absent; and those who were illegally absent. But this last category was relatively small (4.52 percent of all conscripts born between 1854 and 1879), and the absentees were not considered as a source of a (systematic) bias of the mean height of the population of conscripts (see de Rossi 1903, 26–29, 58; Livi 1883, 248–50). The age at whch Italian boys were measured varied over the period between 18 and 22 years. Since changes in the age of measurement obscure the evolution of height of conscripts over time, Costanzo standardized the height of conscripts at an age of 20 years (see A. Costanzo, "La statura degli Italiani ventenni nati dal 1854 at 1920," *Rendiconti dell' Academia Nazionale dei Lincei (classe di Scienze fisiche, matematiche e naturali)* 8 [1947]: 707–12). The standardization was based on the average increase in height between ages 20 and 24 of Danish conscripts listed in a study by Mackeprang (see E. P. Mackeprang, "De vaernepligtiges Legemshojde i Danmark," *Meddedelser om Danmarks Antropologi* 1 [1907–11]: 10–149, esp. 33). For the actual age at which the conscripts were measured see P. Grassivaro Gallo, "L'evoluzione della statura in Italia: Analisi sui conscritti delle leve ta il 1927 e il 1949," *Genus* 28 (1972): 171–203; and L. Terrenato and L. Ulizzi, "Genotype environment relationships: An analysis of stature distribution curves during the last century in Italy," *Annals of Human Biology* 10 (1983): 335–46.

Col. (4), Median heights of French conscripts (standardized to 20-year-old) in millimeters (conscription years): For the basic source on heights of French conscripts, see Annuaire Statistique, *Statistiques Générales de la France 42me Vol. resumé rétrospectif* (Paris, 1926), and the work of J. Ch. M. Boudin, "De l'accroissement de la taille en France," *Mémoires de la Société d'Anthropologie de Paris* 1 (1863): 221–59; P. Broca, "Deuxième discours sur la dégénérescence physiologique des peuples civilisés," *Revue d'Anthropologie* 5 (1875): 605–64. *Mémoires d'Anthropologie* 1 (1871): 498–520; and M. Tschouriloff, "Etude sur la degénérescence physiologique des peuples civilisés," *Revue d'Anthropologie* 5 (1875): 605–64. After 1922, the heights of French conscripts were no longer published by the military authorities. Only a few estimates by anthropologists and medical doctors exist for the period after 1922. The data on (mostly mean) height for this period were found in the work of the following authors: M.-C. Chamla, "L'accroissement de la stature en France de 1880 à 1960: Comparison avec les pays d'Europe Occidentale," *Bulletins et Mémoires de la Société d'Anthropologie de Paris* 6 (1964): 201–78; M.-C. Chamla, "L'Evolution récente de la stature en Europe Occidentale (période 1960–1980)," *Bulletins et Mémoires de la Société d'Anthropologie de Paris* 10 (1983): 195–224; G. Oliver, "The increase of stature in France," *Journal of Human Evolution* 9 (1980): 645–49; G. Olivier and G. Devigne, "Données nouvelles sur la stature et la corpulence en France," *Cahiers d'Anthropologie et de biométrie humaine* 3 (1985): 111–23; P. Sempé and M. Sempé, *Croissance et Maturation Osseuse* (Paris, 1974); and J. Sutter, R. Izac, and T. N. Toan, "L'évolution de la taille des polytechniciens (1801–1954)," *Population* (Paris) 3 (1958): 373–406. See also M. A. van Meerten (1990).

Table 9A.3 Dutch Population (in millions of inhabitants) and Dutch Population Growth (in percentages per year), 1805–1915

Year (1)	Population Netherlands (2)	Yearly Growth (%) (3)	Year (1)	Population Netherlands (2)	Yearly Growth (%) (3)	Year (1)	Population Netherlands (2)	Yearly Growth (%) (3)
1805	2.149651	n.a.	1829	2.620932	0.82	1853	3.205992	0.74
1806	2.161582	0.56	1830	2.646000	0.96	1854	3.230345	0.76
1807	2.163092	0.07	1831	2.660091	0.53	1855	3.239542	0.28
1808	2.156215	−0.32	1832	2.670481	0.39	1856	3.265989	0.82
1809	2.156407	0.01	1833	2.694734	0.91	1857	3.288374	0.69
1810	2.161439	0.23	1834	2.718406	0.88	1858	2.299879	0.35
1811	2.165902	0.21	1835	2.746399	1.03	1859	3.308969	0.28
1812	2.170531	0.21	1836	2.778269	1.16	1860	3.326088	0.52
1813	2.181494	0.51	1837	2.804792	0.95	1861	3.353453	0.82
1814	2.184849	0.15	1838	2.836740	1.14	1862	3.379216	0.77
1815	2.217626	1.50	1839	2.868759	1.13	1863	3.415727	1.08
1816	2.248563	1.40	1840	2.902807	1.19	1864	3.445573	0.87
1817	2.266016	0.78	1841	2.939344	1.26	1865	3.475110	0.86
1818	2.291116	1.11	1842	2.965025	0.87	1866	3.492326	0.50
1819	2.319601	1.24	1843	2.997746	1.10	1867	3.527880	1.02
1820	2.346663	1.17	1844	3.029807	1.07	1868	3.557812	0.85
1821	2.383111	1.55	1845	3.064479	1.14	1869	3.592858	0.99
1822	2.416647	1.41	1846	3.074237	0.32	1870	3.626790	0.94
1823	2.452365	1.48	1847	3.067435	−0.22	1871	3.645118	0.51
1824	2.495136	1.74	1848	3.071164	0.12	1872	3.679189	0.93
1825	2.533014	1.52	1849	3.081118	0.32	1873	3.720699	1.13
1826	2.552483	0.77	1850	3.115421	1.11	1874	3.768703	1.29
1827	2.569405	0.66	1851	3.150484	1.13	1875	3.807338	1.03
1828	2.599737	1.18	1852	3.182526	1.02	1876	3.856362	1.29

(continued)

Table 9A.3   (continued)

Year (1)	Population Netherlands (2)	Yearly Growth (%) (3)	Year (1)	Population Netherlands (2)	Yearly Growth (%) (3)	Year (1)	Population Netherlands (2)	Yearly Growth (%) (3)
1877	3.909692	1.38	1890	4.559247	1.06	1903	5.430942	1.57
1878	3.958700	1.25	1891	4.610839	1.13	1904	5.509660	1.45
1879	4.012693	1.36	1892	4.653772	0.93	1905	5.591412	1.48
1880	4.054591	1.04	1893	4.714154	1.30	1906	5.672232	1.45
1881	4.103159	1.20	1894	4.772655	1.24	1907	5.747263	1.32
1882	4.156988	1.31	1895	4.832527	1.25	1908	5.825198	1.36
1883	4.202759	1.10	1896	4.900232	1.40	1909	5.898429	1.26
1884	4.250151	1.13	1897	4.969566	1.41	1910	5.945525	0.80
1885	4.301200	1.20	1898	5.036267	1.34	1911	6.022476	1.29
1886	4.350137	1.14	1899	5.103979	1.34	1912	6.114300	1.52
1887	4.405526	1.27	1900	5.179233	1.47	1913	6.212701	1.61
1888	4.458704	1.21	1901	5.263232	1.62	1914	6.301760	1.43
1889	4.511415	1.18	1902	5.347190	1.60	1915	6.392237	1.44

Sources: Col. (2), Population of the Netherlands in millions of inhabitants (yearly; end of year): 1805–1900, yearly figures, corrected for frontier changes, constructed by Horlings (1993) on the basis of original ten-year census data, revised by C. A. Oomens, "De loop van de bevollking van Nederland in de negentiende eeuw" (The development of the population of the Netherlands in the nineteenth century), *Statistische Onderzoekingen van het Centraal Bureau voor de Statistiek* (Statistical Research, published by the Dutch Central Bureau of Statistics), no. M35 (1989). These new figures differ considerably from: E. W. Hofstee (1978), *De demografische ontwikkeling van Nederland in de eerste helft van de negentiende eeuw: Een historisch-demografische en sociologische studie* (The demographic development of the Netherlands in the first half of the nineteenth century: A historical-demographic and sociological study) (Deventer: van Loghum Slaterus, 1978); 1900–1915: Dutch Central Bureau of Statistics, *Jaarcijfers voor Nederland* (Statistical yearbook of the Netherlands) (The Hague, 1901–16 eds.).
Col. (3), Yearly growth of the Dutch population in percentages per year: Calculated from col. (2).

Table 9A.4   **Crude Death Rates and Birthrates in the Netherlands (yearly; per 1,000 population), 1805–1915**

Year (1)	Death Rate per 1,000 Population (2)	Birthrate per 1,000 Population (3)	Year (1)	Death Rate per 1,000 Population (2)	Birthrate per 1,000 Population (3)	Year (1)	Death Rate per 1,000 Population (2)	Birthrate per 1,000 Population (3)
1805	31.7	27.0	1828	34.6	25.6	1851	33.2	22.7
1806	31.9	26.2	1829	34.6	29.0	1852	33.9	24.2
1807	32.0	30.9	1830	34.3	25.4	1853	31.9	24.8
1808	30.3	33.3	1831	33.2	27.6	1854	31.8	24.2
1809	29.6	29.4	1832	31.2	26.9	1855	31.4	28.2
1810	31.7	29.0	1833	33.8	25.9	1856	31.9	23.9
1811	33.2	30.9	1834	33.6	25.9	1857	34.0	27.2
1812	32.7	30.4	1835	34.0	24.9	1858	32.0	28.2
1813	32.3	27.5	1836	34.0	23.7	1859	34.5	31.6
1814	32.9	31.3	1837	34.6	25.9	1860	31.3	25.4
1815	35.7	23.6	1838	35.4	25.1	1861	34.7	26.0
1816	35.2	24.1	1839	34.3	23.9	1862	32.9	24.4
1817	32.9	26.9	1840	33.9	24.1	1863	35.8	24.8
1818	33.7	24.9	1841	34.3	23.9	1864	35.3	26.1
1819	35.6	25.6	1842	33.3	26.3	1865	35.9	26.8
1820	33.8	25.0	1843	32.8	23.6	1866	35.4	29.6
1821	35.9	24.0	1844	33.4	24.5	1867	35.0	24.9
1822	36.8	25.9	1845	33.3	23.6	1868	35.0	25.7
1823	35.3	23.4	1846	31.0	28.6	1869	33.8	23.6
1824	36.2	22.3	1847	28.4	31.0	1870	35.1	26.4
1825	35.5	23.2	1848	29.6	29.3	1871	34.8	29.7
1826	35.8	30.5	1849	33.5	31.4	1872	35.1	26.4
1827	32.1	28.0	1850	33.0	22.5	1873	35.3	24.7

(*continued*)

Table 9A.4 (continued)

Year (1)	Death Rate per 1,000 Population (2)	Birthrate per 1,000 Population (3)	Year (1)	Death Rate per 1,000 Population (2)	Birthrate per 1,000 Population (3)	Year (1)	Death Rate per 1,000 Population (2)	Birthrate per 1,000 Population (3)
1874	35.3	23.4	1888	33.3	21.1	1902	31.6	16.1
1875	35.8	26.0	1889	32.6	21.0	1903	31.3	15.5
1876	36.1	24.2	1890	32.0	21.2	1904	31.1	15.8
1877	35.7	22.9	1891	32.8	21.4	1905	30.5	15.2
1878	35.3	23.7	1892	31.4	21.5	1906	30.1	14.7
1879	35.8	23.2	1893	32.8	20.1	1907	29.8	14.5
1880	34.9	24.1	1894	31.6	19.3	1908	29.5	14.9
1881	34.2	22.1	1895	31.9	19.5	1909	29.0	13.6
1882	34.5	21.4	1896	31.7	18.2	1910	28.4	13.5
1883	33.6	22.5	1897	31.4	17.9	1911	27.7	14.4
1884	34.2	23.0	1898	30.9	18.1	1912	27.8	12.2
1885	33.7	21.8	1899	31.0	18.1	1913	27.9	12.2
1886	33.9	22.7	1900	31.4	17.7	1914	27.4	12.8
1887	33.1	20.5	1901	32.0	17.1	1915	26.2	12.5

Sources: Col. (2), Crude death rate of the Netherlands per 1,000 total population (yearly, end of year): See table 9A.3, col. (2).
Col. (3), Crude birthrate of the Netherlands per 1,000 total population (yearly, end of year): See table 9A.3, col. (2).

Table 9A.5   Five-Year Moving Average of Dutch Population Growth (in percentages per year) and Two-Year-Lagged, Five-Year Moving Average of Median Height of Dutch Conscripts (in millimeters), 1817–57

Year (1)	Yearly Growth Percentage of Dutch Population (5-year moving average) (2)	Two-Year-Lagged Median Height (5-year moving average) (3)	Year (1)	Yearly Growth Percentage of Dutch Population (5-year moving average) (2)	Two-Year-Lagged Median Height (5-year moving average) (3)
1817	1.20	n.a.	1838	1.11	1,656.8
1818	1.13	1,644.9	1839	1.13	1,655.1
1819	1.16	1,647.5	1840	1.11	1,653.5
1820	1.29	1,649.4	1841	1.11	1,653.7
1821	1.36	1,651.4	1842	1.09	1,652.8
1822	1.46	1,654.3	1843	1.08	1,651.6
1823	1.54	1,657.4	1844	0.90	1,649.6
1824	1.38	1,659.5	1845	0.68	1,648.1
1825	1.23	1,661.1	1846	0.48	1,645.7
1826	1.17	1,662.8	1847	0.33	1,644.9
1827	0.98	1,662.9	1848	0.33	1,643.3
1828	0.87	1,661.9	1849	0.49	1,643.7
1829	0.82	1,660.5	1850	0.74	1,645.4
1830	0.77	1,660.4	1851	0.86	1,645.9
1831	0.72	1,658.8	1852	0.95	1,644.8
1832	0.73	1,658.1	1853	0.78	1,642.6
1833	0.74	1,658.7	1854	0.72	1,639.8
1834	0.87	1,660.3	1855	0.65	1,637.6
1835	0.98	1,659.3	1856	0.57	1,636.7
1836	1.03	1,658.5	1857	0.48	1,636.7
1837	1.08	1,658.0			

Sources: Col. (2), Five-year moving average of yearly growth of the Dutch population in percentages per year (end of year): Calculated from table 9A.3, col. (3). Col. (3), Five-year moving average of median heights of Dutch conscripts in millimeters, two years lagged: Calculated from table 9A.1, col. (2).

Table 9A.6   Eleven-Year Moving Averages of Crude Death Rate and of Price Index of Agricultural Products (1831–50 = 100) in the Netherlands, 1810–53

Year (1)	Crude Death Rate per 1,000 Population (11-year moving average) (2)	Price Index of Agricultural Products (1831–50 = 100) (11-year moving average) (3)	Year (1)	Crude Death Rate per 1,000 Population (11-year moving average) (2)	Price Index of Agricultural Products (11-year moving average) (1831–50 = 100) (3)
1810	29.05	113.750	1832	26.25	89.836
1811	28.78	112.510	1833	25.99	89.654
1812	28.85	115.420	1834	25.84	90.954
1813	28.30	119.350	1835	25.39	91.681
1814	27.60	119.900	1836	25.25	91.581
1815	27.20	117.980	1837	25.14	92.072
1816	26.75	114.940	1838	24.84	92.218
1817	26.29	112.870	1839	24.71	93.572
1818	25.65	106.740	1840	24.50	97.445
1819	25.18	101.070	1841	24.84	102.330
1820	24.45	98.327	1842	25.50	108.350
1821	25.07	97.654	1843	25.81	110.750
1822	25.43	94.490	1844	26.38	110.300
1823	25.31	87.672	1845	26.25	109.650
1824	25.68	81.745	1846	26.13	110.180
1825	25.66	80.563	1847	26.15	111.100
1826	25.90	82.009	1848	26.02	114.310
1827	26.16	84.363	1849	26.07	120.300
1828	26.16	85.218	1850	26.41	127.840
1829	26.39	86.000	1851	26.44	130.000
1830	26.63	88.490	1852	26.31	130.000
1831	26.67	90.445	1853	26.05	127.650

Sources: Col. (2), 11-Year moving average of the crude death rate of the Netherlands per 1,000 total population (yearly, end of year): Calculated from table 9A.4, col. (2).

Col. (3), 11-Year moving average of the price index for agricultural products in the Netherlands (1830–51 = 100): An 11-year moving average was calculated from a Dutch agricultural price index published by Paping (1995, 406, table G.6). The price index was constructed on the basis of price movements of rye, wheat, oats, barley, potatoes, rape, beans, peas, and buckwheat in the northern part of the Netherlands. See Paping (1995, 364–71).

Table 9A.7 Dutch Real Per Capita Income (different estimates) and Dutch Median Height of Conscripts, 1805–1913

Year (1)	Horlings et al. Real Income per Capita (2)	Brinkman et al. Real Income per Capita (3)	Median Height of Conscripts (mm) (4)
1807	104.08	n.a.	n.a.
1808	n.a.	n.a.	n.a.
1809	n.a.	n.a.	n.a.
1810	n.a.	n.a.	n.a.
1811	n.a.	n.a.	n.a.
1812	n.a.	n.a.	n.a.
1813	n.a.	n.a.	n.a.
1814	n.a.	n.a.	n.a.
1815	n.a.	n.a.	n.a.
1816	n.a.	n.a.	n.a.
1817	n.a.	n.a.	n.a.
1818	n.a.	n.a.	1,637.8
1819	n.a.	n.a.	1,644.5
1820	n.a.	n.a.	1,647.2
1821	n.a.	n.a.	1,647.1
1822	n.a.	n.a.	1,648.0
1823	n.a.	n.a.	1,650.9
1824	n.a.	n.a.	1,653.9
1825	n.a.	n.a.	1,656.9
1826	n.a.	n.a.	1,661.7
1827	n.a.	n.a.	1,663.5
1828	n.a.	n.a.	1,661.5
1829	n.a.	n.a.	1,661.7
1830	n.a.	n.a.	1,665.4
1831	n.a.	n.a.	1,662.6
1832	n.a.	n.a.	1,658.3
1833	n.a.	n.a.	1,654.6
1834	n.a.	n.a.	1,661.1
1835	n.a.	n.a.	1,657.3
1836	n.a.	n.a.	1,659.2
1837	n.a.	n.a.	1,661.1
1838	n.a.	n.a.	1,662.8
1839	n.a.	n.a.	1,656.4
1840	n.a.	n.a.	1,653.3
1841	n.a.	n.a.	1,656.3
1842	n.a.	n.a.	1,655.5
1843	n.a.	n.a.	1,654.0
1844	n.a.	n.a.	1,648.5
1845	n.a.	n.a.	1,654.2
1846	n.a.	n.a.	1,651.9
1847	n.a.	n.a.	1,649.3
1848	n.a.	n.a.	1,644.3
1849	n.a.	n.a.	1,640.7
1850	n.a.	180.67	1,642.5
1851	184.28	203.66	1,647.7
1852	192.38	203.00	1,641.5

(*continued*)

Table 9A.7   (continued)

Year (1)	Horlings et al. Real Income per Capita (2)	Brinkman et al. Real Income per Capita (3)	Median Height of Conscripts (mm) (4)
1853	163.76	202.33	1,646.2
1854	181.05	197.66	1,649.2
1855	171.78	198.33	1,644.8
1856	189.32	185.33	1,642.5
1857	176.38	193.66	1,630.1
1858	187.13	202.66	1,632.4
1859	178.62	224.33	1,638.0
1860	187.15	209.00	1,640.3
1861	189.64	197.33	1,642.9
1862	184.56	200.00	1,646.4
1863	184.68	214.00	1,640.8
1864	177.58	231.00	1,642.7
1865	191.55	226.33	1,646.3
1866	192.63	237.00	1,647.8
1867	199.73	237.66	1,646.7
1868	213.53	258.00	1,648.0
1869	220.49	258.00	1,648.5
1870	215.29	267.66	1,648.4
1871	220.95	251.33	1,649.4
1872	228.78	259.33	1,649.7
1873	226.18	269.00	1,650.7

Year (1)	Horlings et al. Real Income per Capita (2)	Brinkman et al. Real Income per Capita (3)	Median Height of Conscripts (mm) (4)
1884	297.50	285.66	1,663.9
1885	288.86	275.33	1,665.8
1886	291.18	297.00	1,666.9
1887	298.43	301.33	1,668.7
1888	282.08	310.30	1,669.1
1889	294.87	308.66	1,667.5
1890	284.91	322.00	1,668.4
1891	286.11	323.33	1,670.5
1892	290.65	315.33	1,670.0
1893	273.98	320.00	1,668.5
1894	297.76	329.66	1,669.2
1895	300.17	338.00	1,669.4
1896	305.88	330.66	1,672.3
1897	307.94	334.66	1,671.6
1898	317.04	328.00	1,673.5
1899	310.39	311.33	1,675.7
1900	316.90	317.33	1,678.2
1901	304.18	334.66	1,679.4
1902	320.82	359.00	1,680.0
1903	313.02	368.33	1,682.4
1904	317.53	378.00	1,682.0

Year	(2)	(3)	(4)
1874	243.83	267.00	1,650.7
1875	251.51	270.66	1,652.4
1876	246.35	245.33	1,655.0
1877	251.62	258.66	1,656.0
1878	257.83	246.00	1,655.5
1879	248.98	255.66	1,655.3
1880	262.02	251.00	1,657.5
1881	266.58	263.33	1,659.4
1882	277.29	275.33	1,660.5
1883	286.18	275.33	1,662.6
1905	327.06	377.66	1,686.0
1906	339.33	384.66	1,686.2
1907	342.48	381.33	1,685.6
1908	341.81	386.00	1,689.0
1909	347.47	379.00	1,689.4
1910	348.29	379.33	1,687.8
1911	365.90	381.33	1,690.9
1912	377.80	390.66	1,693.0
1913	392.01	n.a.	1,691.3

Sources: Col. (2), Dutch income per capita according to Horlings, Smits, and van Zanden, in constant prices (1900–10 = 100): This series of real per capita income is based on the recently presented figures of nominal GNP at market prices of the Netherlands in Horlings et al. (1995, Bijlage 2: "Het bruto nationaal product tegen marktprijzen, 1850–1913 (lopende prijzen) [Appendix 2: Gross national product at market prices, 1850–1913 (current prices)]. Nominal GNP recalculated on a per capita basis by using population figures of Horlings (1993), reprinted in this appendix (table 9A.3, col. [2]). Nominal national per capita income recalculated at constant (1900–10 = 100) prices by using a price series published by van Stuijvenberg and de Vrijer (1980, 9–12, col. 1).

Col. (3), Dutch income per capita according to Brinkman, Drukker, and Slot, in constant prices (1900–10 = 100): This series is completely derived from median heights of conscripts for the second half of the nineteenth-century, by applying a polynomial distributed, lagged ALMON regression. For details, see Brinkman et al. (1988). Figures originally published in Brinkman et al. (1988, 264, cols. 4 and 5). The series reproduced in this appendix is a three-year moving average of the original Brinkman et al. series.

Col. (4), Median heights of Dutch conscripts in millimeters (conscription years): 1855–62, identical to data in table 9A.1, col. (2); 1863–1913, identical to data in table 9A.1, col. (3).

Table 9A.8   "Unrealistic" Real Income per Capita and Median Height of Conscripts (in millimeters) in the Netherlands, 1807–50

Year (1)	Horlings et al. Real Income per Capita (2)	"Unrealistic" Real Income per Capita (3)	Median Height of Conscripts (mm) (4)
1807	104.08	n.a.	n.a.
1808	n.a.	106.920	n.a.
1809	n.a.	100.300	n.a.
1810	n.a.	99.720	n.a.
1811	n.a.	99.165	n.a.
1812	n.a.	98.607	n.a.
1813	n.a.	97.767	n.a.
1814	n.a.	97.275	n.a.
1815	n.a.	106.020	n.a.
1816	n.a.	97.650	n.a.
1817	n.a.	107.590	n.a.
1818	n.a.	108.840	1,637.8
1819	n.a.	106.160	1,644.5
1820	n.a.	110.590	1,647.2
1821	n.a.	112.950	1,647.1
1822	n.a.	115.310	1,648.0
1823	n.a.	116.300	1,650.9
1824	n.a.	111.090	1,653.9
1825	n.a.	108.270	1,656.9
1826	n.a.	111.360	1,661.7
1827	n.a.	113.110	1,663.5
1828	n.a.	120.420	1,661.5
1829	n.a.	115.950	1,661.7
1830	n.a.	112.990	1,665.4
1831	n.a.	112.640	1,662.6
1832	n.a.	131.820	1,658.3
1833	n.a.	134.640	1,654.6
1834	n.a.	138.470	1,661.1
1835	n.a.	135.930	1,657.3
1836	n.a.	125.230	1,659.2
1837	n.a.	130.940	1,661.1
1838	n.a.	126.750	1,662.8
1839	n.a.	131.960	1,656.4
1840	n.a.	131.480	1,653.3
1841	n.a.	133.130	1,656.3
1842	n.a.	130.430	1,655.5
1843	n.a.	132.610	1,654.0
1844	n.a.	138.940	1,648.5
1845	n.a.	137.790	1,654.2
1846	n.a.	128.200	1,651.9
1847	n.a.	125.650	1,649.3
1848	n.a.	136.270	1,644.3
1849	n.a.	142.200	1,640.7
1850	180	143.370	1,642.5

Sources: Col. (2), Dutch income per capita according to Horlings, Smits, and van Zanden, in constant prices (1900–10 = 100): Identical to data in table 9A.7, col. (2). Col. (3), "Unrealistic" Dutch income per capita, estimated by extrapolating the Horlings et al. (1995) 1807 benchmark up to 1850, on the basis of the yearly growth rate of real value-added in the service sector, in constant prices (1900–10 = 100): The 1807 value of Dutch real income per capita (col. [2]) according to Horlings et al. (1995) was taken as the starting point from which to extrapolate a counter-biased series of Dutch real income per capita, by applying the yearly growth rate of real value-added in the Dutch service sector, as estimated by Horlings (1995). This procedure underestimates the growth of Dutch real income per capita between 1807 and 1850 since there is general agreement that the expansion of the Dutch service sector was lagging severely behind Dutch agriculture and industry during these years. This point is corroborated by the fact that the Horlings et al. (1995) estimate of Dutch real income per capita in 1850 is approximately 25 percent higher than the "unrealistic" estimate for the same year.

Table 9A.9   Five-Year Moving Averages of Crude Death Rates in Traditional Rural, Modern Agricultural, and Urban Regions of the Netherlands (yearly; per 1,000 population), 1803–1911

Year (1)	Traditional Rural (2)	Modern Agricultural (3)	Urban (4)	Year (1)	Traditional Rural (2)	Modern Agricultural (3)	Urban (4)
1803	22.7	26.0	33.8	1826	20.4	30.7	29.3
1804	22.6	25.9	32.7	1827	21.5	32.2	31.2
1805	22.9	27.6	33.0	1828	22.5	32.3	31.3
1806	23.3	29.9	34.2	1829	23.4	28.5	30.5
1807	23.3	31.3	34.6	1830	24.0	26.4	30.5
1808	23.6	32.1	35.4	1831	24.0	25.1	31.1
1809	24.4	33.3	36.5	1832	23.4	23.8	30.6
1810	24.5	32.4	36.8	1833	22.6	23.2	31.5
1811	24.0	30.3	35.4	1834	21.5	22.2	31.2
1812	24.8	29.8	35.8	1835	21.2	22.4	30.9
1813	24.1	28.0	34.5	1836	21.4	22.8	30.2
1814	23.0	26.1	32.8	1837	21.4	22.5	29.2
1815	22.9	24.6	31.8	1838	21.8	22.6	28.1
1816	22.8	24.2	30.7	1839	22.0	22.9	27.8
1817	22.0	23.3	29.0	1840	22.0	23.0	27.9
1818	22.0	23.9	29.3	1841	21.7	22.8	27.5
1819	21.6	23.8	29.6	1842	21.7	23.2	27.7
1820	20.9	24.0	29.3	1843	21.5	23.1	27.7
1821	20.7	23.7	28.8	1844	22.3	24.8	29.1
1822	20.0	23.0	28.0	1845	23.1	26.0	30.7
1823	19.6	22.9	27.6	1846	24.2	27.0	32.2
1824	20.1	27.4	28.7	1847	25.4	27.5	34.8
1825	20.2	29.4	28.8	1848	25.1	27.4	34.7

(*continued*)

Table 9A.9 (continued)

Year (1)	Traditional Rural (2)	Modern Agricultural (3)	Urban (4)	Year (1)	Traditional Rural (2)	Modern Agricultural (3)	Urban (4)
1849	24.0	25.6	33.0	1881	21.4	19.0	24.1
1850	22.9	24.2	30.5	1882	21.3	18.7	24.3
1851	22.1	23.1	29.5	1883	20.9	18.2	23.6
1852	21.2	22.3	26.6	1884	21.0	18.4	23.6
1853	22.2	23.5	28.2	1885	20.9	18.4	23.2
1854	22.5	24.0	28.3	1886	20.9	18.1	22.5
1855	23.0	24.5	29.4	1887	20.7	18.1	21.7
1856	23.5	25.6	30.2	1888	20.7	18.2	21.4
1857	24.1	27.5	32.3	1889	20.6	17.9	20.9
1858	23.6	27.3	31.1	1890	21.0	18.0	21.0
1859	24.0	27.5	31.5	1891	20.8	17.9	20.6
1860	23.7	26.9	30.5	1892	20.7	17.7	20.0
1861	23.3	25.8	29.3	1893	20.5	17.4	19.3
1862	22.9	24.3	27.5	1894	19.9	16.7	18.7
1863	23.4	24.6	27.4	1895	19.1	16.3	17.8
1864	24.4	24.4	28.8	1896	18.6	15.7	17.4
1865	24.3	24.0	29.1	1897	18.2	15.4	17.1
1866	24.7	24.2	29.3	1898	18.0	15.5	16.8
1867	24.3	23.6	28.8	1899	18.1	15.6	16.6
1868	24.2	22.9	28.9	1900	18.0	15.6	16.3
1869	24.0	23.2	28.9	1901	17.8	15.5	15.8
1870	24.4	23.7	29.0	1902	17.6	15.3	15.5
1871	24.1	23.2	28.7	1903	17.2	14.7	14.9
1872	24.0	23.1	28.7	1904	16.7	14.4	14.5

Year	(2)	(3)	(4)
1873	23.8	23.3	28.6
1874	22.8	22.5	26.8
1875	22.2	21.8	26.0
1876	22.1	21.6	25.7
1877	22.1	21.3	25.6
1878	22.0	20.5	25.2
1879	21.7	19.9	24.7
1880	21.6	19.3	24.4
1905	14.1	14.0	16.4
1906	13.9	13.8	16.4
1907	13.5	13.5	15.9
1908	13.1	13.2	15.5
1909	12.9	13.3	15.6
1910	12.5	12.9	15.1
1911	12.0	12.6	14.4

Sources: Col. (2), Five-year moving average of the crude death rate in traditional rural regions of the Netherlands per 1,000 total population (yearly; end of year): The series is derived from Horlings (1993, appendix 2, 18–22). The yearly mortality figures of the traditional rural regions are calculated as weighted averages of the figures for North-Brabant, Gelderland, Utrecht, Overijssel, Drenthe, and Limburg, with yearly total population figures of these provinces as weights. Yearly total population per province from Horlings (1993, appendix 1).

Col. (3), Five-year moving average of the crude death rate in modern agricultural regions of the Netherlands per 1,000 total population (yearly; end of year): For the sources for this series, see col. (2) sources. The yearly mortality figures of the modern agricultural regions are calculated as weighted averages of the figures for Zeeland, Friesland, and Groningen, with yearly total population figures of these provinces as weights.

Col. (4), Five-year moving average of the crude death rate in urban regions of the Netherlands per 1,000 total population (yearly; end of year): For the sources for this series, see col. (2) sources. The yearly mortality figures of the urban regions are calculated as weighted averages of the figures for Zuid-Holland, and Noord-Holland, with yearly total population figures of these provinces as weights.

Table 9A.10   Five-Year Moving Averages of "Guesstimates" of Average Height of Dutch Conscripts (conscription-years): National and for Traditional Rural, Modern Agricultural, and Urban Regions of the Netherlands (in millimeters), 1823–53

Year (1)	National (2)	Modern Agricultural (3)	Traditional Rural (4)	Urban (5)
1823	1,629.0	1,626.3	1,632.6	1,627.0
1824	1,632.6	1,632.5	1,634.2	1,631.3
1825	1,635.8	1,637.9	1,636.1	1,634.5
1826	1,636.9	1,638.8	1,637.7	1,635.2
1827	1,638.6	1,638.7	1,638.7	1,638.4
1828	1,637.7	1,634.6	1,638.1	1,638.3
1829	1,635.4	1,629.5	1,636.9	1,635.9
1830	1,633.9	1,627.4	1,636.0	1,634.1
1831	1,632.5	1,626.2	1,635.4	1,631.6
1832	1,630.1	1,622.1	1,634.7	1,628.1
1833	1,629.8	1,623.2	1,635.1	1,626.3
1834	1,631.1	1,626.5	1,636.8	1,626.5
1835	1,631.7	1,627.6	1,637.8	1,626.7
1836	1,632.4	1,628.4	1,638.4	1,627.7
1837	1,633.1	1,631.6	1,638.5	1,628.0
1838	1,633.2	1,633.4	1,639.3	1,626.6
1839	1,633.3	1,634.0	1,640.5	1,625.0
1840	1,633.3	1,635.6	1,640.4	1,623.7
1841	1,634.1	1,638.4	1,641.2	1,623.2
1842	1,634.9	1,640.1	1,642.6	1,622.5
1843	1,635.4	1,641.7	1,642.8	1,622.8
1844	1,635.3	1,642.1	1,641.6	1,623.2
1845	1,633.7	1,641.1	1,639.5	1,622.0
1846	1,630.9	1,637.4	1,636.6	1,619.7
1847	1,628.1	1,634.0	1,633.4	1,618.1
1848	1,625.5	1,631.3	1,629.7	1,616.7
1849	1,624.0	1,630.1	1,627.8	1,615.5
1850	1,624.5	1,629.3	1,629.1	1,616.4
1851	1,626.8	1,630.8	1,630.2	n.a.
1852	1,627.4	1,630.5	1,630.2	n.a.
1853	1,628.0	1,629.5	n.a.	n.a.

Sources: In table 9A.10 an attempt is made to roughly estimate of both national average heights for Dutch conscripts and three regional series of average heights for the years 1823–53.

Although the surviving Dutch height data for these years is generally considered to be a reliable approximation of all Dutch boys aged 19 3/4 years (see, e.g., B. Koerhuis and W. v. Mulken, "De militieregisters 1815–1922" [The registers of the militia 1815–1922], in *Broncommentaren,* vol. 5 [The Hague, 1986]), the data differ both in availability and quality for the different provinces. For the province of Drenthe, complete individual data are available, so for this particular province average heights, median heights, and percentage of undersized conscripts (both registered and measured) can be derived from the individual data. This was done by Tassenaar for the heights of conscripts in Drenthe in the period 1821–50 on the basis of the "Archive of the Governor of the King," *Provincial Archive of Drenthe* (inv. no. 0040: f 450015–45005). The data for the other provinces are less detailed. For most provinces (Nourd-Holland, Zeeland, and Nourd-Brabant) only the percentage of undersized registered conscripts is available. For the provinces of Utrecht and Groningen, percentages of both measured and registered undersized conscripts are available.

Table 9A.10   (continued)

Essentially, the different series of average heights in table 9A.10 were derived by relating the available series of average heights and percentages of measured and registered undersized conscripts by ordinary regression.

Figures for Groningen from Zeeman (1861, 697, row 11).

Figures for Nourd-Brabant from J. A. Boogaard, "Verslag namens de commissie voor statistiek der Nederlandsche maatschappij tot bevordering van de geneeskunst," *Nederlandsch Tijdschrift voor Geneeskunst* (1859) 3:475, col. 10.

Figures for Nourd-Holland from J. A. Boogaard, "Bijdrage tot de militie-statistiek der provincie Zeeland," *Nederlandsch Tijdschrift voor de Geneeskunst* (1868) 12:317.

Figures for Utrecht were kindly made available through J. J. de Beer. The original data can be found in the Municipal Archive of Utrecht, "Staat der ingeschrevenen in de provincie Utrecht voor de Nationale militie en der vrijgestelden wegens gebrek aan lengte 1824–1851" (inv. no.: 853).

Figures for Zeeland from Boogaard (1868, 315, col. 5).

Col. (2), Five-year moving average of estimated average heights of Dutch conscripts in millimeters (conscription years): The series is a 5-year moving average of a weighted yearly series of data for the provinces of Groningen, Drenthe, Nourd-Brabant, Nourd-Holland, Zeeland, and Utrecht, with the yearly relative number of conscripts per province as weights.

Col. (3), Five-year moving average of estimated average heights of conscripts in millimeters (conscription years) in traditional rural regions: The series is a 5-year moving average of a weighted yearly series of data for the provinces of Drenthe, Nourd-Brabant, and Utrecht, with the yearly relative number of conscripts per province as weights.

Col. (4), Five-year moving average of estimated average heights of conscripts in millimeters (conscription years) in modern agricultural regions: The series is a 5-year moving average of a weighted yearly series of data for the provinces of Groningen and Zeeland, with the yearly relative number of conscripts per province as weights.

Col. (5), Five-year moving average of estimated average heights of conscripts in millimeters (conscription years) in urban regions: The series is a 5-year moving average of a yearly series of data for the province of Nourd-Holland.

References

Brinkman, H.-J., J. W. Drukker, and B. Slot. 1988. Height and income: A new method for the estimation of historical national income series. *Explorations in Economic History* 25:227–64 (a more elaborated version was published in Dutch, in *Economisch- en Sociaal-Historisch Jaarboek* 51 [1988]: 35–79).

Brinkman, H.-J., J. W. Drukker, and S. J. Stuurop. 1989. The representativeness of the Dutch military registers as a source for quantitative history. *Netherlands Economic History Archive: Economic and Social History in the Netherlands* 1:149–70.

Coronel, S., Sr. 1862a. De bevolking van Hilversum in verband tot hare industrie: Eene statistische studie (The population of the village of Hilversum in relation to its industry: A statistical study). *Nederlandsch Tijdschrift voor Geneeskunst* 6:651–64.

———. 1862b. De Hilversumsche industrie: Een hygiënisch-sociale studie (Industry in the village of Hilversum: A hygienistic-social study). *Nederlandsch Tijdschrift voor Geneeskunst* 6:433–47.

———. 1862c. De ligchamelijke ontwikkkeling in verband tot den maatschappelijken toestand en den arbeid der kinderen (The physical development in relation to social conditions and child labor). *Schat der Gezondheid* 5:198.

Cramer, J. S. 1988. De vruchten en de boom (The tree and its fruits). *Economisch-Statistische Berichten* 73:607.

de Meere, J. M. M. 1982. *Economische ontwikkeling en levensstandaard in Nederland gedurende de eerste helft van de 19e eeuw* (Economic development and standard of living in the Netherlands during the first half of the nineteenth century). The Hague: Nijhoff.

de Vries, J. 1974. *The Dutch rural economy in the Golden Age, 1500–1700.* New Haven, Conn.: Yale University Press.

———. 1981. *Barges and capitalism: Passenger transportation in the Dutch economy, 1632–1839.* Utrecht: HES.

de Vries, Joh. 1959. *De achteruitgang der republiek in de 18e eeuw* (The decline of the republic in the eighteenth century). Leyden: Stenfert Kroese.

Griffiths, R. T. 1979. *Industrial retardation in the Netherlands.* The Hague: Nijhoff.

———. 1980. *Achterlijk, achter of anders? Aspecten van de economische ontwikkeling van Nederland in de 19e eeuw* (Retarded, backward or different? Aspects of the economic development of the Netherlands in the nineteenth century). Inaugural lecture, Free University of Amsterdam.

Groote, Peter. 1995. *Kapitaalvorming in infrastructuur in Nederland, 1800–1913* (Capital formation in infrastructure in the Netherlands). Capelle a.d. Ijssel: Labyrint.

Horlings, E. 1993. De ontwikkeling van de Nederlandse bevolking in de negentiende eeuw, 1795–1913 (The development of the Dutch population in the nineteenth century, 1795–1913). Free University of Amsterdam. Unpublished manuscript.

———. 1995. The economic development of the Dutch service sector, 1800–1850 (Reconstruction of national accounts of the Netherlands). Doctoral diss., University of Utrecht.

Horlings, E., J. P. Smits, and J. L. van Zanden. 1995. Het Nederlands Nationaal product, 1807 en 1850–1913: De eerste resultaten (The Dutch national product, 1807 and 1850–1913). University of Utrecht. Unpublished manuscript.

Houwaert, E. S. 1993. Medische statistiek (Medical statistics). In *Geschiedenis van de Techniek in Nederland, De Wording van een Moderne Samenleving.* Vol. 2, *Gezondheid en Openbare Hygiëne; Waterstaat en Infrastructuur; Papier, Druk en Communicatie,* ed. H. W. Lintsen et al. Zutphen: Walburg Pers.

Maddison, A. 1982. *Phases of capitalist development.* Oxford: Oxford University Press.

Mandemakers, C. A., and J. L. van Zanden. 1990. Lengte van lotelingen en nationaal inkomen: Schijnrelaties en misvattingen (Height of conscripts and national income: Spurious relations and fallacies). *Economisch- en Sociaal-Historisch Jaarboek* 53:1–23.

———. 1993. The height of conscripts and national income: Apparent relations and misconceptions. *Explorations in Economic History* 30:81–97.

Mokyr, J. 1975. Capital, labor, and the delay of the Industrial Revolution in the Netherlands. *Economisch- en Sociaal-Historisch Jaarboek* 37:280–99.

———. 1976. *Industrialization in the Low Countries.* New Haven, Conn.: Yale University Press.

———. 1988. Is there still life in the pessimist case? Consumption during the industrial revolution, 1790–1850. *Journal of Economic History* 48:69–92.

Mokyr, J., and C. Ó Gráda. 1994. The heights of the British and the Irish circa 1800–1815: Evidence from recruits to the East India Company's army. In *Stature, living standards and economic development: Essays in anthropometric history,* ed. J. Komlos, 39–59. Chicago: University of Chicago Press.

Noordegraaf, L. 1980. *Daglonen in Alkmaar, 1500–1850* (Daily wages in the town of Alkmaar, 1500–1850). Vol. 9. Apparaat voor de Geschiedenis van Holland. Haarlem: Historische Vereniging Holland.

Nusteling, H. P. H. 1985. *Welvaart en werkgelegenheid in Amsterdam, 1540–1860* (Wealth and employment in Amsterdam, 1540–1860). Amsterdam: Bataafsche Leeuw.

Oppers, V. M. 1963. Analyse van de acceleratie van de menselijke lengtegroei door bepaling van het tijdstip der groeifasen (Analysis of the acceleration of the growth of human stature by the assessment in time of different growth phases). Doctoral diss., University of Amsterdam.

Paping, R. 1995. Voor een handvol stuivers: Werken, verdienen en besteden: De levens-standaard van boeren, arbeiders en middenstanders op de Groninger klei, 1770–1860 (For a handful of dimes: Working, earning, and spending: The standard of living of farmers, laborers and retailers on the alluvial soils of Groningen, 1770–1860). Doctoral diss., University of Groningen.

Rapport der Commissie belast met het onderzoek naar den toestand der kinderen in fabrieken. 1869–72. Second Issue. The Hague: Ministry of Home Affairs.

Sandberg, L., and R. Steckel. 1994. Was industrialization hazardous to your health? Not in Sweden! Paper presented to the NBER preconference on Health and Welfare during Industrialization, Cambridge, Mass., 11–12 July.

Twarog, S. 1994. Heights and living standards in Germany, 1850–1940: The case of Württemberg. Paper presented to the NBER preconference on Health and Welfare during Industrialization, Cambridge, Mass., 11–12 July.

van der Poel, J. M. G. 1972. De Landbouw in de Bataafse Tijd: Illusie en Werkelijkheid (Agriculture in the Batavic period: Illusion and reality). *Economisch- en Sociaal-Historisch Jaarboek* 35:42–76.

van Meerten, M. A. 1990. Développement économique et stature en France, XIXe–XXe siècles (Economic development and stature in France, nineteenth and twentieth centuries). *Annales: Économies, Sociétés, Civilisations* 45:755–77.

van Stuijvenberg, J. H., and J. E. J. de Vrijer. 1980. Prices, population and national income in the Netherlands, 1620–1978. Research Memorandum of the University of Amsterdam no. 8101. Amsterdam: University of Amsterdam.

Vermaas, A. 1995. The development of wages and income inequality in the Netherlands. Doctoral diss., University of Utrecht.

Zeeman, J. 1861. Rapport van de Commissie voor de Statistiek over de lotelingen van de provincie Groningen van 1836–1861 (Report from the Committee for Statistics on the conscripts of the province of Groningen from 1836 to 1861). *Nederlandsch Tijdschrift voor Geneeskunst* 5:691–723.

10 Height, Health, and Economic Growth in Australia, 1860–1940

Greg Whitwell, Christine de Souza, and Stephen Nicholas

Australian economic development in the period 1860–1940 is conventionally divided into two starkly contrasting phases. The first was the long boom of 1860–90. This was a "golden age" of economic progress. Australia acquired the epithet "the workingman's paradise." By 1890, according to Angus Maddison, Australia had the highest real GDP per capita in the world (Maddison 1977, 126). The second phase, from 1890 to 1940, saw things go terribly wrong. In the 1890s Australia experienced a prolonged and deep depression. The end of the decade saw the onset of perhaps the worst drought in recorded Australian history. Recovery eventually began about 1904. Its sudden termination coincided with the outbreak of World War I. Economic growth was disappointing for most of the 1920s. As with just about every other country, the situation deteriorated further and much more markedly during the depression of the 1930s. Only after World War II did Australia begin to enjoy again the sort of prosperity experienced during the first long boom of 1860–90.

When output figures are taken as a guide, living standards improved markedly from 1860 to 1890 but grew much more slowly, or may even have stagnated, in the period from 1890 to 1940. In recent years there has been debate among Australian economic historians about whether living standards did in fact follow such a pattern. Discussion has focused in particular on whether living standards did stagnate between 1890 and 1940.

Greg Whitwell is associate professor in the Department of Business Development and Corporate History, University of Melbourne. Stephen Nicholas is professor and head of the Department of Business Development and Corporate History, University of Melbourne. Christine de Souza was a lecturer in the Department of Economics, Monash University.

This project was funded by the Faculty of Economics and Commerce, University of Melbourne. The authors gratefully acknowledge the support of the Melbourne branches of the Australian Archives and the Department of Veterans' Affairs (DVA), especially the efforts of Len Bergman (DVA), the computer and computing assistance of Doug Belford, and the research assistance of Alexandra Bowen, Geoff Fraser, Phillip Grinter, Sue Kimberley, and Paul Noonan.

379

Inevitably, questions have been raised about the adequacy of real GDP per capita as a measure of economic well-being. It remains true, however, that all those participating in the Australian debate take as their starting point the conventional output or income data. In providing a more accurate measure of changes in living standards, they have chosen to do more than describe trends in a variety of "social indicators." Rather they have produced, by diverse means, an "augmented" output series. This has been done by imputing a money value either to some of the partial indicators (such as infant mortality and improvements in the housing stock) or to the nonmarket activities excluded from the national accounts and then adding these to the output data. Different methods of augmenting the same output series lead to contradictory results: one procedure will show that living standards grew faster than the growth of real GDP per person, while another shows that they rose more slowly than the growth of GDP. Jackson is correct when he says that "this introduces an arbitrary and discretionary element into the scale of the numbers that are produced when an attempt is made to convert GDP into a more direct measure of well-being" (1992, 26).

This chapter makes a novel contribution to the Australian debate by offering an alternative approach to, and index of, changes in living standards. We eschew the conventional economist's measures and their augmented variants. Instead we present anthropometric data on the height of men and women enlisting in the Australian army during the Boer War and World Wars I and II. In doing so we make use of an approach that has attracted increasing interest among social scientists in a number of countries but that, until now, has been little used in analyzing trends in Australian living standards.

10.1   The Workingman's Paradise?

The point has already been made that economic historians conventionally describe the Australian economy between 1861 and 1891 as being remarkably prosperous. Unemployment was low, wages were high by contemporary international standards, and the fruits of prosperity were shared more or less equally by Australians as a whole. Occasionally, economic activity slackened, but recessions were neither deep nor protracted. Overall, it is argued, the Australian economy experienced rapid and sustained growth. Coghlan, in his pioneering work on labor and industry in Australia, argued that while the 1860s were a time of some difficulty for industrial labor, the 1870s and 1880s were years of prosperity. "Wages were rising, and, with few and short intervals, employment was abundant. It appeared as if a certain standard of life had been established definitely for Australian industrial workers, far and above that of Great Britain" (Coghlan [1918] 1969, 1239–40).

Implicit in the notion that Australia was a "workingman's paradise" are three different ideas. First, Australians were thought to be living in greater comfort than working men in comparable occupations in the mother country. Second, the term implied that there were greater opportunities for Australian workers and their families to improve their lot and that these opportunities were achievable with greater ease than in Britain. Third, such opportunities were open to all. The contemporary view, then, was that both relatively and absolutely Australians had a better standard of living. As Shirley Fitzgerald puts it, "In both popular and learned observations about nineteenth century Australian society, two assumptions are firmly entrenched: firstly that the society was wealthy and secondly that it was egalitarian. These two ideas are seen to be compatible, with the one 'causing' the other, through the medium of mobility" (1987, 6). Contemporary observers might have sometimes witnessed the existence of both rural and urban poverty, but this was believed to be temporary.

Macarthy argued that the generally high per capita living standards during the 1860s, 1870s, and 1880s were made possible by "the relationship of scarce labour with the remarkable wealth of Australia's natural endowments" (1970, 56–57). Capital-intensive but non-labor-intensive exploitation of these resources made scarce labor highly productive in the primary industries. The resultant high wages "spread to other groups of workers" because of the unskilled nature of most work (Macarthy 1970, 57). Macarthy insisted that both unskilled and skilled labor received "extraordinarily high" wages. "In the seventies and eighties, railway workers, itinerant pastoral workers and miners were paid 7s or 8s a day," almost twice as much as their British counterparts (Macarthy 1970, 57). He also argued that differentials between skilled and unskilled workers were comparatively narrow. Pre-1850 differentials were broken down by the scarcity of labor (Connell and Irving 1980, 130). More recent research has confirmed these findings. Mark Thomas's assessment is that for "the last quarter of the nineteenth century, at least, Australia was experiencing a reduction in wage dispersion, distorted only by the severity of the depression of the 1890s" (1991, 170).

The concept of the workingman's paradise has been enduring, and research by modern historians and economic historians has tended to perpetuate this rosy view of the second half of the last century. During the past 20 years or so, however, a certain amount of revisionist work has been carried out, although it is not possible to speak of a full-blown standard of living debate. Acknowledging the shortcomings of conventional economic indicators of well-being, the revisionists' work has tended to concentrate on challenging the assumptions underlying the concept of the workingman's paradise. With the exception of Graeme Snooks's work on estimating gross community income (see below), no attempt has been made by the revisionists to rework the output and income data for the period 1860–90.

The level of home ownership was one of the first issues to be tackled. Noel Butlin had argued in 1962 that during the long boom more than 50 percent of houses in Australia were owner occupied (1962, 259–60). More recent research, however, shows that the ideal of home ownership was realized only by a minority of urban dwellers, although it was much more common outside the metropolitan areas (Jackson 1970; Dingle and Merrett 1972; Davison 1978, 175–89). It remains true, however, that from an international perspective Australian home-ownership rates were high; they were certainly higher than in major British cities, and there were few cities in the United States that could match Australian home-ownership rates (see Frost 1991, 123–26).

It could be argued that the level of home ownership is only of peripheral importance in determining trends in living standards. Clearly, home ownership was an important ideal. It signified the acquisition of a certain amount of wealth and status as well as independence. Housing quality, however, is a better indicator of living standards than housing tenure. Would people be better off if they owned or were in the process of paying for houses that were poorly constructed and surrounded by equally insanitary properties?

Urban historians have gathered an impressive amount of evidence on the quality of housing in Australia. For the most part, however, the research has been done in terms of individual cities; few attempts have been made to provide an overview for Australia as a whole. Nevertheless, two things seem reasonably clear. First, great variations in the quality of housing existed both in individual metropolitan areas and in country areas. Second, Australian houses, whether owner occupied or not, were overall much more spacious, and Australian cities tended to be much less crowded, than was the case in other countries (Frost 1991).

In addition to the issue of home ownership, revisionists have questioned whether incomes rose as quickly during the long boom as is commonly assumed. More especially, they have cast doubts on whether the rise in incomes was something experienced by all occupational groups. Before proceeding, it needs to be said that money incomes are a very inadequate proxy for the standard of living. This is so because, among other things, variations in family size, goods and services received in kind from an employer or from family, and the value of the time family members, such as wives and children, spend in nonmarket activities also need to be accounted for (Travers and Richardson 1993, chap. 1). Unfortunately, these other aspects of income are difficult to measure for historical populations. Economic historians have had to make do with information on incomes earned from market activities only. The work of Graeme Snooks (1994), mentioned below, is a notable exception.

Traditionally, economic historians have relied on officially published wage rates for information on incomes during the nineteenth century. Lee and Fahey have argued, however, that such evidence presents a distorted picture in the sense that actual earnings differed markedly from published wage rates. Their work has strongly attacked the conventional assumption that during the long boom labor markets were tight and hence that full employment prevailed (Lee and Fahey 1986, 2). For many workers, they argued, actual earnings varied considerably from what might be deduced from wage rates published in the colonies' yearbooks and statistical registers. Instability and insecurity of employment were major characteristics of most jobs because of the prevalence of casual labor. Shirley Fitzgerald said of Sydney that "within the construction industry the normal fluctuations in the building cycle were accentuated by uneven rates of immigration and by a large erratic public building programme. Much manufacturing was undercapitalized, and used labour on a daily basis. Port work is always seasonal and irregular, but more so if the bulk of the cargo being shipped is primary produce of a limited range, and the pastoral industry impinged on the Sydney economy not only because of its widely varying labour requirements, but because the processing of its raw materials was also seasonal" (1987, 202).

In the country, too, much work was casual. Pastoral stations, for example, might have a small number of more or less permanently employed boundary riders and stockriders, but a large proportion of a station's workforce worked on day or piece rates or on contract (Fox 1991, 35).

Lee and Fahey maintained that the pronounced seasonal variability of work was a fundamental cause of the extent of casual labor. For many industries summer was a time of intense activity. Activity then slackened, and by winter a trough was reached. Lee and Fahey also confirmed the flow-on effects of the seasonal characteristics of the rural production cycle on the demand for labor at the ports and by urban industries. Not all work was subject to seasonal fluctuations to the same extent. The service industries, clerical occupations, and the professions were least affected by it, and in these industries greater security of employment was the norm, although, for example in the case of clerks, not always at better rates of pay than for those of the casual labor force (Kingston 1988, 48).

Apart from seasonal fluctuations, Lee and Fahey also found instability of employment because of the characteristics of Australian manufacturing, which until the late 1880s "was characterised by labour intensity, low levels of capitalisation, short production lead times and small inventories of stock on hand" (1986, 16). On the other hand, industries such as apparel manufacturing houses, large newspapers, highly capitalized food-processing firms, breweries, and big metalworking establishments offered more stable employment opportunities.

The unskilled faced greater job insecurity than the skilled, although skill was found not to be the sole determinant of job security. Long-standing working relationships between employer and worker or family connections were often also important. Nor was the situation static throughout the long boom. By the 1880s changes in urban manufacturing increased job opportunities for unapprenticed, unskilled juveniles and for women, who were frequently employed on a casual basis. These jobs were created often at the expense of skilled tradesmen.

Lee and Fahey suggested that temporary unemployment, or indeed underemployment, was a fact of life for many Australians during the second half of the nineteenth century and that this phenomenon increased in magnitude as the century wore on. Their analysis suggests that even though the differential between published wage rates for the skilled and unskilled may have been narrow, the gap in actual earnings between the two broad groups of workers may have been larger than previously thought.

The large variation in hours and hence earnings emphasized by recent historical work has made any assessment of material living standards much more complex. It has also made generalizations about the living standard experienced by different socioeconomic groups more problematic.

10.2   Inadequacies of the Economist's Measures: The Debate on What Happened to Australian Living Standards, 1890–1940

In 1983 Ian McLean and Jonathon Pincus pointed to a conundrum about Australian economic development in the period 1890–1940.[1] The economist's favored summary measure of economic well-being—real income or product per capita—suggested an extremely poor performance, when compared both to other advanced countries and to Australia's growth performance before and after this 50-year phase. Angus Maddison's estimates suggest that from 1890 to 1940 Australia's growth in real GDP compared favorably with other advanced countries. They indicate also, however, that Australia experienced both the most rapid population growth and the slowest increase in real income *per capita* among the developed countries (Maddison 1977, 103–31). Real GDP per capita, measured in 1966–67 dollars, rose from $915 in 1891 to only $1,045 in 1938–39. Likewise, real consumption expenditure per capita, measured in 1966–67 dollars, reached its peak of $775 in 1889, virtually identical to the $773 achieved 50 years later in 1938–39. While there was much volatility between 1889 and 1938–39, the twentieth-century peak achieved in 1926–27 was a mere 13.5 percent above the 1889 figure (McLean and Pincus 1983, 195).

This evidence suggests that Australian living standards may have stagnated between 1890 and 1940. But if that were so, McLean and Pincus argued, why was it that a host of other indicators indicated unequivocally that living standards had improved substantially during this period? What should we make of the fact, for example, that the life expectancy of an Australian male born in 1890 was only 50 years but that of an Australian male born in 1940 was 65 years? And what about the substantial reduction in the average working week for urban Australians, from 52–54 hours in 1890 to 45 hours in 1939? There was also a marked improvement in the quality of the housing stock. Furthermore, by the late 1930s one in ten Australians had a telephone, one in eight a motor vehicle, and one in six a radio. In 1890 these consumer durables were either nonexistent or at best something to exercise the imagination (McLean and Pincus 1983, 193).[2]

1. An earlier version of the paper, containing a full set of the data on which the 1983 article is based, is McLean and Pincus (1982).

2. In their 1982 paper, McLean and Pincus provide a more comprehensive analysis of these, as well as of a number of other, partial indicators of living standards than is done in the 1983 article.

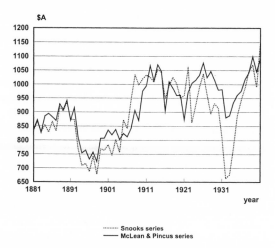

Fig. 10.1   GDP per capita, Australia, 1880–1940
Sources: Adapted from Snooks (1994, 180–81) and McLean and Pincus (1982, 29–30).

McLean and Pincus sought to reconcile two contradictory stories: that told by the economist's measures on the one hand and by the partial indicators of the quality of life on the other. The first step was to revise Noel Butlin's estimates of domestic product. A problem with the Butlin series was that consumption and its deflator had been arrived at residually. By using an alternative and, in their opinion, more appropriate deflator, namely retail price indexes, McLean and Pincus argued that the trend growth in real GDP per person, 1891 to 1938–39, increased by 0.2 percent per annum. (The revised estimates of real GDP per capita are shown in fig. 10.1, where they are compared with another, more recent, reestimate by Graeme Snooks.) The next step was to deal with the reduction in weekly working hours, which they calculated was of the order of 18 percent. By assuming that workers had exchanged leisure for the income they would have earned had they worked longer hours, and hence that leisure was "purchased" at a marginal cost equal to the hourly wage rate, and by generalizing from the paid labor force to the population as a whole, McLean and Pincus argued that real GDP per capita should be increased by 18 percent for the period 1890 to 1938–39, which represented an annual average increase of 0.3 percent. They used a similar procedure in trying to determine the effect on GDP of an apparent decline in retirement ages. The 1891 census showed that the labor force participation rate of males did not fall below 80 percent until age 75, whereas the 1933 and 1947 censuses showed that the fall began at about age 63. McLean and Pincus argued that if the 1939 aged population had had the 1890 labor force participation rate, then labor input would have been about 11 percent higher than it was. This represented an increase in the annual growth rate of real GDP of 0.2 percent. Finally, there was the issue of the increase in life expectancy, which rose for men by about 25 percent in the period from 1890 to 1940. It followed that those men aged 20 in 1940 could consume 25 percent more over their lifetime than their counterparts in 1890 just by living longer. The question was, What was the appropriate rate to discount the value of the extra future years of consumption? If the discount rate is set at 4 percent, McLean and Pincus argued, then the average annual growth in real GDP, 1891 to 1938–39, increased by 0.2 percent. A zero discount rate increased it by 0.4 percent.

Depending on the discount rate used for additional life expectancy, McLean and Pincus's estimates suggest an annual average growth rate in real GDP per capita, 1891 to 1938–39, of either 1.5 or 1.7 percent, which compares with measured real GDP per capita growth of only 0.6 percent. The augmented measure might lead one to conclude that living standards did not stagnate between 1890 and 1940. The difficulty, however, as McLean and Pincus themselves acknowledged, is that the augmented growth rate cannot be compared with growth rates in either the first long boom of 1860–90 or the second long boom of 1940–73. There is a possibility, they said, "that adjustments similar to those we have performed might yield proportionately higher growth rates for the other two periods distinguished, leaving the 1890–1940 period relatively stagnant" (1983, 201).

Not surprisingly, the McLean and Pincus paper has had its fair share of critical commentators. R. V. Jackson pointed to a number of conceptual and technical difficulties in the paper, notably some instances of double counting. His contribution was largely negative, in that he was content to point to weaknesses in McLean and Pincus's analysis but did not offer an alternative measure of changes in living standards. His assessment was that "the characterisation of the decades after 1890 as a period of relatively slow growth in living standards can be allowed to stand, though the relative rate of improvement may have been somewhat greater than is suggested by the conventional national accounting measures" (1992, 44). His overall verdict was that

the prospect of constructing a persuasive summary indicator of wellbeing . . . remains remote. Given the difficulties and arbitrary procedures that are necessarily involved, and given the inevitable partiality of whatever aggregate indicator is developed in this context, it might be more fruitful to attempt something less ambitious. In particular, we would do well to concentrate on the development of measures which aim to do no more than show the change in the volume of economic activity that is relevant to wellbeing. GDP already provides us with an indicator of market output and there is good reason to extend this measure to include an imputation for the nonmarket work which produces output for consumption within the household. This would not pretend to measure the overall level of wellbeing but would serve as an index of both market and nonmarket production of the final goods and services which contribute to wellbeing. (1992, 44)

This is precisely what Graeme Snooks has done. Snooks provided estimates of what he calls "gross community income" (GCI) for the period 1800–1990.

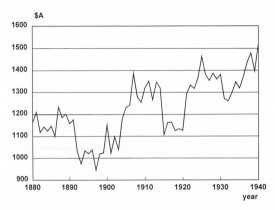

Fig. 10.2   Gross community income per capita, Australia, 1880–1940
Source: Adapted from Snooks (1994, 172–73).

He defines GCI as "a measure of the total economic activity that takes place in both the household and market sectors on an annual basis. It is an extension of the concept of GDP to the Total Economy." The market sector is divided, following convention, into the private and public sectors. The household sector refers to "the production of economic goods and services that could be marketed, but are not" (Snooks 1994, 267).[3] The total economy comprises the household, private, and public sectors.

Snooks is unequivocal about the significance of his estimates of GCI in interpreting economic growth and community living standards in the period 1890–1940: "No matter how much some scholars wish to revive the status of the period 1890 to 1939, particularly in relation to the second half of the nineteenth century, it must be seen as adding little of a permanent nature to average material standards of Australian society" (1994, 25; see also 135). GCI per capita grew by only 0.3 percent per annum from 1889 to 1939, whereas it grew by 1.2 percent per annum from 1861 to 1889, and 2.9 percent per annum from 1946 to 1974. (Fig. 10.2 shows Snooks's estimates of real GCI per capita for the period 1860–1940.) And if one considers GCI *per household,* there was in fact a decline of 0.2 percent per annum from 1889 to 1939, compared with a rise of 1.7 percent per annum from 1861 to 1889. GCI per household, Snooks insisted, is "the most appropriate measure of average living standards" (1994, 25).

Snooks did concede that the quality of life, as indicated by mortality, morbidity, and leisure, improved significantly during this period. But it is important, he argued, "to emphasize the fact that the acquisition of material goods

3. Snooks cited as examples "the preparation of meals and the associated clearing away and dishwashing, laundry, house cleaning, child-care and informal education, the production of clothing and furnishings, garden care, house repairs, and other activities such as shopping, record keeping, and payment of household accounts" (1994, 157, 267).

and services did not much improve, because it is the command over material goods and services that gives human society the resilience to survive in the longrun. In the past, societies that have failed to achieve *economic resilience*—failed to compete successfully in the race for economic power—have not survived. Economic resilience, not the acquisition of non-material gains, is the underlying objective of viable societies." "This critical issue," Snooks suggested, "appears to have been overlooked by previous scholars when discussing the issue of growth and living standards" (1994, 25).

10.3   Height and Living Standards

There is a diversity of opinion on what happened to Australian living standards in both the 1860–90 period and the 1890–1940 period. The evidence provided by some of the partial indicators appears to contradict the trends suggested by data on real income and output per capita. There is the additional difficulty that economic historians have devised a variety of different, and inconsistent, measures of augmented income levels.

An important alternative indicator that captures both the material and non-material aspects of the standard of living is the average nutritional status of a population. For the economic historian it has the virtue of permitting more specific observations about the standard of living experienced by the population as a whole as well as by population subgroups. Average nutritional status can be defined as "the outcome of the nutrient intakes since conception balanced against the demands of those nutrients for health, growth, work, play, warmth and happiness" (Floud, Wachter, and Gregory 1990, 18–19).

A study of average nutritional status, however, presents the researcher with formidable problems. On the supply side, it would require a consistent series of data containing detailed information on food consumption over time. For Australia, as for other countries, such data tend to be rare if available at all, although some valuable work has recently been carried out on the history of food and nutrition in New South Wales by Walker and Roberts (1988). For their research, Walker and Roberts drew on a wide variety of sources such as convict ration scales, rations on convict and immigrant ships, and rations in Sydney infirmaries and asylums. The dietary scales used, however, often represented the minimum nutritional intake and could therefore not say much about actual nutritional intake by individuals. On the demand side, a study of nutritional status would necessitate the construction of an index of various factors that may affect nutritional intake. In practice, this would be a near impossible task, complicated by the question of what weight to attach to the various components of total demand on nutritional intake. These might include demands made on nutritional intake for maintenance and growth of the body, to fight disease, or to maintain a high work intensity.

Fortunately, a convenient proxy exists for average nutritional status, namely, human height. It follows that height-for-age, the change in height between successive ages (velocity or rate of growth), the age at which final height is reached, and final adult height are reliable and important indexes of a country's health and nutrition (Eveleth and Tanner 1976, 1; Fogel et al. 1983). Anthropologists, biologists, and nutritionists have found each of these measures of stature to be sensitive indicators of nutritional inputs and environmental impacts during the growing years. In a sample of developed and underdeveloped countries, average height was found to be highly correlated with the log of per capita income, which suggests that factors correlated with poverty such as poor diet, hard work, and poor medical care are major sources of nutritional deprivation and slow growth (Steckel 1986, 1–7).

Height data, used in conjunction with information on wages, mortality, and morbidity, offer a new way of assessing Australian living standards. Poor nutrition, revealed during wartime shortages, may slow growth, and disease may also retard growth by impeding the absorption of nutrients and diverting nutrition to combat infection. Malnutrition and illness may interact to produce an effect on height larger than the separate effects of each in isolation (Scrimshaw 1975, 22). Catch-up growth (where velocity exceeds the average rate for a given chronological age) may follow brief periods of malnutrition, but if environmental conditions are unsatisfactory, growth may resume at no more than the normal rate. Prolonged but moderate malnutrition tends to delay and diminish the adolescent growth spurt and postpone the age at which adult height is attained. Malnutrition that is severe and chronic may substantially erode the typical growth pattern and result in permanent stunting (Steckel 1986, 1992).

Height provides a net rather than a gross measure of nutrition and depends on the nutrition available for physical growth after claims made by body maintenance, work, and other physical activity. Clearly, the economic historian must investigate work intensity, the disease environment, and the state of public health, as well as nutritional inputs, if the growth spurt and average heights are going to be used to proxy changes in male and female living standards in the past. Unfortunately, it is not possible to determine precisely when during their growing years men and women were affected by changes in their living standards, but environmental factors predominate. While genes are important determinants of individual height, studies of genetically similar and dissimilar populations under various environmental conditions show that differences in average heights across most populations are due to environmental, not genetic, factors (Steckel 1992, 16).

10.4 Data and Findings

In trying to determine trends in height, economic historians have relied principally on military data. This has been our main source as well. We have collected data on 4,676 Australian-born men enlisting for World War I and 7,025 Australian-born men recruited for World War II. We have also collected information on 3,435 Australian-born men who joined the volunteer Common-

Table 10.1   Number of Male Observations Used in Height Profiles

	Australian-Born	Victorian	Non-Victorian
Total sample	10,526	6,456	4,070
Rural	5,936	3,135	2,801
Urban	4,590	3,321	1,269

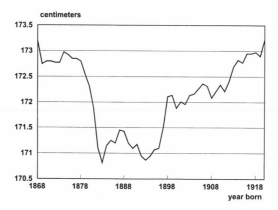

Fig. 10.3   Australian male recruits, five-year moving averages

wealth Boer War contingents of 1902. (Data sources are described in appendix A. Enlistment procedures and practices are discussed in appendix B). Although very few women enlisted in the Australian army during World War I, many thousands did so during World War II. Our data include information on 4,841 Australian-born women recruited during World War II.

Table 10.1 shows that the sample size was reduced to 10,526 once terminal heights had been determined. (Appendix C provides an analysis of the data. It discusses the results of tests for normality and describes our procedure for deciding on terminal heights.) The table also shows that there are a large number of Victorians in our sample. Victoria was, after New South Wales, the most populous colony/state in Australia in the period under review. Its capital city, Melbourne, was the largest Australian city for much of the second half of the nineteenth century and was eventually eclipsed by Sydney only during the twentieth century. The predominance of Victorians arises essentially because the World War II data are derived from the attestation papers of recruits enlisting in that state. This raises questions, of course, about the representativeness of our sample. Clearly, one has to exercise some caution in interpreting the Australia-wide trend in heights (fig. 10.3), although we do contrast the Victorian and non-Victorian trends (see fig. 10.4). There will always be difficulties in interpreting results based on birthplace. The fact that a person was

Fig. 10.4   Victorian and non-Victorian male recruits, five-year moving averages

born in Victoria does not mean, of course, that he or she then stayed there until recruitment. Indeed we know that there was a high degree of geographic mobility in Australia during the period under consideration.

Table 10.1 also provides information on the numbers of people in our sample from rural areas and from urban areas (the latter are defined as towns with 5,000 or more inhabitants in either 1901 or 1921). If it seems that there is a relatively large number of people from urban areas, it has to be remembered, as we will discuss in more detail below, that Australia was already a highly urbanized nation by the late nineteenth century. By 1901, some 51 percent of the population in eastern Australia lived in urban areas (Jackson 1977, 93). Although Victoria was the most highly urbanized state, the non-Victorian rural-born recruits are clearly overrepresented.

Figure 10.3 shows five-year moving averages of final attained height for Australian male recruits.[4] Heights were indexed to the year of birth.[5] Heights were reasonably stable during the 1870s. A dramatic decline in height occurred from 172.8 cm in 1878 to 170.8 cm in 1883. There then occurred a recovery to 171.5 cm in 1885 before a further decline to 170.9 cm in 1892–94. Heights improved rapidly after 1896, reaching a peak of 172.1 cm in 1898–99. From that point the trend continued upward but at a slower rate, reaching 173.2 cm

---

4. Five-year moving averages are used for smoothing purposes. The results do not change using single-year data.

5. More fully, our method is as follows. In the year 1888, to use this as an example, 160 recruits were born. Their average final height was 67.31 inches. We calculate an average height for each year and then smooth it by using five-year moving averages.

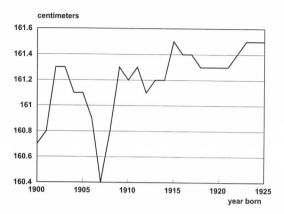

Fig. 10.5   Australian female recruits, five-year moving averages

in 1920, the last year in which we have a suitably large sample size. However, by 1920 heights had only attained the level achieved in 1867–68.[6]

Figure 10.4 shows that the general pattern for the Australian-born males in figure 10.3 was repeated for males born in Victoria and males born outside Victoria (mainly in New South Wales, Queensland, and South Australia). In both cases there is a marked decline in heights during the 1880s and a plateau that lasts until the mid-1890s, followed by a sustained recovery. However, there are also some differences. One is that there was an improvement in height in Victoria until the end of the 1870s, before a sharp fall. Outside Victoria a fall in heights was more gradual and consistent. It also began earlier, dating from the late 1860s. There are differences also in the timing and the extent of the recovery of heights.

Our sample included 4,841 Australian-born women recruited into the army during World War II. The height profile for women in figure 10.5 contrasts sharply with that for males. Heights declined in the first years of twentieth century before experiencing an upward trend, although the improvement in height was very slight and occurred very slowly. Heights rose from 63.28 inches in 1900 to reach a temporary peak of 63.52 inches in 1902 and 1903. They then fell to a minimum of 63.14 inches in 1907. By 1924, the last year for which we have an adequate sample size, a new peak of 63.60 inches had been attained. The profile of female heights suggests that, compared to men, women experienced different access to nutrients, a different disease environment, a different level of work intensity, or some combination of all three.

It is possible that the trends for male and female heights shown in figures

6. It might be argued that the major shifts evident in fig. 10.3 are associated with different recruitment regimes, where the World War I recruits replace the Boer War recruits and where the World War II recruits replace those from World War I. However, when we run five-year moving averages for each individual data set the trends are consistent.

Table 10.2   **Occupational Classification**

Occupational Groups	Occupational Dummies
1. Upper professional	Professional
2. Graziers	Professional
3. Wheat and sheep farmers	Farmers
4. Lower professional	Professional
5. Managerial professional	Professional
6. Self-employed proprietors	Professional
7. Other farmers	Farmers
8. Clerical and related workers	Semiskilled
9. Armed services and police	Semiskilled
10. Craftsmen and foremen	Skilled
11. Shop assistants	Semiskilled
12. Operative and process workers	Semiskilled
13. Drivers	Semiskilled
14. Personal, domestic, and other service worker	Unskilled
15. Miners	Unskilled
16. Farm and rural workers	Unskilled
17. Laborers	Unskilled

Source: Broom and Jones (1976).

10.3, 10.4, and 10.5 are influenced by biases in our sample. Heights may vary with occupations, urban-rural birthplace, and state/colony in which birth occurred, resulting in the height movements in these figures being statistical artifacts of the changing occupational and regional structure of our samples. To cite one of a number of possibilities, a shift in our sample from skilled to unskilled workers could account for the declining heights during the "golden age" of the 1880s. To test this hypothesis, regressions were run on height allowing for occupation, state of birth, urban-rural birthplace, and birth by quinquennia.[7] In table 10.2 occupation dummies were calculated by placing each occupation from the attestation papers into one of the 17 occupational categories from Broom and Jones (1976). These 17 occupational categories were then collapsed into five classes: professional, farmers, skilled, semiskilled, and unskilled. Urban birth location was defined as being born in a town whose population in 1901 or 1921 was greater than 5,000. The state of birth is recorded on the attestation papers.

Regression results on the entire male data set in table 10.3 show that composition effects by occupation and state do not disturb the period effects evident in figures 10.3 and 10.4.[8] The excluded groups in the regression were men born before 1871 in the professional and farmer classes for all states except New South Wales and Victoria. Skilled, semiskilled, and unskilled men were sig-

---

7. The difference in the number of observations in the first and second columns is explained mostly by the exclusion of Boer War recruits from the second column. Part of the difference is due also to a lack of full information.

8. Note that there was no evidence on urban-rural birthplace for Boer War recruits.

Table 10.3 **Regression Model for Composition Effects**

	Regression 1: All Data (1)	World War I and II Males (2)	Females (3)
Urban		−0.19	−0.16
		(0.083)	(0.097)
Skilled	−0.48	−0.39	
	(0.117)	(0.143)	
Semiskilled	−0.40	−0.42	
	(0.105)	(0.126)	
Unskilled	−0.62	−0.66	
	(0.102)	(0.124)	
Farm laborers	−0.38	−0.51	
	(0.134)	(0.182)	
Clerical/office			−0.21
			(0.141)
Birth 71–75	−0.18		
	(0.16)		
Birth 76–80	0.09		
	(0.158)		
Birth 81–85	−0.80		
	(0.195)		
Birth 86–90	−0.62	−0.03	
	(0.178)	(0.158)	
Birth 91–96	−0.85	−0.24	
	(0.163)	(0.138)	
Birth 96–00	−0.19	0.41	
	(0.222)	(0.138)	
Birth 01–05	−0.15	0.45	
	(0.188)	(0.172)	
Birth 06–10	−0.20	0.40	
	(0.171)	(0.151)	
Birth 11–15	0.03	0.49	
	(0.141)	(0.127)	
Birth 15–19			0.23
			(0.158)
Birth 16+	0.19	0.70	
	(0.140)	(0.121)	
Birth 20+			0.11
			(0.1136)
VIC	−0.17	−0.10	0.16
	(0.090)	(0.115)	(0.145)
NSW	−0.13	−0.03	
	(0.106)	(0.142)	
Intercept	68.47	67.92	63.54
	(0.164)	(0.156)	(0.205)
R^2	0.013	0.013	0.011
N	10,364	8,191	3,372

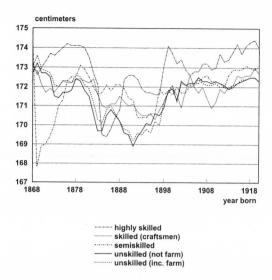

Fig. 10.6   Height by class, five-year moving averages

nificantly shorter than professionals and farmers. This is consistent with figure 10.6, which plots the five-year moving average of each of the occupational dummies. The state dummies were not significant, although recruits born in New South Wales were shorter, and recruits born in Victoria were taller, than recruits from other states. Allowing for occupation and state of birth, the negative and statistically significant quinquennial dummies show declining heights for men born between 1879 and 1893. Although heights rose continuously from 1894, the average height of recruits born after 1894 did not reach the average height of recruits born before 1880 until 1906.

Regressions using the World War I and II data are presented in column (2) of table 10.3. The excluded groups in the regression were rural-born professionals and farmers born before 1886 in all states except New South Wales and Victoria. Men born in urban areas were significantly shorter than those born in rural area. Furthermore, skilled, semiskilled, and unskilled men were significantly shorter than professionals and farmers, the excluded groups. The state dummies were not significant. Allowing for composition effects, the quinquennial dummies are negative (but insignificant) for men born before 1896 and positive and significant for the post-1896 birth year quinquennial coefficients. These results are consistent with the five-year moving averages of World War I and II heights in figure 10.3, where average heights fell before 1896 before rising until 1919.

The final regression in table 10.3 presents results from the female recruits. The urban birthplace coefficient was the expected negative sign, but insignificant. Victorian-born women were taller than women from the rest of Australia, although this coefficient is not statistically significant either. The quinquennial dummies were not significant, with women's heights stagnant through the whole period, which is consistent with the five-year moving averages in figure 10.3.

Allowing for composition effects, all the regressions in table 10.3 confirm the time profiles displayed in figures 10.3, 10.4, and 10.5, which shows that the movements in male and female heights were not an artifact of changes in occupational groupings or the in mix of urban-rural or state birthplace.

10.5   Additional Anthropometric Evidence: Heights of Schoolchildren

Anthropometric work conducted early this century confirms a marked improvement in height in the first two decades of the twentieth century. It also demonstrates, inter alia, that Australian children were taller than their British counterparts and that rural children were taller than those in urban areas. In New South Wales in 1918–19, observations were made of the heights and weights of 112,259 boys and 104,211 girls. One of the things revealed in the survey was the pronounced degree to which children attending schools in rural districts had a bigger physique than those living in metropolitan areas or in large country towns. The children were also classified into parentage groups. It was found that children with "both Australian" parents were both heavier and taller than those with parents "one Australian, one foreign." The latter were in turn heavier and taller than those with parents "both foreign," with "foreign" being defined as outside Australia or New Zealand (Cumpston 1989, 101, 102).

Of particular interest for our purposes are two surveys conducted by the Department of Education of Victoria in 1912 and in 1922. In the former, the heights and weights of 5,833 boys and 5,631 girls were recorded. In the latter, observations were made of 14,561 boys and 11,966 girls. The results are shown in table 10.4. What stands out is that for each of the ages between 4 and 16, the 1922 children were taller than those of 1912.

Drawing on the New South Wales studies of schoolchildren, Sutton went on to call attention to "the curious and important fact that the child born in Australia of Australian born parents is taller and heavier than the boy born in Australia of overseas parents, though both have lived in Australia all their lives. Both definitely exceed the immigrant child in stature and weight, and the immigrant is above the average of the homeland." "In spite of many discussions of Australian characteristics," he continued, "that is almost the only definite fact yet recorded concerning the Australian child. We are growing them bigger and better. . . . The Australian children of overseas parents were in the majority in school in the nineties, the Australian of Australian parentage was in the majority in 1911, while the Australian of Australian grandparents is beginning to make a definite appearance" (1931, 614).

Table 10.4   **Average Height (in inches) of Victorian Schoolchildren, 1912 and 1922**

	1912				1922			
	Elementary School		High School		Elementary School		High School	
Age	Boys	Girls	Boys	Girls	Boys	Girls	Boys	Girls
4					40.4	39.9		
5	41.0	40.5			42.2	42.0		
6	42.7	42.2			44.3	44.0		
7	45.0	44.5			46.5	45.9		
8	47.2	46.5			48.3	47.8		
9	49.0	48.5			50.3	49.9		
10	50.7	50.0			52.2	51.7		
11	52.2	51.5			54.1	53.9	55.4	56.5
12	54.5	54.0			55.5	56.2	55.8	58.3
13	55.5	56.5			57.6	58.3	58.8	60.7
14	57.5	59.0	60.5	61.5	59.6	60.0	61.5	62.0
15			63.2	61.7	61.5	67.5	63.8	63.0
16			64.5	62.0			65.5	63.7
17			65.1	62.6			67.1	63.7
18			66.3	62.7			67.6	65.0

10.6   Mortality and Morbidity

10.6.1   Mortality

It is important to supplement the height data by information on other measures of physical well-being, especially mortality and morbidity data. There are difficulties in interpreting changes in mortality rates over time since death rates are affected by the age structure of the population. Mortality rates as between different social groups for our period are not known, but Ruzicka has argued that

> mortality has taken its toll of lives in an inequitable fashion. Class differentials have existed in Australia as in other Western societies, though the evidence as to the extent of the mortality effect of such differentials is less well documented than, for instance, in the United Kingdom. Although sufficient information and hard data are even more limited, it may be confidently surmised that higher mortality has prevailed among the less privileged, less formally skilled, less educated and less fully-waged people. This area has been so far inadequately explored in Australia although it is likely that the lower social classes are more at risk from occupational diseases and accidents, and have been less quick to relinquish dietary habits and life styles now recognised as hazardous. (1989, 46)

Table 10.5   Australia: Life Expectancy at Selected Ages, 1870–81 to 1932–34

Age	1870–81	1881–90	1891–1900	1901–10	1920–22	1932–34
			Males			
0	46.47	47.20	51.08	55.20	59.15	63.48
10	49.18	48.86	51.43	53.53	56.01	58.02
20	40.80	40.58	42.81	44.74	46.99	48.81
30	33.27	33.64	35.11	36.52	38.44	39.90
40	26.20	26.50	27.65	28.56	30.05	31.11
50	19.80	19.74	20.45	21.16	22.20	22.83
60	13.79	13.77	13.99	14.35	15.08	15.57
70	8.88	8.82	8.90	8.67	9.26	9.60
80	5.39	5.11	5.00	4.96	5.00	5.22
			Females			
0	49.64	50.84	54.76	58.84	63.31	67.14
10	51.67	51.95	54.46	56.38	59.20	61.02
20	43.26	43.43	45.72	47.52	50.03	51.67
30	35.75	36.13	37.86	39.33	41.48	42.77
40	28.95	29.08	30.49	31.47	33.14	34.04
50	22.26	22.06	22.93	23.69	24.90	25.58
60	15.51	15.39	15.86	16.20	17.17	17.74
70	9.69	9.70	9.89	9.96	10.14	10.98
80	5.69	5.27	5.49	5.73	5.61	6.01

Sources: For New South Wales, Victoria, and Queensland only, Burridge (1884); remainder of data are from official life tables for Australia (Young 1976, 3).

We do have, however, estimates of life expectancy at birth for the period being surveyed (table 10.5). These estimates were constructed from generational life tables. It can be seen that a male born, for instance, in 1870–81 could expect to reach age 46.47. By 1920–22 this had increased to 59.15 years. Given the still high level of infant mortality, which was a major component of total mortality, as were accidents and tuberculosis, the rise in life expectancy at birth during the long boom can be interpreted as a positive indication for the standard of living, just as the even more marked rise in life expectancy for those born in the first 40 years of the twentieth century was cited by McLean and Pincus as a sign of a definite improvement in living standards.

Comparing the period 1870–81 with 1920–22, we can observe a marked improvement in survival values for males and females. In the period 1870–81, 59 percent of males and 62 percent of females could expect to survive from birth to 45 years of age. By 1920–22 the proportions had increased to 78 percent and 81 percent (Young 1976, 2). A substantial improvement can be seen also in age-specific mortality rates (table 10.6). In the 50 years surveyed in table 10.6, mortality rates were halved in each of the age groups up to and including those aged 35–44 years. There were significant reductions also in the 55–64 and 65–74 age groups (Young 1976, 7).

Table 10.6   **Australia: Age-Specific Mortality Rates at 1870–72 and 1920–22**

	Males		Females	
Age Group	1870–72[a]	1920–22	1870–72[a]	1920–22
0[b]	126.0	70.1	109.4	54.5
1–4	17.1	7.1	16.2	6.2
5–14	3.9	1.8	3.4	1.5
15–24	5.0	2.6	4.7	2.3
25–34	7.8	3.9	7.4	3.8
35–44	11.1	6.1	10.7	5.2
45–54	17.6	11.3	13.2	7.9
55–64	30.8	23.1	22.8	15.5
65–74	60.2	50.9	46.5	38.6
75+	129.3	146.3	113.9	125.9

Source: Young (1976, 8).

[a]Rates for Victoria.

[b]Rates per 1,000 live births registered.

10.6.2   Infant Mortality

During the second half of the nineteenth century, infant mortality in Australia—at well over 100 deaths per 1,000 births as compared to 10 deaths per 1,000 live births in 1981[9]—was very high by modern standards, though the Australian record compared favorably with that of European countries and the United States. The infant mortality rate displayed considerable variation between the different colonies. In general, this can be related to the pattern of settlement. Close scrutiny of the available statistics reveals that in all the colonies, except Western Australia, infant death rates were rising during the 1880s. Rates started to decline by the end of that decade. However, all colonies experienced a temporary rise in the infant mortality rate during the late 1890s, and this was particularly so for Western Australia, which had previously recorded infant mortality rates below the national average. Tasmania, throughout the period 1870–1900 recorded, with the exception of 1883, consistently lower annual rates than the national average rate. As to the most populous colonies, New South Wales and Victoria, the data show that Victoria's infant mortality rate was on average higher than that in New South Wales, although this differential was eliminated by the 1890s (see Vamplew 1987, 58, table MFM 146–154). The Australia-wide trend is shown in figure 10.7.

The main cause of the still high infant mortality rates is revealed by looking at the main causes of infant deaths, that is, deaths of infants below one year of age. It now seems likely that at least half of all infant deaths were due to infant

9. Statistics on infant mortality are only available from 1870 onward. The records of infant deaths before 1870 are believed to be incomplete (Vamplew 1987, 58). See also Mein Smith (1991, 13) for comments on the shortcomings of the available data.

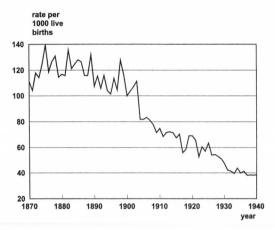

Fig. 10.7   Infant mortality, Australia, 1870–1940
Source: Adapted from Vamplew (1987, 58).

diarrhea associated with a lack of hygiene and contamination of water, milk, and other foods. It has been argued that considerable disparities existed between the infant mortality rates of urban areas and those of rural areas, mainly because "babies in the rapidly growing cities were more susceptible to gut infections" (Mein Smith 1991, 22–23). Within the less healthy urban environment there were also significant differences in infant mortality rates by social class, although no exact statistics are available on this issue.

10.6.3   Morbidity

In an important piece published in the *Medical Journal of Australia* in 1928, J. H. L. Cumpston argued that there are two great indexes of public health, namely, intestinal and respiratory infections, which in turn include enteric fever,[10] diphtheria, scarlet fever, measles, and whooping cough. Death rates from enteric fever showed that the year 1890 represented a dividing line.

Before then, death rates were high, being between 30 and 80 per 100,000. After 1890, however, death rates were lower (never being above 30, with Western Australia being the sole exception) and declining. By 1920 the death rate from enteric fever had fallen to 10 per 100,000. Diphtheria was introduced to Australia in 1858–60. Thereafter, it declined steadily in incidence. The only exception was a marked rise in the period 1887–90. With the introduction of antitoxin in 1895, however, "the biological history of the disease was obscured." There were irregular outbreaks of scarlet fever following its introduc-

---

10. Note that "enteric fever" (and other contemporary names such as "colonial fever") refers in fact to typhoid. Note further that correct diagnoses of typhoid only became possible at the turn of the century with the advent of bacteriology, and hence, until then, typhoid was called many names, even sometimes typhus, which is an entirely different disease spread by fleas.

tion to Australia. Major epidemics occurred at infrequent intervals from 1865 to 1880. The tide began to turn from around 1880 until it ceased to have any importance as a cause of death. This change, Cumpston argued, occurred between 1890 and 1900. After 1900 scarlet fever was at best negligible. For measles the dividing line was 1900. Before then measles epidemics were experienced regularly. During the epidemic years, the incidence of death was high: somewhere between 50 and 200 per 100,000. After 1900, however, the death rate from measles was usually lower than 10 per 100,000. While the disease became less epidemic, it became more endemic, in that the death rate during the interepidemic periods was higher after 1900 than before. Cumpston suggested that the history of whooping cough in Australia could be split into three distinct periods. The first was before 1880, when death rates were high. The second was from 1880 to 1900 (1910 in some states), during which the level of epidemic mortality was generally lower than in the preceding period. The third was the period since 1900, "in which the mortality level has been much lower than before 1900, the fluctuations from year to year are less pronounced and the mortality rate in the interepidemic intervals has not fallen to so low a level as had been the case previously."

The outstanding point to emerge from Cumpston's survey was that "1890 to 1900 was a critical period." "The public health student," he argued, "must inevitably adopt this period as the central point for his examination of Australian public health conditions." "The improvement which occurred at this epoch," he judged, "has not been matched since; little advance has been made on the level of mortalities of the principal public health diseases which was then attained" (1928, 334).

We postpone to the next section the question of what developments led to the 1890s being such a turning point in Australia's history of public health. The point to be made here is that while the 1890s was, from an economic viewpoint, a truly dismal period for the eastern Australian colonies, it was a period of significant improvement in terms of the disease environment. This melioration must have contributed in turn to the improvement in height shown in figures 10.3 and 10.4.

10.7   Explaining Trends in Heights

Floud et al. noted that "height is not determined either by heredity or environment, but always by both" (1990, 5). They went on to argue, however, that "we can attribute relatively greater influence to genetic causes in producing *within-group* variance and relatively greater influence to environmental causes in producing *between-group* variance" (1990, 7). This means that if, for example, we are trying to understand the variation in height of a group of friends born in the same year, we should give primary weight to genetic causes as the explanation. If, however, we are comparing the average height of the group of friends with that of the group of their parents, environmental factors will be the more important causes of the difference. It follows that, in explaining the changes shown in figures 10.3 and 10.4, we need to give particular attention to the environmental factors that contributed to the observed trends, for our interest is in between-group variance.

Our data raise several questions. We have chosen to limit our discussion to what we consider to be the two principal ones. First, why did heights peak as early as 1879 and then fall, before reaching a trough in 1895? What sort of environmental shock produced such a protracted decline? Second, how are we to interpret the improvement in height from the mid-1890s?

10.7.1   Causes of the Decline from 1880

The 1890s Depression

One obvious cause of the fall in heights during the 1880s was the depression of the 1890s. The reason for this lies with the fact, noted earlier, that a person experiences two major growth spurts: one in early infancy and the other in early adolescence. The depression affected some members of the 1880s generation by retarding their adolescent growth spurt. It seems unlikely, however, that the explanation of the 1880s decline in height lies entirely in terms of the depression. What other factors might have contributed? Did it reflect perhaps the influence of industrialization?

Industrialization

Much anthropometric analysis in recent years has been used to contribute to the long-running debate over what happened to living standards during early industrialization. In the Australian case, however, industrialization is likely to be of negligible importance in explaining the trends seen in figure 10.1. Industrialization in Australia was slow and protracted. It is true that in the period 1860–90 manufacturing's share of total product increased. Its share, according to N. G. Butlin, rose from 4–5 percent in 1861 to 10–11 percent in 1891. Allan Thompson, by contrast, argued that manufacturing's share rose much higher, to about 15 percent in 1891.[11] Jackson pointed out that "such large differences in the estimated share of manufacturing in gross domestic product is due partly to measurement difficulties that are themselves revealing about the nature of Australian industrial development in this period." He went on to argue that "some of the measurement problems arise because a considerable amount of Australian manufacturing was carried on in backyard establishments. *There was not much in the way of a recognisable factory system in Australia even at the end of the nineteenth century*" (1977, 115–16; emphasis added). Likewise, Graeme Davison, writing about industrialization in Melbourne in the 1880s, noted that one should not "minimize the continuing significance of small backyard workshops." "Optimistic contemporaries," he points out, "often misjudged the general state of manufacturing by the healthful appearance of a

---

11. The argument is summarized in Jackson (1977, 114–16).

Table 10.7   **Share of Urban in Total Population, Eastern Australia, 1841–1901**

Year	Percentage Urban
1841	30
1851	34
1861	38
1871	41
1881	43
1891	51
1901	52

Source: Jackson (1977, 93).

conspicuous giant." Furthermore, "although the number of clothing factories using steam power doubled during the 1880s, mechanized factories never comprised more than 10 percent of those registered. So far from becoming an industry based on large factories, most firms seem to have employed a diminishing number of hands, at least within the factory itself" (1978, 45).

Urbanization

A much more important environmental factor was the metropolitan nature of the Australian pattern of settlement. Australia during the long boom was already a highly urbanized society by the standards of any continent. According to Vamplew, by 1881, 45.8 percent and, by 1891, 48.9 percent of the Australian population lived in urban areas (1987, 40). We can also consider Jackson's figures presented in table 10.7, which show a sustained rise in urbanization in the second half of the nineteenth century. Table 10.8 demonstrates that, compared to other "regions of recent settlement," Australia had attained a very high level of urbanization by the turn of the century. In addition, a peculiarity of Australian urbanization was that the urban population was concentrated in a handful of relatively large cities: Australia's pattern of urbanization was (and remains) a primate rather than rank distribution. By 1901, 70 percent of the total urban population in Australia lived in towns with a population of 100,000 and over. By contrast, a much lower proportion, 47 percent, lived in such towns in the United States in 1900 (Jackson 1977, 97). Australia's two largest cities, Sydney and Melbourne, had populations of just under half a million by this date.

Melbourne's Typhoid Epidemic: Sinclair's Index of Well-Being

In an important piece published in 1975, Sinclair argued that the typhoid death rate was "an index of a major hazard of nineteenth-century living" and that accordingly it "was an important aspect of well-being" (1975, 154). Sinclair used this index to assess trends in well-being in Melbourne, the capital of Victoria, from 1870 to 1914. As he explained, "Melbourne was a focal point of metropolitan expansion before about 1890 and so contained a large propor-

Table 10.8   **Share of Urban in Total Population in Australia and Other New Countries, circa 1900**

	Year	Minimum Population Counted as Urban	Percentage Urban
Australia	1901	2,500	52
United States	1900	2,500	40
Canada	1901	2,500	35
Australia	1891	10,000	44
Uruguay	1890	10,000	30
Argentina	1890	10,000	28
Chile	1885	10,000	17
Brazil	1888	10,000	10

Source: Jackson (1977, 94).

tion of the population of Australia throughout the period under consideration" (1975, 154). Typhoid fever was a major cause of death in nineteenth-century Australia and was especially prevalent in Melbourne in the 1880s: "In 1889, its deadliest year on record, it was the fifth most important single cause of death in Victoria and was not far behind heart disease, which ranked second.[12] Typhoid was *the* most important cause of death of teenagers and young adults. It was also one of the few diseases of which a resident of Australia was more likely to die in the 1880s than a resident of England. At that time, the English death rate from typhoid was only about half the Victorian" (Sinclair 1975, 154).

Typhoid struck mostly in the warm summer months from December to April–May, a period commonly known as the "typhoid season." Young people in the preadolescent and adolescent age groups were worst affected by the disease. In 1889, for example, those between the ages of 10 and 25 made up 25 percent of all typhoid deaths in Victoria (*Victorian Year Book,* 1889–90, 381). The *Melbourne Argus* referred to typhoid as "the pestilence that walketh in darkness" and as "the annual scourge," thereby attributing to the disease an aspect of inevitability. Typhoid was also known as the "pauperising fever."[13] A man who contracted the disease would lose his job until he recovered, which could take up to six months. In the meantime, his family might be reduced to poverty as a consequence of the loss of the breadwinner's income (Stannage 1979, 252).

In 1889, Melbourne's worst typhoid year, there were 560 reported deaths from the disease in Melbourne and suburbs, and deaths from typhoid made up more than 5 percent of all deaths (de Souza 1988, 23). Yet the typhoid death rate alone does not adequately indicate the full extent of the typhoid problem.

12. The top five causes of death, in descending order, were phthisis (consumption), heart disease, diarrhea, accidents, and typhoid.

13. For an account of perceptions of typhoid in Melbourne, 1855–90, see de Souza (1988).

Typhoid was not a particularly deadly disease in the sense that modern medical knowledge suggests a fatality rate of one in ten, although this can vary according to the virulence of the disease (de Souza 1988, 3, 6). For a one-in-ten fatality rate the number of typhoid cases in Melbourne and suburbs would have been 5,600 in 1889 alone, a much more poignant indicator of how the quality of the urban environment had deteriorated.

At different times, all of Australia's largest cities experienced a sanitary crisis. Even the smallish city of Perth, capital of Western Australia, experienced, albeit a little later than the other Australian capital cities, a number of bad typhoid years during the 1890s following the influx of people attracted by the gold discoveries of that decade. The experience of Perth also illuminates another aspect of the urban sanitary crisis, namely that, while diseases such as typhoid were no respecters of class, inner working-class suburbs suffered more than other suburbs from filth and rubbish (Stannage 1979, 253). Indeed, Fitzgerald (1987) has argued that the increasing degeneration of the environment in Sydney was a major factor in a deteriorating standard of living for large parts of that city's population during the long boom years, 1860–90.

An especially interesting aspect of Sinclair's analysis is his comparison of the typhoid death rate with the annual rate of increase in real GDP per capita for the three decades, 1871–80, 1881–90, and 1900–01 to 1909–10. In both the 1870s and 1880s the typhoid death rate rose, reaching a peak in 1889. There is, however, some confusion about what happened in the 1870s, for the typhoid death rate remained constant for some age groups but rose for others. Further, in the second half of the decade, those aged 20–24 ceased temporarily to be the most vulnerable age group. What is unequivocal about the 1870s, Sinclair argued, is that per capita income rose strongly and this, in the absence of any conclusive evidence that other components of well-being had an offsetting effect, indicated an improvement in general well-being. In the 1880s, by contrast, there occurred both a sharp increase in the incidence of typhoid in Victoria and, for Australia as a whole, a marked slowing down in the annual rate of increase in per capita income: the latter fell from 2.4 percent in the 1870s to only 0.6 percent in the 1880s.[14] Sinclair concluded cautiously that "in view of the small order of magnitude of the rise in average real income, there seem to be no strong grounds for seeing the 1880s as a decade of increased well-being and some reason for regarding them as a period of deterioration" (1975, 158). The typhoid death rate fell sharply in the years 1890–92 and again from 1898, but the beneficial effects this had on well-being were swamped by the loss of real income experienced during the depression. But just as the 1890s witnessed an undeniably pronounced decline in well-being, the period from about 1900

14. Sinclair relied on Butlin's estimates of real GDP per capita. The revised estimates of McLean and Pincus alter the picture, especially when the measure is the average annual increase in real GDP per capita in compound terms. For the decade 1870–79 real GDP per capita increased at an annual average compound rate of 1.7 percent. In the succeeding decade, 1880–89, this slowed to 1.2 percent, a less dramatic change than that suggested by the Butlin series.

to 1914 saw a major reversal of this trend. These years, Sinclair judged, "appear to have been the setting for the most significant advance in well-being of the whole period under consideration. Real income per head rose at least as rapidly as in the 1870s but, in contrast to the position in the 1870s, the typhoid death rate fell to an unprecedentedly low level" (1975, 158).

His conclusions on the period as whole are worth quoting at length:

> The trends in well-being suggested by the joint indicators, income per head and the typhoid death rate, cast a different light on the period 1870–1914 from the conventional one. The 1880s have often been presented as the highlight of the period since 1860, whereas the tendency of economic historians to neglect the first decade of the twentieth century could lead to an impression of near stagnation at the time on the part of the casual observer. It would appear, however, that, considered in the light of key indicators of economic progress, the 1880s may have been a period of relapse whereas the early years after the turn of the century brought rapid and balanced advance. This means a shift in the conventional perspective on post-1860 development such that it reaches its culmination in 1914 rather than comes to an explosive end in the 1890s. (Sinclair 1975, 158–59)

The Urban Disamenities Argument: Further Considerations

Our height data provide some support for Sinclair's assessment, notably his view that the 1880s was "a period of relapse." More generally, our data, like Sinclair's joint indicators, call into question the periodization around which debate has focused. The notion of a long boom reaching a glorious peak in the 1880s is seriously misleading. Likewise, the idea that between 1890 and 1940 there was little improvement in economic well-being does not sit easily with the improvement in height and the reduction in morbidity, nor with the other indicators mentioned by McLean and Pincus.

What is also interesting about Sinclair's work is that it suggests an urban disamenities argument as an explanation for declining heights. More precisely, it could be argued that the evidence provided by infant mortality and typhoid death rates suggests two things: during the long boom urban areas in Australia were becoming progressively less healthy places to live in, and by the 1880s some sort of crisis situation was experienced. A sustained, indeed accelerating, increase in population during the 1870s and the first half of the 1880s placed unbearable pressure on an entirely inadequate sanitary infrastructure.[15]

The rapid pace of urbanization in eastern Australia in the 1880s supports the argument. McCarty points out that Melbourne grew at nearly 6 percent per annum during the 1880s, so that by 1891 four out of ten Victorians lived in the capital. He also notes, however, that Sydney grew just as fast as Melbourne during the 1880s. Adelaide grew at an even faster rate in the 1870s (McCarty 1978, 22).

---

15. Jackson (1977, 33, table 6) showed that the annual increase in population was as follows: 1871–75, 2.9 percent; 1876–80, 3.3 percent; and 1881–85, 3.8 percent.

Just as metropolitan facilities came under increasing strain and the disease environment worsened, so too did the economic environment. We have already noted that although economic growth continued during the 1880s it did so at a markedly slower rate. If we go beyond the aggregate statistics and consider trends in income of different occupational groups, we find further evidence of that 1880s represented a deteriorating economic environment. Recent work by Robert Allen (1994) on real incomes in Sydney, 1879–1913, suggests that the real wages of workers such as bricklayers, laborers, and manufacturing workers tended to stagnate, and in some cases even declined, during the 1880s.

Further support for the urban disamenities argument comes from Alison Pilger in her analysis of the rejected World War I volunteers. She has pointed out that a remarkably high percentage of those who volunteered for service were rejected because they failed to meet the medical and physical standards set for military service. "Of the estimated total of 590,000 men of military service age medically examined during the war, 213,000 were rejected out of hand or discharged shortly afterwards as unfit. Of those passed and sent overseas, a further 17,300 were returned as unfit without seeing active service" (Pilger 1992, 11). Being under the minimum height was a relatively unimportant reason for rejection. The more common causes were things such as poor eyesight, chest diseases or deformity, hernias, dental problems, feet deformities, varicose veins, and poor physique (Pilger 1992, 12, 14).

There was a notable irony here. As Pilger observed, "During the first world war, when thousands were being rejected for war service or discharged after recruitment as unfit and unhealthy, the larger-than-life image of the bronzed digger—fit, athletic, tall and unbeatable, emerged to claim the attention of all and, at the same time, to hide the appalling reality, not only of the French trenches but of the flawed health of Australia's young manhood of the time" (1992, 18).

Pilger was correct in arguing that, in understanding the disabilities that were revealed in the wartime recruiting depots, it is necessary to examine "the familial and environmental influences that were present in late colonial urban society at the birth and during the childhood of the majority of future volunteers" (1992, 16). She pointed to the work of social historians like Fisher, Kelly, and Gandevia, who have revealed the extent of urban poverty as well as the insanitary and unhealthy state of Australian cities during the 1880s and 1890s.[16] "By any standard," she wrote, "urban Australia of the 1880s and 1890s, into which most of the future volunteers for the first world war were born, or were brought as small children, was a poor and unhealthy environment in which to grow and develop" (1992, 16).

Our data on urban and rural heights support the urban externalities argument. Figures 10.8 and 10.9 show that those born in rural areas tended to be

---

16. Another important contributor in this field is Lewis. See, e.g., Lewis (1979) and Lewis and Macleod (1987).

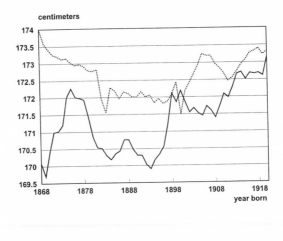

Fig. 10.8   **Urban and rural male recruits, five-year moving averages**

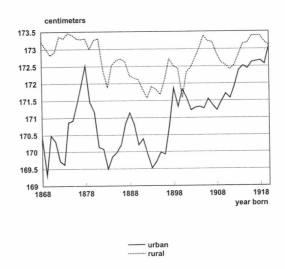

Fig. 10.9   **Victorian urban and rural male recruits, five-year moving averages**

taller than those from urban areas, though figure 10.10 reveals that this was not always the case in the non-Victorian states. Figure 10.8 indicates also that the heights of rural recruits tended downward from at least the late 1860s through to the 1890s. The decline in heights of urban recruits, however, occurred later (from about the mid-1870s) and was much more severe. Another contrast is that the recovery in urban heights occurred earlier. It is clear from figures 10.9

Fig. 10.10   **Non-Victorian urban and rural male recruits, five-year moving averages**

and 10.10 that the fall in heights was largely an urban phenomenon in both Victoria and the non-Victorian states, though this was much more obviously the case in Victoria.[17]

A possible qualification to the urban disamenities argument is that the low-density sprawl of so many Australian cities was conducive to a much less virulent disease environment than in those cities in Europe and parts of the eastern United States characterized by tenement housing and high population density. However, Phillippa Mein Smith and Lionel Frost cast doubt on "the simple assertion that there were intrinsic public health advantages in low-density living" (1994, 261). They did this by examining infant mortality in late-nineteenth-century and early-twentieth-century Adelaide, capital of South Australia. Adelaide had unhealthy "black spots" in which infant mortality was very high, but interestingly, these "black spot" streets were very similar to their neighbors: "There were no obvious physical characteristics which set Adelaide's 'unhealthy' streets apart from its 'healthy' ones" (Mein Smith and Frost 1994, 267). By the turn of the century, Mein Smith and Frost suggested, the level of crowding and cleanliness inside houses was more important than either the closeness of houses or conditions outside houses in determining the health of people living in Adelaide's suburbs (1994, 271). Their analysis of rate books shows that "where new mothers were young and recently married, they were often living with kin, thus affecting the level of crowding inside certain houses.

17. Note that the urban-rural division is based on birthplace: in the absence of evidence on how many rural recruits continued to live in rural areas, there are problems in interpreting figs. 10.8–10.10.

In a particular district or street, the overall population density and number of houses per acre in some cases obscures the population density *within* individual houses" (Mein Smith and Frost 1994, 269). The conclusion is that "a family with adequate income, diet, education, and the knowledge, as well as resources, to practise family planning, hygiene and safe weaning of the baby was just as likely to be able to avoid mortality in a high density as in a low density city" (Mein Smith and Frost 1994, 271).

10.7.2   The Improvement in Height from 1895

Part of the rise in heights from 1895 must reflect the improvement in economic conditions in the decade or so up to 1914. Some people born during the 1890s were able to enjoy a period of catch-up growth because their adolescent growth spurt coincided with an improvement in the economic environment. However, there was a continued rise in height up to our terminal date, 1920, and this occurred despite the poor performance of the Australian economy during World War I and in the early postwar years.

What other factors were at work? We have noted already that the 1890s marked a turning point in Australia's public health record: the disease environment turned decidedly better. Undoubtedly, this contributed to the rise in heights. But this only begs the question: why did the disease environment improve from the 1890s? Cumpston's explanation was that there were two principal factors at work. One was the change in the age distribution of the population that saw a reduction in the proportion of people "at susceptible ages." The other was "the first real introduction of sanitary activities." In his view, organized public health activities did not become general until after 1880. He pointed to the stimulus provided by the passing of the English Public Health Act of 1875. A Royal Commission was appointed in 1888 to inquire into Melbourne's sanitary condition.[18] In New South Wales the Dairies Supervision Act was introduced in 1886, which imposed stringent sanitary conditions on dairies. In Queensland five special inquiries were held between 1884 and 1889 on enteric fever and sanitation. Similar sorts of activities occurred in other colonies (Cumpston 1928, 334).

Cumpston was quick to point out that these initiatives were to a large extent "opportunist in character," in that the primary stimulus was an outbreak of epidemics in the early 1880s. Likewise, continuing public health initiatives required renewed epidemics, notably the Sydney bubonic plague at the beginning of the twentieth century (Cumpston 1928, 334–35). Various acts were introduced in South Australia in 1898, Queensland in 1898 and 1900–1917, New South Wales in 1902, Tasmania in 1903 and 1908, and Victoria in 1907

18. The outcome of the 1888 Royal Commission was the 1889 and 1890 Health Acts. The 1890 Health Act provided for the establishment of the Board of Public Health. Public health administration became more centralized. This was crucial to the 1891 act, which set up the Board of Works, which in turn was charged with the construction of a long overdue underground sewerage system for Melbourne.

and 1915 that established regulations for notifying and controlling infectious diseases: infected children had to be kept away from school, the local authority notified, and if necessary the school premises disinfected (Young 1976, 30). Of importance also were governmental attempts in Australia from the late nineteenth century to improve drainage and sewerage. So too was the development from the end of century of the new field of bacteriology (Young 1976, 30).

There has been debate about why infant mortality experienced a steep decline from the turn of the century. The decline is often attributed to the work of the infant welfare movement, which sought to educate mothers in caring and feeding their babies. J. S. Purdy could argue in 1922 that "without in any way wanting to minimize the effect of improved general sanitation, as represented by purer water supplies, sewerage and a better milk supply, it is worthy of note that the decline in the death-rate at ages under five and more especially among infants under one, synchronizes with the crusade which has been almost universally preached and the work undertaken to secure the better feeding and nurture of infants" (1922, 289).

Purdy drew attention especially to "the efforts of the trained women inspectors appointed in connection with the scheme formulated by the Sydney Municipal Council in 1903 for the preservation of infant health" and to the scheme, formulated in 1904, for home visiting mothers and for issuing a pamphlet on the care and feeding of infants (1922, 294).

Mein Smith, however, has identified several weaknesses in this argument. There is, for example, a temporal mismatch in that the mother and baby movement only flourished in Australia *after* 1918, yet the big fall in infant mortality occurred *before* 1918. Likewise, there is a spatial mismatch in that across Australia the mother and baby movement spread unevenly, while the decline in infant mortality was reasonably even (Mein Smith 1991, 30).

Discussing the history of the Australian public health movement, Mein Smith pointed out that there was "a shift in the critical focus from water and sewage in the late nineteenth century to cleaner milk supplies, adulteration and food legislation around 1900, and then the concern to improve mothers' practices" (1991, 25). Almost certainly, the measures that characterized each of these three phases contributed to an improvement in the disease environment. The difficulty is to judge whether these measures initiated a decline in mortality rates or simply sustained a preexisting downward trend. Just as Mein Smith has cast doubt on the significance of the mothers and babies movement, so too have writers, such as Bryan Gandevia, argued that "there was no close temporal correlation between the introduction of effective sewage systems and the decline in mortality, even from typhoid fever" (Gandevia 1978, 132–33).

The contribution of the public health movement to an improvement in the disease environment has to be seen in the context of the late-nineteenth-century fertility decline. The Australian birthrate began to fall from about 1860. The fall was temporarily halted in Victoria, Queensland, and South Australia during the 1880s. By 1890 the Australian birthrate was 35 births per 1,000 population.

In the period 1862–90 it had declined by about 20 percent. There was an especially steep decline in the birthrate during the 1890s. By 1903, it had fallen to 25.3 births per 1,000 population. The trend continued downward, eventually reaching 16.4 births per 1,000 population in 1934, the lowest level in Australia's demographic history (Ruzicka and Caldwell 1982, 76–81). Accompanying this was a decline in family size. Married women born in 1861–66 bore an average of 5.02 children, those born in 1871–76 an average of 4.02, and those born in 1897–1902 an average of 2.77 (Ruzicka and Caldwell 1982, 206).

There are difficulties in understanding the interrelationship between the decline in infant mortality and the fall in the birthrate. Jackson and Thomas noted that "one view is that the fall in mortality induced a fall in the birth rate by reducing the number of births required for a given number of children to survive infancy. There are also grounds, however, for arguing that the fall in the birth rate itself contributed to the reduction in childhood mortality because individual survival chances were greater in smaller families, where there was less exposure to infection from older siblings and where a given money income would buy more food, clothing, and space for each child" (1995, 10).

Gandevia argued that, indirectly, the decline in the birthrate "gave impetus to measures aimed at preserving the lives of the infants who were born, while, contrariwise, parental realisation of the improved outlook for the survival of their children gave them some confidence in limiting their families. The circle may be completed by suggesting that fewer children meant more time for the mother to care for them effectively, and more money to feed them properly" (1978, 93).

Likewise, Mein Smith's judgment was that "infant survival improved when couples began contracepting. Smaller families and the better spacing of births reduced infant mortality by increasing income per family member, allowing parents more time with their children, reducing overcrowding, and protecting the mother's health. Probably the causal chain went in both directions: from lower fertility to lower infant mortality, and from lower mortality to lower fertility. Both the declines in fertility and infant mortality rates and their perceived causes, then, may be seen part of a larger concept that demographers . . . have begun to call the 'health transition'" (1991, 24–25).

10.8   Conclusion

Anthropometric data provide a useful alternative to standard economic measures of economic well-being. Our data point to several conclusions that are relevant to the debate on living standards in the periods 1860–90 and 1890–1940. First, Australian well-being did not advance continuously upward from 1860 to 1890. Our evidence suggests that the idea that the 1870s and 1880s were some sort of golden age has to be reassessed. To put it another way, the height data indicate that the decline in living standards did not begin, as is commonly assumed, with the onset of the depression of the 1890s; it began at least a decade before that. Second, the data indicate a sustained increase in the living standards of Australian-born males from the mid-1890s through to 1919, the terminal point of our data series. They suggest also a marginal improvement in the living standards of Australian-born women in the first 20 years of the twentieth century. Our analysis indicates that average nutritional status, measured by changes in human height, is influenced not only by changes in average income but, perhaps more important, by changes in the disease environment. The latter improved markedly from the 1890s. The reasons for this are complex and arise from a conjunction of public health initiatives and improved public health education in the context of a marked decline in the birthrate. We concur with McLean and Pincus in arguing that there is a need to reevaluate the course of economic well-being in Australia in the decades following the 1880s. We are cautious, however, in overstating the gains made from 1895 onward, for the fact is that even by 1920 there had not been a return to the peak height experienced 50 years earlier. Nor do we wish to deny the severity of the depression of the 1890s and its effect on material well-being. However, implicit in our analysis is the suggestion that an analysis of living standards based solely on traditional economic measures is likely to be misleading. In situations where GDP per capita is increasing slowly, or even declining, it is possible for living standards to be improving in that average nutritional status is rising. Clearly, the definition of living standards needs to be broadened.

Appendix A
Data Sources

The Boer War data were collected from records of the Commonwealth Boer War recruits held at the Australian Archives, Victorian Regional Office, Brighton, Victoria.[19] The sample size is approximately 95 percent of the total number of records available.

The World War I data are derived from information contained in attestation files held at the Melbourne branch of the Australian Archives.[20] The files are a comprehensive collection of enlistments from each of the Australian states for the years 1914–19. The World War II data, by contrast, are based on information in attestation files held by the Victoria branch of the Department of Veterans' Affairs; these contain information only on those people who enlisted in Victoria (though of course this includes people born in other states and

19. Australian Archives, Victoria, Commonwealth Records Series B4418, Department of the Army, Central Army Records Office, *Dossiers of Boer War Servicemen 1901–1902.* The Victorian Regional Office of the Australian Archives has now moved to Lonsdale Street, Melbourne.
20. The relevant file number is MT 1486/1.

abroad). In both cases, files were selected randomly. The World War I files are grouped in several hundred boxes and organized alphabetically. The World War II files are grouped in tied bundles and organized according to enlistment number.[21]

The attestation papers used for the 1902 Boer War contingent record information on height, place of birth, permanent residence, date and place of enlistment, age in years and months at the time of attestation, marital status, religion, trade or calling, previous military experience, and, where stated, weight.

There are similarities between the attestation papers used in both world wars. The World War I papers record information for each individual on the town in which he was born, whether he was a natural-born British subject or a naturalized British subject, his age and date of birth, his trade or calling, whether he was or had been an apprentice, whether he was married, single, or a widower, the name and address of next of kin, the nature of previous military service, height, weight, chest measurement, complexion, color of eyes and hair, and religious denomination. The World War II papers record information on age, date of birth, birthplace, occupation, religious denomination, height, and weight.

Appendix B
Enlistment Procedures and Requirements

Recruits for the 1902 Boer War contingent had to meet a variety of requirements. For the second Commonwealth contingent (as for the first) the minimum height standard was set at 5 feet, 6 inches. Men also had to be between 20 and 40 years of age, healthy, good shots, and good horsemen. They should have had experience in the management of horses and been used to bush life. Preference was also given to men who had seen service in South Africa or had other military experience. Men were preferably single. Not all these requirements were rigidly adhered to.

Minimum height requirements were set for both World War I and II. In World War I the minimum height was originally set at 5 feet, 6 inches. Another requirement was a chest measurement of at least 34 inches, though those of lighter build could enlist as drivers in the artillery (Bean 1938, 59). An additional restriction was that only those between ages 19 and 38 were allowed to enlist. Initially enlistment centers were restricted to the capital cities, and some recruits traveled up to a thousand miles to reach them. Rejection on medical grounds could be a source of bitter disappointment: "The medical inspection

---

21. The enlistment number is not in accord with the date of enlistment; i.e., the lowest number does not represent the first to enlist. The numbers appear to have been chosen randomly.

was exceedingly severe. 'Many of them,' wrote one medical officer, 'have thrown up good jobs, and have travelled hundreds of miles. They have been fêted as heroes before leaving, and would rather die than go back rejected. Some I have to refuse, and they plead with me and almost break down—in fact some do go away, poor chaps, gulping down their feelings and with tears of disappointment in their eyes'" (Bean 1938, 59).

In 1915, enthusiasm for the war was still high, and many of those who had been rejected did all that was possible to have the decision overturned: "Scores of men rejected because their chests were too small took courses at physical culture schools; short men tried all known methods, and others invented hitherto unknown ones, to increase their height, and the number of men who had disqualifying defects removed by operation was 'legion'" (Robson 1970, 40).

Over time, the enlistment requirements became much more lax. Speaking of the "first contingent" of 1914, Bean says that "at this stage men were rejected for defective or false teeth, who, a year later, were gladly accepted" (1938, 59). As early as January 1915 standards had been lowered to a height requirement of 5 feet, 4 inches and a chest measurement of 34 inches (Pilger 1992, 11). With seeming inexorability, the minimum height requirement was further reduced, so that by April 1917 it was only 5 feet. The age requirement was effectively extended to include all those between 18 and 45 years old. For an interesting analysis of the principal reasons for rejecting World War I volunteers, see Pilger (1992, 11–19).

In World War II the minimum height was again set at 5 feet, 6 inches and again it was subsequently reduced. In this instance, however, it was decided as early as June 1940 to reduce the minimum height to 5 feet. It was simultaneously decided to raise the upper age limit to 40 (Long 1952, 87n).

In both wars there was a distinct ebb and flow in the pattern of enlistment. Hasluck provides a useful comparison:

> The gross monthly recruiting figures for the A.I.F. [Australian Infantry Forces] show that in the first six months of the war [World War II] 21,998 men enlisted, compared with 62,786 in the first six months of the 1914–18 war. . . . As news became worse the enlistments rose. . . . The news of the Dunkirk evacuation on 28th May was followed in June by 48,496 enlistments, the highest monthly total recorded—higher even than the total of 36,575 in July 1915 when news from Gallipoli sent enlistments to the peak for the whole of the 1914–18 war. In October and November [1940] there was another fall in numbers. . . . By September [1941] . . . voluntary enlistment was producing fewer men than the Army staff in Australia regarded as necessary to maintain the A.I.F. . . . In the first two years of war voluntary enlistments had not reached the totals attained in 1914–16. Up to the end of August 1941, the total of enlistments in the A.I.F. from a population of 7,000,000 was 188,587 whereas in the first two years of the 1914–18 war 307,966 had been accepted from a population of 5,000,000. . . . On the other hand Australia had set herself a high standard in this regard in 1914–15, and by the end of 1941 voluntary enlistment had enabled her to form and main-

tain a slightly larger number of divisions in proportion to population than, for example, the United States were to maintain under conscription at any stage of the war. (1952, 399–400)

Conscription was often talked about in both wars. It was a particularly sensitive issue during World War I. A referendum calling for the introduction of conscription was held in 1916 and narrowly lost.[22] One individual who took a prominent role in the anticonscription campaign and indeed against Australia's involvement in the war more generally was the Catholic archbishop of Melbourne, Cardinal Mannix. The cardinal was an influential man, wonderfully articulate and a staunch supporter of Ireland's quest for independence from Britain. He saw the war as a British war and hence one for which Australia should lend no support.

The attitude of Irish Australians to enlistment raises questions about the representativeness of our sample, for such was Cardinal Mannix's hostility to the war and such were his persuasive powers that it might be concluded that a great many Irish Australians chose not to enlist. This in turn would mean that the working classes are underrepresented in the sample, for typically this is the class to which Irish Australians belonged. Lloyd Robson has argued, however, that "no matter what anyone claimed, the constant sectarian strife had not led to a decrease in the number of Catholics who volunteered" (1970, 148). It is true, of course, that not all the Irish Australians were Catholics. Our analysis of the Boer War data demonstrates that one also has to distinguish between the Australian Irish born in Ireland and those born in Australia. The latter showed no reluctance to enlist, whereas the former did. This is significant in that the Boer War was also portrayed by the Catholic Church in Australia as a British war in which Australia should not be involved.

Some analysts have suggested that the 1916 conscription referendum was lost in country districts, specifically the wheat-growing areas. It is clear, however, that in our sample people from country areas are not underrepresented.

It should be noted that about 417,000 men enlisted in the AIF during World War I. This number represented approximately 40 percent of all Australian men aged 18–45 (Robson 1970, 202–3), an astonishingly high proportion.

World War I was very much a man's war. This was less the case for World War II. Up to the beginning of 1941, Australian women played a distinctly minor role in the munitions effort and took even less part in direct war activities. At the end of June 1941 only 1,399 women were in the army, navy, and air force (with 1,181 of these in the army). Most of them were members of the Australian Army Nursing Service (Hasluck 1952, 406–7). According to Hasluck, "The slowness to make better use of women in the war effort seems to have been due very largely to male obtuseness, coupled with a lingering idea that war is a man's work and that a woman in a uniform or a pair of overalls, working in the company of men, would create all sorts of unmentionable diffi-

22. Another was held in 1917 and again was lost by a narrow margin.

culties" (1952, 401). An important breakthrough occurred in the second half of 1941. The Australian prime minister returned from a visit to England and, impressed by the contribution women had made to the British war effort, promoted the idea of establishing three women's services. This was eventually agreed to, if only reluctantly. Accordingly, the Women's Auxiliary Australian Air Force, the Women's Royal Australian Naval Service, and the Australian Women's Army Service (AWAS) were established. By April 1942 the AWAS establishment alone had been set at 6,000. "The Women's Services were thus, once the ice was broken, readily accepted and were to expand" (Butlin and Schedvin 1977, 31). Announcements that additional women would be enlisted for the different services "started a rush of applications" (Hasluck 1970, 61).

Appendix C
Analysis of the Data: Tests for Normality and Determination of Terminal Heights

The standard tests for normality were performed on each of the Boer War, World War I Australian-born male, World War II Australian-born male, and World War II Australian-born female data sets. Figures 10C.1–10C.4, which plot the military heights to the nearest inch, show that there was no truncation due to the enforcement of minimum height standards, nor any evidence of any twisting or other distortion to the height distributions. In table 10C.1, Jarque-Bera tests, which test whether the first four moments of the sample distributions are consistent with the normal distribution, found that the heights of males and females were normal, or Gaussian.

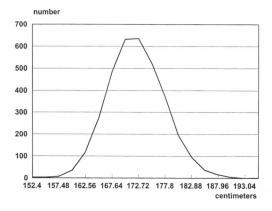

Fig. 10C.1   Height distribution, Boer War male recruits

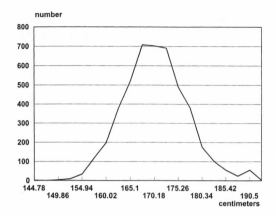

Fig. 10C.2   Height distribution, World War I male recruits

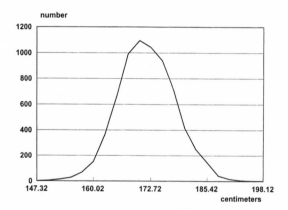

Fig. 10C.3   Height distribution, World War II male recruits

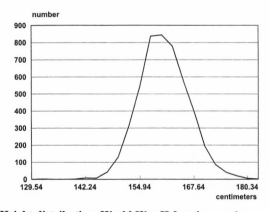

Fig. 10C.4   Height distribution, World War II female recruits

Table 10C.1   **Jarque-Bera Test for Normality**

Sample	Jarque-Bera	Observations	Australian-Born
Australian male Boer War	2.44	4,055	3,435
Australian male WWI	2.80	6,340	4,676
Australian male WWII	3.26	8,029	7,025
Australian female WWII	3.44	5,109	4,841
Total	4.46	23,533	19,977

Note: The critical value at 95 percent confidence is 5.99.

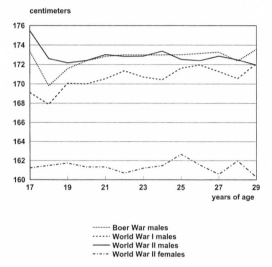

Fig. 10C.5   Average height by age, male and female recruits 17–29 years

There was evidence of height heaping. Heights were measured to the quarter-inch, but heaping at the full and half-inch infected all our military data. Although not a desirable quality, heaping is not uncommon in studies of heights. Simulations suggest that heaping has a relatively minor adverse effect in the estimation of mean heights because its effects tend to cancel out one another (Steckel 1992).

Figure 10C.5 shows the growth spurts of the male and female recruits. These were used to determine at what age the male and female recruits stopped growing. From these graphs, terminal height was obtained for men enlisting in World Wars I and II at age 21, for men enlisting in the Boer War contingent at age 22, and for women enlisting in World War II at age 19. We excluded all men and women under these ages and also all recruits over age 49, when the body begins to shrink.

References

Allen, Robert C. 1994. Real incomes in the English-speaking world, 1879–1913. In *Labour market evolution: The economic history of market integration, wage flexibility and the employment relation,* ed. George Grantham and Mary McKinnon. London: Routledge.

Bean, C. E. W. 1938. *The story of Anzac from the outbreak of war to the end of the first phase of the Gallipoli campaign, May 4, 1915,* 8th ed. Sydney: Angus and Robertson.

Broom, L., and F. L. Jones. 1976. *Opportunity and attainment in Australia.* Canberra: ANU Press.

Burridge, A. F. 1884. On the rates of mortality in Australia. *Journal of the Institute of Actuaries* 24:333–58.

Butlin, N. G. 1962. *Australian domestic product, investment and foreign borrowing 1861–1938/39.* Cambridge: Cambridge University Press.

Butlin, S. J., and C. B. Schedvin. 1977. *War economy 1942–1945.* Canberra: Australian War Memorial.

Coghlan, T. A. (1918) 1969. *Labour and industry in Australia,* vol. 3. Melbourne: Macmillan.

Connell, R. W., and T. H. Irving. 1980. *Class structure in Australian history: Documents, narrative and argument.* Melbourne: Longman Cheshire.

Cumpston, J. H. L. 1928. The development of public health in Australia. *Medical Journal of Australia,* no. 1: 332–36.

———. 1989. *Health and disease in Australia: A history.* Canberra: AGPS.

Davison, Graeme. 1978. *The rise and fall of Marvellous Melbourne.* Melbourne: Melbourne University Press.

de Souza, Christine. 1988. *Typhoid in Melbourne 1855–1890: Perceptions of an invisible enemy.* Unpublished honours research essay, Monash University, Clayton.

Dingle, A. E., and D. T. Merrett. 1972. House owners and tenants in Melbourne 1891–1911. *Australian Economic History Review* 12:21–35.

Eveleth, P. B., and J. M. Tanner. 1976. *Worldwide variation in human growth.* Cambridge: Cambridge University Press.

Fitzgerald, Shirley. 1987. *Rising damp: Sydney 1870–90.* Melbourne: Oxford University Press.

Floud, Roderick, Kenneth Wachter, and Annabel Gregory. 1990. *Height, health and history: Nutritional status in the United Kingdom, 1750–1980.* Cambridge: Cambridge University Press.

Fogel, R., S. Engerman, R. Floud, R. Steckel, J. Trussell, K. Wachter, R. Margo, K. Sokoloff, and G. Villaflor. 1983. Secular changes in American and British stature and nutrition. *Journal of Interdisciplinary History* 14:445–81.

Fox, Charlie. *Working Australia.* Sydney: Allen and Unwin.

Frost, Lionel. 1991. *The new urban frontier: Urbanisation and city building in Australasia and the American West.* Kensington: New South Wales University Press.

Gandevia, Bryan. 1978. *Tears often shed: Child health and welfare in Australia from 1788.* Sydney: Pergamon.

Hasluck, Paul. 1952. *The government and the people 1939–1941.* Canberra: Australian War Memorial.

———. 1970. *The government and the people 1942–1945.* Canberra: Australian War Memorial.

Jackson, R. V. 1970. Owner-occupation of houses in Sydney, 1871–1891. *Australian Economic History Review* 10:138–54.

———. 1977. *Australian economic development in the nineteenth century.* Canberra: ANU Press.

————. 1992. Trends in Australian living standards since 1890. *Australian Economic History Review* 22:24–46.

Jackson, R. V., and Mark Thomas. 1995. Height, weight, and wellbeing of Sydney schoolchildren since 1900. Paper presented to Conference of the Economic History Society of Australia and New Zealand, Melbourne, March.

Kingston, Beverley. 1988. *The Oxford history of Australia.* Vol. 3, *Glad confident morning.* Melbourne: Oxford University Press.

Lee, Jenny, and Charles Fahey. 1986. A boom for whom? Some developments in the Australian labour market, 1870–1891. *Labour History* 50:1–27.

Lewis, M. 1979. Sanitation, intestinal infections, and infant mortality in late Victorian Sydney. *Medical History* 23:325–38.

Lewis, M., and R. Macleod. 1987. A workingman's paradise? Reflections on urban mortality in colonial Australia 1860–1900. *Medical History* 31:387–402.

Long, Gavin. 1952. *To Benghazi.* Canberra: Australian War Memorial.

Macarthy, P. G. 1970. Wages in Australia, 1891–1914. *Australian Economic History Review* 10:56–76.

Maddison, Angus. 1977. Phases of capitalist development. *Banca nazionale de lavoro quarterly review* 30:103–37.

McCarty, J. W. 1978. Australian capital cities in the nineteenth century. In *Australian capital cities: Historical essays,* ed. J. W. McCarty and C. B. Schedvin. Sydney: Sydney University Press.

McLean, Ian W., and Jonathon J. Pincus. 1982. Living standards in Australia 1890–1940: Evidence and conjectures. Working Paper in Economic History no. 6. Canberra: Australian National University.

————. 1983. Did Australian living standards stagnate between 1890 and 1940? *Journal of Economic History* 43:193–202.

Mein Smith, Philippa. 1991. Infant welfare services and infant mortality: A historian's view. *Australian Economic Review,* no. 93: 21–34.

Mein Smith, Philippa, and Lionel Frost. 1994. Suburbia and infant death in late nineteenth- and early twentieth-century Adelaide. *Urban History* 21:251–72.

Pilger, A. 1992. The other lost generation: Rejected Australian volunteers 1914–18. *Journal of the Australian War Memorial,* 21 October, pp. 11–19.

Purdy, J. S. 1922. Infantile mortality in New South Wales. *Medical Journal of Australia,* no. 11: 287–96.

Robson, L. L. 1970. *The first A.I.F.: A study of its recruitment 1914–1918.* Melbourne: Melbourne University Press.

Ruzicka, Lado T. 1989. Long term changes in Australian life expectancies. In *Australia's greatest asset: Human resources in the nineteenth and twentieth centuries,* ed. David Pope and Lee J. Alston. Annandale: Federation.

Ruzicka, Lado T., and John C. Caldwell. 1982. Fertility. In *Population of Australia,* vol. 1, Economic Commission for Asia and the Pacific. New York: United Nations.

Scrimshaw, N. S. 1975. Interactions of malnutrition and infection: Advances in understanding. In *Protein-calorie malnutrition,* ed. R. E. Olsen. New York: Academic Press.

Sinclair, W. A. 1975. Economic growth and well-being: Melbourne 1870–1914. *Economic Record* 51:153–73.

Snooks, Graeme D. 1994. *Portrait of the family within the total economy: A study in longrun dynamics, Australia 1788–1990.* Cambridge: Cambridge University Press.

Stannage, C. T. 1979. *The people of Perth.* Perth: Perth City Council.

Steckel, R. H. 1986. Height and per capita income. *Historical Methods* 16:1–7.

————. 1992. Stature and living standards in the United States. In *American Economic Growth and Standards of Living before the Civil War,* ed. R. Gallman and J. Wallis. Chicago: University of Chicago Press.

Sutton, H. 1931. The Australian child and the progress of child welfare. *Medical Journal of Australia,* no. 2: 603–16.

Thomas, Mark. 1991. The evolution of inequality in Australia in the nineteenth century. In *Income distribution in historical perspective,* Y. S. Brenner, Hartmut Kaelble, and Mark Thomas. Cambridge: Cambridge University Press.

Travers, Peter, and Sue Richardson. 1993. *Living decently: Material well-being in Australia.* Melbourne: Oxford University Press.

Vamplew, Wray, ed. 1987. *Australians, historical statistics.* Broadway: Fairfax Syme and Weldon.

Victorian Year Book. 1889–90. Melbourne: Government Printer.

Walker, Robin, and Dave Roberts. 1988. *From scarcity to surfeit: A history of food and nutrition in New South Wales.* Kensington: New South Wales University Press.

Young, Christabel M. 1976. *Mortality patterns and trends in Australia.* National Population Inquiry, Research Report no. 5. Canberra: AGPS.

11   Conclusions

Richard H. Steckel and Roderick Floud

The papers in this volume present and analyze evidence on health and welfare in diverse settings. The temporal trends, geographic patterns, and socioeconomic differences that they depict help to tell the story of living standards from the preindustrial era to the creation of modern, industrial societies. Their focus is primarily local, with emphasis on changing conditions within particular countries.

In contrast, this concluding chapter adopts a comparative perspective to investigate common patterns across countries. General tendencies appear in the evidence despite substantial differences across countries in dates of industrialization, geographic location, major wars, land availability, government policies, and cultural conditions. While mindful of conditions specific to individual countries, it is those general tendencies that this chapter seeks to elucidate.

11.1   Methodology

As an aid to understanding cross-country patterns, we arrange indicators of the standard of living by country and date (table 11.1) and by country and phase of industrialization (table 11.2). The dates chosen—1800, 1850, 1900, and 1950—encompass the process of industrialization for most countries in the study and provide benchmarks for assessing change.[1]

Though imprecise, the phases of industrialization are also useful concepts for understanding patterns of health and welfare. While economic historians abandoned rigid chronological structures (such as the stages of economic

Richard H. Steckel is professor of economics at Ohio State University and a research associate of the National Bureau of Economic Research. Roderick Floud is provost of London Guildhall University and a research associate of the National Bureau of Economic Research.

1. The exception is England, which started to industrialize before 1800. The date of 1800 is also problematic for Australia, which was colonized only a few years earlier.

Table 11.1   Socioeconomic Indicators by Country and Date

Country	Per Capita GNP (1985 $)	Growth Rate	Men's Height	Life Expectancy	Literacy Rate (%)	Percentage Urban
Date: 1800						
United Kingdom	1,301	0.1	168.9	36.1	52.2	33.6
United States	828	0.5	172.9	46.8	72.4	6.1
France	700	0.3	163.7	34	40	19
Netherlands	876	0.0	167.8	34.1	75	37
Sweden	808	0.1	167.0	39.2	82.5	9.8
Germany				37	83.5	23.3
Australia						
Japan	575	0.1	157.1	36	20	14
Date: 1850						
United Kingdom	1,943	1.6	165.3	39.5	61.3	53.4
United States	1,179	1.5	171.1	39.5	78.0	15.3
France	1,150	1.3	164.7	40	58	26
Netherlands	1,551	0.2	167.4	37.3	75	39
Sweden	871	0.9	168.2	43.9	90.0	10.1
Germany	835	0.0	162.6	37.1	95	32.3
Australia	2,517	1.8	172.7	46	45	34
Japan	606	0.1	155	38	25	34.5
Date: 1900						
United Kingdom	3,792	1.3	169.3	48.0	97	77.7
United States	3,824	2.3	170.0	47.8	89.3	39.7
France	2,250	1.3	166.6	46.8	95	41
Netherlands	2,842	0.9	170.0	49.0	90	49
Sweden	1,895	2.4	172.5	52.9	100.0	21.5
Germany	1,743	1.5	169	44.4	99.9	53.8
Australia	4,100	0.9	170.9	55	80	52
Japan	947	1.0	157	44	75	54.5
Date: 1950						
United Kingdom	5,628	0.9	174.1	69.0	100.0	80.7
United States	8,588	2.1	177.1	68.2	97.4	59.0
France	4,149	4.0	172.3	66.8	99	55
Netherlands	4,706	3.4	178.1	71.3	100	71
Sweden	5,834	2.4	177.9	71.4	100.0	46.6
Germany	2,554	6.4	176.3	66.5	100.0	71.1
Australia	5,931	2.4	173.8	69.5	98	70
Japan	1,563	1.5	162	58	100.0	75.2

Sources: See data appendix.

growth) many years ago, they agree that some order or sequence prevailed in the process. For example, England was clearly the first industrial country, and the process of industrialization tended to spread across Europe from west to east. Industrial activity began in the United States sometime in the early nineteenth century, and economic growth accelerated in Australia near the middle of the century. In Japan the transformation began in the 1880s.

Table 11.2   **Socioeconomic Indicators by Country and Phase of Industrialization**

Country	Approximate Dates	Per Capita GNP (1985 $)	Growth Rate	Men's Height	Life Expectancy	Literacy (%)	Percentage Urban
Phase: Preindustrial							
United Kingdom	1720–60	1,172	0.4	165.1	33.7	48.9	22.6
United States	1800–1820	872	0.4	173	45.3	72.9	6.9
France	1800–20	952	0.1	164.1	36	41	19
Netherlands	1830–50	1,469	0.1	164.0	35	75	38
Sweden	1830–50	832	0.5	168.0	42.1	87.5	9.7
Germany	1830–50				36.9	91	30.5
Australia	1840–60	1,994	1.6	172.5	46	45	30
Japan	1868–80	775	0.2	155.3	36	25	34.5
Phase: Early Industrial							
United Kingdom	1760–1800	1,263	0.2	168.2	36.0	50.2	29.4
United States	1820–50	1,025	0.9	172.4	41.7	75.6	10.5
France	1820–50	976	1.3	164.4	39.3	49	22
Netherlands	1850–70	1,807	0.5	165.9	40	80	44
Sweden	1850–70	980	1.2	169.1	43.9	92.5	11.2
Germany	1850–70	972	1.5	166.2	37.6	95	34.4
Australia	1860–90	3,425	1.8	172	48	55	42
Japan	1880–1900	875	1.0	157	38	70	50
Phase: Middle Industrial							
United Kingdom	1800–1830	1,422	0.6	170.7	38.6	54	38.7
United States	1850–80	1,727	2.5	170.6	40.9	80.3	22.3
France	1850–80	1,400	1.3	165.4	41	67	31
Netherlands	1879–1900	2,453	1.1	168.6	45	85	46
Sweden	1870–1900	1,466	1.8	171.4	49.3	98.2	17.2
Germany	1870–90	1,371	1.6	167.5	38.9	98.5	43.6
Australia	1890–1920	4,263	0.8	172	59.2	80	53
Japan	1900–1920	1,100	2.0	158.8	44	75	60
Phase: Late Industrial							
United Kingdom	1830–70	2,770	2.2	166.9	49.5	64.5	54.1
United States	1880–1910	3,539	2.2	170.2	45.6	87.8	37.2
France	1880–1910	2,050	1.3	166.7	45.5	90	39
Germany	1890–1913	1,885	1.3	169.7	46.8	100.0	56.1
Netherlands	1900–1925	3,718	0.5	172.0	55.2	98	56
Sweden	1900–1925	2,423	2.2	173.5	57.4	100.0	25.7
Australia	1920–40	5,170	0.7	173.2	65.4	90	60
Japan	1920–40	1,320	2.2	160	47	96	75.5

Sources: See data appendix.

The dates assigned here to the phases of industrialization are necessarily imprecise because the character of the process differed across countries. The United Kingdom, the United States, Germany, and Japan developed large manufacturing sectors and heavy industry, whereas the Netherlands (lacking coal and water power) cultivated banking, shipping, and services, and Australia emphasized agriculture and mining. Indeed, it might be more appropriate to call the transformations in Australia and the Netherlands economic modernization rather than industrialization. The term "industrialization" is used here in a broad sense to encompass economic modernization within these countries.

As a result of this variation there is no single indicator of industrialization, such as the percentage of the labor force in manufacturing or the share of GNP originating outside agriculture, that adequately captures the diversity and complexity of the process. Instead, we consider numerous indicators to judge the experiences of various countries against the benchmark of the United States. The categories begin with a short preindustrial period that acts as a backdrop against which the industrial experience is compared. Three phases of industrialization are then identified, beginning with an early industrial period in which the transition to a modern industrial economy began. Industrialization and modernization spread geographically and diversified in the middle period and became widespread and dominant in the late industrial phase.

The phases of industrialization in individual countries are judged relative to developments in the United States. America's early industrial period unfolded in the years 1820 to 1850, a time when economic growth accelerated, a decline in the relative importance of agriculture occurred, and expansion of manufacturing and trade was evident, particularly in the Northeast. In the middle phase, 1850–80, industrialization spread to the Midwest, mechanization and factory methods of production penetrated numerous industries, and regional interdependence became significant. In the late phase, 1880–1910, agriculture was eclipsed by heavy industry, manufacturing, trade and services, and substantial self-sufficiency of the household, which declined throughout industrialization, disappeared as a way of life.[2] Inevitably, the choice of dates for the phases of industrialization in individual countries is imprecise, which is acknowledged by rounding or frequent use of years ending in zero as end points. Given this situation, it is important not to rely too greatly on the results.

11.2   Patterns of Health and Welfare

Table 11.1 shows that the countries varied substantially by income, growth rates, urbanization, health, and literacy at the benchmark dates.[3] In 1800 the

2. These phases of industrialization are least clear in the cases of the United Kingdom and Australia. Numerous researchers emphasize the continuity rather than changes or transitions in the English experience. Moreover, the process of industrialization in the United Kingdom was elongated and drawn out relative to other countries, which poses difficulties in selecting dates. Australia, as noted earlier, had fewer of the hallmarks of industrialization than other countries in the volume. With the possible exception of the United Kingdom, the early phase of industrialization—the transition from agriculture to heavy industry, manufacturing, commerce, and services— is more clearly marked than the later phases.

3. We urge readers to consult the data appendix for sources and qualifications in these data. In general, the estimates for the early period are somewhat fragile relative to the later years, and the per capita GNP data are limited in comparability by reliance on exchange rates. Major conflicts (Napoleonic Wars and World War II) may be an important factor in the results for particular countries in 1800 and 1950.

United Kingdom was ahead of the pack in terms of incomes, but the United States was growing most rapidly. Even at a 0.5 percent annual rate, however, incomes in the United States were doubling every 139 years, an improvement barely noticeable within an individual's working life. Elsewhere, average changes in access to goods and services within a working life span were virtually nil. Americans were the tallest (172.9 cm for males) and the healthiest (life expectancy at birth of approximately 46.8 years) by a wide margin. A substantial majority of the population was literate in the United States, Germany, Sweden, and the Netherlands, but only a small minority could read and write in Japan, which serves as a reminder of the significant educational investments made in that country after the Restoration. The United States, Sweden, Australia, and Japan were thoroughly rural societies, but even the most urban countries (the United Kingdom and the Netherlands) had only one-third of their populations living in cities or towns with populations of 2,500 or more.

By 1850 several countries were growing at nearly 1.0 percent or more, and modest improvements in health had occurred in some countries since 1800. Australia, with its substantial endowment of mineral and grazing resources, led the pack in terms of income, growth rate, stature, and life expectancy. Sweden and Germany had achieved near universal literacy, and the vast majority of residents were literate in the United States, France, and the Netherlands. With over 50 percent of its population living in cities or towns, England was by far the most urbanized country, while Sweden and the United States remained predominantly rural.

All countries in the sample had begun the process of industrialization by the end of the nineteenth century. In 1900 growth rates of real per capita income were more than 2.0 percent in Sweden and the United States, and they were 1.0 percent or more in the United Kingdom, France, Germany, and Japan. Australia and the Netherlands were experiencing temporary economic reversals in which growth rates fell below 1.0 percent. Health had improved substantially since the middle of the nineteenth century, as evidenced by the number of countries in which men's stature was 170.0 cm or more (the United States, the Netherlands, Sweden, and Australia) and life expectancy at birth surpassed 50 years (Sweden and Australia). The Japanese were moderately healthy as measured by life expectancy at birth (44 years), but their stature (156 cm) was remarkably low even after allowing for genetic differences in growth.[4] The vast majority of the population was literate in all countries. In 1900 most residents in the United Kingdom and a majority (or near majority) of those in the Netherlands, Germany, and Australia lived in urban areas. Sweden was the only society in the group under study that remained substantially rural at the turn of the century.

By the middle of the twentieth century the modern industrial economy had

---

4. Today the Japanese have the highest life expectancy in the world, but well-nourished adults in that country fall about one standard deviation (6.5 cm) below modern NCHS height standards. For a discussion of growth in Japan see Tanner et al. (1982).

recently emerged or had existed for some time in all countries in the sample. Although the post–World War II era was generally prosperous, growth rates varied widely at midcentury. The United Kingdom and Japan temporarily languished, but the growth rate reached 3.4 percent in the Netherlands, 4.0 percent in France, and 6.4 percent in Germany. Health had improved substantially over the last half-century. Average adult male stature exceeded 170 cm for seven out of eight countries in the sample, and it equaled or surpassed 175 cm in the United States, France, the Netherlands, Germany, and Sweden. Life expectancy at birth, which was at most 55 years in 1900, exceeded 65 years in seven out of eight countries, and in the Netherlands and Sweden it topped 70 years. Literacy was nearly universal in every country including Japan, which made the remarkable leap from only 25 percent literacy in 1850. The majority of all populations, except residents of Sweden (46.6 percent), lived in urban areas, and the figure exceeded the remarkable level of 80 percent in the United Kingdom.

Table 11.1 highlights the diverse experiences of countries over the long term, but the arrangement of the evidence at particular dates obscures trends that accompanied industrialization. Table 11.2 presents evidence on socioeconomic indicators by country for the preindustrial period and the various phases of industrialization. Given the ambiguities surrounding dates for phases of industrialization that were noted earlier, it is important not to give too much credence to the results that use these categories. Nevertheless, several interesting patterns emerge.

With some notable exceptions, preindustrial life was characterized by poverty, slow growth, poor health, widespread illiteracy, and rural habitation. With its good health and a per capita income and growth rate significantly above those elsewhere, Australia was an outlier. Fueled by mineral and agricultural resources, its economy was well positioned to reap the advantages of a growing demand for fibers and metals that accompanied industrialization elsewhere, and by rising food prices brought on by population growth, wars, or harvest failures near the middle of the century. Good health in Australia was promoted by a sound nutritional base and low population density. With extensive access to land, the United States also had relatively good health in the preindustrial era, but income growth (0.4 percent) was modest by the standards of industrial countries. The vast majority of adults in Germany and Sweden, and to a lesser extent the United States, were literate in the preindustrial period, an investment that helped to catapult these countries along a path of rapid industrialization later in the century.[5]

The countries in table 11.2 are listed in the approximate order in which industrialization unfolded. The United Kingdom was first, followed by the United States and France, and then by a group of three—the Netherlands, Sweden, and Germany. Australia came next, followed by Japan. This configuration

---

5. On the importance of literacy for economic development, see Sandberg (1979).

shows that while income levels varied widely in the early phases of industrialization, growth rates were often higher for the late-comers. Alexander Gerschenkron (1962) noted such a pattern for Europe, but it holds when Japan and Australia are included in the picture. He cited the ability to borrow advanced technology as an important factor that gave late-comers a rapid industrial spurt.

Except in the United States and Australia, stature was substantially below modern height standards in the early industrial period. Life expectancy at birth approached 50 years in Australia, and was nearly 45 years in Sweden. Despite its early industrial success, Germany's life expectancy languished at 37.6 years. Literacy rates improved substantially over those for the preindustrial period in Japan, while France and Australia registered modest improvements. Despite its vast land area, Australia was the most urban country with 42 percent of its population living in cities or towns.

Some departures from the pattern of growth rates appeared in the middle phase of industrialization. In the United Kingdom and Australia, per capita income growth languished, albeit at a high income level in the latter country. Meanwhile, the United States, a relative newcomer, attained the highest growth rate of all countries in the sample.[6] However, stature declined from its level in the early phase, which suggests that the American population may have paid a biological price for aspects of this prosperity. Life expectancy at birth advanced substantially in Australia and Sweden, and large increases in literacy rates were achieved by France and Australia. Australia and Japan became the first countries to have a majority of their populations (53 percent and 60 percent, respectively) reside in urban areas within this phase of industrialization, while the United States and Sweden remained substantially rural.

In the late industrial phase, the United Kingdom, the United States, Sweden, and Japan had annual growth rates of 2.2 percent. Sluggish growth continued in Australia, and the growth rate plummeted to 0.5 percent in the Netherlands. Health measured by life expectancy improved everywhere in the sample, led by an 11-year gain in the United Kingdom, but stature declined from its level in the middle industrial phase in the United Kingdom and the United States. Literacy was virtually universal in Germany, Sweden, and Japan, was very widespread in Australia, France, and the United States, but reached only 64.5 percent in the first industrial country, the United Kingdom. A majority of the population lived in urban areas in Australia, Germany, the Netherlands, the United Kingdom, and Japan, but only one-quarter of the residents in Sweden, the least urban country in the group, lived in cities or towns.

The organization of data by phases of industrialization may disguise declines in health that were not centered on the time periods chosen. Table 11.3 considers whether any meaningful decline in stature occurred during industri-

6. This was a notable achievement in light of the economic penalties associated with destruction of capital during the Civil War of the 1860s and reorganization of the Southern economy thereafter. On the other side of the ledger, inflows from Europe promoted labor force growth and huge amounts of farm land and other resources were made available through westward expansion.

Table 11.3   Stature during Industrialization

Country	Decline in Stature?	Birth Cohorts Approximate Dates	Amount
United Kingdom (men)[a]	Yes	1760–90	0.7 cm
		1820–50	5.4 cm
United Kingdom (women)[b]	Yes	1790–1815	2.5 cm
		1835–55	2.5 cm
United States	Yes	1830–90	4.0 cm
France	No		
Netherlands	No		
Sweden	No		
Germany[c]	Yes	1860–72	2.5 cm
		1879–85	2.0 cm
Australia	Yes	1867–93	3.0 cm
Japan	No		

Sources: See data appendix.

[a]The years 1760 to 1850 embraced two downturns and an upturn from 1790 to 1820 such that the net decline was 2.0 cm over the period. The upturn between 1790 and 1820 was 4.1 cm.

[b]The upturn between 1815 and 1835 was approximately 0.75 cm.

[c]The upturn between 1872 and 1879 was 3.3 cm.

alization.[7] The answer is clearly no in France, Sweden, the Netherlands, and Japan. The results are somewhat ambiguous in Germany; declines were small and short lived, and there was a modest improvement in stature of approximately 1 cm for birth cohorts of the early 1860s through the early 1890s. This leaves the United Kingdom, the United States, and Australia. The deepest decline (about 5.4 cm) occurred for men in the United Kingdom, 1820–50, while the longest—60 years—took place in the United States. Interestingly, the two countries with greatest stature during the nineteenth century—Australia and the United States—experienced declines in this measure of health. However, in neither case did stature at their nadirs approach the level typical of Europe.

11.3 Explanations

If we ask whether the perception of industrialization as seen by Marx, Engels, and Dickens in mid-nineteenth-century England—a world of misery, degradation, and declining quality of life for the working population—was the fate of all industrializing countries, the answer is clearly no. While it may be true that some indicators, such as stature, were deteriorating in England for a portion of the industrializing period, several countries (France, Sweden, the Netherlands, and Japan) witnessed virtually uninterrupted increases in a broad

7. In principle, the question of declines in health could be asked of data on life expectancy. However, the evidence on this measure of health is not so continuous or abundant as it is for stature.

spectrum of measures of the quality of life during industrialization.[8] The situation was more complex in Germany, where downturns in health were cyclical rather than secular, and the long term saw significant improvement in all indicators. Only the United Kingdom, the United States, and Australia experienced significant declines in health.

A comparative international perspective makes clear that no simple relationship existed between various measures of living standards and industrialization. The diversity of experiences—details in the type of indicators, the timing, and the amount of change during industrialization—suggests that some country-specific factors were important. The issue is one of common causal mechanisms, and we find three that were important in the experiences of all countries studied: (1) the timing of industrialization relative to the rise of the germ theory of disease and public health, (2) the extent of urbanization, and (3) diets. Beyond these, numerous characteristics helped to distinguish the experiences of particular countries, including the vigor of public health efforts; the relative abundance of land, or population density; income; inequality of wealth or income; food prices; the nature of industrialization; birthrates; migration and emigration; interregional trade; the rise of public schooling; wars; emancipations; and government policy.[9] The potency and mechanism of these variables for health and nutritional status have been discussed in the literature on stature, including the papers in this volume. Here we provide only a sketch of their relevance.

The germ theory of disease, which came to be widely accepted in the medical profession by the 1880s, and the consequent diffusion of public health measures in the late nineteenth and early twentieth centuries were ultimately effective in preventing infection.[10] The former provided a mechanism for understanding the transmission of pathogens, and its application in the form of public health and personal hygiene led to better health through policies such as waste disposal, clean water supplies, and antiseptic medical procedures. Because congested living in cities or towns provided an environment favorable to the spread of communicable diseases, the percentage of the population living in urban areas was relevant for health prior to the era when public health was effective.

Although urbanization and the germ theory of disease were important for their claims placed on nutritional intakes, as the major input to net nutrition, diets were clearly detrimental to growth and general health. Moreover, diets varied over time and across countries in ways significant for understanding the course of health during industrialization. Abundant land resources improved

---

8. Business cycles and short-term reversals in health were part of the picture.

9. Climate could be on the list, but with the exception of Australia, variations in this factor were modest across the countries in the sample.

10. Some public measures beneficial to health were undertaken before the germ theory was generally accepted by the medical profession (Szreter 1988). In England, for example, Edwin Chadwick's arguments for sanitary reform were based on a different theory of disease causation.

health in three ways: low population density, which reduced the spread of communicable diseases; availability of land to produce food; and the opportunity to choose the best plots for cultivation, which lowered work effort in food production.[11]

Income was important for health because it provided the means to purchase the essentials of life: food, clothing, housing, and medical care. At the level of the individual or household, height was a nonlinear function of income. Extreme poverty resulted in inadequate calories and a lack of vitamins and minerals for health and growth. As income increased from very low levels, a better diet as well as improved clothing and shelter could be purchased. Additional income may have increased the consumption of basic necessities, particularly medical care, but once a person's genetic potential was realized, additional expenditures no longer contributed to growth. The limits to the process are clear from the fact that children from wealthy families are not superhealthy, physical giants. If height is a nonlinear function of income, then the distribution of income or wealth affects average stature and overall health. Assuming that incomes were low enough in some households to constrain health and physical growth, then redistribution of some income from the rich to the poor increased average health and stature of the population because the basic necessities for health for the rich were met even with their lower income.

Exposure to pathogens made substantial claims on health and nutrition, particularly in the era before public health measures. The nature of industrialization affected health through the size of the workplace and associated environmental conditions. The transmission of communicable diseases was greater in large factories as opposed to small workshops, while surrounding conditions such as dust, dampness, ventilation, and lighting affected the prevalence of pathogens. In contrast with the self-paced work on farms or in artisan shops, arduous factory work geared to machines may have been a drain on health. The rise of mass schooling may have contributed to human capital, but at a cost of exposure to communicable diseases in the classroom. Migration, emigration, and interregional trade also increased the exposure of the population to pathogens, as made clear by the diffusion of epidemics along trade routes. Studies of child survival in the mid-nineteenth century indicate that death rates increased with the number of siblings, which indicates that child health and growth varied inversely with the birthrate (Steckel 1988).[12] As recently as the 1960s, among families of unskilled workers in the United Kingdom the stature of children declined by more than 2.5 cm as the number of siblings increased from zero to more than three (Eveleth and Tanner 1990, 202).

Wars and government policy affected the consumption of basic necessities and therefore health and physical growth. Concentrations and turnover of

11. Of course, a measure such as square miles per person is only a crude proxy for available farmland, and population may be far from evenly distributed.

12. The finding that wealth of the household had no systematic effect on survival suggests that the number of siblings was important for its impact on the disease pool.

troops in the American Civil War, for example, spread communicable diseases. This war also disrupted food production and distribution within the country and led to the distress of the cotton famine in Britain. The paper by Gail Honda on Japan shows how government support for the military before and during World War II diverted health resources and lowered nutritional status.

In summary, by reducing exposure to pathogens the germ theory of disease, public health measures, and personal hygiene were significant for the consequences of industrialization. Countries that industrialized and urbanized before these developments paid a biological penalty, as did those places with environments conducive to the spread of infections through high rates of migration, emigration, interregional trade, and early development of public schools. Depending on the country, the costs may have been aggravated by war and perverse government policies. On the other hand, higher incomes, widespread access to land, relatively equitable distribution of resources, and low birthrates could have reduced the penalty.

We also know that significant improvements in mortality and stature occurred before the public health movement of the 1880s, and that countries with relatively greater access to good agricultural land tended to have better diets, larger stature, and lower mortality rates. Stature trended upward from the second quarter of the nineteenth century in France, from the middle of the nineteenth century in the United Kingdom, Sweden, and the Netherlands, and from the 1870s in Germany. Although trends in mortality rates were clouded by subsistence crises near the middle of the century, which is additional testimony to the importance of diets for health, significant improvement was visible by the middle of the century in France and Sweden, by the 1860s in the Netherlands, and by the 1870s in the United Kingdom and Germany. Land-rich countries such as the United States and Australia experienced downturns in heights, but from a relatively high level. A deterioration in diets has been suggested as a contributing factor in the American height decline after 1830 (Komlos 1987).

Although most scholars agree that dietary improvements added to better health prior to the 1880s, they disagree on relative importance. McKeown (1983) has been perhaps the strongest advocate of the dietary position, while Razzell (1993) and Livi-Bacci (1983) have raised doubts or downplayed the contribution of nutritional inputs to health, citing factors such as the independence of many diseases from nutrition, human adaptability to food availability, smallpox inoculation, and changing virulence of diseases. Fogel (1985) estimated that roughly 40 percent of the decline in mortality in England between 1800 and 1980 can be explained by improvements in nutritional status (net nutrition).

We need not resolve the debate over nutrition and the modern rise of population to make the point that health improved during the nineteenth century, and therefore later industrializers had lower biological costs associated with urbanization, congested working conditions, migration, and trade. However, we believe that better diets were important for improving health. Among the papers in the volume, the clearest connection between trends in diet and stature can be seen in David Weir's paper on France. His figure 5.6 shows a rise in meat consumption during the nineteenth century that parallels the rise in stature and the downward trend in mortality. Dietary improvement in nineteenth-century Europe was made possible by technical improvements, such as light iron plows, steam threshers, mechanical harvesters, and commercial fertilizers, as well as by agrarian reforms such as enclosures or emancipation of serfs (Jones 1968; Trow-Smith 1967; Tracy 1964).[13] In the second half of the nineteenth century, diets also received a boost from the free trade movement. This and greater speed and lower transportation costs on long ocean voyages made it feasible to import foodstuffs from Australia and from the land-rich countries in the Western Hemisphere, principally the United States, Canada, and Argentina.

In light of these factors, the questions suggested by cross-country comparisons are: (1) Why did Australia and the United States have relatively tall stature throughout industrialization? (2) Why did some countries (the United Kingdom, the United States, and Australia) experience significant declines or cycles, and another (Germany) only mild fluctuations in stature during industrialization? (3) Why did other countries (France, Sweden, the Netherlands, and Japan) show continuous improvements in health during industrialization? (4) Why did stature and life expectancy remain so low in Japan as late as 1950?

Although the two continental countries had some negative attributes for health, such as early industrialization (the United States) or a relatively large percentage urban (Australia), it is clear that these adverse characteristics were more than outweighed by the enormous benefits of abundant land. Ample land for farming or grazing and excellent waters for fishing provided a strong nutritional base. Moreover, the nutritional costs of disease were less than elsewhere. Epidemics were rare or had minimal consequence for nonindigenous populations before the 1830s in the United States and before the 1860s in Australia. Relative isolation from other parts of the world, at least prior to the middle of the nineteenth century, also helped to reduce disease. Though the share of the Australian population living in urban areas was large, until the late nineteenth century the urban population was widely dispersed in five moderate-sized cities, which were weakly connected by trade and migration.

The height declines during industrialization add new perspective on the standard of living that was once seen primarily through the lenses of per capita income and real wages. The issue is how to reconcile the patterns in these diverse sources of evidence. The outcome depends in part on the definition of the problem. Paul Johnson and Stephen Nicholas demonstrate that women's stature in the United Kingdom declined between 1790 (the date of the earliest evidence) and the mid-nineteenth century, while Roderick Floud and Bernard Harris show that men's stature fell between the 1760s and the 1850s. This sim-

---

13. However, for most of the nineteenth century agrarian reforms were more important as a new, dynamic force in Central or Eastern Europe as opposed to Western Europe.

plified picture might be explained by the United Kingdom's early industrialization and its large and growing share of population living in urban areas that were well connected by migration and trade with other parts of the country and the world. However, this view of the evidence ignores a substantial increase in the stature of military recruits that occurred in the early nineteenth century, which indicates that some beneficial environmental change must have occurred along the way. Likely explanations are income growth, which at 1.0 percent per year was the largest in the sample, and increasing nutritional equality as indicated by a narrowing of occupational differences in stature. These advantages led to a temporary increase in stature, at least for men, which was later offset by the substantial leap in urban population that occurred from 1830 to 1860.

The Americans and the Australians declined in height from the highest levels attained in the early and mid-nineteenth century. Dora Costa and Richard Steckel show that even though the United States was an early industrializer, the share living in urban areas was relatively small and grew slowly. Rising incomes associated with industrialization were beneficial for health, but other costs related to the process outweighed the advantages of income per se. The rise of factories in the era before public health contributed to the height decline, which is consistent with smaller stature in the Northeast where textile mills and other manufacturing plants were located. However, most of the half-century decline after 1830 was rural in nature. The transportation revolution, which began with steamboats on western rivers in 1816 and continued with canals after 1825 and with railroads in the late 1830s, promoted interregional migration and trade that spread communicable diseases among a population whose prior isolation afforded them little immunity to pathogens. The emergence and growth of public schools in the 1840s also contributed to the spread of disease. Over half a century of heavy immigration from Europe, beginning with the Irish potato famine in the late 1840s, churned the disease pool in the United States. Growing inequality of wealth combined with rising food prices, and the falling birthweights of babies of poor women suggest that the quality of life may have decayed for the lower classes. The hardships of the Civil War in the 1860s contributed to the decline in health of those born near the middle of the century, and the struggles of the Southern economy thereafter affected health in that region. In sum, numerous factors contributed to America's deterioration in health, a process that was eventually reversed in the 1880s by growing incomes and by the public health movement acting on the germ theory of disease.

The Australian case parallels that of the United States: residents of both countries were tall and their recovery from the downturn coincided with the rise of the germ theory of disease and public health in the late nineteenth century. Because evidence has yet to be compiled for birth cohorts prior to the 1860s, the timing of the downturn is uncertain. A decline of approximately 3 cm occurred from 1867 to 1893, with most of the drop occurring after 1880.

Why would health decline in a rich country with abundant land and widespread access to resources? Greg Whitwell, Christine de Souza, and Stephen Nicholas observe that the explanation cannot be pinned on the rise of factories and congested working conditions. Instead, the major culprit seems to have been the negative externalities of a large and rapidly growing urban population. As cities grew rapidly in the 1880s, crowd diseases such as typhoid became more prevalent. Those born in the 1880s also experienced, as adolescents, the economic hardships of the depression of the 1890s.

Sophia Twarog argues that the fluctuations in German (Württemberg) stature were not attributable to urbanization. Those born in urban areas were taller during the industrial period, probably due to a vigorous public health movement and government encouragement of breast-feeding in the cities. Instead, the first decline in stature (cohorts born in the 1860s and early 1870s) was related to widening occupational differentials in stature, which were themselves associated with growing inequality and income decline reinforced by the crash of 1873. Economic hardship also lay behind the second dip in stature during the 1880s. The distress in this period led to emigration and to social legislation creating health and accident insurance.

Among the four countries that had sustained increases in health during industrialization—France, the Netherlands, Sweden, and Japan—the first two are particularly intriguing. How did these two countries avoid a decline in health during industrialization, given that France industrialized early and had a moderate-sized urban sector while the Netherlands industrialized later but had a larger share living in urban areas? David Weir's study emphasizes two unusual aspects of French urbanization during industrialization. The first is the slow growth and low overall levels of urbanization, which eased health externalities associated with congestion. The second is the relatively high meat consumption in cities, which apparently improved the diet sufficiently to reduce the negative health consequences of urban living. In addition, he has argued elsewhere that the early decline in fertility in France helped to advance parental investments in child health (Weir 1993). Social, legal, and economic changes of the French Revolution also reallocated resources and reduced inequality compared with other countries. The low French birthrates also improved the health and physical growth of young children by restricting the spread of communicable diseases. J. W. Drukker and Vincent Tassenaar note that in the Netherlands the sustained increase in stature beginning near the middle of the century was matched by a sustained decline in mortality rates. In the early phase of industrialization the modernizing urban sector remained relatively small while much industrial activity occurred in the healthier rural areas, a phenomenon also found in Sweden.

It is easier to explain why industrialization was compatible with improving health in Sweden and Japan. The paper by Lars Sandberg and Richard Steckel notes that Sweden was largely a rural society well into the early twentieth century. Moreover, Sweden had a very high literacy rate that complemented a particularly vigorous public health movement. Japan industrialized rather late, with most of the action occurring after the rise of public health.

Although life expectancy at birth in Japan today is approximately 80 years, health and welfare lagged during industrialization. Between the early phase of industrialization and 1950, average stature grew only 5 cm in Japan compared with 7.4 cm in other countries of the sample.[14] Consistent with this observation, life expectancy at birth grew only 20 years in Japan compared with an average of 28 years elsewhere over these dates. Table 11.2 shows that in 1950 Japan had the lowest life expectancy and the smallest stature (even after allowing 6.5 cm for genetic considerations). Therefore, much of the distance toward exceptional health was achieved along with the phenomenal economic growth of the past few decades. As Honda notes in her paper, stature was higher in the more urban, industrializing areas of the country, which makes it implausible to argue that industrialization per se retarded health. Instead, the answer can be found in government policies that diverted resources from health and nutritional uses to military expansion.

11.4   Epilogue

The papers in this volume expand the range of indicators and apply new methodologies for assessing welfare during industrialization. Once seen primarily through the lenses of per capita income or real wages, here the standard of living is also measured by stature, life expectancy, body mass index, inequality, and education. Among these, stature is the most abundant new source of information on health aspects of the quality of life.

All papers apply the multiple indicators approach to evaluating these measures—an intuitive method for appraising their importance. Several papers also utilize more explicit, but debatable, methods such as the United Nations' Human Development Index or Usher's adjustment for calculating growth rates, and some apply Borda rankings of indicators or Thaler-Rosen estimates of the value of life for adjusting GNP.

Ample research opportunities remain. Several additional countries could be added to the database—Norway, Austria-Hungary, Spain, and Italy come readily to mind in Europe, while in the Western Hemisphere, Canada and several Latin American countries have considerable potential for developing databases on living standards. Study of several Asian countries, which developed in the twentieth century, would provide perspective on events of the eighteenth and nineteenth centuries. In all countries, including those studied in this vol-

---

14. This point does not hinge on a deterioration in Japanese health that occurred during World War II. The results would be essentially unchanged if health conditions in 1940 were substituted for those in 1950.

ume, it may be possible to gather additional information, such as body mass index, stature, inequality, or life expectancy, which will enhance our knowledge of welfare during industrialization.

There may be substantial payoffs to further study of the functional implications of anthropometric measures. Stature and the body mass index are not easily understood in isolation by social scientists who are unfamiliar with biomedical studies or who lack firsthand experience observing malnourished children in poor, developing countries. Therefore, it is important to explain the meaning of these measures in terms of familiar concepts such as income, real wages, educational achievement, productivity, life expectancy, labor force participation, and causes of death. Knowledge of these functional implications will also assist efforts to attach monetary values to nonmonetary indicators of the standard of living, which is important for assessing the net effect of diverse measures on welfare. Several possibilities are explored by the papers in this volume, and we hope that the results will encourage interest in this valuable area of research.

Data Appendix

Australia

(a) Per capita GNP: Interpolated, where necessary, from Maddison (1991, table 1.1).

(b) Stature: Prior to 1950, the source is figure 10.3 of the paper in this volume by Whitwell, de Souza, and Nicholas. The figure cited for 1850 is based on cohorts of the late 1860s and early 1870s. For 1950, the source is Eveleth and Tanner (1976, appendix table 25), which pertains to men aged 18 in Sydney.

(c) Life expectancy at birth: Estimates are based on Vamplew (1987, tables MFM 195–20, MFM 209–220, and MFM 221–232). The figure of 46 years in 1850 is based on Vamplew (MFM 195–201) for males and females in New South Wales for the period 1856–65. Male life expectancy (MFM 209–22), Australia-wide, was 51.06 for the period 1891–1900 and 55.20 for 1901–10, which in turn suggests a figure of about 53 for 1900. For females (table MFM 221–232), the figures are 54.76, 58.84, and 57.0. Averaging the male and female figures (53 and 57) gives a national average of 55. Male life expectancy was 66.07 for the period 1946–48 and 67.14 for the period 1953–55, which suggests a figure of about 66.5 for 1950. The corresponding figures for females are 70.63, 72.75, and 71.7. Averaging the male and female figures for the two periods gives a value of 69.5.

(d) Literacy: Interpolated from Vamplew (1987, 339).

(e) Urbanization: The figures, which include cities or towns with a population of 2,500 or more, are interpolated, where necessary, from Vamplew (1987) and Frost (1990, table 1). The figures in 1850 and 1900 apply to New South Wales, Queensland, South Australia, and Victoria (Western Australia, which was lightly settled, is omitted).

France

Table 11.1 benchmark date estimates are trend values. The data points in table 11.2 are generally averages of annual data.

(a) GDP and growth rates: Estimates in 1985 U.S. dollars were formed by using the real GDP per capita described in the appendix to David Weir's paper in this volume (in 1905–13 francs) and then reflating to 1985 dollars by the ratio of Maddison's (1991) 1985 estimate for French per capita GDP in 1985 dollars to Weir's estimate in 1905–13 francs (ratio = 2.377).

(b) Stature: The average heights are for cohorts born in the years indicated in the tables. Prior to 1922 (cohorts born up to 1902), they are as described in appendix B of Weir's paper. The 1950 cohort is from Olivier et al. (1977, 200).

(c) Life expectancy at birth: The data, which cover both sexes and include civilian mortality only, are based on period life tables from Blayo (1975) for 1740–1829, Vallin (1973) for 1900–60, and unpublished annual life tables constructed by David Weir for 1806–1911.

(d) Literacy: This series is based on signatures for both sexes from new marriages in the years indicated. Data for 1740–1829 are reported by Houdaille (1977), while subsequent periods are taken from annual volumes of the *Annuaire Statistique*.

(e) Percentage urban: The official French census definition of urban is used (communes of at least 2,000 persons in agglomerated areas), following Tugault (1975).

Germany

(a) Per capita GNP: The data on per capita Net National Product (in constant 1913 prices) and average population between 1850 and 1955 were derived from Hoffmann (1965). For 1850–1950, these figures are presented in table 8.3 of Twarog (chap. 8 in this volume). The consumer price indices from Maddison (1991) were used to convert the income data into 1985 marks. The 1985 marks were converted into 1985 dollars using the International Comparison Project benchmark estimates for purchasing power parity (PPP) units in 1985 (DM 2.37162 per dollar), as employed by Maddison (1991). The growth rate for 1950 is the average annual rate between 1950 and 1955. The growth rate for 1900 is the average annual rate between 1895 and 1905.

(b) Stature: The height data for 1850 to 1937 are based on the RSMLE estimates in Twarog (1993), six-year and two-year phases for Württemberg recruits born between 1852 and 1893, and on Harbeck's (1960) finding that the average stature of German 20-year-old recruits born in 1937 was 173.2 cm. Estimates for birth years 1894–1914 were derived via interpolation using the trend between 1892–93 and 1937. The height estimate for 1950 is from Jürgens (1971) and is based on a geographically balanced sample of 7,093 draftable twenty-year-olds born in 1948 and 1949. Since growth generally continues past age 20 in populations subject to adverse environmental conditions, upward adjustments were made to the recruits' average stature as follows: 2 cm for the birth cohort of 1850; 1.5 cm for 1850–71 and 1871–96; 1 cm for 1896–1914 and 1900.

(c) Life expectancy at birth: The figures for life expectancy (average of males and females) after 1871 are derived from Wiegand and Zapf (1982) and given in table 8.12 of Twarog (chap. 8 in this volume). For the periods before 1871, the average mortality rates (from Mitchell 1980) were compared with the mortality rates in those periods for which the life expectancy is known. Based on a comparison of the average life expectancies and mortality rates in 1871–80, 1881–90, and 1891–1900, the assumption used was that a one-point drop in the mortality rate corresponds approximately to a one-year rise in life expectancy in the relevant range. For 1800, the average mortality rate of 1817–19 was used, because earlier data were not available. For 1850, the average mortality rate for 1845–55 was used.

(d) Literacy: Literacy rates are those of army recruits in Prussia (1841–74, available years) and the German Empire (1875–1912). The figures are drawn from table 8.18 in Twarog (chap. 8 in this volume) and Cipolla (1969). For the German army, literacy was defined as being able to write one's name and read sufficiently, a concept that is ambiguous. Moreover, these estimates certainly overestimate the adult population's literacy because women were generally less literate than men. The estimate for 1800 is based on the assumption that the change in the literacy rate between 1800 and 1841 was equal to that between 1841 and 1882 (7.5 percentage points).

(e) Urbanization: Urban refers to communities with over 2,000 residents. These estimates are based on Hoffmann's data as displayed in table 8.2 in Twarog (chap. 8 in this volume). Interpolation and extrapolation were used where necessary. For example, the estimates for 1800–1850 were derived by using the 1852–71 annual rate of change. The percentage urban for each period is the average of the beginning and end year estimated value.

The Netherlands

(a) Per capita GNP: The general source is Maddison (1991), using linear interpolation where necessary: Table A.5, Movement in GDP, 1700–1869 (1913 = 100.0), gives 15.71 for 1820 and 24.5 for 1850; table A.2, Gross Domestic Product in 1985 U.S.-Relative-Prices (million dollars) gives 19.588 for 1913; table B.1, Mid-Year Population, 1500–1860 (thousands), gives 2.355 for 1820 and 3.095 for 1850. So real Dutch GDP per capita in 1820 can be calculated as $(15.71 / 100 * 19.588 * 1000) / 2.355 = 1307$, and in 1850 as $(24.5 / 100 * 19.588 * 1000) / 3.095 = 1551$. Drukker and Tassenaar (chap. 9 in this volume, table 9A.7) give 104.08 for 1807 and 184.28 for 1851.

It is assumed that real income growth was negligible during the years of the French occupation of the Netherlands (1795–1813). If correct, real GNP per capita in 1800 equaled real GNP per capita in 1807. Then (104.08 / 184.28) * 100 = 56.48, so that 56.48 / 100 = real GNP per capita in 1800 / 1551, which implies real GNP per capita in 1800 was 876 in 1985 dollars.

The annual growth rate was assumed to be zero under the French occupation around 1800. Various estimates of the rate are available for the period around 1850, including 1.1 percent as calculated from the per capita GNP data given in table 11.1. However, this estimate is likely to be too high. For the period from 1820 to 1851, Maddison's figures show that the rate was 0.6 percent. Based on Drukker and Tassenaar (chap. 9 in this volume, table 9A.7), the rate was 0.15 percent (col. [2]) to 0.26 percent (col. [3]). Emphasizing the latter figures, a reasonable guess of the growth rate around 1850 is 0.2 percent.

Three sets calculations were considered in estimating the growth rate around 1900. Interpolations from Maddison's figures for the period 1895 to 1905 indicate a rate of 0.7 percent, whereas Drukker and Tassenaar (chap. 9 in this volume, table 9A.7) give rates of 0.9 percent (col. [2]) to 1.11 percent (col. [3]). This collection of estimates suggests a rate of approximately 0.9 percent.

It is somewhat difficult to suggest a growth rate that typifies the period around 1950 since many European economies, including the Netherlands, were recovering from World War II. The annual data on population and GNP in Maddison for the years immediately around 1950 indicate a rate of 3.4 percent.

(b) Stature: (1) The figure for 1800 was estimated from Oppers (1963) using 392 observations in tables 12, 14, 15, 16, 18, and 19. He sampled men's heights from seven geographically spread cities in the Netherlands, ranging in age groups from 19 years up to 34 years, in total more than 14,000 observations, over the period (year of birth) 1794 up to 1877. A number of 382 observations could be used for the estimate of Dutch men's height for 1800. The estimate was calculated as a weighted average of subgroups of applicable observations by Oppers with the number of observations in each subgroup as weights. There is probably a slight underestimation in the figure, due to the facts that his observations were only for city dwellers, who may have been a little bit shorter than country dwellers, and men under 25 years of age may not have reached their final stature. (2) The figure for 1850 was estimated from the same source as for 1800, according to the same procedure, now based on 663 observations of city dwellers. (3) The figure for 1900 was derived from Drukker and Tassenaar (chap. 9 in this volume, table 9A.1) under the assumptions that average height equals median height around 1900, and that adult height was reached by age 19.75. The figure in 1920 was taken as an estimate for average height of the birth cohort in 1900, as the data are for 19.75-year-old year conscripts in the year of measurement. (4) The height of men born in 1950 is from Centraal Bureau voor de Statistiek (1994, 260, table 16, col. [6]). The figure for 1969 (conscription year) was taken, as conscripts were measured in that year at 19 years of age.

(c) Life expectancy at birth: (1) The figure for 1800 was estimated by regressing the crude death rate on average life expectancies for the consecutive periods from 1840–51 to 1900–1909. The life expectancies were obtained from Centraal Bureau voor de Statistiek (1942, 57, table 14) and the average death rates were calculated from Drukker and Tassenaar (chap. 4 in this volume, table 9A.4). The death rate for 1800 was calculated as an average of the yearly death rates between 1795 and 1805, as published by Horlings (1993, appendix 2, 18). The resulting estimate of life expectancy is 34.1 years. (2) Life expectancy in 1850 was estimated as an average for men and women over the years 1840–51 and 1850–59 as published in Centraal Bureau voor de Statistiek (1942, 57, table 14). The value for 1900 was calculated from the same source in a similar manner, while that for 1950 was tabulated in the same way from Centraal Bureau voor de Statistiek (1967, 57, table 14).

(d) Literacy: (1) The figure for 1800 is from van Zanden (1991, 41, table 10), which shows that the percentage of grooms not signing the wedding certificate was 24.6 percent between 1813 and 1819. Supposing that this percentage was more or less constant at least since 1800 gives a figure of approximately 25 percent. From the same table, it can be derived that 25.1 percent of all conscripts in the Netherlands could not read or write between 1846 and 1852, which forms the basis for the figure of 25 percent in 1850. (2) Data in Centraal Bureau voor de Statistiek (1994, 242, table 15, col. [2]; 16, table 1, col. [4]) show that approximately 93 percent of children between ages 6 and 16 attended school in 1900. Since a small percentage of these children were unlikely to master reading and writing skills, a reasonable estimate of the literacy rate is 90 percent around 1900. Of course, older generations alive at the time may have had somewhat lower literacy rates. From the same sources it can be calculated in the same way that the literacy rate around 1950 was very close to 100 percent.

(e) Urbanization: Percentage urban is defined here as the percentage of the population living in municipalities of more than 2,500 inhabitants. (1) 1800: According to De Vries and Van der Woude (1995, 82–83), in 1795 about 40 percent of the total population of the Netherlands lived in cities and 7.1 percent of total city population lived in cities that had fewer than 2,500 inhabitants. Taking conditions in 1795 as a proxy for those in 1800, the percentage urban was approximately $40 - (0.071 \times 40) = 37.2$. (2) 1850: According to the official census of December 1849, 36 percent of the total population of the Netherlands lived in cities. The same source indicates that 0.9 percent of the total population lived in cities that had fewer than 2,500 inhabitants, but not every urban center had the official status of a city. In these places lived 3.4 percent of the total population. So the urbanization rate (percent) was approximately $36.0 - 0.9 + 3.4 = 38.5$. (3) 1900: According to Kooij (1985, 97), 45.2 percent of the population lived in cities and 3.3 percent lived in urban centers without the official title of city. So the percentage living in urban areas was approximately $45.2 + 3.3 = 48.5$. (4) 1950: Kooij (1985, 97) indicates that 54.4 percent of the population lived in cities and 16.2 percent lived in urban centers without the official title of city. So the percentage urban was approximately 54.4 + 16.2 = 70.6.

Japan

(a) Per capita GNP: Interpolated, where necessary, from Maddison (1991, table 1.1).

(b) Growth rates: 1800 and 1850, estimated from growth in per capita grain output, 1750–1850 (Hayami and Miyamoto 1988); 1900 and 1950, Ohkawa and Rosovsky (1973, 25, 28); preindustrial period, estimated from growth in per capita grain output, 1850–72 (Hayami and Miyamoto 1988); early, middle, and late industrial periods, Ohkawa and Rosovsky (1973, 28).

(c) Stature: 1800, based on length of right femur (Hiramoto 1972); 1850, Mosk and Johansson (1986, 429); 1900, Shay (1986, appendix); 1950, Shay (1986, appendix) by extrapolation; preindustrial period, based on length of right femur (Hiramoto 1972); early, middle, and late industrial periods, Shay (1986, appendix).

(d) Life expectancy: 1800, Saitō (1992); 1850 and 1900, Mosk and Johansson (1984); 1950, Taeuber (1958, 294); pre- and early industrial periods, Mosk and Johansson (1986, 429); middle industrial period, Mosk and Johansson (1984); late industrial period, Taeuber (1958, 288).

(e) Percentage urban: Defined in all years as the percentage of the population living in cities or towns of 5,000 or more inhabitants. 1800, Wilkinson (1965, 24); 1850 and 1900, interpolated from Taeuber (1958, 72) and Wilkinson (1965, 24); 1950, Taeuber (1958, 72). The figures for all phases of industrialization were interpolated from Wilkinson (1965, 24) and Taeuber (1958, 72).

(f) Literacy: 1800, Taira (1971, 375); 1850, Nakamura (1983, 48); 1900, Taira (1971, 376); 1950, Taeuber (1958, 66–68); preindustrial, Nakamura (1983, 48); early and middle industrial, Taira (1971, 374–75); late industrial, Taeuber (1958, 66–68).

Sweden

See the data appendix of chapter 4 in this volume, by Lars Sandberg and Richard Steckel, for additional discussion of sources.

(a) Per capita GNP: Maddison (1991) for the period 1820–60 and Krantz and Nilsson (1980) for the period thereafter to 1965. These original numbers were converted from Swedish kronor to U.S. dollars at an exchange rate of 5.18 Skr per dollar.

(b) Stature: Cohorts born before 1820: soldiers of various ages who served in the so-called settled (*indelta*) army (see Sandberg and Steckel 1988). Cohorts born 1820 and thereafter: conscripted militia. These nationwide average data cover the great majority of young men measured in the year they turned age 21 (born 1820–97), age 20 (born 1898–1929), age 19 (born 1930–35), and finally age 18 (born 1936–). Because the age reductions occurred in line with the decline in the age of maturation, the changes had very little effect on the trend in final adult heights. More worrisome was the fact that the military imposed nontrivial height standards on cohorts born between 1819 and 1839. We corrected for the resulting shortfall using the Quantile Bend Estimator (Wachter and Trussell 1982). The fact that data are missing for a few scattered years forced us to interpolate for those years.

(c) Life expectancy at birth: Keyfitz and Fleiger (1968).

(d) Literacy: The numbers we provide are based on the conclusion reported by, although by no means unique to, Cipolla (1969) that Swedish literacy had reached 90 percent by 1850 and that virtually all Swedish youths were then literate. The compulsory education act of 1842 was unquestionably having an effect, although schools were certainly commonplace even before that year. Given a flow of virtually 100 percent literate cohorts reaching adulthood after 1850, a 0.25 annual rate of increase in literacy up to 100 percent in 1890 seems highly reasonable. Similarly, a 0.25 percent rate before 1850 also yields a reasonable result of 82.5 percent in 1820.

(e) Percentage urban: Defined here as cities or towns with populations of 2,500 or more, the source is Statistiska Centralbyrån (1969, 46).

United Kingdom

(a) Per capita GNP: Mitchell's (1988, 837–41) estimates for 1830–1980 were extrapolated backward using the growth rates computed by Crafts (1985, 45). Mitchell's figures in 1900, 1938, 1958, and 1980 were converted to 1980 prices, and the results translated in 1985 sterling prices using the price index for GDP at market prices in Central Statistical Office (1995b, 20–21). The corresponding population figures were obtained from Mitchell (1988, 11–14) for 1801 onward. Backward extrapolation, where necessary, was based on the English population estimates in Wrigley and Schofield (1981, table A3.3). The results were converted from sterling prices into 1985 U.S. relative prices using conversion factors given by Maddison (1991, 197). Average annual growth rates were calculated for the previous five years; e.g., the figure for 1800 is the rate for 1795–1800.

(b) Stature: The basic sources are Floud, Wachter, and Gregory (1990, 142–48) for the eighteenth and nineteenth centuries and Rosenbaum (1988, tables 1, 13, and 19) for 1900 onward. Specifically, the methods are as follows: 1800, average heights of army recruits who were born in 1797.5 and 1802.5, and who were measured between ages 20 and 23; 1850, average height of army recruits who were born in 1847.5 and 1852.5, and who were measured between ages 20 and 23; 1900, the average of the averages of the height of army recruits who were born between 1886 and 1893, and who were measured between ages 20 and 24, and the height of industrial workers who were born between 1905 and 1912, and who were measured between ages 21 and 24; 1950, the average height of army recruits who were born between 1946 and 1954, and who were measured between ages 20 and 24. The figure for 1720–60 is the average for men aged 20–23 who were born in 1742.5, 1747.5, 1752.5, and 1757.5, and for the remaining periods in table 11.2 the figures are based on the averages for the cohorts of 1762.5–1797.5, 1802.5–1827.5, and 1832.5–1867.5. The figures in table 11.3 were calculated as follows: 1760, average of cohorts of 1757.5 and 1762.5; 1790, average of cohorts of 1787.5 and 1792.5; 1820, average of cohorts of 1817.5 and 1822.5; 1850, average of cohorts of 1847.5 and 1852.5.

(c) Life expectancy at birth: Prior to 1871, Wrigley and Schofield (1981, table A3.1); 1871 and after, Office of Population Censuses and Surveys (1987, table 22).

(d) Literacy: Based on Schofield (1973) for 1754–1838, the registrar-general for England and Wales for 1839–1914 (Parliamentary Papers 1840, 1841, 1884, 1916).

(e) Percentage urban: It is defined from the total population of England and Wales inhabiting towns with more than 2,500 residents. Prior to 1800, the figures are based on Thompson (1990, 8); from 1800 to 1900 on Dodghson and Butlin (1978, 370); and that for 1950 on General Register Office (1956, table 5).

United States

Details on most methods and data sources are available from the paper in this volume by Dora Costa and Richard Steckel.

(a) Stature: Compiled from Steckel (1992), Steckel and Haurin (1982), 1959–62 NHES, 1971 NHANES, and from several data sets listed in the appendix to Costa and Steckel (chap. 2 in this volume): Union Army Recruits in White Regiments in the United States, 1861–1865; French and Indian War Army Recruits; American Revolution Army Recruits; United States Army Recruits, 1815–1820; and United States Army Recruits, 1850–1855.

(b) Per capita income: Weiss (1992, table 1.3, variant C) up to 1860, and thereafter U.S. Bureau of the Census (1975, Series F 1–5).

(c) Life expectancy at birth: 1800, based on Pope's (1992, table 9.4) estimate of life expectancy at age 20 (46.8 years, an average for males and females over the years 1780–99 and 1800–1809) and the results by Haines (1994, U.S. model for both sexes of the white population in 1850) that the ratio of life expectancy at birth to life expectancy at age 20 was approximately 1.0. The result hinges on the generality of life expectancy calculated from genealogies by Pope and on the stability over time of the ratio of life expectancy at birth to life expectancy at age 20 (this ratio is slightly greater than one in the Model West tables that Haines estimates for 1850). Given these assumptions, the estimate should be viewed with caution; 1850, Haines (1994, U.S. model of both sexes of the white population in 1850); 1900, Haines (1994, U.S. model for the total population of both sexes); 1950, U.S. Bureau of the Census (1975, Series B 107–115). Values for the preindustrial period and the early industrial period were obtained through linear interpolation of the estimates for 1800 and 1850. Estimates for the middle and late industrial periods are averages of estimates for the relevant years in Haines (1994, U.S. model) and U.S. Bureau of the Census (1975, Series B 107–115).

(d) Literacy: Rates from 1850 onward were taken from the federal censuses as reported in U.S. Bureau of the Census (1975). Literacy rates for the free population to 1800 to 1840 were estimated using reports of literacy by age contained in the 1850 Public Use Micro Sample (PUMS). This procedure may contain biases to the extent that survival rates varied with literacy. The procedure also neglects cohort trends in literacy that may have existed among older generations alive in the early 1800s who did not survive to 1850.

(e) Urbanization: U.S. Bureau of the Census (1975, Series A 57–72). An urban place is defined as a city or town that has a population of 2,500 or more.

References

Blayo, Yves. 1975. La mortalité en France de 1740 à 1829. *Population* 30:123–42.
Centraal Bureau voor de Statistiek. 1942. *Sterftetafels voor Nederland, Afgeleid uit de Waarnemingen over de Periode 1931–1940* (Mortality tables for the Netherlands, derived from observations over the period 1931–1940). The Hague: Rijksuitgeverij.
———. 1967. *Sterftetafels voor Nederland, Afgeleid uit de Waarnemingen over de Periode 1931–1940* (Mortality tables for the Netherlands, derived from observations over the period 1946–1965). The Hague: Rijksuitgeverij.
———. 1994. *Vijfennegentig Jaren Statistiek in Tijdreeksen, 1899–1994* (95 years of statistics in time series, 1899–1994). The Hague: SDU-Uitgeverij.
Central Statistical Office. 1995a. *Economic trends*. London: HMSO.
———. 1995b. *United Kingdom national accounts 1995*. London: HMSO.
Cipolla, Carlo M. *Literacy and development in the West*. Baltimore: Penguin.
Crafts, N. 1985. *British economic growth during the Industrial Revolution*. Oxford: Oxford University Press.
de Vries, J., and A. M. van der Woude. 1995. *Nederland 1500–1815: De Eerste Ronde van Moderne Economische Groei* (The Netherlands 1500–1815: the first phase of modern economic growth). Amsterdam: Balans.
Dodghson, R., and R. Butlin. 1978. *An historical geography of England and Wales*. London: Academic Press.
Eveleth, Phyllis B., and J. M. Tanner. 1976. *Worldwide variation in human growth*. Cambridge: Cambridge University Press.
———. 1990. *Worldwide variation in human growth*, 2d ed. Cambridge: Cambridge University Press.
Floud, Roderick, Kenneth W. Wachter, and Annabel S. Gregory. 1990. *Height, health, and history: Nutritional status in the United Kingdom, 1750–1980*. Cambridge: Cambridge University Press.
Fogel, Robert William. 1985. Nutrition and the decline in mortality since 1700: Some preliminary findings. In *Long-term factors in American economic growth*, ed. Stanley L. Engerman and Robert E. Gallman, 439–555. Chicago: University of Chicago Press.

Frost, Lionel. 1990. *Australian cities in comparative view.* Melbourne: McPhee Gribble.

General Register Office. 1956. *Census 1951: General tables comprising population, ages and marital condition, non-private households, birthplace and nationality, education.* London: HMSO.

Gerschenkron, Alexander. 1962. *Economic backwardness in historical perspective.* Cambridge, Mass.: Harvard University Press.

Haines, Michael R. 1994. Estimated life tables for the United States, 1850–1900. NBER Working Paper Series on Historical Factors in Long Run Growth, no. 59. Cambridge, Mass.: National Bureau of Economic Research.

Harbeck, Rudolf. 1960. Die Körpergrössen 20 jähriger Männer. *Wehrdienst und Gesundheit: Abhandlungen aus Wehrmedizin, Wehrpharmazie und Wehrveterinärwesen,* vol. 1. Darmstadt: Wehr un Wissen Verlagsgesellschaft Mbh.

Hayami, Akira, and Matao Miyamoto. 1988. Gaisetsu 17–18 seiki (An outline of the 17th and 18th centuries). In *Keizai shakai no seiritsu 17–18 seiki* (The development of 17th and 18th century economy and society), ed. Akira Hayami and Matao Miyamoto, 2–84. Tokyo: Iwanami Shoten.

Hiramoto, Yoshisuke. 1972. Jōmon jidai kara kindai ni itaru Kantō chihōjin shinchō no jidaiteki henka (Periodic changes in the heights of Kantō region inhabitants from the Jōmon through the modern period). *Jinrui zasshi* (Journal of the Anthropological Society of Nippon) 80:221–36.

Hoffmann, Walter G. 1965. *Das Wachstum der deutschen Wirtschaft seit der Mitte des 19. Jahrhunderts.* Berlin: Springer.

Horlings, E. 1993. De Ontwikkeling van de Nederlandse Bevolking in de Negentiende Eeuw, 1795–1913 (The development of the Dutch population in the nineteenth century, 1795–1913). Free University of Amsterdam. Unpublished manuscript.

Houdaille, Jacques. 1977. Les signatures au mariage de 1740 à 1829. *Population* 32:65–89.

Jackson, R. V. 1977. *Australian economic development in the nineteenth century.* Canberra: ANU Press.

Jones, E. L. 1968. *The development of English agriculture, 1815–1873.* London: Macmillan.

Jürgens, Hans W. 1971. Gruppenunterschiede des menschlichen Wachstums in zeitlicher und örtlicher Hinsicht. *Zeitschrift für Morphologie und Anthropologie* 63(1).

Keyfitz, N., and W. Fleiger. 1968. *World population: An analysis of vital data.* Chicago: University of Chicago Press.

Komlos, John. 1987. The height and weight of West Point cadets: Dietary change in antebellum America. *Journal of Economic History* 47:897–927.

Kooij, P. 1985. Stad en Platteland (City and countryside). In *De Nederlandse Samenleving sinds 1815, Wording en Samenhang* (Dutch society since 1815, origin and cohesion), ed. F. L. v. Holthoon, 93–118. Assen: Van Gorcum.

Krantz, O., and C. -A. Nilsson. 1980. *Swedish national product, 1861–1970: New aspects on methods and measurement.* Copenhagen: Gleerup.

Livi-Bacci, Massimo. 1983. The nutrition-mortality link in past times: A comment. *Journal of Interdisciplinary History* 14:293–98.

Maddison, Angus. 1991. *Dynamic forces in capitalist development: A long-run comparative view.* New York: Oxford University Press.

McKeown, Thomas. 1983. Food, infection, and population. *Journal of Interdisciplinary History* 14:227–47.

Mitchell, B. R. 1980. *European historical statistics, 1750–1975.* London: Macmillan.

———. 1988. *British historical statistics.* Cambridge: Cambridge University Press.

Mosk, Carl, and S. Ryan Johansson. 1984. Death and development: Mortality decline in Japan 1980–1960. Report to the National Science Foundation.

———. 1986. Income and mortality: Evidence from modern Japan. *Population and Development Review* 12:415–40.
Nakamura, Takafusa. 1983. *Economic growth in prewar Japan,* trans. Robert A. Feldman. New Haven, Conn.: Yale University Press.
Office of Population Censuses and Surveys. 1987. *Mortality statistics: Review of the registrar-general on deaths in England and Wales, 1985.* London: HMSO.
Ohkawa, Kazushi, and Henry Rosovsky. 1973. *Japanese economic growth.* Stanford, Calif.: Stanford University Press.
Olivier, G., Marie-Claude Chamla, G. Devigne, and A. Jacquard. 1977. L'accroissement de la Stature in France. *Bulletins et Mémoires de la Société d'Anthropologie de Paris,* 4 13th ser., 4(2): 197–214.
Oppers, V. M. 1963. *Analyse van de Acceleratie van de Menselijke Lengtegroei door Bepaling van het Tijdstip van de Groeifasen* (Analysis of the acceleration of human growth of height by determination of the timing of growth phases). Doctoral dissertation, University of Amsterdam.
Parliamentary Papers. 1840. (263) xvii, 1. *Second annual report of the registrar-general on births, deaths and marriages in England.*
———. 1841. (II) (345) vi, 1. *Third annual report of the registrar-general on births, deaths and marriages in England.*
———. 1884. C. 4009 xx, 1. *Forty-fifth annual report of the registrar-general on births, deaths and marriages in England (abstracts of 1882).*
———. 1916, Cd. 8206 v, 53. *Seventy-fifth annual report of the registrar-general on births, deaths and marriages in England (1914).*
Pope, Clayne L. 1992. Adult mortality in America before 1900: A view from family histories. In *Strategic factories in nineteenth century American economic history,* ed. Claudia Goldin and Hugh Rockoff, 267–96. Chicago: University of Chicago Press.
Razzell, Peter. 1993. The growth of population in eighteenth-century England: A critical reappraisal. *Journal of Economic History* 53:743–71.
Rosenbaum, S. 1988. 100 Years of heights and weights. *Journal of the Royal Statistical Society A* 151:276–309.
Saitō, Osamu. 1992. Jinkō tenkan izen no Nihon ni okeru mortality (Mortality in Japan before the demographic transition). *Keizai kenkyū* 43:248–67.
Sandberg, Lars G. 1979. The case of the impoverished sophisticate: Human capital and Swedish economic growth before World War I. *Journal of Economic History* 39:225–41.
Sandberg, Lars G., and Richard H. Steckel. 1988. Overpopulation and malnutrition rediscovered: Hard times in nineteenth-century Sweden. *Explorations in Economic History* 25:1–19.
Schofield, R. S. 1973. Dimensions of illiteracy. *Explorations in Economic History* 10:437–54.
Shay, Ted. 1986. The level of living in Japan, 1885–1938: New evidence. Paper presented at the Social Science History Association meetings, St. Louis.
Statistiska Centralbyrån. 1969. *Historisk statistik för Sverige,* del. 1. Befolkning. Stockholm.
Steckel, Richard H. 1988. The health and mortality of women and children, 1850–1860. *Journal of Economic History* 48:333–45.
———. 1992. Stature and living standards in the United States. In *American economic growth and standards of living before the Civil War,* ed. R. E. Gallman and J. J. Wallis. Chicago: University of Chicago Press.
Steckel, Richard H., and Donald R. Haurin. 1982. Height, nutrition, and mortality in Ohio, 1870–1900. Columbus, Ohio. Mimeograph.
Szreter, Simon. 1988. The importance of social intervention in Britain's mortality decline c. 1850–1914: A reinterpretation of the role of public health. *Social History of Medicine* 1:1–37.

Taeuber, Irene B. 1958. *The population of Japan.* Princeton, N.J.: Princeton University Press.

Taira, Koji. 1971. Education and literacy in Meiji Japan: An interpretation. *Explorations in Economic History* 8:371–94.

Tanner, J. M., T. Hayashi, M. A. Preece, and N. Cameron. 1982. Increase in length of leg relative to trunk in Japanese children and adults from 1957 to 1977: Comparisons with British and with Japanese Americans. *Annals of Human Biology* 9:411–23.

Thompson, F. M. L. 1990. Town and city. In *The Cambridge social history of Britain, 1750–1950,* ed. F. M. L. Thompson, 1–86. Cambridge: Cambridge University Press.

Tracy, Michael. 1964. *Agriculture in Western Europe.* New York: Praeger.

Trow-Smith, Robert. 1967. *Life from the land: The Growth of farming in Western Europe.* London: Longmans.

Tugault, Yves. 1975. *Fécondité et Urbanisation.* INED Travaux et Documents Cahier no. 74. Paris: Presses Universitaires de France.

Twarog, Sophia. 1993. *Heights and living standard in industrializing Germany: The case of Württemberg.* Unpublished Ph.D diss., Ohio State University, Columbus.

U.S. Bureau of the Census. 1975. *Historical statistics of the United States, colonial times to 1970.* Washington, D.C.: Government Printing Office.

Vallin, Jacques. 1973. *La Mortalité par Génération en France depuis 1899.* INED Travaux et Documents Cahier no. 63. Paris: Presses Universitaires de France.

Vamplew, Wray, ed. 1987. *Australians: Historical statistics.* Broadway: Fairfax, Syme and Weldon.

van Zanden, J. L., ed. 1991. *"Den Zedelijken en Materiëlen Toestand der Arbeidende Bevolking ten Platten Lande": Een Reeks Rapporten uit 1851 (Fotografische Heruitgave)* ("The moral and material situation of of the working population in the countryside": A series of reports from 1851 [photographic reprint]). Groningen: Nederlands Agronomisch-Historisch Instituut.

Wachter, K. W., and J. Trussell. 1982. Estimating historical heights. *Journal of the American Statistical Association* 77:279–93.

Weir, David R. 1993. Parental consumption decisions and child health during the early French fertility decline, 1790–1914. *Journal of Economic History* 53:259–74.

Weiss, Thomas J. 1992. U.S. labor force estimates, 1800 to 1860. In *American economic growth and the standard of living before the Civil War,* ed. Robert E. Gallman and John Joseph Wallis. Chicago: University of Chicago Press.

Wiegand, Erich, and Wolfgang Zapf. 1982. *Wandel der Lebensbedingungen in Deutschland: Wohlfahrtsentwicklung seit der Industrialisierung.* Frankfurt: Campus.

Wilkinson, Thomas O. 1965. *The urbanization of Japanese labor.* Amherst: University of Massachusetts Press.

Wrigley, E. A., and R. S. Schofield. 1981. *The population history of England, 1541–1871: A reconstruction.* Cambridge: Cambridge University Press.

Contributors

Dora L. Costa
Department of Economics
Massachusetts Institute of Technology
Room E52
Cambridge, MA 02139

J. W. Drukker
Faculty of Economics
University of Groningen
Vakgroep AE-Sectie ESG
POB 800, 9700 AV Groningen
The Netherlands

Stanley L. Engerman
Department of Economics
University of Rochester
Rochester, NY 14627

Roderick Floud
London Guildhall University
31 Jewry Street
London EC3N 2EY
United Kingdom

Bernard Harris
Department of Sociology and
   Social Policy
University of Southampton
Highfield
Southampton SO17 1BJ
United Kingdom

Gail Honda
Department of Sociology
University of Chicago
1155 East 60th Street
Chicago, IL 60637

Paul Johnson
Department of Economic History
London School of Economics
Houghton Street
London WC2A 2AE
United Kingdom

Stephen Nicholas
Department of Business Development
   and Corporate History
University of Melbourne
Parkville, VIC 3052
Australia

Lars G. Sandberg
Department of Economics
Ohio State University
1945 North High Street
Columbus, OH 43210

Richard H. Steckel
Department of Economics
Ohio State University
1945 North High Street
Columbus, OH 43210

Vincent Tassenaar
University of Groningen
Dutch National Foundation of Scientific
    Research NWO.
The Netherlands

Sophia Twarog
Office of the Secretary-General
UNCTAD
Palais des Nations
CH 1211 Geneva 10
Switzerland

David R. Weir
Population Research Center
NORC and University of Chicago
1155 East 60th Street
Chicago, IL 60637

Greg Whitwell
Department of Business Development
    and Corporate History
University of Melbourne
Parkville, VIC 3052
Australia

Author Index

Subject Index

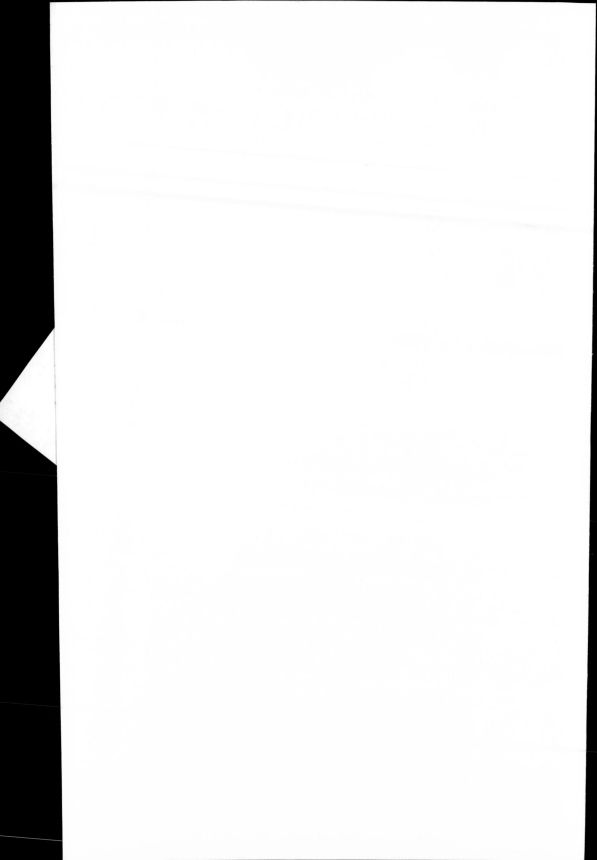

AFR 8698

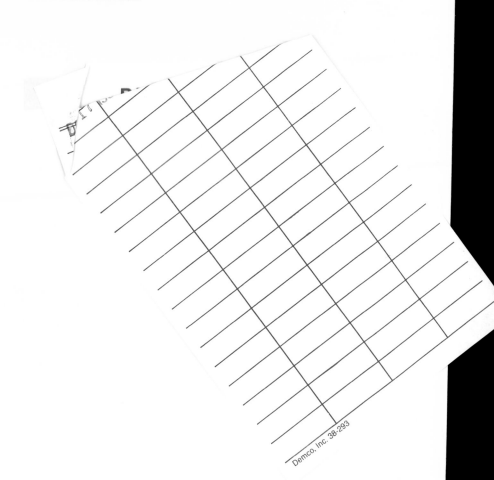

Demco, Inc. 38-293